Komm mit!

HOLT GERMAN

LEVEL 1

HOLT, RINEHART AND WINSTON

A Harcourt Classroom Education Company

Austin • New York • Orlando • Atlanta • San Francisco • Boston • Dallas • Toronto • London

EXECUTIVE EDITOR
George Winkler

SENIOR EDITOR
Konstanze Alex Brown

MANAGING EDITOR
Chris Hiltenbrand

EDITORIAL STAFF
Sara Anbari
Mark Eells,
Editorial Coordinator
Augustine Agwuele,
Department Intern
Sunday Ballew,
Department Intern

EDITORIAL PERMISSIONS
Janet Harrington,
Permissions Editor

ART, DESIGN, & PHOTO
BOOK DESIGN
Richard Metzger,
Design Director
Marta L. Kimball,
Design Manager
Virginia Hassell
Andrew Lankes
Jennifer Trost
Alicia Sullivan
Ruth Limon

IMAGE SERVICES
Joe London,
Director
Tim Taylor,
Photo Research Supervisor
Stephanie Friedman
Michelle Rumpf,
Art Buyer Supervisor
Coco Weir

DESIGN NEW MEDIA
Susan Michael,
Design Director
Amy Shank,
Design Manager
Kimberly Cammerata,
Design Manager
Czeslaw Sornat,
Senior Designer
Grant Davidson

MEDIA DESIGN
Curtis Riker,
Design Director
Richard Chavez

GRAPHIC SERVICES
Kristen Darby,
Manager
Linda Wilbourn
Jane Dixon
Dean Hsieh

COVER DESIGN
Richard Metzger,
Design Director
Candace Moore,
Senior Designer

PRODUCTION
Amber McCormick,
Production Supervisor
Diana Rodriguez,
Production Coordinator

MANUFACTURING
Shirley Cantrell,
Supervisor, Inventory &
Manufacturing
Deborah Wisdom,
Senior Inventory Analyst

NEW MEDIA
Jessica Bega,
Senior Project Manager
Elizabeth Kline,
Senior Project Manager

VIDEO PRODUCTION
Video materials produced by
Edge Productions, Inc.,
Aiken, S.C.

ACKNOWLEDGMENTS

Front Cover: house: Helga Lade/Peter Arnold, Inc

Front Cover: teens: Steve Ewert/HRW Photo

Back Cover: George Winkler/HRW Photo.

For permission to reprint copyrighted material, grateful acknowledgment is made to the following sources:

Baars Marketing GmbH: Advertisement, "Leerdammer Light: Das haben Sie jetzt davon," from *Stern*, no. 27, June 25, 1992.

Bauconcept: Advertisement, "Die Oase in der City!," from *Südwest Presse: Schwäbisches Tagblatt*, Tübingen, July 14, 1990.

KOMM MIT! is a trademark licensed to Holt, Rinehart and Winston, registered in the United States of America and/or other jurisdictions.

Printed in the United States of America

ISBN 0-03-056597-9

5 6 7   48   05 04

ACKNOWLEDGMENTS continued on page R59, which is an extension of the copyright page

AUTHOR
George Winkler
Austin, TX

Mr. Winkler developed the scope and sequence and framework for the chapters, created the basic material, selected realia, and wrote activities.

CONTRIBUTING WRITERS
Margrit Meinel Diehl
Syracuse, NY

Mrs. Diehl wrote activities to practice basic material, functions, grammar, and vocabulary.

Carolyn Roberts Thompson
Abilene Christian University
Abilene, TX

Mrs. Thompson was responsible for the selection of realia for readings and for developing reading activities.

CONSULTANTS
The consultants conferred on a regular basis with the editorial staff and reviewed all the chapters of the Level 1 textbook.

Maria L. Beck
University of North Texas
Denton, TX

Dorothea Bruschke, retired
Parkway School District
Chesterfield, MO

Ingeborg H. McCoy
Southwest Texas State University
San Marcos, TX

REVIEWERS
The following educators reviewed one or more chapters of the Pupil's Edition.

Inge Atkins
Arvada High School
Arvada, CO

Jerome R. Baker
Columbus East High School
Columbus, IN

Jerri Lynn Baxstrom
Smithville High School
Smithville, OH

Angela Breidenstein
Trinity University, previously at Robert Lee High School
San Antonio, TX

Nancy Butt
Washington and Lee High School
Arlington, VA

Kathleen Cooper
Burnsville High School
Burnsville, MN

Frank Dietz
University of Texas at Austin
Austin, TX

Donald R. Goetz
West High School
Davenport, IA

Jacqueline Hastay
Lyndon Baines Johnson High School
Austin, TX

Gerlind Jenkner
Medina High School
Medina, OH

Leslie Kearney
Central High School
Little Rock, AR

LeRoy H. Larson
John Marshall High School
Rochester, MN

Diane E. Laumer
San Marcos High School
San Marcos, TX

Carol Masters
Edison High School
Tulsa, OK

Linnea Maulding
Fife High School
Tacoma, WA

Amy S. McMahon
Parkway Central High School
Chesterfield, MO

David A. Miller
Parkway South High School
Manchester, MO

Linda Miller
Craig High School
Janesville, WI

Douglas Mills
Greensburg Central Catholic High School
Greensburg, PA

Gisela Schubert
New Milford High School
New Milford, CT

Rolf M. Schwägermann
Stuyvesant High School
New York, NY

Esther Spease
Luverne High School
Luverne, MN

Margaret G. Thatcher
Newtown Junior High School
Newtown, PA

Mary Ann Verkamp
Hamilton Southeastern High School
Fishers, IN

Jim Witt
Grand Junction High School
Grand Junction, CO

FIELD TEST PARTICIPANTS
We express our appreciation to the teachers and students who participated in the field test. Their comments were instrumental in the development of this book.

Eva-Maria Adolphi
Indian Hills Middle School
Sandy, UT

Connie Allison
MacArthur High School
Lawton, OK

Dennis Bergren
West High School
Madison, WI

Margaret S. Draheim
Wilson Junior High School
Appleton, WI

Petra A. Hansen
Redmond High School
Redmond, WA

Christa Hary
Brien McMahon High School
Norwalk, CT

Ingrid S. Kinner
Weaver Education Center
Greensboro, NC

Diane E. Laumer
San Marcos High School
San Marcos, TX

Judith A. Lidicker
Central High School
West Allis, WI

Linnea Maulding
Fife High School
Tacoma, WA

Jane Reinkordt
Lincoln Southeast High School
Lincoln, NE

Elizabeth A. Smith
Plano Senior High School
Plano, TX

TO THE STUDENT

Some people have the opportunity to learn a new language by living in another country. Most of us, however, begin learning another language and getting acquainted with a foreign culture in a classroom with the help of a teacher, classmates, and a textbook. To use your book effectively, you need to know how it works.

Komm mit! (*Come along*) is organized to help you learn German and become familiar with the culture of the people who speak German. The Preliminary Chapter presents basic concepts in German and strategies for learning a new language. This chapter is followed by four Location Openers and twelve chapters.

Location Opener Four four-page photo essays called Location Openers introduce different states or cities in Germany.

Chapter Opener The Chapter Opener pages tell you the chapter theme and goals.

Los geht's! (*Getting started*) This illustrated story, which is also on video, shows you German-speaking people in real-life situations, using the language you'll learn in the chapter.

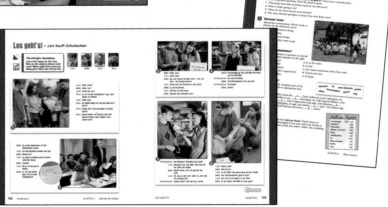

Erste, Zweite, and Dritte Stufe (*First, Second, and Third Step*) After **Los geht's!**, the chapter is divided into three sections called **Stufen**. Within the **Stufe** are **So sagt man das!** (*Here's how you say it*) boxes that contain the German expressions you'll need to communicate and **Wortschatz** and **Grammatik / Ein wenig Grammatik** boxes that give you the German words and grammar structures you'll need to know. Activities in each **Stufe** enable you to develop your skills in listening, speaking, reading, and writing.

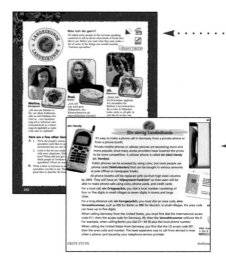

Landeskunde (*Culture*) On this page are interviews with German-speaking people. You can watch these interviews on video or listen to them on the CD-ROM Tutor, then check to see how well you understood by answering some questions about what the people say.

Ein wenig Landeskunde (*Culture Note*) In each chapter, there are notes with more information about the culture in German-speaking countries.

Zum Lesen (*For reading*) The reading section follows the three **Stufen**. The selections are related to the chapter themes and will help you develop your reading skills in German.

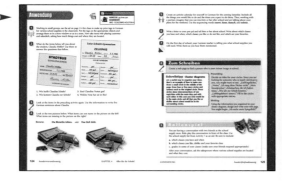

Mehr Grammatikübungen (*Additional grammar practice*) This section begins the chapter review. You will find four pages of activities that provide additional practice on the grammar concepts you learned in the chapter.

Anwendung (*Review*) The activities on these pages practice what you've learned in the chapter and help you improve your listening, reading, and comprehension skills. You'll also review what you've learned about culture. A section called **Zum Schreiben** (*Let's Write*) in chapters 3–12 will develop your writing skills.

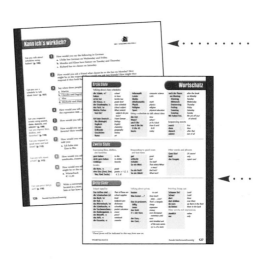

Kann ich's wirklich? (*Can I really do it? . . .*) This page at the end of each chapter contains a series of questions and short activities to help you see if you've achieved the chapter goals.

Wortschatz (*Vocabulary*) On the German-English vocabulary list on the last page of the chapter, the words are grouped by **Stufe**. These words and expressions will appear on quizzes and tests.

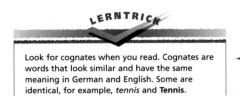

Look for cognates when you read. Cognates are words that look similar and have the same meaning in German and English. Some are identical, for example, *tennis* and **Tennis**.

Und dann noch...

Wir ...

lesen malen kochen schreiben joggen

laufen Ski laufen Rollschuh segeln fahren Rad reiten

You'll also find special features in each chapter that provide extra tips and reminders.

Lerntrick (*Learning Hint*) offers study hints to help you succeed in the foreign language class.

Und dann noch ... (*And then*) lists extra words you might find helpful. These words will not appear on quizzes and tests unless your teacher chooses to include them.

You'll also find German-English and English-German vocabulary lists at the end of the textbook. The words you'll need to know for the quizzes and tests are in boldface type.

At the end of your textbook, you'll find more helpful material, such as:
- a summary of the expressions you'll learn in the **So sagt man das!** boxes
- a summary of the grammar you'll study
- additional vocabulary words that you might want to use
- a grammar index to help you find where grammar is presented

Komm mit! Come along on an exciting trip to a new culture and a new language!

Gute Reise!

Explanation of Icons in *Komm mit!*

Throughout Komm mit! *you'll see these symbols, or icons, next to activities.*
They'll tell you what you'll probably do with that activity.
Here's a key to help you understand the icons.

 Video Whenever this icon appears, you'll know there is a related segment in the *Komm mit! Video Program*.

 Listening Activities This icon indicates a listening activity.

 Pair Work/Group Work Activities

 Writing Activities

 CD-ROM Activities Whenever this icon appears, you'll know there is a related activity on the *Komm mit! Interactive CD-ROM Tutor*.

 Übungsheft, S. 26, Ü. 2

 Grammatikheft, S. 19, Ü. 1-2

Practice Activities These icons tell you which activities from the *Übungsheft* and the *Grammatikheft* practice the material presented.

Mehr Grammatikübungen S. 88, Ü. 1

Mehr Grammatikübungen This reference tells you where you can find related additional grammar practice in the review section of the chapter.

 Internet Activities This icon provides the keyword you'll need to access related online activities at **go.hrw.com**.

Komm mit! Contents

Come along—to a world of new experiences!

Komm mit! *offers you the opportunity to learn the language spoken by millions of people in several European countries and around the world. Let's find out about the countries, the people, and the German language.*

KOMM MIT NACH
Brandenburg!
LOCATION • KAPITEL 1, 2, 3....12

KAPITEL 1
Wer bist du? 16

KAPITEL 2
Spiel und Spaß 42

KAPITEL 3
Komm mit nach Hause!.....68

KAPITEL 4
Alles für die Schule! 100

KAPITEL 5
Klamotten kaufen.....128

KAPITEL 6
Pläne machen 156

IMBISS-KARTE
Café Freizeit
Für den kleinen Hunger und Durst

KLEINE SPEISEN

NUDELSUPPE MIT BROT	€	2,25
KÄSEBROT		2,55
WURSTBROT		2,60
WIENER MIT SENF — 2 PAAR		2,90
PIZZA (15 CM)		
Nr. 1 mit Tomaten und Käse		3,00
Nr. 2 mit Wurst und Käse		3,25
Nr. 3 mit Wurst, Käse und Pilzen		4,25

EIS

FRUCHTEIS KUGEL	€	0,60
SAHNEEIS KUGEL		0,70
EISBECHER		3,40

GETRÄNKE

1 TASSE KAFFEE	€	2,15
1 KÄNNCHEN KAFFEE		3,80
1 TASSE CAPPUCCINO		2,60
1 GLAS TEE MIT ZITRONE		1,60

ALKOHOLFREIE GETRÄNKE

MINERALWASSER	0,5 l	€	1,75
LIMONADE, FANTA	0,5 l		1,80
APFELSAFT	0,2 l		1,25
COLA	0,2 l		1,50

KUCHEN

APFELKUCHEN	STÜCK	€	1,40
KÄSEKUCHEN	STÜCK		3,00

KAPITEL 7
Zu Hause helfen.....188

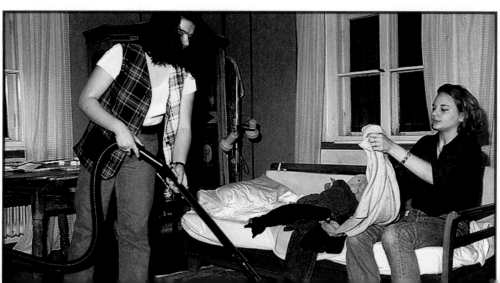

KAPITEL 8
Einkaufen gehen 216

KAPITEL 9
Amerikaner in München.....244

KAPITEL 10
Kino und Konzerte.....276

KAPITEL 11
Der Geburtstag 304

CULTURAL REFERENCES

Nordsee

N

0   50   100 Kilometer
0   50   100 Meilen

DÄNEMARK

Ostsee

NIEDERLANDE

Rhein

BELGIEN

LUX.

FRANKREICH

Ems

Weser

Hamburg

Bremen

Elbe

BUNDESREPUBLIK

DEUTSCHLAND

Havel

Oder

Berlin

Potsdam

POLEN

Oder

Spree

Düsseldorf

Ruhrgebiet

Bonn

Rhein

Mosel

Saale

Leipzig

Elbe

Dresden

Neiße

TSCHECHISCHE REPUBLIK

Frankfurt

Main

Rhein

Schwarzwald

Stuttgart

Neckar

Donau

Isar

München

Inn

Donau

Linz

Traun

Wien

SLOWA

Salzburg

Enns

Eisenstadt

ÖSTERREICH

Basel

Rhein

Aare

Zürich

St. Gallen

Bregenz

Zugspitze

Alpen

Salzach

Großvenediger

Großglockner

Alpen

Graz

UNGAR

Luzern

Vaduz

Chur

LIECHTENSTEIN

Innsbruck

Bern

SCHWEIZ

Alpen

Interlaken

Eiger

Davos

Klagenfurt

Rhône

St. Moritz

Zermatt

Matterhorn

ITALIEN

SLOWENIEN

UNGAR

KROATIEN

Komm mit!

1 Matterhorn, Schweiz

2 Innsbruck, Österreich

3 Wartburg, Deutschland

German is the native language of nearly 100 million people in Austria, Germany, Switzerland, Liechtenstein, and parts of France and Italy. It is an official language of Luxembourg and is used as a second language by many other people in central Europe.

1 **Komm mit!** *Come along!*

You are now going to take a trip to the German-speaking countries of **Deutschland**, **Österreich**, **Schweiz**, and **Liechtenstein**. As you listen to a description of these countries, try to locate on the map the places mentioned. When you have finished, do the following activities.

1. Find and identify:
   a. a non-German-speaking country west of Germany
   b. a river that runs through Germany, Austria, and Hungary
   c. a city in northern Germany; in Austria; in Liechtenstein

2. a. Look at the map on page 2. What three German cities have the status of city-states?
   b. Look at the map on page 3. What is the name of the mountain peak southwest of Zermatt, Switzerland?

Bundesrepublik Deutschland
The Federal Republic of Germany

Übungsheft, S. 1, Ü. 1

DÄNEMARK

Ostsee

0 50 100 Kilometer
0 50 100 Meilen

N

Nordsee

Kiel
SCHLESWIG-HOLSTEIN
Rostock
Lübeck
MECKLENBURG-VORPOMMERN
HAMBURG
Schwerin
Neubrandenburg

BREMEN

NIEDERSACHSEN
BUNDESREPUBLIK
BRANDENBURG
BERLIN
Hannover
Potsdam
Frankfurt a.d. Oder

POLEN

NIEDERLANDE
Braunschweig
Magdeburg
Rhein
Münster
SACHSEN-ANHALT
NORDRHEIN-WESTFALEN
Harz
Spree
Essen Dortmund
DEUTSCHLAND
Halle
Cottbus
Ruhrgebiet
Kassel
Leipzig
Neuss Düsseldorf
SACHSEN
Dresden
Köln
Erfurt
Gera
Chemnitz
Aachen
Erzgebirge
Bonn
HESSEN
Thüringer Wald
THÜRINGEN
Eifel Westerwald
Suhl
BELGIEN
Koblenz
RHEINLAND-PFALZ
Taunus
Frankfurt a. M.
Oberpfälzer Wald
TSCHECHISCHE REPUBLIK
Wiesbaden
Mainz
Würzburg
LUX.
Main
Mannheim
Nürnberg
Böhmerwald
SAARLAND
Heidelberg
Bayerischer Wald
Saarbrücken
BADEN-WÜRTTEMBERG
BAYERN
Karlsruhe
Regensburg
Stuttgart
Donau
Schwäbische Alb
FRANKREICH
Neckar
Ulm
Augsburg
Isar
Schwarzwald
Freiburg
München
Rhein
Bayerische Alpen
Salzburger Alpen
Bodensee
Zugspitze
SCHWEIZ
Rhein
ÖSTERREICH

VORSCHAU

Liechtenstein, Schweiz und Österreich

Liechtenstein, Switzerland, and Austria

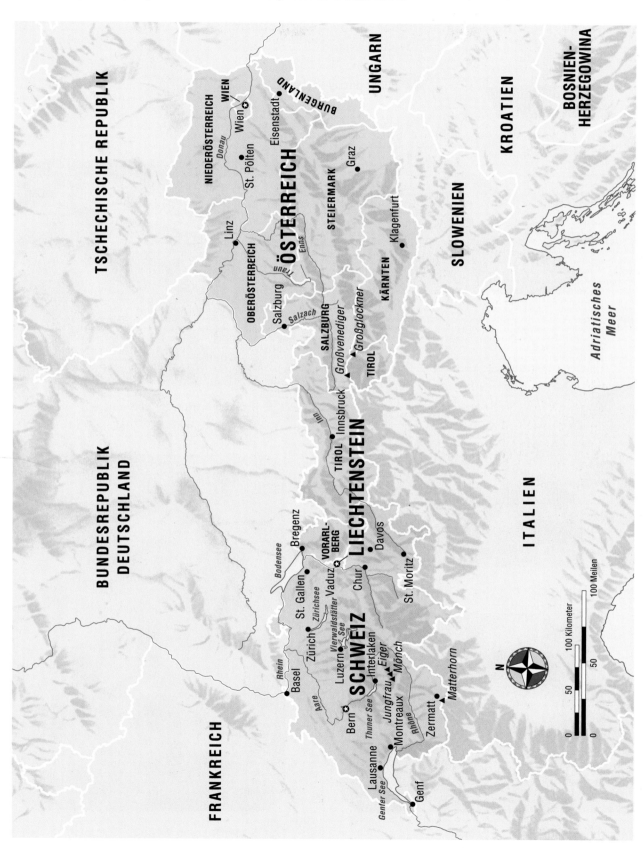

TSCHECHISCHE REPUBLIK

UNGARN

KROATIEN

BOSNIEN-HERZEGOWINA

NIEDERÖSTERREICH

WIEN

Wien

BURGENLAND

Eisenstadt

St. Pölten

Donau

ÖSTERREICH

STEIERMARK

Graz

SLOWENIEN

Linz

Enns

OBERÖSTERREICH

Traun

KÄRNTEN

Klagenfurt

Salzburg

SALZBURG

Salzach

Großvenediger

Großglockner

TIROL

Adriatisches Meer

Innsbruck

Inn

TIROL

LIECHTENSTEIN

BUNDESREPUBLIK DEUTSCHLAND

ITALIEN

Bregenz

VORARL-BERG

Davos

Bodensee

Vaduz

Chur

St. Gallen

Zürichsee

St. Moritz

Zürich

Luzern

Vierwaldstätter See

SCHWEIZ

Basel

Interlaken

Eiger

Mönch

Rhein

Aare

Bern

Thuner See

Jungfrau

Matterhorn

FRANKREICH

Lausanne

Montreux

Rhône

Zermatt

Genter See

Genf

N

100 Meilen

100 Kilometer

50

50

50

0

0

Schon einmal gesehen? · *Seen before?*

There are many things that may come to mind when you hear of places like Germany, Switzerland, Austria, and Liechtenstein. As you can see from these photos, life in these countries ranges from the very traditional to the supermodern.

1 ICE, Intercity-Express

2 Brandenburg Gate in Berlin

3 Liechtenstein

4 Matterhorn, southwest of Zermatt

5 State Opera in Vienna

4 *vier*

VORSCHAU

Bekannte Leute · *Famous people*

Through the centuries, in areas as diverse as science and sports, literature and psychology, German-speaking women and men have made invaluable contributions, both in their own countries and abroad.

1 **Albert Einstein** (1879-1955) revolutionized physics with his theory of relativity. In 1933 he emigrated to the United States and began a lifetime teaching career at the Institute for Advanced Study in Princeton, New Jersey. He received the Nobel Prize for Physics in 1921.

2 **Ludwig van Beethoven** (1770-1827) is perhaps the best-known composer of classical music. Though his hearing became increasingly impaired, he composed his greatest masterpieces during the last years of his life.

3 **Sigmund Freud** (1856-1939) is the founder of modern psychoanalysis. His theories of the unconscious, neuroses, and dreams have had a lasting impact on psychology. His daughter, **Anna Freud** (1895-1982), helped develop the study of child psychology.

4 **Steffi Graf** (1969-), one of the world's greatest tennis players, has won over one thousand career titles, including 7 victories at Wimbledon, 5 French Opens, 5 U.S. Opens, 4 Australian Opens, 21 Grand Slams, and Olympic Gold in 1988.

5 **Annette von Droste-Hülshoff** (1797-1848) was one of the leading writers of nineteenth-century Germany. She is remembered for both her poetry and her prose, her best-known work being the novella **Die Judenbuche**.

6 **Günter Grass** (1927-) is a major figure in contemporary German literature. Many of his works are controversial and deal with such issues as Germany's struggle with its Nazi past. Two well-known works are **Die Blechtrommel** and **Katz und Maus**. In 1998, Grass won the Nobel Prize for Literature for his lifetime achievement in German literature.

Das Alphabet ▪ *The alphabet*

2 **Richtig aussprechen** *Pronounce correctly*

The letters of the German alphabet are almost the same as those in English, but the pronunciation is different. Listen to the rhyme and learn the alphabet the way many children in German-speaking countries learn it. Then pronounce each letter after your teacher or after the recording.

a b c d e,

**der Kopf tut
mir weh,**

f g h i j k,

**der Doktor
ist da,**

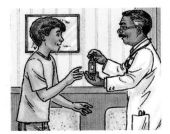

l m n o,

**jetzt bin ich
froh,**

p q r s t,

**es ist wieder
gut, juchhe!**

u v w x,

**jetzt fehlt
mir nix,**

y z,

**jetzt geh ich
ins Bett.**

There are a few more things you should remember about German spelling and pronunciation.

a. The letter ß (Eszett) is often used in place of the "double s" (ss) in German spelling. However, the ß cannot always be substituted for the "double s", so it is important that as you build your German vocabulary you remember which words are spelled with ß.

b. Many German words are spelled and pronounced with an umlaut (¨) over the a, o, or u (ä, ö, ü). The umlaut changes the sound of the vowels, as in **Käse**, **Österreich**, and **grün.** You will learn more about the use of the umlaut in the **Aussprache** sections of the book.

3 **Deutsche Abkürzungen** *German abbreviations*

Listen to how these common abbreviations are pronounced in German.

VW   BMW   USA   BRD   ADAC   BASF

Wie heißt du? · *What's your name?*

4 **Hör gut zu!** *Listen carefully*

a. Listen and try to figure out what these students are saying.

Mädchen: Hallo! Wie heißt du?
Junge: Ich heiße Holger. Und du?
Wie heißt du?
Mädchen: Ich heiße Handan.

b. Below are some popular first names of German girls and boys.
Listen to how they are pronounced.

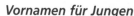

Vornamen für Mädchen	
Daniela	Julia
Marina	Inge
Michaela	Christiane
Nicole	Claudia
Ute	Gisela
Silke	Antje
Ulrike	Kristin
Karin	Katja
Birgit	Sara
Christine	

Vornamen für Jungen	
Mark	Jens
Sven	Peter
Jörg	Daniel
Holger	Andreas
Stefan	Manfred
Jochen	Uwe
Christof	Christian
Michael	Alexander
Benjamin	Sebastian

c. Pick a German name for yourself and practice pronouncing it.

5 **Namenkette** *Name chain*

One student begins the "name chain" by asking the name of the person next to him or her. That student answers and then asks the next person until everyone has had a turn. Students who wish to do so may use the German name they chose in Activity 4c above.

BEISPIEL   **Ich heiße Antje. Wie heißt du?**

6 **Wie heißt mein Partner?** *What's my partner's name?*

In this book you will be asked many times to work with a partner to find out new information and to practice the new things you are learning. Find a partner who sits near you and ask that person his or her name. Then he or she will ask you.

Im Klassenzimmer · *In the classroom*

Übungsheft, S. 2, Ü. 2

7 **Was ist das?** *What's that?*

a. As you look at the picture to the right, listen to the way the names of the classroom objects are pronounced.

b. Pick one of the objects in the illustration and write the German word for it on an index card. When your teacher calls out that object, place your card next to the correct object in your classroom.

c. Take turns asking a partner what the different objects in the classroom are called. As you point to something, you will ask: **Was ist das?** and your partner will answer in German.

das Fenster · die Tür · die Tafel · der Tisch · der Stuhl · das Buch · der Bleistift · der Kuli · ein Stück Papier

Ausdrücke fürs Klassenzimmer
Expressions for the classroom

Here are some common expressions your teacher might use in the classroom:

Öffnet eure Bücher auf Seite …!	*Open your books to page …*
Nehmt ein Stück Papier!	*Take out a piece of paper.*
einen Bleistift!	*a pencil.*
einen Kuli!	*a pen.*
Steht auf!	*Stand up.*
Setzt euch!	*Sit down.*
Hört zu!	*Listen.*
Schreibt euren Namen!	*Write down your names.*
Passt auf!	*Pay attention.*
Geht an die Tafel!	*Go to the chalkboard.*

Here are some phrases you might want to use when talking to your teacher.

Wie sagt man …auf Deutsch?	*How do you say …in German?*
Was bedeutet …?	*What does …mean?*
Wie bitte?	*Excuse me?*

8 **Simon sagt …** *Simon says …*

Look over the classroom expressions for a few minutes. Now your teacher will give everyone in the class instructions in German, but you should do only what your teacher says if he or she first says **Simon sagt …**

BEISPIEL   LEHRER(IN)   **Simon sagt, steht auf!**
Everyone in the class stands up.

VORSCHAU

Die Zahlen von 0 bis 20 · *The numbers from 0 to 20*

9 **Hör gut zu!** *Listen carefully!*

Listen to how the numbers below are pronounced. Then read each number.

Wortschatz

0	1	2	3	4	5	6	7	8	9	10
null	eins	zwei	drei	vier	fünf	sechs	sieben	acht	neun	zehn

11	12	13	14	15	16	17	18	19	20
elf	zwölf	dreizehn	vierzehn	fünfzehn	sechzehn	siebzehn	achtzehn	neunzehn	zwanzig

Ein wenig Landeskunde

Look again at how the numbers are written in German. Pay particular attention to the numbers 1 and 7. When using hand signals to indicate numbers or when counting on their fingers, Germans use the thumb to indicate one, the thumb and the index finger to indicate two, and so on. How do you indicate numbers with your fingers?

10 **Wir üben mit Zahlen!** *Practicing with numbers*

Übungsheft, S. 2, Ü. 3

a. Each person in the class will count off in sequence: first student **eins**, second student **zwei**, etc. When you reach 20, start again with number one.

b. With a partner, count aloud the girls, then the boys in your class.

c. Tell your partner your phone number one digit at a time. Your partner will write it down, say it back to you, and then tell you his or her telephone number.

11 **Zahlenlotto** *Number Game*

Draw a rectangle and divide it into sixteen squares as shown. Number the squares randomly, using numbers between 0 and 20. Use each number only once. Your teacher will call numbers in random order. As you hear each number, mark the corresponding square. The winner is the first person to mark off four numbers in a vertical, horizontal, or diagonal row.

8	2	5	13
7	1	6	4
9	10	3	19
18	11	16	12

Warum Deutsch lernen? ▪ *Why learn German?*

Americans of German-speaking descent

Can you guess how many Americans trace all or part of their ethnic background to Germany, Austria, or Switzerland? — 10 million? 30 million? 50 million? If you guessed 50 million, you were close! Forty-nine million people, or about 20% of the population, reported that they were at least partly of German, Swiss, or Austrian descent.

The early settlers

Germans were among the earliest settlers in the United States. In 1683, the first group arrived from Krefeld and founded Germantown, Pennsylvania. Since 1683 more than seven million German-speaking immigrants have come to this country.

German towns and German words

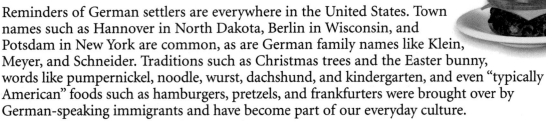

Reminders of German settlers are everywhere in the United States. Town names such as Hannover in North Dakota, Berlin in Wisconsin, and Potsdam in New York are common, as are German family names like Klein, Meyer, and Schneider. Traditions such as Christmas trees and the Easter bunny, words like pumpernickel, noodle, wurst, dachshund, and kindergarten, and even "typically American" foods such as hamburgers, pretzels, and frankfurters were brought over by German-speaking immigrants and have become part of our everyday culture.

German and your career

German might play an important role in your future. Many employers consider knowledge of German to be an asset. You could use German in many professions — as a teacher, professor, librarian, travel agent, lawyer, buyer, economist, publisher, journalist, translator, flight attendant, engineer, doctor — and, of course, tour guide. Many high-tech companies name German as the language they prefer prospective employees to study. More than 1200 American companies have offices in German-speaking countries, and over 140,000 Americans live and work there.

November, 1989: The fall of the Berlin Wall

Berlin today: new buildings on Potsdamer Platz, again the hub of the city

Modern Germany

Above all, NOW is a great time to discover German. With the disappearance of the "iron curtain," you can travel freely in the former German Democratic Republic (East Germany), where travel was restricted for over 40 years. History-making events like the fall of the Berlin Wall and the unification of Germany in 1991 make this an interesting time to study German. Germany, together with most other European countries, has adopted the euro as its currency, opening up new opportunities for commerce and trade. To find out more about German-speaking countries and the language, **Komm mit!** (*Come along*), and learn German.

Tipps fürs Deutschlernen
Tips for studying German

Listen

It's important to listen carefully and take notes in class. Ask questions if you don't understand, even if you think your question is silly. Other people are probably wondering the same thing! You won't be able to understand everything you hear, but don't get frustrated. You're actually absorbing the language even when you don't realize it.

Speak

Practice speaking German every day. Talking with your teachers and classmates is an easy and fun way to learn. Don't be afraid to take risks when speaking! Your mistakes will help you identify problems and will show you important differences between the structure of German and English.

Practice

Learning a new language is like learning to play a sport or an instrument. You can't spend one night practicing and then expect to play perfectly the next morning. You didn't learn English that way either! Short, daily study sessions are more effective than once-a-week cramming sessions. Also, try to practice with a friend or a classmate, since language is all about communication.

Expand

Increase your contact with German outside of class in every way you can. Look for German programs such as **Deutsche Welle** on TV, or rent German-language videos and DVDs. Magazines and newspapers in German are available at libraries and bookstores in the United States. The Internet is another source for German-language material, including German websites with video or radio broadcasts. You won't understand every word, but you can get a lot out of a story or an article by concentrating on words you recognize and doing a little guesswork.

Organize

It's important to be organized and efficient when learning. Throughout the textbook you'll see tips for learning, speaking, reading, and writing (**Lerntrick, Sprachtipp, Lesestrategie, Schreibtipp**) that will help you study smart. For starters, try looking for cognates. Cognates are words that look similar and have the same meaning in German and English, such as **Musik** and *music*. By recognizing which words are cognates, you can then spend your time studying the words that look completely unfamiliar.

Connect

Because English is a Germanic language, your knowledge of English can give you clues about the meanings of German words such as **Bäckerei** (*bakery*) and **schwimmen** (*to swim*). Some German and English words have roots in Latin or Greek, such as **Atmosphäre** and *atmosphere* or **Ökonomie** and *economy*. You may find that learning German will help you in English class!

Have fun!

Above all, remember to have fun! The more you try, the more you'll learn. **Viel Glück!** (*Good luck!*), and **Komm mit!** (*Come along!*)

Komm mit nach Brandenburg!

Population: 2.64 million

Area: 29,056 square kilometers (11,216 square miles), approximately as large as the state of Maryland

Capital: Potsdam (176,000 inhabitants)

Cities: Cottbus, Brandenburg, Frankfurt an der Oder

Rivers: Oder, Havel, Spree

Canals: Oder-Spree-Kanal, Rhinkanal, Oder-Havel-Kanal

Lakes: Ruppiner See, Werbellinsee, Schwielochsee, Plauer See

Industries: Textiles, machinery, cement, porcelain, farming, forestry, petroleum, coal

Favorite local dishes: Lentil soup, chicken fricassee

go.
hrw.
com

WK3 BRANDENBURG

VIDEO

CD-ROM DISC 1

Die Terrassen von Schloss Sanssouci ▶ in Potsdam

Brandenburg

Brandenburg, the heartland of former Prussia, is a state characterized by vast flat sandy lands, hundreds of beautiful lakes, and large wooded areas consisting mostly of fir trees. A trip through the towns in Brandenburg reveals stately buildings and churches in characteristic red brick, waiting to be restored to their former beauty.

1 **Schloss Branitz in Cottbus**
Built in 1772, this castle, now a museum, is located in a beautiful nineteenth-century park.

2 **Eine Marmorstatue Friedrichs des Großen**
Sculpted by Joseph Uphues

3 **Neue Kammern und Historische Mühle**
This new wing of Sanssouci Palace was built in 1747. The Historic Windmill was renovated in 1992.

4 Schloss Cecilienhof
This palace was built for the last German emperor Wilhelm II. between 1913 and 1917. Here the Allied powers signed the Potsdam Agreement in 1945.

5 Schiffshebewerk am Oder-Havel-Kanal in Neufinow
This ship hoist makes it possible for barges to transport bulk goods such as coal, sand, or gravel through a network of canals.

Kapitel 1, 2, 3

The students in the following three chapters live in the Potsdam area. Potsdam is the capital of Brandenburg. In 1993, Potsdam celebrated its 1000th birthday. The city became famous when Frederick the Great decided to establish his summer residence there and built Sanssouci Palace.

6 Ahmet, Jens, Handan, Tara, Holger, and Steffi invite you to Potsdam.

fünfzehn **15**

1
Wer bist du?

Objectives

In this chapter you will learn to

Erste Stufe

- say hello and goodbye
- ask someone's name and give yours
- ask who someone is

Zweite Stufe

- ask someone's age and give yours

Dritte Stufe

- talk about where people are from
- talk about how someone gets to school

 internet

 ADRESSE: go.hrw.com
KENNWORT:
   WK3 BRANDENBURG-1

◀ **Ich bin Holger. Wer bist du?**

siebzehn **17**

Los geht's! · *Vor der Schule*

Strategie Verstehen

Look at the photos for this story. Where and when do you think these scenes are taking place? What clues tell you this?

Jens   **Tara**   **Holger**   **Ahmet**

1

Tara: Hallo, Jens!

Jens: Hallo!

Tara: Ist das dein Moped?

Jens: Ja.

Tara: Super! Klasse!

Jens: Ich komme jetzt immer mit dem Moped zur Schule.

Tara: Ach ja! Du bist jetzt sechzehn!

2

Jens: Hallo! Wer bist du denn? Bist du neu hier?

Holger: Ja, ich bin neu hier.

Jens: Und wie heißt du?

Holger: Ich heiße Holger.

Jens: Ich bin Jens.

3

Jens: Das ist Tara.

Holger: Morgen, Tara!

Tara: Guten Morgen, Holger! Woher kommst du denn?

Holger: Aus Walburg.

Jens: Walburg? Walburg? Wo liegt denn Walburg?

Holger: In Hessen.

Tara: Schau mal! Da kommt der Ahmet. Hallo, Ahmet!

Ahmet: Hallo, Tara! Hallo, Jens! Was gibt's?

Jens: Sag mal, Ahmet, ist morgen Training?

Ahmet: Ja, klar! Um 3 Uhr.

Holger: Ich bin Holger. Wie heißt du?

Ahmet: Ahmet. Ahmet Özkan.

Holger: Wie bitte? Öz …

Tara: Ich buchstabier's für dich. Ö-Z-K-A-N. Stimmt doch, oder?

Ahmet: Ja, das stimmt!

Holger: Also, einfach! Und woher bist du?

Ahmet: Aus der Türkei.

Jens: Ahmet ist der beste Mann bei uns im Team. Die Nummer „Eins"!

Holger: Ja, prima!

Ahmet: Schon gut, tschüs!

Tara: Tschüs!

Holger: Tschüs!

Übungsheft, S. 3

1 Was passiert hier? *What's happening here?*

Do you understand what is happening in **Los geht's!**? Check your comprehension by answering these questions. Don't be afraid to guess.

1. What happens at the beginning of the story?
2. Why is Jens' age important?
3. What do you learn about the new student?
4. What information does Ahmet have for Jens? What "team" do you think they are talking about?

2 Genauer lesen *Reading for detail*

Reread the conversations. Which words or phrases do the characters in **Los geht's!** use to

1. greet each other
2. ask someone's name
3. ask where someone is from
4. ask where a place is
5. say goodbye

3 Stimmt oder stimmt nicht? *Right or wrong?*

Are these statements right or wrong? Answer each one with either **stimmt** or **stimmt nicht**. If a statement is wrong, try to state it correctly.

1. Jens ist jetzt sechzehn und kommt mit dem Moped zur Schule.
2. Ahmet ist neu in der Schule.
3. Walburg ist in Bayern.
4. Tara und Holger haben morgen Training.
5. Ahmet kommt aus der Türkei.

4 Wer macht was? *Who is doing what?*

What have you learned about each of these students? Match the descriptions on the right with the names on the left, then read each completed sentence.

1. Holger
2. Tara
3. Jens
4. Ahmet

a. …ist jetzt sechzehn und kommt mit dem Moped zur Schule.
b. …ist der beste Mann im Team.
c. …buchstabiert den Namen von Ahmet.
d. …ist neu in der Schule.

5 Wer bist du denn? *Who are you?*

Using words from the box, complete this conversation between two new students.

ULRIKE   Hallo! Ich ___1___ Ulrike. Wer bist ___2___ denn? Bist du ___3___ hier?

GUPSE   Ja, ich heiße Gupse. Ich ___4___ aus der Türkei. ___5___ kommst du?

ULRIKE   ___6___ Hessen.

GUPSE   Schau mal! ___7___ ist das?

ULRIKE   Das ist die Birgit. Sie ___8___ sechzehn und kommt ___9___ dem Moped zur Schule. Toll, was?

mit   Woher   Aus
du   Wer   heiße
komme   ist   neu

So sagt man das! *Here's how you say it!*

Saying hello and goodbye

Saying hello:

Guten Morgen! *Good morning!*
Morgen! *Morning!*
Guten Tag! *Hello!*
Tag!
Hallo! } *Hi!*
Grüß dich!

Saying goodbye:

Auf Wiedersehen! *Goodbye!*
Wiedersehen! *Bye!*

Tschüs! }
Tschau! } *Bye!*
Bis dann! *See you later!*

> Übungsheft, S. 4, Ü. 2–3
> Grammatikheft, S. 1, Ü. 1–2

---

6 **Hallo! oder Tschüs!**

Zuhören Listen to the following people greet each other or say goodbye. For each exchange you hear, write whether it is a **hello** or a **goodbye**.

Ein wenig Landeskunde

(About the country and the people)

Guten Morgen! and **Guten Tag!** are standard greetings and can be used in almost any social situation. With whom do you think you might use the abbreviated forms **Morgen!** and **Tag!**? The phrases **Hallo!** and **Grüß dich!** are casual and are generally used with friends and family. **Grüß dich!** is heard more in southern Germany and Austria. **Auf Wiedersehen!**, **Wiedersehen!**, and **Tschüs!** are all ways of saying goodbye. Which of the three do you think would be the most formal? If you were going to greet a fellow student and good friend, and then say goodbye, which phrases would you use?

Grüß dich, Klaus!

Guten Tag, Frau Müller!

Auf Wiedersehen, Herr Kießling!

Tschau, Silvia!

7 Hallo!

Lesen Here you see some friends greeting each other and saying goodbye. Match the exchanges with the appropriate pictures.

a.

b.

c.

d.

1. —Tschüs, Lisa!
    —Tschau, Christian!

2. —Wiedersehen, Frau Weber!
    —Auf Wiedersehen, Peter!

3. —Tag, Alexander! Sebastian!
    —Tag, Julia!

4. —Guten Morgen, Herr Koschizki!
    —Morgen, Elisabeth!

8 Freunde begrüßen *Greeting friends*

Sprechen Make a name tag for yourself, using your own name or one chosen from the list in the **Vorschau**. Get together with a few of your classmates. For more German first names, turn to page R14 in the back of your book. Greet and say goodbye to each other, using the names on the tags. Don't forget to greet and say goodbye to your teacher.

Was sagt Anna zum Monster mit den drei Köpfen?

So sagt man das! *Here's how you say it!*

Asking someone's name and giving yours

When you meet a new student you'll want to find out his or her name.

You ask:

Wie heißt du? *What's your name?*

You might also ask:

Heißt du Holger? *Is your name Holger?*

To ask a boy's name:

Wie heißt der Junge?
Heißt der Junge Ahmet?
    Is that boy's name Ahmet?

To ask a girl's name:

Wie heißt das Mädchen?
Heißt das Mädchen Ulrike?

The student responds:

Ich heiße Holger.

Ja, ich heiße Holger.

Der Junge heißt Ahmet.
Ja, er heißt Ahmet.

Das Mädchen heißt Steffi.
Nein, sie heißt Steffi.

Grammatikheft, S. 2, Ü. 3–4

9 Was sagen sie?

Zuhören To complete these conversations, match each exchange you hear with the correct illustration.

a.

b.

c.

d.

Grammatik

Forming questions

There are several ways of asking questions in German. One way is to begin with a question word (interrogative) such as **wie** (*how*). Some other question words are: **wer** (*who*), **wo** (*where*), and **woher** (*from where*).

Look at the questions below. How are they different from questions such as **Wie heißt der Junge?**[1] What is the position of the verb in these questions?[2]

Heißt du Holger?   **Ja, ich heiße Holger.**
Heißt das Mädchen Kristin?   **Nein, sie heißt Antje.**

Mehr Grammatikübungen
S. 36, Ü. 1–2

Grammatikheft, S. 3, Ü. 5

10 Wie heißt er? Wie heißt sie?

Sprechen How well do you remember the names of your classmates? When someone asks you: **Wie heißt das Mädchen?** or **Wie heißt der Junge?**, give the name of the person referred to. For practice, use complete sentences.

So sagt man das!

Asking who someone is

Grammatikheft, S. 3, Ü. 6

To find out someone else's name you ask: **Wer ist das?**

The response might be:

Das ist die Moni.

Das ist der Stefan.

Das ist Herr Gärtner, der Deutschlehrer.

Das ist Frau Weigel, die Biologielehrerin.

---

1. These questions anticipate *yes* or *no* as a response.
2. The verb is always at the beginning of a *yes/no* question.

The definite articles **der**, **die**, and **das**

German has three words for *the*: **der**, **die**, and **das**, called *definite articles*. These words tell us to which class or group a German noun belongs. Words that have **der** as the article, such as **der Junge** (*the boy*), are masculine nouns. Words that have the article **die**, such as **die Lehrerin** (*the female teacher*), are feminine nouns. The third group of nouns has the article **das**, as in **das Mädchen** (*the girl*), and are neuter nouns. You will learn more about this in **Kapitel 3.**

der-words (*masculine*)	**die**-words (*feminine*)	**das**-words (*neuter*)
der Junge		das Mädchen
der Lehrer	die Lehrerin	
der Deutschlehrer	die Deutschlehrerin	

Mehr Grammatikübungen
S. 36, Ü. 3

Übungsheft, S. 5, Ü. 4–6

11 Grammatik im Kontext

Zuhören Holger is asking Jens and Tara about various people in the class. Listen and decide whether the person they are talking about is male or female.

12 Grammatik im Kontext

Lesen/Schreiben Holger is trying to learn the names of everyone in his class. He asks Tara for help. Rewrite the conversation, filling in the missing definite articles **der**, **die**, or **das.**

HOLGER Wie heißt der Junge?
TARA ___**1**___ Junge heißt Uwe.
___**2**___ Uwe kommt aus München.
HOLGER Und ___**3**___ Mädchen?
TARA ___**4**___ Mädchen heißt Katja. ___**5**___ Katja kommt aus Hamburg.
HOLGER Und wie heißt ___**6**___ Lehrerin?
TARA ___**7**___ Lehrerin heißt Frau Möller.

Ein wenig Landeskunde

In casual speech, the definite articles **der** and **die** are often used with first names (**Das ist die Tara. Das ist der Jens.**). This practice occurs more often in southern Germany, Austria, and Switzerland than in northern Germany. **Der** and **die** are also often used with the last names of celebrities and other well-known people. How would you refer to **Steffi Graf**?

13 Wer sind meine Mitschüler?

Who are my classmates?

Sprechen Now team up with a classmate and ask each other the names of other students in the class. Be sure to use all of the ways of asking you have learned.

14 Ratespiel *Guessing Game*

Sprechen Bring in pictures of well-known people and ask your classmates to identify them.

LERNTRICK

In English, we know that the word "the" signals a noun. In German, we use **der**, **die**, and **das** in much the same way. Remember that in German, every time you learn a new noun, you must also learn the definite article (**der**, **die**, or **das**) that goes with it.

So sagt man das!

Asking someone's age and giving yours

To find out how old someone is, you might ask:

Wie alt bist du?

You might get responses like these:

> **Ich bin vierzehn Jahre alt.**
> *I am 14 years old.*
> **Ich bin vierzehn.**
> **Vierzehn.**

Bist du schon fünfzehn?
Are you already 15?

Nein, ich bin vierzehn.

Wie alt ist der Peter?

Er ist fünfzehn.

Und die Monika? Ist sie auch fünfzehn?

Ja, sie ist auch fünfzehn.

Can you identify the verbs in the different examples?[1]
Why do you think the verbs change?[2]

Grammatikheft, S. 4, Ü. 7

Wortschatz

Do you remember the numbers you learned in the Vorschau?

0 null	1 eins	2 zwei	3 drei	4 vier	5 fünf
6 sechs	7 sieben	8 acht	9 neun	10 zehn	11 elf
12 zwölf	13 dreizehn	14 vierzehn	15 fünfzehn	16 sechzehn	17 siebzehn
18 achtzehn	19 neunzehn	20 zwanzig			

Übungsheft, S. 6, Ü. 7   *Grammatikheft, S. 4, Ü. 8*

---

15 **Wie alt?**

Zuhören Holger wants to get to know his new classmates, so he asks Ahmet how old everyone is. Listen to their conversation and write down the ages of the students below.

Handan: _____   Ahmet: _____   Renate: _____   Jens: _____

16 **Wir stellen vor** *Introducing*

Sprechen Ask your partner's name and age and then introduce him or her to the rest of the class.

---

1. The verbs are **bist**, **bin**, **ist**. 2. The verbs change because the subjects of the sentences change.

Grammatik

Subject pronouns and the verb **sein** (*to be*)

The phrases **ich bin, du bist, er ist, sie ist,** and **sie sind** each contain a subject pronoun corresponding to the English *I, you, he, she,* and *they,* and a form of the verb **sein** (*to be*): *I am, you are, he is, she is, they are.* **Sein** is one of the most frequently used verbs in German.*

Ich	**bin**	dreizehn.
Du	**bist**	auch dreizehn.
Karola Sie	**ist**	vierzehn.
Jens Er	**ist**	sechzehn.
Ahmet und Holger Sie	**sind**	sechzehn.

Mehr Grammatikübungen S. 36–37, Ü. 4–5

Übungsheft, S. 6–7, Ü. 8–11

Grammatikheft, S. 5, Ü. 9–10

---

17 **Grammatik im Kontext**

Zuhören Listen to the following sentences and determine if Ulrike is talking about herself, about one other person, or about more than one person.

	about self	about one person	about more than one person
1			
2			

18 **Grammatik im Kontext**

Lesen/Schreiben Fill in the missing forms of **sein** in this conversation between Ahmet and Holger.

> HOLGER Sag mal, wie alt ___1___ du?
>
> AHMET Ich ___2___ 16.
>
> HOLGER Du ___3___ 16? Ich auch. Und wie alt ___4___ Tara und Jens?
>
> AHMET Tara ___5___ 14, und Jens ___6___ 16.

19 **Wie alt sind die Jungen und Mädchen?**

Sprechen Say who these people are and how old they are.

Steffi, 15

Melanie und Katja, 16

Björn, 16

Karola, 14

20 **Zum Schreiben**

 Schreiben You are preparing for a conversation with an exchange student from Germany. Write in German the questions you want to ask in order to find out the student's name and age. Then write how you would answer those questions yourself.

---

*There are three other forms of **sein** you will learn about and practice later: **wir sind** (*we are*), **ihr seid** (*you are, plural*) and **Sie sind** (*you are, formal*).

21 **Lesen/Schreiben** The **Bundesrepublik Deutschland** (*Federal Republic of Germany*) is made up of **Bundesländer** (*federal states*). Each **Bundesland** has a **Hauptstadt** (*capital*) and its own regional government. The **Bundesrepublik Deutschland** is abbreviated **BRD**.

a. How many **Bundesländer** are there? Make a list of them.

b. Write the **Hauptstadt** beside the name of each **Bundesland.**

c. Which **Bundesland** borders Switzerland? Austria?

d. What are the **Hauptstädte** of Switzerland and Austria?

Kiel
SCHLESWIG-HOLSTEIN

MECKLENBURG-VORPOMMERN
Schwerin

HAMBURG
BREMEN
NIEDERSACHSEN

BRANDENBURG

Wiebke Jansen, 16

Hannover

Magdeburg
SACHSEN-ANHALT

Potsdam
BERLIN

Jörg Schulze, 19

NORDRHEIN-WESTFALEN

Düsseldorf

HESSEN

Erfurt
THÜRINGEN

Dresden
SACHSEN

Kemal Acar, 15

RHEINLAND-PFALZ

Wiesbaden

Brigitte Dennhöffer, 19

Mainz

SAAR-LAND
Saar-brücken

Stuttgart

BAYERN

Wien ⊙

München

Melina Kiritsis, 18

BADEN-WÜRTTEMBERG

Zürich

Bern ⊙   SCHWEIZ   LIECHTENSTEIN

ÖSTERREICH

⊙—Vaduz

So sagt man das!

Talking about where people are from

To find out where someone is from you might ask:

Woher kommst du? *or*
Woher bist du?
Bist du aus Deutschland?

The other person might respond:

Ich komme aus Texas.
Ich bin aus Texas.
Nein, ich bin aus Wisconsin.

To find out where someone else is from you ask:

Und Herr Gärtner, der Deutschlehrer, woher ist er?
Kommt die Inge auch aus Österreich?

Er ist aus Österreich.

Nein, sie kommt aus Thüringen.

Übungsheft,
S. 9, Ü. 14–15

Grammatikheft,
S. 6–7, Ü. 11–13

What do you think the question word **woher** is equivalent to in English?[1]

Schülerausweis I | POTSDAM

gültig bis: 31. 7. 00
00

gültig bis: 31. 7. 01
01

gültig bis: 31. 7. 02
02

Schulstempel/Unterschrift
POTSDAM

Schul II 285-1 – Schülerausweis (2. 92)
Mat. 325. 0 9 8 7 6 5 4 3 2

22 Woher kommen sie?

Zuhören Look at the map on page 27 as you listen to the five students introducing themselves. For each introduction, write the name of the student who is speaking and where he or she is from.

23 Woher sind sie?

a. **Sprechen** Look at the photos of the people on page 27. Take turns asking and telling your partner about each person pictured, mentioning name, age, and where that person is from.

b. **Sprechen** Ask your partner where he or she is from, and your partner will ask you. Be prepared to share your partner's answer with the class.

c. **Sprechen** One student begins by calling on a classmate. That person says his or her name, age, and where he or she is from, then calls on someone else.

---

1. Woher? asks the question *From where?*

24 **Rate mal**

 Sprechen/Schreiben Choose one of the **Landeshauptstädte** from the box below and write it down. The city you choose is your imaginary hometown. Your partner will try to guess where you are from. If he or she guesses incorrectly, you can say **Nein, ich komme nicht aus …** After your partner guesses correctly, switch roles and guess where your partner is from.

Erfurt	Magdeburg	Mainz	Dresden	Berlin	Wiesbaden
Düsseldorf	Saarbrücken	Hamburg	Hannover		
Kiel	Stuttgart	Potsdam	Schwerin	Bremen	München

25 **Woher kommst du?**

 Lesen/Schreiben A classmate, Birgit, slips Holger the following note in class.

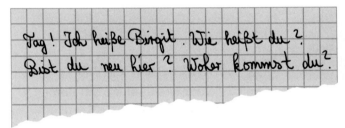

Tag! Ich heiße Birgit. Wie heißt du?
Bist du neu hier? Woher kommst du?

What does Holger write back to her? Write his note.

a. **Schreiben** Choose three of the students shown on the map on page 27 as possible pen pals and write three sentences about each of them, telling their names, ages, and where they are from.

SPRACHTIPP

There are many short words in German that you can use to connect your ideas and to make your German sound more natural. Some of these words are: **und** (*and*), **auch** (*also*), **jetzt** (*now*), and **schon** (*already*).

The teenagers in the **Los geht's!** section also used some other expressions: **Ach so!** (*Yeah, I see!*), **Ach ja!** (*Oh, yeah!*), **Ja, klar!** (*Of course!*), and **Prima!** (*Great!*). Look back at the conversations in **Los geht's!** and see how these words are used.

26 **Zum Schreiben**

 a. **Schreiben** Choose three of the students shown on the map on page 27 as possible pen pals and write three sentences about each of them, telling their names, ages, and where they are from.

 b. **Lesen/Schreiben** Exchange papers with a partner and read your partner's sentences. Is everything written correctly? Make corrections on your partner's paper and he or she will do the same on your paper.

c. **Schreiben** Now write a few sentences about yourself that you might use in a letter to one of these people, giving the same information.

DRITTE STUFE

neunundzwanzig **29**

Wie kommen die Mädchen und Jungen zur Schule?

Annette kommt **mit dem Bus.**

Michael kommt **mit der U-Bahn.**

Philipp kommt **mit dem Rad.**

Sara kommt **zu Fuß.**

Meine Mutter bringt mich **mit dem Auto.**

Und Heike kommt **mit dem Moped.**

27 Stimmt! oder Stimmt nicht!

Zuhören Based on the information given in the **Wortschatz**, determine whether the statements you hear are right or not. List the names you hear and write beside the name **stimmt** if the information is correct or **stimmt nicht** if it is incorrect.

So sagt man das!

Talking about how someone gets to school

To find out how someone gets to school you ask:

Wie kommst du zur Schule?
Kommt Ahmet zu Fuß zur Schule?

Wie kommt Ayla zur Schule?
Und wie kommt der Wolfgang zur Schule?

The responses might be:

Ich komme mit dem Rad.
Nein, er kommt auch mit dem Rad.
Sie kommt mit dem Bus.
Er kommt mit der U-Bahn oder mit dem Bus.

Mehr Grammatikübungen
S. 37, Ü. 6–7

Übungsheft, S. 8, Ü. 12–13

Grammatikheft, S. 8, Ü. 14–16

LANDESKUNDE LANDESKUNDE

CD-ROM DISC 1

VIDEO

Übungsheft, S. 12, Ü. 19

Wie kommst du zur Schule?

In Germany, many people of all ages ride bicycles—to school, to work, even to do their shopping. Why do you think this might be so? In addition to bicycles, there are a number of other possibilities available to German students for getting to and from school. Students who are at least 16 can drive a **Moped,** 14-year-olds can ride **Mofas,** and students 18 or over can get a driver's license for a car. We asked several students around Germany about how they get to school; here are their responses.

Christina, Bietigheim

„Ich heiße Christina, bin 17 Jahre alt und komme mit dem Leichtkraftrad zur Schule."

Johannes, Bietigheim

„Also, ich heiße Johannes Hennicke, bin 12 Jahre alt und fahre jeden Morgen mit dem Fahrrad zur Schule."

Sonja, Berlin

„Ich heiße Sonja Wegener. Ich bin 17 Jahre alt. Ich fahre meistens mit der U-Bahn zur Schule, aber im Sommer fahr ich auch mit dem Fahrrad."

Tim, Berlin

„Mein Name ist Tim Wiesbach. Ich bin 18 Jahre alt und komme mit meinem Moped jeden Tag, wenn das Wetter mitspielt, zur Schule."

Sandra, Berlin

„Also, ich heiße Sandra Krabbel, und ich bin achtzehn Jahre alt, und meistens also, ich geh auf die Max-Beckmann-Oberschule, und meistens fahr ich mit dem Bus. Aber ja manchmal ganz selten auch mit dem Fahrrad, und jetzt neuerdings auch manchmal mit dem Auto, aber nur sehr selten."

A. 1. How do these students get to school? List the names of the students that were interviewed, then beside each name write the way that each student gets to school.

  2. Look at the list you made, and try to determine where these students might live: in a large city? in a suburb? etc. First discuss this question with a partner, then together explain to the rest of the class how you came to the conclusions that you did.

  3. The photo above is fairly typical for a German city. What do you notice about it? Is the German city in the photo similar to or different from a city in the United States? What conclusions can you draw about possible differences in transportation in Germany and in the United States?

B. Ask several of your classmates how they get to school, and decide together if there are differences between the way American students get to school and the way German students get to school. Write a brief essay discussing this question.

28 **Grammatik im Kontext**

Sprechen/Schreiben How many questions and answers can you form?

a. Viele Fragen *A lot of questions*

Wie	kommst kommen kommt	die Sonja der Jens du Ahmet und Holger	zur Schule?

b. Viele Antworten *A lot of answers*

Der Johannes Der Tim Ich Ahmet und Holger	komme kommen kommt	mit dem Rad. mit dem Bus. zu Fuß. mit dem Moped. mit dem Auto. mit der U-Bahn.

29 **Grammatik im Kontext**

Lesen/Sprechen Can you complete this conversation between Susanne and Manfred, two students at Tara's school? (More than one question may be possible!)

SUSANNE	Tag! ═══════?
MANFRED	Ja, ich bin neu hier.
SUSANNE	═══════?
MANFRED	Ich heiße Manfred.
SUSANNE	Und ═══════?
MANFRED	Aus Saarbrücken.

Inge kommt mit dem Moped.

MANFRED	═══════?
SUSANNE	Das ist Inge.
MANFRED	═══════?
SUSANNE	Ja, Inge ist sechzehn und kommt immer mit dem Moped zur Schule. ═══════?
MANFRED	Nein, ich komme mit dem Rad zur Schule.

Which one is the new student? How does he or she get to school?

 Übungsheft, S. 10, Ü. 16–17   Grammatikheft, S. 9, Ü. 17–19

30 **Interview**

Sprechen Write eight questions like the ones you came up with in Activity 29. Be sure to use questions beginning with question words, as well as yes/no questions. Then, working with a partner, use the questions you wrote to interview each other.

31 **Eine Umfrage** *A survey*

a. Sprechen Form small groups. Each of you will take a turn asking the person to your right how he or she gets to school.

b. Sprechen/Schreiben Now take turns reporting to the whole class on how the classmate you asked gets to school. As everyone reports, one person will make a chart on the board. Discuss the survey results with the class.

mit dem Bus	mit dem Rad

32 **Für mein Notizbuch** *For my notebook*

 Schreiben As your first entry in your **Notizbuch**, write something about yourself. Include your name (or your German name), your age, where you are from, and how you get to school.

33
 **Von der Schule zum Beruf**

Schreiben As part of a summer job for your local newspaper, you are asked to visit two businesses to find out how their employees get to work. Prepare a report.

AUSSPRACHE

Richtig aussprechen / Richtig lesen
Pronounce correctly / Read correctly

A. To practice the following sounds, say the words and sentences below after your teacher or after the recording.

1. The letters **ä** and **e:** The long **ä** and **e** are pronounced much like the long *a* in the English word *gate*.
Mädchen, dem, zehn / Das Mädchen kommt mit dem Bus.

2. The letter **ü:** To pronounce the long **ü**, round your lips as if you were going to whistle. Without moving your lips from this position, try to say the vowel sound in the English word *bee*.
Grüß, begrüßen, Tschüs / Grüß dich, Klaus! Tschüs, Ahmet!

3. The letter **ö:** To pronounce the long **ö**, round your lips, then without moving your lips from this position, try to say the vowel sound in the English word *bay*.
Hör, Österreich / Inge kommt aus Österreich.

4. The letter **w:** The letter **w** is pronounced like the *v* in the English word *viper*.
wer, wo, woher, wie / Woher kommt Uwe? Aus Walburg?

5. The letter **v:** The letter **v** is usually pronounced like the *f* in the English word *fish*.
vier, vor, von, viele / Er ist vierzehn, und Volker ist fünfzehn.

Richtig schreiben / Diktat *Write correctly / Dictation*

B. Write down the sentences that you hear.

Zum Lesen

Postkarten aus den Ferien

Lesestrategie

When you read the German texts in this book, you do not need to understand every word. As you progress, you will learn to pay attention to certain things—and you'll be amazed at how much you understand.

Using Visual Clues Certain clues will help you determine in advance what the reading might be about. Before you try to read a text, look at the title and at any visual clues, such as photos or illustrations, as well as at the format of the text. Very often these clues provide you with enough information to figure out what the text is about.

1. Look at the pictures as well as the format of these texts. What kinds of texts are they?

2. What do you think **Postkarten aus den Ferien** means? The format of the texts should help you guess what the word **Postkarten** means. Once you know that, ask yourself: When do people usually write texts like this? How does the answer to this question help you understand what the words **aus den Ferien** mean?

3. Have you ever written to someone while you were on vacation? What did you write about?

4. With a friend, write down some phrases you use when you write to friends on vacation.

5. Which **Postkarte** mentions a lot of activities?

Schwarzwald

Hallo Rita!
Herzliche Grüße aus dem Schwarzwald!
Das Wetter ist prima – warm und sonnig. Wir schwimmen, wandern und spielen Tennis, Volleyball, Minigolf!
Bis bald!

Monika

Rita Meyer
Gartenstraße 21
14482 Potsdam

London

Liebe Frau Polgert!
How do you do? Ich bin in London und finde die Stadt und die Engländer ganz phantastisch! Ich lerne viel Englisch.
Herzliche Grüße!
Ihre Claudia Bach

Fr. Anja Polgert
Vogelsangstr. 39
14478 Potsdam
Germany

Berliner Rathaus

Liebe Omi! Lieber Opi!

Ich bin mit meiner
Schulklasse in Berlin
– eine tolle Stadt, echt
super!
Wir kommen am Freitag
wieder zurück.
Liebe Grüße
          Euer Bernhard

Gerhart u. Friede Schnitzler
Eichenstr. 7
14489 Potsdam

6. Which words in these texts are types of greetings or farewells?

7. To whom are these texts written? What clues tell you how well the writers know the people to whom they are writing? Which **Postkarte** is probably written to a teacher? How can you tell?

8. Where is each person writing from? Why are they there? If they do not state the reason directly, what phrases help you infer why they are there?

9. What is the weather like where Monika is?

10. Why does Claudia use an English expression in her **Postkarte**? Do you think she is enjoying herself? How do you know?

11. Write a postcard in German based on one of the following activities:

   a. You and a friend have stayed with a German family while on vacation. After you leave, write a postcard to your host family, telling them where you are and how you like it.

   b. Assume you are in Germany for the first time. Write a postcard to a friend who knows some German.

Liebe(r) ...

Ich bin in _____.

Hier _____ es sehr

schön. _____ ist eine

interessante Stadt.

Herzliche _____

London Tower Bridge

ZUM LESEN

Übungsheft, S. 11, Ü. 18

Mehr Grammatikübungen

Erste Stufe

Objectives Asking someone's name and giving yours; asking who someone is

1 You are asking someone's name and you get an answer. Complete each of the following exchanges by filling in the blanks with a form of the verb **heißen**. (S. 23)

1. A: Wie _____ du?
   B: Ich _____ Mark.

2. A: _____ du Michael?
   B: Nein, ich _____ John.

3. A: Wie _____ das Mädchen?
   B: Das Mädchen _____ Steffi.

4. A: Wie_____ der Junge?
   B: Der Junge _____ Kurt.

5. A: _____ das Mädchen Brit?
   B: Nein, das Mädchen _____ Anja.

6. A: Und du _____ Stefan?
   B: Ja, ich _____ Stefan.

2 You want to know the names of various boys and girls. Write questions, using the English questions as cues. (S. 23)

1. (Is your name Jack?) _____
2. (Is his name Mark?) _____
3. (What's the boy's name?) _____
4. (His name is Steven.) _____
5. (What's the girl's name?) _____
6. (Her name is Jackie.) _____

3 You want to know the names of various people or at least who they are. Write questions and statements by filling in each blank with the correct form of the definite article. (S. 24)

1. Wie heißt _____ Junge? Und _____ Mädchen?
2. Wie heißt _____ Deutschlehrer? Und _____ Biologielehrerin?
3. Ist das Herr Gärtner, _____ Deutschlehrer?
4. Ist das _____ Steffi? Und das ist _____ Kristin, ja?

Zweite Stufe

Objective Asking someone's age and giving yours

4 You and your friends want to know the ages of various new classmates. Complete the following questions and statements by filling in the blanks with the appropriate form of the verb **sein**. (S. 26)

1. Wie alt _____ der Ahmet? _____ er schon fünfzehn?
2. Der Ahmet und die Karola _____ schon sechzehn.
3. Ich _____ dreizehn. Und wie alt _____ du?
4. Wie alt _____ der Deutschlehrer? _____ er schon 40?
5. Wie alt _____ du? _____ du schon fünfzehn?
6. Ich _____ vierzehn, und du _____ schon sechzehn.

5 One of the new students in class wants to know how old certain people are, and you tell him or her. Complete the following answers by filling in each blank with the appropriate personal pronoun and the appropriate form of the verb **sein. (S. 26)**

1. Wie alt ist die Tara? _____ 14 Jahre alt.
2. Wie alt bist du denn? _____ schon 16 Jahre alt.
3. Wie alt ist der Deutschlehrer? _____ 35 Jahre alt.
4. Und die Biologielehrerin? _____ schon 47 Jahre alt.
5. Wie alt sind Stefan und Moni? _____ 19 Jahre alt.
6. Und wie alt _____ , Michaela?

Dritte Stufe

Objective Talking about how someone gets to school

6 You seem to know how everyone gets to school. Complete the following statements by filling in each blank with the correct form of the verb **kommen** and the means of transportation given in parentheses. **(S. 30)**

1. Wie kommt die Steffi zur Schule? (by bike)   Sie _____ .
2. Wie kommt der Ahmet zur Schule? (he walks)   Er _____ .
3. Wie kommt der Lehrer zur Schule? (by car)   Er _____ .
4. Wie kommt die Annette zur Schule? (by bus)   Sie _____ .
5. Wie kommt der Mark zur Schule? (by subway)   Er _____ .
6. Wie kommt die Heike zur Schule? (by moped)   Sie _____ .

7 At the beginning of the school year, someone reports to the teacher how everyone gets to school. Complete each of the following statements by filling in each blank with the appropriate means of transportation. **(S. 30)**

1. (by bus)   Sandra kommt _____ zur Schule.
2. (on his moped)   Tim kommt _____ zur Schule.
3. (by subway)   Michael kommt _____ zur Schule.
4. (by car)   Sandra kommt _____ zur Schule.
5. (by bike)   Philipp kommt _____ zur Schule.
6. (on foot)   Ich komme _____ zur Schule.

Anwendung

1 Listen to four people talking about themselves. Write their names on a piece of paper, then beside each name write the person's age and where he or she is from.

2 **a.** Say hello to a classmate. Ask his or her name, age, and where he or she is from.

b. Introduce yourself to the class, giving your name, age, and where you are from. Then introduce the classmate you just met.

3 Read the letter below and complete the activities that follow.

Eisenach, den 10. Februar 2002

Lieber Ralph!

Ich heiße Mandy Gerber. Ich bin aus Eisenach. Das ist in Thüringen. Ich bin vierzehn Jahre alt. Wie alt bist du? Bist du auch vierzehn? Bitte, schreib mir und schick auch ein Foto von dir! Viele Grüße

Mandy

a. Make a list of things Mandy tells about herself.

b. What does Mandy want to know? Make a list of her questions.

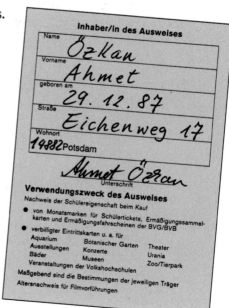

Inhaber/in des Ausweises

Name Özkan
Vorname Ahmet
geboren am 29. 12. 87
Straße Eichenweg 17
Wohnort 14882 Potsdam

Ahmet Özkan
Unterschrift

Verwendungszweck des Ausweises
Nachweis der Schülereigenschaft beim Kauf
• von Monatsmarken für Schülertickets, Ermäßigungssammelkarten und Ermäßigungsfahrscheinen der BVG/BVB
• verbilligter Eintrittskarten u. a. für
Aquarium   Botanischer Garten   Theater
Ausstellungen   Konzerte   Urania
Bäder   Museen   Zoo/Tierpark
Veranstaltungen der Volkshochschulen
Maßgebend sind die Bestimmungen der jeweiligen Träger
Altersnachweis für Filmvorführungen

4 Look at the **Schülerausweis** (*school identification card*) to the right and answer the questions that follow.

a. To whom does this **Schülerausweis** belong?

b. When was this person born?

c. Where does this person live?

5 If you were an exchange student in one of the German-speaking countries, you would receive a **Schülerausweis**. Using the example to the right as a model, create a **Schülerausweis** for yourself, filling in all the required information.

6 Look at the picture below with a partner and take turns with your classmates telling how the people in the illustration get to school.

7 Write a letter to a pen pal in Germany like the one Mandy wrote to Ralph on page 38. Use the information you wrote about yourself from Activity 26c to help you.

8 R o l l e n s p i e l

You and some of your friends have been designated to introduce the "exchange students" on page 31.

a. Working as a group, prepare statements that you can use in your introductions. Remember to give as much information as possible about each student, including name, age, where he or she is from, and how he or she gets to school. Include anything else that might be of interest to the class.

b. Using the pictures, present the visiting exchange students to the class.

Kann ich's wirklich?

WK3 BRANDENBURG-1

Can you greet people and say goodbye? (p. 21)

Can you give your name and ask someone else's? (p. 22)

Can you ask and say who someone is? (p. 23)

1 How would you say hello and goodbye to the following people?
  a. a classmate   **b.** your principal

2 How would you introduce yourself to a new student and ask his or her name?

3 **a.** How would you ask who someone is? Say who these students are.

Tara   **Jens**   **Holger**   **Ahmet**

Can you supply the correct definite articles (der, die, das) for the nouns you have learned in this chapter? (p. 24)

4 Complete Birgit's explanation to Holger about who everyone is, using the articles **der, die,** and **das.**

======= Junge da? Er heißt Helmut. Und ======= Mädchen heißt Monika. ======= Lehrer heißt Herr Becker. Und ======= Deutschlehrerin heißt Frau Hörster.

Can you ask someone's age and tell yours? (p. 25)

5 **a.** How would you ask a classmate his or her age and say how old you are?
  b. Say how old the following students are.
    Silke, 15   Dirk, 13   Marina und Susi, 14

Can you ask where someone is from and tell where you are from? (p. 28)

6 How would you ask a classmate where he or she is from?

7 Say where the following students are from. Make statements with both **kommen** and **sein.**
  a. Nicole, Brandenburg   **c.** Mark, Niedersachsen
  b. Britte und Andreas, Sachsen-Anhalt

8 How would you tell someone where you are from?

Can you say how someone gets to school? (p. 30)

9 How would you ask a classmate how he or she gets to school? How might he or she respond?
  Say how these people get to school:
  a. Steffi, bicycle   **b.** Petra and Ali, moped   **c.** Anna, subway

Erste Stufe

Saying hello and goodbye

Guten Morgen!	Good morning!
Morgen!	Morning!
Guten Tag!	Hello!
Tag!	
Hallo!	Hi!
Grüß dich!	
Auf Wiedersehen!	Goodbye!
Wiedersehen!	Bye!
Tschüs!	
Tschau!	Bye!
Bis dann!	See you later!

Asking someone's name and giving yours

heißen	to be called
Wie heißt du?	What's your name?
Ich heiße …	My name is…
Wie heißt das Mädchen?	What's the girl's name?
Sie heißt …	Her name is …
Wie heißt der Junge?	What's the boy's name?
Er heißt …	His name is …
Heißt sie …?	Is her name …?
ja	yes
nein	no

Asking who someone is

Wer ist das?	Who is that?
Das ist …	That's …
Herr …	Mr …
Frau …	Mrs …
der Lehrer	teacher (male)
die Lehrerin	teacher (female)
der Deutschlehrer	German teacher (male)
die Deutschlehrerin	German teacher (female)
die Biologielehrerin	biology teacher (female)
der Junge	boy
das Mädchen	girl

Definite Articles

der	
die	the
das	

Other Useful Words

und	and
Also, einfach!	That's easy!
Ach ja!	Oh, yeah!
Ja, klar!	Of course!
Prima!	Great!

Zweite Stufe

Asking someone's age and giving yours

sein	to be
Wie alt bist du?	How old are you?
Ich bin 14 Jahre alt.	I am 14 years old.
Du bist …	you are (sing)
Er ist …	He is …
Sie ist …	She is …
Sie sind …	They are …

Die Zahlen von 0 bis 20

See page 25.

Other Useful Words

Bundesland, ¨er	federal state (German)
Hauptstadt, ¨e	capital
jetzt	now
auch	also
schon	already

Dritte Stufe

Talking about where people are from

kommen	to come
Woher bist (kommst) du?	Where are you from?
Ich bin (komme) aus …	I'm from …
Sie ist (kommt) aus …	She's from …
Er ist (kommt) aus …	He's from …
Sie sind (kommen) aus …	They're from …
Deutschland	Germany
Österreich	Austria

Talking about how someone gets to school

Wie kommst du zur Schule?	How do you get to school?
Ich komme …	I come …
mit dem Bus	by bus
mit dem Rad	by bike
mit dem Auto	by car
mit dem Moped	by moped
mit der U-Bahn	by subway
zu Fuß	on foot (I walk)
oder	or

Asking Questions

Wer?	Who?
Wie?	How?
Wo?	Where?
Woher?	From where?

2
Spiel und Spaß

Objectives

In this chapter you will learn to

Erste Stufe

• talk about interests

Zweite Stufe

• express likes and dislikes

Dritte Stufe

• say when you do various activities
• ask for an opinion and express yours
• agree and disagree

🔲 internet

ADRESSE: go.hrw.com
KENNWORT:
    WK3 BRANDENBURG-2

◄ **Was macht ihr jetzt?**

Los geht's! · *Was machst du in deiner Freizeit?*

Strategie Verstehen

Look at the images for this story. What are the students in each picture doing? What do you think Holger might be telling them about himself?

Jens   Tara   Holger   Ahmet   Steffi

1

Holger:	Hallo! Was spielt ihr denn da?
Ahmet:	Was fragst du?
Holger:	Ich frage, was ihr da spielt.
Ahmet:	Karten.
Holger:	Ja, das sehe ich. Aber was spielt ihr?
Tara:	Wir spielen Mau-Mau.
Holger:	Wer gewinnt?
Jens:	Tara und Ahmet, wie immer!

2

Ahmet:	Du gewinnst auch manchmal!
Jens:	Aber ihr mogelt oft.
Tara:	Was? Wir mogeln nicht.
Ahmet:	Du bist nur sauer, weil du verlierst.

3

Jens:	Spielst du auch Karten, Holger?
Holger:	Ja, aber nicht so gern.
Tara:	Was machst du denn sonst noch in deiner Freizeit?
Holger:	Tja, hm … Fußball, ich geh* gern schwimmen, ich …
Ahmet:	Was noch?
Holger:	Im Winter lauf ich Ski.

4

Jens:	Was noch? Hast du andere Interessen?
Holger:	Ich sammle Briefmarken. Und ich höre gern Musik.
Ahmet:	Spielst du auch ein Instrument?
Holger:	Ich spiele Gitarre.

Frequently in spoken German, the **e-ending on the **ich**-form of the verb is omitted.*

5

Tara:	Und spielst du auch Tennis?
Holger:	Nein. Tennis find ich langweilig.
Tara:	Ach, das ist schade!
Holger:	Warum? Spielst du Tennis?
Tara:	Und wie! Mein Lieblingssport.
Holger:	Ich … ich hab …
Tara:	Macht nichts, Holger!

6

Steffi:	Ist Holger nett?
Tara:	Und wie! Und er läuft Ski, spielt Fußball, aber Tennis spielt er nicht gern.
Steffi:	Ach, schade!

Viel später

7

Tara:	Hallo, Holger! Wir gehen Tennis spielen. Aber schade, du spielst ja Tennis nicht gern! Tschüs!
Holger:	He! Ihr … Wartet doch! Ich … ich …

8

Holger:	So ein Mist!

Übungsheft, S. 13

1 Was passiert hier?

Do you understand what is happening in **Los geht's!**? Check your comprehension by answering these questions. Don't be afraid to guess!

1. What are Ahmet, Tara, and Jens doing at the beginning of the story?
2. Which sports does Holger play? What other interests does Holger mention?
3. Why is Tara teasing Holger? What does she say to him?
4. How does Holger feel at the end of the story? What does he say that lets you know how he feels?

2 Genauer lesen

Reread the conversations. Which words or phrases do the characters use to

1. ask what someone likes to do in his or her free time
2. say they like to listen to music
3. ask if someone plays an instrument
4. ask if someone has other interests
5. tell what their favorite sport is
6. say that they do something often
7. say that they find something boring

3 Was passt zusammen? *What goes together?*

Jens and Tara ask Holger what he does in his free time. Match each question on the left with an appropriate response on the right.

1. Spielst du Karten?
2. Was machst du in deiner Freizeit?
3. Hast du auch andere Interessen?
4. Spielst du ein Instrument?
5. Spielst du auch Tennis?

a. Nein, Tennis finde ich langweilig.
b. Ja, ich sammle Briefmarken und höre gern Musik.
c. Ja, aber ich spiele Karten nicht so gern.
d. Ich spiele Fußball, ich geh schwimmen, und im Winter lauf ich Ski.
e. Ja, ich spiele Gitarre.

4 Welches Wort passt? *Which word fits?*

Based on the story you just read and heard, complete each of the sentences below with an appropriate word from the box.

> Karten   Musik   sammelt
> langweilig   spielen   Tennis

Tara, Ahmet und Jens spielen gern ___1___. Holger ___2___ lieber Briefmarken und hört auch gern ___3___. Holger findet Tennis ___4___, aber Tara findet den Sport super. ___5___ ist Taras Lieblingssport. Tara und Steffi ___6___ oft Tennis.

5 Wer macht was?

What have you learned about these students? Match the statements with the people they describe.

1. Tara
2. Ahmet
3. Holger
4. Jens
5. Steffi

a. verliert oft beim Kartenspielen.
b. spielt Karten nicht gern.
c. findet Holger nett.
d. spielt oft mit Tara Tennis.
e. gewinnt oft beim Kartenspielen.

Wortschatz

JENS Was machst du in deiner Freizeit?

UTE Ich mache viel Sport. Ich spiele …

Fußball **Basketball** **Volleyball** **Tennis**

JENS Spielst du auch Golf?

UTE Nein, ich spiele nicht Golf.

JENS Spielst du ein Instrument?

UTE Ja klar! Ich spiele …

JENS Hast du auch andere Interessen?

UTE Ja, ich spiele auch …

Gitarre **Klavier** **Karten** **Schach**

Übungsheft, S. 14, Ü. 2–3   Grammatikheft, S. 10, Ü. 1–2

Und dann noch...

Schlagzeug **Flöte** **Trompete**

LERNTRICK

Look for cognates when you read. Cognates are words that look similar and have the same meaning in German and English. Some are identical, for example, *tennis* and **Tennis**. Others differ slightly in spelling, such as *trumpet* and **Trompete**. How many cognates can you find in the **Wortschatz**?

6 Wer macht was?

Zuhören Using the drawings above as a guide, listen as Holger asks what his classmates do in their free time. First write the name of any activity you hear mentioned. Then, listen again for the students' names. This time, write each student's name beside the activity he or she does.

Bildertext

Sprechen/Schreiben Complete the following description of Ahmet's free time activities, using the pictures as cues.

Ahmet spielt oft ___?___ . Mit Tara und Jens spielt er oft ___?___ , aber

___?___ spielt er nicht so gern. Er spielt auch zwei Instrumente: er spielt

___?___ , und er spielt auch ___?___ aber das spielt er nicht so gut.

So sagt man das!

Talking about interests

If you want to know what a friend does in his or her free time, you might ask:

Was machst du in deiner Freizeit?
Spielst du Volleyball? *Do you play volleyball?*

Was macht Steffi?
Spielt sie auch Volleyball?
Toll! Und Jens? Spielt er auch Volleyball?

You might get these responses:

Ich spiele Gitarre.
Ja, ich spiele Volleyball. *or*
Nein, ich spiele nicht Volleyball.
Sie spielt Tennis und Basketball.
Ja, ich glaube, sie spielt oft Volleyball.
Nein, er spielt nicht Volleyball.

Ein wenig Grammatik

In the sentences above that use **spielen,** the subject pronouns change as different people are addressed or talked about. A question addressed to one person uses **du.** The response to such a question uses **ich.** What pronouns do you use in German when you talk about a female? a male?[1] As the subject pronoun changes, the forms of the verb also change: **ich spiele, du spielst, er/sie spielt.** The part of the verb that does not change is the *stem.* What is the stem of **spielen?**[2]

Mehr Grammatikübungen, S. 62, Ü. 1

Singular

ich	spiel**e**
du	spiel**st**
Jens / er	spiel**t**
Tara / sie	spiel**t**

Übungsheft, S. 15, Ü. 4–6

Grammatikheft, S. 10–11, Ü. 3–7

---

8 **Grammatik im Kontext**

Schreiben Holger wants to know what some of his classmates do in their free time. Supply the correct endings of the verbs.

1. HOLGER Mach ══ du oft Sport?
   HEIKE Ja, ich mach ══ viel Sport!
   HOLGER Was spiel ══ du denn alles?
   HEIKE Ich spiel ══ Fußball, Volleyball und auch Tennis.

2. HOLGER Und Werner? Was mach ══ er gern?
   HEIKE Er spiel ══ gern Klavier.
   HOLGER Spiel ══ Gabi auch Klavier?
   HEIKE Nein. Sie spiel ══ Gitarre.

3. Ich spiel ══ , was du nicht spiel ══ ; Tara spiel ══ Tennis, Holger spiel ══ Gitarre, ich spiel ══ Schach, und du spiel ══ Karten!

---

1. **sie, er** 2. **spiel-**

9 **Fragen und Antworten** *Questions and answers*

Schreiben Steffi is trying to find people to play a game with her. Complete her conversation with Tara by filling in the missing lines with an appropriate question or answer from the boxes. Which game do they decide to play? Do all the girls like that game?

> Spielt die Elisabeth auch?

> Na klar! Basketball ist Klasse!

> Nein, aber sie spielt Volleyball.

> Spielst du auch Volleyball?

STEFFI   Hallo, Tara! Sag mal, spielst du Basketball?

TARA   ⸺

STEFFI   ⸺

TARA   Ja, Elisabeth spielt auch.

STEFFI   Und die Sybille?

TARA   ⸺

STEFFI   Und du? ⸺

TARA   Ja, ich spiele auch Volleyball. Und Elisabeth auch.

STEFFI   Prima! Also spielen wir heute Volleyball!

10 **In meiner Freizeit...**

Schreiben Using the **Wortschatz** shown on page 47, write down three things you do in your free time. Tell these activities to your partner, and then ask if he or she does them, too.

BEISPIEL   **DU**   **Ich spiele ...Und du?**
      PARTNER   **Ja, ich spiele auch ...** *or* **Nein, ich spiele nicht ...**

11 **Ein Interview**

a. Sprechen You are a reporter for the school newspaper and are interviewing students about their interests. Get together with two other classmates and ask them questions in German to find out what they do in their free time. Then switch roles.

Und dann noch...	
Baseball	Tischtennis
Handball	Brettspiele
Videospiele	

b. Schreiben After you talk to two classmates, write what you learned, so that your article can be ready for the next edition.

BEISPIEL   **DU**   **Was ...?**
      (JOHN)   **Ich spiele Fußball und Basketball, und ...**
      YOU WRITE   **John spielt Fußball und Basketball, und ...**

So sagt man das!

Expressing likes and dislikes

To find out what someone likes
or doesn't like to do, you ask:

Was machst du gern, Ahmet?
Schwimmst du gern? *Do you like to swim?*
Steffi, Tara, was macht ihr gern?

The responses might be:

Ich spiele gern Fußball.
Nein, nicht so gern.
Wir schwimmen sehr gern.
We like to swim very much.

To talk about what others like to do, you say:

Tara und Steffi schwimmen gern. *or* **Sie schwimmen gern.**

Ein wenig Grammatik

In the question **Was macht ihr gern?** two
people are addressed directly; the subject
pronoun is **ihr**. The response to this question
is also plural and uses **wir: Wir schwimmen
gern.** The endings added to the verb stem
with **ihr** and **wir** are **-t** and **-en: Schwimmt
ihr? Ja, wir schwimmen gern.**

When you are talking *about* two or more
people, use the plural pronoun **sie**. What
ending is added to the verb stem when the
pronoun **sie** is used?[1]

Plural

wir	spiel**en**
ihr	spiel**t**
Jens und Tara/sie	spiel**en**

In the two boxes below, can you match the
verbs and pronouns correctly?[2]

bist schwimmt machen spielen komme	sie (pl) du ich wir ihr

Grammatikheft, S. 12, Ü. 8–10

Mehr Grammatikübungen,
S. 62, Ü. 2

---

1. **-en** 2. Answers will vary. Possible answers:
**sie machen, du bist, ich komme, wir spielen,
ihr schwimmt**

12 Grammatik im Kontext

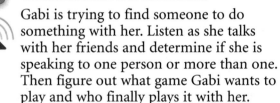

Gabi is trying to find someone to do
something with her. Listen as she talks
with her friends and determine if she is
speaking to one person or more than one.
Then figure out what game Gabi wants to
play and who finally plays it with her.

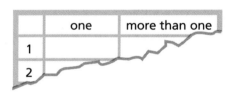

	one	more than one
1		
2		

13 Grammatik im Kontext

Sprechen/Schreiben Complete the following conversation between Ahmet and
Holger with **ihr**, **wir**, or **sie** (pl).

HOLGER   Tag Jens, Ahmet! Was macht
     __1__ jetzt?

JENS UND   __2__ spielen jetzt
AHMET   Fußball. Was machst du?

HOLGER   Steffi, Uwe und ich hören
     Musik. __3__ hören
     Country sehr gern. Ich glaube,
     Tara und Stefan kommen
     auch. __4__ hören Country
     auch gern. Und __5__ ? Hört
     __6__ das gern?

JENS UND   Na klar!
AHMET

CD-ROM DISC 1

UWE Sag mal, was machst du gern?
STEFAN Oh, ich …

sammle Briefmarken und Comics   **zeichne**   **bastle viel**

UWE Und ihr, Christiane und Ulrike?
CHRISTIANE Tja, wir …

besuchen Freunde   **schauen Fernsehen**   **hören Musik**

UWE Und deine Freunde, Katharina und Sven? Was machen sie?
CHRISTIANE Sie …

schwimmen   **tanzen**   **wandern**

Übungsheft, S. 17, Ü. 9–10

Grammatikheft, S.13, Ü. 11–13

Und dann noch…

Wir …

lesen   malen   kochen   schreiben   joggen

laufen Ski   laufen Rollschuh   segeln   fahren Rad   reiten

14 **Mix-Match: Viele Interessen** *A lot of interests*

Sprechen Complete Jutta's description of her and her friends' free time activities by matching the following phrases to form complete sentences.

1. Ich besuche…
2. Und ich spiele…
3. Uwe und ich schauen…
4. Christiane hört…
5. Jörg sammelt…
6. Und Peter und Uwe, sie…

a. Briefmarken.
b. Fernsehen.
c. Freunde.
d. schwimmen sehr gern.
e. Musik gern.
f. Fußball gern.

15 **Wer macht was?**

Zuhören Two of Tara's friends, Claudia and Michael, are trying to figure out what to do today. Listen to their conversation and write down which activities Claudia likes, which ones Michael likes, and what they finally decide to do together.

Grammatik

The present tense of verbs

The statements and questions you have been practicing all refer to the present time and have verbs that are in the present tense. In English there are three ways to talk about the present tense, for example, *I play, I am playing,* or *I do play.* In German there is only one verb form to express the present tense: **ich spiele.**

All verbs have a basic form, the form that appears in your word lists (**Wortschatz**) or in a dictionary. This form is called the *infinitive.* The infinitive of all verbs in German has the ending **-en** as in **spielen** or **-n,** as in **basteln.** When a verb is used in a sentence with a subject, the verb is conjugated. That means that the **-en** (or **-n**) of the infinitive is replaced with a specific ending. The ending that is used depends on the noun or pronoun that is the subject of the verb.

The following chart summarizes these different verb forms using **spielen** as a model.

ich	spiele		wir	spielen
du	spielst		ihr	spielt
Holger / er	spielt			
Tara / sie	spielt	Holger und Tara / sie	spielen

Almost all German verbs follow this pattern. Two verbs that you already know—besides **spielen**—are **kommen** and **machen.**

When speaking to adults who are not family members or relatives, you must use the formal form of address, the pronoun **Sie,** together with the verb form that is used with **sie** plural.

Herr Meyer, spiel**en Sie** Tennis?
Herr und Frau Müller, spiel**en Sie** auch Tennis?

Mehr Grammatikübungen, S. 62, Ü. 3

Übungsheft, S. 18–19, Ü. 11–15

Grammatikheft, S. 14, Ü. 14–15

Ein wenig Landeskunde

Germans tend to be more formal than Americans, and teenagers rarely call adults by their first names. While there are no hard and fast rules about using **du** and **Sie,** it is safer to err in the direction of being too formal. If people want you to call them **du,** they will tell you.

16 Grammatik im Kontext

Zuhören As you listen to these conversations, decide whether the speakers are talking to someone they know well, or someone they don't know so well.

	very well	not very well
1		
2		

17 Grammatik im Kontext

Sprechen/Schreiben Using the photos as cues, take turns with a partner saying what the following people do in their free time.

Wir …
Du …
Sie (*you*, formal) …

Klaus …
Du …
Ihr …

Ahmet und Holger …
Ich …
Sie (pl) …

Das Mädchen …
Der Junge …
Ihr …

18 Frag mal deinen Lehrer!   *Ask your teacher!*

Schreiben Ask your teacher about his or her interests. Work with a partner and write down five questions to ask, for example, **Spielen Sie Tennis? Hören Sie gern Musik?**

> Ich surfe gern im Internet, besonders Sport.

19 Was machst du gern?

Sprechen/Schreiben Look at the vocabulary on pages 47 and 51 again. Tell your partner five things you like to do and two that you do not like to do. Then your partner will do the same. Make a list of your partner's likes and dislikes and circle the items you both like and dislike.

20 Für mein Notizbuch

Schreiben Write down some things you like to do in your **Notizbuch**. For the names of any activities not listed on pages 47 and 51, refer to the Additional Vocabulary section on page R9 in the back of your book. These are words and expressions you can use whenever you're asked about your own interests.

21 Was macht ihr gern?

Sprechen Work with two or four other classmates. Students in your group should pair off, leaving one person to be IT (**ES**). Using German, each pair should decide on one activity they both like to do. The person who is IT has to find out what that activity is by asking questions: **Spielt ihr gern Volleyball? Besucht ihr gern Freunde?** Students should answer truthfully with **Nein, wir … nicht gern …** or, when IT guesses correctly, **Ja, wir … gern …** The person who is IT reports each pair's activity to the class. Take turns being IT.

Was machst du gern?

What kinds of interests do you think German teenagers might enjoy? What sports do you play? What interests do you have? Make a list of the things you like to do in your free time. Then, read what these teenagers said about their free time activities.

Übungsheft, S. 24, Ü. 24

Michael, Hamburg

„Also ich mach am liebsten in meiner Freizeit Basketball spielen oder ausgehen, so in Diskos oder so was mit Freunden und so und auch Fahrrad fahren."

Björn, Hamburg

„Tja, ich sitze eigentlich ziemlich oft vor dem Computer. Ich seh auch gerne fern oder guck mir ein Video an. Dann fahr ich ganz gerne Rad und schwimme auch manchmal ganz gerne."

Christina, Bietigheim

„Ich schwimm gern, ich les gern, ich hör gern Musik und ich fahr gern Moped."

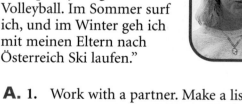

Heide, Berlin

„Ich mach dreimal in der Woche Sport. Da jogg ich vier Kilometer mit Trimm-dich-Pfad, dann fahr ich auch noch Fahrrad, danach so eine Stunde mit einem Freund."

Elke, Berlin

„Ich spiele jetzt gern Volleyball. Im Sommer surf ich, und im Winter geh ich mit meinen Eltern nach Österreich Ski laufen."

A. 1. Work with a partner. Make a list of what each person interviewed likes to do. Organize your answers in a chart with the headings **Sport** and **andere Interessen.** After making your chart, what can you say about the personality of each person interviewed?

2. Answer the following questions with your classmates. Look back at the list of interests you made for yourself before reading. What are some similarities and differences between the free time activities teenagers in the German-speaking countries like to do, and what teenagers like to do where you live? What do you think students in German-speaking countries imagine that teenagers in the United States like to do? Where do they probably get their ideas?

B. You and your partner are exchange students in Potsdam and have been asked to come up with a plan of activities for an afternoon at a local **Jugendzentrum** (youth center). There will also be some other exchange students there, so you will need to plan activities that most everyone will enjoy. Make your plan on a large piece of paper or poster board with a lot of color (you could even cut some pictures out of magazines). Then present your activity plans to the class.

Dritte Stufe

Objectives Saying when you do various activities; asking for an opinion and expressing yours; agreeing and disagreeing

WK3 BRANDENBURG-2

So sagt man das!

Saying when you do various activities

To find out when people do things, you might ask:

Was machst du nach der Schule?
What do you do after school?

They might tell you:

Am Nachmittag mache ich Sport.
In the afternoon I play sports.
Und am Abend mache ich die Hausaufgaben und schaue Fernsehen.
In the evening I do my homework and watch television.

Und am Wochenende? Was machst du am Wochenende?

Tja, am Wochenende besuche ich Freunde.

Was machst du im Sommer?
What do you do in the summer?

Im Sommer wandere ich gern.

What do you notice about the responses in this box? Do they all begin with the subject?[1] What do you observe about the position of the subject in these sentences? What is the position of the verb in all the sentences?[2]

Wortschatz

Wann machst du das?

im Frühling

im Sommer

im Herbst

im Winter

Übungsheft, S. 20, Ü. 16

Grammatikheft, S.15, Ü. 16

---

1. These sentences begin with a time expression, rather than with the subject.
2. The verb is in second position, followed by the subject.

22 Was? und Wann?

Zuhören You will hear one of Holger's new classmates, Uschi, talk about when she does various activities. First, write the activities as you hear them mentioned, then match the activities with the phrases that tell when Uschi does them.

a. im Frühling   c. im Herbst   e. im Sommer

b. am Wochenende   d. am Nachmittag   f. am Abend

23 Wann ...?

Sprechen Based on the page from Tara's weekly planner, answer the following questions.

1. Was macht Tara nach der Schule?
2. Wann wandert sie?
3. Wann besucht sie Steffis Familie?
4. Wann spielt sie Fußball?

24 Wann machst du das?

Schreiben List five activities you like to do and when you do them.

25 Zum Schreiben

Schreiben Using complete sentences, write a description of what activities you like to do and when you like to do them. Use the list you made in Activity 24.

MAI

15. Montag	
16. Dienstag	
17. Mittwoch	7.00 – Steffi u. Ahmet besuchen
18. Donnerstag	2.00 – Basketball
19. Freitag	
20. Samstag	2.00 – Fußball mit Joachim
21. Sonntag	3.00 – wandern mit Ahmet u. Jens

Grammatik

Word order: verb in second position

As you noticed on page 55, German sentences do not always begin with the subject. Often another word or expression (**nach der Schule, im Sommer**) is the first element. What happens to the verb in such cases?[1]

Mehr Grammatikübungen, S. 63, Ü. 4–5

Wir	spielen	nach der Schule	Fußball.
Nach der Schule	spielen	**wir**	Fußball.
Tara und Steffi	besuchen	im Sommer	Freunde.
Im Sommer	besuchen	**Tara und Steffi**	Freunde.

Übungsheft, S. 21–22, Ü. 18–22

Grammatikheft, S. 15, Ü. 17

26 Für mein Notizbuch

Schreiben Exchange the sentences you wrote in Activity 25 with a partner. Check each other's sentences to make sure that the verbs are in second position and that all the verbs have the proper endings. Then trade papers back again, after you and your partner have made corrections or changes. You may want to modify some of your sentences, putting something else besides the subject at the beginning for a little variety. When you have finished, write your corrected sentences in your **Notizbuch**.

---

1. The verb is in second position, even when something other than the subject begins the sentence.

27 Grammatik im Kontext

Sprechen/Schreiben Ask your partner what he or she does at various times. Then switch roles. Use the phrases in the boxes below to help you answer your partner's questions. Be prepared to report your partner's answers to the class.

am Wochenende	im Herbst	Hausaufgaben machen	Karten spielen
am Nachmittag	im Sommer	Freunde besuchen	Basketball spielen
am Abend	im Winter	Fernsehen schauen	Fußball spielen
nach der Schule	im Frühling	Musik hören	schwimmen

So sagt man das!

Asking for an opinion and expressing yours

To find out what someone thinks about something, you might ask:

Wie findest du Tanzen?

Und wie findet Georg Tanzen?

Some possible responses are:

Ich finde Tanzen langweilig. *I think dancing is boring.*
Tanzen ist Spitze! *Dancing is great!*
Tanzen macht Spaß. *Dancing is fun.*
Er findet Tanzen langweilig.

CD-ROM DISC 1

Grammatik

Verbs with stems ending in d, t or n

Finden and other verbs with stems ending in **d**, **t** or **n** do not follow the regular pattern in the **du-** and **er/sie-**forms. These verbs add **-est** to the **du-**form (**du findest**) and **-et** to the **er/sie-** and **ihr-** forms (**er/sie findet, ihr findet**). Another verb that follows this pattern is **zeichnen** (**du zeichnest, er/sie zeichnet, ihr zeichnet**). Compare these verb forms:

	spielen	finden	zeichnen
du	spiel**st**	find**est**	zeichn**est**
er, sie	spiel**t**	find**et**	zeichn**et**
ihr	spiel**t**	find**et**	zeichn**et**

Mehr Grammatikübungen, S. 63, Ü. 6

28 Blöd oder Spitze?

Sprechen Express your opinion about the following activities. You may choose expressions from the list.

1. Ich finde Briefmarkensammeln …
2. Fernsehen ist …
3. Musik hören ist …
4. Basteln finde ich …
5. Wandern finde ich …
6. Volleyball …
7. Freunde besuchen …
8. Schach …

Wortschatz

Degrees of enthusiasm

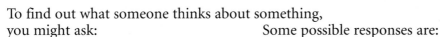

Spitze!
super!
Klasse!
toll!
prima!
interessant!
macht Spaß!
langweilig!
blöd!
macht keinen Spaß!

Übungsheft, S. 20, Ü. 17

Grammatikheft, S. 17, Ü. 20–22

29 **Wie findest du …?**

 **Sprechen** Ask your partner his or her opinion of three activities. Then switch roles. Be prepared to report your partner's opinions to the class.

So sagt man das!

Agreeing and disagreeing

If someone expresses an opinion such as **Ich finde Volleyball langweilig,**
you might agree: Or you might disagree:

> **Ich auch!** *or*   **Ich nicht!** *or*
> **Das finde ich auch.**   **Das finde ich nicht.**

If someone makes a statement like **Basteln ist blöd!**
you might agree: or disagree:

> **Stimmt!**   **Stimmt nicht!**

Grammatikheft, S. 18, Ü. 23–24

Ein wenig Grammatik

Verbs that end in **-eln**, like the verb **basteln**, change in the **ich**-form: the **e** drops from the verb stem, and the verb becomes **ich bastle.** Can you guess what the **ich**-form of **segeln** is?

	seg**eln**	bast**eln**
ich	seg**le**	bast**le**

Grammatikheft, S. 18, Ü. 25

Mehr Grammatikübungen, S. 63, Ü. 7

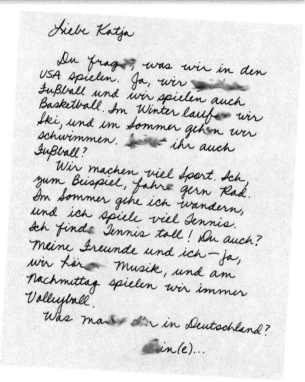

Liebe Katja

Du fragst, was wir in den USA spielen. Ja, wir Fußball und wir spielen auch Basketball. Im Winter laufen wir Ski, und im Sommer gehen wir schwimmen. ___ ihr auch Fußball?

Wir machen viel Sport. Ich, zum Beispiel, fahre gern Rad. Im Sommer gehe ich wandern, und ich spiele viel Tennis. Ich finde Tennis toll! Du auch? Meine Freunde und ich — ja, wir hören Musik, und am Nachmittag spielen wir immer Volleyball.

Was macht ihr in Deutschland?

___ in(e)...

 30 **Stimmt! oder Stimmt nicht!**

Zuhören Listen to the conversation between Ahmet and a friend as they discuss free time activities. Do they agree or disagree? About what?

31 **Grammatik im Kontext**

a. Sprechen/Schreiben Fill in the endings.

Wie find ═══ Holger die Musik? – Er find ═══ sie langweilig. Und du, wie find ═══
═══ du die Musik? Ich find═══ sie prima! – Holger und Steffi, zeichn═══
ihr? – Nein, aber der Jens zeichn═══ , und die Steffi zeichn═══ auch.
Zeichn═══ du? – Nein, ich zeichn═══ nicht. Segel═══ du? Nein, ich
seg═══ nicht, aber ich bast═══ gern. – Bast═══ du auch?

b. Schreiben You have just written the letter above to your pen pal in Germany. Unfortunately, on the way to the post office it started to rain and your letter got a little smeared. Rewrite the letter, fixing all the smeared words.

32 **Und deine Meinung?** *And your opinion?*

1. **Schreiben** List six activities and write your opinion of each one next to it.

2. **Sprechen** Work with a partner. Ask your partner what he or she thinks of each activity on your list. Agree or disagree with your partner's opinion. When you disagree, express your own opinion.

3. **Sprechen** Respond to your partner's list.

4. **Sprechen/Schreiben** Which activities do you and your partner agree on? Which ones don't you agree on? Make a list and be prepared to report to the class.

33 **Zum Schreiben**

Schreiben In this chapter you have learned a lot about how Germans spend their free time. Imagine you are Katja and respond to the letter on page 58. Refer to the **Landeskunde** for ideas.

34  Von der Schule zum Beruf

Schreiben As part of a job application, you are asked to write a brief résumé giving your name, age, and your interests in sports or hobbies.

AUSSPRACHE

Richtig aussprechen / Richtig lesen

A. To practice the following sounds, say the words and sentences below after your teacher or after the recording.

1. The letter combination **ie:** The vowel combination **ie** sounds much like the long *e* in the English word *me.*

   spielen, viel, vier / Sie und ihre sieben Brüder spielen Klavier.

2. The letter combination **ei:** The vowel combination **ei** is pronounced like the long *i* in the English words *mine* and *shine.*

   schreiben, deiner, Freizeit / Heike findet Zeichnen langweilig.

3. The letter **j:** The letter **j** is pronounced like the *y* in the English word *yes.* In words borrowed from other languages, such as **Jeans,** the **j** is pronounced as it is in English.

   Jens, Jürgen, Junge / Wer ist der Junge? Der Junge heißt Jens.

4. The letter **z:** The letter **z** is pronounced like the consonant combination *ts* as in the English word *hits.*

   zur, zehn, zwölf / Zwei und zehn sind zwölf.

Richtig Schreiben / Diktat

B. Write down the sentences that you hear.

Was machen wir am Wochenende?

1. Scan the articles for the following information:

a. the day and time when you can hear a jazz concert in the **HAP-Grieshaber-Halle**

b. the number of hot air balloon clubs in Hessen

c. the three kinds of bands that will perform at the UNI summer festival

Did you have to read every word of the ad in order to find that information?

2. You live in Eningen and have friends visiting for the weekend. They are interested in jazz, so you want to take them to the jazz festival. Now you will need to get more specific information.

a. How many groups can you hear at the festival? Where are the groups from?

b. How much will the tickets cost if you buy them at the **Kreissparkasse** in Reutlingen? How much will they cost if you

Immer mehr machen mit

Immer mehr Leute unterschiedlichen Alters begeistern sich fürs Ballonfahren. Bei den sechs hessischen Ballon-Clubs, die die luftige Fahrt auch für Vereinsgäste anbieten, ist ein Jahr Wartezeit für die Aufnahme in den Club die Regel. Im März dieses Jahres war Stuttgart Ziel des 22. Deutschen Freiballonfahrertages.

Eninger HOT JAZZ Festival

Am 30. Juni 2002 von 17–24 Uhr in der HAP-Grieshaber-Halle

Mit Tante Frieda's Jazz Kränzchen, Reutlingen
All Star Groove, Stuttgart
Royal Garden Ramblers, Stuttgart
Stuttgarter Dixieland All Stars
Budapest Ragtime Orchestra, Ungarn

Hallenbewirtschaftung mit Faßbier und kleineren Speisen.

Eintrittskarten sind zu € 10.– bei allen Zweigstellen der Kreissparkasse Reutlingen und »Sigi's Jazz House«, Im Bebenhäuser Hof, Reutlingen sowie an der Abendkasse zu € 12.– erhältlich.

Hallenöffnung: 16.00 Uhr

Skat

Die Karten in Mittelhand: Kreuz-Bube, Pik-Bube, Herz-Bube, Karo-Bube, Kreuz-As, Herz-As, Dame, Pik-König, Dame, 9
Vorhand paßt nach ausgereiztem Null ouvert Hand. Mittelhand spielt kurzentschlossen Pik Solo Hand, doch das Spiel endet, obwohl es kaum begonnen hat, mit 60:60 Augen. Die Gewinnchancen für einen Grand Hand waren sicher größer, doch käme es hierbei auch auf den Kartensitz bei der Gegenpartei an. Schließlich reizte Vorhand bis 59, und es war nicht auszuschließen, daß Vorhand im Besitz der restlichen Pikkarten sein konnte. Vorhand führt in zwei roten Farben (4+5 K.) 24 Augen, dazu eine schwarze Lusche. Hinterhand führt in zwei schwarzen Farben (1+6 K.) 17, dazu in einer roten Farbe 18 Augen.

Potsminton

BADMINTON-TURNIER

Sonntag, 23. Juni 2001, von 11.00 bis 16.00 Uhr

Vom Freizeitsportler bis zum Aktiven bieten wir für jeden etwas. Hobby-Sportler können alles Wichtige über Federball und Badminton erfahren. Aktiven Spielern verrät unser Fachtrainer **Volker Jürgens** Tricks und Kniffe oder gibt Tipps für das individuelle Training.

Natürlich können Sie auch unsere Courts einfach nur mal testen.

Leihschläger liegen für Sie bereit!

Potsminton/Potsdam Sport-Center
Brandenburger Str. 73
14467 Potsdam
Telefon (003733) 458317

Potsminton

UNI

23. Juni

19.00 Uhr

Sommerfest

- Eintritt frei - Bewirtung -

-Neue Aula-Geschwister-Scholl-Platz

Festsaal
- Workshop Orchester der Tübinger Musiktage
- Tanzband Die Piccolos
- Vorführgruppe Elementarer Tanz
- Die hüpfenden und tanzenden Tonnen
- Modern- und Jazz-Tanzgruppe des Sportinstituts

Neue Aula Foyer
- Big Band Such Over Sky

Geschwister-Scholl-Platz
- Neckartown-Jazzband

Bar
- Karl Springer - Piano

Schach

Nr. 2743 – Dr. Siegfried Brehmer
«Schachexpress» 1948

Matt in zwei Zügen

Weiß: Kb8, De7, Tb7, Ld6, Sd3 (5)
Schwarz: Kc6, De1, Ta5, Th4, Lh2, Lh3, Sc3, Sg3, Ba7, d5, d7, e5, h6 (13)

Liebe(Lieber) ———— !

Morgen habe ich viel vor.
Am Vormittag ————.
Später ————. *Am Abend*
gehe ich zum Sommerfest.
Dort ————. *Bevor ich ins*
Bett gehe, ————.

Dein(e)

---

wait and buy them on the evening of the performance? How early can you enter the concert hall?

3. What would you and your friends probably be interested in if you wanted to attend the **UNI Sommerfest**? Can you figure out who is sponsoring this event? When will the event take place (time and date) and where? How much will it cost to get into the festival?

> **Weißt du noch?** *Remember?* You will often be able to use visual clues to figure out the meaning of a text.

4. List any visual clues on this page that help you determine the meaning of the texts.

5. If your friends would like to learn badminton better, where should they go? What telephone number should they call?

6. With a friend, make a list of places you want to go or activities you want to participate in. Use the ads on these two pages, but feel free to add activities that you particularly enjoy. Are there activities mentioned here that you would not want to do? Write those activities on a separate list.

7. Write a postcard to a friend about what you have planned for tomorrow. Use the partial sentences on the postcard as your guide, filling in the blanks with activities that you enjoy. Use words from the newspaper ads or other words you have learned.

Übungsheft, S. 23, Ü. 23

Mehr Grammatikübungen

Erste Stufe

Objectives Talking about interests

1 You and your friends are talking about your interests and their interests. For each interchange, fill in each blank with an appropriate verb form. **(S. 48)**

1. A: Mark, _____ du Tennis? B: Ja, ich _____ Tennis.
2. A: Was _____ die Steffi? B: Sie _____ Klavier.
3. A: Was _____ der Mark? B: Er _____ Fußball.
4. A: Was _____ du? Schach? B: Ja, ich _____ Schach.
5. A: _____ du ein Instrument? B: Ja, ich _____ Gitarre.

Zweite Stufe

Objectives Expressing likes and dislikes

2 You and your friends are discussing what you like to do and what you dislike. For each interchange, fill in each blank with the appropriate verb form. **(S. 48)**

1. A: Was _____ ihr gern, Heike und Ahmet?
2. B: Wir _____ gern Sport. Fußball, Tennis!
3. A: Tara und Steffi _____ gern Volleyball.
4. B: Und was _____ ihr gern? Tennis?
5. A: Wir _____ gern Klavier. Und was _____ ihr gern?
6. B: Wir _____ gern Gitarre.
7. A: Was _____ ihr nicht gern?
8. B: Wir _____ Golf nicht gern.

3 Ask people about their interests, and they will tell you what they like and what they don't like. Complete each of the following statements and questions by filling in the blanks with the appropriate form of the verb given in parentheses. **(S. 50)**

1. Was (machen) _____ du gern, Ute? (zeichnen) _____ du gern?
2. Ich (zeichnen) _____ gern, und ich (sammeln) _____ Briefmarken.
3. Was (machen) _____ ihr jetzt? (schauen) _____ ihr jetzt Fernsehen?
4. Wir (hören) _____ jetzt Musik, und wir (spielen) _____ Karten.
5. Herr Meier, was (machen) _____ Sie? (spielen) _____ Sie Tennis?
6. Ich (spielen) _____ heute Volleyball.
7. Was (machen) _____ Tara und Stefan? (spielen) _____ sie Karten?
8. Nein, sie (besuchen) _____ Freunde.

4 When are these students doing various activities? Write an answer to each of the following questions, beginning each answer with the underlined part of the question. **(S. 55)**

1. Was machst du <u>nach der Schule</u>? Freunde besuchen? — Ja, _____ .
2. Was macht ihr <u>im Sommer</u>? Viel wandern? — Ja, _____ .
3. Was machen Tara und Eva <u>am Nachmittag</u>? Tennis spielen? — Ja, _____ .
4. Was machst du <u>am Abend</u>? Fernsehen schauen? — Ja, _____ .
5. Was macht ihr <u>am Wochenende</u>? Musik hören? — Ja, _____ .
6. Was machen Bob und Ed <u>am Abend</u>? Moped fahren? — Ja, _____ .

5 You are writing a note to a friend telling what you do after school. Complete the following paragraph by filling in each blank with the appropriate form of a verb. Suggested infinitives are given in the box. **(S. 56)**

besuchen	haben	gehen	hören
schauen	sammeln		spielen

Nach der Schule _____ ich Musik, oder ich _____ Freunde und wir

_____ Karten. Am Nachmittag _____ ich schwimmen, und am Abend

_____ ich Fernsehen. Ich _____ auch andere Interessen: ich _____

Briefmarken und Comics.

6 Ask your friends about their opinions regarding various activities. Then give your opinion. Complete the questions by filling in the blanks with the appropriate form of the verb used to ask for and to express an opinion. **(S. 57)**

1. Basteln macht Spaß. Und wie _____ du Basteln?
2. Schach spielen ist langweilig. Und wie _____ ihr Schach?
3. Volleyball ist Spitze. Und wie _____ Ahmet Volleyball?
4. Wandern ist toll. Und wie _____ Tara und Steffi Wandern?
5. Fußball ist super! Ich _____ Fußball auch super!

7 Someone is expressing an opinion about various activities, and you agree. Complete your agreement by filling in each blank with the correct form of the verb that expresses the activity mentioned. **(S. 56)**

1. Ich finde Segeln Spitze! — Ja, ich _____ auch gern.
2. Ich finde Wandern prima! — Ja, ich _____ auch sehr gern.
3. Ich finde Basteln toll! — Ja, ich _____ auch sehr gern.
4. Ich finde Zeichnen super! — Ja, ich _____ auch gern.
5. Ich finde Schwimmen Spitze! — Ja, ich _____ auch gern.
6. Ich finde Tanzen toll! — Ja, ich _____ auch gern.

MEHR GRAMMATIKÜBUNGEN   *dreiundsechzig*   **63**

CD-ROM DISC 1

internet
ADRESSE: go.hrw.com
KENNWORT:
WK3 BRANDENBURG-2

 1 You will hear several people talk about their interests and activities. Take notes as you listen, then answer the questions **Wer? Was? Wann?** for each conversation.

 2 **a.** Listen to the description of **der Sporti** and **die Sporti** pictured below. Write down any sports and activities that are mentioned but not pictured.

 b. Pick one of the **Sportis** below and tell your partner everything the **Sporti** does. Your partner will tell you about the other **Sporti**.

der Sporti   die Sporti

3 Look at the drawings of **der Sporti** and **die Sporti** above and use them for clues to answer the following questions.

a. Was machst du in deiner Freizeit? Wann machst du das? Was machst du nicht?

b. Wie findest du das alles? Zum Beispiel, wie findest du Fußball, Tennis usw.?

4 Everyone in class will write on a slip of paper the German name for an activity presented in the chapter. Put all the slips of paper into a small box, then get into two teams. Two students, one from each team, together draw a slip of paper from the box. These two "mimes" will act out the activity, and the teams will take turns guessing what they are doing. The first person to guess right wins a point for his or her team. Guesses must be in this form: **Ihr spielt Tennis!**

5 Read the following student profiles. Working with a partner, take turns choosing one of the people pictured below and telling your partner about that person's name, age and interests.

Nicole König, 14
Hamburg
Tennis und Volleyball
spielen, zeichnen,
Freunde besuchen

Martin Braun, 16
Düsseldorf
Fußball und Gitarre
spielen, Briefmarken
sammeln, wandern

Julia Meier, 15
Ludwigsburg
schwimmen, Klavier
spielen, basteln, Schach
spielen, Musik hören

 6 Working in groups of three, interview each member of your group and write descriptions like the ones above. First, decide together which questions you need to ask. Then, while one person interviews another, the third writes down the information on a separate piece of paper, leaving out the person's name. When the whole class is finished, put the descriptions in a box and take turns drawing them and telling the class about that person. Your classmates will guess who is being described.

 7 One of the students pictured above is visiting your school, and you have to introduce him or her at a German club meeting. Write down what you are going to say in complete sentences.

8

Rollenspiel

Get together with two of your classmates and act out the following situation.

It's Friday after school. You and two of your friends are really bored, and you are trying to find something fun to do. Discuss the activities that each of you likes, then try to find several that you can do together. Make a plan that includes several different activities and discuss when you want to do them. Be prepared to report your plans to the class.

Kann ich's wirklich?

Can you ask about someone's interests, report them, and tell your own? (p. 48)

1 How would you ask a classmate about interests, using the verbs **spielen, machen, schwimmen,** and **sammeln?**

2 How would you report someone else's interests?
   a. Susanne: tanzen, wandern, Gitarre spielen
   b. Jörg: Golf spielen, basteln, zeichnen
   c. Johannes: Schach spielen, Freunde besuchen
   d. Uschi: Fernsehen schauen, Musik hören, Karten spielen

Can you ask what others like to do and don't like to do, report what they say, and tell what you and your friends like and don't like to do? (p. 50)

3 How would you tell some of the things you do?

4
   a. How would you say what activities you like and don't like to do?
   b. How would you ask a classmate what he or she likes to do and report that information to someone else?
   c. How would you ask these people what they like to do and then report what they say?
      Katharina und Ute: schwimmen, Schach spielen, Musik hören
   d. How would you ask your teacher if he or she plays basketball or chess, or if he or she collects stamps?

Can you say when you do various activities? (p. 55)

5 How would you say that you
   a. watch TV after school
   b. play soccer in the afternoon
   c. go hiking in the spring
   d. swim in the summer

6 How would you ask a classmate what he or she thinks of
   a. tennis
   b. music
   c. drawing
   d. hiking

Can you ask for an opinion, agree, disagree and express your own opinion? (pp. 57, 58)

7 Agree or disagree with the following statements. If you disagree, express your opinion.
   a. Schach ist langweilig.
   b. Basteln macht Spaß.
   c. Briefmarken sammeln ist interessant.
   d. Tennis ist super!

8 How would you express your opinion of the following activities:
   a. Fußball spielen
   b. Briefmarken sammeln
   c. wandern
   d. schwimmen

Erste Stufe

Talking about interests

Was machst du in deiner Freizeit?	*What do you do in your free time?*
Machst du Sport?	*Do you do sports?*
machen	*to do*
spielen	*to play*
Ich spiele Fußball.	*I play soccer.*
Basketball	*basketball*
Volleyball	*volleyball*
Tennis	*tennis*

Golf	*golf*
Spielst du ein Instrument?	*Do you play an instrument?*
Ich spiele Klavier.	*I play the piano.*
Gitarre	*guitar*
Karten	*cards*
Schach	*chess*
Hast du andere Interessen?	*Do you have other interests?*

Other useful words and phrases

viel	*a lot, much*
nicht	*not, don't*
andere	*other*
Ich glaube …	*I think …*
oft	*often*

Zweite Stufe

Expressing likes and dislikes

gern (machen)	*to like (to do)*
nicht gern (machen)	*to not like (to do)*
nicht so gern	*not to like very much*

Activities

Briefmarken sammeln	*to collect stamps*
Comics sammeln	*to collect comics*
Freunde besuchen	*to visit friends*
Fernsehen schauen	*to watch TV*
Musik hören	*to listen to music*
zeichnen	*to draw*

basteln	*to do crafts*
schwimmen	*to swim*
tanzen	*to dance*
wandern	*to hike*
Spielen Sie Tennis, Herr Meyer?	*Do you play tennis, Mr. Meyer?*

Pronouns

ich	*I*
wir	*we*
du	*you*
ihr	*you (pl)*
er	*he*
sie	*she*

es	*it*
sie	*they*
Sie	*you (formal)*

Other useful words and phrases

so	*so*
sehr	*very*
Sag mal, …	*Say, …*
Tja …	*Hm …*
schreiben	*to write*
Ich gehe schwimmen.	*I go swimming.*

Dritte Stufe

Saying when you do various activities

die Hausaufgaben machen	*to do homework*
Wann?	*When?*
nach der Schule	*after school*
am Nachmittag	*in the afternoon*
am Abend	*in the evening*
am Wochenende	*on the weekend*
im Frühling	*in the spring*
im Sommer	*in the summer*
im Herbst	*in the fall*
im Winter	*in the winter*

Expressing opinions

Wie findest du (Tennis)?	*What do you think of (tennis)?*

Ich finde (Tennis) …	*I think (tennis) is …*
Spitze!	*super!*
super!	*super!*
Klasse! prima! toll!	*great! terrific!*
interessant	*interesting*
langweilig	*boring*
blöd	*dumb*
(Tanzen) macht Spaß.	*(Dancing) is fun.*
(Tennis) macht keinen Spaß.	*(Tennis) is no fun.*

Agreeing and disagreeing

Ich auch.	*Me too.*
Ich nicht.	*I don't./Not me!*
Stimmt!	*That's right! True!*
Stimmt nicht!	*Not true!*
Das finde ich auch.	*I think so too.*
Das finde ich nicht.	*I disagree.*

Other useful phrases

Ich surfe Sport im Internet.	*I surf the 'Net for sports.*
So ein Mist!	*Darn it!*

3

Komm mit nach Hause!

Objectives

In this chapter you will learn to

Erste Stufe

- talk about where you live
- offer something to eat and drink and respond
- say please, thank you, and you're welcome

Zweite Stufe

- describe a room

Dritte Stufe

- talk about family members
- describe people

ADRESSE: go.hrw.com
KENNWORT:
  WK3 BRANDENBURG-3

◀ **Fahr mit mir nach Hause!**

Los geht's! ▪ *Bei Jens zu Hause!*

Strategie Verstehen

Look at the photos on these two pages. Where and when do you think these scenes are taking place? What clues tell you this?

Jens   **Tara**   **Holger**   **Mutter**

1

Jens:	Du gehst zu Fuß nach Hause? Wo wohnst du denn?
Holger:	In der Kopernikusstraße.
Jens:	Wo ist die?
Holger:	In Babelsberg.
Jens:	Ich wohn auch dort in der Nähe. Möchtest du nicht mit mir nach Hause kommen?
Holger:	Prima!

3

Jens:	Hallo, Mutti! Wo bist du?
Mutter:	Hier oben! Ich komme gleich runter.

Jens:	Du, Mutti, das ist Holger, ein Klassenkamerad. Er ist neu.
Holger:	Guten Tag, Frau Hartmann!
Mutter:	Tag, Holger!

4

Mutter:	Möchtet ihr etwas trinken? Oder was essen?
Jens:	Ja, was möchtest du?
Holger:	Ach, ich möchte ... ich trinke eine Cola.
Jens:	Und ich ein Mineralwasser. Haben wir noch Kuchen?
Mutter:	Ich glaube ja.

5

Jens:	Hier, deine Cola und dein Kuchen.
Holger:	Danke!
Jens:	Bitte!

6

Holger: Sag mal, hast du Geschwister?

Jens: Ja, hier, schau! Mein Bruder und meine Schwester.

Holger: Hm, sie sieht nett aus. Wie alt ist sie?

Jens: Bine ist älter, sie ist neunzehn. Mein Bruder ist zwölf.

7

Jens: Ah, übrigens, meine Kusine kommt nachher.

Holger: Deine Kusine? Wie alt ist sie?

Jens: So alt wie ich. Auch sechzehn.

Holger: Ja, wirklich? Wie sieht sie aus?

Jens: Sie ist sehr hübsch. Sie hat braune Haare, braune Augen. Sie ist 1,65 groß und sehr charmant.

Holger: Genau mein Typ.

Jens: Ich weiß. Komm, ich zeig dir jetzt mein Zimmer.

8

Holger: He! Das Poster — Spitze! Wer ist das?

Jens: Na, rate mal!

Holger: Hm, ich weiß nicht.

Jens: Das ist Patricia Kaas!

Holger: Ach so! — Du hast es schön hier. Dein Zimmer ist phantastisch. Die Möbel sind toll! Neu, ja?

Jens: Ja, der Schrank ist neu ...das Regal, das Bett ... und ...

9

Jens: He, das ist bestimmt meine Kusine. — Komm mal mit, Holger!

10

Holger: Was? Tara ist deine Kusine? Das glaub ich nicht.

Tara: Ja, sicher! Ich bin seine Kusine. — Hallo, Tante Monika!

Holger: Und ich denke, Tara ist deine Freundin!

Jens: Mensch, Holger! Du denkst zu viel!

Übungsheft, S. 25 Ü. 1

1 Was passiert hier?

Do you understand what is happening in the story „**Bei Jens zu Hause**"? Check your comprehension by answering these questions. Don't be afraid to guess.

1. Where do Jens and Holger go together after soccer practice?
2. What do the boys do first when they get home?
3. What kinds of photos does Jens show Holger?
4. How does Holger like Jens' room?
5. Who comes to visit? Why do you think Holger is surprised?

2 Genauer lesen

Reread the conversations. Which words or phrases do the characters use to

1. introduce someone else
2. name foods or drinks
3. name family members
4. describe people
5. name or describe furniture

3 Stimmt oder stimmt nicht?

Are these statements right or wrong? Answer each one with either **stimmt** or **stimmt nicht**. If a statement is wrong, try to state it correctly.

1. Holger geht mit Jens nach Hause.
2. Frau Hartmann ist Holgers Mutter.
3. Holger trinkt eine Cola und isst ein Stück Kuchen.
4. Jens hat zwei Geschwister: einen Bruder und eine Schwester.
5. Der Bruder ist neunzehn, und die Schwester ist zwölf.
6. Holger hat auch eine Kusine. Sie heißt Tara.

4 Was passt zusammen?

Match each statement or question on the left with an appropriate response on the right.

1. Wo wohnst du?
2. Mutti, das ist Holger.
3. Möchtest du etwas trinken?
4. Jens, hast du Geschwister?
5. Wie sieht deine Kusine aus?
6. Dein Zimmer ist schön! Sind die Möbel neu?
7. Ich denke, Tara ist deine Freundin!

a. Der Schrank ist neu.
b. Ja, das ist meine Schwester, und das ist mein Bruder.
c. In der Kopernikusstraße.
d. Nein, sie ist meine Kusine.
e. Ich möchte eine Cola, bitte!
f. Sie ist sehr hübsch.
g. Guten Tag, Holger!

5 Nacherzählen

Put the sentences in logical order to make a brief summary of the story.

1. Zuerst fährt Holger mit Jens nach Hause.

Und dann zeigt er Holger sein Zimmer.

Frau Hartmann sagt Holger „Guten Tag".

Und Jens gibt Holger eine Cola und ein Stück Kuchen.

Zuletzt kommt Tara, die Kusine von Jens.

Er zeigt Holger Fotos von der Familie.

Objectives Talking about where you live; offering something to eat and drink and responding; saying please, thank you, and you're welcome

WK3 BRANDENBURG-3

So sagt man das!

Talking about where you live

To find out where someone lives, you ask:

Wo wohnst du?

Wo wohnt der Jens?

How would you ask someone where Tara lives?[1]

The responses might be:

Ich wohne in Los Angeles. *or*
In Los Angeles.

Er wohnt in Babelsberg. *or*
Ich denke, in Babelsberg.

Übungsheft, S. 26, Ü. 2

Wortschatz

AHMET   Wo wohnt Dieter?
JENS   Er wohnt in (Babelsberg).

Michaela

in der Stadt

AHMET   Wohnt ihr **weit von hier?**
GÜNTHER   Nein, ich wohne **in der Nähe.**
ANDREA   Ja, ich wohne **weit von hier.**

Andrea

auf dem Land

Dieter

in Babelsberg, das ist ein Vorort von Potsdam

Günther

in der Brunnenstraße

Grammatikheft, S.19, Ü. 1–2

---

1. Wo wohnt (die) Tara?

6 Wo wohnen die Schüler?

Zuhören You will hear four students talk about where they live. Match each description with one of the pictures below.

a.

b.

c.

d.

 7 Wo wohnen die Schüler?

Sprechen Ahmet wants to know where these students live. Answer his questions using the pictures as cues.

1. Wo wohnt die Sara?

2. Wo wohnt der Georg?

3. Wo wohnen Jürgen und Simone?

4. Wo wohnt die Anja?

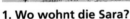 **8 Wer wohnt wo?**

Sprechen Ask your partner where he or she lives, then switch roles. Describe where you live in as much detail as you can, using the phrases you learned in the **Wortschatz** box. Be prepared to tell the class as much as you can about where your partner lives.

So sagt man das!

Offering something to eat and drink and responding

Often, when friends come over, you ask what they would like to eat and drink.
You might ask:

> **Was möchtest du trinken?**
> **Was möchte Holger trinken?**

To offer several friends something to eat, you might ask:

> **Was möchtet ihr essen?**

The response might be:

> **Ich möchte ein Mineralwasser trinken.**
> **Er möchte im Moment gar nichts.**

The response might be:

> **Wir möchten ein Stück Kuchen, bitte.**

Can you figure out what **möchte** means?[1]

---

1. *would like to*

Was möchtet ihr trinken?

Ein Glas Orangensaft.

Eine Cola, bitte!

Ein Mineralwasser.

Ein Glas Apfelsaft.

Und was möchtet ihr essen?

Ein Stück Kuchen, bitte!

Ich möchte Obst.

Ein paar Kekse.

Danke, nichts!

---

9 ### Bei Jens zu Hause

Zuhören Ahmet and Tara come over to Jens' house. Listen to their conversation with Jens and write down what each one would like to eat and drink.

Ein wenig Grammatik

Some of the names for the snack items pictured on this page are preceded by either **ein** or **eine**. What do you think these words mean?[1] Now look at the words below.

ein Junge   eine Limo   ein Stück (Kuchen)

Why are there different forms of **ein**?[2]

Und dann noch...

eine Tasse Kaffee   eine Orange
eine Tasse Tee   ein Stück Melone
eine Banane

Ein wenig Landeskunde

If someone asks for **ein Glas Wasser, ein Glas Mineralwasser** will be served. Germans rarely drink tap water, considering it to be unhealthy. In addition, Germans very rarely use ice cubes in cold drinks, even in cafés and restaurants.

10 ### Grammatik im Kontext

a. Sprechen Look at the pictures in the **Wortschatz** box above and ask your partner what he or she would like to eat and drink.

BEISPIEL   DU   Möchtest du _____ Stück Kuchen?
        PARTNER   Ich möchte jetzt _____ paar Kekse.

b. Schreiben Copy these sentences and fill in the blanks with either **ein** or **eine**.

1. Ich möchte _____ Glas Saft.
2. Wer möchte _____ Stück Kuchen?
3. Holger möchte _____ Cola.
4. Ich möchte _____ Mineralwasser.
5. Wer möchte _____ Banane?
6. Holger möchte _____ Orange.

---

1. Both **ein** and **eine** mean *a, an*. 2. Masculine and neuter nouns are preceded by **ein**, feminine nouns by **eine**.

Grammatik

The *möchte*-forms

The **möchte**-forms express what you *would like* or *would like to do*. They are often used with another verb, but if the meaning is obvious, the second verb can be omitted.

Ich **möchte** ein Glas Orangensaft **trinken**.
Ich **möchte** Obst **essen**. *or* Ich **möchte** Obst.

Here are the forms of **möchte**:

ich	möchte	wir	möchten
du	möchtest	ihr	möchtet
er, sie, es	möchte	sie, Sie	möchten

Mehr Grammatikübungen,
S. 88, Ü. 1–3

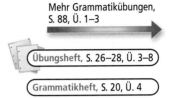

Übungsheft, S. 26–28, Ü. 3–8

Grammatikheft, S. 20, Ü. 4

11 Grammatik im Kontext

a. Sprechen/Schreiben Say what everyone would like using the words and pictures as cues.

| 1. Wir ... | 2. Ihr ... | 3. Er ... | 4. Du ... | 5. Ich ... | 6. Jens und Holger ... |

b. Schreiben Copy these sentences and fill in the blanks with the correct **möchte**-form.

1. Was ===== du essen?   Ich ===== ein Stück Kuchen.
2. Was ===== Holger trinken?   Ich glaube, er ===== ein Mineralwasser.
3. Und ihr, Steffi und Jens, was ===== ihr?   Wir ===== Obst.
4. Frau Weigel, was ===== Sie trinken?   Ach, ich ===== jetzt ein Glas Apfelsaft.

So sagt man das!

Saying please, thank you, and you're welcome

Grammatikheft, S. 21, Ü. 5

To say please, you can simply say **bitte**. You can also add **bitte** to a request:
Ich möchte eine Limo, bitte.

Here are several ways to say thank you:

Danke! Danke sehr! Danke schön!

Here are several ways to say you're welcome:

Bitte! Bitte sehr! Bitte schön!

12 Snacks für deine Freunde

Sprechen Role-play the following situation with three classmates. Use as many forms of **möchte** as possible. You have invited three friends home for a snack after school. One friend will help you get the snack ready by asking the other two "guests" what they would like to eat and drink. After they answer, your helper will tell you what everyone would like. When you have finished, switch roles until everyone has been the "host" and the "helper."

LANDESKUNDE · LANDESKUNDE

Wo wohnst du?

We asked several teenagers where they live. Before you read their interviews, write where you live, using as much detail as you can. Two of these teenagers were not born in Germany. Can you guess who they are?

CD-ROM DISC 1

VIDEO

Übungsheft, S. 36, Ü. 26-31

Dominick, Hamburg

„Ich heiß Dominick Klein. Ich bin zwölf Jahre alt und wohn in Hamburg, also Pinneberg."

Jasmin, München

„Ich heiße Jasmin und bin fünfzehn. Ich geh in die Reichenau-Schule. Und ich wohne in München, und ich komme aus der Türkei."

Thomas, München

„Ich heiße Thomas Schwangart. Ich wohne in München. Ich bin an der Reichenau-Schule und komme aus Italien."

Johanna, Hamburg

„Ich heiß Johanna. Ich bin zwölf Jahre alt und ich wohn in Hamburg."

Ingo, Hamburg

„Ich wohn hier in der Nähe, also in der Gustav-Falke-Straße. Das sind zehn Minuten von hier."

A. 1. Write the name of each person interviewed and what each person says about where he or she lives.

2. Now look at what you wrote earlier. Did any of these teenagers say where they live in the same way you did? If so, which ones? What seems to be the most natural response to the question **Wo wohnst du?** Is this also your first response?

3. Discuss these questions with your classmates: Who are the two teenagers not born in Germany? Where are they from? Did you pick the right people before you read the interviews? What influenced your choice? Considering that two out of these five teenagers were not born in Germany, what can you infer about the ethnic makeup of German society in the large cities?

B. There are many ethnic groups represented in German society: Turks, Italians, Greeks, and many Eastern Europeans, just to name a few. Italian, Greek, Chinese, Indonesian and Thai foods have become very popular with native Germans. Why do you think some of these ethnic groups might be attracted to Germany? How does this compare with the situation in the United States? Discuss these questions with your classmates and then write a brief essay answering these questions.

Wortschatz

Jens zeigt Holger sein Zimmer.

HOLGER   Deine Möbel sind schön!

JENS   Ja, wirklich? Schau!

Das Regal ist schon alt.

Das Bett ist sehr unbequem.

Die Stereoanlage ist kaputt.

Der Schreibtisch ist schön.

Der Stuhl ist sehr bequem.

Der Schrank ist ganz groß.

Die Couch ist ganz neu.

groß – klein
bequem – unbequem
alt – neu
schön – hässlich
kaputt

If **bequem** means *comfortable*, what does **unbequem** mean? What do you think the word **hässlich** means? **Groß** means *large*; what do you think **klein** means? The word **neu** looks like what word in English? What is its opposite?

Übungsheft, S. 29, Ü. 9   Grammatikheft, S. 22, Ü. 8–10

13 Steffis Zimmer

Zuhören Listen as Steffi describes her room to Ahmet, and match each piece of furniture on the left with the appropriate adjective on the right.

1. die Stereoanlage   **a.** bequem
2. der Schrank   **b.** schön
3. das Regal   **c.** groß
4. der Schreibtisch   **d.** neu
5. der Stuhl   **e.** alt
6. das Bett   **f.** klein

So sagt man das!

Describing a room

To describe your room, you might say:

> **Die Stereoanlage ist alt. Sie ist auch kaputt!**
> **Das Bett ist klein aber ganz bequem.** *or* **Das Bett ist klein, aber es ist ganz bequem.**

A friend might ask:

> **Ist der Computer neu?**

You might respond:

> **Ja, er ist neu, aber er ist kaputt.**

What do you think the words **er, sie,** and **es** refer to?[1] What is the English equivalent?[2] Why are there three different words that mean the same thing?[3]

Übungsheft,
S. 29–30, Ü. 10–12

---

14 **Versteckte Sätze**

Sprechen/Schreiben How many sentences can you make using the words in the boxes? Use the picture of Jens' room on page 78 for clues.

BEISPIEL **Die Couch ist neu, aber unbequem.**

Die Couch		bequem		alt
Der Schrank		hässlich		neu
Das Bett		klein		bequem
Das Regal		ganz unbequem		unbequem
Der Schreibtisch	ist	schon alt	aber	schön
Die Stereoanlage		schon kaputt		hässlich
Das Zimmer		neu		groß
Der Stuhl		ganz schön		klein
		sehr groß		kaputt

Grammatik

Pronouns

Er, sie, and **es** are called pronouns. **Er** refers to a masculine noun, **sie** to a feminine noun, and **es** to a neuter noun.

masculine	**Der Schreibtisch** ist neu. *or* **Er** ist neu.
feminine	**Die Stereoanlage** ist kaputt. *or* **Sie** ist kaputt.
neuter	**Das Regal** ist hässlich. *or* **Es** ist hässlich.

The pronoun **sie** is also used to refer to a plural noun.

plural	**Die Möbel** sind schön. *or* **Sie** sind schön.

Mehr Grammatikübungen,
S. 89–90, Ü. 4–7

Übungsheft, S. 30–31, Ü. 13–15

Grammatikheft, S. 23, Ü. 11–12

---

15 **Im Klassenzimmer**

Sprechen Describe your classroom and some of the furniture in it.

---

1. The nouns mentioned in the preceding sentences. 2. Here, **er, sie** and **es** are all equivalent to *it*.
3. The nouns they refer to belong to different noun classes, i.e., masculine, feminine, and neuter.

16 **Grammatik im Kontext**

Lesen/Sprechen Jens has seen Holger's new room and is talking to Steffi about it. Complete his description by filling in the correct article and pronoun.

___1___ Zimmer ist sehr groß, und ___2___ ist ganz schön. ___3___ Couch ist schön, und ___4___ ist auch neu. ___5___ Bett ist ziemlich klein, aber ___6___ ist sehr bequem. ___7___ Schrank ist wirklich alt, und ___8___ ist sehr groß. ___9___ Stereoanlage ist super! ___10___ ist ganz neu. ___11___ Schreibtisch ist groß, aber ___12___ ist leider hässlich. Und dann noch ___13___ Regal. ___14___ ist auch sehr groß. ___15___ Möbel sind wirklich toll. ___16___ sind Klasse!

17 **Wie findest du das Zimmer?**

Sprechen Use one of these adjectives to describe the items below to your partner. Your partner may agree or disagree. Then switch roles.

Du **Der Schreibtisch ist sehr schön.**

Partner **Ja, stimmt! Er ist sehr schön.** *or* **Was? Er ist ganz hässlich!**

bequem kaputt neu hässlich
alt klein groß schön
unbequem

a.

b.

c.

d.

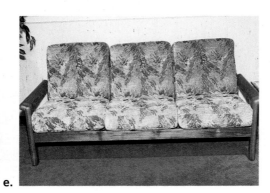

e.

f.

18 **Mein Zimmer**

Schreiben Draw a diagram of your room or a room you would like to have. Label the pieces of furniture. Then write a few sentences describing your room. If you need extra vocabulary, turn to page R9.

Wortschatz

Jens und seine Familie

Grammatikheft, S. 24, Ü. 13

die Großmutter (Oma)
Ella

der Großvater (Opa)
Georg

meine Großeltern

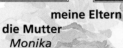

meine Eltern
die Mutter — **der Vater**
Monika — *Dieter*

die Tante — **der Onkel**
Hannelore — *Amir*

Jens

meine Geschwister
die Schwester — **der Bruder**
Sabine — *Andreas*

die Kusine — **der Cousin**
Tara — *Tawan*

die Katze
Fritzi

der Hund
Harras

meine Haustiere

Und dann noch...

Stiefmutter	*stepmother*
Stiefvater	*stepfather*
Stiefschwester	*stepsister*
Stiefbruder	*stepbrother*
Halbschwester	*half sister*
Halbbruder	*half brother*

19 Familienquiz

Lesen/Sprechen Answer the following questions about Jens' family.

1. Wie heißen Sabines Mutter und Vater?
2. Wie heißen die Geschwister von Jens?
3. Wer ist die Schwester von Dieter?
4. Wie heißt Dieters Vater?
5. Wer ist der Onkel von Sabines Bruder?
6. Wer ist die Kusine von Tawan?
7. Wer ist der Bruder von Taras Mutter?
8. Wie heißen die Haustiere?

20 Unsere Familien

Zuhören Make a chart like the one below, listing all of the new vocabulary from Jens' family tree. Then listen as three friends of Jens' describe their families. Every time you hear a family member mentioned put a check next to the correct vocabulary word. After listening to the descriptions, try to answer these questions.

1. Who mentions the most family members?
2. Who does not mention the mother?
3. Who mentions an aunt but not an uncle?
4. Who mentions an uncle but not an aunt?
5. Do any of the three friends mention pets? If so, who mentions them?

	Anja	Werner	Christa
der Vater			
die Mutter			
der Bruder			

So sagt man das!

Talking about family members

To find out about someone's family you might ask:

Ist das deine Schwester?
Wie alt ist sie?
Und dein Bruder? Wie heißt er?
Wie alt ist er?
Und wer ist der Mann?
Und die Frau?
Wo wohnen deine Großeltern?

The responses might be:

Ja, das ist meine Schwester.
Sie ist einundzwanzig.
Mein Bruder heißt Robert.
Er ist schon dreiundzwanzig.
Das ist mein Opa.
Das ist meine Oma.
In Köln.

What is the difference between **dein** and **deine**? **Mein** and **meine**? What do the words mean? When is each one used?

Übungsheft, S. 32, Ü. 16–18

Ein wenig Grammatik

The words **dein** and **deine** (*your*) and **mein** and **meine** (*my*) are called *possessives*.

masculine (**der**)
neuter (**das**) } **mein, dein**

feminine (**die**)
plural (**die**) } **meine, deine**

These words are similar to **ein** and **eine**. Because of this similarity, **mein** and **dein** are often called **ein**-words.

Grammatikheft, S. 24, Ü. 14

Mehr Grammatikübungen, S. 90–91, Ü. 8–9

21 Grammatik im Kontext

Lesen/Sprechen Steffi and Tara are looking at photos of their families. Complete their conversation by filling in the blanks with **mein/meine** or **dein/deine**.

TARA Ist das ___1___ Schwester?

STEFFI Ja, das ist Angelika.

TARA Wie alt ist ___2___ Schwester?

STEFFI ___3___ Schwester ist zwanzig.
Und das ist ___4___ Bruder. Er ist einundzwanzig.

TARA Und sind das ___5___ Großeltern?

STEFFI Ja, das ist ___6___ Oma, und das ist ___7___ Opa. Ist das ___8___ Vater?

TARA Nein, das ist ___9___ Onkel Dieter. Und das hier ist ___10___ Tante.

STEFFI Ist das ___11___ Kusine?

TARA Ja, das ist ___12___ Kusine, die Sabine. Und das ist ___13___ Cousin, Jens.

Grammatikheft, S. 25, Ü. 15

CD-ROM DISC 1

To talk about the ages of various family members, you need to review **die Zahlen von 0 bis 20** and learn **die Zahlen von 21 bis 100**.

21	einundzwanzig	26	sechsundzwanzig	30	dreißig	70	siebzig
22	zweiundzwanzig	27	siebenundzwanzig	40	vierzig	80	achtzig
23	dreiundzwanzig	28	achtundzwanzig	50	fünfzig	90	neunzig
24	vierundzwanzig	29	neunundzwanzig	60	sechzig	100	hundert
25	fünfundzwanzig						

a. With your classmates, count aloud to one hundred, first by tens, then by fives, then by twos. Students take turns leading the counting.

b. Make up simple math problems with no results greater than 100. Working with a partner, ask each other the problems you each wrote down and see how fast you can solve them. Some words you may need are **und** (*plus*), **minus** (*minus*), **mal** (*times*), and **durch** (*divided by*).

22 Steffis Familie

Zuhören Listen as Steffi tells Tara more about her family. First list the names of the family members in the order you hear them. Then listen a second time and write their ages beside their names.

die Kusine Anna   die Mutter   der Vater   der Cousin Bernhard

die Großmutter   der Onkel Florian   der Großvater   die Tante

---

Ein wenig Grammatik

The words **sein** (*his*) and **ihr** (*her*) are also possessives. They take the same endings as **mein** and **dein**.

masculine (**der**)
neuter (**das**) } **sein, ihr**

feminine (**die**)
plural (**die**) } **seine, ihre**

Grammatikheft, S. 25, Ü. 16

Mehr Grammatikübungen, S. 91, Ü. 10–11

23 Grammatik im Kontext

Sprechen Bring some photos of family members to class, or if you like, bring in pictures from magazines and create a make-believe family. Show the photos to your partner, and he or she will ask you questions about them. Then switch roles. When you have finished, tell your class-mates what you learned about one of your partner's relatives.

BEISPIEL   DU   **Das ist Bobs Vater. Sein … heißt …**   *or*

           DU   **Das ist Kristins Kusine. Ihre … ist …**

24 Für mein Notizbuch

Schreiben Write four sentences in which you tell about two of your favorite family members or people who are close to you.

Steffi zeigt Tara ein Fotoalbum. Steffi:

Meine Mutter hat lange, rote Haare und grüne Augen. Sie spielt gern Schach.

Mein Vater hat braune Haare und blaue Augen. Er spielt sehr gut Klavier.

Und mein Bruder Ralf ist einundzwanzig. Er hat kurze, blonde Haare und hat eine Brille. Er schwimmt sehr gern.

Meine Großmutter Marie ist fünfundsechzig. Sie hat weiße Haare und blaue Augen. Sie hört gern Musik.

Und meine Kusine Anna ist zweiundzwanzig. Sie hat kurze, schwarze Haare und braune Augen. Sie geht oft wandern.

Mein Onkel Florian hat eine Glatze und grüne Augen. Er hat auch eine Brille. Er sammelt gern Briefmarken.

Grammatikheft, S. 26–27, Ü. 17–20

25 **Steffis Familie**

Sprechen Working with your partner, create a chart of the characteristics of Steffi's family. Write the names of the various family members across the top and their characteristics underneath using the categories **Alter, Haarfarbe, Augenfarbe,** and **Interessen.**

So sagt man das!

Describing people

Übungsheft, S. 33–34, Ü. 19–23

CD-ROM DISC 1

If you want to know what someone looks like, you might ask:

Wie sieht dein Bruder aus?

The response might be:

Er hat lange, blonde Haare und braune Augen.

If you are asking about more than one person, you say:

Wie sehen deine Großeltern aus?

Mein Opa hat weiße Haare und grüne Augen. Und meine Oma hat graue Haare und blaue Augen.

26 Wie sieht Steffis Familie aus?

Schreiben Referring to the chart you and your partner made for Activity 25, try to answer the following questions about Steffi's family.

1. Wer hat blaue Augen?
2. Wie alt ist Steffis Bruder? Und ihre Kusine?
3. Wie sieht Onkel Florian aus?
4. Was macht die Mutter in der Freizeit? Der Vater? Anna?

5. Wie sehen die Eltern aus?
6. Wer hat schwarze Haare?
7. Wer hat kurze Haare? Lange Haare?
8. Wie alt ist die Großmutter? Wie sieht sie aus?
9. Wer hat eine Brille?

27 Rate mal!

Sprechen Pick one person in the room and think about how you might describe him or her to someone else. Your partner will ask you questions and try to guess whom you have chosen. Then switch roles.

BEISPIEL   PARTNER   **Hat diese Person blonde Haare?**

28

 Von der Schule zum Beruf

Schreiben You work as a police detective. You are trying to apprehend a wanted person. Write a profile of that person, giving name, age, residence, interests, and a physical description.

AUSSPRACHE

Richtig aussprechen / Richtig lesen

A. To practice the following sounds, say the words and sentences below after your teacher or after the recording.

1. The letter **o**: The long **o** is pronounced much like the long *o* in the English word *oboe;* however, the lips are more rounded.

   Obst, Moped, schon / Wo wohnt deine Oma?

2. The letter **u**: The long **u** is similar to the vowel sound in the English word *do;* however, the lips are more rounded.

   Stuhl, super, Kuchen / Möchtest du ein Stück Kuchen?

3. The letters **s, ß, ss**: When the letter **s** begins a word or syllable and is followed by a vowel, it is pronounced like the *z* in the English word *zebra*. In the middle or final position of a syllable, the letter **s** sounds similar to the *s* in the English word *post*. The letters **ß** and **ss** are also pronounced this way.

   so, sieben, Sonja / Deine Kusine sieht sehr hübsch aus.
   aus, das, es   /   Die Couch ist zu groß und ganz hässlich.

Richtig schreiben / Diktat

B. Write down the sentences that you hear.
Note: You write **ß** after a long vowel (**groß**), diphthongs (**weiß**) and **ss** after a short vowel (**hässlich**). Exceptions are some short words, such as **das** and **was,** that are spelled with a single **s** after a short vowel.

Wo wohnst du denn?

> **Lesestrategie** **Using root words to form new words**
> German, like English, uses root words to form new words with related meanings. When you know the root word, you can often guess the meaning of words that are built on that word. An example is the word **wohnen**. A number of words related in meaning can be built on the stem of this word, such as **Wohnung**, **bewohnbar**, and **Eigentumswohnung**.

1. What do you think the classified ads are about? You know the word **wohnen**. Does knowing the meaning of **wohnen** help you understand the ads? Make a list of words built on the stem of **wohnen** (**wohn-/Wohn-**) and try to guess what they mean.

2. Working with a partner, match these German words with their English equivalents. Remember to look for the root words.

   1. Wochenendheimfahrerin
   2. Eigentumswohnung
   3. Einfamilienhäuser
   4. Grundstück

      a. *plot (of land)*
      b. *someone who goes home on the weekend*
      c. *condominium*
      d. *single-family homes*

3. There are two types of ads on this page: ads describing available houses and apartments, and ads placed by people looking for a place to live. Can you figure out which ads fit into each of these categories?

Bauvorhaben
Gösstraße – Tübingen

Die Oase in der City!

z. B. 1½ Zimmer-Wohnung, Südloggia, Garage, großzügiger Grundriß mit 34 m² Wohnfläche:
€ 95 000.–

z. B. 3½ Zimmer-Wohnung, großer Südbalkon, herrliche Aussicht. 62 m² Wohnfläche, Garage:
€ 143 500.–

BAUCONCEPT
Der leistungsstarke Immobilien-Spezialist.

Rufen Sie uns an: Mo – Fr 7.30 bis 20.00 , Sa. 8.00 bis 16.00
Telefon: (0 70 31) 87 70 91

KOMM MIT NACH HAUSE!

Go To: http://www.hause.de

Auf dem Lande
Großzügiges Einfamilienhaus mit Einliegerwohnung in Remmingsheim. Allerbeste Ausstattung mit wertvollen Einbauten und offenem Kamin. Insg. 174 m² Wfl. bei 7½ Zimmern, gepflegtes Grundstück mit 3,5 Ar, Garage und Autoabstellplätze, sofort beziehbar.
€ 229 000.–

2-Zi.-Eigentumswohnung
(Baujahr 1985) in Entringen, sofort beziehbar, 52 m² Wohnfläche, Einbauküche, Balkon, Keller, Stellplatz.
€ 95 000.–

4. Which ads would be most
   interesting to these people:
   a. a large family wanting to buy
      a house
   b. a couple in Tübingen-Lustnau
      looking for a condominium
   c. the owner of several rental
      properties, looking for
      prospective tenants
5. Working with a partner, try to
   find the following information.
   a. the most expensive house or
      apartment
   b. the least expensive house or
      apartment
   c. the house or apartment with
      the most rooms
   d. the house or apartment with
      the most square meters of
      living space
   e. the house or apartment with
      the least amount of living
      space
   f. the places that have either a
      garage or a space to park a car
6. If you were looking for a place
   to live, which of these ads would
   appeal to you the most? Be
   prepared to tell why you would
   choose one place over another.
7. a. Assume that you are going to
      Germany for a year and need
      a place to live. Write an ad in
      German that summarizes
      what you need.
   b. Many Americans and
      Europeans swap houses for
      several weeks at a time, so that
      they can live in a different
      culture without having to pay
      enormous hotel expenses.
      Imagine that you are going to
      take part in such an **Austausch
      (exchange).** Using the format of
      these ads, write a classified ad
      for your home that you could
      place in a German newspaper.

Übungsheft, S. 35, Ü. 24–25

Mehr Grammatikübungen

CD-ROM DISC 1

internet

go.hrw.com

ADRESSE: go.hrw.com
KENNWORT:
WK3 BRANDENBURG-3

Erste Stufe

Objectives Offering something to eat and drink and responding to an offer

1 You have invited friends over, and you are offering food and beverages. Complete each of the following questions and statements by filling in each blank with the appropriate **möchte**-form. (S. 76)

1. Wer _____ ein paar Kekse essen? _____ du Kekse, Holger?

2. Die Tara _____ Obst. Und ihr, _____ ihr auch Obst?

3. Wir _____ Apfelsaft. Und was _____ Tara und Steffi?

4. Der Holger _____ Kuchen, und ich _____ auch Kuchen.

5. Der Jens _____ nichts, aber die Steffi _____ Mineralwasser.

6. Sag, _____ du Kuchen, oder _____ du ein paar Kekse?

7. Was _____ ihr? _____ ihr ein Glas Apfelsaft?

8. Wir _____ eine Cola, und die Tara _____ Orangensaft.

2 Your friends now want something else to eat or drink. Complete each of the following statements and questions by filling in the first blank with a **möchte**-form, and the second blank with the correct form of **ein**. (S. 76)

1. Der Holger _____ jetzt _____ Mineralwasser.

2. Wir _____ jetzt _____ Stück Kuchen, bitte.

3. Wer _____ jetzt _____ Limo trinken? Du, Holger?

4. Der Holger und die Tara _____ jetzt _____ Glas Apfelsaft.

5. Was _____ ihr jetzt? _____ paar Kekse?

6. Was _____ du essen? _____ Stück Kuchen?

7. Ich _____ gern _____ Cola trinken.

3 Ask your friends what they would like to eat or drink. Complete each of the following statements and questions by filling in each blank with the correct form of the pronoun or the **möchte**-form. (S. 76)

1. Was _____ ihr essen? Danke, nichts! _____ möchten jetzt nichts essen.

2. Was _____ du trinken? Ja, _____ möchte jetzt ein Glas Apfelsaft trinken.

3. Was _____ Tara trinken? Ja, _____ möchte Mineralwasser trinken.

4. Was _____ Jens und Ahmet? _____ möchten eine Cola.

5. Ich _____ eine Cola trinken. Was möchtest _____ trinken, Jens?

6. Und ihr? Was _____ ihr trinken? Trinkt _____ Mineralwasser?

4   You are describing to a friend of yours the various pieces of furniture in your room. Complete the following questions and statements by filling in the first blank with the correct form of the definite article, and the second blank with the correct pronoun. (**S. 79**)

1. Wo ist _____ Stereoanlage? Ist _____ kaputt?
2. _____ Schreibtisch ist schön, und _____ ist so groß!
3. Du, _____ Regal ist so alt, und _____ ist auch so hässlich.
4. Ja, _____ Schrank ist schön, und _____ ist sehr groß.
5. _____ Bett ist unbequem, und _____ ist so klein!
6. Ja, _____ Couch ist schon alt, aber _____ ist ganz bequem.
7. _____ Bett ist so klein, und _____ ist so unbequem!
8. Und _____ Stuhl ist so alt, und _____ ist ganz kaputt.
9. Ja, _____ Zimmer ist toll, und _____ ist so groß!
10. _____ Möbel sind schön; _____ sind ganz neu.

5   Your friend is surprised at the condition of your furniture. Complete each of the following questions by filling in each blank with the correct form of the definite article. (**S. 79**)

1. Er ist kaputt. Wirklich? _____ Schreibtisch ist kaputt?
2. Es ist kaputt. Wirklich? _____ Bett ist kaputt?
3. Sie ist schon alt. Wirklich? _____ Couch ist alt?
4. Er ist unbequem. Wirklich? _____ Stuhl ist unbequem?
5. Sie sind ganz neu. Wirklich? _____ Möbel sind ganz neu?
6. Es ist zu klein. Wirklich? _____ Regal ist zu klein?
7. Es ist so groß! Wirklich? _____ Zimmer ist doch nicht groß!
8. Er ist von meiner Oma. Wirklich? _____ Schrank von Oma Helen?
9. Er ist neu. Wirklich? _____ Computer ist neu?
10. Sie ist kaputt. Wirklich? _____ Stereoanlage ist kaputt?

6   You are serving snacks to your friends. Complete the following statements and questions by filling in each blank with the correct pronoun. (**S. 79**)

1. Hier ist die Limo. Danke, _____ ist prima!
2. Bitte, das Stück Kuchen. Hm, _____ ist so gut.
3. Das Obst ist sehr schön. Und _____ ist so gut für dich.
4. Ist das Glas kaputt? Nein, _____ ist nicht kaputt.
5. Hier ist die Cola. Ist _____ gut?
6. Ja, der Kuchen ist so schön! Und _____ ist so gut!

7 Your mother wants to know where all these misplaced items are. Fill in the first blank with the correct German noun and its definite article. Fill in the second blank with the pronoun that refers to that item. (S. 79)

1. (chair)   Wo ist _____ ? Ist _____ in Holgers Zimmer?
2. (furniture) Wo sind _____ ? Sind _____ im Garten?
3. (computer)   Wo ist _____ ? Ist _____ auch in Holgers Zimmer?
4. (shelf)   Wo ist _____ ? Ist _____ kaputt?
5. (desk)   Wo ist _____ ? Ist _____ in Taras Zimmer?
6. (cabinet)   Wo ist _____ ? Ist _____ zu groß für das Zimmer?
7. (couch)   Wo ist _____ ? Ist _____ jetzt in Ahmets Zimmer?
8. (bed)   Wo ist _____ ? Ist _____ wirklich kaputt?
9. (stereo)   Wo ist _____ ? Ist _____ kaputt?

Dritte Stufe

Objectives Talking about family members; describing people

8 You want to find out from a friend what the names of various members of his or her family are. Complete each of the following statements and questions by filling in each first blank with the correct form of the definite article, and each second blank with the correct form of the possessive **dein.** (S. 82)

1. _____ Vater von Andreas heißt Dieter. Wie heißt _____ Vater?
2. _____ Mutter von Andreas heißt Monika. Wie heißt _____ Mutter?
3. _____ Opa von Sabine heißt Georg. Wie heißt _____ Opa?
4. _____ Oma von Sabine heißt Ella. Wie heißt _____ Oma?
5. _____ Onkel von Jens heißt Amir. Und wie heißt _____ Onkel?
6. _____ Tante von Jens heißt Hannelore. Wie heißt _____ Tante?
7. _____ Kusine von Sabine heißt Tara. Wie heißt _____ Kusine?
8. _____ Cousin von Andreas heißt Tawan. Wie heißt _____ Cousin?
9. _____ Eltern von Tara heißen Tehrani. Wie heißen _____ Eltern?

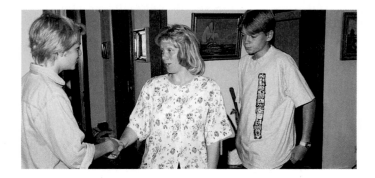

7 **a.** Read each profile that appeared in a magazine for teenagers.

Bettina Schilling, 14 J.
Schulstraße 27
60594 Frankfurt a.M.
Interessen: Musik, Klavier,
Reiten, Schwimmen

Peter Fischer, 15 J.
Körtestraße 8
10967 Berlin
Interessen: Wandern,
Musik, Fußball

Helmut Heine, 16 J.
Königstraße 24
39116 Magdeburg
Interessen: Rad fahren,
Basteln, Comics sammeln

b. Describe one of the persons above using complete sentences.

c. Now listen to Holger's description of a girl named Sonja whom he read about in a magazine. Based on what he says, with which of the students above would Sonja have the most in common?

---

8 ## Zum Schreiben

You have just moved to a different city and attend a new school where you are required to introduce yourself at a newcomer orientation. Draw a personal profile puzzle to introduce yourself, your family, and your home to your new school mates.

> **Schreibtipp** **Arranging ideas spatially** is a useful way to organize information before you write. It's really a way of creating a type of blueprint of how your finished product will look. In this case, the puzzle pieces show different aspects of your life and different parts of your personality.

1. Decide on your categories, for instance: *Activities I enjoy; Me!* (Self-description); *My family; My ideal bedroom.* Jot down as many nouns and adjectives as you can for each category.

2. Now you are ready to create your blueprint. Draw four to six puzzle-shaped areas on a piece of poster board, and label each area with one of the categories you have chosen. Using one puzzle piece per category, complete the puzzle with the items and descriptions you have jotted down.

---

9 ## Rollenspiel

Two friends whom you have not seen for a while come to your house after school. First, offer your friends something to eat and drink, then show them your room. You have recently made some changes, so the three of you talk about your furniture. Then your conversation turns to family. Take turns describing various family members, what they look like, and what their interests are. Write out the conversations and practice them. Then role-play them in front of the class.

Kann ich's wirklich?

Can you talk about where people live? (p. 73)

1 How would you ask a classmate where he or she lives and tell him or her where you live?

2 Say where the following people live:
  a. Thomas (Land)
  b. Britte (Hegelstraße)
  c. Marian und Karl (Brauhausberg, Vorort von Potsdam)
  d. Renate (Köln)
  e. Sabine und Rolf (Stadt: Bismarckstr.)

Can you offer something to eat and drink (using möchte) and respond to an offer? (p. 74)

3 How would you ask a classmate what he or she would like to eat and drink? How would you ask more than one classmate? How would you tell a classmate that you would like a lemon-flavored soda?

4 If you and some of your classmates were at a friend's house, how would you help your friend by telling her or him what everyone was having for a snack?
  a. Anna, eine Cola
  b. Martin und Klaus, ein Stück Kuchen
  c. Nicole und Jörg, ein paar Kekse
  d. Ayla, Obst

Can you say please, thank you, and you're welcome? (p. 76)

5 How would you ask your friend politely for a few cookies? How would you thank him or her? How would he or she respond?

Can you describe a room? (p. 79)

6 How would you describe these pieces of furniture? Make two sentences about each one using the correct pronoun **er, sie, es,** or **sie** (pl) in the second sentence.
  a. der Schrank (*old, ugly, large*)
  b. das Bett (*small, comfortable, new*)
  c. die Möbel (*beautiful, new, large*)
  d. die Couch (*old, ugly, broken*)

Can you talk about family members? (p. 82)

7 How would you tell a classmate about five of your family members, giving their relationship to you, their names, and their ages?

Can you describe people? (p. 84)

8 How would you describe the people below?

a.　　　　　　b.　　　　　　c.　　　　　　d.

9 How would you ask a classmate what his or her brother, sister, grandfather, parents, and cousins (male and female) look like?

Erste Stufe

Talking about where you live

nach Hause gehen	to go home
wohnen	to live
Wo wohnst du?	Where do you live?
in der Stadt	in the city
auf dem Land	in the country
ein Vorort von	a suburb of
weit von hier	far from here
in der Nähe	nearby
in der ...Straße	on ... Street
Wo wohnt Jens?	Where does Jens live?
Ich denke, in/auf ...	I think in ...

Things to eat and drink

möchten	would like (to)
essen	to eat
Was möchtest du essen?	What would you like to eat?
ein Stück Kuchen	a piece of cake
Obst	fruit
ein paar Kekse	a few cookies
trinken	to drink
Was möchtest du trinken?	What would you like to drink?
ein Glas Apfelsaft (Orangensaft)	a glass of apple juice (orange juice)
eine Cola	cola
eine Limo	a lemonade

ein Glas (Mineral) Wasser	a glass of (mineral) water
Nichts, danke!	Nothing, thank you!
Im Moment gar nichts.	Nothing at the moment (right now).

Saying please, thank you, and you're welcome

Bitte!	Please!
Danke!	Thank you!
Danke (sehr) (schön)!	Thank you (very much)!
Bitte (sehr) (schön)!	You're (very) welcome!

Zweite Stufe

Describing a room

das Zimmer, -	room
die Möbel (pl)	furniture
der Schrank, ⸚e	cabinet
der Schreibtisch, -e	desk
die Stereoanlage, -n	stereo
die Couch, -en	couch
das Bett, -en	bed
das Regal, -e	bookcase, shelf
der Stuhl, ⸚e	chair

neu	new
alt	old
klein	small
groß	big
bequem	comfortable
unbequem	uncomfortable
schön	pretty, beautiful
hässlich	ugly
kaputt	broken

Pronouns

er	he, it
sie	she, it
es	it
sie (pl)	they

Other Useful Words and Expressions

ganz	really, quite
aber	but
der Computer, -	computer

Dritte Stufe

Talking about the family

die Familie, -n	family
Das ist ...	That's ...
die Mutter, ⸚	mother
der Vater, ⸚	father
die Schwester, -n	sister
der Bruder, ⸚	brother
die Großmutter, ⸚ (Oma)	grandmother
der Großvater, ⸚ (Opa)	grandfather
die Tante, -n	aunt
der Onkel, -	uncle
die Kusine, -n	cousin (female)
der Cousin, -s	cousin (male)
das Haustier, -e	pet
die Tante, -n	aunt

der Hund, -e	dog
die Katze, -n	cat
der Mann, ⸚er	man
die Frau, -en	woman
Das sind ...	These are ...
die Eltern (pl)	parents
die Geschwister (pl)	brothers and sisters
die Großeltern (pl)	grandparents

Die Zahlen von 21 bis 100

siehe Seite 83	see page 83

Describing People

Wie sieht er aus?	What does he look like?

Wie sehen sie aus?	What do they look like?
lange (kurze) Haare	long (short) hair
rote (blonde, schwarze, weiße, graue, braune) Haare	red (blonde, black, white, gray, brown) hair
blaue (grüne, braune) Augen	blue (green, brown) eyes
eine Glatze haben	to be bald
eine Brille	a pair of glasses

Possessives

dein, deine	your
mein, meine	my
sein, seine	his
ihr, ihre	her

Komm mit nach Schleswig-Holstein!

Einwohner: 2,7 Millionen

Fläche: 16 000 Quadratkilometer (6 177 Quadratmeilen), ungefähr so groß wie Connecticut

Landeshauptstadt: Kiel (240 000 Einwohner)

Große Städte: Lübeck, Flensburg, Neumünster

Flüsse: Elbe, Eider

Inseln: Helgoland, Sylt, Föhr, Fehmarn

Kanäle: Nord-Ostsee-Kanal

Seen: über 300

Industrien: Schiffbau, Ackerbau, Viehzucht

Beliebte Gerichte: Matjes, Krabben, Aale, Räucherspeck, Buttermilchsuppe, Rote Grütze

 go.hrw.com

 VIDEO

 CD-ROM DISC 1

WK3 SCHLESWIG-HOLSTEIN

Das Holstentor in Lübeck, Geburtsstadt ▶ von Thomas Mann (1875-1955)

CONCORDIA DOMI FORIS PAX

Schleswig-Holstein

Schleswig-Holstein is the northernmost German state (**Land**). It is bordered on the west by the North Sea (**Nordsee**), on the east by the Baltic Sea (**Ostsee**), and on the north by Denmark (**Dänemark**). In addition to the dunes, rocky cliffs, tranquil beaches, and fishing villages along its 500-kilometer long coastline, Schleswig-Holstein also has rolling meadows, rich farmland, over 300 lakes and ponds, and beautiful cities, such as Flensburg and Lübeck.

internet

go.hrw.com

ADRESSE: go.hrw.com
KENNWORT:
WK3 SCHLESWIG-HOLSTEIN

1 Ein Friesenhaus
This north Frisian house with thatched roof (**Reetdach**) is typical for the island of Sylt. Thousands of Germans vacation here every year.

2 Kieler Woche
Every year some of the best sailors in the world gather here in Kiel to sail.

3 Westerhaver Leuchtturm
The Westerhaver Lighthouse (**Leuchtturm**) is surrounded by a type of salty marshland that makes up much of Schleswig-Holstein.

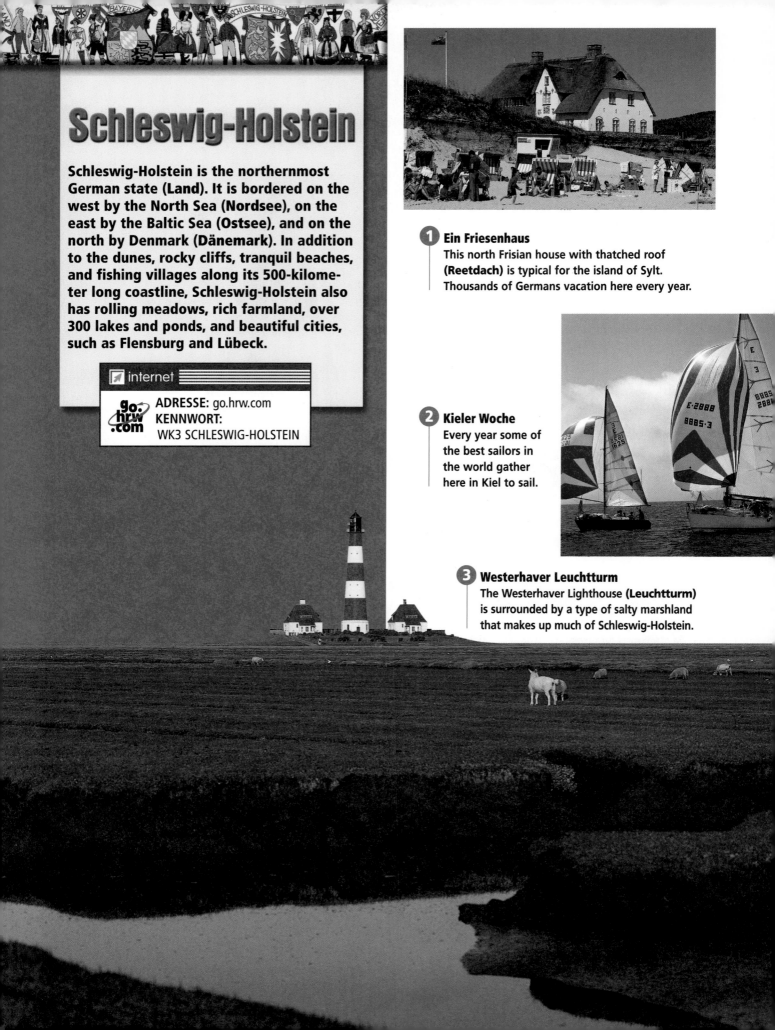

4 Das Reepschlägerhaus
At one time, ropes were manufactured in this Frisian house. Today it is a tearoom (**Teestube**) and is one of Wedel's famous landmarks.

5 Der Roland am Marktplatz
In the open-air market (**Marktplatz**) in Wedel stands a statue of Roland, symbolizing Wedel's ancient rights as a free city.

Kapitel 4, 5, 6

Chapters 4, 5, and 6 take place in the small Holstein town of Wedel. Wedel lies directly on the Elbe, not far from Hamburg, and has a proud heritage as a **Freistadt**, an independent trading town. Among its 30,000 inhabitants are the teenagers you will meet in the next three chapters. They attend the Johann-Rist-Gymnasium in Wedel.

6 Heiko, Alex, Katja, Sonja, Julia, Michael, and Sina say hello and invite you to join them in Wedel.

4
Alles für die Schule!

Objectives

In this chapter you will learn to

Erste Stufe

- talk about class schedules
- use a schedule to talk about time
- sequence events

Zweite Stufe

- express likes, dislikes, and favorites
- respond to good and bad news

Dritte Stufe

- talk about prices
- point things out

 internet

ADRESSE: go.hrw.com
KENNWORT:
WK3 SCHLESWIG-HOLSTEIN-4

◀ **Vor der Schule**

Los geht's! · *Lars kauft Schulsachen*

Lars **Julia** **Sina** **Alex**

Strategie Verstehen

Look at the images for this story. What are the students doing in each scene? Where might these scenes be taking place? What clues tell you this?

Lars: Hallo, Leute!

Julia: Hallo, Lars!

Lars: Suchst du was?

Sina: Ja, wo ist der Stundenplan? Sag, wann haben wir Mathe?

Lars: Weiß nicht.

Alex: Ah, Mathe haben wir nach der Pause um 9 Uhr 45.

Sina: Danke, Alex! Und was haben wir heute zuerst?

Alex: Zuerst haben wir Deutsch, dann Bio, danach Mathe, dann Englisch und zuletzt Sport.

1

Julia: Du, heute bekommen wir die Mathearbeit zurück.

Lars: Ich hab bestimmt wieder eine Vier.

Julia: Meinst du?

Lars: Ja, leider. In Mathe hab ich immer schlechte Noten.

Julia: Schade!

Lars: Na ja, du bist gut in Mathe.

Julia: Ja, ich hab Mathe gern. Das ist mein Lieblingsfach.

2

3

Julia: Hallo, Lars!

Lars: Hallo, Julia!

Julia: Na, was machst du denn hier?—Ach, ich seh's: ein Taschenrechner!

Lars: Schau mal! Der Rechner ist toll, nicht?

Julia: Ja, du hast Recht.

Lars: Und der ist nicht teuer.

Julia: Stimmt! Nur sechzehn Euro!

4

Julia: Entschuldigung! Wo sind bitte die Hefte und die Bleistifte?

Verkäuferin: Die sind da drüben.

Julia: Und Wörterbücher? Wo sind die?

Verkäuferin: Da hinten!

Julia: Danke!

5

Verkäuferin: Der Rechner? Sechzehn Euro, bitte!

Lars: Moment! Ach, wie blöd! Jetzt hab ich nur zehn Euro dabei.

Julia: Macht nichts, Lars! Ich geb dir das Geld.

Lars: Oh, das ist sehr nett, Julia! So, jetzt hab ich zwanzig Euro.

Verkäuferin: Danke schön! Und vier Euro zurück.

6

Lars: Warte, Julia!

Julia: Was ist los?

Lars: So ein Mist! Das ganze Zeug auf der Straße!

Julia: Der Taschenrechner, geht er noch?

Lars: Ach wo! Er ist kaputt! So ein Pech!

Julia: So ein Glück! Die Brille ist noch ganz!

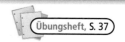

Übungsheft, S. 37

1 Was passiert hier?

Do you understand what is happening in the story? Check your comprehension by answering these questions. Don't be afraid to guess.

1. How is Julia in math? What about Lars?
2. Where do Julia and Lars meet again? What kinds of things are they looking for?
3. What does Lars want to buy? Why does he need it?
4. Lars has both bad luck and good luck on the way home. What happens to him?

2 Genauer lesen

a. Reread the conversations. Which words or phrases do the characters use to

1. name school subjects
2. name school supplies
3. express annoyance
4. point out something
5. express regret
6. express bad luck; good luck

b. In what three ways are numbers used in the conversations?

3 Stimmt oder stimmt nicht?

Are these statements right or wrong? Answer each one with either **stimmt** or **stimmt nicht**. If a statement is wrong, try to state it correctly.

1. Lars hat immer schlechte Noten in Mathe.
2. Sina und Alex haben nach der Pause Deutsch.
3. Julia hat Mathe nicht gern.
4. Der Rechner ist sehr teuer.
5. Julia gibt Lars das Geld.
6. Die Brille ist kaputt.

4 Was passt zusammen?

Match each statement or question on the left with an appropriate response on the right.

1. Was haben wir zuerst?
2. Und wann hast du Mathe?
3. Dieser Taschenrechner ist toll — und nicht teuer.
4. Ich habe nur 10 Euro dabei.
5. Schau mal! Der Taschenrechner ist kaputt!
6. Aber die Brille ist noch ganz.

a. Macht nichts! Ich gebe dir das Geld.
b. Also, zuerst Deutsch, dann Bio.
c. So ein Pech!
d. Das stimmt! Er kostet nur 16 Euro.
e. Nach der Pause.
f. So ein Glück!

5 Nacherzählen

Put the sentences in logical order to make a brief summary of the story.

1. Sina sucht den Stundenplan.

Danach sprechen Julia und Lars über die Mathearbeit und Lars' Noten.

Später kommt Lars in einen Schreibwarenladen. Er möchte einen Taschenrechner.

Auf dem Weg nach Hause fällt Lars' Zeug auf die Straße.

Also gibt Julia Lars das Geld.

Aber er hat nur 10 Euro dabei.

Erste Stufe

Objectives Talking about class schedules; using a schedule to talk about time; sequencing events

Wortschatz

Hier ist Alex' und Sinas Stundenplan *(class schedule)*:

Stundenplan für

NAME _Sina_   KLASSE _9a_

ZEIT	MONTAG	DIENSTAG	MITTWOCH	DONNERSTAG	FREITAG	SAMSTAG
8:00- 8:45	Deutsch	Deutsch	Mathe	–	Physik	frei
8:45-9:30	Deutsch	Bio	Deutsch	Physik	Mathe	
9:30-9:45	Pause	–	–	–	–	
9:45-10:30	Religion	Mathe	Englisch	Bio	Deutsch	
10:30-11:15	Bio	Englisch	Latein	Englisch	Latein	
11:15-11:30	Pause	–	–	–	–	
11:30-12:15	Latein	Sport	Geschichte	Englisch	Kunst	
12:20-13:05	Musik	Sport	Erdkunde	Latein	–	

What do you think the word **Zeit** in the schedule means? What do the other words next to **Zeit** (**Montag**, etc.) refer to? All but four of the class subjects are cognates. Which ones do you recognize?

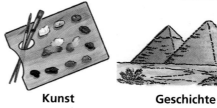

Kunst   Geschichte   Erdkunde

(Übungsheft, S. 38, Ü. 2–3)   (Grammatikheft, S. 28, Ü. 1–3)

6 Alex' und Sinas Stundenplan

Sprechen Look at Alex's and Sina's class schedule and try to answer the following questions in German.

1. On what day(s) do Alex and Sina have religion? And biology?
2. Which subjects do they have on Tuesday? On Wednesday?
3. On which day(s) do they have art? And history?
4. At what times do Alex and Sina have math?* On which day(s)?
5. At what time(s) do they have German?**

---

*To read times from a schedule simply read the numbers and insert **Uhr** between the hour and minutes: **10.30** reads **10 Uhr 30 (zehn Uhr dreißig)**; **8.45** reads **8 Uhr 45 (acht Uhr fünfundvierzig)**.
8:00–8:45 reads: **von acht **bis** acht Uhr fünfundvierzig

Look at the class schedule on page 105. How many different subjects do Alex and Sina have, and when do they have them? How does this compare to your class schedule?

German schools are also different in that Alex, Sina, and their classmates stay together for all their classes and, for the most part, in the same classroom. The teachers move from room to room. What do you think the word **Pause** means, judging by the time allotted for it? Where do you think German students eat lunch? Like you and your friends, students in German-speaking countries have some activities after school: school-sponsored sports, clubs, and social activities. There are, however, fewer such activities in Germany than in the United States.

7 Dein Stundenplan

Schreiben Now make your own class schedule in German. Here are some other subjects you may need to complete your schedule. Turn to page R9 for additional vocabulary.

Und dann noch…

Spanisch, Französisch, Chor, Algebra, Orchester, Werken, Sozialkunde, Technik, Hauswirtschaft

So sagt man das!

Talking about class schedules

If you want to discuss class schedules with your friends, you might ask:

> **Welche Fächer hast du?**
> **Was hast du am Donnerstag?**
> **Was hat die Sina am Donnerstag?**
>
> **Julia, Bernd, welche Fächer habt ihr heute nach der Pause?**
> **Und was habt ihr am Samstag?**

You might get the responses:

> **Ich habe Mathe, Bio, Kunst …**
> **Deutsch, Englisch und Sport.**
> **Sie hat Physik, Bio, Englisch und Latein.**
>
> **Wir haben Chemie und Musik.**
> **Wir haben frei!**

The word **Fächer** used above means *subjects*. What do you think the equivalent of **welche** is?[1] Could you use **welche** in the second, third and fifth questions? The word **am** always precedes the days of the week. What do you think this word means?[2] With what other time expressions have you already used **am**?[3]

8 Welche Fächer hast du?

Sprechen Using the schedule you created in Activity 7, tell your classmates which subjects you have and on what day you have them.

---

1. *which* 2. here: *on* 3. **am Wochenende, am Abend, am Nachmittag**

9 Welche Fächer haben sie?

 Zuhören Listen carefully as Lars asks his classmates when they have various classes. Match the subjects below with the days of the week in the box to the right.

a. Bio   **b. Musik**   **c. Kunst**   **d. Mathe**   **e. Geschichte**

f. Erdkunde   **g. Sport**   **h. Deutsch**

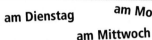

am Dienstag	am Montag
am Mittwoch	am Freitag
am Samstag	am Donnerstag

So sagt man das!

Using a schedule to talk about time

It's the first day of school, and you are curious about when your friends have their classes.

You might ask:

> **Wann hast du Erdkunde?**
> **Was hast du um 11 Uhr 20?**
> **Was hast du von 8 Uhr 45 bis 9 Uhr 30?**
> **Und wann hast du Kunst?**

You might get the responses:

> **Um 11 Uhr 20.**
> **Erdkunde.**
> **Ich habe Informatik.**
> **Um 10 Uhr 30, nach der Pause.**

What do you think **wann** means?[1] How do you answer a question that starts with **wann**?[2] How is the answer to this question different from the answers to questions that begin with **was**? What is the English equivalent of **um**?[3]

Ein wenig Landeskunde

Do any of the times in Alex's and Sina's schedule look unusual to you? When does their last class end? Schedules like this one, and other official schedules like the train schedule to the right, are based on the 24-hour system of telling time. This system starts immediately after midnight (**00.01 Uhr**) and ends at midnight (**24.00 Uhr**). What time would correspond to 2 P.M.? to 3 P.M.? to 8:30 P.M.? What time would you have to board the train in order to get to **Köln**? **Mannheim**?

Bochum ⟶ München
Hauptbahnhof   Hauptbahnhof

Preis pro Person in Euro. Einfache Fahrt. * Bei Benutzung von EC/IC € 3,- Zuschlag.						ICE	Andere Züge*
Mögliche Fahrpreisermäßigungen siehe Kapitel „So günstig fahren Sie Bahn".					Fahrpreis 1. Kl. Fahrpreis 2. Kl.	293,- 188,-	263,- 175,-
ab	Zug	Umsteigen	an	Verkehrstage	Bemerkungen		
14.49	IC 823	Köln IC Stuttgart EC	22.11	1234567			●
14.49	IC 823	Würzburg D	22.29	1234567			●
14.59	S	Duisburg IC Stuttgart EC	22.11	12345--	an Werktagen nicht 24., 31. 12.		●
15.23	IR 2553	Kassel-Wilh. ICE	22.06	1234567		●	
15.49	IC 523	Köln IC Mannheim ICE	22.17	1234567		●	
15.49	IC 523	Köln IC Karlsruhe IR	23.40	1234567			●
16.22	IC 517		23.11	12345-7	nicht 24, 12, -2. 1., 9,- 11.4.		●
16.49	IC 603	Mannheim ICE	23.17	------7	auch 12. 4.,	●	

1. *when* 2. with a time expression 3. here: *at*

10 Welche Fächer hat Klaus?

Zuhören Listen carefully as Klaus, a friend of Sonja's, talks about the busy schedule he has on Wednesdays. Copy the names of the following subjects onto a piece of paper, then complete his schedule by filling in the times as you hear them.

Mathe	Englisch	Latein
Deutsch	Erdkunde	Geschichte

11 Wann hast du Deutsch?

Sprechen Working in small groups, take turns asking each other which subjects each of you has and at what times during the day. Remember, you do not need to answer in complete sentences. Sometimes just a phrase will do:

BEISPIEL   PARTNER **Wann hast du Englisch?**
             DU **Um 10 Uhr.** *oder* **Um 10.**

Grammatik

The verb **haben**, present tense

Look at the conversation below:

    JULIA **Was hat Sina nach der Pause?**
    BEATE **Sie hat Bio. Und was hast du?**
    JULIA **Ich habe Deutsch.**

What do you notice about **haben** that is different from verbs like **spielen** or **wohnen**?[1] Here are the forms of the verb **haben** (*to have*) in the present tense:

Mehr Grammatikübungen
S. 120–121, Ü. 1–3

Übungsheft,
S. 39, Ü. 4–5

Grammatikheft,
S. 29, Ü. 4–6

ich	**habe**		wir	**haben**
du	**hast**		ihr	**habt**
er/sie	**hat**	sie (plural)/Sie (formal)		**haben**

12 Grammatik im Kontext

Sprechen / Schreiben Several students in the **Schulhof** are talking about their schedules. First, fill in each blank with the missing form of the verb **haben,** and then match each conversation with one of the drawings.

1. – ===== Monika und Bernd jetzt Englisch? / Nein, sie ===== jetzt Musik.
2. – Wann ===== du Deutsch? / Nach der Pause ===== ich Deutsch.
3. – Wann ===== Sabine Kunst? / Um 12 Uhr ===== sie Kunst.
4. – Wann ===== ihr Physik? / Am Dienstag ===== wir Physik.

a.

b.

c.

d.

---

1. **haben** is irregular in the **du-** and **er/sie**-forms: **du hast, er/sie hat**

13 Ein Interview

a. **Schreiben** Prepare a list of questions for your partner in order to find out exactly what his or her schedule is for the semester (which classes he or she has, the times of the classes).

b. **Sprechen/Schreiben** Now interview your partner using your list of questions and, as you interview, fill out his or her schedule on another piece of paper. Then your partner will interview you. Compare schedules to see if both of you understood everything correctly.

c. **Lesen/Sprechen** Be prepared to report the information you obtained back to the class.

So sagt man das!

Sequencing events

You might want to know the order in which your friends have their classes on a certain day.

You might ask:

Welche Fächer hast du am Freitag?

If your friend had the schedule on the right he or she would answer:

Zuerst hab ich Deutsch, dann Geschichte, danach Latein, und zuletzt hab ich Sport.

What do the words **zuerst, dann, danach,** and **zuletzt** mean?[1]

Übungsheft, S. 39-40, Ü. 6-8
Grammatikheft, S. 30, Ü. 7-11

Deutsch	8.05
Geschichte	8.55
Latein	9.45
Sport	10.30

14 Was hast du am Mittwoch?

Sprechen/Lesen Alex asks Julia which classes she has on Wednesday. Working with a partner, put these questions and answers in the appropriate order. Then, together with your partner, read the conversation out loud.

ALEX   Julia, was hast du zuerst am Mittwoch?

ALEX   Was hast du danach?

JULIA   Danach hab ich Deutsch um 10 und dann Kunst.

JULIA   Dann hab ich um 9 Uhr Musik.

JULIA   Zuletzt hab ich Informatik.

ALEX   Und zuletzt?

ALEX   Und dann?

JULIA   Zuerst habe ich Sport.

15 Was hast du zuerst? Und zuletzt?

Sprechen Using the sequencing words **zuerst, dann, danach,** and **zuletzt,** tell your classmates the order in which you have your classes on Monday. You can use **dann** and **danach** several times if you have more than four classes.

16 Typisch für einen Samstag!

Schreiben Write a short paragraph describing what you do on a typical Saturday, using some of the activities you learned in **Kapitel 2**, for example, **Tennis spielen, Freunde besuchen,** or **Hausaufgaben machen.** In your description, use the sequencing words you have learned (**zuerst, dann, danach,** and **zuletzt**).

---

1. *first, then, after that, last of all*

So sagt man das!

Expressing likes, dislikes, and favorites

In **Kapitel 2** you learned to say which activities you like and don't like to do using **gern** and **nicht gern**. You might also want to talk about which classes you like and don't like, and which is your favorite.

Your friend might ask you:

> **Welche Fächer hast du gern?**
> **Was hast du nicht so gern?**
> **Und was ist dein Lieblingsfach?**

You might respond:

> **Ich habe Kunst und Englisch gern.**
> **Chemie.**
> **Deutsch, ganz klar!**

Grammatikheft,
S. 31, Ü. 12–13

---

17 Katjas Fächer

Zuhören Listen as Katja describes to Rainer the subjects she is taking. Write down which subjects Katja likes, dislikes, and considers her favorite subjects.

gern	nicht gern	Lieblingsfächer

Ein wenig Grammatik

Lieblings- is a prefix that can be used with many different nouns to indicate favorites. Can you guess what these words mean:

Lieblingsbuch, Lieblingsinstrument, and Lieblingsfilm?

Mehr Grammatikübungen
S. 121, Ü. 4-5

---

18 Und dein Lieblingsfach?

Schreiben/Sprechen Find out which subjects your partner likes and dislikes, and his or her favorite subject. Create a chart like the one you filled out for Activity 17. Using the chart, report the information about your partner back to the class. Remember to use **sein** or **ihr** when you are reporting about your partner's **Lieblingsfach.**

19 Trends: Eine Umfrage

Sprechen/Schreiben Working in small groups, conduct a survey about some of the things teenagers like best. Each member of the group asks two students at least three questions. Use topics from the box to prepare the questions. When you have finished the interviews, prepare a summary in chart form.

Lieblingsbuch	Lieblingsrockgruppe	Lieblingsauto	Lieblingssänger
Lieblingsmusik	Lieblingsfilm	Lieblingslehrer	Lieblingsfarbe

Zeugnis

für **Lars Lehmann**,

geboren am **7. 6. 1988**   Klasse **8b**

Allgemeine Beurteilung: *Muss sich in Latein u. Mathe verbessern!*

Deutsch **3**		Mathematik **4**
mündlich ...... **4** schriftlich...... **4**		Physik **2**
Geschichte/Sozialkunde **2**		Chemie **2**
Geschichte ...... **2** Sozialkd **2**		Biologie **3**
Erdkunde **2**		Musik **4**
1. Fremdsprache: *Englisch* **4**		Bildende Kunst/Werken **2**
mündlich ...... **4** schriftlich...... **4**		Bildende Kunst... **2** Werken........ **2**
2. Fremdsprache: *Latein* **5**		Sport **1**
mündlich ...... schriftlich...... **5**		

Wahlpflichtfach

3. Fremdsprache: *Französisch* **2+**

mündlich ...... **4** schriftlich...... **2**

Freiwillige Unterrichtsveranstaltungen

---

sehr gut *(excellent)*	
gut *(good)*	
befriedigend *(satisfactory)*	
ungenügend *(failing)*	
ausreichend *(just passing)*	
mangelhaft *(unsatisfactory)*	

Ein wenig Landeskunde

Look at Lars's report card. What grades (the numbers) did he get in **Mathe, Erdkunde, Deutsch,** and **Latein?**

He was very happy about his geography grade, not too disappointed with the grade in German, very worried about his math grade, and didn't really want to show his Latin grade to his parents. With this information, can you figure out how the German grading system, which is based on the numbers 1-6 rather than on letters, works? Which numbers go with which descriptions?

20 ## Sonjas Noten

Zuhören Listen as Sonja talks about the grades she received on her last report card. First write down the subjects she mentions in the order you hear them. Then listen again and fill in the **Note** *(grade)* she got for each subject. In which subjects did Sonja do well? In which subjects did she not do so well? Then answer the following questions in German.

1. In which subject did she get the best grade? And the worst?
2. In which subject did Sonja receive a "satisfactory" grade?
3. Judging by her grades, which subject do you think Sonja enjoys the most?
4. In which subject do you think Sonja needs to study more?

Responding to good news and bad news

You will often want to respond to your friends' good news and bad news. Sina is asking Alex about his grades. Notice her responses to his answers.

Sina asks:	Alex answers:	Sina responds:
Was hast du in Musik?	**Eine Eins.**	**Toll! Das ist prima!**
In Physik?	**Eine Drei.**	**Nicht schlecht.**
Und in Englisch?	**Ich habe bloß eine Vier.**	**Schade! So ein Pech!**
Und Mathe?	**Eine Fünf.**	**Schade!**
		Das ist sehr schlecht!

Alex was probably hoping for a better grade in English. What do you think he means by **bloß eine Vier?**[1]

Übungsheft, S. 41–43, Ü. 9–14   Grammatikheft, S. 32, Ü. 14–16

---

21 ## Logisch oder unlogisch?

Lesen/Sprechen Read what these students say about their grades. Does the response in each case make sense? If so, answer **Das ist logisch,** if not, answer **Das ist unlogisch,** and try to think of a response that is more appropriate.

1. —Ich habe eine Fünf in Latein!
   —Toll! Das ist gut!
2. —Du hast eine Vier in Informatik?
   —Ja, das ist blöd, nicht?
3. —Englisch ist mein Lieblingsfach. Ich habe eine Zwei.
   —Super! Das ist wirklich gut!
4. —In Erdkunde habe ich eine Drei.
   —Hm, nicht schlecht!
5. —Und in Deutsch habe ich eine Eins!
   —Ach wie blöd! So ein Pech!

Degrees of enthusiasm

Spitze!
Super!
Toll!
Prima!
Das ist gut!
Nicht schlecht!
Schade!
So ein Pech!
Das ist schlecht!
So ein Mist!

---

22 ## Dein Zeugnis

a. Schreiben Imagine that you are an exchange student in Wedel and have just received your report card for the semester. Design and fill out a German report card for yourself. Write all your subjects and give yourself a grade according to the German grading system.

b. Lesen/Sprechen With your report card in hand, have a conversation with a classmate, asking your partner which grades he or she has in various subjects, responding appropriately, and telling him or her about your classes and grades. Use the phrases above in your responses.

---

23 ## Für mein Notizbuch

Schreiben Schreib ein paar Sätze über dich und deine Schule! Welche Fächer hast du? Welche Fächer hast du gern? Welche Fächer hast du nicht gern? Was ist dein Lieblingsfach? In welchen Fächern sind deine Noten gut? In welchen sind die Noten nicht so gut?

---

1. *only a four* (**ausreichend**)

Was sind deine Lieblingsfächer?

We asked several teenagers in German-speaking countries what school subjects they have and which ones they like and don't like. Before you read the interviews, make a list of your classes and indicate which ones are your favorites and which ones you don't like very much.

Übungsheft, S. 48, Ü. 24–25

Jasmin, München

„Ich hab Arbeitslehre — als Lieblingsfach, und Kunst und Mathe mag ich gar nicht; Physik mag ich auch nicht so gerne. Und sonst Sport mag ich noch und dann Englisch, das mag ich auch — das ist auch mein Lieblingsfach, weil ich sehr gern Englisch lernen will."

Dirk, Hamburg

„Ich bin eigentlich genau das Gegenteil von Michael, weil ich total auf Sprachen mich basier. Ich hab Englisch als Leistungskurs, Spanisch und Französisch hab ich gehabt. Ich will ja auch mit Sprachen mal was machen, Diplomatie oder so. Mal seh'n!"

Michael, Hamburg

„Ich interessiere mich hauptsächlich für Mathe und Physik und Kunst, weil ich also ich Architekt werden will. Chemie mag ich überhaupt nicht. Also ich glaube, es ist auch wichtig. Sonst komm ich mit den meisten Fächern zurecht."

Lugana, Bietigheim

„Okay, ich heiße Lugana, bin Griechin, wurde hier geboren. Bin sechzehn Jahre alt, gehe aufs Ellental-Gymnasium, und Lieblingsfächer sind Englisch und Deutsch."

Björn, Hamburg

„In der Schule mag ich am liebsten Physik, Mathematik und Informatik — das ist mit Computern. Das kommt, weil …ich bin gut in Mathe. Ich arbeite gern an Computern, und ich mag Physik ganz gerne, weil mich die Themen einfach interessieren."

A. **1.** What subjects do these teenagers like and dislike? Make a grid.

    2. Which of these teenagers likes the same subjects you do? What are these subjects?

    3. Several of these teenagers give reasons why they like certain subjects. Work with a partner and decide what these reasons are.

    4. Look at the list you made. Try to think of reasons why you like the subjects you indicated. What do your opinions have to do with your future career plans?

B. Do you think teenagers in German-speaking countries start thinking about their future careers earlier than teenagers in the United States do? What can you find in the interviews to support your answer? Discuss the topic with your classmates and then write a brief essay on this question.

Wortschatz

Was kosten die Schulsachen im Schul-Shop?

EUR 14,90 — **das Wörterbuch**

EUR 40,00 — **die Schultasche**

EUR 5,00 — **die Kassette**

EUR 16,20 — **der Taschenrechner**

EUR 1,20 — **das Heft**

EUR 0,95 — **der Radiergummi**

EUR 0,70 — **der Bleistift**

EUR 2,50 — **der Kuli**

ACHTUNG! SCHULANFANG!

Jetzt kaufen — in Ruhe auswählen

Unser Schul-Spezial-Angebot mit reduzierten Preisen

Bleistifte, 12 Stück	bisher EUR 5,40	jetzt	4,20 €
Hefte	bisher EUR 0,80	jetzt	0,60 €
Kulis, alle Farben	bisher EUR 1,60	jetzt	1,25 €
Jeans-Taschen	bisher EUR 24,50	jetzt	20,00 €
Taschenrechner	bisher EUR 9,75	jetzt	8,10 €
Stundenpläne	bisher EUR 0,85	jetzt	0,65 €
Kassetten, 3 Stück	bisher EUR 9,00	jetzt	7,50 €
Wörterbücher	bisher EUR 8,20	jetzt	7,45 €

Wo? Im Schul-Shop

KAUT-BULLING & Co. GMBH & Co KG

Rolandstr. 30 22880 Wedel - Telefon 04-10-5

Notice the prices that Germans pay for school supplies. How does this compare with the prices you would pay? How many of each of these supplies do you have with you right now in the classroom?

Grammatikheft, S. 33, Ü. 18

---

24 Im Schul-Shop

Schreiben/Lesen Compare the endings of the words in the school supplies ad with the words printed under each illustration. What do you observe? List the differences and compare your list with that of a classmate. Why do you think the words are written differently?

Grammatik

Noun plurals

As you discovered in Activity 24, there are many different plural endings for German nouns. There is no one rule that tells you which nouns take which endings.

Every German dictionary includes the plural ending of a noun next to the main entry, which is the singular form. In the **Vocabulary** in this book beginning on page R29, you will see entries like those above.

Look up the following words and write sentences using the plural forms of these words: **der Stuhl, der Keks, die Kassette.**

das **Wort**, ¨er *word*, 9*
das **Wörterbuch**, ¨er *dictionary*, 4
der **Wortschatz** *vocabulary*, 1
die **Wortschatzübung**, -en *vocabulary exercise, practice*, 1
wunderbar *wonderful*, 11

CD-ROM DISC 1

Mehr Grammatikübungen S. 122, Ü. 6–7

Übungsheft, S. 44–45, Ü. 15–19

---

* ¨er means that the plural form of **Wort** is **Wörter**.

25 Im Schul-Shop

Zuhören Listen to this conversation between Johanna and Daniel in the stationery store. As you listen, put the four pictures in the correct sequence.

a.

b.

c.

d.

So sagt man das!

Talking about prices

If you and your friend are in a store, you might ask one another about the prices of various items.

You might ask:

Was kostet der Taschenrechner?
Was kosten die Bleistifte?

Your friend might respond:

Er kostet nur 16 Euro.
Sie kosten 90 Cent.

After you hear the price you might comment to your friend:

Das ist (ziemlich) teuer!   *That's (quite) expensive!*
Das ist (sehr) billig!   *That's (very) cheap!*
Das ist (sehr) preiswert!   *That's a (really) good deal!*

> Übungsheft, S. 46, Ü. 20–21
> Grammatikheft, S. 34, Ü. 19–20

Ein wenig Landeskunde

As of January 1, 2002 the **Euro** (€) is the national currency in Germany as well as in most European countries. One **Euro** has **100 Cent**. € **1,00** reads **ein Euro**, € **0,90** reads **neunzig Cent**, € **2,30** reads **zwei Euro dreißig**. How would you read € **7,80?** € **1,70?** € **9,10?** € **24,35?**

There are seven euro bills with the following denominations: 5, 10, 20, 50, 100, 200 and 500 euros. And there are eight euro coins: 1, 2, 5, 10, 20 and 50 cents, and a 1 euro and a 2 euro coin. The tails of some coins show German symbols, such as the German Oak Leaf, the Brandenburg Gate, and the Federal Eagle, that are reminders of the beloved German mark.

Mehr Grammatikübungen
S. 123, Ü. 9

Ein wenig Grammatik

Schon bekannt

In **Kapitel 3** you learned that the pronouns **er, sie, es,** and **sie** (pl) can refer to objects:
Die Couch ist neu. Sie ist bequem.
When do you use each of these pronouns?[1]

Mehr Grammatikübungen
S. 122–123, Ü. 8

> Grammatikheft, S. 35, Ü. 21–22

---

1. er refers to masculine nouns, **sie** to feminine nouns, **es** to neuter nouns, **sie** (pl) to plural nouns.

26 **Was kostet ...?**

Schreiben You are starting school and need to buy school supplies. You have 15 euros to spend. Make a list of the things you need to buy. Your partner is the **Verkäufer** (*salesclerk*) at the store and will create a price list, using the items and prices in the **Wortschatz** box as cues. Ask your partner how much the items on your list cost, then figure out how much you must spend. Be sure to be polite!

So sagt man das!

Pointing things out

When you go to a store, you may need to ask the **Verkäuferin** where various items are located.

You might ask:

> **Entschuldigung, wo sind die Schultaschen?**
> **Und Taschenrechner? Wo finde ich sie?**
> **Und die Kulis auch?**
> **Wo sind bitte die Kassetten?**
> **Und dann noch Hefte. Wo sind die, bitte?**

The responses might be:

> **Schauen Sie!* Dort drüben!**
> **Dort!**
> **Nein, sie sind dort drüben!**
> **Kassetten sind da hinten.**
> **Die sind hier vorn.**

How would the salesperson tell you that the pencils are in the front of the store if he or she were also in the front of the store?[1]

_____

*This is the polite form of **Schau!** that is used among friends. In a store, a salesperson would use the polite form **Schauen Sie!**

Übungsheft, S. 46, Ü. 22

Grammatikheft, S. 36, Ü. 23–25

27 **Im Schreibwarenladen**

Schreiben Alex has asked the **Verkäuferin** where various school supplies are located and what they cost. Complete what the **Verkäuferin** says with the items pictured in the drawing. Be sure to use the correct endings for the plural (including umlauts). More than one answer may be possible.

Bitte, ___1___ sind hier vorn. Sie kosten nur € 1,30. ___2___ sind dort drüben und kosten € 14,00. Das ist sehr preiswert. Und ___3___ sind hier vorn. Sie sind im Sonderangebot für nur € 0,35. ___4___ sind auch hier vorn, und ___5___ sind da drüben, ___6___ sind aber weiter hinten. Oh, und ___7___ sind dort drüben. Sie kosten € 1,30.

Mehr Grammatikübungen
S. 123, Ü. 10 ➡

_____

1. Bleistifte sind hier vorn.

28 Eine Werbung *Advertisement*

 Schreiben You are the owner of a store that sells school supplies and you are writing an advertisement to be read over the radio. Make up a name for your store, then pick five school supplies and write an ad describing them.

> **BEISPIEL** **Wir haben Taschenrechner, sie kosten nur 10 Euro 95. Sehr preiswert, nicht? Und Bleistifte nur 45 Cent. Super! Die …**

29 Wir brauchen Schulsachen *We need school supplies*

 a. Lesen Get together with three other classmates and take turns reading the advertisements you wrote in Activity 28. While one person reads, the others will be "listening to the radio" and will write down the various school supplies they hear mentioned and the price of each.

b. Sprechen/Schreiben Decide with your classmates which store your group will visit. The person whose store is chosen will play the **Verkäufer** and should set up his or her store (or draw a floorplan). The others will play the customers. The three customers will make a list of all the things they need from the store.

30

Von der Schule zum Beruf

Schreiben You are an administrator at a German school. Lars's parents have called you to ask about his progress, since his last report card did not meet their high expectations (see his **Zeugnis** on p. 111). Write Lars's parents a letter on school letterhead describing how he is doing in his classes since the last report card.

AUSSPRACHE

Richtig aussprechen / Richtig lesen

A. To practice the following sounds, say the words and sentences below after your teacher or after the recording.

1. The diphthongs **äu** and **eu**: The diphthongs **äu** and **eu** sound similiar to the *oy* sound in the English word *boy*.

   teuer, deutsch, Verkäufer / Der Verkäufer ist Deutscher.

2. The diphthong **au**: The diphthong **au** is pronounced much like the *ow* sound in the English word *cow*.

   Pause, schauen, bauen / Ich schaue Fernsehen nach der Pause.

3. The letters **b, d,** and **g**: At the end of a syllable or word, the consonants **b, d,** and **g** are pronounced as follows: the letter **b** sounds like the *p* in the English word *map;* the letter **d** is pronounced like the letter *t* in the English word *mat;* and the letter **g** is pronounced like the *k* sound in the English word *make*.

   Liebling, gelb, schreib / Schreib dein Lieblingsfach auf!
   Rad, Geld, blöd / Ich finde Radfahren blöd.
   Sag, Montag, Tag / Sag mal, hast du am Montag und Freitag Physik?

Richtig schreiben / Diktat

B. Write down the sentences that you hear.

Lernen macht Spaß!

Lesestrategie

Understanding Compound Words German has many compound words. Often at least one part of a compound word is a cognate that you will recognize from English. Figuring out the meaning of individual words within a compound will often help you determine the meaning of the entire word.

1. Look at the following words and try to determine what they might mean by looking at the cognates within the compounds. You do not have to know the exact meaning of the compound word, but you can probably come close to figuring it out. For example, you can see that the word **Gesangunterricht** (abbreviated **Gesangunterr.** in the ad) has something to do with singing.

   a. **Keyboardschule** ════
   b. **Deutschkurse** ════
   c. **Privatunterricht** ════
   d. **Volksschule** ════
   e. **Schulverbund** ════

2. Work with a partner. Write down the kinds of information you would be looking for if you were looking in the classified ads for a tutor in English.

3. Scan the ads for the following information:

   a. the telephone number you would call if you wanted singing lessons

   b. what the American wants to tutor

Institut Rosenberg

Eine der führenden Schweizer Internatsschulen für Mädchen und Jungen seit 1889

Abitur

Deutsches Abitur im Hause
Vorbereitung für Eidgenössische Maturitätsprüfungen
Vorbereitung für das Studium in England und in den USA
Maturità Italiana

Privatunterricht gewährleistet • Überwachtes Studium
Internationale Atmosphäre

Sportarten:

Tennis • Wasserski • Reiten • Skifahren • Basketball • Volleyball etc.

Auskunft: O. Gademann
Institut Rosenberg • Höhenweg 60 • CH-9000 St.Gallen
Tel. 004171-277 92 91 Fax 004171-277 98 27

SCHULVERBUND PASSAU
Regensburger Straße 8, 94036 Passau, Tel. 0 851/23 26 71

—staatlich anerkannt—

DONAU-GYMNASIUM
Seit Sept. '93 zusätzlicher Schulzweig: SPORTGYMNASIUM

DONAU-REALSCHULE
Klassen 5-10 (Eintritt nach der 4. Klasse der Volksschule)

WIRTSCHAFTSSCHULE
Klassen 7-10 (berufsorientiert)

Passau

DONAU-VOLKSSCHULE
Teilhauptschule II, Klassen 7-9

Diese staatlich genehmigten Schulen bieten Schülern eine individuelle, differenzierte Beurteilung und Förderung.
Es gibt keinen Probeunterricht.Während der Probezeit wird die Eignung der Schüler individuell beurteilt.
Die in den letzten 25 Jahren erzielten überdurchschnittlichen Prüfungserfolge bestätigen unser Konzept.

MAYER-GYMNASIUM
MAYER-REALSCHULE
DONAU-VOLKSSCHULE
Klassen 1-4/Teilhauptschule I
Klassen 5+6 angeschl. Kindergarten

Einschreibung jederzeit möglich!

Ganztagsschulen mit Mittagstisch

Gesangunterr. u. Harmonielehre
☎ (0451) 57328

Dipl.-Physikerin für Mathe, Physik, Chemie
☎ (0451) 13566

Klavier- u. Keyboardschule Müller, Fachlehrer
☎ 89678

Deutschkurse für Ausländer Probestunde
kostenlos, kleine Gruppen, 68 Stunden,
☎ € 250,-
98105 u. 98287.

Amerikaner erteilt qualifizierten
Englischunterricht für Anfänger und
Fortgeschrittene. Auch Übersetzungen.
☎ 98120 ab 13 Uhr

---

c. the address of the **Schulverbund Passau**

4. Read the ads and answer the questions about each ad.

   a. Who might be interested in the programs offered by the **Schulverbund**?

   b. Can students eat at the schools in the **Schulverbund**? What tells you this information? Why would they need to?

   c. What new branch of the **Donau-Gymnasium** has been operating since September 1993?

   d. How much does the German course for foreigners cost? How much does a trial class period cost? How long is the course?

   e. In what country is the **Institut Rosenberg** located? Is it a girls' school? What might it prepare you for?

5. Write some notes that you could use if you wanted to obtain more information from the school that offers German classes to foreigners. You might want to ask, for example, when and where the class meets.

6. With a partner write a short ad to offer tutoring in whatever you do best. It may be an academic class or a skills-oriented class. Use the classified ads on this page as your model.

7. You are going to be an exchange student in Germany. Which one of these schools would you like to attend? Why? Discuss this with a partner.

Übungsheft, S. 47, Ü. 23

Mehr Grammatikübungen

internet
go.hrw.com
ADRESSE: go.hrw.com
KENNWORT:
WK3 SCHLESWIG-HOLSTEIN-4

Erste Stufe Objectives Talking about class schedules; using a schedule to talk about time

1 Sina, Alex, and Julia are talking about their class schedules. Complete the following dialogue by filling in each blank with the correct form of the verb **haben**. (S. 108)

SINA Du, Alex, was _____ wir heute um 8 Uhr?

ALEX Um 8 Uhr _____ wir Mathe, glaube ich.

SINA Hm, die Julia _____ Informatik, sagt sie.

ALEX Sag, Sina, _____ du Informatik gern?

SINA Ich _____ Informatik sehr gern, das ist mein Lieblingsfach.

JULIA Hallo! Was _____ ihr denn morgen um 12 Uhr 20?

ALEX Um 12 Uhr 20 _____ wir Erdkunde.

SINA Und du _____ am Freitag frei. Ein Feiertag!

2 Students are talking about class subjects, what they have on certain days, and when. Complete the following pairs of questions and statements by filling in each blank with the correct form of the verb **haben**. (S. 108)

1. Alex, _____ du heute Physik? — Du, ich _____ heute Physik und Chemie.
2. Was _____ ihr am Samstag? — Am Samstag _____ wir frei.
3. Was _____ Julia und Sina heute? — Sie _____ Deutsch, Latein und Sport.
4. Und was _____ der Alex heute? — Er _____ Physik, Bio und Englisch.
5. Wer _____ heute Kunst? — Ich _____ heute Kunst.
6. Wann _____ du Deutsch? — Deutsch _____ ich um zehn Uhr.
7. Wann _____ ihr denn frei? — Du, wir _____ am Samstag frei.
8. Wann _____ denn die Julia Bio? — Du, sie _____ am Freitag Bio.

3 Ask your classmates the following questions (when they have certain subjects, when they play certain sports, and what subjects they have) by filling in each blank with the correct verb form and pronoun. (S. 108)

Remember: When addressing one classmate, use the **du**-form of the verb.
  When addressing several classmates *(you all)*, use the **ihr**-form.
  When addressing your teacher or a stranger, use the **Sie**-form.
  When addressing several teachers or strangers, use the same **Sie**-form.

1. Sag mal, Frank, wann _____ _____ Biologie?
2. Frank und Mary, wann _____ _____ heute Geschichte?
3. Frau Maier, wann _____ _____ heute frei? Nach der Pause?
4. Frau Meier und Herr Moser, wann _____ _____ heute frei?
5. Wann _____ _____ Tennis, Lisa? Nach der Schule?
6. Wann _____ _____ Fußball, Leute? Heute oder morgen?
7. Wann _____ _____ Golf, Frau Bruschke? Am Wochenende?

8. Wann _____ _____ Volleyball, Herr Meier und Herr Wolff?

9. Welche Fächer _____ _____ heute, Julia?

10. Welche Fächer _____ _____ am Freitag, Lars und Sina?

11. Welche Fächer _____ _____ gern, Herr Moser?

12. Und welche Fächer _____ _____ gern, Frau Maier und Frau Arndt?

Zweite Stufe

Objectives Expressing likes, dislikes, and favorites

4 Try to find out what your friends' favorite subjects in school are. For each response, fill in the first blank with the correct form of the possessive, and the second blank with the correct form of the verb **haben**. (S. 110)

1. Was ist Julias Lieblingsfach? — _____ Lieblingsfach ist Deutsch, aber sie _____ auch Englisch und Biologie gern.

2. Was ist Alex' Lieblingsfach? — _____ Lieblingsfach ist Physik, aber er _____ auch Chemie und Geschichte gern.

3. Was ist dein Lieblingsfach? — _____ Lieblingsfach ist Englisch, aber ich _____ auch Erdkunde und Geschichte gern.

4. Was ist Sinas Lieblingsfach? — _____ Lieblingsfach ist Kunst, aber sie _____ auch Geschichte und Erdkunde gern.

5. Was ist Ahmets Lieblingsfach? — _____ Lieblingsfach ist Sport, aber er _____ auch Latein und Englisch gern.

6. Und was ist dein Lieblingsfach? — _____ Lieblingsfach ist Geschichte, aber ich _____ auch Englisch und Französisch gern.

5 What school subjects don't these students like that much and what are their favorites? Complete each of the following statements by filling in the first blank with a correct form of the verb **haben** and the second blank with an appropriate possessive. (S. 110)

1. Mathe _____ ich nicht so gern, und _____ Lieblingsfach ist Biologie.

2. Alex _____ Bio nicht so gern, und _____ Lieblingsfach ist Physik.

3. Julia _____ Geschichte nicht so gern, und _____ Lieblingsfach ist Kunst.

4. Ich _____ Latein nicht so gern, und _____ Lieblingsfach ist Chemie.

5. Sina _____ Physik nicht so gern, und _____ Lieblingsfach ist Sport.

6. Jens _____ Erdkunde nicht so gern, und _____ Lieblingsfach ist Englisch.

Dritte Stufe **Objectives** Talking about prices; pointing things out

6 You are in the school supply store. You need a lot of supplies for school, but before you buy anything you inquire about the price of all the items on your list. Complete each of the following questions by writing the plural form of the noun in parentheses, together with the plural article. (**S. 114**)

1. (Schultasche) Was kosten _____ ?
2. (Bleistift) Was kosten _____ ?
3. (Kassette) Was kosten _____ ?
4. (Kuli) Was kosten _____ ?
5. (Taschenrechner) Was kosten _____ ?
6. (Radiergummi) Was kosten _____ ?
7. (Heft) Was kosten _____ ?
8. (Wörterbuch) Was kosten _____ ?

7 You are in a school supply store and want to know the prices of various school supplies. Complete each of the following questions by filling in each blank with the correct form of the verb **kosten** and the item given in parentheses (definite article and noun). (**S. 114**)

1. (notebook) Was _____ bitte _____ _____ ?
2. (pencils) Was _____ bitte _____ _____ ?
3. (eraser) Was _____ bitte _____ _____ ?
4. (dictionaries) Was _____ bitte _____ _____ ?
5. (school bag) Was _____ bitte _____ _____ ?
6. (ballpoint pen) Was _____ bitte _____ _____ ?
7. (cassettes) Was _____ bitte _____ _____ ?
8. (calculator) Was _____ bitte _____ _____ ?

8 Still in the school supply store, you want to know how much one item is that you want to buy, and the salesperson tells you. Complete each question and statement by filling in the first blank with the correct form of the definite article, and the second blank with the correct form of the pronoun used to refer to the item. (**S. 115**)

1. Was kostet _____ Wörterbuch? — _____ kostet 10 Euro.
2. Was kostet _____ Schultasche? — _____ kostet 15 Euro.
3. Was kostet _____ Heft? — _____ kostet zwei Euro.
4. Was kostet _____ Taschenrechner? — _____ kostet 20 Euro.
5. Was kostet _____ Kassette? — _____ kostet drei Euro.
6. Was kostet _____ Kuli? — _____ kostet vier Euro.
7. Was kostet _____ Bleistift? — _____ kostet fünfzig Cent.

8. Was kostet _____ Radiergummi? — _____ kostet zwanzig Cent.

9. Was kosten _____ Schulsachen? — _____ kosten 30 Euro.

10. Was kosten _____ Bücher? — _____ kosten zwölf Euro.

9 The new currency in most of Europe, the euro, necessitated adjustments in speaking and writing for hundreds of millions of people. Practice writing out some examples of prices, as shown in the model. Note that the words **Euro** and **Cent** are both singular and plural. (S. 115)

BEISPIEL   € 7,10   **sieben Euro und zehn Cent**   (spoken: sieben Euro zehn)

1. € 1,60	**5.** € 4,70
2. € 3,20	**6.** € 2,90
3. €12,40	**7.** € 7,80
4. €16,30	**8.** €14,50

10 Read the following conversation. Then fill in each blank with an appropriate word from the word box. (S.116)

> Cent   der   die   du   er   Euro   Fächer
> habe   hast   kostet   Er   kosten   kostet   habe
> Cent   ich   Uhr   kosten   ich   zuletzt   sie

– Sag mal, Peter, welche _____ hast _____ denn am Dienstag?

– Zuerst _____ ich Deutsch, dann Mathe und _____ habe _____ Bio.

– Was _____ du nach der Pause um 10 _____ 20?

– Informatik habe _____ , und danach _____ ich frei.

– Sag, _____ Taschenrechner ist toll! Was _____ er?

– Ich glaube, _____ kostet 14 _____ und 50 _____ .

– Was _____ denn _____ Bleistifte?

– Ja, _____ kosten nicht viel, ich glaube 80 _____ .

– Mein Taschenrechner _____ 30 Euro. _____ ist teuer.

CD-ROM DISC 1

internet

go.hrw.com

ADRESSE: go.hrw.com
KENNWORT:
WK3 SCHLESWIG-HOLSTEIN-4

1 Working in small groups, use the ad on page 114 for clues to make up price tags in German for various school supplies in the classroom. Put the tags on the appropriate objects and arrange them as in a store window or as in a store. Now take turns role-playing customer and salesclerk, asking how much things cost and where they are located.

2 What do the items below tell you about the student, Claudia Müller? Use them to answer the questions that follow.

STADTBUS
SCHÜLERAUSWEIS

NAME Claudia Müller

GEBURTSDATUM 7.1.1988

GÜLTIG VON 15.9.02 BIS 30.6.03

Claudia Müller

UNTERSCHRIFT DES SCHÜLERS

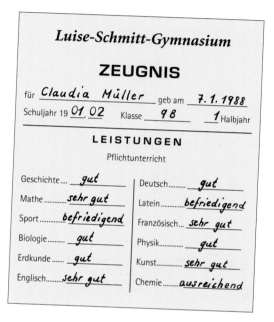

Luise-Schmitt-Gymnasium

ZEUGNIS

für Claudia Müller geb am 7.1.1988
Schuljahr 19 01, 02 Klasse 9 B 1 Halbjahr

LEISTUNGEN
Pflichtunterricht

Geschichte....	gut	Deutsch.........	gut
Mathe.........	sehr gut	Latein.........	befriedigend
Sport.........	befriedigend	Französisch...	sehr gut
Biologie.........	gut	Physik.........	gut
Erdkunde......	gut	Kunst.........	sehr gut
Englisch.........	sehr gut	Chemie........	ausreichend

1. Wie heißt Claudias Schule?

2. Wie kommt Claudia zur Schule?

3. Sind Claudias Noten gut?

4. Welche Note hat sie in Bio?

3 Look at the items in the preceding activity again. Use the information to write five German sentences about Claudia.

4 Look at the two pictures below. What items can you name in the picture on the left? What items are missing in the picture on the right?

BEISPIEL **Die Bleistifte fehlen.** *oder* **Das Heft fehlt.**

5 Create an activity calendar for yourself in German for the coming Saturday. Include all the things you would like to do and the times you expect to do them. Then, working with a partner, imagine that you ran into him or her after school and are talking about your plans for the weekend. Use the sequencing words **zuerst**, **dann**, **danach**, and **zuletzt**.

6 Write a letter to your pen pal and tell him or her about school. Write about which classes you have and when, which classes you like or do not like, and which are your favorites.

7 On the first day of school, your German teacher is telling you what school supplies you will need. Write them as you hear them mentioned.

8

Zum Schreiben

Create a web page to find a person who is your mirror image at school.

Schreibtipp Cluster diagrams are a useful way to organize your ideas. Here's an example of how to make one. Draw a small circle in the middle of the page. Draw four or five more circles and connect each to the original circle. These circles show interconnections of one topic/idea with the main idea and with each other. In this case you (Ich) would be in the main circle and all that you like or dislike about school would be in the surrounding circles.

Prewriting

Decide on titles for your circles. Since you are looking for someone who is nearly identical to you, you might want to use: „Lieblingsfächer," „Noten," „Ich mag diese Fächer nicht," „Mein Stundenplan," „Schulsachen, die ich haben muss," „Wie ich zur Schule komme," „Lieblingslehrer(-innen)." Fill in the circles with appropriate entries.

Writing

Using the information you organized in your cluster diagram, design and write your web page. You might begin: „Ich suche mein Spiegelbild!"

9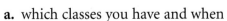

Rollenspiel

You are having a conversation with two friends at the school supply store. Role-play the conversation in front of the class. Use the school supply list from Activity 7 as an aid. Be sure to include:

a. which classes you have and when

b. which classes you like, dislike and your favorite class

c. grades in some of your classes (make sure your friends respond appropriately)

After your conversation, ask the salesperson where various school supplies are located and what they cost.

Can you talk about schedules using haben? (p. 106)

1 How would you say the following in German:
   a. Ulrike has German on Wednesday and Friday.
   b. Monika and Klaus have history on Tuesday and Thursday.
   c. Richard has no classes on Saturday.

2 How would you ask a friend what classes he or she has on Monday? How might he or she respond? How would you ask two friends? How might they respond if they both have the same schedule?

Can you use a schedule to talk about time? (p. 107)

3 Say when these people have these classes.

a. Martin		8.30	Mathe
b. Claudia und Ingrid		9.45	Latein
c. Alex		10.20	Musik
d. Michaela und Manfred		3.00	Kunst

4 How would you tell someone what time you have your German class, using the expression **von …bis …**?

Can you sequence events using zuerst, dann, danach, and zuletzt? (p. 109)

5 How would you tell a classmate the sequence of your classes on Thursday?

Can you express likes, dislikes, and favorites? (p. 110)

6 How would you say which subjects you like, dislike, and which is your favorite? How would you ask your friend for the same information?

Can you respond to good news and bad news? (p. 112)

7 How would you respond if Ahmet, an exchange student at your school, told you:

   a. Ich habe eine Eins in Bio.
   b. Ich habe eine Vier in Latein.
   c. Ich habe eine Zwei in Englisch.

Can you talk about prices? (p. 115)

8 How would you ask a salesperson how much these items cost: calculators, notebooks, erasers, pencils, pens, school bags, dictionaries, and cassettes?

9 How would you tell your friend what each of the following items costs? How might he or she comment on the prices?

   a. Wörterbuch
   € 11,20
   b. Kuli
   € 2,10
   c. Schultasche
   € 10,90

Can you point things out? (p. 116)

10 Write a conversation in which your friend asks you where several things are located in a store. You point them out and give a general location. Then tell him or her how much they cost.

Erste Stufe

Talking about class schedules

die Schule, -n*	school
haben	to have
er/sie hat	he/she has
die Klasse, -n	grade level
der Stundenplan, ⁻e	class schedule
das Fach, ⁻er	(class) subject
Welche Fächer hast du?	What (which) subjects do you have?
Ich habe Deutsch …	I have German …
Bio (Biologie)	biology
Englisch	English
Chemie	chemistry
Erdkunde	geography
Geschichte	history
Kunst	art

Informatik	computer science
Latein	Latin
Mathe (Mathematik)	math
Physik	physics
Religion	religion
Sport	physical education

Using a schedule to talk about time

die Zeit	time
Wann?	when?
um 8 Uhr	at 8 o'clock
von 8 Uhr bis 8 Uhr 45	from 8 until 8:45
heute	today

nach der Pause	after the break
am Montag	on Monday
Dienstag	Tuesday
Mittwoch	Wednesday
Donnerstag	Thursday
Freitag	Friday
Samstag	Saturday
Sonntag	Sunday
Wir haben frei.	We are off (out of school).

Sequencing events

zuerst	first
dann	then
danach	after that
zuletzt	last of all

Zweite Stufe

Expressing likes, dislikes, and favorites

gern haben	to like
nicht gern haben	to dislike
Lieblings-	favorite

Grades

die Note, -n	grade
eine Eins (Zwei, Drei, Vier, Fünf, Sechs)	grades: a 1 (2, 3, 4, 5, 6)

Responding to good news and bad news

gut	good
schlecht	bad
Schade!	Too bad!
So ein Mist!	That stinks!/What a mess!
So ein Pech!	Bad luck!
So ein Glück!	What luck!

Other words and phrases

Ganz klar!	Of course!
bloß	only
das Zeugnis	report card

Dritte Stufe

School supplies

Das ist/Das sind …	That is/Those are
die Schulsachen (pl)	school supplies
das Buch, ⁻er	book
der Kuli, -s	ballpoint pen
das Wörterbuch, ⁻er	dictionary
die Schultasche, -n	schoolbag
der Taschenrechner, -	pocket calculator
der Radiergummi, -s	eraser
der Bleistift, -e	pencil
das Heft, -e	notebook
die Kassette, -n	cassette

Talking about prices

kosten	to cost
Was kostet …?	How much does …cost?
Das ist preiswert.	That's a bargain.
billig	cheap
teuer	expensive
das Geld	money
€ = der Euro	euro (European monetary unit)
der Euro, -	euro
der Cent, -	cent (smallest unit of the euro currency; ¹⁄₁₀₀ of a euro)

Pointing things out

Schauen Sie!	Look!
Schau!	Look!
dort	there
dort drüben	over there
da vorn	up there in the front
da hinten	there in the back

Other words and expressions

ziemlich	rather
nur	only

---

*Plural forms will be indicated in this way from now on.

5
Klamotten kaufen

Objectives

In this chapter you will learn to

Erste Stufe

- express wishes when shopping

Zweite Stufe

- comment on and describe clothes
- give compliments and respond to them

Dritte Stufe

- talk about trying on clothes

🔾 internet

ADRESSE: go.hrw.com
KENNWORT:
   WK3 SCHLESWIG-HOLSTEIN-5

◀ **Wie findet ihr mein T-Shirt?**

Los geht's! ▪ *Was ziehst du an?*

Strategie Verstehen

Look at the images for this story. Who are the people pictured? Where and when do you think these scenes are taking place? What clues tell you this?

Michael   **Katja**   **Julia**

**① **

Katja: Was ziehst du denn zu Sonjas Fete an? Rock? Pulli?

Julia: Ach was! Ich zieh meinen Jogging-Anzug an.

Katja: Und ich meine Shorts. Ich brauche aber etwas, eine Bluse oder ein T-Shirt. Das ist zu alt und gefällt mir nicht.

Julia: Und ich brauche ein Stirnband für meine Haare. Komm, gehen wir zum Sport-Kerner!

②

Katja: Schau, der Michael!

Michael: Hallo, ihr beiden!

Katja: Was hast du denn da in der Tüte?

Michael: Na, wie gefällt euch mein T-Shirt?

Katja: Mensch, scheußlich!

Michael: Wirklich? — Also, ich finde es stark!

③

Verkäuferin: Haben Sie einen Wunsch?

Katja: Ich suche eine Bluse.

Verkäuferin: Blusen haben wir in allen Größen und allen Farben. — Hier haben wir etwas für Sie. Toll, nicht?

Katja: Haben Sie auch Blusen in Blau?

Verkäuferin: Natürlich! Hier, in Blau. Größe 40. Passt bestimmt.

Wortschatz

Mir gefallen alle Klamotten. Mir gefällt/gefallen ...

der Rock   das Hemd   die Stiefel

das Kleid   die Hose   der Gürtel

die Bluse
die Jacke
die Jeans
die Socke
die Shorts
das T-Shirt
der Pulli (Pullover)
der Jogging-Anzug

die Turnschuhe

FÜR DAMEN

Hosen, Leinenstruktur	38.-
Damenhafte Röcke in Leinenoptik	27.-
T-Shirts, bedruckt, mit Perlen und Pailletten	19.-
Coloured Jeans mit Gürtel	30.-
Bedruckte Blusen mit modischen Details	27.-
T-Shirts mit Applikationen	18.-
YOUNG COLLECTIONS Strickkleider in verschiedenen Formen und Farben	14.-

FÜR HERREN

Jacken	42.-
Blouson oder Polo-Shirts, 1/2 Ärmel	25.-
Uni-Socken, Superstretch, 5 Paar	9.-
Seiden-Hemden, sandwashed bedruckt, 1/2 Ärmel	23.-
Streifen-Polo-Shirts, 1/2 Ärmel	24.-
Gymnastik-Shorts	15.-

Many clothing items in this ad are cognates. Which ones do you recognize? Which items are for women, which for men? Which words are used to describe shirts and T-shirts? What do they mean?

Übungsheft, S. 50, Ü. 2

Grammatikheft, S. 37, Ü. 1–2

6   Was ist für Männer? Was ist für Frauen?

Zuhören A certain **Modegeschäft** (*clothing store*) has been doing a lot of advertising lately. As you listen to one of their radio ads, first write down the items in the order you hear them mentioned. Then figure out which items are for men, and which for women. What does this store have for "**die ganze Familie**"?

Ein wenig Landeskunde

When traveling to most countries in Europe, you need to convert dollars (USD) to euros (EUR), since almost all European countries have adopted this new currency. The conversion table (**Umrechnungstabelle**) on the right shows you how many euros you will receive for a certain amount of dollars and vice versa. The rates will vary, and you may want to look up the current rate of exchange in a newspaper or on a web site.

Looking at the clothing ad and using the conversion chart, compare the prices for clothing in Germany to what you pay in the United States. In general, in which country do you think clothes are more expensive? What types of clothes would you expect to be more expensive in Germany than in the United States?

Umrechnungstabelle			Stand: Juni 2001
USA			
EUR	**USD**	**USD**	**EUR**
0,10	0,08	0,10	0,11
0,20	0,17	0,20	0,22
0,50	0,44	0,50	0,56
1,00	0,88	1,00	1,13
5,00	4,42	5,00	5,65
10,00	8,84	10,00	11,31
20,00	44,20	20,00	22,62
50,00	77,68	50,00	56,55
100,00	88,41	100,00	113,10
200,00	176,83	200,00	226,20
500,00	442,08	500,00	565,50
1000,00	884,17	1000,00	1131,00

1 Dollar (USD) = 100 Cents

Diese errechneten Beträge schwanken täglich, da die Kurse für An-und Verkauf von Schecks, Noten und Münzen verschieden sind. Für die Tageskurse siehe Zeitungen und Web Sites.

COMMERZBANK Die Bank an Ihrer Seite

7 **Wie sind die Preise?**

Sprechen/Schreiben Using the **Umrechnungstabelle** for clues, create a price list for the following items listed in the **Wortschatz** but not in the ad: **Gürtel, Jogging-Anzug, Turnschuhe, Pulli,** and **Stiefel.** Your partner will ask you how much these items cost, and you will answer, using your price list and the ad on page 133. Then switch roles. Be polite!

8 **Was gibt es im Modegeschäft?**

Lesen/Sprechen You want to buy something new to wear to your friend's party, but you can't decide what to buy. You have 100€ to spend. Using the ad on page 133 and your price list, put together three different outfits that would be within your budget. With which outfit would you have the most money left over?

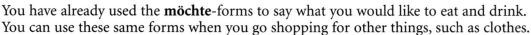

So sagt man das!

Expressing wishes when shopping

Übungsheft, S. 50–51, Ü. 3–4

You have already used the **möchte**-forms to say what you would like to eat and drink. You can use these same forms when you go shopping for other things, such as clothes.

The salesclerk might ask:

Bitte? *or*
Was möchten Sie?
or
Was bekommen Sie?
or
Haben Sie einen Wunsch?

You can respond:

Ich möchte eine Jacke, bitte!
Ich brauche ein T-Shirt.
  I need a T-shirt.
Einen Pulli in Grau, bitte!
  A sweater in gray, please!
Ich suche eine Bluse.
  I'm looking for a blouse.

What is the subject of the sentence in each of the salesclerk's questions? Look at the sentence **Einen Pulli in Grau, bitte!** Is there a subject or verb? What do you think is intended?

Grammatik

Definite and indefinite articles, accusative case

Look at the following sentences:

Der Pulli kostet 15 Euro.
Ein Pulli kostet 15 Euro.

Möchten Sie **de<u>n</u> Pulli?**
Möchten Sie **eine<u>n</u> Pulli?**

Mehr Grammatikübungen
S. 148–149, Ü. 1–3

Übungsheft,
S. 51–52, Ü. 5–6

Grammatikheft,
S. 38, Ü. 3–4

What is the difference between the noun phrases **der Pulli/ein Pulli** on the left and the noun phrases **den Pulli/einen Pulli** on the right?

The noun phrases **der Pulli/ein Pulli** on the left are the *subjects* (nominative case) of the sentences. The noun phrases **den Pulli/einen Pulli** on the right are *direct objects* (accusative case) of the sentences. Only articles for masculine nouns change when they are used as direct objects. The articles for feminine, neuter, and plural nouns stay the same.

	Nominative	Accusative
Masculine	der / ein Pulli	de<u>n</u> / eine<u>n</u> Pulli
Feminine	die / eine Jacke	die / eine Jacke
Neuter	das / ein T-Shirt	das / ein T-Shirt
Plural	die / — Turnschuhe	die / — Turnschuhe

9 **Grammatik im Kontext**

Zuhören Listen carefully to these students commenting on different clothes, and decide whether the item of clothing in each exchange is the subject or direct object of the sentences.

10 **Grammatik im Kontext**

Lesen/Sprechen Read this conversation between Julia and the salesclerk at **Sport-Kerner**. Look carefully at the conversation and determine what the subject and/or direct object is in each sentence. Then answer the questions that follow.

VERKÄUFERIN	Guten Tag! Haben Sie einen Wunsch?
JULIA	Ich suche einen Rock in Blau. Was kostet der Rock hier?
VERKÄUFERIN	Er kostet nur 30 Euro.
JULIA	Und haben Sie vielleicht auch eine Bluse in Weiß?
VERKÄUFERIN	Ja, die Bluse hier kostet 23 Euro. Wir haben auch das weiße T-Shirt hier im Sonderangebot (*a special offer*). Nur 10 Euro. Passt auch schön zu Röcken.
JULIA	Das T-Shirt ist schön, aber ich brauche ein T-Shirt in Schwarz. Also ich nehme nur den Rock und die Bluse. Danke!

1. What is Julia looking for?
2. Why doesn't she want the T-shirt?
3. How much is her final purchase?

11 **Grammatik im Kontext**

a. **Sprechen** Tell some of your classmates what clothes you need, using the indefinite article when appropriate.

b. **Sprechen** Now point to various articles of clothing that your classmates are wearing and say that you would like to have them, using the definite article.

Ich	brauche möchte	Pulli	Turnschuhe
		Rock	Bluse
		Jeans	Kleid
		Hemd	Hose
		T-Shirt	Socken
		Stiefel	Jacke
		Gürtel	

12 **Grammatik im Kontext**

 Schreiben/Sprechen You are in a department store that has many items on sale (**im Sonderangebot**). Make a list of the clothes you would like to buy. Your partner will play the salesperson and ask you what you want and tell you where everything is. In the boxes to the right are some words and phrases you might need.

dort	der/ein
da drüben	den/einen
hier vorn	die/eine
da hinten	das/ein

13 **Haben Sie das auch in …?**

Sprechen You didn't find the colors you like at the last store. Ask the salesperson at the new store on the right if he or she has the items you want in certain colors. Also ask about prices. Then switch roles.

Wortschatz

Farben!

Haben Sie das auch…?

CD-ROM DISC 2

in Blau   in Grün   in Weiß   in Hellblau

in Rot   in Dunkelblau   in Braun   in Gelb

in Grau   in Schwarz

Übungsheft, S. 52, Ü. 8

Grammatikheft, S. 39, Ü. 5–6

 **Ein wenig Landeskunde**

The store hours listed below are typical for small stores in Germany. What are the hours for the different days of the week? Is this different from stores where you live?

In cities stores are allowed to stay open from 6 a.m. until 8 p.m. Stores in smaller communities close at 7 p.m. On Saturdays stores close at 4 p.m.

14 **Alles ist im Sonderangebot!**

 Schreiben Design your own newspaper ad based on four items in the ad on page 133 or cut out pictures from a magazine. Remember, everything is on sale at your store. Be sure to mention prices and colors in stock. Be prepared to share your ads with the class.

So sagt man das!

Commenting on and describing clothes

If you want to know what someone thinks about a particular item of clothing, you might ask:

Wie findest du das Hemd?

You might get positive comments, such as:

Ich finde es fesch.
Es sieht schick aus!
Es passt prima.
Es gefällt mir.

or you might get negative comments, such as:

Ich finde es furchtbar.
Es sieht blöd aus.
Es passt nicht.
Es gefällt mir nicht.

If the person you ask isn't sure, he or she might say:

Ich weiß nicht.   *or*   **Ich bin nicht sicher.**

 Grammatikheft, S. 40, Ü. 7

Ein wenig Grammatik

Look at these sentences:

> **Wie findest du den Rock?**
> **Er gefällt mir.**
> **Und die T-Shirts?**
> **Sie gefallen mir auch.**

What are the subjects in the two responses?[1] When using the verb **gefallen** to say you like something, you need to know only two forms: **gefällt** and **gefallen**.

> **Er/sie/es gefällt mir.** *I like it.*
> **Sie (pl) gefallen mir.** *I like them.*

Grammatikheft, S. 40, Ü. 8

Mehr Grammatikübungen
S. 149, Ü. 4

---

15 Grammatik im Kontext

a. Zuhören Several students are in a store looking at clothes and talking about what they like and don't like. Determine whether the person speaking likes the item of clothing or not.

b. Schreiben Copy these sentences by filling in the blank with the appropriate form of **gefallen**.

1. Die Bluse ═══ mir sehr gut.
2. Die Schuhe ═══ mir auch.
3. Wie ═══ dir die Hose?
4. Sie ═══ mir; sie sieht toll aus.
5. Und wie ═══ dir die Jacke?
6. Sie ═══ mir, aber Jacken wie die hier ═══ mir besser.

 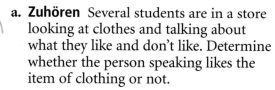    

1.   2.   3.   4.   5.

---

1. er (der Rock), sie (die T-Shirts)

Sprechen Look at the items pictured in Activity 15 and ask your partner if he or she likes each item. Then switch roles.

Nichts passt!

Das Kleid ist zu lang.

Der Pulli ist viel zu weit.

Die Jacke ist zu groß.

Die Hose ist zu kurz.

Das Hemd ist zu eng.

Die Schuhe sind ein bisschen zu klein.

HERRENGRÖSSEN

	USA	BRD
Hemden	13	36
	15	38
	16	40
	17	42
Pullover	S	36-38
	M	39
	L	40-41
	XL	42-44
Anzüge	34	44
	36	46
	40	50
	44	54
	46	56
Schuhe	7, 7½	40
	8	41
	8½	42
	9, 9½	43
	10, 10½	44
	11, 11½	45
	12, 12½	46

DAMENGRÖSSEN

	USA	BRD
Blusen, Pullover	8	36
	10	38
	12	40
	14	42
Kleider, Mäntel	8	38
	10	40
	12	42
	14	44
Schuhe	5	36
	6	37
	7	38
	8	39
	9	40
	10	41

Ein wenig Landeskunde

German sizes are different from American sizes. However, clothes manufactured in the United States and imported to Germany carry U.S. sizes. For example, jeans are often measured in inches, and T-shirts have the designations **S, M, L, XL,** and **XXL.** Look at the size charts on the right. What size would you take if you were buying German clothes or shoes in Germany?

Grammatikheft, S. 41, Ü. 9

17 Was ist los?

Sprechen You and a friend are spending the afternoon **in der Innenstadt** (*downtown*).
You encounter the people pictured below and discuss their clothing. Take turns
describing the clothing pictured to each other.

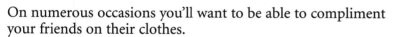

So sagt man das!

Giving compliments and responding to them

On numerous occasions you'll want to be able to compliment
your friends on their clothes.

You could say:

Die Jacke sieht lässig aus! *or* **Ich finde den Pulli echt stark.** *or* **Die Jacke gefällt mir!**

The other person might respond: You could answer:

Ehrlich? *or*   **Ehrlich!**
Wirklich? *or*   **Wirklich!**
Meinst du?   **Ja, bestimmt!**
Nicht zu lang (kurz, groß)?   **Nein, überhaupt nicht!**

Übungsheft, S. 53–54, Ü. 9–11

Grammatikheft, S. 41, Ü. 10

18 Was meinst du?

a. Schreiben Find five pictures of clothing items in your favorite magazine. Write at
least two sentences to describe each item and one sentence to express your opinion
about each picture.

b. Sprechen Show your partner the pictures you
cut out and ask what he or she thinks of your
clothing choices. If your partner compliments
you on your choices, respond appropriately.

fesch	schick	blöd	furchtbar	prima
Spitze	toll	scheußlich	stark	lässig

Direct object pronouns

In **Kapitel 3** you learned that the pronouns **er, sie, es,** and **sie** (pl) can refer to both people and objects. Look at the following sentences:

Der Pulli ist sehr preiswert.
Ja, **er** ist nicht teuer.

Ich finde **den Pulli** toll.
Ich finde **ihn** auch toll.

Mehr Grammatikübungen, S. 149–150, Ü. 5–7

What are the pronouns in these sentences? What do you think **er** and **ihn** refer to? **Er,** the pronoun on the left, is the *subject* (nominative case) of the sentence and refers to **der Pulli.** The pronoun **ihn** on the right is the *direct object* (accusative case) of the sentence and refers to **den Pulli.** Only the masculine pronoun changes when it is used as a direct object. The feminine **sie,** neuter **es,** and plural pronoun **sie** stay the same:

	Subject: Nominative		Direct Object: Accusative	
	Noun Phrase	Pronoun	Noun Phrase	Pronoun
Masculine	der Pulli	er	den Pulli	**ihn**
Feminine	die Jacke	sie	die Jacke	sie
Neuter	das T-Shirt	es	das T-Shirt	es
Plural	die Turnschuhe	sie	die Turnschuhe	sie

Übungsheft, S. 54–55, Ü. 12–15

Grammatikheft, S. 42–43, Ü. 11–12

19 Grammatik im Kontext

a. Zuhören Listen to this conversation between two students who are talking about clothes they want to buy. The first time you hear the conversation, figure out whether the pronouns they mention are subjects or direct objects. Then listen again and match the article of clothing with the words used to describe it.

Subject	Direct object	adjective
0	X	hübsch
1		
2		

BEISPIEL —Ich finde die blaue Bluse sehr schön. Und du?
—Ja, ich finde sie hübsch.

b. Schreiben Copy these sentences by filling in each blank with the correct form of the article and the pronoun.

1. Wie findest du ===== Rock? Ich finde ===== toll!
2. Ich finde ===== Bluse schick. Ja, ===== ist stark!
3. Ich finde ===== T-Shirt prima. Wie findest du ===== ?
4. Ich finde ===== Pulli stark. Wie findest du ===== ?
5. Wie findest du ===== Schuhe? Ich finde ===== teuer.
6. Wie findest du ===== Hemd? Ich finde ===== zu eng!
7. Wie findest du ===== Hose? Ich finde ===== zu klein!
8. Wie findest du ===== Gürtel? Ich finde ===== zu lang!

Ich finde diese Klamotten echt toll!

20 Welcher Satz passt?

 Lesen/Sprechen Katja and Sonja are in a store trying on clothes. Choose the appropriate responses to complete their conversation. Then read the conversation aloud with your partner.

> Ich finde ihn toll, aber er ist viel zu lang für dich.

> Hm, ich finde sie schön, aber sie passt nicht.

> Bist du sicher? Sie sind sehr teuer.

> Ja, es sieht super aus!

SONJA	Wie findest du die Bluse in Rot?
KATJA	══════.
SONJA	Meinst du? Wie findest du den Rock hier in Schwarz?
KATJA	══════.
SONJA	Ehrlich? So ein Mist! Vielleicht kaufe ich das T-Shirt in Blau.
KATJA	══════.
SONJA	Dann kaufe ich das T-Shirt und die Schuhe.
KATJA	══════.
SONJA	Ich weiß, aber sie gefallen mir sehr.

21 Wie findest du …?

 Sprechen Find out what your partner thinks about the clothes that Georg and Beate are wearing to Sonja's party. One of you comments on Georg's clothing, and the other on Beate's. When you have finished, switch roles.

22 Bildbeschreibung

 Schreiben With your partner, write a conversation that could go with the picture below. Practice your conversation and be prepared to share it with the class.

Georg   **Beate**

Welche Klamotten sind „in"?

What do you think German students usually like to wear when they go to a party? We asked many students, and here is what some of them said. Listen first, then read the text.

Übungsheft,
S. 60, Ü. 1–4

Sandra, Stuttgart

„Also, wenn ich zu einer Party gehe, dann ziehe ich am liebsten Jeans an und vielleicht einen Body …und einen weiten Pulli darüber; meistens dann etwas in Blau oder einen weißen Pulli, jetzt, wie grad' eben, denn meine Lieblingsfarben sind doch Blau und Weiß."

Melina, Bietigheim

„Am liebsten mag ich Jeans, vor allem helle, oder ja so lockere Blusen, kurze halt, und jetzt vor allem T-Shirts, einfarbige; und sie sollen halt schön lang sein und ein bisschen locker. Und ja, meine Lieblingsfarben sind Blau, Apricot oder Rot, Lila auch noch."

Alexandra, Bietigheim

„Ja, ich zieh am liebsten Jeans an, und Lieblingsfarben sind dann so Blau oder Pastellfarben, und auf Partys oder so eigentlich immer in Jeans und mal etwas Schöneres oben, in Diskos dann auch, und ab und zu hab ich mal gern einen Rock."

Iwan, Bietigheim

„Also, wenn ich auf eine Party gehe, zieh ich am liebsten ein T-Shirt an und eine kurze Hose. Am liebsten trag ich Schwarz, so einfach, weil es halt schön aussieht und weil es bequem ist."

A. 1. What items of clothing are mentioned most by these students? Make a list of the clothing each student prefers and list the colors he or she seems to like best.

    2. Which of these students would you like to meet and why? Do you and the student you selected have similar tastes in clothes? Explain. What do you generally wear and what are your favorite colors? What do you usually wear to a party?

B. What is your overall impression of the way these German teenagers dress? Compare it with the typical dress for teenagers in the United States. Do you think students in the United States are more or less formal than students in Germany? Why do you think so? Write a brief essay explaining your answer.

23 Was kommt zuerst?

 Zuhören Jürgen goes to a clothing store to find something to wear to Sonja's party. You will hear four short pieces of his conversation with the salesman. On a separate sheet of paper, put the photos in order according to their conversation.

a.

b.

c.

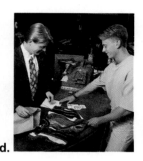
d.

So sagt man das!

Talking about trying on clothes

When you go shopping for clothes, you will want to try them on.

You might say to the salesperson:

Ich probiere das T-Shirt an. *or*   **Ich ziehe das T-Shirt an.**

If you decide to buy it: If not:

Ich nehme es. *or*
Ich kaufe es.

Ich nehme es nicht. *or*
Ich kaufe es nicht.

Grammatik

Separable-prefix verbs

The verbs **anziehen** (*to put on, wear*), **anprobieren** (*to try on*), and **aussehen** (*to look, appear*) belong to a group of verbs that have a separable prefix. The prefix is at the beginning of the verb: **an**ziehen, **an**probieren, **aus**sehen. In the present tense, the prefix is separated from the verb and is at the end of the clause or sentence.

anziehen
Was **ziehe** ich **an**?
Ich **ziehe** Shorts **an**.
Ich **ziehe** Shorts und ein T-Shirt **an**.
Ich **ziehe** heute Shorts und ein T-Shirt **an**.
Ich **ziehe** heute zu Sonjas Fete Shorts und ein T-Shirt **an**.
Ja, zu Sonjas Fete **ziehe** ich ganz bestimmt Shorts und ein T-Shirt **an**!

Mehr Grammatikübungen
S. 151, Ü. 8

Übungsheft, S. 56–57, Ü. 16–19

Grammatikheft, S. 44, Ü. 13–14

24 **Grammatik im Kontext**

Sprechen/Schreiben Build as many sentences as you can. Be sure to use the correct articles.

Ich		Hemd
Er		gut
Bluse	anziehen	blöd
Schuhe	aussehen	scheußlich
Sie	anprobieren	Pulli
Jogging-Anzug		Jacke
Jeans		Jeans
Gürtel		

A number of German verbs have prefixes but not all of them are separable (for example, **gefallen** and **bekommen**). You can usually recognize separable prefixes if they are words that can also stand alone (such as **mit, auf,** and **aus**) and if they carry the main stress of the compound verb. Compare **ánziehen** and **bekómmen**.

Ein wenig Grammatik

The verbs **nehmen** (*to take*) and **aussehen** (*to appear, look*) are called *stem-changing verbs.* In these verbs, the stem vowel changes in the **du-** and **er/sie-**forms. These verbs do not follow the regular patterns of verbs like **spielen.**

Du **nimmst** den Rock.   Du **siehst** gut **aus**!
Er **nimmt** die Jacke.   Sie **sieht** gut **aus**!

You will learn more about these verbs later.

DISC **2**

Mehr Grammatikübungen
S. 151, Ü. 9

Übungsheft, S. 57–58, Ü. 20–22   Grammatikheft, S. 45, Ü. 15–16

25 **Grammatik im Kontext**

 a. Sprechen Look at the pictures of clothing below and ask your partner what Julia, Katja, Michael, and Heiko will wear to Sonja's party. Your partner's responses will be based on the illustrations. Switch roles and vary your responses.

b. Sprechen You and your partner have been invited to Sonja's party. Ask your partner what he or she would wear based on the pictures of clothing. Then switch roles.

26 **Was nimmst du?**

 Sprechen You have picked out five items of clothing that you like. Your partner asks you which items you will try on and which ones you would like to buy. Answer, then switch roles.

Für mein Notizbuch

Schreiben For your **Notizbuch** entry, write a paragraph describing what you and your friends usually wear to a party. Describe the kinds of clothes you like and some that you do not like. Describe some of the latest fashions for teens and write what you think about them.

> Bei Sport-Kerner haben wir alles! T-Shirts ab 15 Euro in Gelb, Grün und Weiß—sehr schön, perfekt für den Sommer. Wie passt das T-Shirt?

> Oh phantastisch! Es gefällt mir sehr! Und so preiswert. Ich kaufe T-Shirts immer bei Sport-Kerner!

28

Im Fernsehen

 You work for an ad agency. Get together with two other classmates and write a TV commercial that will convince your audience to shop at a certain clothing store. Be sure to mention prices, colors, and how well the clothes fit and look.

29

 **Von der Schule zum Beruf**

Schreiben You are employed at an advertising agency. One of your jobs is to write copy for TV commercials. You are to convince your viewers to shop at a certain clothing store. Give your store a name, and be sure to mention in your ad the prices, colors, look, and fit of the items being advertised.

AUSSPRACHE

Richtig aussprechen / Richtig lesen

A. To practice the following sounds, say the words and sentences below after your teacher or after the recording.

1. The letter **i:** When the letter **i** is followed by two consonants, it sounds like the short *i* in the English word *pit*.
   schick, bestimmt, bisschen / Ich finde das Kleid schick. Ehrlich.

2. The letters **ä** and **e:** The letters **ä** and **e** are pronounced as short vowels when followed by two consonants. They sound similar to the short *e* in the English word *net*.
   lässig, hell, gefällt / Das fesche Hemd gefällt mir.

3. The letter **a:** The letter **a** is roughly equivalent to the *a* sound in the English word *father*.
   haben, lang, Jacke / Wir haben Jacken in allen Farben.

4. The letter combinations **sch, st,** and **sp:** The consonant combination **sch** is pronounced like the *sh* in the English word *ship*. When the letter **s** is followed by **p** or **t** at the beginning of a syllable, it is also pronounced in this way.
   schwarz, Turnschuh, Stiefel / Die schwarzen Stiefel sind Spitze!

Richtig schreiben / Diktat

B. Write down the sentences that you hear.

Zum Lesen

KLEIDER MACHEN LEUTE!

Lesestrategie Using what you already know When you are faced with an unknown text, use what you already know to anticipate the kind of information you might expect to find in the text. It is obvious that these texts are about clothing. Though you may see many words that you do not know, you have read clothing ads in English, and you know that they contain information about prices, styles, sizes, types of material, etc. Watch for this kind of information as you read.

1. Look at a clothing ad from a magazine written in English and make a list of some of the words and expressions that you find in the ad.

2. When you look in a newspaper or magazine for some good buys in clothing, what are some words or phrases that tell you that you would be getting a bargain? Write down some of these English words and phrases.

3. Scan these two pages and write any German words or phrases you find that correspond to the words and phrases you listed in Activities 1 and 2 above. Group the words you find in categories (prices, colors, etc.) and list as many words in each category as you can.

4. Look at the prices of the clothing being advertised. Judging from the photos, are these prices reasonable? Are there prices you could afford? Do you think they are the original prices in all cases? What phrase gives you the information to answer that question?

Ohne Shirts und Shorts geht im Sommer nichts. K + L Ruppert hat für Sie die schönsten ausgesucht. Sagenhafte Vielfalt und sommerleichte Qualitäten. Zu Preisen, die Ihnen passen werden!

29.-

39.5

Alex, 16 Jahre
„Ich trage Schwarz. Ich ändere das nie. Andere Sachen habe ich nicht. Ich glaube, mit Mode kann man etwas erklären, ohne zu reden."

Sandra, 16 Jahre
„Zu meinem braunen Kleid trage ich schwarze Strümpfe und schwarze Schuhe mit Klumpabsatz. Ich ziehe mir auch Sachen an, wenn sie nicht 'in' sind. Es gibt wichtigeres als Mode."

3

Manu, 16 Jahre
„Meine Jeans und die Lederjacke sind Markenprodukte, keine billigen Kopien. Ich finde das wichtig."

KRIEGBAUM AKTUELL

Stark Reduziert!

19.90 (3)

12.90 (2)

2) **Kapuzen-T-Shirts**
100% reine Baumwolle, in vielen Farben sortiert, Größe M-XXL **12.90**

3) **Kapuzen-T-Shirts**
100% reine Baumwolle, top Farben, bedruckt **19.90**

Volker, 16 Jahre
„Das sind meine Sachen: Jeans, Sportschuhe, Kapuzen-Shirt. Ich trage sie, weil sie mir gefallen. Mode interessiert mich nicht."

29.-

29.-

QUALITÄTS-GARANTIE
Wenn Sie bei K + L Ruppert einkaufen, stimmt nicht nur der Preis, sondern auch die Qualität. Dafür geben wir Ihnen auf unsere Ware 12 Monate Garantie. Sicher ist sicher.

Amberg, Augsburg, Bayreuth, Deggendorf, Erlangen, Freilassing, Freising, Friedrichshafen, Ingolstadt, Kempten, Kaufbeuren, 2 x in Landshut, Memmingen, Mühldorf/Inn, München/Kauflingerstr. 15, Neumarkt/Opf., Nürnberg, Passau, Ravensburg, Regensburg, Rosenheim, Straubing, Weiden, Weilheim. Irrtmer, Änderungen und Abweichungen vorbehalten. Alle Preise sind DM-Preise.

k+l ruppert

5. Not all the texts on these pages are ads. What other type of text can you identify? What type of magazine would you expect texts like these to come from?

6. What is the age of the students who are describing their clothing? What generalizations can you make about the clothing of these students? Find words in the text that support your answer.

7. In the ad to the left, what kind of guarantee does **K&L Ruppert** offer for its merchandise?

8. What does Volker wear? Where could he buy a shirt like the one he says he likes to wear? How much would it cost? Do you know why it has that name?

9. What does Alex mean when he says „**Ich glaube, mit Mode kann man etwas erklären, ohne zu reden.**"? (**ohne zu reden**- *without speaking*) Work with a partner and come up with some examples that illustrate this statement.

10. How does Manu differ from Sandra and Volker?

11. You are planning a trip to Germany. Your hosts will meet you at the airport, but they have never seen you. Write them a postcard with a short description of what you look like and what you will be wearing (**Ich trage ...**).

12. Your club at school is planning a garage sale. Write an ad for the school or local newspaper in which you describe the kinds of clothing you will sell.

Übungsheft, S. 59, Ü. 23

Erste Stufe   **Objective** Expressing wishes when shopping

1 You and your friend are in a clothing store talking about prices, color, and fit of various items of clothing. Complete your questions and statements by supplying the correct forms of the definite article. **(S. 135)**

1. Was kostet _____ T-Shirt, bitte? Und _____ Jacke da?
2. Ich nehme _____ T-Shirt, ___ Pulli und _____ Jacke da, aber in Grün.
3. Ja, _____ Hose ist preiswert und _____ Gürtel auch.
4. Möchten Sie _____ Hose, und nehmen Sie _____ Gürtel?
5. Du, _____ Rock gefällt mir gut. Ich glaube, ich kaufe ___ Rock.
6. Ich bekomme _____ Hemd, _____ Turnschuhe und _____ Socken.
7. Ich möchte _____ Jeans da und _____ Stiefel.
8. Ich nehme _____ Kleid, und was kostet _____ Bluse da?
9. Möchten Sie _____ Hemd oder _____ Pulli?
10. Ja, _____ Jogging-Anzug ist preiswert, aber _____ Farbe ist nicht schön.

2 You are still in the clothing store, telling the salespersons what you are looking for and asking about the availability of various items of clothing in the colors you want. Complete these questions and statements by supplying the correct form of the indefinite article. **(S. 135)**

1. Ich suche _____ T-Shirt und _____ Pulli. _____ Pulli in Blau, bitte.
2. Dann brauche ich _____ Jeans und _____ Gürtel.
3. Ich möchte _____ Rock in Weiß, bitte, und _____ T-Shirt in Blau.
4. Ich brauche _____ Jogging-Anzug und _____ Shorts.
5. Haben Sie _____ Wunsch? Suchen Sie _____ Kleid oder _____ Bluse?
6. Möchtest du _____ Jeans, _____ Rock oder _____ Kleid?
7. Ich suche _____ Shorts und _____ Jacke, beide in Blau.
8. Ich brauche _____ Hemd, _____ Hose und _____ Gürtel für die Party.

3 You seem to like everything in the clothing store, and you're telling your friend that you need each item. Complete each of the following statements by filling in the first blank with the correct form of the definite article, and the second blank with the correct form of the indefinite article. (S. 135)

1. _____ T-Shirt gefällt mir. Ich brauche _____ T-Shirt.
2. _____ Rock gefällt mir. Ich brauche _____ Rock.
3. _____ Bluse gefällt mir. Ich brauche _____ Bluse.
4. _____ Pulli gefällt mir. Ich brauche _____ Pulli.
5. _____ Hemd gefällt mir. Ich brauche _____ Hemd.
6. _____ Gürtel gefällt mir. Ich brauche _____ Gürtel.
7. _____ Kleid gefällt mir. Ich brauche _____ Kleid.
8. _____ Jacke gefällt mir. Ich brauche _____ Jacke.
9. _____ Jogging-Anzug gefällt mir. Ich brauche _____ Jogging-Anzug.
10. _____ Hose gefällt mir gut. Ich brauche _____ Hose.

Zweite Stufe

Objectives Commenting on and describing clothes; giving compliments

4 You are still in the clothing store. You are asking a friend for comments on the looks and the fit of various items of clothing. Complete each of the following questions and statements, using the correct forms of the definite articles and the verb **gefallen**. (S. 137)

1. Wie findest du _____ Rock? — Prima! Er _____ mir gut.
2. Wie findet Sonja _____ Turnschuhe? — Sie _____ ihr sehr gut.
3. Also, ich finde _____ T-Shirt Spitze. Und _____ Farbe _____ mir sehr gut.
4. Ja, _____ Stiefel _____ mir. Und _____ passen prima.
5. Du, _____ Pulli _____ mir überhaupt nicht. Mir _____ die T-Shirts da!

5 You continue asking for comments on the looks and the fit of various items of clothing. Complete each of the following statements by supplying the correct definite article and pronoun. (S. 140)

1. Ja, du, _____ Rock sieht schick aus, und _____ passt prima!
2. Ich finde _____ Pulli toll; _____ gefällt mir gut.
3. Ja, _____ Pulli sieht gut aus, aber _____ passt dir nicht; _____ ist zu eng.
4. Du, _____ Turnschuhe passen gut, aber _____ sind ein bisschen zu teuer.
5. Ich finde _____ Hemd sehr schick; _____ gefällt mir prima.
6. _____ Stiefel sind toll, aber sind _____ nicht ein bisschen zu groß?
7. Wie findest du _____ T-Shirt? Ist _____ nicht zu weit?
8. Du möchtest _____ Gürtel? Ist _____ nicht zu kurz?
9. Du, _____ Jogging-Anzug passt prima. _____ gefällt mir.
10. Ich finde _____ Jogging-Anzug echt stark, und _____ passt prima.

6 You and your friend are disagreeing about various items of clothing. Your friend finds everything great while you think those items are ugly. Complete each of the following statements by filling in the first blank with the correct form of the definite article, and the second blank with the correct form of the pronoun. (S. 140)

1. Ich finde _____ Pulli toll. – Und ich finde _____ scheußlich!
2. Ich finde _____ Hemd super. – Und ich finde _____ furchtbar!
3. Ich finde _____ Jacke fesch. – Und ich finde _____ scheußlich!
4. Ich finde _____ Stiefel prima. – Und ich finde _____ ganz hässlich!
5. Ich finde _____ Gürtel schick. – Und ich finde _____ scheußlich!
6. Ich finde _____ Bluse prima. – Und ich finde _____ furchtbar!
7. Ich finde _____ Kleid toll. – Und ich finde _____ scheußlich!
8. Ich finde _____ Rock zu lang. – Und ich finde _____ zu kurz!
9. Ich finde _____ T-Shirt zu weit. – Und ich finde _____ zu eng.
10. Ich finde _____ Klamotten zu teuer. – Und ich finde _____ billig!

7 You have decided to buy new clothes and are telling your friend about your decisions. Complete each of the following statements by filling in the first blank with the correct form of the definite article, and the second and third blanks with the correct forms of the pronoun. (S. 140)

BEISPIEL   Ich nehme _____ Bluse. _____ gefällt mir. Ich kaufe _____ .
Ich nehme die Bluse. Sie gefällt mir. Ich kaufe sie.

1. Ich nehme _____ Rock. _____ gefällt mir. Ich kaufe _____ .
2. Ich nehme _____ T-Shirt. _____ gefällt mir. Ich kaufe _____ .
3. Ich nehme _____ Pulli. _____ gefällt mir. Ich kaufe _____ .
4. Ich nehme _____ Hose. _____ gefällt mir. Ich kaufe _____ .
5. Ich nehme _____ Gürtel. _____ gefällt mir. Ich kaufe _____ .
6. Ich nehme _____ T-Shirt. _____ gefällt mir. Ich kaufe _____ .
7. Ich nehme _____ Turnschuhe. _____ gefallen mir. Ich kaufe _____ .
8. Ich nehme _____ Kleid. _____ gefällt mir. Ich nehme _____ .
9. Ich nehme _____ Jacke. _____ gefällt mir. Ich kaufe _____ .
10. Ich nehme _____ Klamotten. _____ gefallen mir. Ich kaufe _____ .

8 You are asking a friend what to wear and what he or she is going to wear to a party. Complete each of the following statements by filling in the blanks with the correct form of the separable-prefix verb given in parentheses. **(S. 143)**

1. Sag, was _____ du denn zur Fete _____? (anziehen)
2. Die Sonja und die Katja _____ heute sehr schick _____. (aussehen)
3. Warum _____ du den Pulli nicht mal _____? (anprobieren)
4. Der Michael _____ das T-Shirt mit dem Texas-Motiv _____. (anziehen)
5. Wie _____ ihr denn heute _____! Fesch! (aussehen)
6. Du sagst, sie sind zu groß? Ich _____ mal die Stiefel _____. (anprobieren)
7. Was _____ die Katja zur Party _____? Jeans und T-Shirt? (anziehen)
8. Wie _____ wir heute nur _____? Scheußlich! (aussehen)
9. Wer _____ den Jogging-Anzug _____? (anprobieren)

9 You are asking your friends why they are taking or not taking various items of clothing by commenting on their looks. Complete each of the statements by using the correct forms of the verbs **nehmen** and **aussehen. (S. 144)**

1. Warum _____ du den Rock nicht? Er _____ doch sehr fesch _____.
2. Wer _____ die Jacke? Du, Sonja? Sie _____ toll _____!
3. Du _____ heute so fesch _____! Warum _____ du nur dieses T-Shirt?
4. Die Sonja _____ den Pulli; er _____ einfach toll _____!
5. Ihr _____ die Stiefel, ja? Sie _____ doch gut _____.
6. Wer _____ die Klamotten? Sie _____ furchtbar _____.
7. Ich _____ den Pulli; er _____ doch fesch _____!
8. Der Michael _____ das T-Shirt, und es _____ so scheußlich _____!

Anwendung

1 You have been hired to write for a German fashion magazine on trends among teens today. Interview your partner about his or her taste in clothes. When you have finished, switch roles and then interview one other person. Find out what clothes they like to wear, what they wear to a party, their favorite color, and their favorite article of clothing. Take notes and write an article in German based on your interviews.

2 Look at the two display windows for **Mode-Welt.** With a partner compare the two windows and take turns telling each other which items are missing (**fehlen**) from the second window.

3 Read the fashion review to the right, then answer these questions.

1. What clothing item is the fashion editor talking about?
2. Is he or she enthusiastic or skeptical about the item?
3. What does he or she say about the clothing being reviewed?

DAS WEISSE HEMD

Ein weißes Hemd ist das, was Modekenner einen „all time classic" nennen: schick, aber trotzdem leger—ein Basisstück für jede Garderobe. In dieser Saison ist das weiße Hemd das Lieblingskind der Designer, die sich in ihren Variationen gegenseitig übertreffen. Asymmetrisch, geknotet oder aus Leinen, lang oder kurz—zu Jeans, Shorts oder Röcken: alles geht.

4 You are in a store looking for some new clothes and your partner, a pushy salesperson, tries to convince you to try on and get clothes that are the wrong color and don't fit. You try them on, and he or she tells you how good they look and how well they fit. You're not so sure. Express your uncertainty and hesitancy. Will you succumb to the pressure in the end and buy the clothes? Develop a conversation based on this scenario and practice it with your partner.

5 You will hear some conversations in a clothing store. In each case the customer has decided not to buy the item. Determine the reason. Is it the price, the color, or the fit?

6

Zum Schreiben

Plan, write (and videotape) a German Club fashion show spotlighting appropriate party wear. The show is being sponsored by a local clothing store.

> **Schreibtipp** **Arrange your thoughts logically by using an outline form.** To make an outline, first put your ideas in related groups. Then put these groups in the order you want to write about them. Within each group, you might add sub-groups to develop your ideas in more detail.

Prewriting

Draw up your outline: in this case the introduction could be used for information about the store. Then, beginning with the most casual party possible, continue on to dress for more formal occasions (a formal wedding, etc.), and end with a fancy-dress party (Roman numerals I, II, etc.).

Writing

Now you are ready to begin your show commentary. Give a brief description of the clothing store, including the store's name, where it is located, and what a great bargain everything is. After placing each ensemble in the correct category, use some of the many descriptive words you've learned to talk about each ensemble. Be sure to give prices. Descriptions can be inserted beneath the name of the outfit in your outline.

7

Rollenspiel

You and two friends are at home trying to find something to wear to a party.

a. One of you is trying on clothes, but you can't find anything that fits or is the right color. Your friends comment on the clothes you try on.

b. Unsuccessful, in the end you all decide to go to the store. Look at the display windows in Activity 2 on page 152 again. Choose one window on which to base your conversation. This time one of you is the salesperson. The other two will be the customers. Ask for items in specific colors. The salesperson will tell you what's available. Will you try the clothes on? How do they look? Will you buy them? Role-play your scene in front of the class using props.

Kann ich's wirklich?

Can you express wishes when shopping? (p. 134)

1 How would a salesperson in a clothing store ask what you would like?

2 How would you answer, saying that you were looking for the following? (Be sure to practice using the articles correctly, and watch out for direct objects.)

a. a sweater **c.** pants in red **e.** a jacket in light gray

b. boots in black **d.** a shirt in brown **f.** a dress in blue

Can you comment on and describe clothing? (p. 137)

3 How would you ask a friend what he or she thinks of these clothes:

a. **b.** **c.** **d.**

4 How might your friend respond positively? Negatively? With uncertainty?

5 How would you disagree with the following statements by saying the opposite? Use the correct pronoun.

a. The jacket is too short. **e.** I think the belt is terrible.

b. The shoes are too tight. **f.** I like the tennis shoes.

c. The jogging suit is too small. **g.** I think the dress is too long.

d. The shirt fits just right. **h.** The skirt looks stylish.

Can you compliment someone's clothing and respond to compliments? (p. 139)

6 How would you compliment Katja, using the cues below?

a. blouse **b.** sweater **c.** T-shirt **d.** skirt

7 **a.** How might Katja respond to your compliments?

b. What would you say next?

8 How would you tell a friend what the following people are wearing to Sonja's party? (Remember to use **anziehen!**)

a. Julia **b.** Katja **c.** Heiko

> Jeans Bluse T-Shirt Jogging-Anzug
>
> Shorts Turnschuhe Gürtel

Can you talk about trying on clothes? (p. 143)

9 How would you tell the salesperson that you would like to try on a shirt in red, pants in white, a sweater in yellow, and a jacket in brown?

10 How would you tell your friend that you will get the shirt, the sweater, and the jacket? (Use **nehmen** or **kaufen**.)

Wortschatz

Erste Stufe

Expressing wishes when shopping

Bitte?	Yes? Can I help you?
Was bekommen Sie?	What would you like?
Haben Sie einen Wunsch?	May I help you?
Ich möchte …	I would like …
Ich brauche …	I need …
Ich suche …	I'm looking for …
Einen Pulli in Grau, bitte.	A sweater in gray, please.
Haben Sie das auch in Rot?	Do you also have that in red?
die Farbe, -n	color
in Rot	in red
in Blau	in blue

in Grün	in green
in Gelb	in yellow
in Braun	in brown
in Grau	in gray
in Schwarz	in black
in Weiß	in white
in Dunkelblau	in dark blue
in Hellblau	in light blue
die Klamotten (pl)	casual term for clothes
die Bluse, -n	blouse
der Rock, ⸚e	skirt
das Kleid, -er	dress
das Hemd, -en	shirt
die Jeans, -	jeans
der Gürtel, -	belt

die Hose, -n	pants
die Jacke, -n	jacket
der Pulli, -s (Pullover,-)	sweater
der Jogging-Anzug, ⸚e	jogging suit
das T-Shirt, -s	T-shirt
der Turnschuh, -e	sneaker, athletic shoe
der Stiefel, -	boot
die Socke, -n	sock
die Shorts, -	shorts

Masculine articles: accusative case

den	the
einen	a, an

Zweite Stufe

Commenting on and describing clothes

Er/Sie/Es gefällt mir.	I like it.
Sie gefallen mir.	I like them.
Der Rock sieht … aus.	The skirt looks …
hübsch	pretty
lässig	casual
schick	chic, smart
fesch	stylish, smart
scheußlich	hideous
furchtbar	terrible, awful
Der Rock passt prima!	The skirt fits great!

Ich finde den Pulli echt stark!	I think the sweater is really awesome!
Ich bin nicht sicher.	I'm not sure.
Ich weiß nicht.	I don't know.
die Größe, -n	the size
zu	too
viel zu	much too
ein bisschen	a little
weit	wide
eng	tight
lang	long
kurz	short

Giving and responding to compliments

Meinst du?	Do you think so?
ehrlich	honestly
wirklich	really
überhaupt nicht	not at all
bestimmt	definitely
Nicht zu lang?	Not too long?

Masculine Pronoun: accusative case

ihn	it; him

Dritte Stufe

Talking about trying on clothes

aussehen (sep)*	to look (like), appear
er/sie sieht aus**	he/she looks
anprobieren (sep)	to try on

anziehen (sep)	to put on, wear
nehmen	to take
er/sie nimmt	he/she takes
kaufen	to buy

*Verbs with separable prefixes will be indicated with (sep) **For verbs with stem-vowel changes, the third person singular form will be listed to show you the vowel change that occurs.

6
Pläne machen

Objectives

In this chapter you will learn to

Erste Stufe

- start a conversation
- tell time
- talk about when you are doing things

Zweite Stufe

- make plans

Dritte Stufe

- order food and beverages
- talk about how something tastes
- pay the check

 internet

go. hrw .com

ADRESSE: go.hrw.com
KENNWORT:
WK3 SCHLESWIG-HOLSTEIN-6

◀ **Was bekommst du?**

Los geht's! ▪ *Wollen wir ins Café gehen?*

VIDEO

Strategie Verstehen
Look at the images for this story. Where and when do you think these scenes are taking place? What clues tell you this? What do you think will happen in this story?

Heiko   **Julia**   **Katja**   **Michael**

1

Julia: Hallo, Heiko! Wie geht's denn so?

Heiko: Hm …So lala. Was machst du jetzt so hier? Wohin gehst du?

Julia: Zu Katja. Wir machen zuerst Hausaufgaben, und dann wollen wir ins Café Freizeit gehen, ein Eis essen. Willst du mitkommen?

Heiko: Gern! Wann wollt ihr gehen?

2

Julia: Wie spät ist es jetzt?

Heiko: Viertel nach drei.

Julia: Ja, so um halb fünf?

Heiko: Okay!

Julia: Bis dann, tschüs!

Heiko: Tschüs!

3

Kellner: Guten Tag! Was bekommt ihr?

Julia: Ich bekomme einen Eisbecher. Fruchteis.

Katja: Ich möchte einen Cappuccino, bitte.

Heiko: Hm …Ich will im Moment gar nichts. Ich esse später etwas.

Michael: Und ich esse jetzt eine Pizza. Nummer eins, bitte!

IMBISS—KARTE

Café Freizeit
Für den kleinen Hunger und Durst

KLEINE SPEISEN
NUDELSUPPE MIT BROT	EUR 2,25
KÄSEBROT	2,60
WURSTBROT	2,55
WIENER MIT SENF — 2 PAAR	2,90
PIZZA (15CM)	
Nr. 1 mit Tomaten und Käse	3,00
Nr. 2 mit Wurst und Käse	3,25
Nr. 3 mit Wurst, Käse und Pilzen	4,25

EIS
FRUCHTEIS	KUGEL EUR	0,60
SAHNEEIS	KUGEL	0,70
EISBECHER		3,40

4

Kellner:	Cappuccino?
Katja:	Ich bekomme den. Er ist für mich. Danke!
Kellner:	Eisbecher?
Julia:	Den Eisbecher bekomme ich.
Kellner:	Bitte sehr!
Julia:	Danke!
Kellner:	Die Pizza kommt gleich.
Michael:	Schon gut!

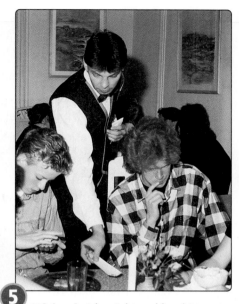

5

Michael:	Ich möchte zahlen, bitte.
Kellner:	Eine Pizza, drei Euro; ein Wurstbrot, zwei Euro sechzig; eine Cola, ein Euro fünfzig. Macht zusammen sieben Euro zehn.
Michael:	Stimmt schon!
Kellner:	Danke!

6

Michael:	Und nun trinke ich meine Cola aus und gehe.
Katja:	Du, pass auf! Pass doch auf!

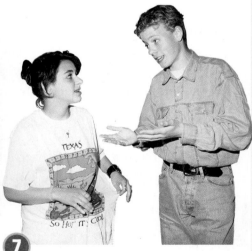

7

Michael:	Oje! Katja, es tut mir Leid!
Katja:	Macht ja nichts! Es ist ja nur mein T-Shirt!

Übungsheft, S. 61

1 Was passiert hier?

Do you understand what is happening in **Los geht's!**? Check your comprehension by answering these questions. Don't be afraid to guess.

1. What plans have Julia and Katja made for the afternoon?
2. What is Heiko going to do?
3. Where do the three friends meet Michael?
4. Why does Michael apologize to Katja? How does Katja react?

2 Genauer lesen

Reread the conversations. Which words or phrases do the characters use to

1. ask how someone is doing
2. talk about time
3. name foods and drinks
4. tell a waiter they want to pay
5. apologize

3 Was passt zusammen?

Match each statement or question on the left with an appropriate response on the right.

1. Wie geht's denn?
2. Wohin gehst du?
3. Wie spät ist es jetzt?
4. Wer bekommt den Cappuccino?
5. Ich möchte zahlen.

a. Er ist für mich.
b. So lala.
c. Das macht zusammen sieben Euro zehn.
d. Viertel nach drei.
e. Zu Katja.

4 Was fehlt hier?

Based on **Los geht's!**, complete each of the sentences below with an appropriate item from the list.

bekommt   Eis   einen Eisbecher   möchte
zahlen   Hausaufgaben   Stimmt   halb

Katja und Julia machen zuerst die ___1___. Dann wollen sie in ein Café gehen, ein ___2___ essen. Sie wollen so um ___3___ fünf gehen. Im Café fragt der Kellner: „Was ___4___ ihr?" Katja ___5___ einen Cappuccino. Julia sagt: „Ich bekomme___6___, Fruchteis." Michael will gehen. Er sagt: „Ich möchte ___7___, bitte." Der Kellner sagt: „Sieben Euro zehn." Und Michael antwortet: „ ___8___ schon."

5 Und du?

Look at the menu from the **Café am Markt**. Which items are foods, and which are beverages? If you were with your friends at the **Café am Markt**, what would you order? Make a list, including the prices.

Café am Markt

Nudelsuppe	EUR 2,25
Käsebrot	2,60
Wurstbrot	2,80
Wiener mit Senf	2,90
Pizza	4,00
Apfelkuchen	1,20
Eis	0,60
Mineralwasser	1,80
Kaffee	2,40
Cola	1,60

So sagt man das!

Starting a conversation

If you want to find out how someone is doing, you ask:

Wie geht's? *or* **Wie geht's denn?**

The person might respond in one of these ways, depending on how he or she is doing.

Sehr gut! Prima!	Danke, gut! Gut!	Danke, es geht. So lala. Nicht schlecht.	Nicht so gut. Schlecht.	Sehr schlecht. Miserabel!

Sven	Silke	Nadja	Kemal	Jörg

Übungsheft, S. 62, Ü. 2   Grammatikheft, S. 46, Ü. 1

6 ## Wie geht's?

Zuhören You will hear several students respond to the question **Wie geht's?** As you listen, look at the faces in the box above and determine who is speaking.

7 ## Hallo! Wie geht's?

Sprechen Greet several students around you and ask them how they are doing.

8 ## Was hast du um ...?

Sprechen Get together with your partner, greet him or her, and ask how he or she is doing. Then take turns asking each other what classes you have at the times shown below.

BEISPIEL DU Was hast du um ...?

a.　　　　　b.　　　　　c.　　　　　d.

Die Uhrzeit

You already know how to express time when referring to schedules: **um acht Uhr dreißig, um acht Uhr fünfundvierzig.** Now you will learn a more informal way of telling time.

neun Uhr

zehn vor zehn

zehn nach neun

vor

nach

Viertel vor zehn

zwanzig vor zehn

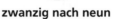

zwanzig nach neun

Viertel nach neun

halb zehn

Grammatikheft, S. 46–47, Ü. 2–5

So sagt man das!

Telling time and talking about when you do things

You might ask your friend:

Wann gehst du ins Café?
Und um wie viel Uhr gehst du schwimmen?
Wie spät ist es?
Wie viel Uhr ist es? ∫

The responses might be:

Um halb fünf.
Um Viertel nach drei.

Es ist Viertel vor zwei.

What specific information does each question ask for?

Mehr Grammatikübungen
S. 176–177, Ü. 1–3

Übungsheft, S. 62–64, Ü. 3–8

9 Wie viel Uhr ist es, bitte?

Sprechen Using the clocks in the **Wortschatz** box, take turns asking and telling your partner what time it is.

10 Was fehlt hier?

Sprechen Katja is trying to find Heiko. His mom explains where he will be this afternoon. Complete what she says by filling in the blanks according to the times given. Use the words and phrases in the box to the right.

fünf Uhr   nach vier   sechs
Viertel   zwanzig nach sieben   halb

Um ══ drei (2.30) geht er ins Einkaufszentrum. Dann hat er um Viertel ══ (4.15) Fußballtraining. Danach geht er mit Michael um ══ (5.00) ins Schwimmbad. Um ══ vor ══ (5.45) gehen die zwei Jungen ins Café Freizeit. Und dann kommt Heiko um ══ (7.20) nach Hause.

11 Wie spät ist es?

Sprechen You are making plans to meet friends. Ask your partner what time it is. Take turns.

1.

2.

3.

Grosse Hafenrundfahr
Erwachsene 7,00€
Kinder 3,50€
Gruppen - Sonderpreise
Nächste
Abfahrt

4.

5.

Nächster Zug
nach München
Gleis 5

6.

12 Wann macht Ulrike alles?

Sprechen/Schreiben Work with a partner to reorder these statements into a chronological description of how Ulrike spends a typical Monday.

1. Jeden Montag um acht Uhr gehe ich zur Schule.

Und am Abend schaue ich Fernsehen.

Dann um halb elf, direkt nach der Pause, habe ich Bio.

Um Viertel nach neun habe ich Mathe.

Um drei Uhr oder um halb vier esse ich Kuchen oder vielleicht etwas Obst.

Und jeden Montag um vier Uhr gehe ich schwimmen.

Danach mache ich so um fünf Hausaufgaben.

Nach der Schule gehe ich nach Hause.

13 Was machen sie zu dieser Zeit?

Zuhören Match what these students say with the illustrations below.

a. **b.** **c.**

d. **e.** **f.**

14 Wann? Wer? Was?

Schau die Zeichnungen an!

1. **Schreiben** Make a list of the times and corresponding activities shown in Activity 13.

2. **Schreiben** Choosing your own activities, write six sentences stating what you do at the times shown above.

15 Um wie viel Uhr …?

Sprechen Ask your partner at what time he or she does various activities or has certain classes.

Denn, mal, halt, and **doch** are words that you've seen a lot throughout this book. None of these words has a direct translation, but they are often used in everyday conversations to give emphasis to a question, command, or statement. For example, **Wie sieht er denn aus? Sag mal, wann gehst du? Das hat halt nicht jeder.** and **Wir gehen doch um vier.** Using these words in your conversations will help your German sound more natural.

Wortschatz

Wohin gehen?   Was machen?

Lies, was Katja und Julia planen! Julia sagt: „Katja und ich, wir wollen …"

in ein Café gehen,
ein Eis essen

ins Schwimmbad gehen,
baden gehen

ins Kino gehen,
einen Film sehen

in eine Disko gehen,
tanzen und Musik hören

in die Stadt gehen,
Klamotten kaufen

ins Rockkonzert gehen,
Musik hören

(Übungsheft, S. 65, Ü. 9–11)   (Grammatikheft, S.48, Ü. 6–8)

16 ### Wohin geht ihr?

Zuhören You will hear two students talk about their plans for the weekend. List all of the places they want to go in the order you hear them mentioned.

17 ### Was wollen wir machen?

Wir wollen …

ins Schwimmbad
ins Kino
in ein Café
in die Stadt
in eine Disko
ins Rockkonzert

gehen und …

tanzen
Klamotten kaufen
Musik hören
schwimmen
einen Film sehen
ein Eis essen

18 ### Für mein Notizbuch

Schreiben In your **Notizbuch** write some of the places you go and some of the things you do after school and on weekends. Look on page R9 for additional words you might want to use.

Making plans

You have been using the **möchte**-forms (*would like to*) to express your intentions:
Er möchte Musik hören. You can also use **wollen** (*to want to*).

Talking to someone:

Heiko, was willst du machen?

Talking about yourself:

Ich will in ein Café gehen.

Talking about someone:

Wohin will Birte gehen?

Sie will ins Schwimmbad gehen.

Grammatik

The verb **wollen**

Wollen means *to want* or *to want to do*. The forms of this verb — and of other modal
verbs — are different from those of regular verbs. Here are the forms:

ich	will	wir	wollen
du	willst	ihr	wollt
er, sie, es	will	sie (pl), Sie	wollen

What do you notice about the **ich** and **er/sie** forms?[1] Like the **möchte**-forms
you learned in **Kapitel 3**, **wollen** is also a modal auxiliary verb. It is often used
with another verb, although the second verb can be omitted if the meaning
is obvious:

Ich will ins Schwimmbad gehen.
Ich will ins Schwimmbad.

Note the position of the verb **wollen** and the second verb, the infinitive.

Mehr Grammatikübungen,
S. 177, Ü. 4–6

Übungsheft, S. 66, Ü. 12–14

Grammatikheft, S. 49, Ü. 9–10

19 Grammatik im Kontext

Lesen/Schreiben Julia and her friend Sonja are talking about
their plans for the day. Complete their conversation with the
correct forms of **wollen**.

JULIA   Was ___1___ du heute machen?

SONJA   Ich ___2___ nach Hamburg fahren.
Die Katja ___3___ mitkommen.

JULIA   Und Michael? ___4___ er auch mitkommen?

SONJA   Ich glaube, ja. Katja, Heiko und Michael
___5___ alle mitkommen.

JULIA   Um wie viel Uhr ___6___ ihr fahren?

SONJA   So um drei. Wir ___7___ um sieben
wieder zu Hause sein.

Fischmarkt in Hamburg

---

1. Though the pronouns are different, the verb forms are alike.
They have no endings.

20 Grammatik im Kontext

Schreiben/Sprechen Wie viele Sätze kannst du bauen?

BEISPIEL **Katja will um vier Uhr ins Kino gehen.** *oder*
Um vier Uhr will Katja ins Kino gehen.

ich Katja du wir ihr die Jungen	wollen willst will wollt	am Nachmittag nach der Schule um vier Uhr von 3 bis 5 Uhr am Abend	in ein Café gehen ins Kino gehen tanzen gehen in die Stadt gehen ins Konzert gehen Musik hören

26	Montag	Fußball 16³⁰ Schach mit Sven 19⁰⁰ Arbeitsgruppe Umwelt 20³⁰
27	Dienstag	Kino 14⁴⁵
28	Mittwoch	?
29	Donnerstag	schwimmen mit Michael 17⁴⁵
30	Freitag	16⁰⁰ – 18⁰⁰ zu Hause helfen
31	Samstag	13⁰⁰ Klavierstunde Disko 19³⁰
1	Sonntag	13³⁵ segeln

21 Heikos Pläne für nächste Woche

1. Sprechen Look at Heiko's plans for next week. Take turns saying what Heiko plans to do each day.

BEISPIEL **Am Dienstag will er ins Kino gehen.**

2. Sprechen Take turns asking each other when Heiko plans to do each of his activities.

22 Grammatik im Kontext

1. Schreiben Write your own plans for the coming week on a calendar page. For each day write what you want to do and at what time you plan to do it.

2. Sprechen Your partner will ask you about your plans. Tell him or her what you want to do and at what time. Then switch roles. Be prepared to share your partner's plans with the class.

3. Schreiben/Sprechen Restate each of the following sentences, beginning each one with a time expression.

  a. Ich habe am Samstag Klavierstunde.
  b. Ich gehe um 19 Uhr 30 in die Disko.
  c. Wir gehen am Montag ins Kino.
  d. Der Film beginnt um 14 Uhr 45.
  e. Wir gehen am Sonntag ins Konzert.
  f. Es beginnt um 8 Uhr 30.
  g. Julia will um 3 Uhr ins Café gehen.
  h. Sie will am Abend Hausaufgaben machen.

Ein wenig Grammatik

Schon bekannt
Monika could say of Katja:

Katja will am Freitag in die Stadt gehen.
or
Am Freitag will Katja in die Stadt gehen.

You saw this type of word order before in **Kapitel 2**, when you learned about German word order:

Wir spielen um 2 Uhr Fußball.
Um 2 Uhr spielen wir Fußball.

What is the position of the conjugated verbs in the above sentences[1]?

Mehr Grammatikübungen, S. 178, Ü. 7

Übungsheft, S. 67, Ü. 15–16   Grammatikheft, S. 50, Ü. 11–12

---

1. The conjugated verb is in second position.

23 Monikas Pläne fürs Wochenende

Lesen/Sprechen Read the letter that Monika has written to Katja, then answer the questions that follow.

Liebe Katja,

Es freut mich, dass du am Donnerstag kommst. Hier sind meine Pläne fürs Wochenende: Am Freitag will ich mit dir in die Stadt gehen — zuerst ein paar Klamotten kaufen (ich brauche Tennisschuhe!), dann etwas essen, danach ins Kino gehen.

Samstag ist immer mein Sporttag. Am Vormittag können wir Rad fahren, baden gehen (wir haben ein prima Schwimmbad!), und später am Abend will Vati für uns ein Grillfest machen. Neun Klassenkameraden kommen! Was willst du am Sonntag machen? Willst du wieder in die Stadt fahren? In ein Museum gehen? In ein Café gehen? Oder willst du faulenzen?

Mach's gut und bis bald.

Deine Monika

1. Why is Monika writing to Katja? How do you know?
2. When will Katja visit Monika?
3. How long will she stay? How do you know?

24 Monikas Pläne

Schreiben List Monika's plans for Friday and Saturday and her suggestions for Sunday. Include all the words that indicate the sequence of the plans.

Am Freitag: **in die Stadt gehen**
             Zuerst ...
             Dann ...

25 Ihr macht Pläne

Sprechen You and two of your friends are discussing your plans for the weekend. All of you are very busy, but you want to get together. Decide on several things you could do and places you could go together, then create a conversation discussing your plans.

LANDESKUNDE ◄ ► LANDESKUNDE

Was machst du in deiner Freizeit?

What do you think students in Germany like to do when they have time to spend with their friends? We have asked a number of students from different places this question, but before you read their responses, write down what you think they will say. Then read these interviews and compare your ideas with what they say.

CD-ROM DISC 2

VIDEO

Übungsheft, S. 72, Ü. 26

Sandra, Stuttgart

„Also, meine Freizeit verbringe ich am liebsten mit ein paar Freundinnen oder Freunden. Dann gehen wir abends in die Stadt Eis essen, oder wir gehen tanzen, oder wir setzen uns einfach in ein Café rein und reden. Aber am liebsten gehen wir halt tanzen."

Annika, Hamburg

„Ich bin bei den Pfadfindern; da fährt man halt am Wochenende auf Fahrt, und ja, mit denen mach ich auch hauptsächlich ziemlich viel, auch mal außerhalb, ins Kino gehen und so —und sonst spiel ich noch Klavier."

Marga, Bietigheim

„Ja, das ist sehr unterschiedlich. Wenn ich heimkomme, mach ich eigentlich erst einmal meine Hausaufgaben, dann gehe ich noch mit Freunden weg oder spiel Tennis und Gitarre, ja und ich mach auch Ballet und tänzerisch sehr viel. Ja, da ist meine Freizeit schon ausgebucht."

Karsten, Hamburg

„Also, ich mach als Erstes natürlich Hausaufgaben notgedrungen und dann irgendetwas mit Sport, oder ich geh in die Stadt einkaufen, oder meistens treff ich mich mit meiner Freundin."

A. 1. Working with a partner, write beside each student's name where he or she likes to go and what he or she likes to do.

   2. Compare the lists you have prepared for the four German students. Which activities do they have in common?

   3. Discuss with your classmates which activities you and your friends like to do that are similar to those done by the students in Germany. Which are different?

B. Look at the list you made before you read the interviews. Does what you wrote match what the students say? If it is different, how? Where do your ideas about German students come from? How do you think students in Germany might describe a "typical" American student? Where might they get their ideas? Write a brief essay discussing these questions.

26 Im Café Freizeit

Lesen/Schreiben Read the menu of **Café Freizeit**, then list what you would order for yourself. Add up the cost of your snack. With a partner, compare your order and the amount each of you would spend.

IMBISS-KARTE
Café Freizeit
Für den kleinen Hunger und Durst

KLEINE SPEISEN

NUDELSUPPE MIT BROT	€	2,25
KÄSEBROT		2,55
WURSTBROT		2,60
WIENER MIT SENF — 2 PAAR		2,90
PIZZA (15 CM)		
Nr. 1 mit Tomaten und Käse		3,00
Nr. 2 mit Wurst und Käse		3,25
Nr. 3 mit Wurst, Käse und Pilzen		4,25

EIS

FRUCHTEIS KUGEL	€	0,60
SAHNEEIS KUGEL		0,70
EISBECHER		3,40

GETRÄNKE

1 TASSE KAFFEE	€	2,15
1 KÄNNCHEN KAFFEE		3,80
1 TASSE CAPPUCCINO		2,60
1 GLAS TEE MIT ZITRONE		1,60

ALKOHOLFREIE GETRÄNKE

MINERALWASSER	0,5 l	€	1,75
LIMONADE, FANTA	0,5 l		1,80
APFELSAFT	0,2 l		1,25
COLA	0,2 l		1,50

KUCHEN

APFELKUCHEN	STÜCK	€	1,40
KÄSEKUCHEN	STÜCK		3,00

27 Was essen und trinken sie?

Zuhören You will hear four students saying what they want to eat and drink. Listen and decide what each one is ordering.

So sagt man das!

Ordering food and beverages

Here are some expressions you can use when you order something in a café or restaurant.

The waiter asks for your order:

> **Was bekommen Sie?**
> **Ja, bitte?**
> **Was essen Sie?**
> **Was möchten Sie?**
> **Was trinken Sie?**

You order:

> **Ich möchte ein Wurstbrot.**
> **Ich möchte ein Stück Kuchen, bitte.**
> **Einen Eisbecher, bitte!**
> **Ich trinke eine Limonade.**
> **Ich bekomme einen Kaffee.**

You might ask your friend:

> **Was nimmst du?**
> **Was isst du?**

Your friend might respond:

> **Ich nehme ein Käsebrot.**
> **Ich esse ein Eis.**

HEIKO: **Was nimmst du?**

MICHAEL: **Ich nehme …**

eine Nudelsuppe

ein Wurstbrot

ein Käsebrot

eine Pizza

ein Eis/einen Eisbecher

ein Stück Apfelkuchen

eine Tasse Kaffee

ein Glas Tee

Übungsheft,
S. 68, Ü. 17–19

Grammatikheft,
S. 51, Ü. 13–15

---

28 Du hast Hunger!

Sprechen Imagine that you are in **Café Freizeit**. You are very hungry and order a lot of food. Your partner plays the waiter, writing down everything you order, then tells the class what you have ordered. Switch roles.

BEISPIEL   **Was bekommen Sie?**

DU   **Ich esse … dann … und danach …**

Grammatik

Stem-changing verbs

Remember the verb **nehmen** that you used in **Kapitel 5**? **Nehmen** has a change in the stem vowel of the **du-** and **er/sie** forms: **du nimmst, er/sie nimmt.** Another verb in this group is **essen** (*to eat*). Here are the forms of **essen:**

ich	esse	wir	essen
du	**isst**	ihr	esst
er, sie, es	**isst**	sie, Sie	essen

Mehr Grammatikübungen,
S. 178–179, Ü. 8–10

Übungsheft, S. 69–70, Ü. 20–24

Grammatikheft, S. 53, Ü. 19

---

29 Grammatik im Kontext

a. **Sprechen** Du hast großen Hunger! Schau auf die Speisekarte von Café Freizeit auf Seite 170.

   1. Was isst du?
   2. Was isst dein Partner? Frag ihn!

b. **Schreiben** Schreib die Sätze ab und setz die richtige Form von **essen** ein.

   1. Was ===== du? – Ich ===== ein Wurstbrot.
   2. Was ===== denn die Julia? – Sie ===== nichts.
   3. Was ===== der Michael? – Er ===== Kuchen.
   4. Was ===== ihr? – Wir ===== Eis.

> **LERNTRICK**
>
> **Listening for gender cues.** It is important to listen not only for meaning, but also for other cues that may be helpful. If someone asks: **Nimmst du einen Apfelsaft?** the **einen** tells you that **Apfelsaft** is a masculine noun. You can have your response ready immediately: Ja, **einen Apfelsaft, bitte.** *or* Ja, bitte! Der Apfelsaft ist wirklich gut.

Talking about how something tastes

If you want to ask how something tastes, you ask:

Some possible responses are:

Wie schmeckt's?

> **Gut! Prima! Sagenhaft!**
> **Die Pizza schmeckt lecker!** (*tasty, delicious*)
> **Die Pizza schmeckt nicht.**

Schmeckt's?

> **Ja, gut!**
> **Nein, nicht so gut.**
> **Nicht besonders.** *Not especially.*

Mehr Grammatikübungen, S. 179, Ü. 11

Grammatikheft, S. 53, Ü. 20

30 Wie schmeckt's?

1. **Sprechen** Your partner was really hungry and ordered a lot to eat. Everything looks great! Ask him or her how the different dishes taste. (React to the foods ordered in Activity 29.)

2. **Sprechen** The food doesn't taste very good. Ask your partner about different dishes that she or he has ordered. Then switch roles.

Paying the check

Calling the waiter's attention	**Hallo!**
Asking for the check	**Hallo! Ich will/möchte zahlen.**
Totaling up the check	**Das macht (zusammen)…**
Telling the waiter to keep the change	**Stimmt schon!**

Grammatikheft, S. 54, Ü. 21–22

31 Zahlen, bitte!

Zuhören After Heiko and his friends eat, the waiter brings them the check. Listen as he adds up the bill, then write down each individual price you hear, the total, and what they round it off to as a tip.

32 Du willst zahlen

Sprechen You have finished your meal. Tell the waiter you want to pay. Before you pay the check, the waiter mentions every item you ordered and adds up the total. Role-play this situation with a partner, using the orders below and the menu on page 170. Be polite!

1. Nudelsuppe mit Brot, Mineralwasser
2. Tasse Cappuccino, Käsekuchen, Sahneeis
3. Wurstbrot, Cola, Tee mit Zitrone

Café Freizeit

geöffnet: Mo-Sa 10-10 Uhr
Sonntag: Ruhetag

2,25
2,90
2,60
1,40
———
9,15

33 Kommst du mit?

Sprechen Get together with two other classmates and role-play the following situations.

1. Your German pen pal is visiting you while you are in Wedel. Treat him or her to dinner at **Café Freizeit**. Talk about what both of you want to eat and drink. Order for the two of you. A waiter will take the order.

2. The waiter brings the order but can't remember who ordered what. Help him out.

3. While you are eating, you comment to each other about how the food tastes.

4. Your friend wants to order something else. Call the waiter over and tell him what else you want.

5. It is time to pay. Call the waiter and ask for the check. The waiter will name everything you ordered and add up the bill. You pay and leave a tip.

Ein wenig Landeskunde

The prices on German menus include the tip. However, most people will round the check up to the next euro or to the next round sum, depending on the total of the bill.

Stimmt schon!

34  Von der Schule zum Beruf

Schreiben You are the new owner of a small restaurant. Wanting to attract customers, you decide to design an unusual menu, listing items your chef can prepare. You also price the items. Give your restaurant a name, an address, a telephone number, and any other information that you consider appropriate.

AUSSPRACHE

Richtig aussprechen / Richtig lesen

A. To practice these sounds pronounce after your teacher or after the recording the words and sentences in bold.

1. The letter combination **ch**: The consonant combination **ch** can be pronounced two different ways. When preceded by the vowels **i** and **e**, it sounds similar to the *h* in the English word *huge*. When preceded by the vowels **a, o** or **u,** it is produced farther back in the throat.

   ich, Pech, dich / So ein Pech! Ich habe es nicht.
   ach, doch, Buch / Was macht Heiko am Wochenende? Spielt er Schach?

2. The letter **r**: The German **r** sound does not exist in English. To produce this sound, put the tip of your tongue behind your lower front teeth. Then tip your head back and pretend that you are gargling.

   rund, recht, Freizeit / Rolf, Rudi, und Rita gehen ins Café Freizeit.

3. The letter combination **er**: At the end of a word the letter combination **er** sounds almost like a vowel. It is similar to the *u* in the English word *but*.

   super, Lehrer, Bruder / Wo ist meine Schwester?

Richtig schreiben / Diktat

B. Write down the sentences that you hear.

Wohin in Hamburg?

People who live in Wedel often go into Hamburg for a day of entertainment.

1. What are the two main types of ads on these pages?

2. **a.** Use context clues to guess the meaning of these German words. Match each word with its English equivalent.

   1) **lädt**   a) enjoy
   2) **genießen**   b) meeting place
   3) **Treffpunkt** c) a dish of ice cream
   4) **Bratkartof-** d) invites
      felgerichte
   5) **Eisbecher**   e) fried potato dishes

   b. What kinds of foods are advertised here? Which restaurant ad interests you the most?

HAMBURG
Kulinarische Highlights

Jeden **Dienstag** lädt Don Diego Gonzales zur **Fiesta Mexicana**: Ein buntes Spezialitäten-Buffet und feurige Gitarrenklänge sorgen für einen stimmungsvollen mexikanischen Abend.

Donnerstags und **freitags** entführt Sie Neptun in sein Reich der sieben Meere: Genießen Sie sein lukullisches **Seafood-Buffet!**

LIBERTY IM MOTORAMA 21.00–3.00

Liberty
DISKOTHEK · CAFÉ

Oldie Disco
Hits der 60er u. 70er Jahre

NACHTEULE
DISCOTEK

FREITAG:
OLDIES bis 3 Uhr

Täglich ab 20 Uhr   Montag Ruhetag

Dienstag, 26. Januar
Martha Argerich, Klavier
Guy Tourvton, Trompete
Württembergisches Kammerorchester Heilbronn
Dirigent: **Jörg Faerber**
Haydn: Konzert für Klavier und Orchester D-Dur
Janácek: Suite für Streichorchester
Hindemith: Fünf Stücke für Streichorchester op. 44
Schostakowitsch: Konzert für Klavier, Trompete und Streichorchester op. 35

Dienstag, 25. Mai
Murray Perahia, Klavier
Mozart: Sonate F-Dur KV 332
Brahms: Rhapsodie h-Moll op. 79, Intermezzo es-Moll op. 118
Capriccio h-Moll op. 76, Rhapsodie Es-Dur op. 119
Beethoven: Sonate B-Dur op. 106 (Hammerklavier)

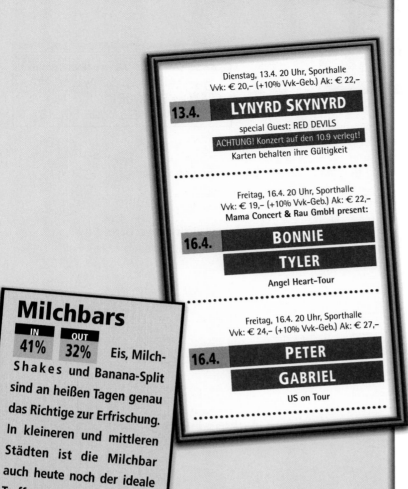

Dienstag, 13.4. 20 Uhr, Sporthalle
Vvk: € 20,– (+10% Vvk-Geb.) Ak: € 22,–

13.4. **LYNYRD SKYNYRD**

special Guest: RED DEVILS

ACHTUNG! Konzert auf den 10.9 verlegt!

Karten behalten ihre Gültigkeit

- -

Freitag, 16.4. 20 Uhr, Sporthalle
Vvk: € 19,– (+10% Vvk-Geb.) Ak: € 22,–
Mama Concert & Rau GmbH present:

16.4. **BONNIE**
TYLER

Angel Heart-Tour

- -

Freitag, 16.4. 20 Uhr, Sporthalle
Vvk: € 24,– (+10% Vvk-Geb.) Ak: € 27,–

16.4. **PETER**
GABRIEL

US on Tour

- -

Milchbars

IN	OUT
41%	32%

Eis, Milch-Shakes und Banana-Split sind an heißen Tagen genau das Richtige zur Erfrischung. In kleineren und mittleren Städten ist die Milchbar auch heute noch der ideale Treffpunkt für die jungen Leute.

c. Where can you eat Mexican food? On what day?

d. Where can you get "**tolle Eisbecher**"? Where is this place located?

3. a. Where can you hear music? What kinds of music can you hear?

 b. What are the names of the discos? How long is the **Liberty** open?

 c. When (day and time) can you see Bonnie Tyler? Peter Gabriel? Will Lynyrd Skynyrd fans get to hear them on 13.4.? If not, why not?

4. What is the social purpose of the **Milchbar**? What word supports your opinion?

5. Remembering the word you learned for "juice," find the word that means "juicy."

6. Assume you and your family are in Wedel. You want to go to Hamburg for two or three days.

 a. To which places would you more likely go with your parents?

 b. To which places would you more likely go with your friends?

 c. Write a postcard to a friend telling of your plans for your weekend in Hamburg. Be sure to use sequencing words appropriately.

Tag u. Nacht

deftige Bratkartoffelgerichte

Tag und Nacht warme Küche,
Frühstück zu jeder Zeit,
saftige Steaks,
das ganze Jahr Eisbergsalat,
tolle Eisbecher

gestern & heute treff
Kaiser-Wilhelm-Straße 55

Bahrenfelder Forsthaus

Hamburger Küche und feine Spezialitäten
Besondere Sonntagsmenüs

Restaurant, Romantischer Wintergarten, Café und Café-Terrasse
Von-Hutten-Str. 45 · Hamburg 22761 · Telefon (0 40) 89 40 21

Übungsheft, S. 71, Ü. 25

Mehr Grammatikübungen

Erste Stufe   **Objective** Telling time and talking about when you do things

1   You and your friends are at the mall. You seem to be the only person with a watch, and a lot of people ask you what time it is. Rewrite the time statements by filling in each blank with the time given in parentheses. **(S. 162)**

1. Wie spät ist es, bitte?   Es ist (3:15) _____ .
2. Wie viel Uhr ist es?   Es ist (3:30) _____ .
3. Wie spät ist es jetzt?   Es ist (3:45) _____ .
4. Wie viel Uhr ist es?   Es ist (4:55) _____ .
5. Wie spät ist es, bitte?   Es ist (7:10) _____ .
6. Wie viel Uhr ist es?   Es ist (8:20) _____ .

2   You are in Munich, Stuttgart, and Besigheim. Look at these clocks and write out what time it is. **(S. 162)**

Auf dieser Bahnhofsuhr ist es _____ .

Die Uhr an einer Münchner Apotheke zeigt _____ .

Diese schöne Uhr am Turm des Stuttgarter Rathauses zeigt _____ .

Auf dieser Rathausuhr in Besigheim ist es _____ .

3 You are telling your parents when you and your friends are going to do various activities. Complete the following statements by filling in the blanks with the time given in parentheses. (S. 162)

1. (9:45) Um _____ spielen wir Fußball.
2. (12:10) Um _____ wollen wir mit dem Bus in die Stadt fahren.
3. (4:15) Wir kommen um _____ nach Hause.
4. (4:30) Heute um _____ möchten wir Volleyball spielen.
5. (5:50) Um _____ möchten wir Fernsehen schauen.
6. (6:00) Und um _____ kommt ein Fußballspiel!

Zweite Stufe   Objective Making plans

4 During recess, you and your friends are planning activities for the afternoon. Complete each question or statement by filling in each blank with the correct form of the verb **wollen**. (S. 166)

1. Wer _____ heute Tennis spielen?
2. Heiko und Julia _____ ins Café Freizeit gehen.
3. Wohin _____ du gehen, Katja? _____ du ins Café gehen?
4. Ich _____ Musik hören. Und du, was _____ du machen?
5. _____ ihr ein Eis essen, Heiko und Julia?
6. Julia _____ ins Kino gehen, und Katja _____ ins Konzert.
7. Und was _____ wir jetzt machen? Was meinst du?

5 You are trying to find out from your friends when they want to do certain activities. Complete the following questions by filling in the first blank with the correct form of the verb **wollen** and the second one with an appropriate infinitive. (S. 166)

1. Um wie viel Uhr _____ ihr ins Kino _____?
2. Warum _____ du heute nicht Musik _____?
3. Wer _____ jetzt ein Eis _____?
4. Warum _____ du nicht mit Michael baden _____?
5. Wir _____ heute mal einen Film _____.
6. Warum _____ ihr nicht die Klamotten _____?
7. Katja und Sonja _____ jetzt Tennis _____.

6 Rephrase these sentences using a form of **wollen**. (S. 166)

1. Ich gehe heute ins Kino.
2. Wer spielt heute Tennis?
3. Warum hörst du nicht Musik?
4. Michael zieht den Pulli nicht an.
5. Probierst du die Jacke an?
6. Wir fahren heute in die Stadt.

7 Begin each sentence with the underlined part. **(S. 167)**

1. Wir gehen <u>um drei Uhr</u> ins Café.
2. Ich höre <u>jetzt</u> Musik aus Deutschland.
3. Sonja spielt <u>nach der Schule</u> Tennis.
4. Ich will <u>am Abend</u> ins Kino gehen.
5. Julia will <u>am Freitag</u> in die Stadt fahren.
6. Der Michael will <u>im Moment</u> gar nichts.
7. Tom und Julia möchten <u>heute</u> ein Eis essen.
8. Wir möchten <u>am Nachmittag</u> ins Café gehen.
9. Ich möchte <u>danach</u> in die Disko gehen.

Dritte Stufe

Objectives Ordering food and beverages; talking about how something tastes; paying the check

8 You and your friends are in a snack bar ordering food and beverages. What does everyone want? Complete the sentences and questions by supplying the correct indefinite articles. **(S. 171)**

1. Ich bekomme _____ Eisbecher. Und du? Nimmst du _____ Käsebrot?
2. Wir möchten _____ Pizza, _____ Apfelsaft und _____ Glas Tee.
3. Michael nimmt _____ Käsebrot, und er trinkt _____ Cola.
4. Ich esse _____ Stück Kuchen und trinke _____ Tasse Kaffee.
5. Michael isst _____ Nudelsuppe und trinkt _____ Limo.
6. Sonja nimmt _____ Wurstbrot und _____ Mineralwasser.

9 You are in a restaurant, talking about food and what you want to order. Complete each of the following questions and statements with the correct form of the verb **essen**. **(S. 171)**

1. Ja, was _____ du denn? Du _____ ein Käsebrot?
2. Ich _____ ein Eis, und die Julia _____ einen Eisbecher.
3. Und was _____ ihr? Auch was wir _____, Pizza?
4. Heiko und Michael _____ Nudelsuppe.
5. Wer _____ ein Stück Apfelkuchen?
6. Heiko, du _____ doch gern Apfelkuchen, nicht?

10 You are offering your friend different items of food and telling how good everything tastes. Complete each of the following questions and statements by filling in the first blank with the correct form of the indefinite article, and the second blank with the correct form of the pronoun. Note: If no indefinite article is required, write 0 in the space provided. **(S. 171)**

1. Möchtest du _____ Eis? _____ schmeckt prima!
2. Willst du _____ Pizza? _____ schmeckt prima!
3. Möchtest du _____ Eisbecher? _____ schmeckt gut!
4. Isst du _____ Nudelsuppe? _____ schmeckt sehr gut!
5. Nimmst du _____ Käsebrot? _____ schmeckt bestimmt gut!
6. Trinkst du _____ Limo? _____ schmeckt prima!
7. Oder trinkst du _____ Apfelsaft? _____ schmeckt auch gut!
8. Isst du _____ Obst? _____ ist so gut!

11 You and your friend are ordering a meal in a restaurant. Complete the following dialogue by filling in each blank with the correct verb form. The verb to be used is indicated in parentheses. **(S. 172)**

Kellner	(to get)	Was _____ Sie, bitte?
Michael	(to take)	Ich _____ eine Suppe, die Nudelsuppe.
Julia	(to eat)	Und ich _____ eine Pizza, die Nummer 2.
Kellner	(to drink)	Was _____ Sie?
Julia	(to drink)	Ich _____ eine Limo.
Michael	(would like)	Und ich _____ ein Glas Mineralwasser.
(später)		
Kellner	(to taste)	Wie _____ die Suppe?
Michael	(to be)	Sie _____ wirklich gut.
Julia	(to taste)	Meine Pizza _____ phantastisch!
(später)		
Michael	(to pay)	Wir möchten _____ , bitte. Zusammen!
Kellner	(to make)	Das _____ zusammen 6 Euro 40.

internet

ADRESSE: go.hrw.com
KENNWORT:
WK3 SCHLESWIG-HOLSTEIN-6

1 Express the times shown in as many different ways as you can.

2 In each of the following reports, an activity is mentioned. If the activity mentioned is shown in the photos below, match the activity with the appropriate photo.

a.

b.

c.

d.

e.

f.

g.

h.

3 Look at the photos. Your partner will ask you what you want to do. Choose three activities from above and tell your partner which ones you want to do and at what time you want to do them. Then switch roles.

4 Write in German a conversation you might have had when you last ate a meal or a snack in a restaurant. Include ordering your food, some comments on how it tasted, and paying for it.

5 # Zum Schreiben

Write a letter to a friend describing your plans for the week. This letter should be so intriguing that it will convince your friend to come for a visit during spring break.

> **Schreibtipp Arranging your ideas chronologically** is helpful when planning activities for a week.

Prewriting

To arrange items chronologically, take a sheet of paper, turn it sideways, and divide it into seven columns. Write one day of the week at the top of each column, and *morning, afternoon,* and *evening* down the left side. Next, decide on activities you would like to do and at which times. Place this information in the appropriate column. (One of your activities might be to go to an **Imbissstand** where they have the best **Wurst** in town!)

Writing

Now, using the information you have organized on your chart, write a letter convincing your friend that the activities you have planned are so great that he or she absolutely has to come for a visit during spring break.

6 # Rollenspiel

Du bist mit einem Freund in Hamburg. Ihr habt Hunger und möchtet etwas essen.

Verkauf am Fenster

Sensationell

1/2 Hähnchen	2,20
Käsebrot	1,50
Wurstbrot	1,45
La Flute m. Schinken & Ananas	3,30
Gr. Fladenbrot (Giros/Kochschinken/ Schinken/Spießbraten)	4,20
	4,75
Giros mit Krautsalat	gr. 2,00
Currywurst, kl. 1,85	0,95
Rostbratwurst	0,95
Bockwurst	1,35
Schokoladeneis	1,35
Vanilleeis	1,40
Fruchteis	

Cola	Becher 0,3	0,75	0,4	0,85
Milchshake	0,3	0,90	0,4	1,10
Apfelsaft	0,3	0,90	0,4	1,20
Orangensaft	0,3	0,90	0,4	1,20
Mineralwasser				1,00
Fanta	0,3	0,65	0,4	0,90

You are in a hurry for the Peter Gabriel concert, so you decide to put dinner off until later and just grab a snack at an **Imbissstand.** You also don't want to spend very much money—each of you is limited to six euros.

a. Create a conversation in which you discuss the possibilities that are available, decide what each of you wants, and figure out how much it will cost.

b. One partner can then play the role of vendor, and you can order the food and drink that each of you decided upon. After you receive your food, pay for it.

Kann ich's wirklich?

Can you start a conversation? (p. 161)

1 How would you greet a friend and ask how he or she is doing? If someone asks how you are doing, what could you say?

Can you tell time? (p. 162)

2 How would you ask what time it is? Say the times shown below, using expressions you learned in this chapter.

1. 1.00 2. 11.30 3. 9.50 4. 2.15 5. 7.55

Can you talk about when you do things? (p. 162)

3 Using the time expressions above, say when you and your friends intend to

a. go to the movies

c. go to the swimming pool

b. go to a café

4 How would you ask a friend when he intends to do the activities in Activity 3?

Can you make plans using wollen? (p. 166)

5 Say you intend to go to the following places and tell what you plan to do there. Establish a sequence: *first …, then …*

a. café

d. department store

b. swimming pool

e. disco

c. movies

6 How would you say that the following people want to go to a concert?

1. Michael 3. ihr 5. Peter und Monika

2. Silke 4. wir

Can you order food and beverages? (p. 170)

7 You are with some friends in a café. Order the following things for yourself.

a. (noodle) soup

c. a cheese sandwich

b. a glass of tea with lemon

8 Say that these people are going to eat the foods listed. Then say what you are going to eat (using **ich**). How would you ask your best friend what he or she is going to eat (using **du**)?

a. Michael - Käsekuchen

d. Ahmet und ich - Wiener mit Senf

b. Holger und Julia - Apfelkuchen

e. Ich …

c. Monika - Käsebrot

f. Und du? Was …?

Can you talk about how something tastes? (p. 172)

9 How would you ask a friend if his or her food tastes good? How might he or she respond?

Can you pay the check? (p. 172)

10 Ask the waiter for the check, then tell him to keep the change.

Erste Stufe

Starting a conversation

Wie geht's (denn)?	*How are you?*
Sehr gut!	*Very well!*
Prima!	*Great!*
Gut!	*Good/Well!*
Es geht.	*Okay.*
So lala.	*So-so.*
Schlecht.	*Bad(ly).*
Miserabel.	*Miserable.*

Telling time

Wie spät ist es?	*What time is it?*
Wie viel Uhr ist es?	*What time is it?*
Um wie viel Uhr ...?	*At what time ...?*
Viertel nach	*a quarter after*
halb (eins, zwei, usw.)	*half past (one, two, etc.)*
Viertel vor ...	*a quarter to ...*
(zehn) vor ...	*(ten) till ...*
um (ein) Uhr ...	*at (one) o'clock*
um Viertel nach ...	*at a quarter past ...*

Zweite Stufe

Making plans

Wohin?	*Where (to)?*
in ein Café/ins Café	*to a café*
ein Eis essen	*to eat ice cream*
in die Stadt gehen	*to go downtown*
ins Schwimmbad gehen	*to go to the (swimming) pool*
baden gehen	*to go swimming*
ins Kino gehen	*to go to the movies*
einen Film sehen	*to see a movie*
in eine Disko gehen	*to go to a disco*
tanzen gehen	*to go dancing*
ins Konzert gehen	*to go to the concert*
in ein Konzert gehen	*to go to a concert*
wollen	*to want (to)*
er/sie will	*he/she wants (to)*

Dritte Stufe

Ordering food and beverages

Was bekommen Sie?	*What will you have?*
Ich bekomme ...	*I'll have ...*
eine Tasse Kaffee	*a cup of coffee*
ein Glas Tee mit Zitrone	*a (glass) cup of tea with lemon*
eine Limonade	*a lemon-flavored soda*
eine Limo	*short for* **Limonade**
eine Nudelsuppe mit Brot	*noodle soup with bread*
ein Käsebrot	*cheese sandwich*
einen Eisbecher	*a dish of ice cream*
ein Wurstbrot	*sandwich with cold cuts*
eine Pizza	*pizza*
Apfelkuchen	*apple cake*
ein Eis	*ice cream*
essen	*to eat*
er/sie isst	*he/she eats*

Talking about how food tastes

Wie schmeckt's	*How does it taste?*
Schmeckt's?	*Does it taste good?*
Sagenhaft!	*Great!*
Lecker!	*Tasty! Delicious!*
Nicht besonders.	*Not really.*

Paying the check

Hallo! Ich möchte/ will zahlen!	*The check please!*
Das macht (zusammen) ...	*That comes to ...*
Stimmt (schon)!	*Keep the change.*

Other words and phrases

Pass auf!	*Watch out!*
nun	*now*

Note: Both **jetzt** and **nun** mean *now*. While **jetzt** can be used in all situations indicating a point in time, **nun** is used more to indicate a point in sequence. On p. 159, Michael says: **Und nun trinke ich meine Cola aus und gehe**, indicating that he has been doing other things before, such as ordering various dishes, and now he's ready to leave.

Komm mit nach München

Landeshauptstadt von Bayern

Einwohner: 1,3 Millionen

Fluss: München liegt an der Isar

Berühmte Gebäude: Frauenkirche, Rathaus, Maximilianeum, Theatinerkirche

Museen: Alte und Neue Pinakothek, Deutsches Museum, Glyptothek

Industrien: Elektrotechnik und Elektronik, Automobilindustrie, Brauereien, Verlage, Filmindustrie

Bedeutende Münchner: Josef von Fraunhofer (1787-1826, Physiker); Moritz von Schwind (1804-1871, Maler); Karl Valentin (1882-1948, Komiker); Annette Kolb (1870-1967, Schriftstellerin)

Typische Gerichte: Schweinshaxe, Leberkäs, Weißwürste

go.hrw.com

WK3 MUENCHEN

 VIDEO

 CD-ROM DISC 2

Ein Blick über die Dächer von München ▶

München

München ist die Hauptstadt Bayerns. Die Stadt ist bekannt für ihre vielen Museen, Theater, Musikstätten und Sportanlagen. Hier haben 1972 die Olympischen Spiele stattgefunden. München ist auch ein Zentrum der Autoindustrie (BMW, MAN), Computer-Industrie (Siemens), High-Tech-Industrie, Raumfahrtindustrie, Medienindustrie und auch der Sitz von vielen anderen, sogenannten „sauberen" Firmen.

 internet

ADRESSE: go.hrw.com
KENNWORT:
WK3 MUENCHEN

1 Bayrische Tracht
Die Lederhose und der Gamsbart auf dem Hut gehören zur bayrischen Männertracht. Auch heute sieht man noch Tracht in Dörfern und Städten und besonders zu festlichen Anlässen.

2 In der Neuhauserstraße
Die Neuhauserstraße ist eine Fußgängerzone mit vielen Geschäften und Straßenlokalen, wo sich die Einkäufer und Touristen vom Einkaufen und Bummeln ausruhen können.

3 Ein Maibaum
Maibäume sieht man überall in Bayern. Dieser Maibaum auf dem Viktualienmarkt zeigt das bayrische Wappen, das weiß-blaue Rautenmuster, sowie Münchens Wahrzeichen, das Münchner Kindl, und zwei schwarz-gelbe Stadtfahnen.

4 Auf dem Marienplatz
Der Marienplatz im Herzen Münchens ist ein Treffpunkt für Jung und Alt. Links ist die Mariensäule, im Hintergrund das Alte Rathaus mit dem Rathausturm.

5 Auf dem Viktualienmarkt
Drei Minuten vom Marienplatz entfernt ist der Viktualienmarkt, wo viele Münchner täglich ihre Lebensmittel und Obst und Gemüse einkaufen.

Kapitel 7, 8, 9

Kapitel 7, 8 und 9 finden in München statt. Die Schüler in diesen Kapiteln gehen auf verschiedene Schulen. Flori besucht das Einstein-Gymnasium, Markus und Claudia gehen aufs Theodolinden-Gymnasium und Mara besucht die Rudolf-Diesel Realschule.

6 Mara, Flori, Markus und Claudia heißen euch in München willkommen.

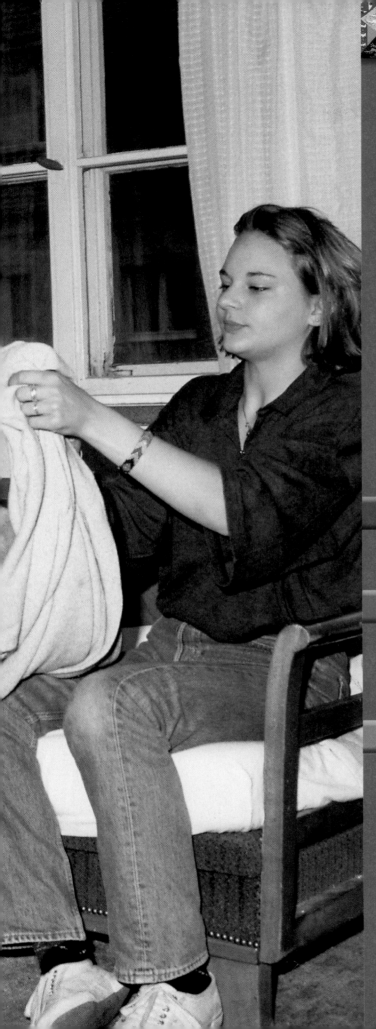

7
Zu Hause helfen

Objectives

In this chapter you will learn to

Erste Stufe

- extend and respond to an invitation
- express obligations

Zweite Stufe

- talk about how often you have to do things
- ask for and offer help and tell someone what to do

Dritte Stufe

- talk about the weather

internet

ADRESSE: go.hrw.com
KENNWORT:
   WK3 MUENCHEN-7

◀ **Mara hilft beim Aufräumen.**

Los geht's! • *Was musst du machen?*

Strategie Verstehen

Look at the images for this story. Who are these students? What are they doing? Where and when do you think these scenes are taking place? What clues tell you this?

 Claudia   Flori   Markus   Mara

1

Mara:	Claudia, hallo!
Claudia:	Wohin geht's?
Mara:	In den Englischen Garten. Komm doch mit!
Claudia:	Das geht heute nicht. Ich muss zu Hause helfen.
Flori:	Schade, dass du nicht mitkommen kannst! Es ist heute so schönes Wetter zum Radeln.
Markus:	Was musst du denn tun, Claudia?

Claudia: Ich muss mein Zimmer aufräumen, Müll sortieren, das …

Flori: Einen Moment! Ich hab eine Idee. Fahren wir alle zur Claudia und helfen ihr.

Mara: Prima Idee! — Ja, dann ist sie schnell fertig und kann mitkommen.

Claudia: Das ist lieb von euch.

Bei Claudia

2

Claudia: Markus, du und der Flori, ihr könnt den Müll sortieren. Die Flaschen kommen hier rein, die Dosen kommen da rein.

Markus: Und die Zeitungen?

Claudia: Die Zeitungen kommen in den Korb da.

Miau!

Mara: Deine Klamotten musst du selber aufräumen.

Claudia: Mach ich schon! — Willst du für mich Staub saugen?

Mara: Das muss ich auch immer zu Hause machen.

Flori: So, wir sind fertig!

Mara: Wir auch.

Markus: Also, gehen wir! Die Sonne scheint noch immer.

Claudia: Ich muss nur noch die Katze füttern.

Flori: Wer weiß denn, wie morgen das Wetter wird?

Mara: Morgen regnet es.

Flori: Ach, Quatsch! Es bleibt schön.

Mara: Was sagt denn der Wetterbericht?

Markus: Ich weiß nicht. Der stimmt aber sowieso nie!

Claudia: Micki! Micki! Wo bist du?

Flori: Ist die Katze schon wieder weg?

Claudia: Ja. Und sie muss ins Haus!

Markus: Also los, Kinder! Wir müssen die Katze suchen.

Übungsheft, S. 73

1 Was passiert hier?

Do you understand what is happening in **Los geht's!**? Check your comprehension by answering these questions. Don't be afraid to guess.

1. Where do Claudia's three friends (Mara, Markus, and Flori) invite Claudia to go?
2. Does Claudia go along? Why or why not?
3. What does Flori suggest?
4. What are some things the friends do at Claudia's house?
5. Is the weather good enough for an outing in the park? What about tomorrow's weather?
6. At the end of the story, there is still a problem. What is it?

2 Genauer lesen

Reread the conversations. Which words or phrases do the characters use to

1. invite someone   2. express obligation   3. name chores   4. describe the weather

3 Was ist richtig?

Was ist die beste Antwort, a., b. oder c.?

1. Claudia muss ══.
   a. in den Englischen Garten gehen   **b.** zu Hause helfen   **c.** radeln
2. Claudias Freunde wollen helfen. Das findet Claudia ══.
   a. furchtbar   **b.** nicht schlecht   **c.** lieb
3. Mara will ══.
   a. die Katze füttern   **b.** den Müll sortieren   **c.** Claudias Klamotten nicht aufräumen
4. Die Katze ist ══.
   a. schon im Haus   **b.** nicht zu Hause   **c.** im Englischen Garten

4 Was passt zusammen?

Match each statement or question on the left with an appropriate response on the right.

1. Wohin geht's?   a. Das geht nicht.
2. Komm doch mit!   b. Gut! Mach ich!
3. Was musst du tun?   c. In den Englischen Garten.
4. Du kannst den Müll sortieren.   d. Ich muss zu Hause helfen.
5. Was sagt der Wetterbericht?   e. Ja. Wir müssen sie suchen.
6. Ist die Katze wieder weg?   f. Morgen regnet es.

5 Nacherzählen

Put the sentences in a logical order to make a brief summary of **Los geht's!**.

1. Mara, Markus und Flori wollen in den Englischen Garten gehen.

Dann wollen sie gehen, aber Micki ist weg.

Sie müssen zuerst die Katze suchen.

Sie müssen den Müll sortieren, das Zimmer aufräumen, Staub saugen und die Katze füttern.

Aber Claudia kommt nicht mit, denn sie muss zu Hause helfen.

Claudias Freunde wollen helfen.

Wortschatz

Was musst du zu Hause tun? — Ich muss ...

mein Zimmer aufräumen

das Bett machen

meine Klamotten aufräumen

die Katze füttern

den Tisch decken

den Tisch abräumen

das Geschirr spülen

die Blumen gießen

den Müll sortieren

den Rasen mähen

Staub saugen

die Fenster putzen

Übungsheft, S. 74, Ü. 2–3   Grammatikheft, S. 55, Ü. 1–2

6 ### Was muss Claudia tun?

Schreiben Claudia muss eine Liste machen und alles aufschreiben, was sie zu Hause tun muss. Du kannst ihr dabei helfen: Schreib das passende Verb hinter jeden nummerierten Ausdruck.

1. das Zimmer
2. das Bett
3. den Rasen
4. die Katze
5. den Tisch
6. das Geschirr
7. den Müll
8. die Blumen

spülen	füttern	aufräumen
machen		mähen
decken	gießen	sortieren

7 **Was kommt zuerst?**

Zuhören Jürgen has a few chores to do before he and Peter can go to the movies. Listen to their conversation and put the illustrations below in the correct order.

a.   b.   c.   d.   e.

So sagt man das!

Extending and responding to an invitation

In **Kapitel 6** you learned to make plans. How would you invite someone to come along with you?

You might ask:

> **Willst du in den Englischen Garten?** *or*
> **Wir wollen in den Englischen Garten. Komm doch mit!** *or* **Möchtest du mitkommen?**

Your friend might accept: Or decline:

> **Ja, gern!** *or*
> **Toll! Ich komme gern mit.**

> **Das geht nicht.** *or*
> **Ich kann leider nicht.**

8 **Kommst du oder kommst du nicht?**

 Zuhören Listen to the following conversations and decide if the person being invited is accepting or declining the invitation. What is each person being invited to do?

So sagt man das!

Expressing obligations

If you decline an invitation, you might want to explain your prior obligations.

You might say:

> **Ich habe keine Zeit. Ich muss zu Hause helfen.**

Your friend might ask: You might respond:

> **Was musst du denn tun?**   **Ich muss den Rasen mähen.**

What do you think the phrase **keine Zeit** means?[1]

---

1. *no time*

9 Kommst du mit?

Sprechen Du lädst deine Freunde zu verschiedenen Aktivitäten ein. Was sagen die Freunde, die mitgehen, und was sagen die Freunde, die nicht mitgehen können?

ins Kino gehen   in ein Konzert gehen

Tennis spielen   ein Eis essen

in die Disko gehen   schwimmen gehen

10 Was ist los?

Sprechen Der kleine Junge tut etwas, was er nicht tun soll! Was sagst du zu ihm? (**Du musst …**)

a.   b.   c.   d.   e.

11 Ich muss zu Hause …

Schreiben/Sprechen Mach eine Liste und schreib darauf alles, was du zu Hause machen musst. Frag danach deine Klassenkameraden, was sie zu Hause tun müssen, und berichte, was du tun musst.

Grammatik

The verb müssen

The verb **müssen** expresses obligation and means that you *have to* or *must* do something. Here are the forms of **müssen**:

ich	muss	wir	müssen
du	musst	ihr	müsst
er, sie, es	muss	sie, Sie	müssen

Müssen is usually used with a second verb (an infinitive), although the second verb can be omitted if the meaning is obvious. Ich **muss** nicht (**helfen**).

Mehr Grammatikübungen, S. 208, Ü. 1–2

Übungsheft, S. 75–76, Ü. 4–8

Grammatikheft, S. 56, Ü. 3–4

12 Grammatik im Kontext

Sprechen/Schreiben Einige Klassenkameraden sind zu Thomas gekommen, um ihm zu helfen. Was muss jeder tun? Was sagt Thomas? Schreibe die Sätze zu Ende.

  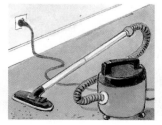 

1. Zuerst muss ich …   **2. Mara und ich, wir …**   **3. Du …**   **4. Und die Nikki …**

13 Grammatik im Kontext

Sprechen/Schreiben Nimm die Liste von Übung 11 zur Hand und such dir einen Partner. Frag ihn, was er zu Hause tun muss und schreib es auf. Danach fragt dein Partner dich und schreibt auf, was du tun musst. Tauscht (exchange) dann eure Listen. Stimmt alles?

Ein wenig Grammatik

Schon bekannt

In **Kapitel 5** you learned the separable prefix verbs **anziehen**, **anprobieren**, and **aussehen**. Note that **aufräumen**, **abräumen**, and **mitkommen** are also verbs with separable prefixes. Compare the sentences below:

Ich räume den Tisch ab.
Ich muss den Tisch abräumen.

In the first sentence, the prefix **ab** is in last position. Now look at the second sentence. As with other verbs, when a separable prefix is used with a modal, like **müssen**, the conjugated form is in second position, and the second verb is in infinitive form in final position.

Grammatikheft, S. 57, Ü. 5–6

Mehr Grammatikübungen, S. 208–209, Ü. 3–4

14 Und meine Familie ...

Sprechen Wer muss in deiner Familie zu Hause helfen? Wer muss was tun? Sag das deinen Klassenkameraden.

15 Grammatik im Kontext

a. **Schreiben** Was möchtest du heute Nachmittag tun und wann? Mach eine Liste.

b. **Sprechen** Frag dann deine Partnerin, ob sie mitkommen möchte. Sie akzeptiert oder sagt dir, warum sie nicht mitgehen kann. Tauscht dann die Rollen. Schreibt danach auf eine Liste, was ihr zusammen tun möchtet und teilt das euren Klassenkameraden mit.

16 Ein Brief

a. **Lesen/Sprechen** Lies Markus' Brief an Roland. Beantworte dann die Fragen.

1. Wer kommt am Wochenende nach München?

2. Was wollen Markus und Flori am Freitag machen?

3. Was muss Markus am Samstag machen?

4. Gefällt es Markus, dass er zu Hause helfen muss? Woher weißt du das?

b. **Schreiben** Schreib Markus einen Brief und lade ihn für das Wochenende ein. Schreib ihm, was du für ihn planst. Schreib ihm auch, dass du dieses Wochenende zu Hause helfen musst. Du hoffst, dass ihr trotzdem viel Zeit für eure Pläne habt.

---

4. März 2001

Lieber Roland!

Mensch, das freut mich, dass du am Wochenende hier in München bist!

Flori und ich wollen am Freitag ins Konzert. Die „Jungen Katzen" spielen! Toll, nicht! Willst du auch mitkommen?

Am Samstag muss ich wie immer zu Hause helfen. Wie blöd! Ich muss den Rasen mähen, mein Zimmer aufräumen, die Blumen gießen und auch Staub saugen. Ach, das ist zu viel, nicht? Musst du auch zu Hause so viel tun?

Na ja, macht nichts. Am Sonntag hab ich frei. Du, Flori und ich machen alles, was wir wollen.

Bis dann!
Dein Markus

LANDESKUNDE LANDESKUNDE

Was tust du für die Umwelt?

In both the old and new states, Germans today are very aware of the need to protect the environment. Young people all over Germany are involved in projects that range from recycling to cleaning up rivers and forests. We asked several students what they do for the environment, and here is what they told us.

Marga, Bietigheim

„Also bei uns zu Hause wird jeder Müll sortiert, eben in Plastik, Aluminium, Papier und so weiter. Das halten wir also ziemlich streng ein. Ja, und wenn schönes Wetter ist und es sich vermeiden lässt, mit dem Auto zu fahren, nehme ich lieber das Fahrrad."

Fabian, Hamburg

„Wir tun für die Umwelt, dass wir einmal Müll vermeiden, dass wir unser Altpapier wegbringen, Glas sammeln und möglichst auch Glas, was wiederverwertet werden kann, kaufen, also sprich Mehrwegflaschen, und dass wir halt möglichst wenig Putzmittel oder so sparsam brauchen."

Elke, Berlin

„Ich habe mit meinen Eltern angefangen, Flaschen zu sortieren und regelmäßig zum Container zu bringen. Der Müll wird meistens auch separat sortiert und dann, ja, einzeln weggebracht. Jetzt zähl ich dazu, dass man mit dem Bus zur Schule fährt und nicht mit dem Auto.

A. 1. Write the names of the students interviewed, and beside each name, write what that student does for the environment. What things do they have in common?

2. Think about what you have learned about Germany. Do you think the environmental concerns of the Germans are the same as those of Americans? Why or why not?

3. Compare what you and your friends do for the environment with what these German students do. Is there anything you do that was not mentioned in these interviews?

B. a. Discuss with your classmates what you think the biggest environmental concerns in Germany and in the United States are.

b. Write in German your answer to the question **Was tust du für die Umwelt?**

Zweite Stufe

Objectives Talking about how often you have to do things; asking for and offering help and telling someone what to do

WK3 MUENCHEN-7

So sagt man das!

Talking about how often you have to do things

You might want to ask a friend how often he or she has to do certain things, such as chores.

You might ask:

> **Wie oft musst du Staub saugen?**
> **Und wie oft musst du den Tisch decken?**
> **Und wie oft musst du den Rasen mähen?**

Your friend might respond:

> **Einmal in der Woche.**
> **Jeden Tag.**
> **Ungefähr zweimal im Monat.**

Look at the words **einmal** and **zweimal**. What words do you recognize within each of these words?[1] What do you think the phrases **einmal in der Woche** and **zweimal im Monat** mean?[2] How would you say "three times a week"?[3] "Four times a month"?[4] What does the expression **jeden Tag** mean?[5] (*Hint: Look at the chore the speaker above does **jeden Tag**. How often would you do that task?*)

> Übungsheft, S. 77, Ü. 9–10

Wortschatz

Wie oft ... ?

einmal, zweimal, dreimal
...in der Woche
...im Monat

immer *always*	**oft** *often*	**manchmal** *sometimes*	**nie** *never*

> Grammatikheft, S. 58, Ü. 7–8

17 Grammatik im Kontext

Sprechen/Schreiben Wie viele Sätze kannst du bauen? Wann und wie oft machst du das alles?

Im Herbst Im Frühling Im Winter Im Sommer Am Montag Am Wochenende Nach der Schule Am Nachmittag Am Abend	spiele spüle putze gehe decke räume...auf	ich	(ein)mal in der Woche (zwei)mal im Monat nie oft manchmal immer	Karten Gitarre Klavier Geschirr die Fenster ins Konzert den Tisch Fußball Basketball in eine Disko mein Zimmer

---

1. ein(s), zwei 2. *once a week, twice a month* **3. dreimal in der Woche 4. viermal im Monat**
5. *every day*

18 Wie oft tut Markus das?

Zuhören Listen as Markus describes when and how often he does things. First make a calendar page for one month and then fill in a possible schedule for his activities.

So sagt man das!

Asking for and offering help and telling someone what to do

CD-ROM DISC 2

If your friend has a lot to do, you might offer to help. Then he or she could explain what to do.

You might ask:

> **Was kann ich für dich tun?** *or*
> **Kann ich etwas für dich tun?**

Your friend might answer:

> **Ja, du kannst den Müll sortieren.** *or*
> **Willst du für mich Staub saugen?**

You agree:

> **Gut! Mach ich!**

What are the English equivalents of the phrases **für dich** and **für mich?**[1]

SPRACHTIPP

Often, other elements besides the subject are placed at the beginning of a sentence to give them special emphasis. For example, if someone asks you: **Kannst du heute Volleyball spielen?**, you might respond: **Nein, heute muss ich zu Hause helfen, aber morgen kann ich sicher spielen.** The time expressions are placed first, because time is the most important issue in this conversation. By putting something other than the subject in first position, you not only add variety to your conversations, but also express yourself more exactly.

Ein wenig Grammatik

The words **kann** and **kannst** are forms of the verb **können**, a modal auxiliary verb. **Kann** is a cognate. What does it mean?[2] Here are the forms of **können**:

ich	kann	wir	können
du	kannst	ihr	könnt
er, sie, es	kann	sie, Sie	können

Übungsheft, S. 77, Ü. 11

Grammatikheft, S. 59, Ü. 9–10

Mehr Grammatikübungen, S. 209, Ü. 5–7

19 Grammatik im Kontext

Schreiben Deine Freunde wollen dir zu Hause helfen. Schreib Gespräche, die zu den Zeichnungen *(sketches)* passen.

BEISPIEL **Können wir etwas für dich tun? Ja, ihr könnt den Rasen mähen. Danke!**

---

1. *for me/for you;* 2. *can*

20 **Peter macht ein Geschäft**

Lesen/Sprechen Katrin und ihr Bruder Peter haben am Wochenende viel zu tun. Lies die folgenden Gespräche und beantworte die Fragen.

KATRIN Ach, ich hab heute viel zu tun. He, du Peter! Kannst du etwas für mich tun?

PETER Vielleicht.

KATRIN Kannst du die Blumen gießen?

PETER Ja, gern. Was kann ich noch für dich tun?

KATRIN Müll sortieren?

PETER Okay, aber das kostet drei Euro. Danke!

Ayla und Mario kommen vorbei.

MARIO Na, Katrin und Peter, was macht ihr? Können wir etwas für euch tun?

PETER Sicher! Ihr könnt für uns die Blumen gießen und dann den Müll sortieren. Geht das?

MARIO Klar. Wir helfen gern!

1. Compare the following sentences from the conversations above: **Was kann ich noch für dich tun?** and **Können wir etwas für euch tun?** To whom do the pronouns **dich** and **euch** refer in the conversations?

2. Now compare these sentences: **Kannst du etwas für mich tun?** and **Du kannst für uns die Blumen gießen.** To whom do the pronouns **mich** and **uns** refer?

3. Which of these pronouns are used for talking to others? Which ones are used to talk about yourself?

4. What is the English equivalent for each of these pronouns?

Grammatik

The accusative pronouns

CD-ROM
DISC **2**

In **Kapitel 5** you learned the accusative forms of the third person pronouns **er**, **sie**, **es**, and **sie** (pl). They are **ihn**, **sie**, **es**, and **sie**. The first and second person pronouns are in boldface in the summary chart below.

Person	Nominative Singular	Accusative Singular	Nominative Plural	Accusative Plural
First	ich	**mich**	wir	**uns**
Second	du	**dich**	ihr	**euch**
Third	er sie es	ihn sie es	sie	sie
Formal	Sie	**Sie**	Sie	**Sie**

Mehr Grammatikübungen
S. 210, Ü. 8–9

The accusative forms are used as direct objects, as in **Ich besuche dich morgen**, or as objects of prepositions such as **für**, as in **Du kannst für mich den Müll sortieren.** To ask for whom someone is doing something, use **für wen**: **Für wen** machst du das?

Übungsheft,
S. 78–79, Ü. 12–14

Grammatikheft,
S. 60, Ü. 11–12

21 Grammatik im Kontext

Sprechen/Schreiben Mara is going to the **Schreibwarenladen** to buy a few things for herself. Before she leaves she asks some friends if she can buy anything for them. Create an exchange for each picture, telling what Mara would ask, and how the person or people pictured would respond.

BEISPIEL   MARA   **Kann ich etwas für dich kaufen?**
                MARKUS   **Ja, bitte. Du kannst für mich einen Bleistift kaufen.**

1.   2.   3.   4.

22 Zu Hause helfen

Schreiben/Sprechen Two of your friends are coming over to help you with your chores so that you can go swimming together. Before they arrive, make a list of six chores you have to do today. Then, with your partners, develop a conversation in which your friends offer to help and you discuss together who will do each of the chores. Be creative!

23 Arbeit suchen

Schreiben Du brauchst Geld und willst dir einen Job suchen. Schreib auf einen Zettel, was du alles tun kannst und wann und wie oft du arbeiten kannst. Wie viel Geld möchtest du verdienen? Vergiss deine Telefonnummer nicht!

BABYSITTER
Ich bin 15 und will
Montag u. Mittwoch von 17-21 Uhr
als Babysitter arbeiten.
Ich verlange 4 € pro Stunde.
Petra Müller Tel. 245476

24 Für mein Notizbuch

Schreiben Schreib, was du zu Hause alles machen musst! Wann und wie oft machst du das? Was machst du gern? Was machst du nicht gern? Hast du ein Haustier? Wie heißt es? Wer füttert das Tier?

Und dann noch...

der Vogel   die Maus

das Meerschweinchen   der Fisch

das Kaninchen   der Hamster

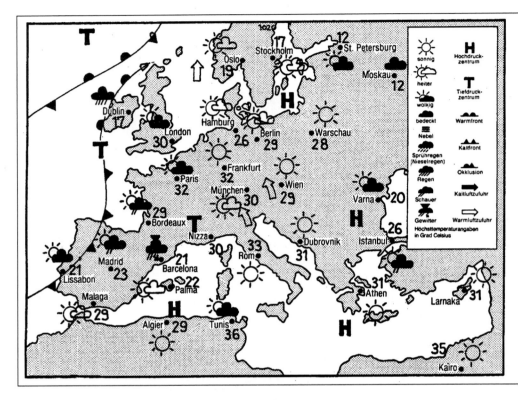

Wettervorhersagekarte für Europa 13. Juni 2001

Lage: Deutschland liegt am Rande eines umfangreichen Hochs über dem östlichen Mitteleuropa. Dabei ist es teils sonnig und warm.

Vorhersage: Am Montag überwiegend sonnig, nur vereinzelt auch wolkig. Höchsttemperaturen 28 bis 32 Grad. In der Nacht auf Dienstag Abkühlung auf 20 Grad. Schwacher bis mäßiger Wind aus Nordwest.

Aussichten: Am Dienstag sonnig und heiter mit Temperaturen von 26 bis 32 Grad. Tiefstwerte um 15 Grad. Schwacher, örtlich auch mäßiger Wind aus dem Norden.

25 Was sagt der Wetterbericht?

Sprechen Beantworte die folgenden Fragen zu der Wetterkarte.

1. What area of the world is this weather map for?
2. What kinds of information can you get from the map?
3. Look at the table of symbols and the words that go with them. Can you figure out what each word means?
4. Which cities are the coldest? What do you think the reason for this is?
5. Name three cities where you might need an umbrella.
6. Name three cities where you might do outdoor activities.
7. List the words in the weather forecast that describe the weather for Monday and Tuesday.

Wortschatz

Das Wetter

Regen
Gewitter
nass
wolkig

Schnee
Eis

sonnig
trocken

C	F	
35	95	heiß
27	80	warm
13	55	kühl
0	32	kalt

Talking about the weather

For some plans you make with your friends, you might first need to know about the weather.

You could ask:

Wie ist das Wetter heute?

Or you might want to ask about tomorrow:

Wie ist das Wetter morgen?

Or you might want to ask for specific information:

Regnet es heute?
Schneit es heute Abend?
Wie viel Grad haben wir heute?

Some possible responses are:

Heute regnet es.
Wolkig und kühl.

Sonnig, aber kalt.

Ich glaube schon.
Nein, es schneit nicht.
Ungefähr 10 Grad.

Übungsheft,
S. 80–82, Ü. 15–21

Grammatikheft,
S. 61, Ü. 13–14

What do you think the word **Grad** means?[1] Look at the response for a clue. When you tell someone the temperature, you might not know exactly what it is, so you say **ungefähr ...** What do you think **ungefähr** means?[2]

---

26 Was machst du bei diesem Wetter?

Listen to the following weather reports from German radio. For each report determine which activity fits best with the weather described.

a.

b.

c.

d.

Ein wenig Grammatik

What do you notice about the verb that is used to ask and tell about the weather for tomorrow? The present tense is often used when referring to the near future. The meaning is made clear with words such as **morgen**. How would you invite a German friend to go to the movies tomorrow?[3]

Grammatikheft, S. 62, Ü. 15-16

Mehr Grammatikübungen,
S. 211, Ü. 10–11

27 Grammatik im Kontext

Sprechen Sprich mit einer Partnerin über das Wetter in eurer Stadt. Sprecht über folgende Themen. Zusätzliche (additional) Wörter findet ihr auf Seite R9.

1. Wie ist das Wetter heute?
2. Wie viel Grad haben wir heute?
3. Und was sagt der Wetterbericht für morgen?
4. Wie ist das Wetter im Januar? Und im Juli?
5. Und im April? Und im Oktober?

---

1. *degree* 2. *approximately* 3. **Ich gehe morgen ins Kino. Kommst du mit?**

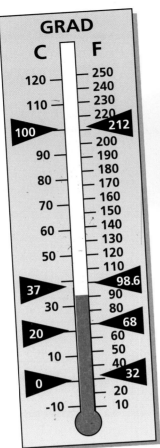

GRAD

C	F
120	250
110	240
	230
	220
100	212
	200
90	190
	180
80	170
	160
70	150
60	140
	130
50	120
	110
37	98.6
	90
30	80
20	68
	60
10	50
	40
	32
0	
	20
-10	10

Ein wenig Landeskunde

Weather in the German-speaking countries is extremely variable, depending on the latitude and seasons. These countries usually get a lot of rainfall. Summers are often rainy, and winters can be cold, especially in the Alps. As in other European countries, German-speaking countries use the Celsius system of measuring temperature, rather than the Fahrenheit system. Look at the thermometer. If it were 35°C would you need a jacket? If the temperature fell below 0°C would you expect rain or snow? What is a comfortable room temperature in Celsius? Look at the weather map on p. 202. If you were in Moscow, what kinds of clothes would you be wearing? In Athens?

Übungsheft, S. 84, Ü. 1–2

Wortschatz

Wie ist das Wetter im ...?

Januar	Juni	November
Februar	Juli	Dezember
März	August	
April	September	
Mai	Oktober	

Grammatikheft, S. 63, Ü. 17–18

28 Gespräche

Lesen/Sprechen Ordne die Sätze für jede Zeichnung.

1. BRITTE   Hallo, Gupse! Gehen wir morgen schwimmen?

Toll! Also, bis morgen!

Ja, klar. Aber was sagt der Wetterbericht?

Gut! Dann gehen wir schwimmen.

Morgen ist es sonnig und warm.

1. HANNES   Tag, Jörg! Ich geh ins Kino. Kommst du mit?

Nein, ich kann nicht. Ich muss den Rasen mähen.

Gut! Mach ich! Aber schau mal, Hannes! Es regnet jetzt!

Gern! Du kannst für mich die Blumen gießen.

Ach, dann gehen wir doch ins Kino!

Brauchst du Hilfe, Jörg?

29 **Ein Wetterbericht für …**

Schreiben Schau auf die Wetterkarte auf Seite 202. Wähle eine Stadt aus und schreib einen Wetterbericht für diese Stadt.

30 **Pläne machen**

Sprechen With a partner, pretend that you are meeting tomorrow in the city that you chose for Activity 29. You would like to invite your friend to do something special that is appropriate for the expected weather. Create a conversation in which you invite your partner to do something. He or she will ask about the weather, and you say what you know about it. Your partner can either accept or decline the invitation. Then switch roles and create another conversation, using your partner's city.

31  Von der Schule zum Beruf

Schreiben You have been hired by a local radio station to be the weather reporter. Your job is to write the weather report for today and tomorrow. Give the conditions, temperature, and forecast for your area.

AUSSPRACHE

Richtig aussprechen / Richtig lesen

A. To practice the following sounds, say the words and sentences below after your teacher or after the recording.

1. The letter **o**: In **Kapitel 3** you learned how to pronounce the letter **o** as a long vowel, as in **Oma**. However, when the letter **o** is followed by two or more consonants, it is pronounced as a short vowel, like the *o* in the English word *cot*.

   wolkig, Sonne, Woche / Im Oktober ist es sonnig und trocken.

2. The letter **u**: In **Kapitel 3** you learned how to pronounce the letter **u** as a long vowel, as in **super**. However, when the letter **u** is followed by two or more consonants, it is pronounced as a short vowel, like the *u* in the English word *put*.

   uns, muss, putzen / Mutti, ich muss die Fenster putzen.

3. The letter **l**: The letter **l** is pronounced like the *l* in the English word *million*. It is much more tense than the *l* sound in the English word *bill*.

   Müll, kühl, April / Der Lehrer kann im Juli mit dem Müll helfen.

4. The consonant combination **th**: The combination **th** within the same syllable is pronounced the same as the letter **t** in German.

   Theater, Mathe, Theatinerkirche / Wie komme ich zur Theatinerkirche und zum Theater?

5. The letter combination **pf**: The consonant combination **pf** sounds similiar to the *pf* combination in English, as in the word *cupful*. However, in German this letter combination often occurs at the beginning of a word and is pronounced as one sound.

   Pfennig, Pfund, Kopfsalat / Zwei Pfund Pflaumen kosten neunundneunzig Pfennig.

Richtig schreiben / Diktat

B. Write down the words and sentences that you hear.

Wem hilfst du?

Lesestrategie **Finding relationships between ideas.** Subordinating conjunctions (words such as *if, when, because,* or *although* in English) indicate the relationship of the idea in the dependent clause to the idea in the main clause. For example, they may indicate when or under what conditions (**wenn**), a reason (**weil**), a concession (**obwohl**), or introduce an opinion or fact (**dass**). Knowing the meaning of a conjunction can help you guess the meaning of a sentence, even if you do not understand each word.

Weißt du noch? Using visual clues, such as illustrations or photos, will give you advance information about a text before you try to read it.

1. Before you try to read these three interviews, look at the title and at the photos. What do you expect the articles to be about?

2. What do these three texts have in common? What kind of texts do you think they are?

3. You probably figured out that these articles have to do with young people helping others. Working in groups of three or four students, write as many German phrases as you can that have to do with offering to help people.

4. Read the interview questions. Even though you may not know all the words in each question, you can probably figure out what is being asked. With a partner, write what you think is being asked in each question.

WEM
Helfen Jugendliche ihren Eltern und Freunden? Verdienen sie dabei Taschengeld?

HILFST
Oder bieten sie Hilfe freiwillig an? JUMA— Reporter Bernd hat sich umgehört.

DU?

Hallo Heiko!

Wem hilfst du? Ich helfe meiner Mutter.

Und wobei hilfst du? Ab und zu bei der Hausarbeit. Zum Beispiel helfe ich meiner Mutter beim Staubsaugen oder beim Wäscheaufhängen. Mein Zimmer räume ich allerdings seltener auf. Dazu habe ich meistens keine Lust. Und das Auto wäscht mein Vater lieber selbst. Dann wird es sauberer als bei mir.

Bekommst du etwas für deine Hilfe? Nein. Aber wenn ich längere Zeit nichts mache, schimpfen meine Eltern. Natürlich haben sie damit recht, wenn ich faul bin.

Gibt es Menschen oder besondere Organisationen, denen du gerne helfen würdest? Ich weiß jetzt nichts Spezielles. Aber ich weiß, wem ich nicht gerne helfen würde: aufdringlichen Freunden.

Warum hilfst du anderen Menschen? Ich finde es wichtig, daß man anderen eine Last abnimmt. Außerdem ist Mithilfe eine nette Geste, über die sich wahrscheinlich jeder freut.

Hallo Tina!

Wem hilfst Du? Meiner Familie, meinen Freunden und meinen Bekannten.

Und wobei hilfst Du? Ich passe auf Kinder auf oder helfe meiner Schwester bei den Hausaufgaben. Im Haushalt mache ich eigentlich alles: Spülen, Bügeln oder Putzen.

Bekommst Du etwas für Deine Hilfe? Ich helfe freiwillig, obwohl ich meiner Schwester die Hausaufgaben nicht so gerne erkläre. Meinen Eltern und Bekannten biete ich auch schon mal Hilfe an.

Gibt es Menschen oder besondere Organisationen, denen Du gerne helfen würdest? Ja. Ich möchte gerne einmal in einem Kinderhort mitarbeiten. Das ist bestimmt anstrengend, aber interessant.

Warum hilfst du anderen Menschen? Wichtig für mich ist es, Pflichten zu erfüllen. Anderen zu helfen, ist eine Pflicht.

Hallo Sven!

Wem hilfst du? Ich helfe meistens meinen Freunden.

Und wobei hilfst du? Eigentlich bei allem, was mit Schule zu tun hat. Meistens aber bei Hausaufgaben und Prüfungsvorbereitungen. Nachhilfestunden in Biologie oder Chemie gebe ich ziemlich regelmäßig, weil ich in diesen Fächern ganz gut bin.

Bekommst du etwas für Deine Hilfe? Ja, manchmal. Ich bessere mein Taschengeld mit Nachhilfe auf.

Gibt es Menschen oder besondere Organisationen, denen du gerne helfen würdest? Allen netten Leuten helfe ich gerne.

Warum hilfst du anderen Menschen? Es ist schön, wenn sie sich über Mithilfe freuen.

5. Scan the articles and list any subordinating conjunctions that you find. Using the information in the **Lesestrategie**, determine what you expect each of the clauses introduced by these conjunctions to contain: a condition, a reason, a concession, an opinion, or a statement of fact. Write your guess beside the corresponding conjunction.

6. Read each clause that begins with a subordinating conjunction. Can you determine what the clause means? Now read the entire sentence. What does each sentence mean?

7. Now read the articles for the following information:

   a. Whom do these young people help? What are some of the things they do to help?

   b. When do Heiko's parents complain? Does Heiko think they have a right to complain? How do you know? What does Heiko say about "taking a burden from others"?

   c. What does Tina not like to do? Where does she want to work someday? What does she say is a "duty"?

   d. Why does Sven tutor other students in biology and chemistry? Whom does he like to help?

8. If you had been asked these questions by *JUMA*, how would you have answered them?

9. Imagine that you will spend the next year as an exchange student with a German family. Write a letter to your host family and include an explanation of some of the chores you regularly do at home. Offer to do them for your German family while you are there.

Übungsheft, S. 83, Ü. 22

Mehr Grammatikübungen

CD-ROM
DISC **2**

☑ internet

ADRESSE: go.hrw.com
KENNWORT:
WK3 MUENCHEN-7

Erste Stufe **Objective** Expressing obligations

1 Du und deine Freunde, ihr habt heute viel zu tun. Setze die richtigen Formen von **müssen** ein *(insert)*. **(S. 195)**

1. Was _____ du jetzt tun? — Ich _____ jetzt die Katze füttern.
2. Was _____ die Mara tun? — Sie _____ Staub saugen.
3. Was _____ ihr heute tun? — Wir _____ heute den Müll sortieren.
4. Was _____ die Jungen tun? — Sie _____ den Rasen mähen.
5. Was _____ der Flori tun? — Er _____ sein Zimmer aufräumen.
6. Was _____ wir jetzt tun? — Ihr _____ jetzt den Tisch abräumen.

2 Alle müssen heute etwas tun. Vervollständige *(complete)* die folgenden Aussagen *(statements)* und benutze dabei die richtige Form von **müssen** und die Ausdrücke in Klammern *(parentheses)*. **(S. 195)**

1. (das Geschirr spülen) Der Flori _____ .
2. (die Fenster putzen) Der Markus _____ .
3. (den Tisch decken) Ich _____ .
4. (Staub saugen) Du _____ .
5. (den Müll sortieren) Ihr _____ .
6. (den Rasen mähen) Wir _____ .
7. (die Blumen gießen) Mara und Claudia _____ .

3 Wer macht was? Beantworte die folgenden Fragen und setze dabei die richtige Form von **müssen** in die erste Lücke *(blank)* und eine passende Infinitivform in die zweite Lücke. **(S. 196)**

1. Wer räumt den Tisch ab? — Der Markus _____ den Tisch _____ .
2. Wer räumt die Klamotten auf? — Die Mara _____ die Klamotten _____ .
3. Wer kommt mit? — Du _____ _____ .
4. Wer probiert die Stiefel an? — Ihr _____ die Stiefel _____ .
5. Wer zieht Turnschuhe an? — Die Mara _____ Turnschuhe _____ .

4 Dein Freund hat viele Fragen. Schreib die folgenden Sätze ab *(copy)* und schreib dabei die richtige Verbform und das richtige Präfix in die Lücken. (**S. 196**)

1. (abräumen) Wer _____ heute Abend den Tisch _____ ?
2. (aufräumen) Wer _____ heute das Wohnzimmer _____ ?
3. (mitkommen) Wer _____ in die Stadt _____ ?
4. (anprobieren) Wer _____ die Klamotten _____ ?
5. (anziehen) Wer _____ die alten Klamotten _____ ?
6. (aussehen) Wer _____ in den Klamotten gut _____ ?

Zweite Stufe

Objective Asking for and offering help and telling someone what to do

5 Ihr helft euren Freunden. Was könnt ihr für sie tun? Schreib die richtige Form von **können** in die Lücken. (**S. 199**)

1. Was _____ ich tun? — Du _____ den Rasen mähen.
2. Was _____ Mara tun? — Sie _____ die Katze füttern.
3. Was _____ wir tun? — Ihr _____ den Müll sortieren.
4. Was _____ die Jungen tun? — Die Jungen _____ die Blumen gießen.
5. Was _____ der Flori tun? — Der Flori _____ den Tisch decken.
6. Was _____ ich tun? — Du _____ zu Hause helfen.
7. Was _____ ich tun? — Herr Meier, Sie _____ die Katzen füttern.
8. Und was _____ die Mädchen tun? — Sie _____ Mutti helfen.

6 Alle müssen helfen. Schreib die richtige Form von **können** und den Ausdruck in Klammern in die Lücken. (**S. 199**)

1. (das Geschirr spülen) Mara, du _____ .
2. (das Zimmer aufräumen) Der Flori _____ .
3. (den Tisch abräumen) Wir _____ .
4. (den Müll sortieren) Ihr _____ .
5. (die Fenster putzen) Die Claudia _____ .
6. (Staub saugen) Und ich _____ .

7 Deine Freunde wollen dir helfen, und du sagst ihnen, was sie für dich tun können. Schreib die folgenden Sätze ab *(copy)* und schreib die richtige Verbform von **können** in die erste Lücke, die richtige Verbform von **müssen** in die zweite Lücke und die richtige Verbform von **wollen** in die dritte Lücke. (**S. 199**)

1. Was _____ ich für dich tun? – Ich _____ einkaufen gehen. _____ du mitkommen?
2. Was _____ wir für euch tun? – Mein Bruder _____ den Rasen mähen. _____ ihr ihm helfen?
3. Was _____ Flori für uns tun? – Wir _____ den Müll sortieren, und vielleicht _____ er uns helfen.
4. Du _____ etwas für uns tun. – Ich _____ die Fenster putzen, und du _____ bestimmt die Garage aufräumen.
5. Ihr _____ uns helfen. Die Claudia _____ in der Küche helfen, und ich _____ heute ins Kino gehen.

8 Alle wollen helfen. Was können sie tun? Vervollständige *(complete)* die folgenden Sätze und schreib dabei das richtige Pronomen (**mich, dich, uns, euch**) in die Lücken. (**S. 200**)

1. Mara, was kann ich für _____ tun? — Du kannst für _____ den Müll sortieren.
2. Flori und Jens, was kann ich für _____ tun? — Du kannst für _____ Staub saugen.
3. Markus, was können wir für _____ tun? — Ihr könnt für _____ den Rasen mähen.
4. Mara und Jens, was können wir für _____ tun? — Ihr könnt nichts für _____ tun.

9 Du willst deinen Freunden helfen und fragst sie, was du für sie tun kannst. Deine Freunde geben dir zwei Aufgaben *(tasks)*. Schreib die Antworten ab und schreib dabei die richtige Form von **können** in die erste Lücke, das richtige Pronomen in die zweite Lücke und ein passendes Verb aus dem Kasten *(box)* in die dritte und vierte Lücke. (**S. 200**)

füttern	abräumen	gießen	mähen
putzen	saugen	sortieren	spülen

1. Was kann ich jetzt für euch tun? Die Blumen gießen? — Ja, du _____ jetzt für _____ die Blumen _____ und den Rasen _____ .
2. Was kann ich jetzt für dich tun? Den Tisch abräumen? — Ja, du _____ jetzt für _____ den Tisch _____ und das Geschirr _____ .
3. Was können wir jetzt für euch tun? Staub saugen? — Ja, ihr _____ jetzt für _____ Staub _____ und die Katze und den Hund _____ .
4. Was können wir jetzt für dich tun? Den Müll sortieren? — Ja, ihr _____ jetzt für _____ den Müll _____ und die Fenster _____ .

10 Du willst wissen, wie das Wetter heute, morgen, und heute Abend ist. Schreib Fragen und benutze dabei die gegebene Information. **(S. 203)**

BEISPIEL **You want to know whether it is going to snow today.**
Schneit es heute? *or* **Wird es heute schneien?**

You want to know whether it is going to:

1. rain tomorrow.
2. snow tonight.
3. be cloudy today.
4. be cool tonight.
5. be dry tomorrow.

11 Sieh dir die Wetterkarte an, und beantworte die folgenden Fragen. **(S. 203)**

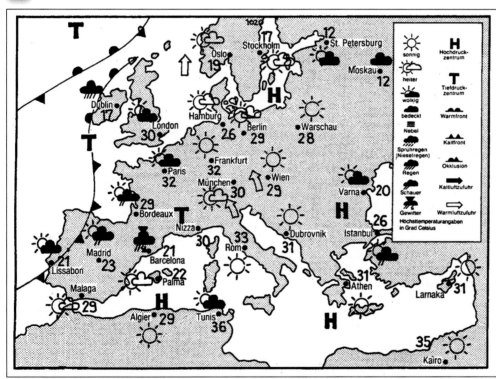

1. Wo regnet es? _____
2. Wie ist das Wetter in Rom und in Wien? _____
3. Wie hoch ist die Temperatur in Paris? _____
4. Wie ist das Wetter in Moskau? _____
5. Wie ist das Wetter in Lissabon? _____

CD-ROM DISC 2

internet

go.hrw.com
ADRESSE: go.hrw.com
KENNWORT:
   WK3 MUENCHEN-7

1 You will hear five students invite their friends to do something. Sometimes their friends accept, and sometimes they decline and give a reason. Listen to the exchanges and write the information you hear. Compare your notes with those of a classmate. The chart to the right will help you organize your information.

Invitation	accept/decline	reason
BEISPIEL schwimmen gehen	kommt nicht	muss Zimmer aufräumen

2 Below is a page from Flori's calendar for the month of **März**. Take turns asking and telling your partner when and how often Flori does the activities. Now make your own calendar page. Fill in all the activities you do in a typical month. Describe to your partner the things you wrote on your calendar, and he or she will try to find out when and how often you do them. Then switch roles.

März

Mo	Di	Mi	Do	Fr	Sa	So
	1 Staub saugen	2	3	4 Müll sortieren	5 Fenster putzen 4:00 Fußball spielen	6
7 9:30 mit Michael ins Konzert	8 Staub saugen	9 3:30 Klavier= unterricht 7:00 Volleyball	10	11 9:00 Disko	12 Rasen mähen 4:00 Fußball spielen	13
14 8:30 Kino mit Sabine	15 Staub saugen	16 3:30 Klavier= unterricht	17	18 Müll sortieren	19 Fenster putzen 4:00 Fußball spielen	20
21 4:00 Schwimmen	22 Staub saugen	23 3:30 Klavier= unterricht	24	25 9:00 Disko	26 Rasen mähen 4:00 Fußball spielen	27
28	29 Staub saugen	30 3:30 Klavier= unterricht	31			

3 Ask your partner when and how often he or she does the activities shown in the photos below. Does he or she enjoy each activity? Then your partner will ask you the same questions.

a.

b.

c.

d.

e.

4 Look at the weather map and answer the following questions in German.

1. Which cities are expecting rain?

2. In which cities could you probably go swimming?

3. Which city will be the warmest?

4. What kinds of activities might you plan in **Berlin** for Monday, April 7?

5. Where might you go skiing?

6. Claudia is planning to drive to the **Zugspitze,** and then to have a picnic in the **Englischer Garten.** What would she say if she wanted to invite you? Would you accept or decline?

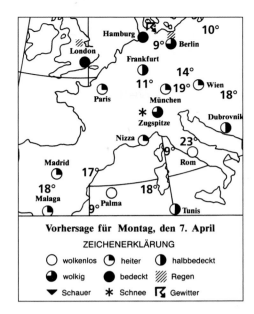

Vorhersage für Montag, den 7. April
ZEICHENERKLÄRUNG

○ wolkenlos ◑ heiter ◐ halbbedeckt
◕ wolkig ● bedeckt ░ Regen
▼ Schauer ✳ Schnee ⚡ Gewitter

5

Zum Schreiben

Write a TV script for your portion of the school "Teen Show," a program that reports on planned school activities. You represent the German club and give a summary of all the activities this club has planned for the semester.

Schreibtipp Making a writing plan before you begin is important. Think about your topic carefully. Do you know all the vocabulary you'll need? If not, use a bilingual dictionary or ask your teacher for help. Will your topic require you to use certain grammatical structures frequently? If you are not sure you can use them correctly, consult your textbook or your teacher.

1. Brainstorm types of activities and types of weather expressions with your group. Activities might include helping out with chores some afternoon at the local home for the elderly (**Altersheim**) or a French Club/German Club soccer match. Activities, however, are dependent on the weather, so you need to give alternatives for some of the outdoor activities in case of rain or other bad weather. How many creative activities can your "club" sponsor?

Remember also the expression, „**Guten Tag, liebe Zuschauer!**" which is used at the beginning of many weather reports and other information shows.

2. Using your list of activities and weather expressions, write your script. Videotape your program and show it to the class.

6

Rollenspiel

It's raining today, so you are at home doing your chores. Your friends show up and offer to help. As you and your friends work around the house, you decide to invite your friends to go somewhere tomorrow. Great crashes of thunder turn your conversation to the weather for tomorrow. What will you do? Create a conversation with two other classmates. Be prepared to act it out in front of the class with props that will convey the idea of doing chores around the house.

Can you extend and respond to an invitation? (p. 194)

1 How would you invite a friend to go
  a. to a movie **b.** to a café **c.** shopping **d.** swimming

2 Accept or decline the following invitations. If you decline, give a reason why you can't go.
  a. Wir gehen jetzt in eine Disko. Komm doch mit!
  b. Ich muss in die Stadt gehen. Möchtest du mitkommen?
  c. Wir spielen jetzt Tennis. Kannst du mitkommen?

Can you express obligation using müssen? (p. 194)

3 Say that the people below have to do the things indicated.

Bernd　　　　**Leyla**　　　**Pedro und Felipe**　　　**Karin**

Can you talk about how often you have to do things? (p. 198)

4 How would you ask a classmate how often he or she has to
  a. wash the windows　　　　**c.** clear the table
  b. vacuum　　　　**d.** do the dishes

5 How would you tell a classmate how often you have to do each of the things above?

Can you offer help and tell someone what to do using expressions with für? (p. 199)

6 How would you ask a classmate if you could help him or her? How would you ask two classmates?

7 Using **können**, explain to each of these people what they can do to help you:
  a. Sara: das Geschirr spülen
  b. Silke und Peter: das Zimmer aufräumen
  c. Markus: das Bett machen
  d. Claudia und Daniel: den Tisch decken

8 How might a friend respond if he or she agreed to do some chores for you?

Can you talk about the weather? (p. 203)

9 How would you tell a classmate what the weather is like today? How would you tell him or her the weather forecast for tomorrow?

10 How would you tell someone new to your area what the weather is like in
  a. January　　**c.** June　　　**e.** December
  b. March　　　**d.** October

Erste Stufe

Extending and responding to invitations

mitkommen (sep)	to come along
Komm doch mit!	Why don't you come along!
Ich kann leider nicht.	Sorry, I can't.
Das geht nicht.	That won't work.

Expressing obligation

tun	to do
helfen	to help
zu Hause helfen	to help at home
müssen	to have to

ich muss …	I have to …
mein Zimmer aufräumen (sep)	clean up my room
Staub saugen	vacuum
den Müll sortieren	sort the trash
den Rasen mähen	mow the lawn
die Katze füttern	feed the cat
den Tisch decken	set the table
den Tisch abräumen (sep)	clear the table
das Geschirr spülen	wash the dishes

die Blumen gießen	water the flowers
das Bett machen	make the bed
meine Klamotten aufräumen	pick up my clothes
die Fenster putzen	clean the windows
Ich habe keine Zeit.	I don't have time.

Zweite Stufe

Saying how often you have to do things

Wie oft?	How often?
nie	never
manchmal	sometimes
immer	always
einmal, zweimal, dreimal …	once, twice, three times …
in der Woche	a week
im Monat	a month
jeden Tag	every day

Asking for and offering help and telling someone what to do

können	can, to be able to
Was kann ich für dich tun?	What can I do for you?
Kann ich etwas für dich tun?	Can I do something for you?
Du kannst …	You can …
Gut! Mach ich!	Okay! I'll do that!
für	for
Für wen?	For whom?

mich	me
dich	you
uns	us
euch	you (pl)

Other useful words and expressions

ungefähr	about, approximately

Dritte Stufe

Talking about the weather

Was sagt der Wetterbericht?	What does the weather report say?
Wie ist das Wetter?	How's the weather?
Es ist …	It is …
heiß	hot
warm	warm
kühl	cool
kalt	cold
trocken	dry
nass	wet
sonnig	sunny
wolkig	cloudy

der Schnee	snow
Es schneit.	It's snowing.
der Regen	rain
Es regnet.	It's raining.
das Eis	ice
das Gewitter	thunderstorm
Die Sonne scheint.	The sun is shining.
heute	today
morgen	tomorrow
heute Abend	this evening
Wie viel Grad haben wir?	What's the temperature?
der Grad	degree(s)
zwei Grad	two degrees

der Monat, -e	month
der Januar	January
im Januar	in January
Februar	February
März	March
April	April
Mai	May
Juni	June
Juli	July
August	August
September	September
Oktober	October
November	November
Dezember	December

8
Einkaufen gehen

Objectives

In this chapter you will learn to

Erste Stufe

- ask what you should do
- tell someone what to do

Zweite Stufe

- talk about quantities
- say that you want something else

Dritte Stufe

- give reasons
- say where you were and what you bought

 internet

ADRESSE: go.hrw.com
KENNWORT:
WK3 MUENCHEN-8

◀ **Ich war beim Gemüsehändler.**

Los geht's! ▪ *Alles für die Oma!*

Strategie Verstehen

Look at the images for this story. Who are the people pictured? What are they doing? Where and when do you think these scenes are taking place? What clues tell you this?

Flori

Omi

1

Flori:	Hallo, Omi!
Omi:	Hallo, Flori!
Flori:	Hm, Omi, was kochst du denn? Es riecht so gut! Kaiserschmarren? Super!
Omi:	Den isst du doch so gern!
Flori:	Und wie!

2

Flori:	Hm, Omi, der Kaiserschmarren war gut! Wie immer!
Omi:	Wirklich? Nicht zu süß?
Flori:	Nein, überhaupt nicht. Er war gerade richtig!
Omi:	Na, das freut mich!

3

Flori:	Und was soll ich heute für dich einkaufen?
Omi:	Hier ist der Einkaufszettel.
Flori:	Wo soll ich denn die Tomaten kaufen?
Omi:	Die kaufst du im Supermarkt. Dort sind sie nicht so teuer.
Flori:	Und das Brot? Kann ich es auch gleich da kaufen?
Omi:	Hol das Brot lieber beim Bäcker! Dort ist es immer frisch und schmeckt besser.

4

Omi: Hier sind hundert Euro. Verlier das Geld nicht!

Flori: Keine Sorge, Omi! Ich pass schon auf!

5

Flori: Hm…ein Pfund Hackfleisch, bitte!

Verkäuferin: Hast du noch einen Wunsch, bitte?

Flori: Dann noch hundert Gramm Aufschnitt.

Verkäuferin: Sonst noch einen Wunsch?

Flori: Nein, danke! Das ist alles.

6

Verkäuferin: Bitte schön?

Flori: So ein Brot, bitte!

Verkäuferin: Dieses hier?

Flori: Ja, genau das.

Verkäuferin: Sonst noch etwas?

Flori: Und dann noch zwei Semmeln.

Verkäuferin: Alles dann?

Flori: Danke, das ist alles.

Verkäuferin: Macht zwei Euro neunzig, bitte!

Flori: Einen Moment! Dann noch bitte so eine Brezenstange für mich. Nein, die brauchen Sie nicht einpacken, die ess ich gleich.

Verkäuferin: Alles dann? Drei Euro vierzig dann, bitte!

7

Flori: So, Omi, hier bin ich wieder. Hier sind noch ein paar Blumen für dich!

Omi: Das ist aber nett!

Flori: So, jetzt packen wir erst mal aus! Die Eier, die Butter …Tja, wo ist denn das Portemonnaie?

Omi: Wo warst du denn zuletzt?

Flori: Einen Moment, Omi, ich bin gleich wieder da! Tschau!

Übungsheft, S. 85

1 **Was passiert hier?**

Do you understand what is happening in the story? Check your comprehension by answering these questions. Don't be afraid to guess.

1. What does Flori do when he first arrives at his grandmother's house?
2. What does Flori offer to do for his grandmother?
3. Why does she give him money? What else does she give him for his errand?
4. What types of stores does Flori go to?
5. Why do you think Flori rushes out of his grandmother's house at the end of the story?

2 **Genauer lesen**

Reread the conversations. Which words or phrases do the characters use to

1. express satisfaction or praise
2. refer to different kinds of stores
3. name foods
4. express quantities in weight
5. ask if someone wants more

3 **Wo war Flori?**

Flori went to several different stores when he was shopping for his grandmother. In which of the places listed might he have made these statements?

1. Ein Pfund Hackfleisch, bitte!
2. Jetzt bekomme ich noch zwei Semmeln.
3. Ein Kilo Tomaten, bitte!
4. Ich möchte bitte ein paar Rosen.

a. beim Bäcker
b. beim Metzger
c. im Blumengeschäft
d. im Supermarkt

4 **Was passt zusammen?**

You can use the word **denn** (*since, for, because*) to show the relationship between two sentences that express an action and the reason for that action: **Hol das Brot beim Bäcker, denn dort ist es immer frisch!** Connect the following pairs of sentences in this way to logically explain some of the actions in the story.

1. Es riecht sehr gut bei Omi,
2. Flori kauft Tomaten im Supermarkt,
3. Flori kauft Brot beim Bäcker,
4. Omi gibt Flori einen Einkaufszettel,
5. Flori geht schnell weg,

a. er geht für sie einkaufen.
b. dort ist es immer frisch.
c. dort sind sie nicht so teuer.
d. er kann das Portemonnaie nicht finden.
e. sie kocht Kaiserschmarren.

5 **Nacherzählen**

Put the sentences in logical order to make a brief summary of the story.

1. Zuerst kocht die Großmutter Kaiserschmarren für den Flori.

Dann gibt sie Flori auch das Geld.

Dann fragt Flori die Großmutter, was er für sie einkaufen soll.

Zuletzt kauft er auch Blumen für die Großmutter.

Die Tomaten kauft er im Supermarkt, das Brot beim Bäcker und das Hackfleisch beim Metzger.

Sie gibt Flori den Einkaufszettel.

Nach dem Einkaufen kommt Flori wieder zurück.

Aber er kann das Portemonnaie nicht finden und geht es suchen.

Wortschatz

Einkaufen gehen

Schau dir die Werbung an. Welche Geschäfte werben hier? Was kannst du in diesen Geschäften kaufen?

Beim Bäcker Motz

Brot 1 kg 1,70

Semmel Stück -,30

Brezeln Stück -,55

Torte Stück 1,40

BEIM METZGER SEIBT

Hackfleisch 1 kg 2,98

Hähnchen 4,20

Aufschnitt 100 g 1,19

Bratwurst 100 g 0,69

Im Obst- und Gemüseladen Frisch

Tomaten 1 kg 2,40

Kartoffeln 1 kg 0,98

Äpfel 1 kg 1,60

Salat St. -,59

Trauben 1 kg 1,98

IM SUPERMARKT KRAUS

Milch l 1,10

Eier 10 St. 1,10

Kaffee 1 Pfd. 4,49

Butter 250 g 1,19

Fisch 100 g 0,89

Zucker 1 kg 2,10

Käse 100 g 0,99

Mehl 500 g Beutel 0,79

LEBENSMITTEL • GANZ PREISWERT!

Übungsheft, S. 86–87, Ü. 2–4   Grammatikheft, S. 64, Ü. 1–2

Ein wenig Landeskunde

Although there are many large, modern supermarkets in Germany, many people still shop in small specialty stores or at the open-air markets in the center of town. Many Germans shop frequently, buying just what they need for one or two days. Refrigerators are generally much smaller than in the United States, and people prefer to buy things fresh.

6 Flori und Claudia gehen einkaufen

Zuhören Flori and Claudia are at a café discussing their plans for the day. They decide to do their shopping together. Make a list of the things they are going to buy at each of the following kinds of stores.

    im Supermarkt   beim Bäcker

    beim Metzger   im Obst- und Gemüseladen

Milch	Kuchen		Wurst
		Aufschnitt	
Fisch	Hackfleisch	Brot	Äpfel
Butter	Bratwurst	Semmeln	Brezeln

7 Was möchtest du kaufen?

Schreiben Schau dir die Artikel auf Seite 221 an und schreib auf eine Einkaufsliste, was du in den verschiedenen Geschäften kaufen möchtest. Addiere die Preise. Gibst du zu Hause mehr aus? Weniger *(less)*?

8 Was möchte dein Partner?

Schreiben Gebrauche deinen Einkaufszettel von Übung 7 und frag deine Partnerin, was sie kaufen möchte. Mach dir Notizen. *(Take notes.)* Tauscht dann die Rollen. Sag dann der Klasse, was deine Partnerin kaufen möchte.

    Beispiel   Du   **Beim Bäcker möchte er/sie …**

So sagt man das!

Asking what you should do

If you were going to help a friend or relative run errands, you would first ask what you should do:

The responses might be:

Was soll ich für dich tun?	**Du kannst für mich einkaufen gehen.**
Wo soll ich das Brot kaufen?	**Beim Bäcker.**
Soll ich das Fleisch im Supermarkt holen?	**Nein, du holst das besser beim Metzger.**
Und die Tomaten? Wo soll ich sie kaufen?	**Im Gemüseladen, bitte.**

What do you think the word **soll** means? In the sentences with **soll** and **kannst,** what happens to the word order? Where is the main verb?

The verb **sollen**

Sollen is used to express what you *should* or *are supposed to* do.

> Du **sollst** das Brot beim Bäcker **kaufen.**

What verbs do you already know that are similar to **sollen?** In what ways are they similar? Here are the forms of **sollen.**

ich	soll	wir	sollen
du	soll**st**	ihr	soll**t**
er, sie, es	soll	sie, Sie	sollen

Mehr Grammatikübungen, S. 236, Ü. 1–3

Übungsheft, S. 87, Ü. 5–6   Grammatikheft, S. 65, Ü. 3–4

---

9 **Grammatik im Kontext**

Schreiben/Sprechen Wie viele Fragen kannst du bauen? (Be sure to match the food items with the correct store.)

Sollen Sollt Sollst Soll	ich wir er ihr du Flori und Claudia

holen?
kaufen?

---

10 **Wo soll ich … kaufen?**

Lesen/Sprechen Du bist Austauschschüler *(exchange student)* bei einer deutschen Familie. Deine Gastmutter gibt dir einen Einkaufszettel, und du sollst für sie einkaufen gehen. Gebrauche die Einkaufsliste auf der rechten Seite und frag deine Partnerin, wo du diese Lebensmittel kaufen sollst. Tauscht dann die Rollen.

> Wurst
> Käse
> Brot
> Äpfel
> Semmeln
> Salat
> Mineralwasser
> Zucker
> Aufschnitt

So sagt man das!

Telling someone what to do

You have learned one way to tell someone what he or she can do to help you using **können.** Here are some other ways to express the same thing:

Someone might ask:	The response might be:
Was soll ich für dich tun?	**Geh bitte einkaufen!**
Was sollen wir für dich tun?	**Geht bitte einkaufen!**

What would be the English equivalent of the first response?[1] What would be the English equivalent of the second response?[2] What is the difference?[3]

[1.] *Go shopping, please.* [2.] *Go shopping, please.* [3.] The first is a singular command, the second is a plural command.

The **du**-command and the **ihr**-command

Look at the following commands:

du-command		**ihr**-command	
Kauf	Brot für die Oma!	**Kauft**	Brot für die Oma!
Komm	doch mit!	**Kommt**	doch mit!
Nimm	das Geld mit!	**Nehmt**	das Geld mit!

The above sentences are commands. These command forms are used to tell a person or persons you know well what to do. The **du**-command is formed by using the **du**-form of the verb without the **-st** ending. The **ihr**-command uses the **ihr**-form of the verb.

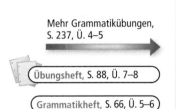

Mehr Grammatikübungen, S. 237, Ü. 4–5

Übungsheft, S. 88, Ü. 7–8

Grammatikheft, S. 66, Ü. 5–6

11 Grammatik im Kontext

Zuhören Flori's grandmother is preparing lunch on Saturday for him and his friends, Markus and Mara. She needs help and tells everyone what to do. Listen and decide what each person is supposed to do. Under each of their names (Markus, Mara, Flori) list their tasks.

12 Grammatik im Kontext

a. Sprechen/Schreiben Welche Verbformen sind richtig?

1. Flori, ══════ jetzt zum Bäcker und ══════ ein Brot!
2. Und Flori, ══════ das Geld mit und ══════ es nicht!
3. Und ihr, Markus und Mara, ══════ bitte die Blumen für mich!
4. Und, Markus und Mara, ══════ dann die Katze und ══════ das Geschirr!

b. Sprechen Frank hat zu Hause schon lange nicht mehr geholfen. Schau dir die Zeichnung mit einer Partnerin an und sagt, was Franks Eltern ihm wohl sagen werden.

13 Eine Fete

Sprechen You are having a party and two friends are helping you get ready. You've already gone shopping but have forgotten some of the things you need. Get together with two other classmates and, using your lists from Activity 7, each of you chooses six things you still need to buy. First you are the host, and your partners will ask what they can do to help. Tell each person to buy three items and where to buy them. Then switch roles so that each person plays the host once.

LANDESKUNDE LANDESKUNDE

Was machst du für andere Leute?

How do you think students in German-speaking countries help others? We asked several students whom they help and in what ways they help them. Before you read, try to guess what they might say.

Sandra, Stuttgart

„Bei uns in der Nachbarschaft gibt's grad' ältere Leute. Und unter uns wohnt eine Frau, die …für die mach ich manchmal kleine Einkäufe oder geh einfach nur hin und rede mit ihr, damit sie halt nicht grad' so allein ist, und besuch sie einfach oder bring ihr halt mal was rüber, wenn wir zum Beispiel Obst aus dem Garten haben."

Brigitte, Bietigheim

„Also, ich hab mit Kindern zu tun. Ich hab mal Kinderkirche sonntags, und da beschäftigt man sich mit kleinen Kindern und spielt mit denen, und das mach ich aber unregelmäßig. Also ich habe das auch schon lange Zeit nicht mehr gemacht."

Silvana, Berlin

„Zweimal in der Woche gebe ich Nachhilfe. Da hab ich einen kleinen Schüler. Der ist in der dritten Klasse, und dem geb ich Nachhilfe in Rechtschreibung und Lesen und Mathematik."

Iwan, Bietigheim

„Also meistens da helf ich zum Beispiel meinem Bruder irgend-wie, wenn er irgend-welche Probleme in der Schule hat. Und wenn ich bei meiner Oma bin, dann helf ich auch meiner Oma."

A. 1. Write each student's name. Then write whom each student helps.

2. The people whom the students help fall into two groups. What are they? With a partner, make a chart for these two groups and list the ways in which the students help each one.

3. Now make a list of the people you help and how you help them. Ask your partner what he or she does to help others: **Was machst du für andere Leute?** Then switch roles.

B. With your classmates, discuss some of the ways you help other people. Do you do any of the same things the German students do? What is your impression: Do people help others more in Germany than in the United States? What are your reasons for deciding one way or the other? When you have finished your discussion, write a brief essay explaining your answers.

Wortschatz

Und wie viel?

wiegen ungefähr
1 Kilo (kg)
= 1000 Gramm (g)
= (*2.2 lb.*)

wiegen ungefähr
1/2 (ein halbes) Kilo
= 500 Gramm
= 1 (deutsches)
Pfund (Pfd.)

wiegt ungefähr
100 Gramm

1 Liter (l) ist
ein bisschen mehr
als 1 *quart*
= (*1.057 quarts*)

2 Pfund = 1 Kilo = 1000 Gramm

Das amerikanische
Pfund hat nur 453 g.

Das deutsche
Pfund hat 500 g.

Übungsheft,
S. 89–90, Ü. 9–10

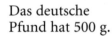
Grammatikheft,
S. 67, Ü. 7–8

So sagt man das!

Talking about quantities

When shopping for groceries in Germany, you will need to know how much to ask for
using weights. For example, at the butcher's the salesperson
might ask you: You might respond:

Was bekommen Sie?   **Aufschnitt und Hackfleisch, bitte.**
Wie viel Hackfleisch?   **500 Gramm Hackfleisch.**
Und wie viel Aufschnitt?   **100 Gramm, bitte!**

14 ### Was kaufen sie und wie viel?

Zuhören You are standing in line at the **Gemüseladen** and overhear other customers
asking the salesperson for specific amounts of certain items. First, listen to the conversations and write down what the customers are asking for. Then listen again and decide
how much of each item they want.

Ein wenig Landeskunde

Übungsheft,
S. 96, Ü. 24

Look back at the ads on page 221 and find the abbreviations that are used to describe quantities. What do they stand for? How many different units of measurement are listed? How does this compare with measures in the United States? In German-speaking countries, the metric system is used for weights and measures. At the open-air markets and in many specialty stores, such as the bakery and the butcher shop, you will have to ask the salesperson for certain foods rather than serve yourself. You will need to be able to tell the vendor how much of each item you would like.

15 **Was bekommen Sie?**

Lesen/Sprechen Du bist mit deiner Einkaufsliste (siehe rechts) in einem Laden. Dein Partner, der Verkäufer, fragt dich, was du kaufen möchtest. Du nennst vier Dinge, die auf deiner Liste stehen und sagst, wie viel du brauchst. Tauscht dann die Rollen.

VERKÄUFER	**Was …?**
DU	**Ich brauche …**
VERKÄUFER	**Wie viel?**
DU	**…**

1 kg Tomaten
250 g Kaffee
350 g Butter
1 l Milch
100 g Käse
200 g Aufschnitt
500 g Hackfleisch

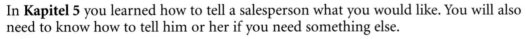

So sagt man das!

Saying that you want something else

In **Kapitel 5** you learned how to tell a salesperson what you would like. You will also need to know how to tell him or her if you need something else.

The salesperson might ask:

Sonst noch etwas?
or
Was bekommen Sie noch?
or
Haben Sie noch einen Wunsch?
Ist das alles?

You might respond:

Ja, ich brauche noch ein Kilo Kartoffeln.
Ich bekomme noch sechs Semmeln.
Nein, danke. *or*
Danke, das ist alles.

Mehr Grammatikübungen, S. 237–238, Ü. 6–7

Übungsheft,
S. 90–91, Ü. 11–14

Grammatikheft,
S. 68, Ü. 9-11

In several of the questions and answers, the word **noch** appears. Can you guess what it means?

16 **Logisch oder unlogisch?**

Zuhören Listen to these conversations in various food stores and determine whether the response in each case is logical or not.

	logisch	unlogisch	
1			
2			

17 Noch einen Wunsch?

Sprechen You are trying out new recipes tonight, and you still need to buy several things. Make shopping lists for the two recipes below. Then get together with two other classmates. One will play the salesperson at the supermarket, and the other will be another customer shopping for the second recipe. The salesperson will ask the customers what and how much they need and if they need something else.

Salami-Riesenpizza

Pizzateig (32 cm ⊘) für 2 Personen mit 4–6 Esslöffeln Tomatenstückchen belegen. 125 g Pizzakäse in Streifen schneiden, gitterförmig darüber legen.

10–12 Scheiben Salami und 6–8 blättrig geschnittene Champignons auf der Pizza verteilen.

Mit 1/2 Teelöffel Pizzagewürz bestreuen und bei 250 Grad 14 Minuten im Ofen backen.

Pikanter Quark

Zutaten:

250 g Quark
• etwa 4 Esslöffel Sahne
• etwa 4 Esslöffel Milch
• 1 Knoblauchzehe
• 1 Teelöffel Kümmel
• Salz

Insgesamt etwa 2370 Joule/565 Kalorien

18 Das Angebot der Woche

Schreiben Pick a specific kind of food store and make your own ad. Either cut pictures from a newspaper or draw your own pictures. You may want to refer to page 221 for a model. Below are some additional grocery items you may want to include. Remember to include prices per unit (**Kilo, Gramm, Pfund,** or **Liter**).

Und dann noch...

Bananen	**Apfelstrudel**
Erdnussbutter	**Joghurt**
peanut butter	**Ananas** *pineapple*
Marmelade *jam, jelly*	**Birnen** *pears*
Erdbeeren	**Melonen**
strawberries	**Müsli**

LERNTRICK

When you are learning a lot of new words, group them together in meaningful categories: group baked goods under **die Bäckerei**, meat items under **die Metzgerei**, etc. Putting the words in context will help you recall them more easily.

19 Für mein Notizbuch

Schreiben Schreib in dein Notizbuch, wo du gern einkaufst! Was kaufst du? Was kaufst du gern? Was ist dein Lieblingsgericht (*favorite dish*)? Welches Essen schmeckt dir und welches Essen schmeckt dir nicht?

SPAR *supermarkt*

Die elegante Fassade fällt auf, weil sie frei von jeglichen Preisplakaten ist.

Milch veredelt den Geschmack und ist gut für Ihr Wohlbefinden, denn Milch bringt erst die Wirkung des Koffeins in Einklang mit dem Geschmack des Kaffees!

20 **Warum?**

Lesen/Sprechen Schau dir die drei Werbungen an und beantworte die Fragen.

1. Using the reading strategies you have learned so far, try to get the gist of each ad. What is each ad promoting? What reason does each ad give to persuade you to buy the product or to shop at a particular store?
2. Identify the words **weil** and **denn**. What do they mean? How do you know?
3. In the **SPAR Supermarkt** ad, what is the position of the verb in a clause that starts with **weil**? How does this compare with clauses starting with **denn**?

So sagt man das!

Giving reasons

In **Kapitel 7** you learned how to make an excuse and express obligation using **müssen**:
Claudia kommt nicht mit. Sie muss zu Hause helfen. You can also do this with
expressions beginning with **weil** or **denn**.

A friend might ask you:

**Kannst du für mich
einkaufen gehen?**

You might respond giving a reason:

Es geht nicht, denn ich mache die Hausaufgaben. *or*
Ich kann jetzt nicht (gehen), weil ich die Hausaufgaben mache.

---

21 **Wer kommt zur Party?**

Zuhören Mara is having a party on the
weekend. Listen to the messages left on her
answering machine and take down the following information: the name of the person who called, if that person is coming to
the party, and if not, the reason why not.

wer	ja oder nein?	warum (nicht)?
BEISPIEL Markus	nein	geht ins Kino

22 **Grammatik im Kontext**

Sprechen Sag deinen Klassenkameraden,
was du dieses Wochenende machen
kannst. Sag ihnen danach, was du nicht
machen kannst und warum das nicht geht.
Gebrauche das Beispiel unten. Beachte die
Wortstellung *(word order)* nach der
Konjunktion **weil**.

BEISPIEL

Du Am Wochenende kann ich
ins Kino gehen.
Am Wochenende kann ich
nicht ins Konzert gehen,
weil ich keine Zeit habe.

Am Wochenende

Ein wenig Grammatik

**The conjunctions denn
and weil**

Denn and **weil** are called *conjunctions.*
Using them will help your German sound
more natural. Both words begin clauses that
give reasons for something (for example,
why you can or can't do something).
Clauses beginning with **denn** have the regular word order pattern, that is, the conjugated verb is in second position. However, in
clauses that begin with **weil**, the conjugated
verb is in final position.

Ich gehe nicht ins Kino, **denn** ich **habe**
kein Geld.
Ich gehe nicht ins Kino, **weil** ich kein Geld
habe.

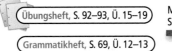

Übungsheft, S. 92–93, Ü. 15–19

Grammatikheft, S. 69, Ü. 12–13

Mehr Grammatikübungen,
S. 238, Ü. 8

Was?	**Warum?**
Baseball spielen	ich habe keine Zeit
ins Kino gehen	ich habe kein Geld
tanzen gehen	ich muss zu Hause helfen
Klamotten kaufen	ich mähe den Rasen
wandern	ich putze die Fenster
ins Café gehen	ich lerne für die
Freunde besuchen **weil**	(Mathe)prüfung
Volleyball spielen	ich mache Hausaufgaben
Pizza essen	die Großeltern besuchen uns
?	?

23 Grammatik im Kontext

Schreiben/Sprechen Look at the following statements. Agree or disagree and give a reason why. First write your answers, then discuss your opinions with your classmates.

> **BEISPIEL** Ich bin damit einverstanden, weil/denn …
> Ich bin nicht damit einverstanden, weil/denn …

1. Jugendliche sollen das ganze Jahr in die Schule gehen.
2. Jugendliche sollen nicht Auto fahren, bevor sie 18 sind.
3. Wir sollen mehr Geld für die Umwelt (*environment*) ausgeben.
4. Jugendliche müssen vor 10 Uhr abends zu Hause sein.

So sagt man das!

Saying where you were and what you bought

If a friend wants to find out where you were or what you bought, he or she might ask:

Wo warst du heute Morgen?

You might respond:

Zuerst war ich beim Bäcker und dann beim Metzger. Danach war ich im Supermarkt und zuletzt war ich im Kaufhaus.

Und was hast du beim Bäcker gekauft?
Wo warst du gestern?

Ich habe Brot gekauft.
Ich war zu Hause.

What do the phrases **ich war** and **du warst** mean? What are their English equivalents? What other words or expressions in these sentences indicate the past?

Grammatikheft, S. 70, Ü. 14–15

Wortschatz

gestern *yesterday*
vorgestern *day before yesterday*
gestern Abend *yesterday evening*

heute Morgen *this morning*
heute Nachmittag *this afternoon*
letztes Wochenende *last weekend*

Grammatik

The past tense of sein

War and **warst** are past tense forms of the verb **sein** (*to be*) and are used to talk about events in the past.

Wo **warst** du denn?   Ich **war** beim Bäcker.

Here are the past tense forms of **sein**:

ich	**war**	wir	**waren**
du	**warst**	ihr	**wart**
er, sie, es	**war**	sie, Sie	**waren**

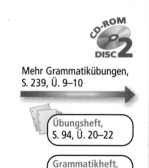

Mehr Grammatikübungen, S. 239, Ü. 9–10

Übungsheft, S. 94, Ü. 20–22

Grammatikheft, S. 71–72, Ü. 16–18

24 **Grammatik im Kontext**

 Zuhören Listen to the following exchanges as Claudia talks with her friends. For each conversation, decide if the person Claudia is talking to has already done the activity mentioned or plans to do it in the future.

	already done	plans to do
1		
2		

25 **Grammatik im Kontext**

Sprechen Look at the pages out of Mara's and Flori's lists of things to do. Your partner will ask you where Flori was during the day. Use his schedule to answer your partner's questions. Then switch roles and ask your partner about Mara's day. Remember to use **zuerst, dann, danach,** and **zuletzt** to organize your answers.

> *Mara*
> 10:00 Supermarkt für Mutti
> 12:00 mit Markus im Café essen
> 13:00 ins Einkaufszentrum gehen, Klamotten kaufen
> 14:30 Zimmer aufräumen

> *Flori*
> 9:30 Brot und Äpfel für die Omi kaufen
> 13:00 zu Hause Mittag essen
> 13:30 Omis Fenster putzen
> 15:00 Kaufhaus, Fußball kaufen

26 **Grammatik im Kontext**

Schreiben Claudia hat viele Pläne. Aber sie kann ihre Freunde nicht erreichen *(contact)*.

a. Schreib die vier Dialoge ab und setze dabei die richtige Vergangenheitsform *(past tense form)* von **sein** in die Lücken.

b. Welches Bild passt zu welchem Dialog?

a.

b.

c.

d.

1. CLAUDIA Sag mal, Petra, wo ===== du denn heute Morgen?

   PETRA Ich ===== in der Stadt. Zuerst ===== ich beim Bäcker, dann im Obstladen. Heute Abend essen meine Tante und mein Onkel bei uns.

2. CLAUDIA Und wo ===== denn die Michaela? Weißt du das? Sie ===== auch nicht zu Hause.

   PETRA Na, sie ===== im Eiscafé mit Gabi und Susanne. Die drei essen immer nur Joghurteis! Ingo hat sie später in der Disko gesehen.

3. CLAUDIA Tag, Oma! Wo ===== du denn heute Morgen? Ich bin vorbeigekommen, und du ===== nicht da.

   OMA Die Tante Dorle ===== da, und wir haben im Café am Markt zu Mittag gegessen. Ach, Kind, das Essen ===== köstlich!

4. CLAUDIA Hallo, ihr zwei! Wo ===== ihr am Samstagabend?

   HEIKE Robert und ich, wir ===== im Kino — im neuen Cinedom. Mensch, das ===== echt toll! Wir haben den Film *Metro* gesehen. Unheimlich spannend!

27 Einkaufsbummel

Sprechen Your partner just got back from shopping on a rainy Saturday. Your partner will decide on three items that he or she bought at each of the stores pictured. Ask your partner what he or she bought at each store. Switch roles, and be prepared to tell the class about your **Einkaufsbummel.**

Sometimes you don't know the exact word for something even in your own language. One way you can get your message across is by describing what you can't remember. Use a phrase like **Es ist etwas …** and then tell what it does, how it's used, or where it is. As practice, look around your classroom and pick three things you don't know how to say in German. How could you describe them so a German speaker would understand? Test your skills on a classmate! Look at these two drawings. Can you describe these items to a friend?

28 Von der Schule zum Beruf

Schreiben You have advanced to the position of store manager at a large food chain. Your job is to work with the marketing department, creating colorful and descriptive flyers that advertise the specials of the week for your various departments, such as produce, bakery, milk, cheese, etc.

AUSSPRACHE

Richtig aussprechen / Richtig lesen

A. To practice or review the following sounds, say the words and sentences below after your teacher or after the recording.

1. The letters **ü** and **ö**: In **Kapitel 1** you learned how to pronounce the letters **ü** and **ö** as long vowels, as in **Grüß** and **Österreich.** However, when the letters **ü** and **ö** are followed by two or more consonants, they are pronounced as short vowels.

   müssen, Stück, Würste / Wir müssen fünf Stück Kuchen holen.
   können, köstlich, Wörterbuch / Könnt ihr für mich ein Wörterbuch kaufen?

2. The letter combinations **ei** and **ie**: The letter combination **ei** is pronounced like the *i* in the English word *mine*. The combination **ie** is pronounced like the *e* in the English word *me*.

   Bäckerei, Eier, Fleisch / Kauf das Fleisch in der Metzgerei!
   wieder, wie viel, lieber / Wie viel bekommen Sie? Vier Stück?

3. The letter **z**: In **Kapitel 2** you learned that the letter **z** is always pronounced like the *ts* sound in the English word *hits*, although in German, this sound often occurs at the beginning of a word.

   Zeit, zahlen, ziehen / Ich habe keine Zeit, in den Zoo zu gehen.

Richtig schreiben / Diktat

B. Write down the sentences that you hear.

Zum Lesen

Richtig essen!

1. Before you read these ads, think about what foods you like to eat. Which of the food items you eat on a regular basis are really good for you?

2. Compare your weekly diet to a partner's and try to figure out together what percentage of your diet is carbohydrate, fat, and protein.

3. Look at the illustrations in the ads, then try to figure out the meaning of the boldfaced titles and subtitles. Judging from what you learned from these two sources, what do you think these ads are about?

   a. snack foods

   b. healthful foods

   c. ways to make sandwiches

4. You have figured out the general topic of these articles. Now skim the ads to get the gist. What information are these ads trying to get across to you?

Das Thema im Juli:

Die herzhaften Fünf – Original Mühlbacher Bauernbrote

Nur wenige Brote verdienen den Namen Bauernbrot. Was darf rein, was nicht? Der bekannte Ernährungsexperte und Fernsehkoch Armin Roßmeier sagt Ihnen alles, was Sie schon immer über Brot wissen wollten: Rufen Sie ihn an. Jeden ersten Mittwoch im Monat: 7. Juli, 4. August, 1. September

Das haben Sie jetzt davon.

Alle wollen Leerdammer, nur:

Manche mögen's leicht. Na gut.

Dann nehmen manche jetzt eben den

Leerdammer Light. Und wer's nicht

leicht nimmt, läßt sich den

Leerdammer so schmecken wie bisher.

GOURMETS GENIESSEN PUR.

Der Leichte
Almenrausch
WEICHKÄSE
NEU
150 g e · Fettstufe · Nur 20% Fett

SAHNIGER GESCHMACK
AUF DIE LEICHTE ART.

Der Leichte Almenrausch. Eine Weichkäse-Spezialität mit dem sahnig-milden Geschmack, den Gourmets noch pur zu genießen verstehen. Almenrausch gibt es auch extrasahnig als de Luxe und mit feinem Knoblauch.

GUTER GESCHMACK AUS TRADITION.

Der Mensch ist, wie er ißt.

Körperliche Fitness und Leistungsvermögen beruhen in erster Linie auf einer ausgewogenen Ernährung. Das gilt für den Spitzensport ebenso wie für den alltäglichen Lebens-„Marathon".

Wir alle benötigen bestimmte Mengen an Kohlehydraten, Proteinen, Vitaminen und Mineralstoffen, um gesund und in Form zu bleiben.

Wichtigste Voraussetzung für Leistungsvermögen und körperliche Fitness ist die richtige Kombination der drei Hauptnahrungsgruppen.

Als Faustregel für den Wochendurchschnitt gilt: 50% Kohlehydrate, 30% Fett und 20% Eiweiß sind ideal für 100%iges Wohlbefinden.

Auf das Frühstück kommt es an.

Besonders wichtig ist es, wie Sie den Tag beginnen: Das „richtige" Frühstück ist die wichtigste Mahlzeit des Tages. Dafür serviert Ihnen Müller-Brot auf den folgenden Seiten wertvolle Tips: Gesunden Appetit!

Beispielhafte Fitmacher für den Start in den Tag:

Die Vollkorn-Spezialitäten von Müller-Brot – Fitness, die man essen kann.

---

5. Based on your knowledge of German, match these compound words with the most logical English equivalent.

> **Weißt du noch?** Remember that knowing the meaning of root words can help you guess the meaning of many compound words.

1. Mahlzeit	**a.** daily
2. Fernsehkoch	**b.** soft cheese
3. alltäglich	**c.** whole-grain bread
4. Ernährungs-experte	**d.** television chef
5. Vollkornbrot	**e.** meal
6. der Weichkäse	**f.** nutrition expert

6. Read the ad for **Vollkornbrot**. Which word in the ad means "well-being"? According to the ad, in order to have 100% physical well-being, what is the percentage of carbohydrates you should eat on the average in a week? What is the percentage of fat? And what is the percentage of protein?

7. According to the ad, what is the most important meal of the day?

8. What is the name of the person who has the hotline? When can you call him? What kind of information would he give you?

9. Scan the articles for the following information.

   a. Who can enjoy **Almenrausch** soft cheese?

   b. What kind of **Leerdammer** do some people want to eat?

   c. What company advertises itself as a whole-grain specialist?

10. You are an exchange student in Germany. You and your friends are opening up a student-run snack stand at school, and you plan to have plenty of healthful snacks. Write an article for the school newspaper describing the foods you will offer at your stand.

Übungsheft, S. 95, Ü. 23

Mehr Grammatikübungen

CD-ROM
DISC 2

☑ internet

go.
hrw
.com

ADRESSE: go.hrw.com
KENNWORT:
WK3 MUENCHEN-8

Erste Stufe   **Objectives** Asking what you should do; telling someone what to do

1 Du und deine Freunde, ihr wollt zu Hause helfen. Ihr fragt, was jeder *(everyone)* tun soll. Setze die richtige Form von **sollen** ein. **(S. 223)**

1. Omi, _____ ich für dich zum Supermarkt gehen?
2. Was _____ wir für euch tun, Mara und Flori?
3. Wer _____ für die Mutti zum Metzger gehen?
4. Du _____ nach der Schule nach Hause gehen.
5. Ich sage euch, ihr _____ mit dem Bus zur Schule fahren.
6. Was _____ die Schüler nach der Schule tun?
7. Wir _____ zum Bäcker gehen und Brot kaufen.
8. Was _____ der Flori für die Omi tun? Zum Supermarkt gehen?

2 Jeder soll etwas tun. Setze die richtige Form von **sollen** in die erste Lücke und eine passende Verbform in die zweite und dritte Lücke. **(S. 223)**

1. Der Flori _____ für mich zum Metzger _____ und Wurst _____ .
2. Du _____ für die Omi zum Bäcker _____ und Brot _____ .
3. Ihr _____ für Vati den Rasen _____ und den Müll _____ .
4. Mara _____ für mich einkaufen _____ , etwas Obst _____ .
5. Wir _____ nach Hause _____ , die Hausaufgaben _____ .
6. Wohin _____ ich _____ ? Was _____ ich für dich _____ ?

3 Du und deine Freunde, ihr fragt deine Mutter, wo ihr die Lebensmittel kaufen sollt, die *(that)* sie braucht. Schreib die folgenden Sätze ab und schreib die richtige Verbform von **sollen** in die erste Lücke und die richtige Form des bestimmten Artikels *(definite article)* in die zweite und dritte Lücke. **(S. 223)**

BEISPIEL   Wo _____ wir denn _____ Limo und _____ Kuchen kaufen?
Wo **sollen** wir denn **die** Limo und **den** Kuchen kaufen?

1. Wo _____ ich denn _____ Aufschnitt und _____ Hähnchen kaufen?
2. Wo _____ wir denn _____ Hackfleisch und _____ Wurst kaufen?
3. Wo _____ Flori denn _____ Salat und _____ Tomaten kaufen?
4. Wo _____ du denn _____ Zucker und _____ Kaffee kaufen?
5. Wo _____ ihr denn _____ Milch und _____ Käse kaufen?
6. Wo _____ Claudia denn _____ Fisch und _____ Gemüse kaufen?
7. Wo _____ Vati denn _____ Eier und _____ Mehl kaufen?
8. Wo _____ ich denn _____ Obst und _____ Kartoffeln kaufen?

4 Was sollst du tun? Was sollen deine Freunde tun? Beantworte die folgenden Fragen und gebrauche dabei den **du**-Imperativ. (S. 224)

1. Soll ich das Brot beim Bäcker kaufen? — Ja, _____ das Brot beim Bäcker!
2. Wo soll Flori die Milch holen? — Flori, _____ die Milch im Supermarkt!
3. Soll ich zum Metzger gehen? — Klar, _____ zum Metzger!
4. Soll ich jetzt den Tisch decken? — Ja, _____ jetzt den Tisch!
5. Wann soll ich die Kartoffeln kochen? — Du, _____ sie heute Abend!
6. Soll ich jetzt den Müll sortieren? — Ja, _____ jetzt den Müll!
7. Wann soll ich die Fenster putzen? — Ach, _____ die Fenster morgen!

5 Flori und seine Freunde wollen für seine Mutter einkaufen gehen. Floris Mutter sagt ihnen, wo sie die Lebensmittel kaufen sollen. Beginn jede Antwort mit einem Imperativ. Benutze das richtige Pronomen in der Antwort. (S. 224)

BEISPIEL **Wo soll ich die Butter kaufen? Im Supermarkt?**
<u>**Ja, kauf sie doch im Supermarkt!**</u>
Wo sollen wir das Eis kaufen? Im Eiscafé?
<u>**Ja, kauft es doch im Eiscafé!**</u>

1. Wo soll ich den Fisch kaufen? Im Fischladen?
2. Wo sollen wir das Obst kaufen? Im Obstladen?
3. Wo soll ich die Kartoffeln holen? Auf dem Markt?
4. Wo sollen wir den Salat kaufen? Im Gemüseladen?
5. Wo soll ich das Brot kaufen? Beim Bäcker?
6. Wo sollen wir den Käse kaufen? Im Supermarkt?
7. Wo soll ich die Milch kaufen? Im Milchladen?
8. Wo sollen wir das Fleisch kaufen? Beim Metzger?

Zweite Stufe

Objectives Talking about quantities; saying that you want something else

6 Was weißt du über Kilo, Pfund, Gramm und Liter? Beantworte die folgenden Fragen. Schreib einen ganzen Satz für Fragen 1 - 5. Achte darauf, dass Kilo, Pfund, Gramm und Liter in Sätzen wie diesen keine Pluralform haben. (S. 226)

1. Wie viel Gramm hat ein Kilo?
2. Wie viel Pfund hat ein Kilo?
3. Wie viel Gramm hat ein halbes Pfund?
4. Wie viel Gramm hat ein amerikanisches Pfund?
5. Was ist mehr Wasser, ein Liter oder ein Quart?
6. Was sind die Abkürzungen für:
   a. Kilogramm? _____
   b. Pfund? _____
   c. Gramm? _____
   d. Liter? _____

7 Du bist in einem Laden und kaufst ein. Schau auf die Einkaufsliste und schreib auf, was du kaufen willst. Vervollständige *(complete)* die Sätze und schreib dabei in die Lücke, was und wie viel du kaufen willst. **(S. 226)**

1. (2 lbs. of apples)   Ich bekomme _____ .
2. (500 grams of butter)   Ich möchte _____ .
3. (1 lb. of tomatoes)   Ich brauche _____ .
4. (100 grams of cheese)   Ich bekomme noch _____ .
5. (1 liter of milk)   Ich möchte _____ .
6. (2 liters of mineral water) Ich bekomme _____ .

Dritte Stufe

Objectives Giving reasons; saying where you were and what you bought

8 Warum kannst du das nicht tun? Schreib die folgenden Sätze zweimal um. Der Nebensatz *(clause)* soll einmal mit **denn** beginnen und einmal mit **weil**. Achte auf die Stellung des Verbs. **(S. 230)**

BEISPIEL   **Ich esse das Eis nicht. Es ist zu kalt.**
    a. Ich esse das Eis nicht, *denn* es **ist** zu kalt.
    b. Ich esse das Eis nicht, *weil* es zu kalt **ist**.

1. Ich kann nicht ins Café gehen. Ich habe keine Zeit.
2. Ich kann nicht ins Kino gehen. Ich habe kein Geld.
3. Flori geht zum Bäcker. Er muss Brot kaufen.
4. Mara geht zum Metzger. Sie muss Fleisch kaufen.
5. Jens möchte die Trauben. Sie sind so gut.
6. Wir essen viel Fisch. Er ist so lecker.

9 Du fragst deine Klassenkameraden, wo sie waren. Beantworte die folgenden Fragen mit der Antwort in Klammern. **(S. 231)**

1. Wo warst du heute Morgen? (in der Stadt)   Ich _____ .
2. Wo war Flori? (im Supermarkt)   Er _____ .
3. Wo waren die Schüler? (in der Schule)   Sie _____ .
4. Wo war ich? (zu Hause)   Du _____ .
5. Wo waren wir gestern? (im Kino)   Ihr _____ .
6. Wo wart ihr? (beim Bäcker)   Wir _____ .

10 Lies das folgende Telefongespräch. Schreib es ab und setze die Vergangenheit (*past tense*) von **sein** in die Lücken. **(S. 231)**

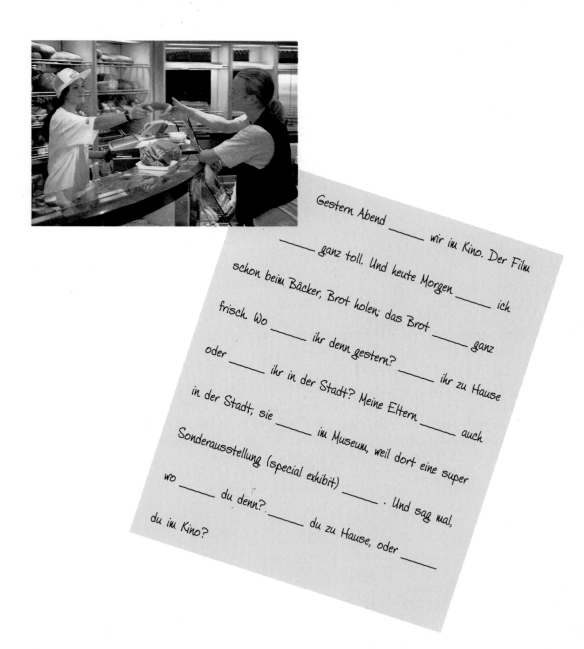

Gestern Abend _____ wir im Kino. Der Film _____ ganz toll. Und heute Morgen _____ ich schon beim Bäcker, Brot holen; das Brot _____ ganz frisch. Wo _____ ihr denn gestern? _____ ihr zu Hause oder _____ ihr in der Stadt? Meine Eltern _____ auch in der Stadt; sie _____ im Museum, weil dort eine super Sonderausstellung (special exhibit) _____ . Und sag mal, wo _____ du denn? _____ du zu Hause, oder _____ du im Kino?

Anwendung

 CD-ROM DISC 2

internet
go.hrw.com
ADRESSE: go.hrw.com
KENNWORT:
WK3 MUENCHEN-8

1 Flori's mother would like him to go shopping for her. Listen as she tells him what to get, and make a shopping list for Flori. Be sure to include the amounts she needs.

2 You and a friend are about to go grocery shopping. You have only 12 euros and want to get the most for your money. **Kaufmarkt** always has great daily specials. Look at the ads on the right and tell your partner eight things you want to buy and how much of each you are buying. Your partner will make a list and add up the cost for you. When finished, switch roles.

Fleisch

Schweine-Kotelett
zart 1kg **3,24**

Schweinebraten
ohne Knochen,
mit Kruste 1kg **2,49**

Schweine-Schulter
wie gewachsen 1kg **1,49**

Schweine-Halsgrat
saftig 1kg **3,74**

Schweine-Brustspitzen
frisch 1kg **2,98**

Hals-Steaks
vom Schwein 1kg **4,99**

Sur-Hax'n
mild gesalzen 1kg **1,98**

Holzfällersteak
gewürzt 1kg **2,98**

Konditorei

Erdbeerkuchen
mit frischen
Früchten Stück **1,25**

Gemischter
Obstkuchen
auf zartem
Wiener Biskuit Stück **1,10**

Himbeerkuchen
mit Mandeln nach
Hausfrauenart Stück **0,95**

Bamberger
Butterhörnchen
mit reiner Butter
gebacken Stück **0,45**

Schwäbischer
Käsekuchen
mit bestem Konditorquark
und mit Sahne verfeinert
Stück **0,95**

Fleisch

Schweinswürstel
frisch 100g **0,54**

Wollwurst 100g **0,49**

Kalbsbratwürstl
gebrüht 100g **0,59**

Kalbsbrust 1kg **4,98**

Kalbsrücken
(Lende ohne
Knochen) 1kg **16,45**

Frische
Putenschnitzel
1kg **4,98**

Neuseeland
Hirschkalb-Steak
frisch,
Spitzenqualität 1kg **14,98**

Lammsteak
gefr. 1kg **5,98**

3 Could you convince someone to buy a specific product? Bring in pictures of several food or clothing items from a magazine, or use props, and create a commercial to convince your classmates to buy one or more of the products. Use statements with **denn** and **weil** to persuade them. Then present your commercial to the class.

4 You and two of your friends work with a local organization that helps elderly people around the house. Your team has been assigned three people to help. The team leader goes over each list with each volunteer and tells him or her what to do. Switch roles, so that each person on the team is the leader once.

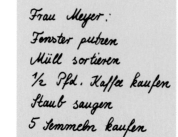

Frau Meyer:
Fenster putzen
Müll sortieren
½ Pfd. Kaffee kaufen
Staub saugen
5 Semmeln kaufen
375 g Wurst kaufen

Herr Schmidt:
Wohnzimmer aufräumen
500 g Aufschnitt kaufen
250 g Butter kaufen
Müll sortieren
400 g Hackfleisch holen

Frau Heppner:
Blumen gießen
1 Kilo Kartoffeln kaufen
Staub saugen
Fisch holen
Rasen mähen
1 Pfd. Tomaten kaufen

5 Zum Schreiben

Do you and your classmates have good nutrition habits? Take a nutrition survey of your classmates using the **"Six-W questions"** - **"Wer? Was? Wann? Wo? Warum?** and **Wie?"** to find out.

Schreibtipp

Have you thought about how reporters collect information for their news stories? They often use the **"Five-W How?" questions:** Who? What? Where? When? Why? How? Remember though, not every question applies to every topic, and sometimes you can think of more than one good question for a question word. For example, you can ask: "What do you eat for breakfast?" or "What happens if you don't eat breakfast?"

Prewriting

First, decide which questions best fit the information you would like to gather about the food habits of the group with which you are working. You might choose to ask about buying food, about preparing food, or about food habits.

Writing

Write your survey questions in complete sentences. Choose a category of questions and ask 10 questions from this category. Ex: Where do you buy your food? when? how? (cash, credit card, check), or "Who shows up for dinner in your family? What meals does your family prefer?" Compile your answers (ex: six students eat dinner at 6 p.m.; 4 eat at 7 p.m.) and present to your group or class.

6 Rollenspiel

Get together with a classmate and role-play the following scenes.

OBSTSALAT

1 Apfel, 2 Bananen, 1 Birne,

1 Kiwi, 150 g Trauben (blau),

1 Orange, 2 EL Zitronensaft,

3 EL Honig, 2 EL Rosinen,

2 EL Walnusskerne, gehackt

Zubereitung: 20 Minuten

185 Kalorien

a. You and a friend are preparing lunch. Read the recipe for **Obstsalat** and tell your friend what you need, where to get it, and how much you need based on the recipe. Your friend will make a shopping list.

b. With your list in hand, go to the store to get what you need. Your partner plays the salesperson and will ask what you need, how much, and if you need anything else.

Can you ask someone what you should do using sollen?
(p. 222)

1 How would you ask someone what you should do for him or her? How might he or she answer using the following items?
   a. bread: at the baker's
   b. ground meat: at the butcher's
   c. milk: at the supermarket
   d. apples: at the produce store

Can you tell someone what to do using a du-command?
(p. 223)

2 How would you tell someone where to buy the food items above?

3 How would you tell a friend to
   a. mow the lawn
   b. buy 500 grams of tomatoes
   c. clean the room
   d. get 6 apples

Can you ask for specific quantities?
(p. 226)

4 How would you tell a salesperson you need the following things?
   a. 500 Gramm Hackfleisch
   b. Brot
   c. 1 Liter Milch
   d. 1 Pfd. Tomaten
   e. 2 Kilo Kartoffeln

Can you say that you want something else?
(p. 227)

5 How would a salesperson ask you if you wanted something else? How would you respond using the following items?
   a. 10 Semmeln   **b.** 100 Gramm Aufschnitt   **c.** 200 Gramm Käse

Can you give reasons using denn and weil? (p. 230)

6 How would you say that you can't do each of the following and give a reason why not?
   a. go to a movie   **b.** go shopping   **c.** go to a café

Can you say where you were (using sein) and what you bought?
(p. 231)

7 How would you ask someone where he or she was yesterday? How would you ask two friends? Can you say where you were using the following cues?
   a. at the baker's in the morning
   b. at the supermarket yesterday
   c. at the butcher's yesterday morning
   d. at home this afternoon

8 How would you ask your friend what he or she bought? How would you say that you bought the following items?
   a. bread
   b. a shirt
   c. a sweater
   d. cheese
   e. pants

Erste Stufe

Asking what you should do; telling someone what to do

sollen	should, to be supposed to	das Hackfleisch	ground meat (mixture of beef and pork)	der Salat, -e	lettuce
				der Supermarkt, ⸚e	supermarket
einkaufen gehen	to go shopping	die Wurst, ⸚e	sausage	im Supermarkt	at the supermarket
einkaufen (sep)	to shop	der Aufschnitt	cold cuts	die Milch	milk
holen	to get, fetch	das Hähnchen,-	chicken	die Butter	butter
der Laden, ⸚	store	der Obst- und	fresh produce store	der Käse	cheese
die Lebensmittel (pl)	groceries	Gemüseladen, ⸚		das Ei, -er	egg
die Bäckerei, -en	bakery	im Obst- und	at the produce	der Kaffee	coffee
beim Bäcker	at the baker's	Gemüseladen	store	der Zucker	sugar
das Brot, -e	bread	das Obst	fruit	das Mehl	flour
die Semmel, -n*	roll	die Traube, -n	grape	der Fisch, -e	fish
die Brezel, -n	pretzel	der Apfel, ⸚	apple		
die Torte, -n	layer cake	das Gemüse	vegetables	**Other Useful Words**	
die Metzgerei, -en	butcher shop	die Kartoffel, -n	potato	besser	better
beim Metzger	at the butcher's	die Tomate, -n	tomato	frisch	fresh
das Fleisch	meat				

(handwritten note in left margin: das Brötchen)

Zweite Stufe

Talking about quantities

				Saying you want something else	
Wie viel?	How much?	der Liter	liter	Sonst noch etwas?	Anything else?
wiegen	to weigh	ein bisschen mehr	a little more	Haben Sie noch	Would you like
das Pfund	pound	ungefähr	approximately	einen Wunsch?	anything else?
das Gramm	gram			Ich brauche noch …	I also need …
das Kilo	kilogram			Das ist alles.	That's all.

Dritte Stufe

Giving reasons

denn	because, for	Was hast du gekauft?	What did you buy?	vorgestern	day before yesterday
weil	because	Ich habe Brot gekauft.	I bought bread.	letztes Wochenende	last weekend
				letzte Woche	last week

Saying where you were and what you bought

Time expressions

war	was (see p. 231)	heute Morgen	this morning
Wo warst du?	Where were you?	heute Nachmittag	this afternoon
Ich war beim Bäcker.	I was at the baker's. I went to the bakery.	gestern	yesterday
		gestern Abend	yesterday evening

*In northern Germany these are called **Brötchen,** and in Baden-Württemberg and in other areas in southern Germany they are called **Wecken.**

Objectives

In this chapter you will learn to

Erste Stufe

- talk about where something is located

Zweite Stufe

- ask for and give directions

Dritte Stufe

- talk about what there is to eat and drink
- say you do or don't want more
- express opinions

 internet

ADRESSE: go.hrw.com
KENNWORT:
  WK3 MUENCHEN-9

◀ **Im Zentrum von München**

Los geht's! · *München besuchen*

VIDEO

Strategie Verstehen
Look at the images for this story. Who are the people? What are they doing? Where are they? What do you think they are talking about? What do you suppose will happen in the story?

Amerikaner   **Markus**   **Mara**

1

Mara:	Die Säfte hier sind doch wirklich Spitze!
Markus:	Ja, und vor allem gesund!

2

Amerikaner:	Entschuldigung!
Markus:	Ja?
Amerikaner:	Wie kommen wir zum Marienplatz?
Markus:	Ganz einfach! Immer geradeaus bis zur Ampel und dann nach rechts.

3

Mara:	Das stimmt doch gar nicht! An der Ampel nach links!
Markus:	Klar, nach links! Dann kommt ihr direkt zum Marienplatz.
Amerikaner:	Ah, vielen Dank!
Markus:	Bitte, gern geschehen.

4

Mara:	Ihr seid Amerikaner, nicht?
Amerikaner:	Ja, wir sind aus Wisconsin.
Mara:	Wirklich? Was macht ihr hier?
Amerikaner:	Ja …wir wohnen in Rosenheim, und heute besuchen wir München.

5 **Mara:** Prima! Na dann, viel Spaß!

6 **Markus:** Noch einen Saft?
Mara: Nein, danke! Keinen Saft mehr.

Später

7 **Mara:** Schau, da kommen die Amerikaner.
Markus: Hallo, Wisconsin! Wohin geht's?
Amerikaner: Was esst ihr hier?
Mara: Schau, hier gibt's Bratwurst, Weißwurst, Leberkäs …
Markus: Der Leberkäs ist hier echt gut.
Amerikaner: Was ist Leber …Leberkäs?
Markus: Eine bayrische Spezialität. Die musst du mal probieren!

8 **Markus:** So, schmeckt's?
Amerikaner: Wirklich gut.

9 **Markus:** Ich ess jetzt noch eine Bratwurst. Wer möchte auch noch etwas? Noch einen Leberkäs?
Amerikaner: Nein, danke! Ich habe genug.

10 **Mara:** Weißt du was, Markus? Wir zeigen den Amerikanern jetzt die Stadt. Was meint ihr?
Amerikaner: Gute Idee!

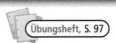
Übungsheft, S. 97

1 Was passiert hier?

Verstehst du die Gespräche in „München besuchen"? Versuche, die folgenden Fragen zu beantworten.

1. Where are Mara and Markus at the beginning of the story? What are they doing?
2. Who approaches Mara and Markus? What kind of information do these people need?
3. What does Markus recommend to eat? Why do you think he recommends this?
4. What do Markus and Mara decide to do at the end of the story?

2 Genauer lesen

Lies die Gespräche noch einmal. Welche Wörter gebraucht man, um:

1. to start conversations or get someone's attention
2. to end conversations
3. to name foods and drinks
4. to ask for and give directions
5. to ask if someone would like more of something

3 Stimmt oder stimmt nicht?

Sind die folgenden Aussagen richtig oder falsch? Sag „stimmt", wenn sie richtig sind, sag „stimmt nicht", wenn sie falsch sind. Gib die richtige Antwort für jede falsche Aussage.

1. Zuerst trinken Markus und Mara Kaffee.
2. Der Amerikaner möchte zum Marienplatz gehen.
3. Mara und Markus besuchen Amerika.
4. Dann wollen der Amerikaner und seine Freunde etwas essen, denn sie haben Hunger.
5. Aber Markus isst Leberkäs nicht gern.
6. Leberkäs ist eine bayrische Spezialität.
7. Dann wollen Markus und Mara den Amerikanern die Stadt München zeigen.

4 Was passt zusammen?

Welche Aussagen in der rechten Spalte (column) passen zu den Fragen in der linken Spalte?

1. Wie kommen wir zum Marienplatz?
2. Vielen Dank!
3. Was macht ihr hier?
4. Was esst ihr hier?
5. Isst du noch eine Bratwurst?
6. Schmeckt's?

a. Wir besuchen die Stadt München.
b. Gern geschehen!
c. Ihr müsst an der Ampel nach links.
d. Ja, wirklich gut!
e. Hier gibt's Leberkäs und Weißwurst.
f. Nein, danke! Ich habe genug.

5 Nacherzählen

Put the sentences in a logical order to make a brief summary of **Los geht's!**

1. Am Saftstand trinken Mara und Markus einen Saft.

Dann probiert er den Leberkäs.

Später wollen der Junge und seine Freunde wissen, was Mara und Markus essen.

Er wohnt in Rosenheim und besucht heute München.

Danach zeigen Mara und Markus den Amerikanern München.

Ein Junge kommt vorbei und möchte wissen, wie er zum Marienplatz kommt.

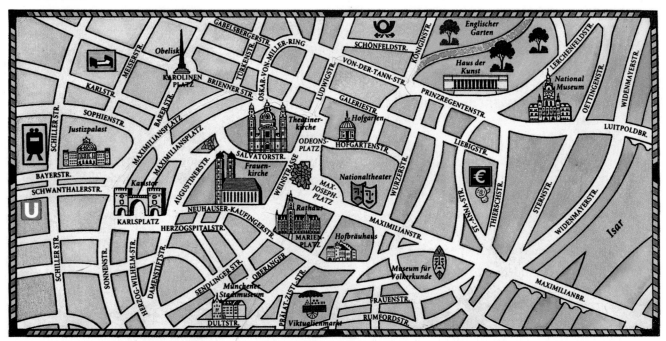

What kinds of places are pictured on this map of **München**? What do you think a **Kirche** is? And the **Rathaus**? How many museums can you find? And parks? Judging by the types of buildings on this map, what part of the city do you think this is?

Wortschatz

In der Innenstadt

Wo ist … ?

CD-ROM DISC 3

das Hotel   die Kirche   das Rathaus   der Marktplatz

die Bank   die Post   das Museum   der Bahnhof

das Theater   der Garten   die U-Bahnstation

Übungsheft, S. 98, Ü. 2–3   Grammatikheft, S. 73, Ü. 1–2

Ein wenig Landeskunde

Many cities in Germany were originally built around the **Marktplatz,** with the **Rathaus** and the main **Kirche** nearby. A wall surrounded the city and offered protection to the inhabitants. In a number of cities, parts of the original city wall are still standing around the **Innenstadt** (*downtown*). In many cities the main streets through downtown are closed to traffic and are designated as a **Fußgängerzone** (*pedestrian zone*).

Talking about where something is located

Grammatikheft,
S. 75, Ü. 5–6

If you are in a new city, you might need to ask where things are located.

You might ask a passerby:

> **Verzeihung! Wissen Sie, wo das Rathaus ist?**
> **Und wo ist das Karlstor?**
> **Entschuldigung! Weißt du, wo der Bahnhof ist?**
> **Und wo ist hier ein Café?**

You might get the responses:

> **In der Innenstadt am Marienplatz.**
> **In der Neuhauser Straße.**
> **Es tut mir Leid. Das weiß ich nicht.**
>
> **Keine Ahnung! Ich bin nicht von hier.**

What is the position of the second verb in questions that begin with **wissen** and **weißt**? Which expression might you use to ask someone older than yourself? To ask a person your own age? Which responses were probably made by someone who does not live in Munich?

6 Stimmt? oder Stimmt nicht?

Zuhören At the tourist information center in **München,** you overhear a conversation between an American tourist and someone who doesn't know the city very well. Using the map on page 249, decide whether the information the tourist is given for each of the places listed below is correct or incorrect.

1. ein Hotel
2. die Post
3. eine Bank
4. eine U-Bahnstation
5. das Stadtmuseum
6. der Englische Garten
7. die Frauenkirche

The verb wissen

The verb **wissen** means *to know* (a fact, information, etc.). Here are the forms:

ich	**weiß**	wir	wissen
du	**weißt**	ihr	wisst
er, sie, es	**weiß**	sie, Sie	wissen

Mehr Grammatikübungen,
S. 264, Ü. 1–3

Übungsheft,
S. 99–100, Ü. 4–8

Grammatikheft,
S. 74, Ü. 3–4

Look at the sentences below.

> Wo ist das Museum?
> Weißt du, wo das Museum **ist**?

> Ich weiß nicht.
> Ich weiß nicht, wo das Museum **ist**.

What is the position of the verbs in the clauses introduced by **wo**? Used in this way, **wo** introduces a dependent clause. The verb is in final position.

7 Grammatik im Kontext

a. Sprechen Mara und ihre Familie fahren heute in die Innenstadt. Sie möchten sich viel ansehen, und sie müssen auch viel einkaufen *(to shop)*. Wissen sie, wo alles ist? Ergänze Maras Aussagen mit der richtigen Form von **wissen**!

b. Schreiben Schreib die Antworten!

BEISPIEL   **Mutti weiß, wo das Theater ist.**

1. Ich …   **2. Vater und ich …**   **3. Ali …**   **4. Du …**   **5. Ihr …**   **6. Leyla und Jasmin …**

8 Amerikaner treffen Engländer in München

Sprechen Eine amerikanische Schülergruppe hat sich in München verlaufen. Die Schüler fragen eine Gruppe von Leuten, aber das sind Touristen aus England und sie wissen auch nicht, wo sie sind. Schreibe ein Gespräch und benutze dabei die richtigen Verbformen von „wissen".

9 Entschuldigung! Wissen Sie, wo …?

Sprechen Du hast deinen Stadtplan verloren. Wie kannst du jetzt diese Sehenswürdigkeiten *(sights)* in München finden? Schau auf die Stadtkarte auf Seite 249 und such dir fünf Sehenswürdigkeiten aus. Setz dich jetzt mit zwei Klassenkameraden zusammen. Ein Partner ist ein Fußgänger, ungefähr 50 Jahre alt, der andere Partner eine junge Person in deinem Alter. Frag jetzt beide Partner nach den Orten, die du sehen möchtest. Tauscht dann die Rollen.

10 Wie sieht deine Stadt aus?

Schreiben Ein deutscher Austauschschüler möchte wissen, wo die Sehenswürdigkeiten in deinem Ort sind. Zeichne mit einer Klassenkameradin einen Stadtplan, der alle Sehenswürdigkeiten in deinem Ort zeigt. Wo kann der Austauschschüler etwas zum Anziehen oder zum Essen kaufen? Beschrifte *(label)* alle Straßen und wichtigen Sehenswürdigkeiten. Mehr Wörter findest du auf Seite R9.

LANDESKUNDE
LANDESKUNDE

Was isst du gern?

We asked some people in the German-speaking countries to tell us about what kinds of foods they like to eat. Before you read what they said, make a list of some of the things you would consider "German specialties."

CD-ROM
DISC 3

VIDEO

Übungsheft, S. 108, Ü. 24

Uli,
München

Würstchen

„Dafür lieb ich Würstchen, jeglicher Art, besonders die Berliner Currywürstchen, die es hier in München leider nicht so oft gibt. Ja und das ist so das, was ich gern esse."

Rosi,
Berlin

Kaiserschmarren

„Ach, ich esse auch gern Süßspeisen, also Kaiserschmarren als österreichisches [Gericht] oder Eierkuchen — ja, also eigentlich alles Mögliche!"

Melina,
Bietigheim   Schweineschnitzel

„Ich esse am liebsten so Eis, vor allem Erdbeereis oder so, mit Früchten drin. Und so…von Gerichten mag ich ja Schnitzel oder Linseneintopf. Ja, trinken mag ich eigentlich so mehr Cola oder so Apfelsaft."

Here are a few other German specialties.

Scholle, Hamburg

Maultaschen, Baden-Württemberg

A. 1. Write the people's names and list the German specialties each likes to eat. Are there any foods mentioned that are not German specialties?

2. Look at the list you made before reading and discuss the following questions with your classmates. Did your guesses differ from what the people said? If so, how? Where did you get your ideas about German specialties? What do you think people in German-speaking countries would name as American specialties? Where do you think they get their ideas?

B. Write a letter in German to one of the people interviewed telling her about the local specialties you like to eat. The person may not know what they are, so it might be a good idea to describe the foods in as much detail as you can.

11 Den Weg zeigen

Sprechen Hier ist ein Teil einer Karte von Mittersendling, einem Stadtteil in München. Beginne an der U-Bahnstation und folge den Richtungsangaben *(directions)* im Wortschatz. Wohin kommst du, wenn du diesen Richtungsangaben folgst?

Wortschatz

Gehen Sie ...

nach rechts	bis zum Krüner Platz	dann geradeaus	bis zur Ampel, dann nach rechts	dann die erste (zweite, dritte) Straße nach rechts
die nächste Straße nach links	bis zur Herrschinger Str.	und wieder nach rechts	dann geradeaus. Da ist ...	Grammatikheft, S. 76–77, Ü. 7–10

Stimmt die Richtung?

An American exchange student is trying to find the produce store, shopping center, and the bakery in Mittersendling. He is standing in front of the butcher's asking a passerby for directions. Listen to their conversation several times and determine whether the directions given will take him where he wants to go or not. If not, where do they lead him?

13 Du gehst nach links, dann nach ...

Zeig den Weg zu den folgenden Orten (*places*) in Mittersendling! Fang beim Hotel an! Tausche die Rolle mit deinen Klassenkameraden aus!

a. vom Hotel bis zur Post

b. von der Post bis zum Supermarkt

c. von der Bank bis zum Hotel

So sagt man das!

Asking for and giving directions

To find out where things are located, you will want to be able to ask for directions.

You might ask a passerby:

> **Verzeihung! Wie komme ich zum Hotel am Bahnhof?**
>
> **Und wie kommt man* zur Bäckerei?** **Entschuldigung! Wie kommen wir zum Einkaufszentrum?**
>
> **Und wie kommen wir zur U-Bahnstation?**

The responses might be:

> **Gehen Sie geradeaus bis zur Alpseestraße, dann nach links!**
>
> **Die nächste Straße nach rechts.** **Fahren Sie geradeaus bis zur Ampel, dann nach links!**
>
> **Sie fahren hier nach rechts, dann die zweite Straße wieder nach rechts.**

What do you think the words **zum** and **zur** mean?[1] Why is there a difference and what does it depend on?[2] In two of the responses, the verb is in first position. Can you figure out why?

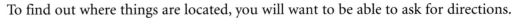
Übungsheft, S. 101–102, Ü. 9–11

---

1. *to the* 2. It depends on the noun that follows: masculine/neuter nouns > **zu dem (zum)**; feminine nouns > **zu der (zur)**.
*man means *one*, *you* (in general), *people*; it is used with the **er/sie**-form of the verb: **man geht, man fährt.**

Lesen/Sprechen Du stehst vor der Post in Mittersendling, und du musst heute noch viel erledigen. Du musst noch Semmeln kaufen, Geld umtauschen (du warst in den USA) und ein T-Shirt kaufen. Danach willst du deine Freunde im Jugendclub treffen. Schau dir den Stadtplan auf Seite 253 an, wähle zwei Orte aus und frag deinen Partner, wie du am besten dorthin kommst. Tauscht dann die Rollen.

zum Einkaufszentrum	zur Bank
zur Bäckerei	zum Jugendclub

Ein wenig Grammatik

In the **So sagt man das!** box on page 254, both **gehen** and **fahren** are used. How is **fahren** different in meaning from **gehen**? **Fahren** is used whenever someone is using a vehicle to go somewhere, such as **ein Auto, ein Bus,** or **ein Fahrrad. Fahren** has a stem-vowel change in the **du-** and **er/sie-** forms: **Du fährst mit dem Bus, und sie fährt mit dem Auto.** However, with **du-** commands, the umlaut is not used: **Fahr jetzt nach Hause!**

Übungsheft, S. 102, Ü. 12–13

Mehr Grammatikübungen, S. 265, Ü. 4

Grammatik

The formal commands with Sie

In **Kapitel 8** you learned how to use commands with people you know well: **Kauf ein Kilo Kartoffeln, bitte!** In this chapter you have seen how you would give a command to a person whom you do not know well and who is older than yourself. Look at the following sentences:

Fahren Sie nach links!   **Gehen Sie geradeaus!**

What do you notice about the word order in formal commands?[1] How would you give a command to someone your own age using **fahren** and **gehen**?[2] To two strangers older than yourself?[3]

Mehr Grammatikübungen, S. 265–266, Ü. 4–6

Übungsheft, S. 103, Ü. 14–15

Grammatikheft, S. 78, Ü. 11–12

15 **Grammatik im Kontext**

a. **Zuhören** At the information counter at the main train station in Munich, a friend of yours is asking how to get to the **Viktualienmarkt.** Listen to the directions given several times and jot down some notes as you listen.

b. **Lesen** Check your notes with the map on page 249. Did you understand the directions?

c. **Sprechen** Now use your notes to explain in your own words to another friend how he or she can get to the **Viktualienmarkt.**

16 **Grammatik im Kontext**

Schreiben Your parents are having a party for you. You decided to e-mail an invitation to a classmate and to one of your teachers, giving directions to your home. Write the directions by filling in the command forms of the verbs given in parentheses.

Hallo: (warten) ===== am Bahnhof auf einen Bus. (einsteigen) ===== in die # 3 =====, und (fahren) ===== bis zur Meisestraße. (aussteigen) ===== =====und (gehen) ===== immer geradeaus bis zur Ampel. An der Ampel (gehen) ===== rechts in die Drosselstraße. Unser Haus ist das dritte Haus rechts. (gehen) ===== nicht ins Haus, sondern (kommen) ===== gleich in den Garten. Hier ist die Party.

---

1. The verb is in first position and is followed by **Sie. 2. Fahr/Geh …! 3. Fahren/Gehen Sie …!**

17 Wohin?

Lesen Your friend wants you to see some famous places in Munich and has left behind a set of directions from the **Bahnhof** to somewhere in Munich. However, he forgot to tell you what you will see. Read his directions and use the map of Munich (page 249) to find out where they lead. Match the destination with one of the photos.

a.

b.

c.

> Also, du kommst aus dem Bahnhof, gehst über die Straße und dann in Richtung Karlsplatz. Du gehst durchs Karlstor, und hier kommst du in die Neuhauser und Kaufingerstraße. Die führen zum Marienplatz. Am Marienplatz musst du links in die Weinstraße einbiegen. Geh jetzt immer geradeaus, bis du zum Odeonsplatz kommst. Auf der linken Seite ist ein großes Gebäude. Da bin ich!

18 Also, fahren Sie ...

Sprechen Role-play the following situation with two classmates. One of you will be a German student at the **Rathaus** where several people ask you for directions. Another will be an American high school teacher sightseeing in Munich by car, and the third classmate will be a young student from Los Angeles on a bike. Each tourist will think of two places he or she wants to see in downtown **München** and will ask you for directions. Use the map on page 249 to help them. Then switch roles.

BEISPIEL Wie komme ich ...?

> zum Hofbräuhaus
> zum Haus der Kunst
> zum Münchner Stadtmuseum
> zum Karlstor
> zum Hofgarten
> zum Nationalmuseum
> zum Bahnhof
> zum Englischen Garten
> zur Theatinerkirche
> zum Nationaltheater
> zur Frauenkirche

19 Für mein Notizbuch

Schreiben Ein deutscher Austauschschüler möchte dich besuchen. Beschreib in deinem Notizbuch den Weg von deiner Schule bis zu deinem Haus! Fährst du mit dem Bus oder vielleicht mit der U-Bahn? Das kannst du auch beschreiben.

BEISPIEL Du gehst ... *oder*
Du fährst mit dem Bus/der U-Bahn Nummer ... bis ..., dann ...

So sagt man das!

Talking about what there is to eat and drink

If you go to a restaurant for the first time, you might ask your friend or a waiter what there is to eat or drink.

You might ask:

Was gibt es hier zu essen?

Und zu trinken?

The response might be:

Es gibt Leberkäs, Vollkornsemmeln, Weißwurst …
Cola, Apfelsaft und auch Mineralwasser.

What do you think the expressions **Was gibt es?** and **Es gibt …** mean?

Übungsheft, S. 104, Ü. 16–17

Ein wenig Grammatik

The phrase **es gibt** (*there is, there are*) is a fixed expression that stays the same despite the number of objects referred to. In the example **Gibt es hier in der Nähe einen Supermarkt?** is **Supermarkt** in the nominative or accusative case? How can you tell? What can you say about noun phrases following **es gibt**?[1]

Grammatikheft, S. 79, Ü. 13–14

Mehr Grammatikübungen, S. 266, Ü. 7

IMBIẞSTUBE am Rathaus

Leberkäs mit Senf	4,00	Brezel	1,00
mit Semmel	4,50	Käsebrot	3,20
Hähnchen vom Grill	6,00	Milch	2,00
Gyros	4,50	Mineralwasser	1,00
mit Salat	7,50	Apfelsaft	2,40
Weißwurst	3,80	Tee, Glas	2,50
Volkornsemmel	-,50		

 20 **Grammatik im Kontext**

a. Sprechen Du kannst dich nicht entscheiden (*to decide*), was du in der **Imbissstube am Rathaus** bestellen (*order*) möchtest. Frag deinen Partner, was es zu essen und zu trinken gibt! Sag deinem Partner, was du möchtest! Tauscht dann die Rollen aus!

b. Schreiben Was fehlt? Schreib es in die Lücken!

MARK   Was gibt ▭▭▭ hier zu essen?

SARA   Es ▭▭▭ …

MARK   Und was ▭▭▭ hier zu trinken?

SARA   ▭▭▭ Milch, Mineralwasser, und so.

Ein wenig Landeskunde

Leberkäs is a Bavarian specialty of ground beef or pork liver, pork, and spices. Most people eat it with a **Semmel** or **Brezel** and sweet mustard. How would you tell a German friend about specialties available in your area?

---

1. Noun phrases that follow **es gibt** are always in the accusative case.

Saying you do or don't want more

In **Kapitel 8** you learned how to ask if someone wants something else when shopping. When eating at a café or at your friend's house, you may also be asked what else you would like.

The host or your friend might ask:

> **Möchtest du noch etwas?**

> **Möchtest du noch einen Saft?**

> **Noch eine Semmel?**

You might respond:

> **Ja, bitte, ich nehme noch eine Brezel.** *or*
> **Nein, danke! Ich habe keinen Hunger mehr.** *or*
> **Nein, danke! Ich habe genug.** *or*
> **Danke, nichts mehr für mich.**
> **Ja, bitte. Noch einen Saft.** *or*
> **Nein, danke, keinen Saft mehr.**
> **Ja, gern!**

Übungsheft,
S. 105, Ü. 18

Grammatikheft,
S. 80, Ü. 15

What do you think the phrases **noch einen Saft** and **keinen Saft mehr** mean?[1] What subject and verb might be understood in the question **Noch eine Semmel?**[2]

---

21 **Wollt ihr noch etwas?**

Zuhören Markus is having a **Grillfest**. His friends have just finished eating, and he asks them if they want more. Listen to the conversations and decide what each person had to eat or drink. Then listen again and determine whether each person wanted more or not.

	Mara	Silvia	Thomas	Flori	Claudia	Frank
zu essen						
zu trinken						
noch mehr?						

22 **Logisch oder unlogisch?**

Lesen/Sprechen Sind die folgenden Aussagen logisch oder unlogisch? Wenn sie unlogisch sind, ändere die Aussagen, damit sie logisch sind!

1. Ja, bitte, ich möchte noch einen Leberkäs. Ich habe keinen Hunger.
2. Nein, danke! Nichts mehr für mich. Ich möchte noch eine Weißwurst.
3. Ja, ich habe Hunger. Ich möchte noch eine Semmel.
4. Ja, bitte, ich trinke noch einen Saft. Ich habe Apfelsaft gern.
5. Ich habe noch Hunger. Ich nehme noch ein Käsebrot.
6. Ja, bitte, noch eine Tasse Tee. Ich trinke Tee nicht gern.

Ein wenig Grammatik

Schon bekannt

In **Kapitel 5** you learned about the indefinite article **ein** (*a, an*). If the noun is a subject, **ein** is used with masculine and neuter nouns, and **eine** with feminine nouns. When the noun following **ein** is used as a direct object, the masculine form is **einen**. The possessive pronouns **mein, dein, sein,** and **ihr** also have these same endings.

When **noch** precedes the indefinite article **ein**, it has the meaning of *another*.

Übungsheft, S. 105, Ü. 19

Mehr Grammatikübungen,
S. 266, Ü. 8

---

1. *another juice, no more juice* 2. **Möchtest du**

Grammatik

Negation of indefinite articles with kein

You have already learned some expressions using **kein: Ich habe keinen Hunger. Ich habe keine Zeit.** What does **kein** mean?[1] What do you notice about the endings that **kein** takes?[2] **Kein** is used to negate a noun, rather than an entire statement. Often when people say that they want more, they say **Ja, noch ein** (Käsebrot). If they don't want more, they simply say: **Keinen** (Kaffee) **mehr, danke.**

Mehr Grammatikübungen, S. 267, Ü. 9

Übungsheft, S. 105, Ü. 20

Grammatikheft, S. 80, Ü. 16–17

---

23 **Grammatik im Kontext**

Sprechen Are there some things that you refuse to eat or drink? Take turns asking and telling your classmates about these things, using **kein** in your answers, for example, **Ich trinke keine Limo.** Use the box for ideas or turn to page R9 for additional words.

> (der) Blumenkohl (cauliflower)
> (der) Rosenkohl (Brussels sprouts)
> (die) Zwiebel (onion)
> (die) Milch
> (der) Spinat (spinach)
> (der) Haferbrei (oatmeal)
> (die) Wurst
> (die) Leber (liver)

---

24 **Grammatik im Kontext**

Schreiben Nach der Schule sind einige Freunde bei Mara zu Hause und essen etwas. Ergänze das Gespräch mit den Wörtern im Kasten und der richtigen Form von **kein** und **noch ein**!

MARA   Wer möchte noch was trinken oder essen? Du, Flori, möchtest du ___1___?

FLORI   Ja, gern, Äpfel esse ich sehr gern.

MARA   Und mehr Orangensaft?

FLORI   Nein, danke. ___2___ mehr.

MARA   Und du Claudia, du hast nur ein Stück Kuchen gegessen. Möchtest du noch etwas?

> (die) Semmel   (der) Orangensaft
> (die) Brezel   (der) Hunger
> (das) Stück Kuchen   (der) Apfel

CLAUDIA   Ja, ___3___ bitte und auch ein Mineralwasser.

MARA   Und Markus? Willst du auch noch eine Semmel?

MARKUS   Nein, ___4___ mehr. Danke! Ich habe ___5___.

MARA   Und du, Rolf? Hast du noch Hunger?

ROLF   Ja, ein bisschen. Ich hab nur eine Brezel gegessen. Ich möchte ___6___. Brezeln esse ich immer gern!

CLAUDIA   Das weiß ich!

---

25 **Möchtest du noch ein ...?**

Sprechen Du machst jetzt ein Grillfest. Es gibt noch viel zu essen und zu trinken. Frag deinen Partner, ob er noch etwas haben möchte! („Dein Partner") sagt ja (mit **noch ein**) oder nein (mit **kein ...mehr**). Dann tauscht ihr die Rollen aus!

LERNTRICK

Take note of words that are similar and follow the same grammatical patterns. For example, **ein** and **kein** look and sound alike and have the same endings before nouns. Can you think of other words you have learned that look and sound like **ein** and **kein**?[3]

---

1. *not, not any, or no*   2. **Kein** has the same endings as **ein**.   3. **mein, dein,** and **sein.**

26 Ein Leserbrief

Lesen/Schreiben Lies diesen Brief an die Zeitschrift **Jugend** und beantworte die Fragen!

a. 1. Woher kommt Eva?

   2. Wann ist sie geboren?

   3. Welches Hobby hat Eva?

   4. Wie finden die Eltern Evas Hobby?

   5. Was hofft Eva? (**hoffen** *to hope*)

b. Lesen Find the two sentences in which the word **dass** is used. What is Eva trying to express in these sentences? What is the English equivalent of **dass**? What is the position of the verb in the clauses that begin with **dass**?

Hobby

Ich heiße Eva Hörster und bin am 17.10.88 in München geboren. Ich laufe mit den Rollschuhen auf der Straße oder auf der Rollschuhbahn. Meine Eltern finden es gut, dass ich Sport treibe. Sie begleiten mich immer zum Training und Langlauf. Ich hoffe, dass Rollschuhlaufen eine olympische Sportart wird. Das Foto ist nach meinem ersten Pokalsieg aufgenommen worden.

Viele Grüße,
Eva Hörster, München

So sagt man das!

Expressing opinions

In **Kapitel 2** you learned to express opinions such as: **Ich finde Tennis super**! You can also use a **dass**-clause to elaborate on your opinions.

Your friend might ask:

   Wie findest du München?

You might respond:

   Super! Ich finde es toll, dass es hier so viele Parks und Museen gibt. Und ich glaube, dass die Leute sehr freundlich sind. Aber ich finde es schlecht, dass das Essen so teuer ist.

What are the different phrases that begin the sentences expressing opinions? What is the subject in each **dass**-clause? What opinion is being expressed in each sentence?

Grammatik

The conjunction dass

Look again at the responses in the **So sagt man das!** box. Name the verbs in the **dass**-clauses.[1] What is the position of these verbs?[2] The conjunction **dass** often begins clauses that express opinions: **Ich finde, dass … Ich glaube, dass …** In clauses that begin with **dass**, the conjugated verb is at the end of the clause.

   München **ist** sehr schön.
   Ich glaube, **dass** München sehr schön **ist**.

What other conjunction do you know that affects the word order in the same way?[3]

Mehr Grammatikübungen, S. 267, Ü. 10

Übungsheft, S. 106, Ü. 21–22

Grammatikheft, S. 81, Ü. 18–19

CD-ROM DISC 3

---

1. gibt, sind, ist 2. at the end of the clause **3. weil**

27 Wer spricht im Radio?

Zuhören You're listening to a radio talk show as several teenagers call in to give their opinion on different topics. Listen to the four call-ins and for each one write the name and the age of the person calling and the general topic on which he or she is expressing an opinion.

28 Grammatik im Kontext

Sprechen/Schreiben Sag deinen Klassenkameraden, was du glaubst! Schreib danach deine Meinungen *(opinions)*.

BEISPIEL   Die Münchner sind sehr freundlich.
DU   **Ich glaube, dass die Münchner sehr freundlich sind.** *oder*
         Ich glaube nicht, dass die Münchner sehr freundlich sind.

1. Kinokarten sind zu teuer.
2. Politik ist interessant.
3. Hausaufgaben machen macht Spaß.
4. Fernsehen macht klug *(smart)*.
5. Schüler sind faul *(lazy)*.
6. Pizza essen ist gesund *(healthy)*.

29

Von der Schule zum Beruf

Schreiben You have been hired to work at your city's Chamber of Commerce. One of your first assignments is to design and describe an area of your city that is a family tourist attraction. As part of your assignment, you are to draw a plan of the area, place the buildings, and label them. Underneath your city plan, give a brief description of the various sights.

AUSSPRACHE

Richtig aussprechen / Richtig lesen

A. To practice the following sounds, say the words and sentences below after your teacher or after the recording.

1. The long vowels **ü** and **ö**: In **Kapitel 1** you learned how to pronounce the letters **ü** and **ö** as long vowels.

   führen, für, spülen / Kannst du für mich das Geschirr spülen?
   blöd, hören, Österreich / Ich höre gern Rock, aber Disko finde ich blöd.

2. The letters **s, ss,** and **ß**: At the beginning of a syllable, the letter **s** is pronounced much like the *z* in the English word *zebra*. However, if it is followed by the letters **t** or **p,** it sounds like the *sh* combination in the English word *shine*. In the middle or at the end of a syllable, the letter **s** is pronounced the same as the *s* in the English word *post;* the letters **ß** and **ss** are always pronounced this way as well.

   Senf, super, Semmel / Sonja will eine Wurst mit Senf und eine Semmel.
   Straße, Innenstadt, Spaß / Wo ist die Spatzenstraße? In der Innenstadt?
   Wurst, besser, Imbiss / Die Wurst ist besser in der Imbissstube hier rechts.

Richtig schreiben / Diktat

B. Write down the sentences that you hear.

Ein Bummel durch München

> **Lesestrategie Reading for a purpose** When you read for information, it is a good idea to decide beforehand what kind of information you want. If you simply want an overview, a general reading will suffice. If you need specific information, a close reading will be required.

1. These articles are from a book called **Merian live! München**. What kind of book do you think it is?

   a. a history book

   b. a book about parks and gardens

   c. a travel guide

2. When you read a travel guide, you generally have one of two specific purposes: to gather general information about what is going on, or to find specific information about an event — cost, time, date, etc. In which case would you skim to get the gist, and in which case would you scan for specific information?

3. How is information in a travel guide organized? Group the places listed below under one of these three general headings: **Essen und Trinken, Einkaufen, Sehenswertes.**

   Sportmode, Deutsches Museum, Cafés, Restaurants, Geschenkwaren, Alte Pinakothek, Peterskirche, Stehimbisse, Kaufhäuser, Englischer Garten, Konditoreien, Fotogeschäfte

	Durchschnittstemperaturen in °C		Sonnenstunden pro Tag	Regentage
	Tag	Nacht		
Januar	1,4	-5,6	1,8	11
Februar	3,4	-5,1	2,9	10
März	8,7	-1,5	3,9	9
April	13,5	2,8	5,4	10
Mai	18,0	6,6	6,0	12
Juni	21,3	10,0	7,5	14
Juli	23,2	12,1	7,8	13
August	22,7	11,4	6,7	12
September	19,6	8,4	6,0	10
Oktober	13,3	3,7	4,5	9
November	6,6	0,1	1,9	9
Dezember	2,3	-3,8	1,2	10

Quelle: Deutscher Wetterdienst, Offenbach

Lebensmittel

Dallmayr

In den heiligen Hallen der Gaumenfreuden wird sogar der Kauf einer banalen Kiwi zum gastronomischen Ereignis. Münchens ältestes Feinkosthaus ist nicht zuletzt seines aromatischen Kaffees wegen weit über die Grenzen der Stadt hinaus bekannt geworden.
2 Dienerstr. 14/15
U-/S-Bahn: Marienplatz

Januar
Fasching

Die »närrische Saison« beginnt in München mit dem 7. Januar und endet in der Nacht zwischen Faschingsdienstag und Aschermittwoch. In diesen Wochen quillt das städtische Veranstaltungsprogramm über von Faschingsbällen aller Art – exklusiven und volkstümlichen, intimen und massenhaften.

Als gesellschaftliche Höhepunkte der Faschingssaison gelten der Chrysanthemenball, Magnolienball, Madameball, Filmball und Presseball. Die phantasievollsten oder auch aufwendigsten Kostüme und Dekorationen sind beim Karneval in Rio im Bayerischen Hof, bei den Festen der Damischen Ritter, den Weißen Festen und der Vorstadthochzeit zu sehen.

Seiner Tradition nach findet der Münchner Fasching im Saal statt, nicht auf der Straße wie etwa der Rheinische Karneval. Nur während der drei letzten Faschingstage – von Sonntag bis Dienstag – tummelt sich das närrische Volk auch im Freien, vor allem in der Fußgängerzone, am Marienplatz und auf dem Viktualienmarkt, wo am Faschingsdienstag ab 6 Uhr in der Früh die Marktfrauen tanzen.

Englischer Garten

Münchens vielgeliebte »grüne Lunge« – etwa 5 km lang, bis zu 1 km breit und mit einer Gesamtausdehnung von nahezu 4 km². Entstanden ist der Englische Garten aus einer Anregung des unter Kurfürst Karl Theodor amtierenden Ministers Benjamin Thompson (später Graf Rumford), einen Volkspark in der Art der englischen Landschaftsgärten in den Isarauen anzulegen. 1789 begannen die Arbeiten am Park, die ab 1804 vom Gartenarchitekten Ludwig von Sckell geleitet wurden. Am auffälligsten unter den Bauten im Park sind der Chinesische Turm (1790), nach der Zerstörung im Krieg 1952 originalgetreu wiederaufgebaut, der Monopteros, ein klassizistischer Rundtempel nach einem Entwurf Leo von Klenzes im Auftrag Ludwigs I. (1837/38), das Japanische Teehaus, das Mitsuo Nomura 1972 anläßlich der Olympischen Spiele in München als Geschenk Japans an die Olympia-Stadt erbaut hat. Hinzu kommt der künstlich angelegte Kleinhesseloher See mit drei kleinen Inseln, einem Bootsverleih und dem Seehaus (Restaurant und Biergarten).

Zugänge zum Park gibt es am Haus der Kunst, an der Veterinärstraße (Nähe Universität), Gunezrhainerstraße (Nähe Münchner Freiheit), am Seehaus (Ausfahrt Mittlerer Ring) sowie an der Tivolistraße (Nähe Max-Joseph-Brücke). (→ Spaziergänge)

Olympiapark

Auf dem ehemaligen Oberwiesenfeld wurde für die XX. Olympischen Spiele 1972 von der Architektengemeinschaft Günter Behnisch und Partner dieser Park entworfen.

Der 52 m hohe Olympiaberg wurde auf zusammengetragenen Ruinentrümmern des Zweiten Weltkrieges angelegt und mit voralpiner Vegetation begrünt.

Als weitere Sportstätten gibt es das Eissportstadion, die Schwimmhalle (»Europas schönstes Garten-Hallenbad«) und das Radstadion. Die Olympiahalle selbst dient auch Kongressen, Ausstellungen und Konzerten.

Kaufhäuser

Ludwig Beck

Eine Münchner Institution. Auf vier Stockwerken gibt es vom Lodenmantel bis zum Gaultier-Jäckchen vor allem Mode zu kaufen; man findet aber auch den passenden Schmuck dazu, Tisch- und Bettwäsche, originelles Küchenzubehör, eine riesige Jazz-Auswahl auf CD – sowie Münchens netteste Verkäufer! Für das leibliche Wohl empfehlen sich drei Restaurants, darunter eine Sushi-Bar.
Marienplatz 11
U-/S-Bahn: Marienplatz

Medizinische Versorgung

Bitte wenden Sie sich an den Hotelportier.

Auskunft dienstbereiter Apotheken:
Tel. 59 44 75

Große Apotheken im Zentrum:
Internationale Ludwigs-Apotheke
Neuhauser Str. 8
Von Mendel'sche Apotheke
(große Abteilung für homöopathische Medikamente)
40 Leopoldstr. 58

Peterskirche, St. Peter

Erste und lange Zeit einzige Pfarrkirche der Stadt, deren erster Bau (erste Hälfte 11. Jh.) älter als die Stadt selbst ist. In der Folgezeit erlebte das Gotteshaus zahlreiche Erweiterungen und Modernisierungen in den Stilen der Gotik, der Renaissance und des Barock. Die Bombenzerstörungen der Jahre 1944/45 waren so schwer, daß man die Kirche beinahe gänzlich gesprengt hätte.

Der **Turm »Alter Peter«** ist – neben den Türmen der Frauenkirche – das Wahrzeichen der Stadt geblieben. 302 hölzerne Stufen führen an den vier Glocken vorbei zur Aussichtsgalerie.

Der Besondere Tip

Isar-Floßfahrt Floßfahrten auf der Isar zwischen Wolfratshausen und München sind eine bei Alt und Jung sehr beliebte »Gaudi«. Die Fahrt selbst dauert etwa sieben Stunden; eine Mittagspause wird an Land eingelegt. Zu einer Floßfahrt kann man sich freilich nicht spontan entschließen: Die meisten Termine sind (von Firmen, Vereinen, Freundeskreisen) schon lange im voraus gebucht. Einzelpassagiere wenden sich an das Amtliche Bayerische Reisebüro (ABR), das sich ein Kontingent für »Individualisten« zu sichern pflegt.

Feuchtfröhliche Gaudi ohnegleichen: Isarfloßfahrten

4. What general types of information appear in these texts? Which excerpts can you classify, using the categories you developed in Activity 3?

5. What are the names of some places to go shopping for fine foods? For fashionable clothes?

6. Where would you go in these situations?

   a. It's the middle of January and you want to go dancing.

   b. You want to go for a long relaxing walk.

   c. You have a sore throat and you need throat lozenges.

   d. You have been invited to someone's home and you want to buy a special coffee for them.

7. If you had a whole day free and wanted to do something out of the ordinary, what special tip does the guidebook give? Could you do it on the spur of the moment, or do you have to plan ahead? How do you know?

8. Read the excerpts **Peterskirche, St. Peter,** and **Olympiapark** and see if you can answer these questions. How old is the **Peterskirche**? What would you see if you climbed the steps of the **Alter Peter**? When was the **Olympiapark** built? How high is the mountain in the **Olympiapark**, and what is it made out of?

9. You are going to be in Munich for a day in June. Plan what you would do. How will the weather chart help you in making your plans? What can you do in June that you could not have done in January? What could you have done in January that you cannot do in June?

Übungsheft, S. 107, Ü. 23

Mehr Grammatikübungen

 CD-ROM DISC 3

internet

go.hrw.com

ADRESSE: go.hrw.com
KENNWORT:
WK3 MUENCHEN-9

Erste Stufe

Objective Talking about where something is located

1 Du bist zum ersten Mal in dieser Stadt und willst wissen, wo verschiedene öffentliche Gebäude *(public institutions)* sind. Schreib die folgenden Sätze ab und schreib dabei die richtige Form von **wissen** in die Lücken. **(S. 250)**

1. _____ du, wo das Hotel ist? — Nein, ich _____ es nicht.
2. _____ die Mara, wo das Café ist? — Ja, sie _____ es.
3. _____ ihr, wo die Bank ist? — Nein, wir _____ es nicht.
4. Wer _____ , wo das Museum ist? — Ich _____ es!
5. Die Schüler _____ nicht, wo das Theater ist, aber der Markus _____ es.

2 Frag diese Leute, ob sie wissen, wo diese Gebäude *(buildings)* sind. Schreib Fragen zu den Antworten. Gebrauche die richtige Form von **wissen**. Achte auf die Form der Anrede. **(S. 250)**

> **BEISPIEL**   deine Schwester sagt: Die U-Bahnstation ist am Marienplatz.
> **Weißt du, wo die U-Bahnstation ist?**

1. ein Klassenkamerad: Die Bank ist in der Karlstraße.
2. zwei Freunde: Die Post ist in der Ottostraße.
3. dein Lehrer: Das Theater ist in der Maxstraße.
4. dein Onkel: Das Museum ist in der Georgenstraße.
5. deine Eltern: Der Bahnhof ist am Bahnhofsplatz.
6. eine Lehrerin: Das Rathaus ist am Marienplatz.

3 Schreib eine Verbform von **wissen** in die erste Lücke und den abgebildeten Ort in die zweite Lücke. **(S. 250)**

1. Wer _____ , wo _____ ist?

2. Ihr _____ nicht, wo _____ ist?

3. Du musst doch _____ , wo _____ ist!

4. _____ du, wo _____ ist?

5. Alle Leute _____ , wo _____ ist!

6. Ich _____ nicht, wo _____ ist.

4 Du fragst und sagst, wie man am besten dorthin kommt. Schreib die richtigen Verbformen von **fahren** in die Lücken. (S. 255)

1. Wie _____ ich am besten zur Schule? — Ja, du _____ am besten geradeaus bis zur Alpseestraße und dann _____ du nach links bis zur Schulstraße.

2. Wie _____ denn die Mara zur Schule? _____ sie mit dem Bus oder _____ sie mit dem Rad? Weißt du, wie sie zur Schule _____ ?

3. Wie _____ ihr denn zur Schule? _____ du mit dem Rad, Flori, oder _____ du mit dem Moped? Und wie _____ du, Markus?

4. Ich _____ mit der U-Bahn zur Schule. Und Sie, Herr Meier, wie _____ Sie zur Schule? _____ Sie auch mit der U-Bahn?

5 Schreib die richtige Befehlsform (command form) von **fahren** in die erste Lücke und die Information, die im Piktogramm abgebildet ist, in die zweite Lücke. (S. 255)

 1. Herr Maier, _____ immer _____ !

 2. Mark, _____ geradeaus bis _____ !

 3. Lisa und Ann, _____ geradeaus und dann _____ !

Krüner Platz **4.** Rick, _____ doch mit bis _____ !

 5. Frau Abb, _____ die nächste Straße _____ !

Mehr Grammatikübungen

CD-ROM
DISC 3

go.
hrw
.com

WK3 MUENCHEN-9

6 Du bist in der Stadt und gibst verschiedenen Erwachsenen *(adults)* Auskünfte und Ratschläge *(advice)*. Gebrauch die korrekte Befehlsform. **(S. 255)**

1. (fahren) _____ immer geradeaus bis zur Ampel!
2. (gehen) _____ die nächste Straße nach rechts!
3. (kaufen) _____ das Brot und die Semmeln beim Bäcker!
4. (holen) _____ das Obst im Obst- und Gemüseladen!
5. (vergessen) _____ nicht die grünen Bohnen!
6. (probieren) _____ doch mal eine bayrische Spezialität!
7. (essen) _____ doch den Leberkäs! Er ist so gut!
8. (trinken) _____ doch mal einen Apfelsaft!

Dritte Stufe

Objectives Talking about what there is to eat and drink; saying you do or don't want more; expressing opinions

7 Du bist mit einer Freundin in einer Imbissstube und sagst ihr, was es hier zu essen und zu trinken gibt. Schreib den Ausdruck *(expression)* **es gibt** *(there is, there are)* in die Lücken. **(S. 257)**

Ja, in dieser Imbissstube _____ so viele kleine Gerichte. _____ zum

Beispiel Leberkäs und Hähnchen, und dann _____ Gyros, und _____

Semmeln, Brötchen, und _____ auch viel zum Trinken. Da _____

Mineralwasser, und _____ auch Milch.

8 Du bist in einer Imbissstube und willst von allem noch etwas bestellen. Schreib die richtige Form von **noch ein** zusammen mit dem Ausdruck in Klammern in die Lücken. **(S. 258)**

BEISPIEL (ein Eis) **Hallo! Ich möchte _____ , bitte.**
Hallo! Ich möchte <u>noch ein Eis</u>, bitte.

1. (ein Leberkäs) Hallo! Ich möchte _____ .
2. (eine Semmel) Hallo! Ich möchte _____ , bitte.
3. (ein Brötchen) Hallo! Für mich _____ , bitte.
4. (ein Apfelsaft) Bitte, _____ für mich.
5. (eine Weißwurst) _____ , bitte!
6. (ein Mineralwasser) Ich möchte _____ , bitte.

9 Du bist zu Hause und hast Hunger und Durst. Du fragst deine Eltern, was es noch zu essen und zu trinken gibt. Aber es gibt nichts mehr! Schreib die richtige Form von **kein** in die Lücken. (**S. 259**)

1. Gibt es noch Semmeln? — Nein, es gibt _____ Semmeln mehr.
2. Gibt es noch Kaffee? — Nein, es gibt _____ Kaffee mehr.
3. Gibt es noch Milch? — Nein, es gibt _____ Milch mehr.
4. Gibt es noch Kuchen? — Nein, es gibt _____ Kuchen mehr.
5. Gibt es noch Obst? — Nein, es gibt _____ Obst mehr.
6. Gibt es noch Weißwurst? — Nein, es gibt _____ Weißwurst mehr.
7. Gibt es noch Leberkäs? — Nein, es gibt _____ Leberkäs mehr.
8. Gibt es noch Mineralwasser? — Nein, es gibt _____ Mineralwasser mehr.

10 Jemand (someone) hat viele Fragen, und du gibst deine Meinung (opinion) dazu. Schreib in jede Lücke die Antwort zu jeder Frage. Beachte die Wortstellung (word order)! (**S. 260**)

1. Ist das Essen hier teuer? — Ich glaube, dass _____ .
2. Gibt es noch Leberkäs? — Ich glaube, dass _____ .
3. Ist der Salat gut? — Ich finde, dass _____ .
4. Ist das Brot frisch? — Ich glaube, dass _____ .
5. War die Mara beim Bäcker? — Ich glaube, dass _____ .
6. Ist München sehr schön? — Ich finde, dass _____ .

ADRESSE: go.hrw.com
KENNWORT:
WK3 MUENCHEN-9

1 Listen to some American students tell their friends back in Rosenheim about their day in **München** with Mara and Markus. Make a list of where they were and what they bought.

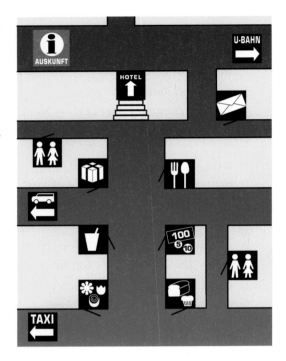

2 You work at the information desk in the train station, and several people need your help. Take turns with your partner asking for and giving the requested information. Use the cues below to formulate your questions. Different people want to know:

where a bank is

where the post office is

where a restaurant is

if there is a hotel here

if there's a subway station here

where to buy flowers

3 Lies die Postkarte unten und beantworte die folgenden Fragen!
   a. Wie findet Jörg die Stadt München? Was sagt er?
   b. Warum isst er soviel Leberkäs und so viele Weißwürste?
   c. Was besichtigt (besichtigen: *to sightsee*) Jörg in München?

4 In this chapter you have learned a lot about Munich. Write a postcard either to your parents or to a friend giving your opinions about the city or write a postcard about some other place you have visited. Use the postcard here as a model for your salutation and closing.

Hallo Bärbel!
Einen kurzen Gruß aus
München, wo ich kaum was
anderes als Leberkäs und
Weißwurst esse, weil sie hier
sagenhaft gut sind. Ich mache
aber auch hier einen echten
Kulturtrip mit Frauenkirche,
Rathaus usw. Ich finde, dass
München eine unheimlich starke
Stadt ist, weil es hier eine gute
Szene gibt, viele junge Leute,
viel zu tun.
Mehr wenn wir uns wieder
sehen. Bis dann, Alles Gute
Jörg

Bärbel Hörster
Eichenwegstr. 35
48161 Münster

5 You have learned your way around Mittersendling but your visiting American friend has not. Your friend will tell you three things he or she needs to do or buy. Tell your friend where he or she needs to go (bakery, butcher shop, etc.) and how to get there. Decide together on a starting point and use the map on page 253. Then switch roles.

> Du   **Ich brauche …** *oder* **Ich muss … kaufen.**
>
> Partner   **Also, du musst zum/zur … gehen!** *oder* **Geh …!**

6

Zum Schreiben

Your German pen pal wants to know about your after-school and weekend activities. He is especially interested in hearing about your neighborhood and about the places you go and what you do there. Write several paragraphs describing these activities.

Schreibtipp **Drawing a map** and including on this map places you frequently go and activities you do at each of these places is a good way to organize your thoughts about where things are located in your neighborhood.

Prewriting

In order to organize your thoughts before you begin writing, draw a map of your area and indicate at least 5 places you frequently go. Then think of an activity you do in each place, list the activity under each location, and under each activity list some adjectives to describe these activities.

Writing

Use your drawing to help you write a paragraph describing where your favorite places are located in relation to where you live, and to describe what you like to do in each place. Be sure to include a restaurant or snack bar on your map. You might also include others' opinions of the restaurant, i.e. „**Mein Vater sagt, dass ….**"

7 ## Rollenspiel

Get together with two classmates and role-play the following scene.

Design a menu for an **Imbissstube** and write it on a piece of paper or poster board. Then, with three other classmates, develop a conversation at the snack stand that is based on this situation.

a. You are discussing with your friends what's available at the stand. Then each of you orders something. Ask what it costs and pay the person behind the counter. Be polite!

b. As you enjoy the food, discuss how the food tastes and if someone wants more or not. If so, order more. Discuss with your friends some of your opinions about the city of Munich, which you are visiting today.

Kann ich's wirklich?

Can you talk about where something is located? (p. 250)

1 How would you ask an older passerby where the following places are using **wissen**? How would you ask someone who is your own age? How would you answer?

    a. Frauenkirche (… Straße)

    b. Rathaus (Marienplatz)

    c. Museum (Maximilianstraße)

Can you ask for and give directions? (p. 254)

2 How would you ask for directions from the **X**-mark to the following places?

    a. Bahnhof

    b. Theater

    c. Marktplatz

    d. Bank

3 How would you tell an older person to get to the following places using the command forms? Someone your own age? Use the **X**-mark as the starting point.

By vehicle:

    a. to the train station

    b. to the town hall

On foot:

    a. to the supermarket

    b. to the café

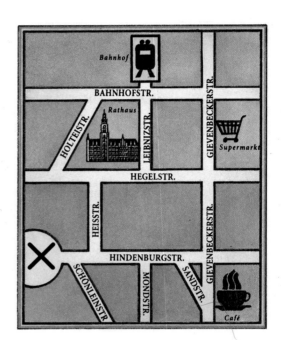

Can you talk about what there is to eat and drink? (p. 257)

4 How would you ask what there is to eat? And to drink? How would you tell someone what there is to eat or drink, using the items below?

    a. Leberkäs   **c.** apple juice   **e.** salad

    b. whole wheat rolls   **d.** tea   **f.** grilled chicken

Can you ask or tell someone that you do or don't want more? (p. 258)

5 How would you ask someone if he or she wants more? How would you tell someone that you want more of the items below or that you don't want more, using **noch ein** and **kein … mehr?**

    a. piece of cake   **c.** mineral water

    b. roll   **d.** ice cream

Can you express opinions using dass-clauses? (p. 260)

6   **a.** How would you give your opinion about the following statement? How would you agree with it? And disagree?

      Autofahren ist gefährlich.

    b. State your opinions about school in general. Write at least two sentences using **dass**-clauses.

Erste Stufe

In der Innenstadt

die Stadt, ¨e	city
das Rathaus, ¨er	city hall
der Marktplatz, ¨e	market square
die Post	post office
der Bahnhof, ¨e	railroad station
die Bank, -en	bank
die Kirche, -n	church
das Hotel, -s	hotel
der Garten, ¨	garden, yard

das Museum, die Museen	museum
das Theater, -	theater
die U-Bahnstation, -en	subway station

Talking about where something is located

in der Innenstadt	downtown

die Straße, -n	street
am ... Platz	on ...Square
wissen	to know (a fact, information, etc.)
Entschuldigung! Verzeihung! }	Excuse me!
Es tut mir Leid.	I'm sorry.
Keine Ahnung!	I have no idea!

Zweite Stufe

Asking for and giving directions

Wie komme ich zum (zur) ...	How do I get to ...
nach links	to the left
nach rechts	to the right
geradeaus	straight ahead
bis zur Ampel	until you get to the traffic light
bis zur ... Straße	until you get to ... Street

bis zum ... Platz	until you get to ... Square
die nächste Straße	the next street
die erste (zweite, dritte, vierte) Straße	the first (second, third, fourth) street
wieder	again

fahren	to go somewhere, ride, drive (using a vehicle)
er/sie fährt	he/she drives/is driving/is going
Vielen Dank!	Thank you very much!
Gern geschehen!	My pleasure!

Dritte Stufe

Talking about what there is to eat and drink

die Imbissstube, -n	snack bar
Was gibt's zu essen?	What's there to eat?
Es gibt ...	There is/are ...
der Leberkäs	Bavarian specialty (see p. 257)
mit Senf	with mustard
die Weißwurst, ¨e	Southern German sausage specialty (see p. 257)
die Vollkornsemmel, -n	whole grain roll
das Gyros	gyros

Saying you do or don't want more

Möchtest du noch etwas?	Would you like anything else?
Ich möchte noch ein(e)(en) ...	I'd like another ...
Ich möchte kein(e) (en) ... mehr.	I don't want another .../ anymore
noch ein(e) (en)	more, another one
genug	enough
kein	no, none, not any
kein (en) ... mehr	no more ...
Nichts mehr, danke!	No more, nothing else, ...thanks!

Ich habe genug.	I've had enough.
Ich habe keinen Hunger mehr.	I'm not hungry anymore.

Expressing opinions

dass	that
Ich finde, dass ...	I think that ...
Ich finde es gut/ schlecht, dass ...	I think it's good/ bad that ...
die Leute (pl)	people

Other words and phrases

probieren	to try
mal	(short for einmal) once

Komm mit nach Baden-Württemberg!

Einwohner: 10 000 000

Fläche: 36 000 Quadratkilometer (13 896 Quadratmeilen), etwa halb so groß wie Südkarolina

Landeshauptstadt: Stuttgart (570 000 Einwohner)

Große Städte: Mannheim, Karlsruhe, Freiburg, Heilbronn, Heidelberg, Pforzheim

Flüsse: Donau, Rhein, Neckar, Jagst, Kocher

Seen: Bodensee

Berge: Feldberg (1493 Meter hoch), Belchen (1414 Meter hoch)

Industrien: Maschinenbau, Automobilindustrie, Elektrotechnik, Chemie, Feinmechanik, Optik

Beliebte Gerichte: Spätzle, Schwarzwälder Kirschtorte, Maultaschen, Schinken

go.hrw.com

WK3 BADEN-WUERTTEMBERG

VIDEO

CD-ROM DISC 3

Das Alte Schloss in Meersburg am Bodensee ▶

Baden-Württemberg

Baden-Württemberg ist bekannt für seine reizvolle Landschaft und für seine Hightechindustrie. Der Schwarzwald (Black Forest) mit seinen traditionsreichen Bauernhöfen und Häusern ist eine der beliebtesten Touristenattraktionen Deutschlands.

Im Umkreis von Stuttgart, der Hauptstadt Baden-Württembergs, findet man wichtige Automobil- und Elektronikkonzerne, sowie viele mittelgroße Unternehmen, die Textilien, Uhren und optische Geräte herstellen.

◢ internet

go.hrw.com

ADRESSE: go.hrw.com
KENNWORT:
WK3 BADEN-WUERTTEMBERG

1 **Dorf im Schwarzwald**
Ein typisches Schwarzwalddorf

2 **Hexenloch Mühle**
Diese alte Mühle in Märgen ist typisch für Schwarzwälder Holzbauten.

3 **Besigheim**
Das einzigartige Stadtbild von Besigheim an der Enz, mit dem Schloss im Hintergrund

4 **Am Hexenwegle**
Hexen dekorieren viele
Häuser am Hexenwegle.

5 **Bietigheimer Rathaus**
Das Bietigheimer Rathaus
stammt aus dem Jahre 1507.

6 Martin, Andreas, Thomas, Sabine,
Sandra und Nicole laden euch zu
einem Besuch in Bietigheim ein.

Kapitel 10, 11, 12

**Die Szenen in diesen letzten drei Kapiteln
kommen aus Bietigheim-Bissingen, einer
historischen Stadt an der Enz, nördlich von
Stuttgart. Die Schüler in diesen Kapiteln
gehen aufs Ellental Gymnasium in Bietigheim.**

10
Kino und Konzerte

Objectives

In this chapter you will learn to

Erste Stufe

- express likes and dislikes
- express familiarity

Zweite Stufe

- express preferences and favorites

Dritte Stufe

- talk about what you did in your free time

 internet

 ADRESSE: go.hrw.com
KENNWORT:
WK3 BADEN-WUERTTEMBERG-10

◀ **Wie war der Film?—Cool!**

Los geht's! · *Wie verbringt ihr eure Freizeit?*

Strategie Verstehen

Look at the images that accompany the interviews. What are the students doing and what clues help you determine what they might be talking about?

Thomas Sandra Martin Nicole Sabine

Thomas: Wir sind eine Clique, drei Jungen und drei Mädchen, und—na ja—wir machen viel zusammen, besonders Sport. Wir joggen zusammen, wir fahren Rad, einmal im Monat gehen wir kegeln. Aber sonst hat jeder auch seine eigenen Interessen. Ich zum Beispiel gehe oft in Konzerte. Rockkonzerte höre ich am liebsten.

Sandra: Ab und zu gehe ich auch in ein Rockkonzert. Aber die Karten sind so furchtbar teuer und, ehrlich gesagt, höre ich lieber Country. Die Clique kommt manchmal zu mir, und jeder bringt eine Kassette oder eine CD. Wir hören dann Musik und spielen Karten oder Brettspiele.

Martin: Ich muss sagen, ich mag Rock überhaupt nicht. Ich mag auch die meisten Country Sänger nicht. Ich mag am liebsten klassische Musik, Brahms, Ravel und so. Ich gehe sehr gern ins Konzert und auch in die Oper.

Nicole: Was ich am liebsten mache? Ganz einfach! Ich geh am liebsten ins Kino. Fantasyfilme und Komödien sind meine Lieblingsfilme. Was ich nicht mag? Ich hasse Actionfilme. Die sind meistens so brutal. Mein Lieblingsfilm ist und bleibt *Kevin—Allein zu Haus*, und meine Lieblingsschauspieler sind Joe Pesci und Whoopi Goldberg.

Sabine: Ja, unsere Clique ist toll. Es stimmt, wir sind viel unterwegs, sehen viel. Wir kommen aber oft zusammen und diskutieren über Filme, Musik, Stars und so. Ich selbst bin auch gern zu Hause. Ich lese furchtbar gern. Ich habe viele Bücher.

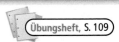

Übungsheft, S. 109

1 **Was passiert hier?**

Verstehst du, worüber die fünf Schüler sprechen? Beantworte die folgenden Fragen so gut du kannst.

1. What is the main idea of each of the five interviews?
2. What is each student's main interest or interests?
3. Which of the students mention something they don't like? What do they mention?

2 **Mix und Match: Interessen**

Welcher Schüler hat welche Interessen? Welche Aussage *(statement)* passt zu welchem Namen?

1. Thomas
2. Sandra
3. Martin
4. Nicole
5. Sabine

a. klassische Musik hören und in Konzerte und in die Oper gehen
b. joggen, Rad fahren, kegeln
c. über Filme, Musik, Stars usw. diskutieren, Bücher lesen
d. Musik hören, Karten und Brettspiele spielen
e. ins Kino gehen, besonders Fantasyfilme und Komödien sehen

3 **Erzähl weiter!**

Wer von den Schülern hat wahrscheinlich *(most likely)* die folgenden Aussagen gemacht?

1. Heute Abend, zum Beispiel, gehe ich ins Beethovenkonzert.
2. Mein Lieblingsbuch ist *Die unendliche Geschichte.*
3. Und ich habe alle Filme mit Steve Martin gesehen.
4. Meine Freunde hören auch gern Country.
5. Ach ja! Wir segeln auch gern.

4 **Genauer lesen**

Reread the interviews. Which words or phrases do the students use to

1. name sports
2. name different kinds of music
3. name other free-time activities
4. name different kinds of films
5. express likes and dislikes
6. say that something is their favorite

Frühkonzert in einer Halle auf dem Hamburger Fischmarkt

5 **Und du?**

Now write your own interview. First choose the interview that most closely describes the free-time activities you like to do. Then rewrite the interview, replacing any information with your own particular interests.

Wortschatz

SANDRA Wie verbringst du deine Freizeit?

MARTIN Ich gehe gern mit Freunden ins Kino und sehe …

CD-ROM
DISC 3

Actionfilme — Der Terminator 2

Horrorfilme — Dracula

Krimis — Eine Frage der Ehre

Abenteuerfilme — Indiana Jones–und der letzte Kreuzzug

Liebesfilme — Entscheidung aus Liebe

Kriegsfilme — Das Boot

Komödien — Kevin - Allein in New York

Western — Zwölf Uhr mittags

Sciencefictionfilme — Star Trek 6 - Das unbekannte Land

Grammatikheft, S. 82, Ü. 1

6 **Welche Filme erkennst du?** *Which films do you recognize?*

Sprechen Welche Filme auf Seite 281 kennst du? Wie heißen sie auf Englisch? Was bedeuten Wörter wie, zum Beispiel, Horrorfilme oder Krimis? Wie heißen diese Filmarten auf Englisch?

So sagt man das!

Expressing likes and dislikes

You have learned several ways of expressing likes and dislikes, using **gern** and **nicht gern** with various verbs, and using the verb **gefallen**. Another way to express what you like or don't like is with the present tense of the verb **mögen**.

You might ask:

Was für Musik magst du?
Und Filme?
Magst du auch Abenteuerfilme?
Magst du Kevin Costner?

The responses might be:

Ich mag Rock und auch Jazz.
Horrorfilme mag ich sehr gern.
Ja, furchtbar gern! *or* **Nein, überhaupt nicht.**
Ja, ich mag ihn besonders gern.

Übungsheft,
S. 110–111, Ü. 2–4

Grammatikheft,
S. 82, Ü. 2

What do you think the phrase **Was für ...** means?[1]

7 **Was seht ihr gern?**

Zuhören Listen to the following interviews about the kinds of movies these German teenagers enjoy seeing. For each interview, write the name of the person being interviewed. Then, beside each name, write the kinds of movies the person likes and does not like.

Grammatik

The verb mögen

The verb **mögen** (*to like, care for*) is used in sentences such as:

Magst du Krimis?   Nein, aber ich **mag** Horrorfilme.

Here are the forms
of **mögen**:

ich	mag	wir	mögen
du	magst	ihr	mögt
er, sie, es	mag	sie/Sie	mögen

Mehr Grammatikübungen,
S. 296–297, Ü. 1–3

Übungsheft, S. 111–112, Ü. 5–8

Grammatikheft, S. 83, Ü. 3

8 **Grammatik im Kontext**

Schreiben Schreib einem Freund die folgende E-Mail und setze dabei die richtige Form von **mögen** in jede Lücke.

Lieber Ralph: Viele Klassenkameraden und auch ich, wir ≡ Abenteuerfilme. Aber die Sara und die Amy ≡ Komödien lieber. Und der Rolf ≡ nur Sciencefiction. Was können wir zusammen sehen? Ich ≡ auch Kriegsfilme. Schreib mir, welche Filme du am liebsten ≡ . Welche Filme ≡ ihr in eurer Familie am liebsten? Tschüs, John

1. *what kind of ...*

Wortschatz

You can use these expressions to talk about how much you like or don't like someone or something.

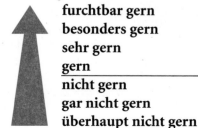

furchtbar gern
besonders gern
sehr gern
gern
nicht gern
gar nicht gern
überhaupt nicht gern

UTOPIA - KINO
Reihe 1-3
Spätvorstellung
2,50 €
Aufbewahren und auf
Verlangen vorzeigen
Landgrabenstr. 9
053890 053890
Abriss

Alba 252 25 45 Central	3/5/7/9 **BALTO—Ein Hund mit dem Herzen eines Helden** Als mitverantwortlicher Produzent für dieses Zeichentrickabenteuer bleibt Steven Spielberg seinem Stil treu—actionsgeladen, gefühlvoll und dramatisch.
Capitol 2 251 37 00 beim Central	2.45/4.45/6.45/8.45 Fr/Sa 22.45 8. Woche **DER DUMMSCHWÄTZER** Ab 6 J. —eine ebenso intelligente, wie turbulente Familienkomödie. Jim Carrey spielt einen Anwalt, der es mit der Wahrheit nicht allzu genau nimmt, weder vor Gericht noch privat.
Radium 251 18 07 Mühlengasse 7	3/5/7/9 **DAS ATTENTAT** Rob Reiners eloquent erzähltes und spannend inszeniertes Gerichtsdrama. Ab 12 Jahren

Judging by the excerpt of movie listings from Germany to the left, from which country do you think most foreign films come? Think about how movies are rated in the U.S. Then scan the movie listing and see if you can find the rating system used in Germany. (*Hint: Look for something that has to do with age.*) How is it different from the one in the U.S.? How much does admission for one person cost in Germany? As you discovered, American movies are very popular in German-speaking countries. Most movies are dubbed into German; however, larger cities usually have at least one movie theater that shows foreign movies with the original sound track.

Übungsheft, S. 120, Ü. 24

9 Eine Umfrage

a. Sprechen Ask your partner what kinds of movies he or she likes and does not like. Then ask what kinds of movies he or she especially likes. Switch roles.

b. Schreiben/Sprechen Working with your classmates, conduct a survey about the most popular kinds of movies (**Abenteuerfilme, Krimis usw.**). Take turns going to the front of the room and asking someone **Was für Filme mag (Susan) besonders gern?** Write the answers you get in an ongoing chart on the chalkboard. When everyone has been asked, discuss together which types of movies are most popular.

BEISPIEL   (Cathy) **mag ...besonders gern.**

Wortschatz

Rock and Roll	Jazz
Heavy Metal	Disko
klassische Musik	Oper
Country	

Grammatikheft, S. 83, Ü. 4

Herbert Grönemeyer

Looking at the pop chart from a well-known magazine for young people, what can you say about popular music among teenagers in Germany? Where does most of it come from? There are many well-known German singers, such as Herbert Grönemeyer, Marius Müller-Westernhagen, and Ina Deter.

in DEUTSCHLAND
10 TOP
SINGLES

1 (3)	**Ms. Jackson** OutKast	
2 (1)	**Stan** Eminem	
3 (7)	**Overload** Suababes	
4 (9)	**Operation Blade** Public Domain	
5 (6)	**Gravel Pit** Wu-Tang Clan	
6 (2)	**Ich Geh Nicht Ohne Dich** Walter	
7 (10)	**What A Feeling** DJ Bobo & Irene Cara	
8 (5)	**La Passiont** Gigi D' Agostino	
9 (4)	**Who Let The Dogs Out** Baha Men	
10 (8)	**Götterfunken** Tanzwut	

10 Ein Interview

a. Sprechen/Schreiben Create a list of questions to ask your partner about his or her taste in music. Be sure to obtain the following information: name, age, what kind of music the person likes or dislikes, how much he or she likes or dislikes the music mentioned; if he or she goes to concerts, when, and how often. Take notes using a chart like the one below. Then switch roles.

wer?	wie alt?	was für Musik?	gern/ nicht gern?	Konzerte?	wie oft/ wann?

b. Schreiben Schreib einen Bericht über deinen Partner! Verwende dabei die Information aus dem Interview oben (*above*)!

Wortschatz

Kennst du ...?

die Gruppe *DAF*
den Film *Wayne's World*
das Lied *America*
den Sänger *Udo Lindenberg*
die Sängerin *Nina Hagen*
den Schauspieler *Harrison Ford*
die Schauspielerin *Julia Roberts*

So sagt man das!

Expressing familiarity

You may want to find out if your friend is familiar with the films, songs, and groups that you like. You might ask:

Kennst du den Film *Das Russlandhaus?*

Your friend might respond positively:

Ja, sicher! *or*
Ja, klar!

Or negatively:

Nein, den Film kenne ich nicht. *or*
Nein, überhaupt nicht.

11 Kennst du die Gruppe?

Zuhören Listen to some students talking about movies and music with their friends. For each exchange decide whether the person they are speaking to is or is not familiar with the groups, songs, or films mentioned.

12 Kennst du die neuste Gruppe aus Amerika?

Sprechen List three lesser-known films, songs, or groups that you like (for example, local musicians). Ask your partner if he or she is familiar with them. If not, he or she will ask questions to find out what kind of movie/music you are talking about. Describe it to your partner. Then switch roles.

Ein wenig Grammatik

Schon bekannt

In **Kapitel 7** you learned the verb **wissen** (*to know a fact, information*). The verb **kennen** means *to know* as in *to be acquainted or familiar with* someone or something:

Ja, ich kenne Udo Lindenberg.
Kennst du das Lied „Sonderzug nach Pankow"?

The forms of **kennen** are regular in the present tense.

Mehr Grammatikübungen, S. 297, Ü. 4

Grammatikheft, S. 84, Ü. 6

So sagt man das!

Expressing preferences and favorites

When discussing music groups and movies, your friend might ask you about your
preferences and favorites.

He or she might ask:

Siehst du gern Horrorfilme?

**Siehst du lieber Abenteuerfilme
oder Sciencefictionfilme?**

**Und du, Gabi? Was siehst
du am liebsten?**

You might respond:

**Ja, aber Krimis sehe ich lieber. Und
am liebsten sehe ich Western.**

**Lieber Sciencefictionfilme. Aber
am liebsten sehe ich Liebesfilme.**

Am liebsten sehe ich Komödien.

What is the idea expressed by **gern**, **lieber**, and **am liebsten**?[1] What other
way can you express that something is your favorite?[2]

---

13 **Grammatik im Kontext**

a. Zuhören Listen to the following students tell you what they like and don't
like, what they prefer, and what they
like most of all. Make a chart like the
one below and fill in the information.

	likes	doesn't like	prefers	likes most of all
Marianne				
Stefan				

b. Sprechen Using the chart you've just
completed, take turns with your classmates reporting back in your own
words the information from Marianne's
and Stefan's interviews.

Ein wenig Grammatik

The words **lieber** and **am liebsten** express
preferences and favorites. They are used
with **haben** and other verbs in the same
way **gern** is used.

**Ich sehe gern Actionfilme, aber ich sehe
Komödien lieber.
Am liebsten sehe ich Krimis.**

Mehr Grammatikübungen,
S. 297–298, Ü. 5–6

Grammatikheft, S. 85, Ü. 7

Ein wenig Grammatik

In **Kapitel 5** you learned that the verb
aussehen (*to look, appear*) is irregular in the
du- and **er/sie-**forms. The verb **sehen** (*to
see*), of course, follows this same pattern:

**Siehst du gern Horrorfilme?
Er sieht Abenteuerfilme am liebsten.**

How would you answer
the question **Siehst du
gern Horrorfilme?**

Grammatikheft,
S. 86, Ü. 8–9

---

1. *like; prefer; like best of all* 2. **Lieblings-**

ZWEITE STUFE

zweihundertfünfundachtzig **285**

14 Was wollen wir tun?

Sprechen Du willst heute Abend mit deinem Partner etwas tun. Du wählst etwas von der linken Seite aus, dein Partner von der rechten. Er sagt dir, was er lieber tun möchte. Dann tauscht die Rollen aus!

DU **Wir können …**
PARTNER **Ich möchte lieber …**

Jerry Maguire
Vorstellungen um:
16.00
18.30
20.30

15 Grammatik im Kontext

Sprechen Stell Fragen an einen Klassenkameraden! Dann beantworte die Fragen selbst (*yourself*)! Verwende die Wörter im Kasten (*in the box*) unten mit verschiedenen (*different*) Verben!

Frag deinen Partner:

a. Was hast du oder was machst du gern?

b. Was hast du oder was machst du nicht gern? Was hast du oder was machst du lieber?

c. Was hast du oder was machst du am liebsten?

Western	Country and Western	Kuchen	Pizza	Heavy Metal	Basketball
Rock'n'Roll	Fußball	Tennis		Klavier	Cola
Oper	Lied Kaffee	schwimmen	Mathe		
Horrorfilme				Karten	Schach
Technik	Gitarre kegeln	Apfelsaft sammeln	angeln	Jazz	

16 Und du? Wie steht's mit dir?

a. **Schreiben/Sprechen** Create a chart in German similar to the one you used in Activity 13 and fill in the following information about yourself: the music you like, prefer, or like the best, and the music you do not like at all. Then get together with your partner and ask him or her questions in order to find out the same information. Take notes using your chart. Then switch roles. Use the chart to help you organize your answers.

b. **Lesen/Sprechen** You must introduce your partner at the next German Club meeting, where the topic of the afternoon is music. Use the notes you took on your partner's preferences and favorites in music and write a paragraph introducing him or her and describing his or her interests in music.

17 Das Kinoprogramm

Lesen/Sprechen Schau dir die Werbung an und beantworte die Fragen.

Mittwoch, 7. 7.
20:00 Uhr
Olympia Bissingen

Absolute Power
mit Clint Eastwood und
Gene Hackman
Regie: Clint Eastwood

Donnerstag, 8. 7.
21:00 Uhr
Delta Bietigheim

DO 27.05.
FR 28.05.
SA 29.05.
SO 30.05.
MO 31.05.
DI 1.06.
MI 2.06.

21.30 *Filmkritikers Liebling*

**Jerry Maguire—
Spiel des Lebens**
von Cameron Crowe,
mit Tom Cruise und Kelly
Preston

USA 1996

IMAX
ALASKA
Ruf der Wildnis

deutsche Fassung

Mo: 12,18,21 Uhr   Fr: 14,17,20 Uhr
Di: 13,17,21 Uhr   Sa: 11,19,21 Uhr
Mi: 11,18,21 Uhr   So: 11,21 Uhr
Do: 10,16,21 Uhr
Schwanthalerstr. 3   Tel. 55 57 54 - ab 6 J.
14.45, 17.30, 20,15, Fr./Sa. a. 23.00

☎ 55 75 40

16.00 **MICHAEL COLLINS**
mit Liam Neeson, Julia Roberts
12. Wo./ab 16 J.

18.00 / 20.15 **DER GEIST UND DIE DUNKELHEIT**
mit Michael Douglas, Val Kilmer
26. Wo./ab 16 J.

22.30 **DIEBE DER NACHT**
mit Catherine Deneuve
10. Wo./ab 12 J.

EIN FILM VON SIDNEY LUMET
NACHT ÜBER MANHATTAN
ANDY GARCIA
RICHARD DREYFUSS
LENA OLIN
3. Woche
im Verleih der tobis Filmkunst
Internet: http://www.tobis.de
14.00/16.00/18.00/20.00 Fr./Sa. auch 22.00

„DIE LUSTIGSTE KOMÖDIE
AUS DEUTSCHLAND
SEIT ÜBER 10 JAHREN"

Hollywood Reporter

13. Wo.

GÖTZ GEORGE · UWE OCHSENKNECHT
SCHTONK!
DER FILM ZUM BUCH VOM FÜHRER
RIO-PALAST
Rosenheimer Platz, Tel. 48 69 79
18.15, 20.30, Di./Mi. auch 16.00

NEUES REX
Agricolastraße 16, Tel. 56 25 00
Täglich 20.30 Uhr

Mittwoch, 7. 8.
20:00 Uhr
Olympia Bissingen

Jack
mit Robin Williams
und Diane Lane
Regie: Francis Ford
Coppola

Donnerstag, 8. 8.
21:00 Uhr
Delta Bietigheim

1. What kind of ads are these?

2. Which films do you recognize? Using the pictures and cognates as cues, try to guess what the English titles are for all the different movies listed.

3. What specific kinds of information can you find in these ads?

4. At what times on Friday can you see the movie *Nacht über Manhattan*?

5. What telephone number do you need to call to find out what day *Diebe der Nacht* is showing? Figure out how long *Diebe der Nacht* has been showing.

6. Is the movie *Schtonk* showing in more than one movie theater? If so, what are the addresses of the theaters?

7. Look at the listing for *Absolute Power*. What does **Regie** mean?

8. How would you describe these movies using the movie categories you learned on page 281 (for example, **Horrorfilme**)?

LERNTRICK

In the expression **am liebsten,** the part of the word that expresses the superlative (= most of all) is the suffix **-sten.** Watching for this suffix will frequently help you understand the meaning of new words. In the ad for *Schtonk* you see the phrase: **die lustigste Komödie. Lustig** means *funny.* What is the ad saying about the film *Schtonk?* What kind of film are you talking about if you say **der traurigste Film?** You will learn more about the superlative forms later.

18 Wie findest du ...?

Schreiben/Sprechen From the films listed on page 287, choose three that you've already seen or three other movies. Write them on a piece of paper and give it to your partner. He or she will do the same. Now ask your partner his or her opinion of the movies on the list. Then switch roles. Use **weil**-clauses and the adjectives below to express why you do or don't like the movie.

> **BEISPIEL**   **PARTNER**   **Wie findest du den Film *Vater der Braut?***
> **DU**   **Den Film mag ich gar nicht, weil er zu doof ist.**

Wortschatz

Gut!
phantasievoll
lustig
spannend
sensationell

Schlecht!
grausam
zu brutal
zu schmalzig *(corny, mushy)*
dumm
zu traurig
doof *(stupid)*

Übungsheft, S. 113–115, Ü. 9–15   Grammatikheft, S. 87, Ü. 10–11

CD-ROM DISC 3

Don't forget these words that you already know:

Spitze	toll	langweilig
interessant	blöd	prima

> Komödien sind lustig.
>
> Horrorfilme sind grausam, aber Krimis sind spannend.
>
> Liebesfilme können traurig oder oft sehr schmalzig sein.

19 Welchen Film sehen wir heute Abend?

Sprechen You and your partner are using the movie listings on page 287 to select a movie to see tonight. Discuss the types of movies each of you prefers, then make a suggestion and see if your partner agrees. Once you agree on a movie, decide on a time. Share your plans with your classmates.

20 Rate mal!

a. Schreiben Write a paragraph describing your favorite film or rock star using the new vocabulary and phrases you've learned in this chapter. Refer to your favorite star as **mein Lieblingsstar** or **mein(e) Lieblingssänger(in)**. Here are some questions you will want to answer in your paragraph.

1. Woher kommt er/sie?

2. Wie sieht er/sie aus?

3. Was für Filme macht er/sie? (Was für Lieder singt er/sie?)

4. Was ist sein/ihr neuster Film? (Was ist sein/ihr neustes Lied?)

b. Lesen/Sprechen Now read your description to the class. Your classmates will take turns asking questions and guessing who the mystery person is.

Welche kulturellen Veranstaltungen besuchst du?

We asked several teenagers in the German-speaking countries what cultural events they usually go to for entertainment. What do you think they might have said? Before you read the interviews, make a list of the types of cultural events that you think German-speaking teenagers might find interesting.

Silvana, Berlin

„Also, kulturelle Veranstaltungen …geh ich manchmal ins Ballett mit meiner Mutter, also uns interessiert das Ballett: *Schwanensee* war ich schon, *Nussknacker* von Tschaikowsky, und ab und zu gehen wir mit der Schule ins Museum oder zu irgendwelchen Ausstellungen, aber eigentlich nicht so oft."

Silke, Hamburg

„Ich geh auch gern ins Theater, ich kuck mir auch mal Shakespeare an oder so und auch mal so witzige Theaterstücke, und ich geh auch sehr gern ins Museum. Und es gab da hier vor kurzem die Picasso-Ausstellung, und die war auch ganz gut."

Tim, Berlin

„Also, ich versuch's so oft wie möglich—bei jeder Chance—in ein Theater oder in eine Oper zu gehen, sobald ich günstig Karten bekomme, das heißt über die Schule krieg ich Vergünstigung, oder dass meine Eltern mich halt einladen oder was sponsern, dass ich dann ins Theater gehe."

Rosi, Berlin

„Ich geh nicht oft zu kulturellen Veranstaltungen, weil …meine Eltern wollen mich da immer mitnehmen, aber ich hab dann andere Sachen vor, dann bin ich verabredet und hab keine Lust. Aber meine Eltern sind schon dafür, dass ich dahin gehen würde."

A. 1. What events do these teenagers like to attend? Make a list of the events each one attends.

2. With your partner, write answers for the following questions. Are all of these teenagers interested in cultural events? If not, what reasons are given for not going to the events? What does the person say? Now look at Tim's interview. What do you think might keep Tim from attending a play or an opera?

3. Compare the list you made before reading the text with what the teenagers actually said. Do teenagers in the German-speaking countries like the same types of cultural events as teenagers where you live? What are some of the differences? Do you think teenagers in the German-speaking countries are more or less interested in cultural events than teenagers where you live? Why do you think this is so? Discuss these answers with your classmates and then write a brief essay in German about the topic.

B. What would you say if you were interviewed about the kinds of cultural events you like? Write your answer in German giving reasons for why you do or don't like particular events.

Hanns-Martin-Schleyer-Halle

Sonntag, 1. März
Peter Maffay

Montag, 2. März
Joe Cocker

Sonntag, 8. März
Musikantenstadl

Samstag, 14. März
Udo Jürgens

Sonntag, 15. März
Placido Domingo und Julia Migenes

Samstag, 28. März
Schöller Oldie Night

Vor und nach der Vorstellung!

Der Treff • für Leute von heute!

WÜRTTEMBERGER-STUBEN
- Dieter Franke -

70174 Stuttgart 10, Schloßstraße 33 (bei der Liederhalle) ☎ 0711/29 03 14

Täglich von 11-24 Uhr geöffnet. | **Küche bis 24 Uhr.**
Sonn - u. feiertags geschlossen.

TOP 10 Leihvideos

1 **Nur noch 60 Sekunden**	6 **Haunted Hill**
2 **Gladiator**	7 **Crazy**
3 **Scream3**	8 **Mission to Mars**
4 **Der Sturm**	9 **Harte Jungs**
5 **Bats-Fliegende Teufel**	10 **Ein Herz und eine Kanone**

TOP 10 Sachbücher

1 Haffner, Sebastian
Geschichte eines Deutschen
Deut. Verlgs. Anst. EUR 20,35

2 Schwanitz, Dietrich
Bildung
Eichborn Verlag EUR 25,45

3 Kohl, Helmut
Mein Tagebuch 1998-2000
Droemer Knaur EUR 23,00

4 The Beatles Anthology
Ullstein GMBH EUR 65,45

5 Illies, Florian
Generation Gold
Argon Verlag EUR 18,40

6 Armstrong, Lance/ Jenkins, Sally
Tour des Lebens
Luebbe EUR 18,40

7 Henkel, Hans-Olaf
Die Macht der Freiheit
Econ Verlag EUR 20,40

8 Schäuble, Wolfgang
Mitten im Leben
Bertelsmann EUR 21,50

9 Carnegie, Dale
Sorge dich nicht-lebe!
Scherz Verlag EUR 23,50

10 Reich-Ranicki, Marcel
Mein Leben
Deut. Verlagsanst. EUR 25,45

TOP 10 Belletristik

1 Rowling, Joanne K.
Harry Potter und der Stein des Weisen
Carlsen Verlag EUR 14,35

2 Rowling, Joanne K.
Harry Potter und der Feuerkelch
Carlsen Verlag EUR 22,50

3 Rowling, Joanne K.
Harry Potter und die Kammer des Schreckens
Carlsen Verlag EUR 14,35

4 Rowling, Joanne K.
Harry Potter und der Gefangene von Askaban
Carlsen Verlag EUR 15,35

5 Pilcher, Rosamunde
Wintersonne
Wunderlich Verlag EUR 25,50

6 Link, Charlotte
Die Rosenzüchterin
Blanvalet Verlag EUR 24,50

7 Mankell, Henning
Mittsommermord
Zsolnay-Verlag EUR 23,00

8 Grisham, John
Das Testament
Heyne Wilhelm EUR 23,50

9 Leon, Donna
In Sachen Signora Brunetti
Diogenes Verlag EUR 20,40

10 Marai, Sandor
Die Glut
Piper Verlag EUR 18,40

---

21 ### Was machen die Jugendlichen in ihrer Freizeit?

Lesen/Sprechen Sieh dir die Anzeigen (*ads*) zur Freizeitplanung an!

1. Was für Anzeigen siehst du hier?

2. Welche Bücher, Filme oder Stars kennst du schon? Mach eine Liste!

3. Lies die Buchtitel auf den Bestsellerlisten! Was bedeuten „Sachbuch" und „Belletristik"?

4. Wenn du Konzerte magst, welche Anzeige interessiert dich? Wann ist das Konzert von Udo Jürgens? Wo ist es?

5. Welche Leihvideos kennst du schon? Was kannst du im Allgemeinen (*in general*) über den deutschen Videomarkt sagen?

JOACHIM Was liest du?

UTE Oh, ich lese viel, zum Beispiel …
Romane
Krimis
Gruselromane
Liebesromane
Fantasyromane
Sciencefictionromane
Hobbybücher

Zeitungen

Sachbücher

JOACHIM Und worüber sprichst du mit deinen Freunden?

UTE Wir sprechen oft über …
Politik, Mode, die Umwelt

Zeitschriften

Übungsheft, S. 116–117, Ü. 16–18

Grammatikheft, S. 88, Ü. 12–14

---

22 **Was liest du?**

Sprechen Beantworte die folgenden Fragen mit deinen Klassenkameraden!

1. Liest du gern? Wenn nicht, warum nicht?
2. Was liest du am liebsten?
3. Was ist dein Lieblingsbuch? Was für ein Buch ist das?
4. Worüber sprichst du mit deinen Freunden?

Stem-changing verbs

You have learned that some verbs, such as **nehmen** and **essen,** change their stem vowel in the second and third persons singular (see page 171). Here are two more: **lesen** *(to read)* and **sprechen** *(to speak).*

	lesen	**sprechen**
ich	lese	spreche
du	**lie**st	spr**i**chst
er, sie, es	**lie**st	spr**i**cht

The verb phrase **sprechen über** means *to talk about* or *to discuss.* When you use **sprechen über,** the noun phrase or pronoun following the preposition **über** must be in the accusative case.

Wir sprechen über **den Deutschlehrer.**—Wir sprechen auch über **ihn.**

When you want to find out what topic people are talking about, use **worüber** to begin your sentence.

Worüber sprecht ihr?—Wir sprechen über **den Film.**

Mehr Grammatikübungen, S. 298, Ü. 7

Übungsheft, S. 117, Ü. 19–20

Grammatikheft, S. 89, Ü. 15–16

---

23 **Grammatik im Kontext**

a. Lesen/Sprechen Vervollständige das Gespräch von Nicole mit ihren Freunden und wähle dabei eins der gegebenen Wörter aus.

REPORTER Was für Bücher ____1____ du am liebsten? (lese, sprecht, liest)

NICOLE Tja, normalerweise ____2____ ich Fantasybücher oder Krimis. (lesen, lest, lese)

REPORTER ____3____ du auch die Zeitung? (Liest, Sprechen, Lesen)

NICOLE Na klar! Aber Zeitschriften ____4____ ich lieber. (lese, sprecht, spricht)

REPORTER Und worüber ____5____ du mit deinen Freunden? (spreche, lesen, sprichst)

NICOLE Hm…normalerweise ____6____ wir über Klamotten oder über einen Film, aber manchmal auch über Politik oder die Umwelt. (sprechen, lesen, spreche)

REPORTER Und ihr zwei, was ____7____ ihr am liebsten? (sprechen, lest, lesen)

MONIKA Ganz einfach! Wir beide haben Gruselromane furchtbar gern. Wir ____8____ sie immer! (sprechen, liest, lesen)

b. Schreiben Kopiere die Sätze und schreib die richtigen Formen von **lesen** oder **sprechen** in die Lücken.

1. Der Thomas ══ über den Krimi. – Und worüber ══ du?

2. Ich weiß, dass du gern Zeitschriften ══ . Mein Bruder ══ sie auch gern.

3. Meine Mutter ══ Deutsch, und mein Vater ══ Spanisch. Was ══ du?

4. Ich ══ hier, dass unser Präsident gern Krimis ══ .

24 **In einer Buchhandlung**

Sprechen You are the salesperson in a bookstore and your partner is a customer. Using the cues below, ask questions to find out what type of book to recommend. Make your recommendation, then switch roles.

Was für Bücher …? Was für Interessen …?

Worüber sprechen Sie …? Lieblingsbuch?

25 **Was machst du heute Abend?**

Sprechen Diskutiere mit deinem Partner, was du heute machen willst! Was macht dein Partner? Wenn du Ideen brauchst, verwende die vier Anzeigen auf Seite 290.

So sagt man das!

Talking about what you did in your free time

To find out what someone did last weekend you ask:

Was hast du am Wochenende gemacht?

The response might be:

Am Samstag war ich im Herbert-Grönemeyer-Konzert. Und ich war am Sonntag zu Hause. Am Nachmittag habe ich gelesen, und am Abend habe ich mit Thomas und Martin das Video „Der mit dem Wolf tanzt" gesehen. Danach haben wir über den Film gesprochen.

Mehr Grammatikübungen, S. 299, Ü. 8–9

Übungsheft, S. 118, Ü. 21–22

Grammatikheft, S. 90, Ü. 17–19

26 **Logisch oder unlogisch?**

Zuhören Schüler erzählen, was sie letztes Wochenende gemacht haben. Sind die Antworten zu jedem Gespräch logisch oder unlogisch?

27 Sätze bauen

Sprechen/Schreiben Was hast du letztes Wochenende gemacht? Wie viele Sätze kannst du bauen?

| Ich war … | im Konzert
im Kino
zu Hause
bei meinen Freunden | und ich/wir habe(n) … | den Film …
die Gruppe …
das Buch …
das Video …
über (die Hausaufgaben) | gemacht
gesprochen
gesehen
gelesen |

28 Hat es Spaß gemacht? *Was it fun?*

Schreiben/Sprechen Was hast du am Wochenende gemacht? Mach eine Liste! Dann frag deinen Partner, was er gemacht hat! Danach tauscht ihr die Rollen aus!

29 Für mein Notizbuch

Schreiben Beschreib in deinem Notizbuch dein Lieblingswochenende! Wo warst du? Was hast du alles gemacht? Was hast du gesehen, gelesen oder gekauft?

30

Von der Schule zum Beruf

Schreiben You have become the manager of a movie theater. As part of your duties, you send the local newspaper a listing of movies that will be shown at your theater in the coming week. In order to attract moviegoers, you have decided to describe the movies briefly, along with giving any other details useful to the viewer.

AUSSPRACHE

Richtig aussprechen / Richtig lesen

A. To review the following sounds, say the sentences below after your teacher or after the recording.

1. The long and short **o**: The long **o** sounds similar to the long *o* in the English word *toe*. When the letter **o** is followed by two or more consonants (except when followed directly by **h**), it is pronounced as a short vowel, as in the English word *on*.
Wo wohnt die Monika? In der Bodenstraße?
Mein Onkel Otto kommt oft in der Woche zu Besuch.

2. The long and short **u**: The long **u** is pronounced much like the vowel sound in the English word *do*. However, when the letter **u** is followed by two or more consonants, it is pronounced as a short vowel like the *u* in the English word *put*.
Ich find die Musik super. Du auch, Uwe?
Ulrike mag die Gruppe „Untergrund" furchtbar gern. Und ihr?

3. The letter combination **ch**: When the consonant combination **ch** follows the vowels **e, i, ä, ö,** and **ü,** it is pronounced like the *h* in the English word *huge*. Following the vowels **a, o,** and **u,** it is pronounced further back in the throat.
So ein Pech! Ich möchte gern mit Michaela ins Kino, aber ich kann nicht.
Jochen geht doch lieber nach Hause und liest ein Buch und macht Hausaufgaben.

Richtig schreiben / Diktat

B. Write down the sentences that you hear.

Was sagen die Kritiker?

Lesestrategie **Watch for false cognates** Remember to look for cognates as individual words as well as in compound words to help you determine meanings. Occasionally, you will encounter false cognates (words that look alike in both languages but have totally different meanings). Context clues can sometimes help you recognize false cognates. (A good example of a false cognate is the English word *gift*. You will find the same word in German (**Gift**), but you would hardly want to give it to someone you care about: it means *poison*!)

1. Write the English equivalents for the following cognates:
   a. exklusiv
   b. militärisch
   c. desillusioniert
   d. Radio-Meteorologe
   e. zynisch

2. You already know a couple of false cognates. Try to determine (from the choices given) what the false cognates in the following sentences might mean.

   a. Wenn du wissen möchtest, welche Themen in Deutschland **aktuell** sind, musst du eine deutsche Zeitung lesen.
   1. *actual* 2. *out of date*
   3. *current*

   b. Wer einmal diesen Krimi zu lesen begonnen hat, kann **die Lektüre** nicht unterbrechen, weil das Buch so spannend ist.
   1. *lecture* 2. *lesson* 3. *reading*

3. a. With a partner, write down all the cognates you can find in these selections. Include those cognates that are in compound words, even if part of the compound is not a cognate.

Groundhog Day
(UND TÄGLICH GRÜSST DAS MURMELTIER)

Phil ist ein Ekel. Doch eines Tages wird der zynische und oberflächliche Radio-Meteorologe verzaubert: Die Zeit steht still. Wieder und wieder muß er den von ihm so gehaßten GROUNDHOG DAY, ein Frühlingsfest, in den skurrilsten und wahnwitzigsten Situationen erleben, bis aus ihm endlich ein liebenswerter Mensch geworden ist.

GROUNDHOG DAY von Harold Ramis, mit Bill Murray, Andie MacDowell, Chris Elliott, Stephen Tobolowski u.a.
Englische Originalfassung   103 Min.

John Grisham
Die Firma

Etwas ist faul an der exklusiven Kanzlei, bei der Mitch McDeere arbeitet. Der hochbegabte junge Anwalt wird auf Schritt und Tritt beschattet, er ist umgeben von tödlichen Gefahren. Als er dann noch vom FBI unter Druck gesetzt wird, erweist sich der Traumjob endgültig als Alptraum…

Roman. 544 Seiten.
Gebunden mit Schutzumschlag.

Nr. 02001 6
Club-Preis   **17.45**

OK-PUR TAGESTIP

The Romeos
Nicht aus dem New Yorker Italo-Distrikt, sondern aus Bremen und Oldenburg kommen die Mitglieder der Band. Weniger banal die Musik der Jungs. Bei einer großen Plattenfirma unter Vertrag gelten sie als vielleicht eines der größten Talente der deutschen Popszene.
29.4. Marquee, 21:00 Uhr

JURASSIC PARK™

Spielbergs spektakulärster Film seit Jahren. Gen-Ingenieure haben für einen Freizeitpark Dinosaurier zum Leben erweckt. Eines Tages wird aus dem Spiel mit der Vorzeit blutiger Ernst...

Mit: Sam Neill, Laura Dern, Richard Attenborough
Regie: Stephen Spielberg
Verleih: UIP

FREITAG, 9. JULI 1993

DER MIT DEM WOLF TANZT

USA 1990, 180 Minuten, CinemaScope, Dolby-Stereo;
Ein Film von Kevin Costner.
Mit Kevin Costner, Mary MacDowell und anderen.

Vom Bürgerkrieg und militärischem Drill desillusioniert, läßt sich Lieutenant John J. Dunbar, ein Offizier der Nordstaaten im äußersten Westen, am Rand der Zivilisation, im Sioux-Gebiet nieder. In einem abgelegenen Blockhaus bezieht er Stellung und knüpft behutsamen Kontakt mit den Indianern, deren Kultur er langsam zu begreifen und zu schätzen lernt. Er nimmt ihre Sitten und Gebräuche an, und sie beginnen, ihn als einer der ihren zu akzeptieren. Sie geben ihm den Namen "der mit dem Wolf tanzt". Doch die scheinbare Idylle findet ein jähes Ende, als eine Einheit der US-Kavallerie anrückt, die den verschollen geglaubten Dunbar aufspüren soll.

b. List any false cognates that you find. Were you able to figure out the meaning? If so, how?

4. What do these reading selections have in common? Where do you think you might find them?

5. How many of the selections mention something or someone you are familiar with? How does being familiar with the topics help you read the selections?

6. Read the articles and see if you can figure out

    a. what Jo Backe did to ease the difficulties in making his new video

    b. where Harry McBride thinks he has more fans: in Germany or in Ireland

    c. the name of the group regarded as one of the most talented on the German pop scene

7. In groups of two to four, read the articles about the movies and the book, then answer these questions. Be prepared to share your findings with the class.

    a. What do you think **Original-fassung** means at the end of the article on *Groundhog Day*? What is the German word for groundhog?

    b. What do you think the word **Bürgerkrieg** means in the article on *Der mit dem Wolf tanzt?*

    c. What do you think **Traumjob** means in the article on *Die Firma*? Knowing the story, what do you think then that **Alptraum** means?

8. Your German pen pal wants to know what movies or books you have seen or read recently and would recommend. Write a two or three sentence response in German, recommending one movie or book that you like.

Übungsheft, S. 119, Ü. 23

Mehr Grammatikübungen

☐ internet

go.
hrw
.com

ADRESSE: go.hrw.com
KENNWORT:
WK3 BADEN-WUERTTEMBERG-10

Erste Stufe   **Objectives** Expressing likes and dislikes

1 Welche Musik hast du gern, und welche Musik haben deine Freunde gern? Schreib
die folgenden Sätze ab und schreib dabei die richtige Form von **mögen** in
die Lücken. **(S. 282)**

1. Was für Musik _____ du gern? — Ich _____ Country gern.
2. Und was _____ dein Bruder? — Er _____ nur Rock.
3. Deine Eltern, was _____ sie? — Sie _____ klassische Musik.
4. Die Sabine, was _____ sie gern? — Sie _____ alles gern.
5. Was _____ ihr gern, Eva und Bob? — Wir _____ gern Jazz.

2 Welche Filme magst du nicht und welche Filme haben deine Freunde nicht gern?
Schreib die folgenden Sätze und Fragen ab und schreib dabei die richtige Form von
mögen, kein und die Art des Filmes in die Lücken. **(S. 282)**

BEISPIEL   (Sciencefictionfilme)   Wir _____ _____ _____ .
            Wir <u>mögen</u> <u>keine</u> <u>Sciencefictionfilme</u>.

1. (Horrorfilme)   Also, ich _____ .
2. (Western)   Und du _____ , nicht?
3. (Kriegsfilme)   Wir _____ .
4. (Krimis)   Ihr _____ , nicht wahr?
5. (Liebesfilme)   Meine Freunde _____ .
6. (Komödien)   Der Martin _____ .

3 Ihr sprecht über Filme. Wer mag welchen Film am liebsten? Schreib Sätze und gebrauche dabei alle Wörter, wie im Beispiel. (**S. 282**)

BEISPIEL **wir / Horrorfilme / am liebsten / mögen**
<u>**Wir mögen Horrorfilme am liebsten.**</u>

1. ich / Western / am liebsten / mögen

2. Paul / Kriegsfilme / am liebsten / mögen

3. die Schüler / Krimis / am liebsten / mögen

4. ihr / Actionfilme / am liebsten / mögen

5. Mary / Komödien / am liebsten / mögen

6. die Kinder / Videos / am liebsten / mögen

4 Für das englische Verb „*to know*" gibt es im Deutschen zwei Verben, **wissen,** *to know a fact* und **kennen,** *to know a person* oder *to be familiar with something.* Schreib die folgenden Sätze ab und schreib dabei die richtige Verbform in die Lücken. (**S. 284**)

1. Sag mal, _____ du, wann der Film „Das Boot" beginnt, und _____ du den Schauspieler? Ich möchte _____ , wie er heißt.

2. Ich _____ den Schauspieler nicht, aber ich _____ , wo er wohnt.

3. Martin und Sandra, _____ ihr, wo wir diese Rockgruppe hören können, und _____ ihr den Sänger der Gruppe? ___ ihr, wie er heißt?

4. Sag, _____ der Martin dieses Lied, und _____ er, wo ich eine CD mit diesem Lied finden kann? — Du, ich frag meinen Bruder. Der _____ das!

Zweite Stufe

Objective Expressing preferences and favorites

5 Was hast du und was haben deine Freunde gern, lieber, am liebsten? Schreib die folgenden Sätze ab und schreib dabei die richtige Form von **sehen** und **gern, lieber,** oder **am liebsten** in die Lücken. (**S. 285**)

1. Ich _____ _____ Krimis, aber Kriegsfilme _____ ich _____ ; und _____ _____ ich Abenteuerfilme.

2. Was _____ du _____ ? Krimis? Oder _____ du Komödien _____ ? Was _____ du denn _____ ?

3. Wir _____ Western _____ , aber der Martin _____ Krimis _____ . Ja, aber er _____ doch Komödien _____ .

6 Du sagst deinen Freunden, was du gern tust und was du am liebsten tust. Schreib Sätze mit einem Verb und „gern" und „am liebsten" und suche dir dabei passende Wortpaare aus dem Kasten aus. (S. 285)

BEISPIEL   **gern trinken [Kaffee / Cola]**
            Ich trinke gern Kaffee, aber Cola trinke ich am liebsten.

Cola   Deutsch   Fußball   Hamburger   Krimis

Hemden   Horrorfilme   Jazz

Mathe   meine Tante

Limo   meine Oma

Pizza   Rock

Pullis   Volleyball

1. gern haben
2. gern sehen
3. gern hören
4. gern spielen
5. gern besuchen
6. gern anziehen
7. gern essen
8. gern trinken

Dritte Stufe

Objectives Telling about what you do or did in your free time

7 Worüber lesen und sprechen deine Freunde in ihrer Freizeit? Schreib die folgenden Sätze ab und schreib dabei die richtige Verbform von **lesen** oder **sprechen** in die Lücken. (S. 291)

1. Also, ich _____ gern Romane. Und du, was _____ du gern?
2. Mein Bruder _____ gern Krimis, und mein Vater _____ sie auch gern.
3. Was _____ ihr denn gern, Sandra und Michael? _____ ihr auch Krimis?
4. Worüber _____ ihr in der Deutschklasse? _____ ihr über Mode?
5. Ich weiß, worüber du gern _____ . Politik. Ich _____ auch über Politik.
6. Wir _____ gern über die Umwelt. _____ ihr auch über die Umwelt?

8 Du sagst jemandem, was du in deiner Freizeit gemacht hast. Schreib die folgenden Sätze ab und schreib dabei eine passende Verbform in die Lücken. **(S. 292)**

1. Am Samstag _____ ich in einem super Konzert.
2. Am Sonntag habe ich einen prima Film _____ .
3. Am Nachmittag habe ich ein Buch _____ .
4. Danach habe ich mit meiner Freundin über Mode _____ .
5. Ja, und was hast du am Wochenende _____ ?

9 Schreib, was du mit deinen Freunden letztes Wochenende gemacht hast. **(S. 292)**

BEISPIEL   Wir _____ im Kino, und wir _____ einen _____ _____ .
Wir <u>waren</u> im Kino und wir <u>haben</u> einen <u>Western gesehen</u>.

Actionfilm	Gruselroman	Politik
Hausaufgaben	Pandabär	Video

1. Ich _____ im Kino, und ich _____ einen _____ _____ .
2. Peter _____ zu Hause. Er __ einen _____ _____ .
3. Ich _____ mit Mark im Zoo. Wir _____ einen _____ _____ .
4. Wir _____ in der Schule und _____ über _____ _____ .
5. Ich _____ am Abend zu Hause und _____ _____ _____ .
6. Ann _____ zu Hause, und sie _____ mit Monika ein _____ _____ .

internet

go. ADRESSE: go.hrw.com
hrw KENNWORT:
.com WK3 BADEN-WUERTTEMBERG-10

1 You will hear four students talk about how they spend their free time. Make a chart like the one here and fill in the information for each student as you listen.

Name	wohin?	was?	wann?	wie oft?
1				
2				

2 Now interview two classmates, asking them where they go and what they do in their free time, and when and how often they do these things. Continue the above chart, filling in the appropriate information for your classmates. Then switch roles.

3 Read the text of this movie ad and answer the following questions about it:

1. What is the name of the main character in the ad?

2. What is this character's profession?

3. Where does he settle?

4. What change is taking place in this man?

5. Is he being accepted by the Indians?

6. Why doesn't he stay with the Indians?

4 Working in pairs, write a review of a movie expressing your feelings about a specific movie that you have seen.

5 Write down the nine different kinds of films you learned on page 281, each on a separate slip of paper, and put them into a container. The class will divide up into two teams. Partners from each team will take turns drawing a movie type and acting that movie type out in front of the class. The two teams will take turns guessing what kind of movie it is.

FREITAG, 9. JULI 1993

DER MIT DEM WOLF TANZT

USA 1990, 180 Minuten, CinemaScope, Dolby-Stereo;
Ein Film von Kevin Costner.
Mit Kevin Costner, Mary MacDowell und anderen.

Vom Bürgerkrieg und militärischem Drill desillusioniert, läßt sich Lieutenant John J. Dunbar, ein Offizier der Nordstaaten im äußersten Westen, am Rand der Zivilisation, im Sioux-Gebiet nieder. In einem abgelegenen Blockhaus bezieht er Stellung und knüpft behutsamen Kontakt mit den Indianern, deren Kultur er langsam zu begreifen und zu schätzen lernt. Er nimmt ihre Sitten und Gebräuche an, und sie beginnen, ihn als einer der ihren zu akzeptieren. Sie geben ihm den Namen "der mit dem Wolf tanzt". Doch die scheinbare Idylle findet ein jähes Ende, als eine Einheit der US-Kavallerie anrückt, die den verschollen geglaubten Dunbar aufspüren soll.

6 Zum Schreiben

You are a famous talent agent with a hot new German rock group to publicize during the "Summer Rock" festival in your town. Write a publicity blurb for a local newspaper and design an eye-catching poster to publicize the group.

> **Schreibtipp Using a topic sentence** at the beginning of a paragraph lets the reader know what to expect in the rest of the paragraph. A topic sentence also helps focus your writing. The **summary** sentence at the end of the paragraph helps pull all the details in the paragraph together.

Prewriting

The rock group needs a name and a type of rock music. **Brainstorm** with your group/class for rock group names and other necessary information for your advertisement. Your publicity blurb should include (but not be limited to) the group's song titles, the places they have played, the movies they have made, and the stars with whom they made the movies. Also include any future movie plans, book rights the group may own, and the date and location the group will be featured at the festival. Include the movie houses/video rental stores which will feature their movies during the coming festival to help convince your audience that this is the group to see. Include this information on your poster.

Writing

Using this information, begin your writing with a **topic sentence** that will introduce your subject and focus your writing, then develop your publicity, and end with a **summarizing sentence.**

Revising

- After writing your paragraph, set it aside for a day and then reread it.
- Assess its strengths and weaknesses.
- Make changes, then read your paper aloud, listening for confusing statements and awkward wording. Have a peer evaluate strengths and weaknesses of your paragraph.
- Revise, proofread, and submit your paragraph to your teacher.

7 Rollenspiel

Get together with two or three other classmates and create an original scene for one of the following situations. Role-play your scene in front of the class.

a. You are in front of a movie theater and want to see a film. Talk about the different movies and say which ones you like, dislike, and strongly dislike, and which one(s) you have already seen. Then decide together which movie you will see.

b. You and your friends are at the video store to rent (**ausleihen**) a movie. Talk about what kinds of movies each of you likes and decide on a movie everyone will enjoy. Don't forget to mention any movies you have already seen.

Kann ich's wirklich?

Can you express likes and dislikes using mögen? (p. 282)

1 How would you ask a friend what type of movie he or she likes? How might he or she respond?

2 How would you say that
  a. Thomas likes horror films a lot
  b. Julia really doesn't like rock music at all
  c. Sabine and Nicole like fantasy films
  d. We don't care for romance movies

Can you express familiarity using kennen? (p. 284)

3 How would a friend ask if you are familiar with
  a. the movie *Air Force One*
  b. the singer Ina Deter
  c. the group R.E.M.
  d. the film star Clint Eastwood

4 How would you respond to each of your friend's questions?

Can you express preferences and favorites? (p. 285)

5 How would you tell a friend what type of movies you like to see, what type of movies you prefer, and what type of movies you like best of all?

6 How would you say that
  a. Martin likes adventure movies, but prefers movies about romance.
  b. Sandra likes horror films best of all.
  c. Sabine doesn't like to read magazines and prefers to read newspapers.

Can you talk about what you did in your free time? (p. 292)

7 How would you ask a friend what he or she did on the weekend? How would your friend respond if he or she
  a. saw the movie *The Lost World* on Saturday evening
  b. read a newspaper on Sunday
  c. saw the movie *Michael Collins* on video on Friday evening
  d. read the book *The Horse Whisperer* on Saturday
  e. was at the Billy Joel concert on Friday evening
  f. bought clothes and talked about fashion with his or her friends

8 Write a short paragraph describing what you saw, read, or talked about with your friends last weekend.

Erste Stufe

Expressing likes and dislikes

verbringen	to spend (time)	der Science-fictionfilm, -e	science fiction movie	der Sänger, -	singer (male)
mögen	to like, care for			die Sängerin, -nen	singer (female)
Was für Filme magst du gern?	What kind of movies do you like?	der Western, -	western (movie)	die Gruppe, -n	group
		Was für Musik hörst du gern?	What kind of music do you like?	das Lied, -er	song
der Film, -e	movie			**Degrees of liking and disliking**	
der Abenteuerfilm, -e	adventure movie	klassische Musik	classical music	besonders gern	especially like
der Actionfilm, -e	action movie	die Oper, -n	opera	furchtbar gern	like a lot
der Horrorfilm, -e	horror movie	**Expressing familiarity**		gar nicht gern	not like at all
die Komödie, -n	comedy			überhaupt nicht gern	strongly dislike
der Kriegsfilm, -e	war movie	kennen	to know, be familiar or ac- quainted with	sehr gern	very much
der Krimi, -s	detective movie, crime drama				
der Liebesfilm, -e	romance	der Schauspieler, -	actor		
		die Schauspielerin, -nen	actress		

Zweite Stufe

Expressing preferences and favorites

lieber (mögen)	prefer	spannend	exciting, thrilling	schmalzig	corny, mushy
am liebsten (mögen)	like most of all	sensationell	sensational	traurig	sad
		lustig	funny	doof	dumb
sehen	to see	zu grausam	too cruel		
er/sie sieht	he/she sees	dumm	dumb, stupid		
phantasievoll	imaginative	brutal	brutal, violent		

Dritte Stufe

Talking about what you did in your free time

Was hast du am Wochenende gemacht?	What did you do on the week- end?	der Fantasyroman, -e	fantasy novel	er/sie spricht über ...	he/she talks about ...
		der Sciencefiction- roman, -e	science fiction novel	Worüber habt ihr gesprochen?	What did you (pl) talk about?
lesen	to read	der Krimi, -s	detective novel		
er/sie liest	he/she reads	das Sachbuch, ¨er	nonfiction book	die Politik	politics
Was hast du gelesen?	What did you read?	die Zeitung, -en	newspaper	die Mode	fashion
		die Zeitschrift, -en	magazine	die Umwelt	environment
der Roman, -e	novel	das Hobbybuch, ¨er	hobby book	Was hast du gesehen?	What did you see?
der Gruselroman, -e	horror novel	sprechen über	to talk about		
der Liebesroman -e	love story			das Video, -s	video (cassette)

11
Der Geburtstag

Objectives

In this chapter you will learn to

Erste Stufe

- use the telephone in Germany

Zweite Stufe

- invite someone to a party and accept or decline
- talk about birthdays and express good wishes

Dritte Stufe

- discuss gift ideas

internet

go.
hrw
.com

ADRESSE: go.hrw.com
KENNWORT:
WK3 BADEN-WUERTTEMBERG-11

◀ **Was schenkst du deiner Freundin?**

Los geht's! · *Geschenke aussuchen*

Strategie Verstehen
Look at the images for the story. Where are the girls? What are they doing? What do you think they are talking about?

Sabine   **Nicole**

①

Frau Kroll: Kroll.

Nicole: Guten Tag, Frau Kroll! Hier ist die Nicole. Ist die Sabine da?

Frau Kroll: Nein, Sabine ist mit ihrem Vater weg. Kann ich ihr etwas sagen?

Nicole: Ja, hm …sagen Sie ihr bitte, dass der Martin am Samstag Geburtstag hat! Und ich möchte für ihn eine Fete organisieren.

Frau Kroll: Na, prima! Ich sag es Sabine. Tschüs!

Nicole: Wiederhören, Frau Kroll!

②

Sabine: Was schenkst du dem Martin?

Nicole: Kein Problem! Ich kaufe ihm eine Kassette.

Sabine: Aber er hat doch schon so viele Kassetten.

Nicole: Na und?

Sabine: Warum kaufst du ihm keine CD?

Nicole: Er hat doch noch keinen CD-Player.

3

Sabine:	Was soll ich ihm bloß schenken? Was meinst du? Du kennst ihn besser. Eine Idee?
Nicole:	Kauf ihm doch ein Buch! Er liest auch gerne.
Sabine:	Bücher sind so teuer.

4

Nicole:	Dann schenk ihm halt ein T-Shirt mit einem Komponisten drauf! Das mag er bestimmt auch.
Sabine:	Eine prima Idee! — Schau mal, Nicole! Die Karte ist lustig, nicht?
Nicole:	Wahnsinn! Und lies mal den Vers!
Sabine:	Die schenk ich dem Martin!

Zu Hause bei Nicole

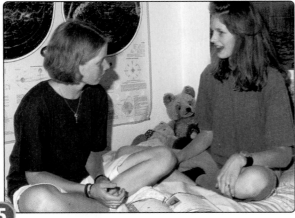

5

Sabine:	Übrigens, weißt du, wann der Thomas Geburtstag hat?
Nicole:	Irgendwann im Sommer. Ich glaub, im August.
Sabine:	An welchem Tag?
Nicole:	Warum fragst du? Willst du …?
Sabine:	Nein, nein. Seinen Geburtstag feiern wir nie.

6

Nicole:	Im August haben wir immer Ferien.
Sabine:	Zeig her!
Nicole:	Schau, hier: am elften August!
Sabine:	Hier steht: „Martin am achtzehnten". Er hat also nicht diesen Samstag Geburtstag!
Nicole:	Was? Das kann doch nicht wahr sein! Was soll ich jetzt machen? Die kommen alle diesen Samstag!

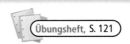

Übungsheft, S. 121

1 Was passiert hier?

Do you understand what is happening in **Los geht's!**? Check your comprehension by answering these questions. Don't be afraid to guess.

1. Why does Nicole call Sabine?
2. What do they discuss when they get together later?
3. What suggestions does Nicole make to Sabine? Which one does Sabine like the best?
4. What does Sabine discover when she looks up Thomas's birthday? What is Nicole's predicament?

2 Genauer lesen

Reread the conversations. Which words or phrases do the characters use to

1. begin and end a phone conversation
2. name gift ideas
3. ask for advice and opinions
4. say when someone's birthday is
5. express disbelief

3 Was ist richtig?

Was ist die beste Antwort, a., b., oder c.?

1. Nicole ruft Sabine an. Sie will ihr sagen, ══.
   a. dass sie eine Kassette gekauft hat
   b. dass sie für Martin eine Party geben will
   c. dass sie mit Martin ausgeht

2. Nicole kauft dem Martin keine CD, ══.
   a. weil er so viele Kassetten hat
   b. weil er keinen CD-Player hat
   c. weil er gern liest

3. Sabine schenkt Martin auch ══ zum Geburtstag.
   a. eine CD   b. ein Buch   c. eine Karte

4. Nicole und Sabine feiern nie den Geburtstag von Thomas, ══.
   a. weil sie Martin eine Karte schenken möchten
   b. weil alle im August Ferien haben
   c. weil Martin am 18. Geburtstag hat

5. Am Ende weiß Nicole nicht, was sie tun soll, ══.
   a. denn Martin hat am 18. Geburtstag, nicht diesen Samstag
   b. denn Thomas gibt Martin ein Buch
   c. denn sie hat Ferien

4 Nacherzählen

Put the sentences in logical order to make a brief summary of **Los geht's!**.

1. Nicole ruft Sabine an. Sie möchte über Martins Geburtstag sprechen.

Aber Sabine weiß nicht genau, was sie Martin kaufen soll.

Sabine findet, dass das T-Shirt die beste Idee ist.

Aber die Sabine ist nicht zu Hause.

Nicole will Martin eine Kassette kaufen.

Am Ende sieht Sabine in ihrem Adressbuch, dass Martin am 18. Geburtstag hat.

Dann hat Nicole eine Idee: vielleicht ein Buch oder ein T-Shirt.

Später sprechen die zwei Mädchen über Martins Geschenk.

Danach findet Sabine eine tolle Geburtstagskarte für Martin.

5 Und du?

Was möchtest du zum Geburtstag? Mach eine Liste! Dann frag deinen Partner, was er zum Geburtstag haben möchte!

den Hörer abheben   Münzen einstecken   die Nummer wählen   wieder auflegen

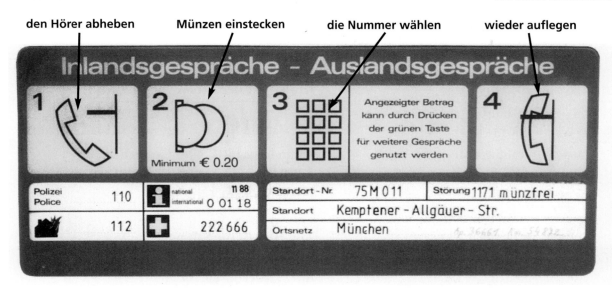

Inlandsgespräche – Auslandsgespräche

1

2 Minimum € 0.20

3 Angezeigter Betrag kann durch Drücken der grünen Taste für weitere Gespräche genutzt werden

4

Polizei Police	110	ℹ️ national international	11 88 0 01 18	Standort - Nr.	75 M 0 11	Störung 1171 m ünzfrei
🔥	112	✚	222 666	Standort	Kemptener - Allgäuer - Str.	
				Ortsnetz	München	

6 In der Telefonzelle

Lesen/Sprechen Schau dir die obige Information an und beantworte die Fragen.

1. What kind of information is this? Where would you expect to find it?
2. What number could you call to find out someone else's number in Germany?
3. Which emergency numbers are provided?
4. How would you tell a German exchange student (in German) how to use a phone booth in the United States? Use the four steps pictured above.

Wortschatz

Telefonieren ist nicht schwer!

Grammatikheft, S. 91–92, Ü. 1–2

CD-ROM DISC 3

der Apparat/ das Telefon

der Hörer

telefonieren/anrufen

den Hörer abheben
die Münzen einstecken
die Telefonnummer wählen
den Hörer auflegen
besetzt (busy)

die Telefonzelle

So sagt man das!

Using the telephone in Germany

Mehr Grammatikübungen
S. 324, Ü. 1

Here are some phrases you will need to know in order to talk on the phone in German:

Übungsheft, S. 122–124, Ü. 2–7

Grammatikheft, S. 92, Ü. 3

The person who answers says his or her name:	**Kroll.** *or* **Hier Kroll.**
The person calling says who he or she is:	**Hier ist die Nicole.**
The person calling asks to speak to someone:	**Ich möchte bitte Sabine sprechen.** *or* **Kann ich bitte Sabine sprechen?**
The person who answered says:	**Einen Moment, bitte.**
After the person comes to the phone, he or she might say:	**Tag! Hier ist die Sabine.**
The conversation may end with:	**Wiederhören!** *or* **Auf Wiederhören!** *or* **Tschüs!**

How are these phrases different from the ones you use when talking on the phone?

---

7 Was passt?

Zuhören Listen to the four telephone conversations and match each one with an appropriate illustration.

a.

c.

b.

d.

8 Tag! Hier ist ...

Sprechen Get together with a classmate and practice "calling" a friend on the telephone. Your partner will be the parent of the friend you are calling. Use the expressions you have learned so far. Then practice saying good-bye. When you are finished, switch roles.

9 Willst du einen Film sehen?

Sprechen Ruf deinen Partner an und frag ihn, ob er heute Abend mit dir ins Kino gehen will. Besprich mit ihm, was ihr euch ansehen wollt. Gebraucht dabei die Wörter in den Kästen.

person answering

Was für Filme magst du?   Tschüs!

Ja, prima!   Hier ist …   Tag …!

person calling

Hier …   Tag …!   Ich mag Liebesfilme sehr gern.

Willst du einen Film sehen?   Wiederhören!

10 Ich möchte bitte … sprechen

Sprechen You worked in the office at the youth center today, and a lot of people called in and left messages for their friends. Work with a partner to create the telephone conversations you would have as you attempt to pass along the messages to the appropriate people. Take turns playing the role of the office worker.

1. Call Stefan (who is not at home; you reach his mother) and let him know that Petra wants to play tennis tomorrow at 4 P.M.
2. Call Ulrike and remind her that the biology class on Tuesday is at 9 A.M. instead of (**anstatt**) at 10 A.M.
3. Call Holger and tell him that soccer practice is at 3 P.M. on Tuesday.
4. Monika is not home yet, but you need to let her know that Ulla called and wants to go shopping with her on Saturday morning at 9 A.M.

ein Kartentelefon

ein Handy

Ein wenig Landeskunde

It's easy to make a phone call in Germany from a private phone or from a phone booth.

Private mobile phones or cellular phones are becoming more and more popular, since many access providers have lowered the prices to be more competitive. A cellular phone is called **ein (das) Handy** (pl. **Handys**).

Public phones can be accessed by using coins, but most people use phone cards **(Telefonkarten)** that can be bought in various amounts at post offices or newspaper kiosks.

All phone booths will be replaced with six-foot high steel columns by 2005. They will have an **"Allpayment-Funktion"** so that users will be able to make phone calls using coins, phone cards, and credit cards.

For a local call, **ein Ortsgespräch,** you dial a local number consisting of four or five digits in small villages to seven digits in towns and large cities.

For a long distance call, **ein Ferngespräch,** you must dial an area code, **eine Vorwahlnummer,** such as 030 for Berlin or 089 for Munich. In small villages, the area code can have up to five digits.

eine Telefonkarte

When calling Germany from the United States, you must first dial the international access code 011, then the access code for Germany, 49, then the **Vorwahlnummer** without the 0. For example, when calling Berlin you dial 011 49 30 plus the local phone number.

When calling the United States from Germany, you first dial the US access code 001, then the area code and number. The least expensive way to call from abroad is most often a phone card issued by your telephone service provider.

Übungsheft, S. 132, Ü. 24

Mehr Grammatikübungen, S. 324, Ü. 2

Gesprächs-Notiz

		Uhrzeit
		7 | 8 | 9 | 10 | 11 | 12
		Tag
mit		20
		13 | 14 | 15 | 16 | 17 | 18

Straße
Ort
Vorwahl   Ruf
Betreff:

Unterschrift:

11 Gesprächs-Notiz

Sprechen Beantworte die folgenden Fragen.

1. What do you think the page on the left is used for? Which words are the clues for your answer?

2. Where would you record the date and time?

3. Where would you record the information about the person who called? What specific information is asked for in this section?

4. Where would you write the message?

5. Where would you sign the page if you took the call?

Übungsheft, S. 125, Ü. 8

12 Schreib auf, was du hörst!

Zuhören/Schreiben At your host family's home in Germany, someone calls while one of the family members is out. Make a German phone message page like the one pictured above. Then take down all the information asked for on the **Gesprächs-Notiz**. For the actual message, just write down a few notes. What phrase did the person answering the phone use at the beginning of the conversation? What is its English equivalent?

13 Deine Gesprächs-Notiz

Schreiben Using your notes from Activity 12, rewrite the message in neat sentences so that it can be easily understood by the person receiving it. Then switch papers with a partner and check whether your partner wrote his or her message correctly.

14 Ruf mal an!

Sprechen Decide on a free time activity that you would like to do with your partner. Call your partner and invite him or her to come along. Then switch roles. Here are a few possibilities:

> **Ich mache am Samstag eine Party. Kannst du kommen?**
> **Ich möchte heute in die Stadt fahren. Kommst du mit?**

Zweite Stufe

Objectives Inviting someone to a party and accepting or declining; talking about birthdays and expressing good wishes

WK3-BADEN-WUERTTEMBERG-11

15 Eine Einladung

Lesen/Sprechen Schau die Einladung an und beantworte die folgenden Fragen!

1. Wer schickt die Einladung?
2. Für wen ist die Fete? Warum?
3. Wann ist die Fete? An welchem Tag? Um wie viel Uhr?
4. Wo ist die Fete?
5. Welche Nummer kannst du anrufen, um Information zu bekommen?
6. Was musst du tun, um zu sagen, ob (*whether*) du kommen kannst?

> **Fete!** **Ich lade dich ein!** **Fete!**
>
> _Wann?_ am Samstag, den 11. Juni
> _Um wie viel Uhr?_ 19 Uhr
> _Wo?_ Martin-Luther-Strasse 8
> _Telefon:_ 07142 / 6376
> Martin hat Geburtstag! Wir wollen feiern!
> Ruf mich bitte an, wenn du kommen kannst.
> Deine Nicole

So sagt man das!

Inviting someone to a party and accepting or declining

You invite a friend:

> **Ich habe am Samstag eine Party.**
> **Ich lade dich ein.**
> **Kannst du kommen?**

Your friend might respond:

> **Ja, gern!** *or*
> **Aber sicher!** *or*
> **Natürlich!** *or*
> **Leider kann ich nicht.**

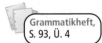

Grammatikheft, S. 93, Ü. 4

Which response would you use if you already had a previous engagement?[1]

16 Eine Einladung

Schreiben Schreib eine Einladung! Was für eine Fete ist das? An welchem Tag ist die Fete? Um wie viel Uhr beginnt sie? Wo ist sie? Wenn man nicht kommen kann, soll man anrufen?

17 Ich möchte dich einladen!

Sprechen You are having a party and want to invite several of your friends. "Call" two other classmates and invite each of them to the party. They will ask you for information about the party and then tell you whether they can come. If not, they should give you a reason. You should respond appropriately. End your conversation, then switch roles so that each person takes a turn extending the invitations.

---

1. Leider kann ich nicht.

Talking about birthdays and expressing good wishes

If you want to find out when a friend has his or her birthday, you ask:

Wann hast du Geburtstag?

Wann hat Martin Geburtstag?

Your friend might respond:

Ich habe am 28. Oktober* Geburtstag. *or*
Am 28. Oktober.
Bald. Nächste Woche.

There are a number of things you can say to express good wishes:

Alles Gute zum Geburtstag!
Herzlichen Glückwunsch zum Geburtstag!

_____
*Read as: **am achtundzwanzigsten Oktober.**

 Grammatikheft, S. 94, Ü. 5–6

Wortschatz

Wann hast du Geburtstag?

am 1. = am ersten (Juli)
am 2. = am zweiten
am 3. = am dritten
am 4. = am vierten
am 5. = am fünften
am 6. = am sechsten
am 7. = am siebten
am 8. = am achten
am 9. = am neunten
am 10. = am zehnten
am 11. = am elften
        usw.
am 20. = am zwanzigsten
am 21. = am einundzwanzigsten
        usw.

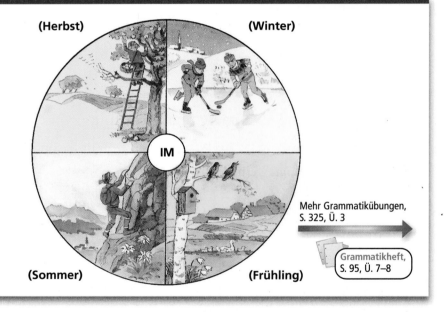

(Herbst)   (Winter)

IM

(Sommer)   (Frühling)

Mehr Grammatikübungen, S. 325, Ü. 3

Grammatikheft, S. 95, Ü. 7–8

18 Geburtstagskette

Sprechen One person in the class begins the chain by asking another: **Wann hast du Geburtstag?** That person answers and asks someone else. Continue until everyone has been asked.

19 Wann haben Anjas Freunde Geburtstag?

Zuhören Das Schuljahr ist bald zu Ende. Anja will wissen, wer im Sommer Geburtstag hat. Sie fragt ihre Klassenkameraden und schreibt dann die Geburtstage in ihr Adressbuch. Schreib, wann Anjas Freunde Geburtstag haben!

1. Bernd   **2.** Maja   **3.** Benjamin   **4.** Katrin   **5.** Mario

20 Für mein Notizbuch

Schreiben Schreib, wann du Geburtstag hast! Welches Geschenk hast du am liebsten? Schreib auch, wann deine Eltern, deine Geschwister und deine Freunde Geburtstag haben!

Ein wenig Landeskunde

Birthdays are important occasions in German-speaking countries and are usually celebrated with family and friends. In some areas of Germany (primarily in the strongly Catholic areas) and in Austria, the **Namenstag,** or Saint's Day, is also celebrated. Children in these areas are named after certain saints, such as **Johannes, Josef,** and **Maria.** There is a saint's day for each day of the year. Anyone named for a saint also celebrates on the day that honors that saint. The **Namenstag** celebration is similar to a birthday celebration, with a party, gifts, and flowers for the honoree.

Namenstag im Juli

10. Erich/Erika
13. Margarete
15. Heinrich
24. Christine
25. Jakob
26. Anne Marie
29. Martha

Gratulieren Sie mit Blumen!

Wortschatz

Feiertage

Weihnachten:
Fröhliche Weihnachten!

Chanukka:
Frohes Chanukka-Fest!

Ostern:
Frohe Ostern!

Vatertag:
  Alles Gute zum
  Vatertag!

Muttertag:
  Alles Gute zum
  Muttertag!

Mehr Grammatikübungen,
S. 325, Ü. 4

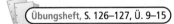

Übungsheft, S. 126–127, Ü. 9–15

---

21 Was passt?

Zuhören You will hear four conversations about four different holidays. Match each conversation to the most appropriate card.

22 Eine Geburtstagskarte

Schreiben Design a German birthday card or a card for another special occasion to send to a friend or family member. Below are some common German good luck symbols.

Schornsteinfeger

Glücksschwein

Glücksklee

Hufeisen

Marienkäfer

CD-ROM
DISC 3

VIDEO

Was schenkst du zum Geburtstag?

We asked several teenagers what they usually give as birthday presents. Before you read the interviews, write what you give your friends and relatives for their birthdays.

Melanie, Hamburg

„Ich geh mit Freunden essen oder lade sie zu mir ein. Und dann sitzen wir zusammen und unterhalten uns nett oder Ähnliches, … ansonsten gar nichts weiter. Bei Familienmitgliedern ist es ähnlich, da feiern wir auch in der Familie. Und schenken tu ich dann meiner Schwester zum Beispiel, die hört ziemlich gerne Musik, und der schenk ich dann Kassetten oder CDs oder Ähnliches. Und ansonsten eben schenk ich Bücher oder eben andere Kleinigkeiten, für die sich die Freunde oder Familienmitglieder interessieren."

Eva, Berlin

„Eigentlich hass ich Geburtstage, weil ich nie weiß, was ich schenken soll. Es ist irgendwie immer dasselbe, Bücher oder Kassetten oder CDs. Und na ja, dann sucht man sich immer was aus. Meistens verschenkt man Gutscheine, weil … da kann man nichts falsch machen."

Rosi, Berlin

„Also wenn ich auf Geburtstage gehe von Freunden oder Freundinnen, die ich gut kenne, dann geb ich auch mal mehr Geld aus. Dann kriegen sie schon persönliche Geschenke, wo sie sich auch darüber freuen. Und wenn ich auf Geburtstage gehe von Leuten, die ich nicht so gut kenne, dann nehme ich nur Kleinigkeiten mit. Aber ich nehm eigentlich immer was mit, wenn ich auf Geburtstage gehe."

Jutta, Hamburg

„Ich hab einen kleinen Bruder, und er ist elf, und der spielt unheimlich gern mit Lego,™ und dem schenk ich dann was zum Spielen oder eine Musikkassette. Und wenn ich bei Freunden eingeladen bin, meistens was Selbstgemachtes, ein bemaltes T-Shirt, ja auch eine Musikkassette, ein Buch oder ein gemaltes Bild."

A. 1. Make a list of the gifts these teenagers give as birthday presents and to whom they give them. What do you think **Gutscheine** might be? *Hint: they are available for many different things, such as cassettes, CDs, and books.*

2. Rosi has two categories of people she buys gifts for. What are they? What are some of the differences in the types of gifts she buys for each one?

3. Why does Eva not care much for birthdays? Do you agree or disagree with her?

4. Of the four people interviewed, who do you think puts the most thought and time into giving just the right gift? What statements support your answer?

B. Use the list you made earlier to write an answer to the questions **Was schenkst du zum Geburtstag, und wem schenkst du das?** Share your answers with your classmates and decide which of the interviews above most closely resembles your own. Are there any differences in the things teenagers give as gifts in the German-speaking countries and in the United States? If so, what are they and why do you think this is so? If not, why not?

23 Im Geschenkladen

Lesen/Sprechen Here is an excerpt from an article in the teen magazine *JUMA.* Look at the photo and read the caption. Then answer the questions that follow.

1. Using the photo as a clue, what do you think a **Geschenkladen** is? What do you think the topic of this article is?

2. Reread the caption. Do you think Martina is finding a lot of things she could buy? Why or why not?

3. What gift does Martina decide to buy for her friend? Do you think she buys anything else? If so, what?

4. Was für Geschenke schenkst du Verwandten (*relatives*) und Freunden? Wo kaufst du gewöhnlich Geschenke? Fünf Euro sind ungefähr sechs Dollar. Was kannst du für sechs Dollar kaufen?

Martina, 14, will ihrer Freundin etwas zum Namenstag schenken. Im Geschenkladen sucht sie lange nach einer Kleinigkeit. Die meisten Sachen kosten mehr als fünf Euro. Martina entscheidet sich für eine Kerze. Dann geht sie in ein Süßwarengeschäft.

Wortschatz

Geschenkideen

Bärbel: Was schenkst du Jutta zum Geburtstag?
Berndt: Ich weiß noch nicht. Vielleicht …

eine Armbanduhr

Pralinen

einen Blumenstrauß

einen Kalender

ein Poster

eine CD

Parfüm

Schmuck

Was schenkst du zu verschiedenen Feiertagen, z. B. zum Muttertag?

Grammatikheft, S. 96, Ü. 9

So sagt man das!

Discussing gift ideas

When talking about birthdays and holidays with friends, you'll also want to be able to discuss gift ideas.

You might ask your friend:

> **Schenkst du deinem Vater einen Kalender zum Geburtstag?**

> **Und was schenkst du deiner Mutter zum Muttertag?**

> **Kauf ihr doch ein Buch!**

> **Wem schenkst du den Blumenstrauß?**

Your friend might respond:

> **Nein, ich schenke ihm wahrscheinlich eine CD, weil er doch Musik so gern hört.**

> **Ich weiß noch nicht. Hast du eine Idee?**

> **Prima Idee! Das mach ich!**

> **Der Nicole schenke ich den Strauß.**

Can you find the subject and the verb in each of these sentences? What is the item being given (the direct object) in the first question?[1] Who is the person receiving the gift (the indirect object)?[2] In the first response, you see the word **ihm**. To whom does it refer?[3] To whom does the word **ihr** refer in the sentence **Kauf ihr doch ein Buch!**?[4]

Übungsheft,
S. 128–129, Ü. 16–18

Grammatikheft,
S. 96, Ü. 10

---

24 ## Was soll man schenken?

Lesen/Sprechen Mechtild Kaldenkirchen and Gothild Thomas of Essen offer a unique information service. Read the article on the right, then answer these questions.

1. Wie heißt der Informationsservice von Mechtild und Gothild? Was für Information können sie uns geben? Gib ein oder zwei Beispiele!

2. Was muss man machen, um die Information zu bekommen?

3. Wie sagt man den letzten Satz auf Englisch?

25 ## Welches Geschenk?

Zuhören You call **Interkulturelle Beratung und Information** to find out the proper gift or gifts for families you'll visit on your trip to France, Italy, Spain, and Austria. On a separate piece of paper, write the gift(s) they advise you to give in each country: **Frankreich, Italien, Spanien,** and **Österreich.**

GESCHENKE
Hilfe per Telefon

Was bringt man als Gast einer Familie in Frankreich mit – Blumen, Pralinen oder Getränke? Wer viel reist, hat solche Probleme öfter. Helfen kann ein Bürgertelefon in Essen. Mechtild Kaldenkirchen und Gothild Thomas leiten die „Interkulturelle Beratung und Information": Sie informieren Anrufer aber nicht nur über Gastgeschenke im Ausland. Man kann nämlich auch erfahren, wie man sich im Ausland richtig benimmt. Denn eines ist ja allgemein bekannt: andere Länder, andere Sitten.

---

1. **einen Kalender** 2. **deinem Vater** 3. **ihm = Vater** 4. **ihr = Mutter**

Introduction to the dative case

You have learned that the subject of a sentence is in the nominative case and that the direct object is in the accusative case. A third case, the dative case, is used for indirect objects, which express the idea of "to someone" or "for someone." Look at the following sentences:

Robert, was schenkst du **deinem Opa**?
Und was schenkst du **deiner Oma**?

Ich schenke **ihm** einen Taschenrechner.
Ich schenke **ihr** ein Buch.

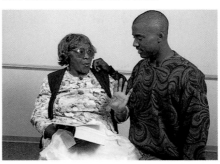

How would you say each of the above sentences in English?[1] Look at the photos for clues. You have already seen several examples of the dative case with definite articles after prepositions: **mit dem Bus, mit der U-Bahn.** Definite articles may also be used with proper names in the dative case:

Was kaufst du **dem Martin**?
Gibst du **der Sandra** das Geld?

Ich kaufe **ihm** ein T-Shirt.
Ja, ich gebe **ihr** morgen das Geld.

To ask the question "To whom …?" or "For whom …?" you use the dative form "**Wem** …?"

Wem schenkst du die Blumen?
Wem kaufst du das Buch?

To whom are you giving the flowers?
For whom do you buy the book?

Dative Case

masculine ⎱
neuter ⎰ **dem, ihm, deinem, meinem**
feminine ⎰ **der, ihr, deiner, meiner**

What pattern do you notice in the formation of the dative case? Make a chart of the definite articles, pronouns for *he* and *she*, and the possessive **mein** for all the cases you have learned so far. What patterns do you notice?

Mehr Grammatikübungen,
S. 325–326, Ü. 5–7

(Übungsheft, S. 129–130, Ü. 19–22) (Grammatikheft, S. 97–98, Ü. 11–14)

---

26 ### Grammatik im Kontext

Zuhören You're visiting Germany during the holiday season and would like to send something to your friends and family members. You ask your German friend for gift ideas. Your friend makes suggestions for specific family members and friends. Write down which gift he suggests for each person.

---

1. *Robert, what are you giving your grandfather? I'm giving him a calculator. And what are you giving your grandmother? I'm giving her a book.*

27 Grammatik im Kontext

Schreiben/Lesen Put the following sentence elements in the correct order to express what you and others are planning to give as presents at an upcoming party.

1. kaufe
   eine Bluse
   Ich
   meiner Oma

2. eine CD
   Peter
   schenken
   Wir

3. meiner Mutter
   ein Handy
   Mein Vater
   kauft

4. Und ich
   ihm
   schenke
   auch ein Buch

5. Sie
   dem Opa
   kauft
   einen Kalender

6. schenken
   ein Buch über Musik
   Wir
   meiner Mutter

7. eine Telefonkarte
   schenke
   meiner Freundin
   Ich

Grammatik

Notice the word order when you use the dative case. The indirect object (dative case) comes before the direct object (accusative case):

Ich schenke meiner Mutter ein Buch.
Ich schenke ihr ein Buch.

Grammatikheft, S. 99, Ü. 15

Mehr Grammatikübungen,
S. 326–327, Ü. 8–10

28 Grammatik im Kontext

Sprechen/Schreiben Take turns with your classmates asking and telling who is getting which gift. Practice replacing the noun phrases with the appropriate pronoun in the response. Use the drawings below as cues.

BEISPIEL　DU　**Was schenkst du deinem Bruder?**
MITSCHÜLER　**Ich schenke ihm einen Kuli.**

dein Bruder　　dein Vater　　deine Kusine　　deine Oma　　deine Lehrerin　　dein Onkel　　deine Schwester

29 Memory-Spiel

Sprechen Wem schenkst du ein Buch?

BEISPIEL　DU　**Ich schenke meiner Mutter ein Buch.**
MITSCHÜLER　**Ich schenke meiner Mutter und meinem Freund ein Buch.**

LERNTRICK

When you use indirect objects in your conversations, they must be in the dative case. It helps to remember that the dative forms for masculine and neuter articles and pronouns always end in **-m: dem, ihm, meinem, deinem.** The dative forms for feminine articles and pronouns always end with **-r: der, ihr, meiner, deiner.**

30 Eine Geschenkliste

Schreiben/Sprechen Make a list of what you would like to buy for three of your friends or family members for their birthdays. Give your partner a list with just the names of the people receiving gifts. Your partner will ask you what you plan to give them. Respond according to your list. Then switch roles. Jot down your partner's answers, then compare lists to see if you understood everything.

31 **Deine Europareise**

 Schreiben You're going to Europe! Decide which three countries you would like to visit. On a card write down the countries you choose, the souvenir you would buy from each, and the name of the person to whom you would like to give each souvenir.

Österreich

ein Buch   eine CD von Mozart

Schweiz (in der Schweiz)

Pralinen   eine Armbanduhr

Spanien

einen Fächer   Kastagnetten

Italien

Schuhe   ein Halstuch

Deutschland

einen Pulli   eine Kerze

32 **Ein Brief aus Europa**

 Schreiben Schreib einem Freund oder deiner Familie einen Brief über deine Europareise! Schreib, wo du warst, was du gekauft hast und wem du die Andenken (*souvenirs*) schenkst! Benutze deine Information von Übung 31!

33 **Von der Schule zum Beruf**

Schreiben You are the advertising manager of a souvenir shop chain in Germany. Your glossy advertising brochure has to be revised because many new items have been added to your inventory. Describe these items and target them for a particular audience.

AUSSPRACHE

 ### Richtig aussprechen / Richtig lesen

A. To review the following sounds, say the sentences below after your teacher or after the recording.

1. The letters **r** and **er:** The letter **r** is pronounced by placing the tip of the tongue behind your lower front teeth and then tipping the head back and pretending to gargle. The combination **er** at the end of a syllable or word is pronounced like the *a* in the English word *sofa.*

   Ich schenke meinem Bruder Rolf und seiner Frau ein Radio.
   Und ich schenke meiner Mutter Bücher und einen Kalender.

2. The letter **a:** The letter **a** is pronounced much like the *a* sound in the word *father.*

   Kaufst du dem Vater eine Armbanduhr oder eine Jacke zum Vatertag?

3. The diphthongs **eu, äu,** and **au:** The vowel combinations **eu** and **äu** sound similar to the *oy* sound in the English word *toy.* The diphthong **au** is pronounced like the *ow* sound in the English word *how.*

   Heute war der Verkäufer am Telefon ganz unfreundlich.
   Ich kaufe der Claudia einen Blumenstrauß.

Richtig schreiben / Diktat

B. Write down the sentences that you hear.

Billig einkaufen gehen

1. You are invited to a party and need to bring a gift. What can you buy for $5.00?

2. A foreign exchange student is also invited to the party. Where would you suggest that person should go to buy a gift for $5.00? What would you suggest might be a good gift for the foreign exchange student to buy?

3. Look at the title, the pictures, and the captions. Without actually reading the texts, what would you say is the type of reading selection on these pages? Are they ads, postcards, poems, or articles?

4. Judging by the title, what kind of information do you expect to find in these selections?

5. Read the article about Stefan through without stopping to ask about words you don't know. Then summarize the article in two or three sentences.

Was gibt's heute noch für 5 Euro?

Im Supermarkt läuft Ben durch die Regalreihen und vergleicht Preise. Viele Dinge nimmt er zuerst aus dem Regal und stellt sie wieder zurück, nachdem er den Preis gelesen hat. Er kauft Orangensaft und Cola.

▶ „Ich möchte etwas Sinnvolles kaufen. Etwas, das ich auch brauchen kann." Stefan lebt in der kleinen Stadt Schwalmtal nahe der niederländischen Grenze. Dort gibt es nicht viele Läden. Darum entscheidet er sich für ein kleines Schreibwarengeschäft am Marktplatz. Dort kauft er einen Zeichenblock, zwei Buntstifte, einen Anspitzer, ein Radiergummi und eine Geburtstagskarte. Die Geburtstagskarte ist das teuerste Teil seines Einkaufs: 1,75 Euro. Insgesamt hat er 5,02 Euro ausgegeben. Zwei Cent zu viel! „Es ist fast unmöglich, für genau 5 Euro einzukaufen."

Stefan ist mit seinem Einkauf zufrieden. „Nur die Geburtstagskarte fand ich ganz schön teuer. Aber insgesamt konnte ich doch einige nützliche Dinge kaufen. Einen dicken Filzschreiber für 1,40 Euro fand ich übertrieben teuer. Den habe ich nicht gekauft." Stefan bekommt 25 Euro Taschengeld im Monat. Den Betrag findet er „in Ordnung", obwohl das Geld selten reicht. In den Ferien verdient Stefan etwas dazu. „Dann räume ich in einem Lebensmittelgeschäft Ware in Regale ein." Von seinem Taschengeld kauft Stefan Süßigkeiten, Musik-CDs, kleine Geschenke wie Notizbücher oder Stifte und Pflanzen. Schulsachen muss er nicht kaufen. „Die bezahlen meine Eltern." Sein größter Wunsch: „Wenn ich Geld zu verschenken hätte, würden es Tierschutz- und Umweltorganisationen bekommen."

Stefans Freund Ben wohnt in der Kleinstadt Brüggen. Er entscheidet sich für den Einkauf in einem Supermarkt. „Wenn man nur 5 Euro zur Verfügung hat, bekommt man in einem Supermarkt wahrscheinlich die meisten Dinge. Außerdem gibt es in Supermärkten viele nützliche Sachen, die man für das tägliche Leben braucht." Im Supermarkt geht Ben durch die Regalreihen und vergleicht Preise. Die Auswahl fällt ihm schwer. Manche Dinge stellt er wieder ins Regal zurück. Ben bekommt für 5,05 Euro eine Zahnbürste, eine Flasche Orangensaft, eine Dose Cola, einen Sportdrink und einen Lippenpflege-Stift. Der Lippenpflege-Stift ist teuer. Er kostet 1,35 Euro. Ben glaubt, daß er gut eingekauft hat. „Ich habe mehr bekommen, als ich dachte. Einen Riesen-Unterschied gab es allerdings bei den Preisen für Getränkedosen. Das Marken-Getränk aus der Werbung kostete 99 Cent. Die Dose Cola war dagegen spottbillig: nur 25 Cent."

Ben bekommt pro Woche 4 Euro Taschengeld. Ihm reicht der Betrag. „Ich kann sogar ein bisschen Geld sparen, denn Schulsachen oder Kleidung muss ich nicht bezahlen. Diese Dinge kaufen meine Eltern." Von seinem Taschengeld kauft Ben ab und zu eine Compact Disc für sich oder ein kleines Geschenk, zum Beispiel ein Taschenbuch, für seine Freunde. Was würde Ben mit viel Geld machen? „Ich würde sofort eine Taucherausrüstung kaufen. Tauchen ist mein Hobby. Und wenn ich Geld verschenken könnte, dann würde ich es zum Schutz der Weltmeere und zum Schutz der Umwelt einsetzen."

Stefan wird im Schreibwarengeschäft von der Verkäuferin beraten. Sie zeigt ihm verschiedene Dinge und nennt ihm die Preise. Stefan braucht einige Zeit, bis er möglichst viele Sachen für fünf Euro gekauft hat.

6. Read the article about Ben through without stopping to ask about words you don't know. Then summarize the article in two or three sentences. In both articles, notice how much you can understand without knowing every word!

7. Read the article about Stefan again and try to answer these questions.
   a. What kind of store did Stefan shop in? What did he buy? What was his total bill?
   b. How much is Stefan's allowance per month? What does he buy with that money? What do his parents buy for him?
   c. What would Stefan do if he had money to give away?

8. Read the article about Ben again and try to answer these questions.
   a. Where does Ben think he can find the largest selection of useful items for 5 euros? How does he define "useful"?
   b. What do Ben's parents buy for him? For what does he use his own money?
   c. If Ben had a lot of money, what would he buy? To what cause would he give?

9. You are planning a trip to a German-speaking country in the summer and are going to stay with a family. Write a short note asking them what small items you might bring them.

Übungsheft, S. 131, Ü. 23

Erste Stufe

Objective Using the telephone

1 Was machst du, wenn du telefonieren willst? Schreib den folgenden Absatz *(paragraph)* ab und schreib dabei die fehlenden Wörter in die Lücken. Benutze die Wörter im Kasten. **(S. 310)**

anrufen	Apparat	Handy	Hörer
Münzen	Nummer	Telefonkarte	Telefonzelle

Du bist in der Stadt beim Einkaufen. Du willst zu Hause _____ , aber

du hast keine _____ . Was machst du? Du gehst in eine _____ . Du

nimmst den _____ ab und du schiebst eine _____ ein. Dann wählst

du die _____ . Aber du hörst *tüt, tüt, tüt:* der _____ ist besetzt.

2 Es gibt noch immer Münztelefone in Deutschland, und hier sind einige Anweisungen *(instructions)* für den Gebrauch solcher Telefone. Schreib den folgenden Absatz ab und schreib dabei passende Verbformen und passende Wörter in die Lücken. **(S. 310)**

Also, zuerst _____ du in die Telefonzelle _____ . Du _____ den Hörer

_____ und die Münzen _____ . Dann _____ du die Nummer _____ .

Wenn es besetzt ist, _____ du den Hörer wieder _____. — Wenn aber

jemand an den Apparat kommt, dann sagst du: _____ ich bitte Sabine

_____ ? Oder du _____ auch sagen: Ich _____ Sabine _____ , bitte.

Ist sie zu Hause?

Wenn du aber von einem Telefon mit einer „Allpayment-Funktion"

anrufst, so kannst du auch eine_____ benutzen. Aber vielleicht

brauchst du kein öffentliches Telefon mehr, weil du ein _____ hast.

Das ist bequem!

3 An welchem Tag finden diese Geburtstage und Feiertage statt? Schreib die richtigen Daten in die Lücken. (**S. 314**)

> **BEISPIEL**   **Mein Vater, 17. Mai**   Am ___ .
>   Am <u>siebzehnten Mai</u>.

1. Wer hat wann Geburtstag?
   a. George Washington, February 22   Am _____ .
   b. Susan B. Anthony, June 16   Am _____ .
   c. Martin Luther King Jr., January 15   Am _____ .
2. Wann sind diese Feiertage?
   a. Weihnachten, 25. Dezember   Am _____ .
   b. Ostern, 7. April   Am _____ .
   c. Tag der Arbeit, 3. September   Am _____ .

4 Schreib Grüße zu diesen Feiertagen! (**S. 315**)

Was schreibst du:
1. zu Weihnachten?
2. zum Muttertag?
3. zu Ostern?
4. zu Chanukka?
5. zum Namenstag?
6. zum Geburtstag?

5 Du sprichst über Geschenke für verschiedene Familienmitglieder. Schreib die folgenden Fragen ab und schreib dabei die richtige Form des bestimmten Artikels (**der, die, das**) in die Lücken. (**S. 319**)

1. Was schenkst du _____ Opa zum Geburtstag?
2. Was schenkst du _____ Tante Helene?
3. Was schenkst du _____ Mama zum Muttertag?
4. Was schenkst du _____ Papa zum Vatertag?
5. Was schenkst du _____ Beatrice zum Namenstag?
6. Was schenkst du _____ Mark zu Weihnachten?

6 Jetzt sprichst du über Geschenkideen für andere Leute. Schreib die folgenden Fragen und Antworten ab und schreib dabei die richtige Form des Possessivpronomens in die Lücken. (S. 319)

1. Was schenkst du _____ Mutter und _____ Vater zu Weihnachten?
2. Ich schenke _____ Vater und _____ Mutter zwei CDs.
3. Was schenkst du _____ Onkel und _____ Tante?
4. Ich schenke _____ Onkel ein Buch und _____ Tante Pralinen.
5. Was schenkst du _____ Oma und _____ Opa zum Hochzeitstag?
6. Ich schenke _____ Opa Blumen und _____ Oma Pralinen.

7 Jetzt sprichst du wieder über Geschenkideen für deine Familienmitglieder. Lies die Fragen und schreib das richtige Pronomen in die Lücken. (S. 319)

1. Was schenkst du dem Vati?—Ich schenke _____ ein Buch.
2. Was schenkst du der Mutti?—Ich schenke _____ eine CD.
3. Was schenkst du dem Opa?—Ich schenke _____ eine Armbanduhr.
4. Was schenkst du der Oma?—Ich schenke _____ Blumen.
5. Was schenkst du dem Bernd?—Ich schenke _____ ein Poster.
6. Was schenkst du der Erika?—Ich schenke _____ Parfüm.

8 Du sagst einem Freund, was du deinen Verwandten (relatives) schenken willst. Schreib die folgenden Sätze ab und schreib dabei das richtige Possessivpronomen in die erste Lücke und das richtige Pronomen in die zweite Lücke. (S. 320)

1. Ich schenke _____ Bruder ein Buch, und ich schenke _____ auch eine CD.
2. Ich schenke _____ Oma Blumen, und ich schenke _____ auch Pralinen.
3. Ich schenke _____ Mutter ein Poster, und ich schenke _____ auch Parfüm.
4. Ich schenke _____ Opa Pralinen, und ich schenke _____ auch eine CD.
5. Ich schenke _____ Onkel ein Poster, und ich schenke _____ auch ein Buch.
6. Ich schenke _____ Tante Pralinen, und ich schenke _____ auch ein Poster.

9 Du hast viele Geschenkideen. Sag, welche Ideen du hast. Schreib Sätze, die ein indirektes und ein direktes Satzobjekt enthalten. **(S. 320)**

> **BEISPIEL** **Was schenkst du deinem Bruder? (CD) Ich schenke _____ .**
> **Ich schenke <u>meinem Bruder eine CD</u>.**

1. Was schenkst du deiner Mutter? (Buch)   Ich schenke _____ .
2. Was schenkst du deinem Opa? (CD)   Ich schenke _____ .
3. Was schenkst du deiner Oma? (Blumen)   Ich schenke _____ .
4. Was schenkst du deinem Vater? (Hemd)   Ich schenke _____ .
5. Was schenkst du deinem Onkel? (Uhr)   Ich schenke _____ .
6. Was schenkst du deiner Tante? (Rock)   Ich schenke _____ .

10 Was gibst du den Leuten zum Geburtstag oder zum Namenstag? Schreib die folgenden Antworten ab und gebrauche dabei ein passendes Pronomen und den unbestimmten Artikel für jedes Hauptwort *(noun)*. **(S. 320)**

1. Was schenkst du deiner Freundin zum Namenstag?
   (Buch; Blumenstrauß) — Ja, ich schenke _____ .
2. Was schenkst du deinem Großvater zum Namenstag?
   (Hemd; Kalender) — Ja, ich schenke _____ .
3. Was schenkst du deiner Mutter zum Namenstag?
   (Armbanduhr; Pralinen) — Ja, ich schenke _____ .
4. Was schenkst du denn deiner Biolehrerin zum Namenstag?
   (Poster; Blumen) — Ja, ich schenke _____ .
5. Was schenkst du deinem Freund Kurt zu Weihnachten?
   (T-Shirt; Gürtel) — Ja, ich schenke _____ .
6. Was schenkst du deinem Bruder zum Geburtstag?
   (Hobbybuch; Roman) — Ja, ich schenke _____ .

1 Listen to Helene and Volker's conversation about what they are buying their friends as birthday presents. Write down who's giving what to whom as a present.

2 Drei Schüler sprechen darüber, was sie am liebsten zum Geburtstag bekommen möchten und warum.

a. Read the interviews and decide what each of the three teenagers would like to have and why. Write down the information.

„Du fragst, was ich am liebsten zum Geburtstag haben möchte? — Ganz einfach! Du weißt doch, dass ich gern lese. Du kannst mir also ein Buch kaufen, vielleicht etwas über gefährdete Tiere in Afrika, oder — ich hab da noch eine Idee. Du kannst mir zum Geburtstag ein Karl-May-Buch schenken, denn seine Bücher sind wieder ganz populär. Und ich lese Karl May furchtbar gern."

Ingo, 17

„Ja, am liebsten möchte ich irgendetwas, was mit Musik zu tun hat. Eine prima Kassette, Mathias Reim vielleicht, oder eine CD. Du weißt, ich höre auch klassische Musik gern. Und unter den Klassikern gibt es eine wirklich große Auswahl, zum Beispiel etwas von ...nein, ich hab's: die schönsten Arien aus den populärsten Opern. Das ist etwas für mich!"

Margot, 16

„Du kannst mir eine große Freude machen und mir eine Karte zum nächsten Rockkonzert schenken. Die „Toten Hosen" kommen nächsten Monat hierher, und die möchte ich unbedingt hören. Natürlich sind die Karten furchtbar teuer, ich weiß. Aber du kannst dich vielleicht mit zwei andern Leuten zusammentun, und ihr könnt mir gemeinsam eine Karte kaufen. Dann ist es für jeden nicht so teuer."

Clarissa, 16

3 Gabriele und Philipp sprechen über Bernhards Geburtstag und machen Pläne. Was wollen sie zuerst machen? First look at the pictures and decide what Gabriele and Philipp are doing in each one. Then listen to their conversation and put the following drawings in the correct order.

a.

b.

c.

d.

4 Ihr möchtet der Lehrerin oder dem Lehrer etwas schenken. Macht eine Liste von Geschenkideen! Dann sprecht darüber, was ihr schenken möchtet. Fragt alle in der Gruppe, was sie schenken wollen. Wie sind ihre Ideen? Toll oder blöd?

5 # Zum Schreiben

Write a dialogue in which you call a friend to discuss a birthday party that will take place soon. Agree to buy a gift together.

> **Schreibtipp** Think about the **logical order** in which you will build the conversation. Be sure to make the conversation flow in a logical way, building from saying hello, asking questions in a logical order, and saying good-bye.

Prewriting

Make **lists** of gift ideas, clothing to wear to a party, and dates and times.

Writing

Create your **dialogue** using the following sentences: Say hello, and ask your friend's mother (who answers the phone) if you may talk to your friend. Greet the friend; ask if he/she is going to the party. Discuss what you both will wear. Ask if she/he wants to go in with you to buy a gift. After discussing several choices, decide on a gift. Decide on a day and time to go shopping. Say good-bye.

Revising

- Read the conversation aloud with a partner, looking for strengths and weaknesses. Are your questions and responses clear? Are the ideas well organized? Check over spelling and grammar and make changes. Set the conversation aside and go back to it later.
- Proofread your dialogue once more as a final check for spelling and grammar errors, making corrections as necessary.
- Revise and submit it to your teacher. You might ask two of your classmates to present this dialogue to the class.

6 # Rollenspiel

Role-play the following situation with two or three classmates:

Each group picks one type of store you have learned about (**Metzgerei, Modegeschäft, Schreibwarenladen ...**). Write it on a card, and put the cards in a box. One person from each group draws a card from the box. Your group has just been hired by the store you drew to write some commercials to help boost sales for the holidays. Write a commercial to convince people to buy the items at your store as gifts. Suggest people in the family to give the gifts to. (You will have to be pretty persuasive in order to convince people to buy gifts at a **Metzgerei**!) Bring in props and perform your commercial in front of the class.

Kann ich's wirklich?

Can you use the telephone in Germany? (p. 310)

1 If you were calling someone in Germany, how would you
a. say who you are
b. ask to speak to someone
c. say hello to the person you want to speak with
d. say goodbye

2 If you were answering the phone in Germany, how would you
a. identify yourself   b. ask the caller to wait a minute

3 How would you tell someone how to use a public telephone to make a call? (Use **zuerst, dann, danach,** and **zuletzt.**)

Can you invite someone to a party and accept or decline? (p. 313)

4 How would a friend invite you to his or her birthday party on Saturday evening at 8:00?

5 How would you respond if
a. you can come
b. you can't come because a relative is coming to visit
c. you can't come because you are going to a concert
d. you can't come because you have to do your homework

Can you talk about birthdays and express good wishes? (p. 314)

6 How would you ask a friend when he or she has a birthday?

7 How would your friend respond if he or she has a birthday on
a. May 29   b. March 9   c. February 16   d. July 7

8 How would you express good wishes for the following occasions?
a. birthday   b. Christmas   c. Hanukkah

Can you discuss gift ideas? (p. 318)

9 How would you ask a friend what he or she is getting another friend for his or her birthday? How might your friend respond?

10 How would you tell a friend that you are going to give these items to various relatives for their birthdays?

a.   b.   c.   d.

mein Vater   **meine Tante**   **meine Oma**   **mein Bruder**

Erste Stufe

Using the telephone in Germany

telefonieren	to call on the phone	abheben (sep)	to pick up (the phone)	Hier (ist) …	This is …
anrufen (sep)	to call	auflegen (sep)	to hang up (the phone)	Hier bei …	The …residence
der Apparat, -e	telephone			Kann ich bitte … spechen?	Can I please speak to …?
das Telefon, -e	telephone	die Nummer wählen	to dial the number	Auf Wiederhören!	Goodbye!
der Hörer, -	receiver			Wiederhören!	Bye!
die Telefonzelle -n	telephone booth	besetzt	busy		
die Telefonnummer, -n	telephone number	Einen Moment, bitte!	Just a minute, please.	**Other useful words**	
Münzen einstecken (sep)	to insert coins			das Handy, -s	cell phone
				die Telefonkarte, -n	phone card

Zweite Stufe

Inviting someone to a party

einladen (sep)	to invite	Wann hast du Geburtstag?	When is your birthday?	Fröhliche Weihnachten!	Merry Christmas!
er/sie lädt …ein	he/she invites	am ersten (1.), zweiten (2.), dritten (3.), usw.	on the first, second, third, etc …	Chanukka	Hanukkah
Accepting or declining				Frohes Chanukka-Fest!	Happy Hanukkah!
Natürlich!	Certainly!	bald	soon	Ostern	Easter
Ja, gern!	Sure!	nächste Woche	next week	Frohe Ostern!	Happy Easter!
Aber sicher!	Sure!	Alles Gute zum Geburtstag!	Happy Birthday!	der Muttertag	Mother's Day
Talking about birthdays and expressing good wishes		Herzlichen Glückwunsch zum Geburtstag!	Best wishes on your birthday!	Alles Gute zum Muttertag!	Happy Mother's Day!
der Geburtstag, -e	birthday			der Vatertag	Father's Day
die Party, -s	party	der Feiertag, -e	holiday	Alles Gute zum Vatertag!	Happy Father's Day!
Ich habe am … Geburtstag.	My birthday is on …	Weihnachten	Christmas		

Dritte Stufe

Discussing gift ideas

schenken	to give (a gift)	das Poster, -	poster	wem?	whom? to whom? for whom?
geben	to give	die CD, -s	compact disc		
er/sie gibt	he/she gives	das Parfüm, -e	perfume	**Articles, dative case**	
die Geschenkidee, -n	gift idea	der Schmuck	jewelry	dem	the (masc.)
das Geschenk, -e	gift	deinem Vater	to/for your father	der	the (fem.)
die Praline, -n	fancy chocolate	meinem Vater	to/for my father	**Other useful words**	
die Armbanduhr, -en	(wrist)watch	deiner Mutter	to/for your mother		
		meiner Mutter	to/for my mother	wahrscheinlich	probably
der Kalender, -	calendar	**Pronouns, dative case**		vielleicht	maybe
der Blumenstrauß, ¨e	bouquet of flowers	ihm	to/for him	verschieden	different
		ihr	to/for her		

12
Die Fete

Objectives

In this chapter you will review and practice how to

Erste Stufe

- offer help and explain what to do
- ask where something is located and give directions

Zweite Stufe

- make plans and invite someone to come along
- talk about clothing
- discuss gift ideas

Dritte Stufe

- describe people and places
- say what you would like and whether you do or don't want more
- talk about what you did

 internet

 ADRESSE: go.hrw.com
KENNWORT:
WK3 BADEN-WUERTTEMBERG–12

◀ **Was möchtet ihr essen?**

Los geht's! · *Die Geburtstagsfete*

Strategie Verstehen

Look at the images for this story. What big event is taking place? What preparations are being made? Who is helping? What is everyone doing?

Nicole **Andreas** **Thomas** **Sabine** **Mutter** **Vater** **Martin**

Nicoles Freunde sind da. Sie wollen ihr helfen.

Andreas: So, Nicole, was können wir für dich tun?

Nicole: Zuerst müssen wir einkaufen gehen. Wer will mitkommen? Ich muss zum Supermarkt.

Andreas: Wir können ja beide mit den Rädern fahren.

Nicole: Lieb von dir! Aber wir müssen so viel einkaufen. Die Mutti fährt uns mit dem Auto hin. — Aber du kannst mitkommen, wenn du willst.

Andreas: Klar!

Nicole und Andreas kommen vom Einkaufen zurück.

Thomas: Und was mache ich?

Nicole: Thomas, du kannst dem Vati im Garten helfen, und dann müssen wir noch das Gemüse waschen.

Andreas: Okay! Wir können das ja machen, wenn wir zurückkommen.

Vater: Was habt ihr mitgebracht? Oh, die Bratwurst sieht gut aus! Hm …ganz frisch. Und, was habt ihr sonst noch?

Nicole: Wir haben noch Eier, Mehl, Zucker …Andreas und ich, wir backen dann einen Kuchen.

Vater: Schön!

Die Fete beginnt. Martin kommt.

Nicole: Vati! Das ist Martin!

Vater: Hallo Martin! Herzlich willkommen bei uns!

Martin: Guten Tag! Vielen Dank für die Einladung!

Vater: Schon gut! Wir freuen uns, wenn wir einmal im Jahr Nicoles Freunde zu uns einladen können. — Was willst du trinken? — Andreas, willst du Martin etwas zu trinken geben? Ich muss zum Grill.

Andreas: Okay, Martin, was möchtest du denn haben?

Nicole: Die Bowle schmeckt gut.

Martin: Gut, dann probier ich die Bowle.

Andreas: Prost!

Martin: — Hm, die ist wirklich gut!

Mutter: So, wer möchte was? Es gibt Kartoffelsalat, Krautsalat, Gurkensalat, Tomatensalat … Thomas? Möchtest du Kartoffelsalat?

Thomas: Ja, bitte! — Die Wurstbrote sehen auch ganz lecker aus!

Mutter: Nimm doch gleich zwei! — Und eine Brezel!

Thomas: Okay. — Wo ist denn der Kuchen?

Mutter: Pst! Der Kuchen kommt erst nachher.

Thomas: Ach so!

Happy Birthday to you...

Martin: Was für eine Überraschung! Vielen, vielen Dank!

Übungsheft, S. 133

1 **Was passiert hier?**

Do you understand what is happening in the story? Check your comprehension by answering these questions. Don't be afraid to guess.

1. Why are Nicole's friends at her house? What does Nicole tell them they can do to help?
2. Why does Nicole need **Eier, Mehl,** and **Zucker**?
3. Why does Nicole's mother tell Thomas to keep his voice down?
4. What do you think might happen next in the story?

2 **Welche Beschreibung passt zu welcher Person?**

Match each person from the story with the most appropriate description.

1. Martin
2. Thomas
3. Nicole
4. Andreas
5. Nicoles Vater

   a. geht mit Nicole einkaufen.
   b. hilft Nicoles Vater im Garten und fragt Nicoles Mutter, wo der Kuchen ist.
   c. bekommt heute einen Geburtstagskuchen.
   d. lädt ihre Freunde zur Fete ein, geht einkaufen und bäckt den Kuchen.
   e. findet es super, dass Nicoles Freunde kommen, steht am Grill und grillt die Bratwurst.

3 **Nacherzählen**

Put the sentences in logical order to make a brief summary of the story.

1. Andreas, Sabine und Thomas kommen vorbei, um Nicole zu helfen.

Als letzter kommt der Martin.

Zuerst gehen Andreas und Nicole zum Supermarkt, und Thomas hilft Nicoles Vater im Garten.

Später am Nachmittag kommen die Gäste.

Andreas gibt Martin etwas zu trinken.

Es gibt Bowle zu trinken, und es gibt viel zu essen: Kartoffelsalat, Tomatensalat, Krautsalat, Gurkensalat und Bratwurst.

Nach dem Essen bringen Nicole und Thomas den Geburtstagskuchen, und die Freunde singen „Happy Birthday!"

4 **Und ihr?**

Du und dein Partner habt heute Abend eine Fete. Was gibt's zu essen? Und zu trinken? Macht eine Liste! Schreibt alles auf, was ihr braucht! Dein Partner sagt dir, was er bringt, dann sagst du ihm, was du bringst. Dann besprich mit deinem Partner, wen ihr eingeladen habt und wer kommt!

BEISPIEL	PARTNER	Ich bringe ...mit. Was bringst du?
	DU	Ich bringe ...
	PARTNER	Und wen hast du eingeladen?
	DU	Ich habe ...eingeladen.

So sagt man das!

Offering help and explaining what to do

Schon bekannt

You are having a party! Your friends come over to help you get things ready.

A friend might ask:

Kann ich etwas für dich tun?

or

Was kann ich für dich tun?

Was kann ich für euch tun?

You could respond:

Du kannst für mich das Geschirr spülen.

Geh bitte einkaufen! Hol ein Pfund Bratwurst und 10 Semmeln!

Holt die Bratwurst beim Metzger und kauft das Brot beim Bäcker!

> Übungsheft, S. 134–136, Ü. 2–7

---

5 **Die Fete**

Zuhören Nicole hat viel zu tun, denn sie muss alles für die Fete vorbereiten. Schau ihre Arbeitsliste an! Hör dir das Gespräch gut an und schreib auf, was jede Person macht, um Nicole zu helfen!

Ein wenig Grammatik

Schon bekannt

The preposition **für** is always followed by an accusative case form: **Kannst du für mich 200 Gramm Aufschnitt kaufen?** See page R18 to review the accusative pronouns. To review **du/ihr**-commands, see page R22. If you need to review the forms of **können,** see page R21.

> Grammatikheft, S. 100–101, Ü. 1–3

Mehr Grammatikübungen, S. 352–353, Ü. 1–3 →

Arbeitsliste für die Fete
Müll sortieren
Rasen mähen
Staub saugen
Fenster putzen
Zimmer aufräumen
Tisch decken
Geschirr spülen
Einkaufen gehen — Tomaten, Brot, Semmeln, Bratwurst, Hackfleisch, Eier, Mehl, Zucker, Äpfel, Orangen, Kartoffeln, Mineralwasser, Cola kaufen

---

6 **Grammatik im Kontext**

a. Schreiben Heute Abend hast du eine Fete für eine Freundin. Schreib einen Einkaufszettel und eine Arbeitsliste!

b. Sprechen Dein Partner fragt dich, wie er dir helfen kann. Sag ihm, was er für dich kaufen und machen kann! Sag deinem Partner auch, wo er die Lebensmittel kaufen soll! Dann tauscht ihr die Rollen aus!

Spätzle and Apfelküchle are specialties of Baden-Württemberg. Spätzle ("little sparrow" in the local dialect) are thick, round noodles made by spreading dough onto a board, then cutting it into small strips or pieces, and dropping them into boiling water.

Apfelküchle is a dessert made of apple slices dipped in a pancake batter and fried. The apples are then sprinkled with sugar and cinnamon. Apfelküchle is often served with vanilla sauce or vanilla ice cream.

7 ## Soll ich backen oder kochen?

Lesen/Sprechen Some friends are coming over for dinner. You and your partner are planning to make **Apfelküchle** and **Spätzle,** two popular southern German dishes. Each of you picks one recipe. Tell your partner what to buy for your recipe and how much. Then switch roles.

Käsespätzle

Für 4 Personen

400 g Mehl
2 Eier
etwas Salz
1/8 - 1/4 l Wasser
(oder Milch verdünnt)
1 EL Öl
200 g Emmentaler
4 Zwiebeln
50 g Butter
1 Spatzenbrett

Apfelküchle

Für 4 Portionen

200 g Mehl
3 Eier
1/4 l Milch
1 Prise Salz
4 möglichst säuerliche
   Äpfel (groß)
1 Zitrone
1 EL Zucker
1 EL Zimt
Butterschmalz zum Ausbacken

Wortschatz

das Salz
der Zimt *cinnamon*
das Butterschmalz *shortening*

(die) Zwiebel   (die) Zitrone   (das) Öl

8 ## Am nächsten Tag

Sprechen What a party! You and your friends had a great time last night, but now it's time to clean up the mess. You also promised your parents that you would do some other things around the house. Look at the picture of the house on the right and tell your partner what he or she can do to help. Then switch roles.

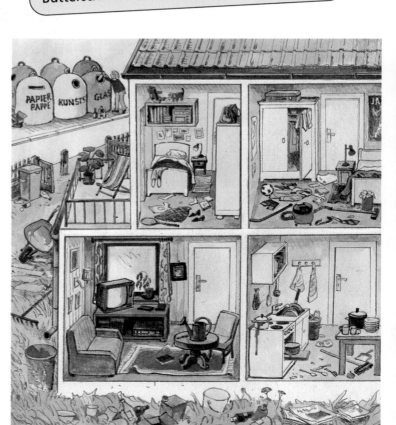

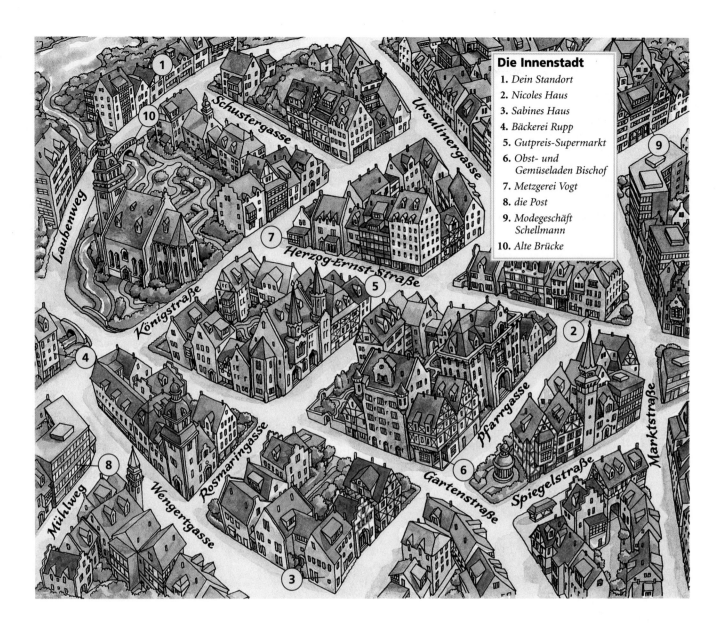

Die Innenstadt

1. *Dein Standort*
2. *Nicoles Haus*
3. *Sabines Haus*
4. *Bäckerei Rupp*
5. *Gutpreis-Supermarkt*
6. *Obst- und Gemüseladen Bischof*
7. *Metzgerei Vogt*
8. *die Post*
9. *Modegeschäft Schellmann*
10. *Alte Brücke*

So sagt man das!

Asking where something is located and giving directions   Schon bekannt

If your friend asks you to pick up a few things at the butcher shop, you might first have to ask someone:

Weißt du, wo die Metzgerei ist?

The response might be:

In der Herzog-Ernst-Straße.

After you leave the house, you realize that you don't know how to get to **Herzog-Ernst-Straße.**

You ask a passerby:

Entschuldigung! Wie komme ich zur Metzgerei?

The response might be:

Gehen Sie geradeaus bis zur Schustergasse, dann nach rechts, dann die nächste Straße nach links.

9 Grammatik im Kontext

Zuhören Following Nicole's party on Saturday, Sabine has invited everyone over on Sunday afternoon for a little get-together. Listen as both Sabine and Nicole give directions over the phone from where you are (**dein Standort**) to their houses. Write each set of instructions so that you know how to get to both parties. Check your directions on the map to see if you got them right.

10 Grammatik im Kontext

Sprechen You are at the **Bäckerei Rupp** and your partner is at Nicole's house. Tell your partner how to get to the bakery. Then switch roles: Now you're at Sabine's house, and your partner will give you directions to the **Modegeschäft Schellman**.

11 Ihr habt Hunger

Lesen/Sprechen Du und deine Partnerin, ihr seid bei Sabine. Ihr habt Hunger. Wähl zwei von den folgenden Lebensmitteln aus und erzähl deiner Partnerin, wo sie die kaufen kann und wie sie dahin kommt. Schau auf den Stadtplan auf Seite 339!

die nächste Straße nach …   nach links
nach rechts   an der Ampel nach …
bis zum …platz   geradeaus   bis zur …straße
die (erste, zweite …) Straße nach …

Ein wenig Grammatik

Schon bekannt
See pages R24 and R19 to review the forms of **wissen** and word order following **wissen**. To review formal commands, see page R22.

Übungsheft, S. 136, Ü. 8

Grammatikheft, S. 102, Ü. 4–5

Mehr Grammatikübungen, S. 353, Ü. 4–5

LERNTRICK

When you are learning or reviewing vocabulary, remember to use the word or phrase in a sentence or conversation that gives it meaning. For example, when trying to learn the phrase **zur Bäckerei**, use it in an imaginary conversation:

— **Wie komme ich zur Bäckerei? Ich muss Brot kaufen.**
— **Die nächste Straße nach links.**

Musst du zu Hause helfen?

You've already discovered how German students like to spend their free time, and you know that they enjoy planning and going to parties. However, life isn't all fun! Often before they go out or meet with their friends, they have to help around the house. What chores do you think German students have to do? Make a list of chores that the following German students might mention. Then read the interviews.

Übungsheft, S. 144, Ü. 25–26

Heide, Berlin

„Ich muss zweimal in der Woche die Toilette sauber machen, und dann ab und zu halt den Geschirrspüler ausräumen oder die Küche wischen und halt mein Zimmer aufräumen."

Monika, Berlin

„Also, ich muss fast jeden Tag den Mülleimer runterbringen und ab und zu mal Waschmaschine an, Waschmaschine aus, Wäsche aufhängen …Dann ab und zu Staub saugen, wischen — also wir haben in der Küche so Fliesen *(tiles)* und — aber meistens, wenn meine Eltern keine Zeit dazu haben. Abwaschen muss ich nicht, also, wir haben einen Geschirrspüler."

Silvana, Berlin

„Zu Hause helf ich meistens so beim Abwaschen, Spülmaschine ausräumen, oder die Wäsche aufhängen oder abnehmen, zusammen-legen, immer so, was anfällt."

Gerd, Bietigheim

„Ich saug halt ab und zu Staub, räum die Spülmaschine aus, bring Müll raus, hol halt teilweise Getränke und so, mäh manchmal den Rasen — kommt ganz darauf an."

A. 1. Make a list of the chores that are mentioned by each of the students. Do they have chores in common? How do the chores they mention compare to those you listed before reading the interviews?

2. Which of these students do the same kinds of things that you do at home?

3. Which of the chores mentioned do you like or dislike? Give a reason in English.

B. You and your friends probably have chores to do at home. Make a list in German, indicating what you have to do and for whom, and report it to your class. Keep track of which chores your classmates do. How do the chores that American students do at home compare to those of German students? Write a brief essay in which you discuss this question, pointing out the differences and similarities.

So sagt man das!

Making plans and inviting someone to come along

Schon bekannt

There are many times when you will want to make plans with your friends and invite them to go places with you. You could say:

Ich will um halb drei ins Einkaufszentrum gehen, Klamotten kaufen. Willst du mitkommen? *or* **Kommst du mit?**

Your friend might accept:

Ja gern! *or*
Super! Ich komme gern mit!

Or decline and give a reason:

Das geht leider nicht, denn ich muss am Nachmittag die Hausaufgaben machen.

Übungsheft, S. 137, Ü. 9–11

Wortschatz

THOMAS **Wohin willst du gehen? Was willst du tun?**

SABINE **Ich will ...**

die Stadt besichtigen

in den Park gehen

in den Zoo gehen

CD-ROM DISC 3

Schlittschuh laufen

joggen

ein Brettspiel spielen

Grammatikheft, S. 103, Ü. 7

Ein wenig Grammatik

Schon bekannt

See page R21 to review the forms of **wollen** and **müssen**. In German the conjugated verb in a main clause of a statement is always in second position. If there is a second verb, it is at the end of the sentence or clause and is in the infinitive. To review German word order, see page R19.

CD-ROM DISC 3

Übungsheft, S. 138, Ü. 12

Grammatikheft, S. 103, Ü. 6

Mehr Grammatikübungen, S. 353, Ü. 6

Grammatik im Kontext

  Zuhören A youth magazine recently interviewed four teens in the German-speaking countries about what they like to do in their free time. Match each person interviewed with the activity below that best fits that person's interests.

1. …in den Zoo gehen
2. …jeden Tag joggen
3. …Brettspiele spielen, z. B., Monopoly®
4. …die Altstadt besichtigen

13 **Grammatik im Kontext**

Lesen/Sprechen Du und dein Partner, ihr seid Austauschschüler in der Stadt Bietigheim. Heute besucht ihr das Jugendzentrum. Schaut auf die Tafel, dann wählt vier Tätigkeiten, die ihr zwei gern macht, und sagt, wann ihr diese Tätigkeiten machen könnt.

Tennis spielen	14⁰⁰–15³⁰
joggen	12¹⁵–13¹⁵
Schach spielen	13⁰⁰–17⁰⁰
Tanzunterricht	16⁰⁰–17⁰⁰
schwimmen	14⁰⁰–16³⁰
Film: "Der mit dem Wolf tanzt"	12⁰⁰–14¹⁵
basteln	15⁴⁵–17⁴⁵
Karten spielen (Skat)	13⁴⁵–15³⁰
Gitarrenunterricht	14³⁰–15³⁰
Zeichenunterricht	17⁰⁰–18⁰⁰
Basketballturnier	13⁰⁰–14³⁰

14 **Willst du mitkommen?**

a. **Lesen/Sprechen** Schau die Fotos an und lies den Text! Dann beantworte die Fragen!

1. Was spielen die Jungen hier?
2. Wo spielen sie?
3. Warum nennt (*to name*) man den Sport „Polo mit Eskimorolle"?
4. Glaubst du, dass dieser Sport Spaß macht?
5. Möchtest du „Polo mit Eskimorolle" spielen? Warum oder warum nicht?

b. **Schreiben/Sprechen** Hast du Freizeitinteressen, die so ungewöhnlich sind, wie „Polo mit Eskimorolle"? Mach eine Liste mit drei Aktivitäten, die du gern machst, und lad dazu deinen Partner ein! Tauscht dann die Rollen aus!

Kein Sport für Wasserscheue: Manchmal muss man mit dem Kopf ins Wasser. In der Fachsprache heißt das „Eskimorolle".

Wo ist der Ball? Besonders geschickte Spieler führen ihn mit ihrem Paddel unter Wasser.

Wo ist das Tor? Der Ball muss zwei Meter über dem Wasser in einen Korb.

Talking about clothing

Schon bekannt

You might have the following conversation with the salesperson in a clothing store:

VERKÄUFERIN:	**Haben Sie einen Wunsch?**
DU:	**Ich brauche einen Pulli, in Gelb, bitte! Oh, und ich suche auch ein T-Shirt. Der Pulli dort drüben sieht sehr fesch aus. Ich probiere ihn mal an.**
VERKÄUFERIN:	**Wie passt er? Nicht zu lang oder zu eng?**
DU:	**Nein, überhaupt nicht. Er passt prima, und er gefällt mir.**
VERKÄUFERIN:	**Ja, er sieht phantastisch aus.**
DU:	**Wirklich?**
VERKÄUFERIN:	**Wirklich!**
DU:	**Ja, das finde ich auch. Ich nehme ihn.**

Grammatikheft, S. 104, Ü. 8–9

15 In welchem Geschäft kaufst du deine Klamotten?

Zuhören Heute gibt es viele neue Modegeschäfte in Bietigheim. Leute in einem Eiscafé sprechen über diese Geschäfte. Welches Gespräch passt zu welchem Schaufenster?

a.

b.

c.

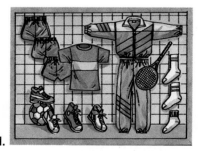

d.

Wortschatz

aus Seide	*made of silk*
aus Baumwolle	*made of cotton*
aus Leder	*made of leather*
gestreift	*striped*
gepunktet	*polka-dotted*

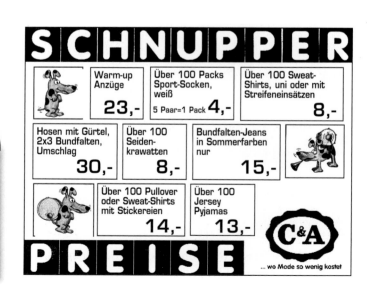

16 Grammatik im Kontext

Schreiben Make a window display for a clothing store. Either draw the items of clothing or cut pictures out of magazines and newspapers, then add price tags to your items. Name your store and write an advertisement for it. Look at the **C & A** ad on page 344 for ideas.

 17 Grammatik im Kontext

Sprechen You are looking for one of the items to the right in a clothing store. Your partner is the salesclerk. Find out if his or her store has the exact item you want. Find out the cost and where the item is located in the store. Then switch roles.

Ein wenig Grammatik

Schon bekannt

To review the nominative and accusative pronouns, see page R18. To review the definite and indefinite articles in the nominative and accusative cases, see pages R15–R16.

Übungsheft, S. 138, Ü. 13

So sagt man das!

Discussing gift ideas *Schon bekannt*

In **Kapitel 11** you learned to talk about giving gifts on special occasions.

A friend might ask:

> **Was schenkst du deinem Bruder zum Geburtstag?**
> **Und was schenkst du deiner Kusine zu Weihnachten?**

You might respond:

> **Ich schenke ihm eine Armbanduhr.**
> **Ich schenke ihr ein Buch.**

 18 Grammatik im Kontext

Sprechen Unten sind ein paar typische Geschenke aus Deutschland und der Schweiz. Schau dir die Geschenke an. Dann erzähl deinem Partner, wem du sie schenkst (z.B. dem Vater, der Mutter). Dann erzählt dir dein Partner, wem er was schenkt.

die Kuckucksuhr   der Krug

das Poster   ein Stück von der   die Armbanduhr
                Berliner Mauer

Ein wenig Grammatik

Schon bekannt

Do you remember the dative pronouns **ihm** (*to him*) and **ihr** (*to her*) and the definite articles **dem** and **der**? Don't forget the dative endings for **dein** and **mein**.

masculine
dein-
mein- } em

feminine
dein-
mein- } er

Übungsheft, S. 139, Ü. 14–15

Grammatikheft, S. 105, Ü. 10–11

Mehr Grammatikübungen, S. 354, Ü. 7–8

Dritte Stufe

Objectives Describing people and places; saying what you would like and whether you do or don't want more; talking about what you did

WK3-BADEN-WUERTTEMBERG-12

So sagt man das!

Describing people and places

Schon bekannt

You will probably meet people at parties who will ask you about yourself, your friends, and your family.

Someone might ask:

Woher kommst du, Lisa?

Und wo wohnst du jetzt?

Ist das deine Schwester?

Und was machst du in deiner Freizeit?
Wer ist denn Michael?
Wie sieht er aus?

You might respond:

Aus Kalifornien.

Ich wohne jetzt in Berlin, in der Schönleinstraße.

Ja, das ist meine Schwester. Sie heißt Jennifer.

Ich spiele oft Schach mit Michael.
Mein Freund.
Er hat lange, braune Haare und grüne Augen und er hat eine Brille.

You'll also want to be able to describe places, like your own room:

Mein Zimmer, das ist wirklich toll! Die Möbel sind echt schön, das Bett sogar ganz neu, ja und auch der Schreibtisch. Dann habe ich auch eine Couch. Die Farbe, na ja, das Grün ist nicht sehr schön, aber sonst ist die Couch wirklich sehr bequem.

> Übungsheft, S. 140–141, Ü. 16–20
>
> Grammatikheft, S.106, Ü. 12

Ein wenig Grammatik

Schon bekannt

CD-ROM DISC 3

When you refer to people and places, you will use the nominative pronouns **er**, **sie**, **es**, and **sie** (pl), for example, **Das ist mein Vater. Er heißt Gerd.** To review these pronouns, look at page R18. To review possessives like **mein** and **dein**, see page R16.

Mehr Grammatikübungen, S. 354, Ü. 9 →

19 Grammatik im Kontext

Sprechen Cut out magazine photos of two famous people and bring them to class. Place the photos in a container. Each student will take out a photo. Describe the person in the photo you picked with as much detail as possible so that your partner can guess who it is. Switch roles.

20 Grammatik im Kontext

Schreiben/Sprechen Dein Freund hat eine Fete, und du bist eingeladen. Du möchtest auf der Fete andere Leute kennen lernen (*meet*). Mach eine Liste mit acht Fragen, z.B. **Wo wohnst du? Was machst du in deiner Freizeit?** Frag deine Partnerin, und schreib ihre Antworten auf! Dann tauscht ihr die Rollen aus.

21 Deine Partnerin vorstellen *Introducing your partner*

Sprechen Heute tagt (*meets*) der Deutsch-Club. Du musst deine Partnerin vorstellen. Erzähl der Klasse alles, was du über deine Partnerin weißt! (Verwende Information von Übung 20.)

Wortschatz

Welche Möbel habt ihr im Wohnzimmer?

Wir haben ...

- ein Sofa
- einen Tisch
  - aus Holz
  - aus Kunststoff
- eine Lampe

einen Teppich   einen Sessel

rund
eckig (*with corners*)
modern

Und in der Küche gibt es ... einen Esstisch

einen Kühlschrank   einen Herd

einen Ofen   ein Spülbecken

Grammatikheft, S. 107, Ü. 13–15

22 Beschreib den Raum!

Sprechen/Schreiben Beschreib deinem Partner die Möbel im Wohnzimmer! Frag ihn, wie er die Möbel findet! Sag ihm, wie du die Möbel findest! Jetzt beschreibt dein Partner die Möbel in der Küche.

23 Für mein Notizbuch

Schreiben Beschreib dein Wohnzimmer und deine Küche! Was für Möbel gibt es da? Wie sehen diese Möbel aus? Du kannst auch eine Skizze machen.

Saying what you would like and whether you do or don't want more

Schon bekannt

When eating at a friend's house,
you may be asked by your host:

You could respond:

> **Was möchtest du trinken?**

> **Ich möchte eine Limo, bitte!**

Later your host might ask if you want more of something:

> **Möchtest du noch etwas?**
> **Und noch eine Semmel?**

> **Ja, bitte! Noch einen Saft.**
> **Nein, danke! Keine Semmel mehr.**

Übungsheft,
S. 142, Ü. 21–23

Ein wenig Grammatik

Schon bekannt

Mehr Grammatikübungen,
S. 355, Ü. 10–11

To review the **möchte** forms, see page R21. To review the use of **kein ... mehr**, see page R16.

Grammatikheft,
S. 108, Ü. 16–17

24 **Grammatik im Kontext**

Sprechen Spiel mit zwei oder drei Klassenkameraden die folgende Szene vor der Klasse: Ihr seid auf einer Geburtstagsfete. Ein Schüler spielt den Gastgeber *(host)*. Er fragt die Gäste, was sie essen und trinken möchten. Später sagen die Gäste, wie das Essen schmeckt. Dann fragt der Gastgeber, wer noch etwas möchte.

25 **Eine Imbissstube in Bietigheim**

Lesen/Schreiben Du besichtigst heute mit zwei Klassenkameraden die Stadt Bietigheim. Ihr habt Hunger und wollt etwas essen. Schaut auf die Speisekarte und schreibt ein Gespräch! Was gibt es zu essen? Was bestellt ihr? Was kostet das Essen? Wie schmeckt das Essen? Wollt ihr noch mehr?

So sagt man das!

Talking about what you did

Schon bekannt

You will often want to describe to friends or family what you did in the past, for example, last week or over the weekend.

A friend might ask: **Was hast du am Wochenende gemacht?**

Your response might be:

Am Samstag war ich in der Innenstadt. Zuerst habe ich Klamotten gekauft, dann war ich im Supermarkt, danach im Eiscafé mit Andreas und zuletzt bei Andreas zu Hause. Am Sonntag war ich die ganze Zeit zu Hause. Am Nachmittag habe ich gelesen, und am Abend habe ich ein Video gesehen. Danach haben Antje, Jörg und ich über Filme und Musik gesprochen.

Grammatikheft, S. 108, Ü. 18

---

26 **Hast du ein schönes Wochenende gehabt?**

Sprechen Frag deine Partnerin, was sie am Wochenende gemacht hat! Dann fragt dich deine Partnerin. Verwende die Vorschläge (*suggestions*) hier rechts.

Wo warst du am Wochenende?
- im Kaufhaus
- beim Bäcker
- zu Hause
- bei Freunden
- in der Stadt
- im Konzert

Was hast du gemacht?
- gekauft?
- gelesen?
- gesehen?
- Worüber habt ihr gesprochen?

27 **Von der Schule zum Beruf**

Schreiben You have been hired as copy writer for your local newspaper. Your boss wants to print a special insert for newcomers to your town, an insert familiarizing them with the local attractions, theaters, stores, etc. Your boss lets you choose which topic you want to cover.

AUSSPRACHE

 Richtig aussprechen / Richtig lesen

A. To review the following sounds, say the sentences below after your teacher or after the recording.

1. The letter **w**: The letter **w** is always pronounced like the *v* in the English word *vent*.
   Weißt du, wann Werners Geburtstag ist? Am Mittwoch?

2. The letter **j**: The letter **j** is pronounced the same as the *y* in the English word *you*.
   Die Julia besucht Jens im Juli, nicht Juni.

3. The letters **ä** and **e**: The letters **ä** and **e** are pronounced as short vowels when followed by two consonants. When followed by one consonant or the letter **h** the **ä** and **e** are usually pronounced as long vowels.
   Ich finde den Sessel hässlich. Er gefällt mir nicht.
   Peter kauft Käse. Das Mädchen mäht den Rasen.

Richtig schreiben / Diktat

B. Write down the sentences that you hear.

Mahlzeit!

Lesestrategie Combining reading strategies You can often derive the main idea of a text by looking at visual clues and format, and then searching for cognates and words you already know. In trying to figure out the meaning of unknown words, look at the context in which they occur. Often the surrounding text will give you clues about the meaning of the unknown word.

1. Judging by their form, what kinds of texts are these? What kinds of expressions do you expect to find in them? List in English the words and expressions you would find in typical recipes at home.

2. Recalling what you know about cognates and compound words, what do the following words mean in English?
   gefüllte Eier
   Kartoffelsalat
   Mandelkuchen
   (**Mandeln**=*almonds*)

3. Since German recipes often use infinitives in the directions, you need to look at the end of the sentences to determine what to do with the ingredients. Make an educated guess about the meaning of the verbs in these phrases.

1. mit Salz und Pfeffer **abschmecken**
2. die Eier **halbieren**
3. die Dotter **herausnehmen**
4. Essig **dazugeben**
5. Speck in kleine Würfel **schneiden**
6. mit fein gehackter Zwiebel **anrösten**

a. *take out*
b. *season*
c. *brown lightly*
d. *halve*
e. *cut*
f. *add*

Kartoffelsalat mit Speck

Kartoffelsalat mit Speck

1Pfd. gekochte Kartoffeln
50g Speck
1 Zwiebel
3 Esslöffel Essig
Salz
Pfeffer
4 Esslöffel Brühe

Kartoffeln in Scheiben schneiden. Warm halten. Etwas Speck in kleine Würfel schneiden und mit fein gehackter Zwiebel anrösten. Essig dazugeben und die Kartoffeln und den Speck mit Salz und Pfeffer abschmecken. Die heiße Fleischbrühe dazugeben.

gefüllte Eier

Mandelkuchen

Mandelkuchen

150 g Butter oder Margarine
200 g Zucker
1 Päckchen Vanillin-Zucker
5 Eier
3 Tropfen Bittermandelöl
100 g Weizenmehl
50 g Maisstärke
1 Teelöffel Backpulver

Aus den Zutaten einen Rührteig bereiten, dann 150 g Mandeln, gemahlen und 150 g Schokoladenstücke unterheben und alles in eine gefettete Kastenform füllen. Bei 175 Grad etwa 60-70 Minuten backen.

Gefüllte Eier

Hart gekochte Eier, nach Bedarf
Butter
Salz
fein gehackte Kräuter
   (Thymian, Majoran,
   Basilikum, Estragon)

Die Eier halbieren, die Dotter herausnehmen und in einer Schüssel mit der Butter, dem Salz und den fein gehackten Kräutern gut verrühren. Die Masse wieder in die Eihälften füllen.

4. Scan the lists of ingredients. How are most of the ingredients measured? How does that compare to recipes in the United States?

5. What ingredients will you need to make the deviled eggs? What do you think **Kräuter** means? (*Hint: look at the words in parentheses that follow.*)

6. What ingredients will you need to make **Kartoffelsalat**? How does this differ from the way you would make potato salad?

7. What steps will you need to follow to make the **Kartoffelsalat?**

8. What ingredients will you need to make the **Mandelkuchen**? What do you think **Bittermandelöl** is?

9. What cooking temperature is given for the cake? The baking temperature for electric ovens is 175°. This number is much lower than the usual temperature needed for baking cakes. How can you explain this? (Remember what you learned in **Kapitel 7** about how temperature is measured in German-speaking countries.)

10. What are the steps in making deviled eggs?

11. Assume you are in Germany, and you have been asked to bring your favorite food to a party, along with the recipe. Choose something that is not too complicated to make and write out the recipe.

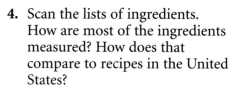

Übungsheft, S. 143, Ü. 24

Mehr Grammatikübungen

Erste Stufe   Objectives Offering help and explaining what to do

1 Vor der Party gibt es so viel zu tun! Vervollständige die folgenden Anweisungen und schreib dabei die passende Form von **können** in die erste Lücke, das passende Possessivpronomen in die zweite Lücke und ein passendes Verb in die dritte Lücke. **(S. 337)**

Was können wir für euch tun?

1. Peter, du _____ für _____ Vater den Rasen _____ .

2. Heike, du _____ für _____ Mutter das Geschirr _____ .

3. Uwe und Eva, ihr _____ für _____ Opa den Müll _____ .

4. Klaus und Antje, ihr _____ für _____ Tante den Tisch _____ .

5. Hans und Grete, ihr _____ für _____ Oma einkaufen _____ .

6. Du und ich, wir _____ für _____ Kusine Staub _____ .

2 Es gibt so viel Arbeit, und deshalb hat Nicoles Mutter eine Arbeitsliste gemacht. Wer kann was für sie tun? Lies die Liste und schreib Nicoles Mutters Anweisungen. **(S. 337)**

BEISPIEL THOMAS **Garage aufräumen**
Thomas, <u>du kannst für mich die Garage aufräumen.</u>

> ### Arbeitsliste für die Fete
>
> **wer?**
> Nicole / Sabine
> Thomas
> Andreas / Thomas
> Sabine
> Nicole / Sabine
> Andreas
>
> **was?**
> einkaufen gehen
> Rasen mähen
> Müll sortieren
> Staub saugen
> Geschirr spülen
> Fenster putzen

1. Nicole und Sabine, _____ .

2. Thomas, _____ .

3. Andreas und Thomas, _____.

4. Sabine, _____.

5. Nicole und Sabine, _____ .

6. Andreas, _____ .

3 Du sagst zuerst einem Freund, was er tun soll. Danach sagst du zwei Freunden dasselbe. Schreib also das erste Mal den **du**-Imperativ in die Lücken, das zweite Mal den **ihr**-Imperativ. (S. 337)

1. _____ bitte zuerst den Müll und _____ danach den Rasen!

2. _____ bitte einkaufen und _____ Milch, Brot und Obst!

3. _____ bitte zuerst die Fenster und _____ danach Staub!

4. _____ bitte das Geschirr und _____ dann den Tisch!

5. _____ doch zu Hause und _____ ein Buch!

6. _____ mit ins Café Freizeit und _____ einen Apfelsaft!

4 Jeder weiß etwas. Schreib die folgenden Fragen und Sätze ab und schreib dabei die korrekte Form von **wissen** in die erste Lücke und eine passende Verbform in die zweite Lücke. (S. 340)

1. Herbert, _____ du, wann unser Deutschlehrer Geburtstag _____ ?

2. Wer _____ , wann der Namenstag von Erika _____ ?

3. Eva und Jörg, _____ ihr, wie der Ahmet zur Schule _____ ?

4. Wir _____ nicht, wer heute Abend eine Fete _____ .

5. Ich _____ , was ich meinem Opa zum Geburtstag _____ .

6. Meine Eltern _____ , dass ich gern Gruselromane _____ .

5 Du sagst verschiedenen Erwachsenen *(various adults)*, was sie tun sollen. Schreib den **Sie**-Imperativ in die Lücken. (S. 340)

1. _____ nicht diesen Liebesroman! Er ist viel zu schmalzig.

2. _____ die Brötchen lieber beim Bäcker! Dort sind sie immer frisch.

3. _____ Ihrer Großmutter einen Blumenstrauß! Sie hat Blumen gern.

4. _____ doch mal über Mode und nicht immer über Politik!

5. _____ doch mal Schach und nicht immer Karten!

6. _____ doch mal Orangensaft und nicht immer nur Apfelsaft!

Zweite Stufe **Objectives** Making plans and inviting someone to come along; talking about clothing; discussing gift ideas

6 Du und deine Freunde, ihr wollt heute so viel tun. Aber zuerst müsst ihr die Arbeiten fertig machen, die ihr angefangen habt. Schreib die folgenden Sätze ab und schreib dabei die richtige Form von **wollen** in die erste Lücke und die richtige Form von **müssen** in die zweite Lücke. (S. 342)

1. Peter, _____ du ins Kino gehen? — Ja, aber zuerst _____ ich Staub saugen.

2. _____ ihr Schach spielen? — Klar, aber zuerst _____ wir alles aufräumen.

3. Karl _____ ins Café gehen, aber zuerst _____ er den Hund füttern.

4. Die Kinder _____ lesen, aber zuerst _____ sie das Zimmer aufräumen.

5. Ich _____ mit Peter Tennis spielen, aber er _____ zuerst einkaufen gehen.

6. Eva und Kurt, _____ ihr Musik hören, oder _____ ihr nach Hause gehen?

7 Du fragst eine Freundin, was du für sie und ihre Familie tun kannst. Schreib die folgenden Fragen ab und schreib dabei die richtige Form von **dein** in die erste Lücke und das richtige Personalpronomen in die zweite und dritte Lücke. (S. 345)

1. _____ Bruder, wie heißt _____ ? Was kann ich für _____ tun?
2. _____ Schwester, wie heißt _____ ? Was kann ich für _____ tun?
3. _____ Opa, wie heißt _____ ? Was kann ich für _____ tun?
4. _____ Großmutter, wie heißt _____ ? Was kann ich für _____ tun?
5. _____ Kusine, wie heißt _____ ? Was kann ich für _____ tun?
6. _____ Cousin, wie heißt _____ ? Was kann ich für _____ tun?

8 Was schenkst du? Du fragst einen Freund, was er seinen Familienmitgliedern schenkt. Schreib die folgenden Fragen und Antworten ab und schreib dabei die richtige Form von **dein** in die erste Lücke, die richtige Form von **mein** in die zweite Lücke und das richtige Pronomen in die dritte Lücke. (S. 345)

1. Was schenkst du _____ Oma?   _____ Oma? Ich schenke _____ ein Buch.
2. Was schenkst du _____ Opa?   _____ Opa? Ich schenke _____ Pralinen.
3. Was gibst du _____ Kusine?   _____ Kusine? Ich gebe _____ eine Uhr.
4. Was gibst du _____ Cousin?   _____ Cousin? Ich gebe _____ ein Poster.
5. Was kaufst du _____ Mutti?   _____ Mutti? Ich kaufe _____ Parfüm.
6. Was kaufst du _____ Vati?   _____ Vati? Ich kaufe _____ einen Roman.

Dritte Stufe

Objectives Describing people and places; saying what you would like and whether you do or don't want more; talking about what you did

9 Du schaust mit einer Freundin das Familienalbum an und sprichst über deine Familienmitglieder. Schreib den folgenden Absatz ab und schreib dabei die richtigen Possessivpronomen und Pronomen in die Lücken. (S. 346)

Den Mann hier, kennst du _____ ? Das ist _____ Vater. _____ ist 40

Jahre alt. _____ hat braune Haare und grüne Augen. Ich habe _____

sehr gern. _____ spielt immer Ball mit mir. Am Samstag hat _____

Geburtstag und ich schenke _____ Blumen, weil _____ Blumen so

gern hat. Die Frau hier ist _____ Oma. _____ ist schon 70 Jahre alt.

_____ hat graue Haare und _____ hat eine Brille. Ich habe _____

Oma gern. Nächste Woche hat _____ Oma Namenstag, und ich

schenke _____ Pralinen zum Namenstag und vielleicht gebe ich

_____ auch einen Blumenstrauß.

10 Auf einer Party bietet man den Gästen mehr zu essen und zu trinken an. Aber alle sagen nein. Schreib die folgenden Fragen und Antworten ab und schreib dabei die richtige Form von **möchte** in die erste Lücke und die richtige Form von **kein** in die zweite Lücke. (S. 348)

1. Claudia, _____ du noch Kuchen? — Nein, danke, _____ Kuchen mehr.
2. Frau Bär, _____ Sie noch Obst? — Nein, danke, _____ Obst mehr.
3. _____ ihr noch Milch? — Nein, danke, _____ Milch mehr.
4. _____ die Kinder noch Leberkäs? — Nein, danke, _____ Leberkäs mehr.
5. Wer _____ noch Saft? — Nein, danke, _____ Saft für mich.
6. _____ du noch ein Wurstbrot? — Nein, danke, _____ Wurstbrot mehr.

11 Du hast eine kleine Wohnung und brauchst verschiedene Möbel und Geräte. Du gehst in ein Geschäft, und fragst den Verkäufer nach den Dingen, die links abgebildet sind. (S. 348)

1. – Wie teuer ist _____ _____ ?
   – _____ kostet 200 Euro.
   – Ich suche _____ _____ für ungefähr 120 Euro.
   – Für 120 Euro finden Sie _____ _____ . Bestimmt nicht!

Teppich

2. – Wie teuer ist _____ _____ ?
   – _____ kostet 150 Euro.
   – Ich suche _____ _____ für ungefähr 80 Euro.
   – Für 80 Euro finden Sie _____ _____ . Bestimmt nicht!

Couch

3. – Wie viel kostet _____ _____ ?
   – _____ kostet 300 Euro.
   – Ich suche _____ _____ für ungefähr 200 Euro.
   – Für 200 Euro finden Sie _____ _____ . Bestimmt nicht.

Ofen

4. – Wie teuer ist _____ _____ ?
   – _____ kostet 50 Euro.
   – Ich suche _____ _____ für ungefähr 30 Euro.
   – Für 30 Euro finden Sie _____ _____ . Bestimmt nicht!

Handy

5. – Wie teuer ist _____ _____ ?
   – _____ kostet 700 Euro.
   – Ich suche _____ _____ für ungefähr 200 Euro.
   – Für 200 Euro finden Sie _____ _____ . Bestimmt nicht!

Computer

 1 You will hear five different conversations taking place at Martin's party. Listen and decide which of the five topics below belongs with which conversation.

   a. Filme   **b.** Musik   **c.** Essen   **d.** Sport   **e.** Schule

2 Wer ist deine Lieblingsperson? Schreib alles über deine Lieblingsperson in dein Notizbuch. Wer ist diese Person? Wie alt ist sie? Wo wohnt sie? Wie sieht diese Person aus? Was macht diese Person in der Freizeit? Was für Interessen hat sie?

3 Du gehst bald zu einem Familientreffen (*family reunion*). Du willst den Verwandten etwas schenken. Was schenkst du ihnen? Zum Beispiel, was schenkst du deinem Onkel? Und deiner Kusine? Erzähl es deinem Partner! Danach sagt er dir, was er schenkt.

4 You are taking a day trip to Stuttgart and would like to visit some interesting places. Go to the information center and find out how to get to the following places. Your partner will give you directions at the information counter.

1. ins Theater in der Altstadt   3. zum Alten Schloss
2. zum Rathaus   4. zur tri-bühne

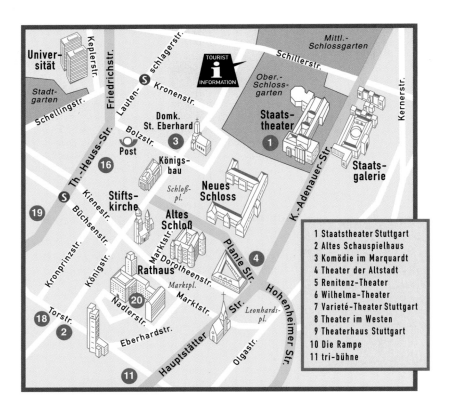

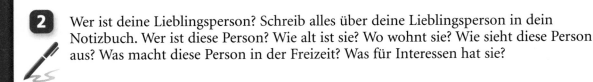

1 Staatstheater Stuttgart
2 Altes Schauspielhaus
3 Komödie im Marquardt
4 Theater der Altstadt
5 Renitenz-Theater
6 Wilhelma-Theater
7 Varieté-Theater Stuttgart
8 Theater im Westen
9 Theaterhaus Stuttgart
10 Die Rampe
11 tri-bühne

5 Zum Schreiben

Klaus, your school's exchange student from Germany, returned home just before the surprise party to celebrate John's birthday and the end of school. Write a letter telling him all about the party. In your letter, tell Klaus who did chores to help out before the party, who could not come and why, who brought which gift, what there was to eat and drink, and describe any comical birthday cards guests brought.

Schreibtipp Combining sentences is a good way to improve your paragraphs. Short, choppy sentences tend to break up the reader's thoughts. If you use words like "and," "but," and "because," your ideas will flow more naturally.

Prewriting

Make lists of chores that need to be done before a party, of food and drink necessary for a party, of gifts one might bring for a birthday, and of reasons for which one might not be able to attend a party.

Writing

For your first draft, use the writing strategies you've practiced this year. Think about what verbs and grammar structures you will need to describe party activities. Ask your teacher if you are uncertain about a grammar point. Combine sentences to give your paragraphs a natural flow. In describing a chain of events, such as what was done first, later and last during the party preparation, the terms **zuerst, dann, danach,** and **zuletzt** are helpful. End with a conclusion summing up the party.

Revising

- Reread your letter several times, listening for confusing statements and awkward wording. Check over spelling and grammar, make changes, then read your letter aloud.

- Set the letter aside and go back to it later. Reread it again, then switch letters with a classmate and check the strengths and weaknesses of each other's paper.

- Read the conclusion. Does it review or summarize the main idea? Proofread your letter once more for spelling and grammar errors, making any corrections necessary.

- Revise your letter and submit it to your teacher.

6 Rollenspiel

Everyone writes the name of the store that he or she created in Activity 16 on page 345 on a slip of paper and puts it into a small box. Draw out five stores. The people whose stores were chosen will line up at the front of the class with their store windows and play the **Verkäufer.** Bring in old clothing for the customers to try on. The rest of the class will divide into pairs and take turns visiting the stores on the **Einkaufsstraße.** When you are finished, draw more store names and continue your shopping spree. Remember to ask the salesperson about color and price. Try the clothes on and discuss the fit. Comment on your friend's clothing when he or she tries something on.

Can you offer help and explain what to do? (p. 337)

1 How would you offer to help a classmate do some chores around the house?

2 How would he or she respond if he or she needed you to
a. pick up clothes
b. clean the windows
c. go to the store
d. buy some tomatoes

Can you ask directions and say where something is located? (p. 339)

3 How would you tell a classmate how to get to school from your house? How would you tell him or her where your school is located?

Can you make plans and invite someone to come along? (p. 342)

4 How would your friend invite you to go to a concert at 8:30 on Saturday evening? How would you respond if
a. you accept
b. you decline because you're going to a movie at 8:00

Can you talk about clothes in a clothing store? (p. 344)

5 Write a conversation you would have with a salesperson in a clothing store. Talk about particular items of clothing, price, color, fit, and make some comments about how the clothing looks on you.

Can you discuss gift ideas? (p. 345)

6 How would you tell a classmate what you plan to give two family members for their birthdays?

Can you describe people and places? (p. 346)

7 How would you describe your partner: how he or she looks, his or her interests, and where he or she lives?

8 How would you describe your living room and your kitchen?

Can you say what you would like and that you do or don't want more? (p. 348)

9 How would you say that you do or don't want more of the following items?
a. eine Semmel
b. ein Apfel
c. ein Apfelsaft
d. ein Käsebrot

Can you talk about what you did? (p. 349)

10 How would a friend ask you what you did last weekend? How would you respond, telling where you were, what you bought, what movies you saw, or what books you read?

Erste Stufe

Ingredients for a recipe

das Salz	salt
das Öl	oil
die Zwiebel, -n	onion

die Zitrone, -n	lemon
der Zimt	cinnamon
das Butterschmalz	shortening
der Salat, -e	salad

Zweite Stufe

Making plans

die Stadt besichtigen	to visit the city
in den Park gehen	to go to the park
in den Zoo gehen	to go to the zoo
Schlittschuh laufen	ice skate
joggen	to jog
ein Brettspiel spielen	to play a board game

Talking about clothing

die Seide	silk
aus Seide	made of silk
die Baumwolle	cotton
aus Baumwolle	made of cotton
das Leder	leather
aus Leder	made of leather
gestreift	striped
gepunktet	polka-dotted

Dritte Stufe

Describing places

im Wohnzimmer	in the living room
das Sofa, -s	sofa
der Tisch, -e	table
aus Holz	made of wood
aus Kunststoff	made of plastic
die Lampe, -n	lamp

der Teppich, -e	carpet
der Sessel, -	armchair
die Küche, -n	kitchen
in der Küche	in the kitchen
der Esstisch, -e	dining table
der Kühlschrank, ¨e	refrigerator

der Herd, -e	stove
der Ofen, ¨	oven
das Spülbecken, -	sink
rund	round
eckig	with corners
modern	modern

Reference Section

Functions are probably best defined as the ways in which you use a language for specific purposes. When you find yourself in specific situations, such as in a restaurant, in a grocery store, or at school, you will want to communicate with those around you. In order to do that, you have to "function" in the language so that you can be understood: you place an order, make a purchase, or talk about your class schedule.

Such functions form the core of this book. They are easily identified by the boxes in each chapter that are labeled SO SAGT MAN DAS! These functions are the building blocks you need to become a speaker of German. All the other features in the chapter—the grammar, the vocabulary, even the culture notes—are there to support the functions you are learning.

Here is a list of the functions presented in this book and the German expressions you will need in order to communicate in a wide range of situations. Following each function is the chapter and page number where it was introduced.

Socializing

Saying hello Ch. 1, p. 21
Guten Morgen!
Guten Tag!
Morgen! } *shortened forms*
Tag!
Hallo! } *informal*
Grüß dich!

Saying goodbye Ch. 1, p. 21
Auf Wiedersehen!
Wiedersehen! *shortened form*
Tschüs!
Tschau! } *informal*
Bis dann!

Offering something to eat and drink Ch. 3, p. 74
Was möchtest du trinken?
Was möchte *(name)* trinken?
Was möchtet ihr essen?

Responding to an offer Ch. 3, p. 74
Ich möchte *(beverage)* trinken.
Er/Sie möchte im Moment gar nichts.
Wir möchten *(food/beverage)*, bitte.

Saying please Ch. 3, p. 76
Bitte!

Saying thank you Ch. 3, p. 76
Danke!
Danke schön!
Danke sehr!

Saying you're welcome Ch. 3, p. 76
Bitte!
Bitte schön!
Bitte sehr!

Giving compliments Ch. 5, p. 139
Der/Die/Das *(thing)* sieht *(adjective)* aus!
Der/Die/Das *(thing)* gefällt mir.

Responding to compliments Ch. 5, p. 139
Ehrlich?
Wirklich?
Nicht zu *(adjective)*?
Meinst du?

Starting a conversation Ch. 6, p. 161
Wie geht's? } *Asking how someone is doing*

Wie geht's denn?
Sehr gut!
Prima!
Danke, gut!
Gut!
Danke, es geht.
So lala. } *Responding to* **Wie geht's?**
Nicht schlecht.
Nicht so gut.
Schlecht.
Sehr schlecht.
Miserabel.

Making plans Ch. 6, p. 166
Was willst du machen?   Ich will *(activity)*.
Wohin will *(person)* gehen?   Er/Sie will in(s) *(place)* gehen.

Ordering food and beverages Ch. 6, p. 170

Was bekommen Sie?	Ich bekomme (food/beverage).
Ja, bitte?	
Was essen Sie?	Ein(e)(n) (food), bitte.
Was möchten Sie?	Ich möchte (food/beverage), bitte.
Was trinken Sie?	Ich trinke (beverage).
Was nimmst du?	Ich nehme (food/beverage).
Was isst du?	Ich esse (food).

Talking about how something tastes Ch. 6, p. 172

Wie schmeckt's?	Gut!
	Prima!
	Sagenhaft!
	Der/die/das (food/beverage) schmeckt lecker!
	Der/die/das (food/beverage) schmeckt nicht.
Schmeckt's?	Ja, gut!
	Nein, nicht so gut.
	Nicht besonders.

Paying the check Ch. 6, p. 172

Hallo!
Ich will/möchte zahlen.
Das macht (zusammen) (total).
Stimmt schon!

Extending an invitation Ch. 7, p. 194; Ch. 11, p. 313

Willst du (activity)?
Wir wollen (activity). Komm doch mit!
Möchtest du mitkommen?
Ich habe am (day/date) eine Party. Ich lade dich ein. Kannst du kommen?

Responding to an invitation Ch. 7, p. 194; Ch. 11, p. 313

Ja, gern! ⎫
Toll! Ich komme gern mit. ⎬ accepting
Aber sicher! ⎪
Natürlich! ⎭
Das geht nicht. ⎫ declining
Ich kann leider nicht. ⎭

Expressing obligations Ch. 7, p. 194

Ich habe keine Zeit. Ich muss (activity).

Offering help Ch. 7, p. 199

Was kann ich für dich tun? ⎫
Kann ich etwas für dich tun? ⎬ asking
Brauchst du Hilfe? ⎭
Gut! Mach ich! — agreeing

Asking what you should do Ch. 8, p. 222

Was soll ich für dich tun?	Du kannst für mich (chore).
Wo soll ich (thing/things) kaufen?	Beim (Metzger/Bäcker). In der/Im (store).
Soll ich (thing/things) in der/im (store) kaufen?	Nein, das kannst du besser in der/im (store) kaufen.

Telling someone what to do Ch. 8, p. 223

Geh bitte (action)!
Geht (thing/things) holen, bitte!

Getting someone's attention Ch. 9, p. 250

Verzeihung!
Entschuldigung!

Offering more Ch. 9, p. 258

Möchtest du noch etwas?
Möchtest du noch ein(e)(n) (food/beverage)?
Noch ein(e)(n) (food/beverage)?

Saying you want more Ch. 9, p. 258

Ja, bitte. Ich nehme noch ein(e)(n) (food/beverage).
Ja, bitte. Noch ein(e)(n) (food/beverage).
Ja, gern.

Saying you don't want more Ch. 9, p. 258

Nein, danke! Ich habe keinen Hunger mehr.
Nein, danke! Ich habe genug.
Danke, nichts mehr für mich.
Nein, danke, kein(e)(n) (food/beverage) mehr.

Using the telephone Ch. 11, p. 310

Hier (name). ⎫
Hier ist (name). ⎪
Ich möchte bitte (name) sprechen. ⎬ starting a conversation
Kann ich bitte (name) sprechen? ⎪
Tag! Hier ist (name). ⎭
Wiederhören! ⎫
Auf Wiederhören! ⎬ ending a conversation
Tschüs! ⎭

Talking about birthdays Ch. 11, p. 314

Wann hast du Geburtstag?	Ich habe am (date) Geburtstag. Am (date).

Expressing good wishes Ch. 11, p. 314

Alles Gute zu(m)(r) (occasion)!
Herzlichen Glückwunsch zu(m)(r) (occasion)!

Exchanging Information

Asking someone his or her name and giving yours Ch. 1, p. 22

Wie heißt du?	Ich heiße *(name)*.
Heißt du *(name)*?	Ja, ich heiße *(name)*.

Asking and giving someone else's name Ch. 1, p. 22

Wie heißt der Junge?	Der Junge heißt *(name)*.
Heißt der Junge *(name)*?	Ja, er heißt *(name)*.
Wie heißt das Mädchen?	Das Mädchen heißt *(name)*.
Heißt das Mädchen *(name)*?	Nein, sie heißt *(name)*.

Asking and telling who someone is Ch. 1, p. 23

Wer ist das?	Das ist der/die *(name)*.

Asking someone his or her age and giving yours Ch. 1, p. 25

Wie alt bist du?	Ich bin *(number)* Jahre alt. Ich bin *(number)*. *(Number)*.
Bist du schon *(number)*?	Nein, ich bin *(number)*.

Asking and giving someone else's age Ch. 1, p. 25

Wie alt ist der Peter?	Er ist *(number)*.
Und die Monika? Ist sie auch *(number)*?	Ja, sie ist auch *(number)*.

Asking someone where he or she is from and telling where you are from Ch. 1, p. 28

Woher kommst du?	Ich komme aus (place).
Woher bist du?	Ich bin aus (place).
Bist du aus (place)?	Nein, ich bin aus (place).

Asking and telling where someone else is from Ch. 1, p. 28

Woher ist *(person)*?	Er/sie ist aus *(place)*.
Kommt *(person)* aus *(place)*?	Nein, sie kommt aus *(place)*.

Talking about how someone gets to school Ch. 1, p. 30

Wie kommst du zur Schule?	Ich komme mit der/dem *(mode of transportation)*.
Kommt Ahmet zu Fuß zur Schule?	Nein, er kommt auch mit der/dem *(mode of transportation)*.
Wie kommt Ayla zur Schule?	Sie kommt mit der/dem *(mode of transportation)*.

Talking about interests Ch. 2, p. 48

Was machst du in deiner Freizeit?	Ich *(activity)*.
Spielst du *(sport/ instrument/game)*?	Ja, ich spiele *(sport/ instrument/game)*. Nein, *(sport/instrument/ game)* spiele ich nicht.
Was macht *(name)*?	Er/Sie spielt *(sport/ instrument/game)*.

Saying when you do various activities Ch. 2, p. 55

Was machst du nach der Schule?	Am Nachmittag *(activity)*. Am Abend *(activity)*.
Und am Wochenende?	Am Wochenende *(activity)*.
Was machst du im Sommer?	Im Sommer *(activity)*.

Talking about where you and others live Ch. 3, p. 73

Wo wohnst du?	Ich wohne in *(place)*. In *(place)*.
Wo wohnt der/die *(name)*?	Er/Sie wohnt in *(place)*. In *(place)*.

Describing a room Ch. 3, p. 79

Der/Die/Das *(thing)* ist alt.
Der/Die/Das *(thing)* ist kaputt.
Der/Die/Das *(thing)* ist klein, aber ganz bequem.
Ist *(thing)* neu? Ja, er/sie/es ist neu.

Talking about family members Ch. 3, p. 82

Ist das dein(e) *(family member)*?	Ja, das ist mein(e) *(family member)*.
Und dein(e) *(family member)*? Wie heißt er/sie?	Er/Sie heißt *(name)*.
Wo wohnen deine *(family members)*?	In *(place)*.

Describing people Ch. 3, p. 84

Wie sieht *(person)* aus?	Er/sie hat *(color)* Haare und *(color)* Augen.

Talking about class schedules Ch. 4, p. 106

Welche Fächer hast du?	Ich habe (classes).
Was hast du am (day)?	(Classes).
Was hat die Katja am (day)?	Sie hat (classes).
Welche Fächer habt ihr?	Wir haben (classes).
Was habt ihr nach der Pause?	Wir haben (classes).
Und was habt ihr am Samstag?	Wir haben frei!

Using a schedule to talk about time Ch. 4, p. 107

Wann hast du (class)?	Um (hour) Uhr (minutes).
Was hast du um (hour) Uhr?	(Class).
Was hast du von (time) bis (time)?	Ich habe (class).

Sequencing events Ch. 4, p. 109

Welche Fächer hast du am (day)?	Zuerst hab ich (class), dann (class), danach (class) und zuletzt (class).

Talking about prices Ch. 4, p. 115

Was kostet (thing)?	Er/Sie kostet nur (price).
Was kosten (things)?	Sie kosten (price).
Das ist (ziemlich) teuer!	
Das ist (sehr) billig!	
Das ist (sehr) preiswert!	

Pointing things out Ch. 4, p. 116

Wo sind die (things)?	Schauen Sie!
	Dort!
	Sie sind dort drüben!
	Sie sind da hinten.
	Sie sind da vorn.

Expressing wishes when shopping Ch. 5, p. 134

Was möchten Sie?	Ich möchte ein(e)(n) (thing) sehen, bitte.
	Ich brauche ein(e)(n) (thing).
Was bekommen Sie?	Ein(e)(n) (thing), bitte.
Haben Sie einen Wunsch?	Ich suche ein(e)(n) (thing).

Describing how clothes fit Ch. 5, p. 137

Es passt prima.
Es passt nicht.

Talking about trying on clothes Ch. 5, p. 143

Ich probiere den/die/das (item of clothing) an.
Ich ziehe den/die/das (item of clothing) an.

If you buy it:	*If you don't:*
Ich nehme es.	Ich nehme es nicht.
Ich kaufe es.	Ich kaufe es nicht.

Telling time Ch. 6, p. 162

Wie spät ist es jetzt?	Es ist (time).
Wie viel Uhr ist es?	Es ist (time).

Talking about when you do things Ch. 6, p. 162

Wann gehst du (activity)?	Um (time).
Um wie viel Uhr (action) du?	Um (time).
Und du? Wann (action) du?	Um (time).

Talking about how often you do things Ch. 7, p. 198

Wie oft (action) du?	(Einmal) in der Woche.
Und wie oft musst du (action)?	Jeden Tag.
	Ungefähr (zweimal) im Monat.

Explaining what to do Ch. 7, p. 199

Du kannst für mich (action).

Talking about the weather Ch. 7, p. 203

Wie ist das Wetter heute?	Heute regnet es. Wolkig und kühl.
Wie ist das Wetter morgen?	Sonnig, aber kalt.
Regnet es heute?	Ich glaube schon.
Schneit es am Abend?	Nein, es schneit nicht.
Wie viel Grad haben wir heute?	Ungefähr 10 Grad.

Talking about quantities Ch. 8, p. 226

Wie viel (food item) bekommen Sie?	500 Gramm (food item).
	100 Gramm, bitte.

Asking if someone wants anything else Ch. 8, p. 227

Sonst noch etwas?
Was bekommen Sie noch?
Haben Sie noch einen Wunsch?

Saying that you want something else Ch. 8, p. 227

Ich brauche noch ein(e)(n) (food/beverage/thing).
Ich bekomme noch ein(e)(n) (food/beverage/thing).

Telling someone you don't need anything else Ch. 8, p. 227

Nein, danke.
Danke, das ist alles.

Giving a reason Ch. 8, p. 230

Jetzt kann ich nicht, weil ich (reason).
Es geht nicht, denn ich (reason).

Saying where you were **Ch. 8, p. 231**
Wo warst du heute Morgen?   Ich war *(place)*.
Wo warst du gestern?   Ich war *(place)*.

Saying what you bought **Ch. 8, p. 231**
Was hast du gekauft?   Ich habe *(thing)* gekauft.

Talking about where something is located
Ch. 9, p. 250
Verzeihung, wissen Sie, wo
der/die/das *(place)* ist?   In der Innenstadt.
    Am *(place name)*.
    In der *(street name)*.
Wo ist der/die/das *(place)*?   Es tut mir Leid. Das weiß ich nicht.
Entschuldigung! Weißt du,
wo der/die/das *(place)* ist?   Keine Ahnung! Ich bin nicht von hier.

Asking for directions **Ch. 9, p. 254**
Wie komme ich zu(m)(r) *(place)*?
Wie kommt man zu(m)(r) *(place)*?

Giving directions **Ch. 9, p. 254**
Gehen Sie geradeaus bis zu(m)(r) *(place)*.
Nach rechts/links.
Hier rechts/links.

Talking about what there is to eat and drink
Ch. 9, p. 257
Was gibt es hier
zu essen?   Es gibt *(foods)*.
Und zu trinken?   Es gibt *(beverage)* und auch *(beverage)*.

Talking about what you did in your free time
Ch. 10, p. 292
Was hast du *(time phrase)* gemacht?   Ich habe *(person/thing)* gesehen.
    (book, magazine, etc.) gelesen.
    mit *(person)* über *(subject)* gesprochen.

Discussing gift ideas, **Ch. 11, p. 318**
Schenkst du *(person)*
ein(e)(n) *(thing)*
zu(m)(r) *(occasion)*?   Nein, ich schenke ihm/ihr ein(e)(n) *(thing)*.
Was schenkst du *(person)*
zu(m)(r) *(occasion)*?   Ich weiß noch nicht. Hast du eine Idee?

Wem schenkst du
den/die/das *(thing)*?   Ich schenke *(person)* den/die/das *(thing)*.

Expressing Attitudes and Opinions

Asking for an opinion **Ch. 2, p. 57; Ch. 9, p. 260**
Wie findest du *(thing/activity/place)*?

Expressing your opinion **Ch. 2, p. 57;**
Ch. 9, p. 260
Ich finde *(thing/activity/place)* langweilig.
(Thing/Activity/Place) ist Spitze!
(Activity) macht Spaß!
Ich finde es toll, dass ...
Ich glaube, dass ...

Agreeing **Ch. 2, p. 58; Ch. 7, p. 199**
Ich auch!
Das finde ich auch!
Stimmt!
Gut! Mach ich!

Disagreeing **Ch. 2, p. 58**
Ich nicht!
Das finde ich nicht!
Stimmt nicht!

Commenting on clothes **Ch. 5, p. 137**
Wie findest du den/die/
das *(clothing item)*?   Ich finde ihn/sie/es *(adjective)*.
    Er/Sie/Es gefällt mir *(nicht)*.

Expressing uncertainty, not knowing
Ch. 5, p. 137; Ch. 9, p. 250
Ich bin nicht sicher.
Ich weiß nicht.
Keine Ahnung!

Expressing regret **Ch. 9, p. 250**
Es tut mir Leid.

Expressing Feelings and Emotions

Asking about likes and dislikes **Ch. 2,**
p. 50; Ch. 4, p. 110; Ch. 10, p. 282
Was *(action)* du gern?
(Action) du gern?
Magst du *(things/activities)*?
Was für *(things/activities)* magst du?

Expressing likes Ch. 2, p. 50; Ch. 4, p. 110;
Ch. 10, p. 282
> Ich *(action)* gern.
> Ich mag *(things/activities)*.
> *(Thing/Activities)* mag ich (sehr/furchtbar) gern.

Expressing dislikes Ch. 2, p. 50; Ch. 10, p. 282
> Ich *(action)* nicht so gern.
> Ich mag *(things/action)* (überhaupt) nicht.

Talking about favorites Ch. 4, p. 110
> Was ist dein
>   Lieblings*(category)*?   Mein Lieblings*(category)*
>   ist *(thing)*.

Responding to good news Ch. 4, p. 112
> Toll!
> Das ist prima!
> Nicht schlecht.

Responding to bad news Ch. 4, p. 112
> Schade!
> So ein Pech!
> So ein Mist!
> Das ist sehr schlecht!

Expressing familiarity Ch. 10, p. 284
> Kennst du
>   *(person/place/thing)*?   Ja, sicher!
>   Ja, klar! or
>   Nein, den/die/das
>   kenne
>   ich nicht.
>   Nein, überhaupt nicht.

Expressing preferences and favorites
Ch. 10, p. 285
> (Siehst) du gern ...?   Ja, aber ... (sehe) ich
>   lieber.
>   Und am liebsten (sehe)
>   ich ...
>
> (Siehst) du lieber
>   ... oder ...?   Lieber ... Aber am liebsten
>   (sehe) ich ...
>
> Was (siehst) du
>   am liebsten?   Am liebsten (sehe) ich ...

This list includes additional vocabulary that you may want to use to personalize activities. If you can't find the words you need here, try the German–English and English–German vocabulary sections beginning on page R29.

Sport und Interessen
(Sports and Interests)

angeln	to fish
Baseball spielen	to play baseball
Brettspiele spielen	to play board games
fotografieren	to take photographs
Gewichte heben	lift weights
Handball spielen	to play handball
joggen	to jog
kochen	to cook
malen	to paint
Münzen sammeln	to collect coins
nähen	to sew
Rad fahren	to ride a bike
reiten	to ride (a horse)
Rollschuh laufen	to roller-skate
segeln	to sail
Skateboard fahren	to ride a skateboard
Ski laufen	to (snow) ski
stricken	to knit
Tischtennis spielen	to play table tennis
Videospiele spielen	to play video games

Instrumente (Instruments)

die Blockflöte, -n	recorder
das Cello (Violoncello), -s	cello
die Flöte, -n	flute
die Geige, -n	violin
die Harfe, -n	harp
die Klarinette, -n	clarinet
der Kontrabass, ¨e	double bass
die Mandoline, -n	mandolin
die Mundharmonika, -s	harmonica
die Oboe, -n	oboe
die Posaune, -n	trombone
das Saxophon, -e	saxophone
das Schlagzeug, -e	drums
die Trompete, -n	trumpet
die Tuba, (pl) Tuben	tuba

Getränke (Beverages)

die Limo, -	lemon-flavored drink
ein Glas Milch	a glass of milk
ein Glas Tee	a glass of tea
eine Tasse, -n Kaffee	a cup of coffee

Speisen (Foods)

die Ananas, -	pineapple
der Apfelstrudel, -	apple strudel
die Banane, -n	banana
die Birne, -n	pear
der Chip, -s	potato chip
der Eintopf	stew
die Erdbeere, -n	strawberry
die Erdnussbutter	peanut butter
das Gebäck	baked goods
die Gurke, -n	cucumber
die Himbeere, -n	raspberry
der Joghurt, - or Jogurt	yogurt
die Karotte, -n	carrot

die Marmelade, -n	jam, jelly
die Mayonnaise	mayonnaise
die Melone, -n	melon
das Müsli	muesli (cereal)
die Nuss, ¨e	nut
die Orange, -n	orange
das Plätzchen, -	cookie
die Pommes frites (pl)	french fries
der Spinat	spinach
die Zwiebel, -n	onion

Möbel (Furniture)

das Bild, -er	picture
der Computer, -	computer
die Lampe, -n	lamp

der Sessel, -	armchair
das Sofa, -s	sofa
der Teppich, -e	carpet, rug
der Tisch, -e	table
der Vorhang, ¨e	curtain

Familie (Family)

der Halbbruder, ¨	halfbrother
die Halbschwester, -n	halfsister
der Stiefbruder, ¨	stepbrother
die Stiefmutter, ¨	stepmother
die Stiefschwester, -n	stepsister
der Stiefvater, ¨	stepfather

Fächer (School Subjects)

Algebra	algebra
Band	band
Chor	chorus
Französisch	French
Hauswirtschaft	home economics
Informatik	computer science
Italienisch	Italian
Japanisch	Japanese
Orchester	orchestra
Russisch	Russian
Spanisch	Spanish
Sozialkunde	social studies
Werken	shop
Wirtschaftskunde	economics

Kleidungsstücke (Clothing)

der Anzug, ¨e	suit
der Badeanzug, ¨e	swimsuit
der Blazer, -	blazer
das Halstuch, ¨er	scarf
der Handschuh, -e	glove
der Hut, ¨e	hat
die Krawatte, -n	tie
der Mantel, ¨	coat
die Mütze, -n	cap
die Sandalen (pl)	sandals
der Schal, -s	shawl
die Strumpfhose, -n	panty hose
die Weste, -n	vest

Farben (Colors)

beige	*beige*
bunt	*colorful*
gepunktet	*polka-dotted*
gestreift	*striped*
golden	*gold*
lila	*purple*
orange	*orange*
rosa	*pink*
silbern	*silver*
türkis	*turquoise*

Hausarbeit (Housework)

das Auto polieren	*to polish the car*
das Auto waschen	*to wash the car*
den Fußboden kehren	*to sweep the floor*
den Müll wegtragen	*to take out the trash*
putzen	*to clean*

Staub wischen	*to dust*
sauber machen	*to clean*
die Wäsche waschen	*to do the laundry*
trocknen	*to dry*
aufhängen	*to hang*
legen	*to fold*
bügeln	*to iron*
einräumen	*to put away*

Haustiere (Pets)

die Eidechse, -n	*lizard*
der Fisch, -e	*fish*
der Frosch, ⸚e	*frog*
der Hamster, -	*hamster*
der Hase, -n	*hare*
der Kanarienvogel, ⸚	*canary*
die Maus, ⸚e	*mouse*
das Meerschweinchen, -	*guinea pig*
der Papagei, -en	*parrot*
das Pferd, -e	*horse*
die Schildkröte, -n	*turtle*

die Schlange, -n	*snake*
das Schwein, -e	*pig*
der Vogel, ⸚	*bird*

Wetter (Weather)

feucht	*damp*
gewittrig	*stormy*
halbbedeckt	*partly cloudy*
heiter	*bright*
kühl	*cool*
neblig	*foggy*
nieslig	*drizzly*
trüb	*dreary*
windig	*windy*

Computer (Computer)

abrufen (die E-mail abrufen) (sep)	*to check the e-mail*
Bildschirm, der	*screen*
CD-ROM, die	*CD-ROM disc*
CD-ROM Laufwerk, das	*CD-ROM drive*
Computer, der	*computer*

E-mail, die	e-mail
Eingabemarke, die	cursor
Eingabetaste, die	return key
einloggen (sep)	to log on
entfernen	to delete
Entferntaste, die	delete key
Festplatte, die	hard drive
herunterladen (sep)	to download
Internet, das	Internet
Lesezeichen, das	bookmark
Maus, die	mouse

Modem, das	modem
Monitor, der	monitor
Netz, das (das Internet)	Internet
neu starten	to reboot, restart
speichern	to save
suchen	to search
Suchmaschine, die	search engine
surfen (im Internet surfen)	to surf (the Net)
Tastatur, die	keyboard

Zentraleinheit, die	CPU (central processing unit)
ziehen (auf Symbole)	to drag

In der Stadt (Places around Town)

die Brücke, -n	bridge
die Bücherei, -en	library
der Flughafen, (pl) Flughäfen	airport

das Fremdenverkehrsamt, (pl) Fremdenverkehrsämter	tourist office
der Frisiersalon, -s	beauty shop
das Krankenhaus, (pl) Krankenhäuser	hospital
der Park, -s	park
die Polizei	police station
der Zoo, -s	zoo

Zum Diskutieren (Topics to Discuss)

die Armut	poverty
die Gesundheit	health
der Präsident	the president
die Politik	politics
die Reklame	advertising
die Umwelt	the environment
das Verbrechen	crime
der Wehrdienst	military service
der Zivildienst	alternate service

Geschenkideen (Gift Ideas)

das Bild, -er	picture
die Kette, -n	chain
der Ohrring, -e	earring
die Puppe, -n	doll
das Puppenhaus, -er	dollhouse
der Ring, -e	ring
... aus Silber	made of silver
... aus Gold	made of gold
die Schokolade	chocolate
das Spielzeug, -e	toy

ERDKUNDE *(GEOGRAPHY)*

Here are some terms you will find on German-language maps:

Länder *(States)*

Most of the states in the United States (**die Vereinigten Staaten**) have the same spelling in German that they have in English. Listed below are those states that have a different spelling.

Kalifornien	*California*
Neumexiko	*New Mexico*
Nordkarolina	*North Carolina*
Norddakota	*North Dakota*
Südkarolina	*South Carolina*
Süddakota	*South Dakota*

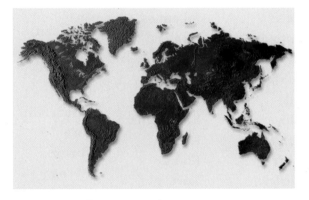

Staaten *(Countries)*

Ägypten	*Egypt*
Argentinien	*Argentina*
Brasilien	*Brazil*
Indien	*India*
Indonesien	*Indonesia*
Kanada	*Canada*
Mexiko	*Mexico*
Russland	*Russia*
die Vereinigten Staaten	*The United States*

Kontinente *(Continents)*

Afrika	*Africa*
die Antarktis	*Antarctica*
Asien	*Asia*
Australien	*Australia*
Europa	*Europe*
Nordamerika	*North America*
Südamerika	*South America*

Meere *(Bodies of Water)*

der Atlantik	*the Atlantic*
der Golf von Mexiko	*the Gulf of Mexico*
der Indische Ozean	*the Indian Ocean*
das Mittelmeer	*the Mediterranean*
der Pazifik	*the Pacific*
das Rote Meer	*the Red Sea*
das Schwarze Meer	*the Black Sea*

Geographical terms

der Breitengrad	*latitude*
die Ebene, -n	*plain*
der Fluss, ¨e	*river*
das ... Gebirge	*the ... mountains*
die Grenze, -n	*border*
die Hauptstadt, ¨e	*capital*
der Kontinent, -e	*continent*
das Land, ¨er	*state*
der Längengrad	*longitude*
das Meer, -e	*ocean, sea*
der Nordpol	*the North Pole*
der See, -n	*lake*
der Staat, -en	*country*
der Südpol	*the South Pole*
das Tal, ¨er	*valley*

DEUTSCHE NAMEN *(GERMAN NAMES)*

Some German names are listed in the **Vorschau**, but here are some additional ones that you will hear when you visit a German-speaking country.

Mädchen *(girls)*

Andrea	Elke	Jutta
Angela,	Erika	Karin
Angelika	Eva	Katharina
Anja	Gabriele	Katja
Anna	(Gabi)	Katrin
Anneliese	Gertrud	Kirstin
Annette	(Trudi(e))	Liselotte
Antje	Gisela	(Lotte)
Barbara	Grete	Marie
Bärbel	Gudrun	Marta
Beate	Hannelore	Martina
Birgit	Heidi/	Meike
Brigitte	Heidemarie	Michaela
Britta	Heike	Monika
Christa	Helga	Nicole
Christiane	Hilde	Petra
Christine	Hildegard	Regina
Claudia	Ilse	Renate
Connie	Ina	Roswitha
Cordula	Inge	Rotraud
Dorothea	Ingrid	Sabine
Dorothee	Irmgard	Sara
Elfriede	Jennifer	Silke
Elisabeth	Julie	Simone
(Lisa)		Stephanie
		Susanne
		Silvia
		Tanja
		Ulrike (Uli)
		Ursel
		Ursula (Uschi)
		Ute
		Veronika
		Waltraud

Jungen *(boys)*

Alexander	Heinz	Rainer
Andreas	Heinz-Dieter	(Reiner)
Axel	Helmar	Ralf
Bernd(t)	Helmut	Reinhard
Bernhard	Ingo	Reinhold
Bruno	Jan	Rolf
Christian	Jens	Rudi
Christoph	Joachim	Rüdiger
Daniel	Jochen	Rudolf
Detlev(f)	Johann	Sebastian
Dieter	Johannes	Stefan
Dietmar	Jörg	(Stephan)
Dirk	Josef	Thomas
Eberhard	Jürgen	Udo
Erik	Karl	Ulf
Felix	Karl-Heinz	Ulrich (Uli)
Frank	Klaus	Uwe
Franz	Konrad	Volker
Friedrich	Kurt	Werner
Fritz	Lars	Wilhelm
Georg	Lothar	(Willi)
Gerd	Lutz	Wolfgang
Gerhard	Manfred	
Gottfried	Markus	
Gregor	Martin	
Günter	Mathias	
Gustav(f)	Max	
Hannes	Michael	
Hans	Norbert	
Hans-Georg	Otto	
Hans-Jürgen	Patrick	
Hartmut	Paul	
Hauke	Peter	
Heinrich	Philipp	

NOUNS AND THEIR MODIFIERS

In German, nouns (words that name a person, place, or thing) are grouped into three classes or genders: masculine, feminine, and neuter. All nouns, both persons and objects, fall into one of these groups. There are words used with nouns that signal the class of the noun. One of these is the definite article. In English there is one definite article: *the*. In German, there are three, one for each class: **der, die,** and **das**.

THE DEFINITE ARTICLE

SUMMARY OF DEFINITE ARTICLES

	Nominative	Accusative	Dative
Masculine	der	den	dem
Feminine	die	die	der
Neuter	das	das	dem
Plural	die	die	den

When the definite article is combined with a noun, a noun phrase is formed. Noun phrases that are used as subjects are in the nominative case. Nouns that are used as direct objects or the objects of certain prepositions (such as **für**) are in the accusative case. Nouns that are indirect objects, the objects of certain prepositions (such as **mit, bei**), or the objects of special verbs that you will learn about in Level 2, are in the dative case. Below is a summary of the definite articles combined with nouns to form noun phrases.

SUMMARY OF NOUN PHRASES

	Nominative	Accusative	Dative
Masculine	der Vater der Ball	den Vater den Ball	dem Vater dem Ball
Feminine	die Mutter die Kassette	die Mutter die Kassette	der Mutter der Kassette
Neuter	das Mädchen das Haus	das Mädchen das Haus	dem Mädchen dem Haus

THE INDEFINITE ARTICLE

Another type of word that is used with nouns is the *indefinite article:* **ein, eine, ein** in German, *a, an* in English. There is no plural form of **ein**.

SUMMARY OF INDEFINITE ARTICLES

	Nominative	Accusative	Dative
Masculine	ein	einen	einem
Feminine	eine	eine	einer
Neuter	ein	ein	einem
Plural	—	—	—

THE NEGATING WORD **KEIN**

The word **kein** is also used with nouns and means *no, not,* or *not any.* Unlike the **ein-** words, **kein** has a plural form.

	Nominative	Accusative	Dative
Masculine	kein	keinen	keinem
Feminine	keine	keine	keiner
Neuter	kein	kein	keinem
Plural	keine	keine	keinen

THE POSSESSIVES

These words also modify nouns and tell you *whose* object or person is being referred to (*my* car, *his* book, *her* mother). These words have the same endings as **kein**.

SUMMARY OF POSSESSIVES

	Before Masculine Nouns			Before Feminine Nouns		Before Neuter Nouns		Before Plural Nouns	
	Nom	Acc	Dat	Nom & Acc	Dat	Nom & Acc	Dat	Nom & Acc	Dat
my	mein	meinen	meinem	meine	meiner	mein	meinem	meine	meinen
your	dein	deinen	deinem	deine	deiner	dein	deinem	deine	deinen
his	sein	seinen	seinem	seine	seiner	sein	seinem	seine	seinen
her	ihr	ihren	ihrem	ihre	ihrer	ihr	ihrem	ihre	ihren

Other possessive adjectives that you will learn more about in Level 2 are:

unser	*our*
euer	*your* (informal, plural)
ihr	*their*
Ihr	*your* (formal)

NOUN PLURALS

Noun class and plural forms are not always predictable. Therefore, you must learn each noun together with its article (**der, die, das**) and with its plural form. As you learn more nouns, however, you will discover certain patterns. Although there are always exceptions to these patterns, you may find them helpful in remembering the plural forms of many nouns.

Most German nouns form their plurals in one of two ways: some nouns add endings in the plural; some add endings and/or change the sound of the stem vowel in the plural, indicating the sound change with the umlaut (¨). Only the vowels **a, o, u,** and the diphthong **au** can take the umlaut. If a noun has an umlaut in the singular, it keeps the umlaut in the plural. Most German nouns fit into one of the following five plural groups.

1. Nouns that do not have any ending in the plural. Sometimes they take an umlaut.
   NOTE: There are only two feminine nouns in this group: **die Mutter** and **die Tochter.**

der Bruder, die Brüder	der Schüler, die Schüler	das Fräulein, die Fräulein
der Lehrer, die Lehrer	der Vater, die Väter	das Mädchen, die Mädchen
der Onkel, die Onkel	die Mutter, die Mütter	das Poster, die Poster
der Mantel, die Mäntel	die Tochter, die Töchter	das Zimmer, die Zimmer

2. Nouns that add the ending **-e** in the plural. Sometimes they also take an umlaut. **NOTE:** There are many one-syllable words in this group.

der Bleistift, die Bleistifte	der Sohn, die Söhne	das Jahr, die Jahre
der Freund, die Freunde	die Stadt, die Städte	das Spiel, die Spiele

3. Nouns that add the ending **-er** in the plural. Whenever possible, they take an umlaut, i.e., when the noun contains the vowels **a, o,** or **u,** or the diphthong **au. NOTE:** There are no feminine nouns in this group. There are many one-syllable words in this group.

das Buch, die Bücher	das Haus, die Häuser
das Fach, die Fächer	das Land, die Länder

4. Nouns that add the ending **-en** or **-n** in the plural. These nouns never add an umlaut.
   NOTE: There are many feminine nouns in this group.

der Herr, die Herren	die Klasse, die Klassen	die Tante, die Tanten
der Junge, die Jungen	die Karte, die Karten	die Wohnung, die Wohnungen
die Briefmarke, die Briefmarken	der Name, die Namen	die Zahl, die Zahlen
die Familie, die Familien	der Vetter, die Vettern	die Zeitung, die Zeitungen
die Farbe, die Farben	die Küche, die Küchen	
die Frau, die Frauen	die Schwester, die Schwestern	

   Feminine nouns ending in **-in** add the ending **-nen** in the plural.

die Freundin, die Freundinnen	die Verkäuferin, die Verkäuferinnen
die Lehrerin, die Lehrerinnen	

5. Nouns that add the ending **-s** in the plural. These nouns never add an umlaut. **NOTE:** There are many words of foreign origin in this group.

der Kuli, die Kulis	das Auto, die Autos
die Kamera, die Kameras	das Hobby, die Hobbys

SUMMARY OF PLURAL ENDINGS

Group	1	2	3	4	5
Ending:	-	-e	-er	-(e)n	-s
Umlaut:	sometimes	sometimes	always	never	never

PRONOUNS

PERSONAL PRONOUNS

		Nominative	Accusative	Dative
Singular				
1st person		ich	mich	mir
2nd person		du	dich	dir
3rd person	*m.*	er	ihn	ihm
	f.	sie	sie	ihr
	n.	es	es	ihm
Plural				
1st person		wir	uns	uns
2nd person		ihr	euch	euch
3rd person		sie	sie	ihnen
you (formal, sing. & pl.)		Sie	Sie	Ihnen

DEFINITE ARTICLES AS DEMONSTRATIVE PRONOUNS

The definite articles can be used as demonstrative pronouns, giving more emphasis to the sentences than the personal pronouns **er, sie, es.** Note that these demonstrative pronouns have the same forms as the definite articles:

Wer bekommt *den* Cappuccino? *Der* ist für mich.

	Nominative	Accusative
Masculine	der	den
Feminine	die	die
Neuter	das	das
Plural	die	die

INTERROGATIVES

INTERROGATIVE PRONOUNS

	People		Things	
Nominative	**wer?**	*who?*	**was?**	*what?*
Accusative	**wen?**	*whom?*	**was?**	*what?*
Dative	**wem?**	*to, for whom?*		

OTHER INTERROGATIVES

wann?	*when?*	**wie viele?**	*how many?*	**welche?**	*which?*
warum?	*why?*	**wo?**	*where?*	**was für (ein)?**	*what kind of (a)?*
wie?	*how?*	**woher?**	*from where?*	**(eine)**	
wie viel?	*how much? how many?*	**wohin?**	*to where?*	**(einen)**	

WORD ORDER

POSITION OF VERBS IN A SENTENCE

The conjugated verb is in **first** *position in:*	*yes/no questions (questions that do not begin with an interrogative)* **Trinkst du Kaffee?** **Spielst du Tennis?** **Möchtest du ins Konzert gehen?** *both formal and informal commands* **Kommen Sie bitte um 2 Uhr!** **Geh doch mit ins Kino!**
The conjugated verb is in **second** *position in:*	*statements with normal word order* **Wir spielen heute Volleyball.** *statements with inverted word order* **Heute spielen wir Volleyball.** *questions that begin with an interrogative* **Wohin gehst du?** **Woher kommst du?** **Was macht er?**
The conjugated verb is in **second** *position and the infinitive or past participle is* **final** *in:*	*statements with modals* **Ich möchte heute ins Kino gehen.** *statements in conversational past* **Ich habe das Buch gelesen.**
The conjugated verb is in **final** *position in:*	*clauses following the verb* **wissen** **Ich weiß, wo das Hotel ist.** *clauses that begin with* **weil** *or* **dass** **Ich gehe nicht ins Kino, weil ich kein Geld habe.** **Ich glaube, dass er Rockmusik gern hört.**

NOTE: In Level 2 you will learn more about word order in clauses with modals and verbs with separable prefixes:

> **Ich komme morgen nicht, weil ich zu Hause helfen muss.**
> **Ich weiß nicht, wer heute Morgen angerufen hat.**

POSITION OF **NICHT** IN A SENTENCE

To negate the entire sentence, as close to end of sentence as possible:	Er fragt seinen Vater	nicht.	
Before a separable prefix:	Ich rufe ihn	nicht	an.
Before any part of a sentence you want to negate, contrast, or emphasize:	Er kommt	nicht	heute. (Er kommt morgen.)
Before part of a sentence that answers the question **wo?**	Ich wohne	nicht	in Berlin.

VERBS

PRESENT TENSE VERB FORMS

		Regular	-eln Verbs	Stem Ending with t/d	Stem Ending with s/ß
INFINITIVES		spiel -en	bastel -n	find -en	heiß -en
PRONOUNS		stem + ending	stem + ending	stem + ending	stem + ending
I	ich	spiel -e	bastl -e	find -e	heiß -e
you	du	spiel -st	bastel -st	find -est	heiß -t
he *she* *it*	er sie es	spiel -t	bastel -t	find -et	heiß -t
we	wir	spiel -en	bastel -n	find -en	heiß -en
you (plural)	ihr	spiel -t	bastel -t	find -et	heiß -t
they	sie	spiel -en	bastel -n	find -en	heiß -en
you (formal)	Sie	spiel -en	bastel -n	find -en	heiß -en

NOTE: There are important differences between the verbs in the above chart:

1. Verbs ending in -eln (**basteln, segeln**) drop the **e** of the ending -**eln** in the **ich**-form: **ich bastle, ich segle** and add only -**n** in the **wir**-, **sie**-, and **Sie**-forms. These forms are always identical with the infinitive: **basteln, wir basteln, sie basteln, Sie basteln.**

2. Verbs with a stem ending in **d** or **t,** such as **finden,** add an **e** before the ending in the **du**-form (**du findest**) and the **er**- and **ihr**-forms (**er findet, ihr findet**).

3. All verbs with stems ending in an **s**-sound (**heißen** or **müssen**) add only -**t** in the **du**-form: **du heißt, du musst.**

VERBS WITH A STEM-VOWEL CHANGE

There are a number of verbs in German that change their stem vowel in the **du-** and **er/sie-** forms. A few verbs, such as **nehmen** (*to take*), have a change in the consonant as well. You cannot predict these verbs, so it is best to learn each one individually. They are usually irregular only in the **du-** and **er/sie-** forms.

	e → i			e → ie		a → ä	
	essen	geben	nehmen	lesen	sehen	fahren	einladen
ich	esse	gebe	nehme	lese	sehe	fahre	lade ein
du	isst	gibst	nimmst	liest	siehst	fährst	lädst ein
er, sie	isst	gibt	nimmt	liest	sieht	fährt	lädt ein
wir	essen	geben	nehmen	lesen	sehen	fahren	laden ein
ihr	esst	gebt	nehmt	lest	seht	fahrt	ladet ein
sie	essen	geben	nehmen	lesen	sehen	fahren	laden ein
Sie	essen	geben	nehmen	lesen	sehen	fahren	laden ein

SOME IMPORTANT IRREGULAR VERBS: **HABEN, SEIN, WISSEN**

	haben	sein	wissen
ich	habe	bin	weiß
du	hast	bist	weißt
er, sie	hat	ist	weiß
wir	haben	sind	wissen
ihr	habt	seid	wisst
sie	haben	sind	wissen
Sie	haben	sind	wissen

MODAL (AUXILIARY) VERBS

The verbs **können, müssen, sollen, wollen, mögen** (and the **möchte**-forms) are usually used with an infinitive at the end of the sentence. If the meaning of that infinitive is clear, it can be left out: **Du musst sofort nach Hause!** (**Gehen** is understood and omitted.)

	können	müssen	sollen	wollen	mögen	möchte
ich	kann	muss	soll	will	mag	möchte
du	kannst	musst	sollst	willst	magst	möchtest
er, sie	kann	muss	soll	will	mag	möchte
wir	können	müssen	sollen	wollen	mögen	möchten
ihr	könnt	müsst	sollt	wollt	mögt	möchtet
sie	können	müssen	sollen	wollen	mögen	möchten
Sie	können	müssen	sollen	wollen	mögen	möchten

VERBS WITH SEPARABLE PREFIXES

Some verbs have *separable prefixes:* prefixes that separate from the conjugated verbs and are moved to the end of the sentence.

	Infinitive: aussehen
ich sehe ... aus	Ich sehe heute aber sehr schick aus!
du siehst ... aus	Du siehst heute sehr fesch aus!
er/sie/es sieht ... aus	Sieht sie immer so modern aus?
	Sieht dein Zimmer immer so unordentlich aus?
wir sehen ... aus	Wir sehen heute sehr lustig aus.
ihr seht ... aus	Ihr seht alle so traurig aus.
sie sehen ... aus	Sie sehen sehr schön aus.
Sie sehen ... aus	Sie sehen immer so ernst aus.

Here are the separable-prefix verbs you learned in Level 1.

abheben	anziehen	einkaufen
abräumen	auflegen	einladen
anprobieren	aufräumen	einstecken
anrufen	aussehen	mitkommen

COMMAND FORMS

Regular Verbs	gehen	kommen
Persons you address with **du** (singular) with **ihr** (plural) with **Sie** (sing & pl)	Geh! Geht! Gehen Sie!	Komm! Kommt! Kommen Sie!

Separable-prefix Verbs	mitkommen	anrufen	einladen	anziehen	ausgehen
	Komm mit! Kommt mit! Kommen Sie mit!	Ruf an! Ruft an! Rufen Sie an!	Lad ein! Ladet ein! Laden Sie ein!	Zieh an! Zieht an! Ziehen Sie an!	Geh aus! Geht aus! Gehen Sie aus!

Stem-changing Verbs	essen	nehmen	geben	sehen	fahren
	Iss! Esst! Essen Sie!	Nimm! Nehmt! Nehmen Sie!	Gib! Gebt! Geben Sie!	Sieh! Seht! Sehen Sie!	Fahr! Fahrt! Fahren Sie!

Note: The vowel changes **e → i** and **e → ie** are maintained in the **du**- form of the command. The umlaut vowel change **a → ä** does not occur in the command form.

EXPRESSING FUTURE TIME

You can use the present tense with a time expression to talk about events that will take place in the future:

Wir fahren morgen nach Berlin.

Am Wochenende besuche ich meine Großeltern.

PAST TENSE VERB FORMS

In this book, you learned the following verbs to express past time:

Weak Verbs		Strong Verbs	
Present Tense Form	**Past Tense Form**	**Present Tense Form**	**Past Tense Form**
Er macht das. Sie kauft das.	Er hat das gemacht. Sie hat das gekauft.	Er spricht oft. Sie sieht das nicht. Du liest gern.	Er hat oft gesprochen. Sie hat das nicht gesehen. Du hast gern gelesen.

In addition you learned the simple past form of the verb **sein**:

THE SIMPLE PAST OF SEIN

ich	war
du	warst
er, sie	war
wir	waren
ihr	wart
sie	waren
Sie (formal)	waren

THE CONVERSATIONAL PAST

In Level 2 you will learn more about how to express past events. In general, German verbs are divided into two groups: weak verbs and strong verbs. Weak verbs usually follow a regular pattern, as do the English verb forms *play, played, has played.* In German, weak verbs add a **ge-** and a **-t** to the verb stem to form the past participle. Strong verbs usually have irregularities, like the English verb forms *run, ran, has run* and *go, went, has gone.* Look at the past tense verb forms chart above and compare the present tense forms of the verbs on the left with the past tense forms on the right. As a rule of thumb, verbs that are irregular (stem-changing verbs) in the present tense are irregular, or strong, in the past tense.

In Level 1 you have learned that **haben** is used as the helping verb with the past participle. In Level 2 you will also learn some verbs that use **sein** as their helping verb, such as the verb **gehen** in the following example:

Ich gehe oft ins Kino.   **Ich bin gestern ins Kino gegangen.**

PRINCIPAL PARTS OF THE VERBS PRESENTED IN LEVEL 1*

This list includes all verbs included in the **Wortschatz** sections of this textbook. Both strong and weak verbs, including verbs with separable prefixes, stem-vowel changes, and other irregularities, are listed. Though most of the verbs in this list form the conversational past with **haben**, a few of the verbs you have learned take **sein** in the present perfect tense. You will work with these verbs and learn more about them in Level 2.

STRONG VERBS

Infinitive	Present (stem-vowel change and/or separable prefix)	Past Participle	Meaning
abheben	hebt ab	abgehoben	to lift (the receiver)
anrufen	ruft an	angerufen	to call up
anziehen	zieht an	angezogen	to put on (clothes)
aussehen	sieht aus	ausgesehen	to look, appear
bekommen	bekommt	bekommen	to get, receive
einladen	lädt ein	eingeladen	to invite
essen	isst	gegessen	to eat
fahren	fährt	(ist) gefahren	to drive, ride
finden	findet	gefunden	to find
geben	gibt	gegeben	to give
gefallen	gefällt	gefallen	to like, be pleasing to
gehen	geht	(ist) gegangen	to go
gießen	gießt	gegossen	to pour; to water
haben	hat	gehabt	to have
heißen	heißt	geheißen	to be called
helfen	hilft	geholfen	to help
kommen	kommt	(ist) gekommen	to come
lesen	liest	gelesen	to read
mitkommen	kommt mit	(ist) mitgekommen	to come along
nehmen	nimmt	genommen	to take
scheinen	scheint	geschienen	to shine
schreiben	schreibt	geschrieben	to write
schwimmen	schwimmt	(ist) geschwommen	to swim
sehen	sieht	gesehen	to see
sein	ist	(ist) gewesen	to be
sprechen	spricht	gesprochen	to speak
trinken	trinkt	getrunken	to drink
tun	tut	getan	to do
wissen	weiß	gewusst	to know

*The past participles in this chart are for reference only. Most of them will be taught in Level 2.

WEAK VERBS

abräumen	räumt ab	abgeräumt	to clear away
anprobieren	probiert an	anprobiert	to try on
auflegen	legt auf	aufgelegt	to hang up (receiver)
aufräumen	räumt auf	aufgeräumt	to pick up/clean room
basteln	bastelt	gebastelt	to do arts and crafts
besichtigen	besichtigt	besichtigt	to sightsee
besuchen	besucht	besucht	to visit
brauchen	braucht	gebraucht	to need
decken	deckt	gedeckt	to set (the table)
füttern	füttert	gefüttert	to feed
einkaufen	kauft ein	eingekauft	to shop
einstecken	steckt ein	eingesteckt	to insert (coin)
glauben	glaubt	geglaubt	to believe
holen	holt	geholt	to get
hören	hört	gehört	to hear
kaufen	kauft	gekauft	to buy
kennen	kennt	*gekannt	to know
kosten	kostet	gekostet	to cost
machen	macht	gemacht	to do or make
mähen	mäht	gemäht	to mow
meinen	meint	gemeint	to think, be of the opinion
passen	passt	gepasst	to fit
putzen	putzt	geputzt	to clean
regnen	regnet	geregnet	to rain
sagen	sagt	gesagt	to say
sammeln	sammelt	gesammelt	to collect
schauen	schaut	geschaut	to look (at)
schenken	schenkt	geschenkt	to give (a gift)
schmecken	schmeckt	geschmeckt	to taste
sortieren	sortiert	sortiert	to sort
spielen	spielt	gespielt	to play
spülen	spült	gespült	to wash dishes
suchen	sucht	gesucht	to look for
tanzen	tanzt	getanzt	to dance
telefonieren	telefoniert	telefoniert	to call (on the phone)
verbringen	verbringt	*verbracht	to spend time
wählen	wählt	gewählt	to dial
wandern	wandert	(ist) gewandert	to hike
wohnen	wohnt	gewohnt	to live
zahlen	zahlt	gezahlt	to pay
zeichnen	zeichnet	gezeichnet	to draw

*Although weak, these verbs have a vowel change in the past participle.

Learning to pronounce new and different sounds can be one of the most challenging aspects of learning a new language. You must first learn to hear new sounds. Then you have to learn to use your tongue, lips, jaw, and facial muscles in new ways to produce the sounds. Pronunciation can also be a very important aspect of learning a language; poor pronunciation can often interfere with communication. Although it is not necessary to learn to speak "like a native," it is important that you learn to make the sounds in order to communicate clearly and effectively.

The pronunciation features treated in this book are intended to be as helpful as possible. The descriptions of the German sound system used throughout this book focus on spelling and how different letters or letter combinations are usually pronounced. The **Aussprache** sections are meant to familiarize you with the German sound system, to help you recognize individual sounds when they occur, and to enable you to "sound out" new words and pronounce them correctly. Luckily, in German there is a much closer relationship between spelling and pronunication than there is in English. There are, of course, exceptions, and for the most conspicuous ones, we have provided examples to remind you that these pronunciation rules are usually true, but not always.

Whenever possible, a familiar sound in an English word is compared to the German sound being introduced. All German sounds are designated by boldfaced print, and all English sounds are designated by italics. For sounds not occurring in English, we have provided brief descriptions of how to produce the sounds. In general, German vowels require more tension in the facial muscles and less movement of the tongue than English. The vowels usually do not glide, which means the sounds are more pure or continuous.

The thought of learning a whole new sound system might be intimidating at first, but practice will be your key to success. Here are some hints that might make learning pronunciation seem a little easier:

Don't be afraid to guess the pronunciation of an unfamiliar German word!

In general, German words are pronounced just like they are written. By looking at the spelling of a German word, you can often guess the pronunciation. Regardless of whether you are dealing with a short word, like **Katze,** or a much longer word, such as **Donaudampfschifffahrtsgesellschaftskapitän,** you should be able to sound out the word using the spelling as a guide.

Don't be afraid to make pronunciation mistakes!

Learning a foreign language takes time, and you are going to make some mistakes along the way. Making German sounds requires the use of different facial muscles and, just like riding a bike, it takes practice to get it right.

Pronunciation and dictation exercises are found at the end of the **Dritte Stufe** in each chapter. The symbols within slashes below, for example /e/, are from the *International Phonetic Alphabet* and represent sounds.

CHAPTER PAGE	LETTER/COMBINATION	IPA SYMBOL	EXAMPLE
Ch. 1 p. 33	the long vowel **ä**	/e/	Mädchen
	the long vowel **e**	/e/	zehn
	the long vowel **ü**	/y/	Grüß
	the long vowel **ö**	/ø/	hören
	the letter **w**	/v/	wer
	the letter **v**	/f/	vier
Ch. 2 p. 59	the vowel combination **ie**	/i/	spielen
	the diphthong **ei**	/ai/	schreiben
	the letter **j**	/j/	Junge
	the letter **z**	/ts/	zur
Ch. 3 p. 85	the long vowel **o**	/o/	Obst
	the long vowel **u**	/u/	Stuhl
	the letter **s**	/z/	sieben
	the letter **s**	/s/	Preis
	the letters **ss**	/s/	müssen
	the letter **ß**	/s/	Straße
Ch. 4 p. 117	the diphthong **eu**	/ɔy/	teuer
	the diphthong **äu**	/ɔy/	Verkäufer
	the diphthong **au**	/au/	bauen
	the final **b**	/p/	gelb
	the final **d**	/t/	Rad
	the final **g**	/k/	sag
Ch. 5 p. 145	the short vowel **i**	/ɪ/	schick
	the short vowel **ä**	/ɛ/	lässig
	the short vowel **e**	/ɛ/	Bett
	the long vowel **a**	/a/	haben
	the letter combination **sch**	/ʃ/	Schule
	the letter combination **st**	/ʃt/	Stiefel
	the letter combination **sp**	/ʃp/	Spitze
Ch. 6 p. 173	the letter combination **ch**	/ç/	ich
	the letter combination **ch**	/x/	doch
	the letter **r**	/r/	rund
	the final **er**	/ɐ/	super
Ch. 7 p. 205	the short vowel **o**	/ɔ/	wolkig
	the short vowel **u**	/ʊ/	uns
	the letter **l**	/l/	Lehrer
	the letter combination **th**	/t/	Mathe
	the letter combination **pf**	/pf/	Pfennig
Ch. 8 p. 233	the short vowel **ö**	/œ/	können
	the short vowel **ü**	/Y/	Stück
	review diphthong **ei**	/ai/	Eier
	review vowel combination **ie**	/i/	wieder
	review letter **z**	/ts/	Zeit
Ch. 9 p. 261	review long vowel **ü**	/y/	für
	review long vowel **ö**	/ø/	blöd
	review letter **s**	/z/	Senf
	review letter **s**	/s/	es
	review letters **ss**	/s/	besser
	review letter **ß**	/s/	Spaß
Ch. 10 p. 293	review short vowel **o**	/ɔ/	Onkel
	review long vowel **o**	/o/	Oma
	review short vowel **u**	/ʊ/	Gruppe
	review long vowel **u**	/u/	Musik
	review combination **ch**	/ç/	Pech
	review combination **ch**	/x/	Buch
Ch. 11 p. 321	review **r**	/r/	Bruder
	review **er**	/ɐ/	meiner
	review long vowel **a**	/a/	Vater
	review diphthong **eu**	/ɔy/	heute
	review diphthong **äu**	/ɔy/	Verkäufer
	review diphthong **au**	/au/	Strauß
Ch. 12 p. 349	review letter **w**	/v/	weiß
	review letter **v**	/f/	viel
	review letter **j**	/j/	Juli
	review short vowel **ä**	/ɛ/	hässlich
	review short vowel **e**	/ɛ/	Sessel
	review long vowel **ä**	/e/	Käse
	review long vowel **e**	/e/	dem

This vocabulary includes almost all words in this textbook, both active (for production) and passive (for recognition only). Active words and phrases are practiced in the chapter and are listed in the **Wortschatz** section at the end of each chapter. You are expected to know and be able to use active vocabulary. An entry in black, heavy type indicates that the word or phrase is active. All other words—some in the opening dialogs, in exercises, in optional and visual material, in the **Landeskunde, Zum Lesen** and **Kann ich's wirklich?** sections—are for recognition only. The meaning of these words and phrases can usually be understood from the context or may be looked up in this vocabulary.

With some exceptions, the following are not included: proper nouns, forms of verbs other than the infinitive, and forms of determiners other than the nominative.

Nouns are listed with definite article and plural form, when applicable. The numbers in the entries refer to the chapter where the word or phrase first appears or where it becomes an active vocabulary word. Vocabulary from the preliminary chapter is followed by a page reference only. Vocabulary from the location openers is followed by a "Loc" and the chapter number directly following the location spread.

The following abbreviations are used in this vocabulary: adj (adjective), pl (plural), pp (past participle), sep (separable-prefix verb), sing (singular), and conj (conjunction).

A

ab *from, starting at,* 4; **ab und zu** *now and then,* 10

der Abend, -e *evening,* 2; **am Abend** *in the evening,* 2; **jeden Abend** *every evening,* 10

der Abendhauch *evening breeze,* 10

abends *evenings,* 6

der Abenteuerfilm, -e *adventure movie,* 10

aber *but,* 3; **Aber sicher!** *Sure!,* 11

die Abfahrt, -en *departure,* 6

abgelegen *remote,* 10

abheben (sep) *to pick up,* 11; **den Hörer abheben** *to pick up the receiver,* 11

das Abitur, -e *final examination in high school,* 4

abräumen (sep) *to clean up, clear off,* 7; **den Tisch abräumen** *to clear the table,* 7

der Absatz, ⁼e *paragraph,* 11

abschmecken (sep) *to taste,* 12

abschreiben *to copy,* 8

die Abschrift, -en *transcript,* 8

die Abteilung, -en *section,* 9

abwaschen (sep) *to wash dishes,* 12

Ach *Oh!,* 2; **Ach ja!** *Oh yeah!,* 1; Ach so! *Oh, I see!,* 1; Ach was! *Give me a break!,* 5; Ach wo! *Oh no!,* 4

acht *eight,* 1

achten *to pay attention (to),* 9

Achtung! *Attention!,* 6

achtzehn *eighteen,* 1

achtzig *eighty,* 3

der Ackerbau *agriculture,* Loc 4

der Actionfilm, -e *action movie,* 10

actionsgeladen *full of action,* 10

addieren *to add,* 8

das Adressbuch, ⁼er *address book,* 11

der Affe, -n *ape; monkey,* 10

ähnlich *similar,* 11

die Ahnung: **Keine Ahnung!** *I have no idea!,* 9

das Akkordeon, -s *accordion,* 10

aktiv *active,* 12

die Aktivität, -en *activity,* 7

aktuell *current,* 10

akzeptieren *to accept,* 7

die Algebra *algebra,* 4

alle *all, everyone,* 2

allein *alone,* 8

aller *of all,* 8

allerdings *admittedly,* 7

alles *everything,* 2; **Das ist alles.** *That's all.* 8; Alles klar! *O.K.!,* 10; **Alles Gute zum Geburtstag!** *Best wishes on your birthday!,* 11; **Alles Gute zum Muttertag!** *Happy Mother's Day!,* 11

allgemein *general,* 4; im Allgemeinen *in general,* 10

alltäglich *daily,* 8

allzu *overly,* 10

der Alptraum, ⁼e *nightmare,* 10

als *as,* 6; als letzter *the last,* 12

also *well then,* 2; Also, auf geht's! *Well, let's go!,* 9; **Also, einfach!** *That's easy.* 1

alt *old,* 3; **Wie alt ...?** *How old ...?,* 1

älter *older,* 3

das Altpapier *recycled paper,* 7

die Altstadt, ⁼e *historical part of downtown,* 12

das Alter: in deinem Alter *your age,* 9

das Aluminium *aluminum,* 7

am=an dem *at the,* 2; **am ...platz** *on ... Square,* 9; **am Abend** *in the evening,* 2; **am ersten (Juli)** *on the first (of July),* 11; **am liebsten** *most of all,* 10; **Am liebsten sehe ich Krimis.** *I like detective movies the best.,* 10; **am Montag** *on Monday,* 4; **am Nachmittag** *in the afternoon,* 2; **am Wochenende** *on the weekend,* 2

der Amerikaner, - *American (male),* 9

die Amerikanerin, -nen *American (female),* 9

amerikanisch *American (adj),* 8

die Ampel, -n *traffic light,* 9; an der Ampel *at the traffic light,* 9; **bis zur Ampel** *until you get to the traffic light,* 9

amtlich *official,* 9

an *to, at,* 4; an der Ampel *at the traffic light,* 9; ansonsten *otherwise,* 11; an welchem Tag? *on which day?,* 11

die Ananas, - *pineapple,* 8

anbieten, *to offer,* 8

das Andenken, - *souvenir,* 11

andere *other,* 7

ändern *to change,* 9

anerkannt *recognized,* 4

anfallen (sep): alles was anfällt *anything that comes up,* 12

der Anfänger, - *beginner*, 4
angefangen (pp) *started*, 7
angeln *to fish*, 10
ankommen: es kommt darauf an *it depends on*, 12
der Anlass, ̈e *occasion*, Loc 7
anprobieren (sep) *to try on*, 5
anrösten (sep) *to brown*, 12
anrücken *to advance*, 10
anrufen (sep) *to call* (phone), 11; Ruf mal an! *Give me a call!*, 11
anschauen (sep) *to look at*, 6
ansehen (sep) *to look at*, 9
ansonsten *otherwise*, 11
anstrengend *exhausting*, 7
die Antwort, -en *answer*, 1
antworten *to answer*, 2
der Anwalt, ̈e *lawyer*, 10
die Anweisung, -en *instruction*, 9
die Anwendung, -en *application*, 1
die Anzeige, -n *ad*, 10
anziehen (sep) *to put on, wear*, 5
der Anzug, ̈e *suit*, 5
der Apfel, ̈e *apple*, 8
der Apfelkuchen, - *apple cake*, 6
das Apfelküchle, - *(see p. 298)*, 12
der Apfelsaft, ̈e *apple juice*, 3; **ein Glas Apfelsaft** *a glass of apple juice*, 3
der Apfelstrudel, - *apple strudel*, 8
der Apparat, -e *telephone*, 11
die Applikation, -en *appliqué*, 5
das Apricot *apricot (color)*, 5
der April *April*, 7
das Aquarium, die Aquarien, *aquarium*, 10
die Arbeit *work*, 7
die Arbeitslehre, -n *work-study class*, 4
die Arbeitsliste, -n *work list*, 12
der Architekt, -en *architect*, 4
ärgerlich *annoying*, 6
die Arie, -n *aria*, 11
die Armbanduhr, -en *wristwatch*, 11
der Ärmel, - *sleeve*, 5
aromatisch *aromatic*, 9
der Artikel, - *article*, 8
die Asche, -n *ash*, 10
der Aschermittwoch *Ash Wednesday*, 9
der Ast, ̈e *branch*, 8
die Atmosphäre, -n *atmosphere*, 4
das Attentat, -e *assassination*, 10
auch *also*, 1; **Ich auch.** *Me too.*, 2
auf *on; to*, 1; Also, auf geht's! *Well, let's go!*, 9; **auf dem Land** *in the country*, 3; auf dem Weg *on the way*, 6; auf der Straße *on the street*, 9; auf einer Fete *at a party*, 12; auf Englisch *in English*, 10; auf Schritt und Tritt *all the time*, 10; **Auf Wiederhören!** *Goodbye! (on the telephone)*, 11; **Auf Wiedersehen!** *Goodbye!*, 1; auf Deutsch *in German*, 9; auf der rechten Seite *on the right (hand) side*, 9
aufdringlich *pushy*, 7
der Aufdruck, -e *design*, 5

auffällig *conspicuous*, 9
die Aufgabe, -n *task*, 7
aufhängen (sep) *to hang up*, 12; die Wäsche aufhängen *to hang up the laundry*, 7
aufhören (sep) *to stop*, 3
auflegen (sep) *to hang up (the telephone)*, 11; **den Hörer auflegen** *to hang up (the receiver)*, 11
die Aufnahme, -n *admittance*, 2
aufpassen: **Pass auf!** *Watch out!*, 6; **Passt auf!** *Pay attention!*, p. 8
aufräumen (sep) *to clean up*, 7; **mein Zimmer aufräumen** *to clean my room*, 7; **meine Klamotten aufräumen** *to pick up my clothes*, 7
der Aufschnitt *cold cuts*, 8
aufschreiben *to write down*, 7
aufspüren *to track down*, 10
das Auge, -n: *eye*; **blaue (braune, grüne) Augen** *blue (brown, green) eyes*, 3
der August *August*, 7
aus *from*, 1; *made of*, 9; **aus Baumwolle** *made of cotton*, 12; **aus Holz** *made of wood*, 12; **aus Kunststoff** *made of plastic*, 12; **aus Leder** *made of leather*, 12; **aus Seide** *made of silk*, 12
ausarbeiten *to work out*, 7
ausbacken (sep) *to bake until done*, 12
der Ausdruck, ̈e *expression*, p. 8
ausgeben (sep) *to spend (money)*, 8
ausgehen (sep) *to go out*, 11
die Auskunft, ̈e *information*, 4
das Ausland *foreign country*, 11
der Ausländer, - *foreigner*, 9
das Auslandsgespräch, -e *international telephone call*, 11
ausleihen (sep) *to rent*, 10
auspacken (sep) *to unpack*, 8
ausräumen (sep) *to clean, clear out*, 12; den Geschirrspüler ausräumen *to unload the dishwasher*, 12
ausreichend *sufficient, passing (grade)*, 4
ausruhen (sich) *to rest* Loc 7
die Aussage, -n *statement*, 9
aussehen (sep) *to look like, to appear*, 3; **der Rock sieht ... aus.** *The skirt looks...*, 5; **er/sie sieht aus** *he/she looks like*, 5; **Wie sieht er aus?** *What does he look like?*, 3; **Wie sehen sie aus?** *What do they look like?*, 3
außerdem *in addition*, 7
außerhalb *outside of*, 6
aussprechen (sep) *to pronounce*, 1; richtig aussprechen *to pronounce correctly*, 1
die Ausstellung, -en *exhibit*, 10
aussuchen, (sich) *to select, pick*, 8
austauschen *to exchange*, 7

der Austauschschüler, - *exchange student*, 9
die Auswahl *selection*, 11
auswählen (sep) *to select*, 4
auswandern *to emigrate*, 11
das Auto, -s *car*, 1; Auto fahren *to drive (a car)*, 9; **mit dem Auto** *by car*, 1

backen *to bake*, 8
der Bäcker, - *baker*, 8; **beim Bäcker** *at the baker's*, 8
die Bäckerei, -en *bakery*, 8
das Backpulver *baking powder*, 12
das Bad, ̈er *pool*, 12
baden *to swim*, 6; **baden gehen** *to go swimming*, 6
der Badepark, -s *park with swimming facilities*, 12
der Bahnhof, ̈e *train station*, 9
bald *soon*, 11
der Ball, ̈e *ball*, 12
das Ballett, -e *ballet*, 10
der Ballon, -s *balloon*, 11
banal *trivial*, 10
die Banane, -n *banana*, 3
die Bank, -en *bank*
der Baseball *baseball*, 2
basieren (auf) *to be based on*, 4
das Basilikum *basil*, 12
das Basisstück, -e *basic item*, 5
der Basketball, ̈e *basketball*, 2
basteln *to do crafts*, 2
bauen *to build*, 5
das Bauernbrot, -e *(coarse) brown bread*, 8
das Bauernhaus, ̈e *farm house*, Loc 10
die Baumwolle *cotton*, 12; **aus Baumwolle** *made of cotton*, 12
die Baustelle, -n *construction site*, 10
bayrisch *Bavarian* (adj), 9
beantworten *to answer*, 9
der Becher, - *cup*, 6
der Bedarf *need*, 12
bedeckt *cloudy*, 7
bedeuten *to mean*, 10; Was bedeutet ... ? *What does...mean?*, p. 8
bedeutend *important*, Loc 7
bedruckt *printed*, 5
befriedigend *satisfactory (grade)*, 4
beginnen *to begin*, 11
begleiten *to accompany*, 9
begonnen (pp) *begun*, 10
begreifen *to understand*, 10
begrüßen *to greet*, 1
behalten *to keep*, 6
behutsam *cautious*, 10

bei *at,* 1; bei meinen Freunden *at my friends',* 10; **beim Bäcker** *at the baker's,* 8; **beim Metzger** *at the butcher's,* 8; **Hier bei ...** *The ...residence.,* 11
beide *both,* 5
beim=bei dem *at the,* 2
das **Beispiel, -e** *example, model,* p. 5; zum Beispiel *for example,* 10
der **Bekannte** *acquaintance (male),* 7
bekannt (für) *known (for),* Loc, 7
bekommen *to get, to receive,* 5; **ich bekomme ...** *I'll have...,* 6; **Was bekommen Sie?** *What would you like?,* 5; *What will you have?* 6
belegen: mit Tomaten belegen *to top with tomatoes,* 8
beliebt *popular,* Loc 4
die **Belletristik** *fiction,* 10
bemalt *painted,* 11
die **Bemerkung, -en** *remark,* 4
benehmen (sich) *to behave,* 11
benutzen *to use,* 9
Benutzung, -en *use,* 4
bequem *comfortable,* 3
beraten *to consult,* 11
die **Beratung, -en** *advice,* 11
bereit *ready,* 10
bereiten *to prepare,* 12
der **Berg, -e** *mountain,* 10
der **Bericht, -e** *report,* 10
berichten, *to report,* 7
der **Berliner, -** *here: jelly-filled roll,* 9
die **Berliner (pl)** *residents of Berlin,* 9
berufsorientiert *career-oriented,* 4
berühmt *famous,* Loc 7
beschäftigt *occupied, busy,* 8
beschäftigt sein *to be busy,* 8
beschattet *tailed, shadowed,* 10
beschreiben *to describe,* 9
die **Beschreibung, -en** *description,* 12
besetzt *busy (telephone),* 11
besichtigen *to visit, to sightsee,* 9; **die Stadt besichtigen** *to visit the city,* 12
besonder- *special,* 7
besonders *especially,* 8; **Nicht besonders.** *Not really.* 6; **besonders gern** *especially like,* 10
besprechen *to discuss,* 11
besser *better,* 8
best *best,* 1
bestimmt *certainly, definitely,* 5
bestimmt *definite,* 8
bestreuen *to sprinkle,* 8
der **Besuch** *visit,* Loc 10
besuchen *to visit,* 2; **Freunde besuchen** *to visit friends,* 2
besuchen (eine Schule) *to attend,* Loc 7
der **Betrag, ̈e** *amount,* 11
das **Bett, -en** *bed,* 3; **das Bett machen** *to make the bed,* 7
die **Bettwäsche** *bed linen,* 9

die **Beurteilung, -en** *evaluation,* 4
der **Beutel, -** *bag,* 8
bevor *before,* 2
bewohnbar *inhabitable,* 3
die **Bewölkung** *cloudiness,* 7
bieten *to offer,* 4
bieten: anbieten (sep) *to offer,* 7
das **Bild, -er** *picture,* 11
billig *cheap,* 4
bin: ich bin *I am,* 1
die **Biologie (Bio)** *biology,* 4
die **Biologielehrerin, -nen** *biology teacher (female),* 1
die **Birne, -n** *pear,* 8
bis *until,* 1; **Bis bald!** *See you soon!,* 9; **Bis dann!** *Till then! See you later!,* 1; **bis zum ...platz** *until you get to ... Square,* 9; **bis zur ...straße** *until you get to ... Street,* 9; **bis zur Ampel** *until you get to the traffic light,* 9
bisschen: ein bisschen *a little,* 5; **ein bisschen mehr** *a little more,* 8;
bist: du bist *you are,* 1
bitte *please,* 3; **Bitte?** *Excuse me?,* 1; **Bitte (sehr, schön)!** *You're (very) welcome!,* 3; **Bitte?** *Yes? Can I help you?,* 5
das **Bittermandelöl, -e** *almond flavor,* 12
blättrig *flaky,* 8
blau *blue,* 3; **in Blau** *in blue,* 5
bleiben *to stay,* 7
der **Bleistift, -e** *pencil,* 4
der **Blick, -e** *view,* Loc 7
blöd *dumb,* 2
blond *blonde,* 3
bloß *only,* 4
der **Blouson, -s** *short jacket,* 5
die **Blume, -n** *flower,* 7; **die Blumen gießen** *to water the flowers,* 7
das **Blumengeschäft, -e** *florist shop,* 8
der **Blumenkohl** *cauliflower,* 8
der **Blumenstrauß, ̈e** *bouquet of flowers,* 11
die **Bluse, -n** *blouse,* 5
blutig *bloody,* 10
die **Bockwurst, ̈e** *smoked and cooked sausage,* 6
die **Bowle, -n** *punch,* 12
braten *to roast,* 8
die **Bratkartoffeln (pl)** *fried potatoes,* 6
die **Bratwurst, ̈e** *bratwurst,* 8
brauchen *to need,* 5; **ich brauche ...** *I need...,* 5; **ich brauche noch ...** *I also need...,* 8
die **Brauerei, -en** *brewery,* 7
braun *brown,* 3; **in Braun** *in brown,* 5
das **Brettspiel, -e** *board game,* 2; **ein Brettspiel spielen** *to play a board game,* 12
die **Brezel, -n** *pretzel,* 8

die **Brezenstange, -n** *pretzel stick,* 8
der **Brief, -e** *letter,* 2
die **Briefmarke, -n** *stamp,* 2; **Briefmarken sammeln** *to collect stamps,* 2
die **Brille, -n** *a pair of glasses,* 3
bringen *to bring,* 1
das **Brot, -e** *bread,* 8; **Ich habe Brot gekauft.** *I bought bread.,* 8
das **Brötchen, -** *hard roll,* 8
die **Brücke, -n** *bridge,* 10
der **Bruder, ̈** *brother,* 3
die **Brühe, -n** *broth,* 12
brutal *brutal, violent,* 10
brutalste *the most brutal,* 10
das **Buch, ̈er** *book,* 4
die **Buchhandlung, -en** *bookstore,* 10; **buchstabieren** *to spell,* 1
bügeln *to iron,* 7
der **Bummel** *stroll,* 9
das **Bundesland, ̈er** *federal state (German),* 1
bunt *colorful,* 6
der **Buntstift, -e** *colored pencil; crayon,* 11
der **Bürgerkrieg, -e** *civil war,* 10
das **Bürgertelefon** *help line,* 11
der **Bus, -se** *bus,* 1; **mit dem Bus** *by bus,* 1
die **Butter** *butter,* 8
das **Butterschmalz** *shortening,* 12

das **Café, -s** *café,* 6; **in ein Café/ins Café gehen** *to go to a/the café,* 6
der **Cappuccino, -s** *cappuccino,* 6
die **CD, -s** *compact disc,* 11
der **Cent, -** *cent (smallest unit of the euro; 1/100th of a euro),* 4
der **Champignon, -s** *mushroom,* 8
die **Chance, -n** *chance,* 10
Chanukka *Hanukkah,* 11; **Frohes Chanukka-Fest!** *Happy Hanukkah!,* 11
charmant *charming,* 3
Chemie (die) *chemistry,* 4
chic *smart (looking),* 12
der **Chor, ̈e** *choir,* 4
die **Clique, -n** *clique,* 10
der **Club, -s** *club,* 2
die **Cola, -s** *cola,* 3
die **Comics (pl)** *comic books,* 2; **Comics sammeln** *to collect comics,* 2
der **Computer, -** *computer,* 3
die **Couch, -en** *couch,* 3
der **Cousin, -s** *cousin (male),* 3
die **Currywurst, ̈e** *curry sausage,* 6

D

da *there*, 1; da drüben *over there*, 4; **da hinten** *there in the back*, 4; **da vorn** *there in the front*, 4
dabei *with*, 4
dabei *at the same time*, 8
das Dach, ⸚er *roof*, Loc 7
dafür *for it*, 5
dahin *there*, 10
der Dalmatiner, - *Dalmatian*, 10
die Dame, -n *lady*, 5
damenhaft *ladylike*, 5
damit *with it; so that*, 7
danach *after that*, 4
Danke! *thank you!*, 3; **Danke (sehr, schön)!** *Thank you (very much)!*, 3
dann *then*, 4
darauf *on it*, 7
darüber *about it*, 5
das *the* (n); *that*, 1; **Das ist ...** *That's...*, 1; **Das ist alles.** *That's all.*, 8; **Das sind...** *These are...* (with plurals), 3
dass *that* (conj), 9; **ich finde es gut/schlecht, dass ...** *I think it's good/bad that...*, 9; **ich finde, dass ...** *I think that...*, 9; ich glaube, dass ... *I think that...*, 9
dasselbe *the same*, 11
dauern *to last*, 9
davor *in front*, Loc 10
dazugeben *to add*, 12
decken: den Tisch decken *to set the table*, 7
deftig *hearty*, 6
dein *your*, 3; **deinem Vater** *to, for your father*, 11; **deiner Mutter** *to, for your mother*, 11
dem *the* (masc, neuter, dat case), 11
den *the* (masc, acc case), 5
denken *to think*, 3
denn (particle), 1; 6
denn *because, for* (conj), 8
der *the* (m), 1; *to the* (fem, dat case), 11
des *of the*, 4
desillusioniert *disillusioned*, 10
deutsch *German* (adj), 9
Deutsch *German* (language), p. 4; (school subject), 4; **Ich habe Deutsch.** *I have German.*, 4
der Deutsche, -n *German (male)*, 2
die Deutsche *German (female)*, 2
die Deutschen (pl) *German people*, 2
Deutschland (das) *Germany*, 1
der Deutschlehrer, - *German teacher (male)*, 1
die Deutschlehrerin, -nen *German teacher (female)*, 1
der Dezember *December*, 7
dich *you* (acc), 7

die *the*, 1
der Dieb, -e *thief*, 10
dienen *to serve*, 9
der Dienstag *Tuesday*, 4
dienstbereit *ready for service*, 9
dies- *this, these*, 2
diesmal *this time*, 10
das Diktat, -e *dictation*, 1
der Dinosaurier, - *dinosaur*, 10
die Diplomatie *diplomacy*, 4
dir *to you*, 3
direkt *direct(ly)*, 6
der Dirigent, -en *conductor (music)*, 6
die Disko, -s *disco*, 6; **in eine Disko gehen** *to go to a disco*, 6
diskutieren *to discuss*, 10
DM = Deutsche Mark *German mark* (former monetary unit)
doch (particle), 6
Doch! *Oh yes!*, 2
der Donnerstag *Thursday*, 4
donnerstags *Thursdays*, 6
doof *dumb*, 10
dort *there*, 4; **dort drüben** *over there*, 4;
dorthin *there*, 9
die Dose, -n *can*, 7
das Dotter, - *egg yolk*, 12
dramatisch *dramatic*, 10
drei *three*, 1
dreimal *three times*, 7
dreißig *thirty*, 3
dreiundzwanzig *twenty-three*, 3
dreizehn *thirteen*, 1
der Drill -s *drill*, 10
drin *in it*, 9
dritte *third*, 8
der Druck: jemanden unter Druck setzen *to put pressure on somebody*, 10
du *you* (sing), 2
dumm *dumb, stupid*, 10
der Dummschwätzer *silly prattler*, 10
dunkel *dark*, 10
dunkelblau *dark blue*, 5; **in Dunkelblau** *in dark blue*, 5
durch *through*, 9; *divided by*, 3
die Dunkelheit *darkness*, 10
die Durchschnittstemperatur, -en *average temperature*, 9
der Durst *thirst*, 6

E

eben (particle), 5
ebenso...wie *just as...as*, 10
ebenso wie *as well as*, Loc 10
echt *real, really*, 5
echt super! *great!*, 1
eckig *with corners*, 12
ehemalig *former*, 9
ehrlich *honestly*, 5

das Ei, -er *egg*, 8; gefüllte Eier *deviled eggs*, 12
der Eierkuchen, - *pancake* 9
eigen *own* (adj), 10
eigentlich *actually*, 5
die Eigentumswohnung, -en *condominium*, 3
ein *a, an*, 3; **ein paar** *a few*, 3; **eine Eins (Zwei, Drei, Vier, Fünf, Sechs)** (German grades), 4
einbiegen (in eine Straße) *to turn onto (a street)*, 9
einen *a, an* (masc, acc case), 5; **Einen Pulli in Grau, bitte.** *A sweater in gray, please.*, 5
einfach *simple, easy*, 1; **Also, einfach!** *That's easy!*, 1
das Einfamilienhaus, ⸚er *single-family house*, 3
einfarbig *solid color*, 5
eingeladen (pp) *invited*, 11
eingelegt (pp): eine Mittagspause einlegen *to take a lunch break*, 9
die Einheit, -en *unit*, 10
einige *some*, 9
der Einkauf, ⸚e *purchase*, 8
einkaufen *to shop*, 8; **einkaufen gehen** *to go shopping*, 8
der Einkäufer, - *shopper*, Loc 7
der Einkaufsbummel *shopping trip*, 8
das Einkaufszentrum, die Einkaufszentren *shopping center*, 6; ins Einkaufszentrum gehen *to go to the shopping center/mall*, 6
der Einkaufszettel, - *shopping list*, 8
der Einklang, ⸚e *unison, harmony*, 8
einladen (sep) *to invite*, 11; **er/sie lädt ... ein** *he/she invites*, 11
die Einladung, -en *invitation*, 11
einmal *once*, 7
eins *one*, 1; **eine Eins** *an A*
die Einschreibung, -en *registration*, 4
einsetzen *to insert*, 8
der Eintritt, -e *admission*, 4
einundzwanzig *twenty-one*, 3
einverstanden *agreed*, 8
der Einwohner, - *inhabitant*, Loc 4
die Einwohnerzahl, -en *population*, 1
einzeln *single, individual*, 7
der Einzelpassagier, -e *individual passenger*, 9
einzigartig *unique*, Loc 10
das Eis *ice cream*, 6; *ice*, 7; **ein Eis essen** *to eat ice cream*, 6
der Eisbecher, - *a dish of ice cream*, 6
das Eiscafé, -s *ice cream parlor*, 8
die Eissporthalle, -n *skating rink*, 12
das Ekel, - *nasty person*, 10
EL=Esslöffel, - *tablespoon*, 8
die Elektronik *electronics*, 7
die Elektrotechnik *electrical engineering*, Loc 10
elf *eleven*, 1
eloquent *eloquent*, 10
die Eltern (pl) *parents*, 3

der Emmentaler *Emmentaler (cheese)*, 12
emotional *emotional*, 10
das Ende *end*, 5
Ende: zu Ende schreiben *to finish writing*, 7
endgültig *final*, 10
eng *tight*, 5
engagiert *occupied*, 10
der Engel, - *angel*, 10
die Engländer (pl) *English people*, 1
der Engländer, - *English person (male)*, 9
die Engländerin, -nen *English person (female)*, 9
Englisch *English (adj)*, 4; auf Englisch *in English*, 10
Englisch *English (school subject)*, 4; (language), 9
entfernt *away*, Loc 7
entführen *to carry off*, 6
entscheiden *to decide*, 9; sie entscheidet sich für *she decides on*, 11
die Entscheidung, -en *decision*, 10
entschließen *to decide*, 9
Entschuldigung! *Excuse me!*, 9
er *he*, 2; *it*, 3
die Erdbeere, -n *strawberry*, 8
das Erdbeereis *strawberry ice cream*, 9
der Erdbeerkuchen, - *strawberry cake*, 8
die Erdkunde *geography*, 4
die Erdnussbutter *peanut butter*, 8
die Erfrischung *refreshment*, 6
erfüllen *to fulfill*, 7
ergänzen *to complete*, 9
erkennen *to recognize*, 10
erklären *to explain*, 5
erleben *to experience*, 9
erledigen *to accomplish*, 9
ermittelt von *compiled by*, 10
der Ernährungsexperte, -n *nutrition expert*, 8
der Ernst *seriousness*, 10; im Ernst? *seriously?*, 10
erst *first*, 6
ersten: **am ersten (Juli)** *on the first (of July)*, 11
erteilen *to give*, 4
erwarten *to expect*, 12
erwecken *to awaken*, 10
erweisen *to grant*, 10
die Erweiterung, -en *expansion*, 9
erzählen *to tell*, 10; Erzähl weiter! *Keep on talking!*, 10
es *it*, 3
essen *to eat*, 3; **er/sie isst** *he/she eats*, 6
der Essig *vinegar*, 12
der Esslöffel, - *tablespoon*, 8
der Esstisch, -e *dining table*, 12
der Estragon *tarragon*, 12
etwa *approximately*, 12
etwas *something*, 7; **Sonst noch etwas?** *Anything else?*, 8

etwas: etwas zum Anziehen *something to wear*, 9; etwas zum Essen *something to eat*, 9
euch *you* (pl, acc case), 7
der Euro, - *euro (the national currency of most European countries)*, 4
europäisch *European (adj)*, 10
die Europareise, -n *trip to Europe*, 11
exclusiv *exclusive*, 10

F

das Fach, ⸚er *school subject*, 4
der Fächer, - *fan*, 11
der Fachlehrer, - *subject teacher*, 4
die Fachsprache, -n *technical lingo*, 12
fahren *to go, ride, drive (using a vehicle)*, 9; **er/sie fährt** *he/she drives*, 9; Auto fahren *to drive (a car)*, 9; in die Stadt fahren *to go downtown (by vehicle)*, 11; wir fahren Rad *we're riding bikes*, 10
der Fahrpreis, -e *fare*, 4
die Fahrpreisermäßigung, -en *reduced fare*, 4
das Fahrrad, ⸚er *bicycle*, 7
die Fahrt, -en *drive* 2
falsch *false*, 11
falsch *wrong*, 10
die Familie, -en *family*, 3
die Familienkomödie, -n *family comedy*, 10
das Familienmitglied, -er *family member*, 11
das Familientreffen, - *family reunion*, 12
Fang mit ... an! *Begin with...*, 9
das Fantasybuch, ⸚er *fantasy book*, 10
der Fantasyfilm, -e *fantasy film*, 10
der Fantasyroman, -e *fantasy novel*, 10
die Farbe, -n *color*, 5; Wir haben das in allen Farben. *We have that in all colors.*, 5
der Fasching *carnival*, 9
die Fassade, -n *facade*, 8
fast *almost*, 12
faul *lazy*, 7
faulenzen *to be lazy; to take it easy*, 6
die Faustregel, -n *rule of thumb*, 8
der Februar *February*, 7
fehlen *to be missing*, 4; Was fehlt hier? *What's missing?*, 5
fehlend- *missing*, 11
feiern *to celebrate*, 11
der Feiertag, -e *holiday*, 11
feiertags *holidays*, 10
fein gehackt *finely chopped*, 12
das Feinkosthaus, ⸚er *delicatessen*, 9
die Feinmechanik *precision mechanics*, Loc 10

das Fenster, - *window*, p. 8; **die Fenster putzen** *to clean the windows*, 7
die Ferien (pl) *vacation*, 1
das Ferngespräch, -e *long distance call*, 11
das Fernsehen *television*, 2; **Fernsehen schauen** *to watch television*, 2; im Fernsehen *on television*, 5
der Fernsehkoch, ⸚e *television chef*, 8
die Fernsehsendung, -en *television show*, 9
fertig *finished*, 7
fertig machen *to finish*
fesch *stylish, smart*, 5
das Fest, -e *festivity*, 11
festlich *festive*, Loc 7
die Fete, -n *party*, 5; auf einer Fete *at a party*, 12
feurig *fiery*, 6
der Film, -e *movie*, 10; **einen Film sehen** *to see a movie*, 6
die Filmart, -en *type of movie*, 10
der Filmkritiker, - *film critic*, 10
der Filmverleih, -e *movie rental*, 10
der Filzschreiber, - *felt-tip pen*, 11
finden *to think of, to find*, 2; **Das finde ich auch.** *I think so, too.*, 2; **Das finde ich nicht.** *I disagree.*, 2; **ich finde es gut/schlecht, dass ...** *I think it's good/bad that...*, 9; **ich finde (Tennis) ...** *I think (tennis) is...*, 2; **Ich finde den Pulli stark!** *The sweater is awesome!*, 5; Ich finde es toll! *I think it's great!*, 9; **Wie findest du (Tennis)?** *What do you think of (tennis)?*, 2
die Firma, die Firmen *firm, company*, 9
der Fisch, -e *fish*, 8
die Fläche, -n *surface, area*, Loc 4
das Fladenbrot *pita bread*, 6
die Flasche, -n *bottle*, 7
das Fleisch *meat*, 8
die Fleischbrühe, -n *meat broth*, 12
die Fliese, -n *tile*, 12
die Floßfahrt, -en *rafting trip*, 9
die Flöte, -n *flute*, 2
das Fluchtstück, -e *flight scene*, 10
der Fluss, ⸚e *river*, Loc 4
folgen *to follow*, 7
folgende *following*, 9
Folgendes *the following*, 7
die Folgezeit, -en *following period*, 9
die Form, -en *form*, 5
der Fortgeschrittene, -n *advanced person*, 4
das Foto, -s *photo*, 3
das Fotoalbum, die Fotoalben *photo album*, 3
das Fotogeschäft, -e *photo store*, 9
die Frage, -n *question*, 1
fragen *to ask*, 9
Französisch *French (school subject)*, 4
Frau *Mrs.*, 1
die Frau, -en *woman*, 3
frei: **Wir haben frei.** *We are off (out of school).*, 4

die Freiheit, -en *liberty*, 10
freilich *of course*, 9
der Freitag *Friday*, 4
freitags *Fridays*, 6
freiwillig *voluntary*, 7
der Freiwillige, -n *volunteer*, 4
die Freizeit *free time, leisure time*, 2
das Freizeitinteresse *free time interest*, 12
der Freizeitpark, -s *amusement park*, 10
das Freizeitvergnügen, - *enjoyment of leisure time*, 12
die Fremdsprache, -n *foreign language*, 4
die Freude, -n *joy, happiness*, 11
freuen *to be happy, glad*, 7; **Freut mich!** *It's a pleasure!*, 8; Sie freut sich darüber. *She is happy about it.*, 11; wir freuen uns *we're very happy, pleased*, 12
der Freund, -e *friend (male)*, 2; **Freunde besuchen** *to visit friends*, 2
der Freundeskreis, -e *peer group*, 9
die Freundin, -nen *friend (female)*, 1
freundlich *friendly*, 9
frisch *fresh*, 8
fritieren *to fry*, 8
froh *happy*, 11
fröhlich *happy, cheerful*, 11
die Frucht, ⁻e *fruit*, 8
das Fruchteis *ice cream with fruit*, 6
der Frühling *spring* (season), 2; **im Frühling** *in the spring*, 2
das Frühstück *breakfast*, 6
führen *to lead*, 12
füllen *to fill*, 12
fünf *five*, 1
fünfundzwanzig *twenty-five*, 3
fünfzehn *fifteen*, 1
fünfzig *fifty*, 3
für *for*, 7
Für wen? *For whom?*, 7
furchtbar *terrible, awful*, 5; **furchtbar gern haben** *to like a lot*, 10
fürs=für das *for the*, 2
der Fuß, ⁻e *foot*, 1; **zu Fuß** *on foot*, 1
der Fußball *soccer*, 2; **Ich spiele Fußball.** *I play soccer.*, 2
der Fußgänger, - *pedestrian*, 9
die Fußgängerzone, -n *pedestrian area*, Loc 7
füttern *to feed*, 7; **die Katze füttern** *to feed the cat*, 7

der Gamsbart, ⁻e *chamois beard*, Loc 7
ganz *really, quite*, 3; *not broken*, 4; *whole*, 9; die ganze Zeit *the whole time*, 12; Ganz einfach! *Quite* simple!, 9; **Ganz klar!** *Of course!*, 4
gänzlich *completely*, 9
die Ganztagsschule, -n *all-day school*, 4
gar (particle), 3; **gar nicht gern** *not to like at all*, 10
die Garantie, -n *guarantee, warranty*, 5
die Garderobe, -n *wardrobe*, 5
der Garten, ⁻ *yard, garden*, 9
der Gast, ⁻e *guest*, 12
die Gastmutter, ⁻ *host mother*, 8
der Gastgeber, - *host*, 12
die Gaudi *fun*, 9
das Gebäude, - *building*, Loc 7
geben *to give*, 11; **er/sie gibt** *he/she gives*, 11; **es gibt ...** *there is/are ...*, 9; **Was gibt es hier zu essen?** *What is there to eat here?*, 9; Was gibt's? *What's up?*, 1
geboren *born*, 4
der Gebrauch, ⁻e *practice*, 10; *use, operation*, 11
gebrauchen *to use*, 8
gebrüht *simmered*, 8
gebucht *booked*, 9
gebunden *bound*, 10
das Geburtsdatum (pl -daten) *date of birth*, 4
die Geburtsstadt, ⁻e *place of birth*, 6
der Geburtstag, -e *birthday*, 11; **Alles Gute zum Geburtstag!** *Best wishes on your birthday!*, 11; **Herzlichen Glückwunsch zum Geburtstag!** *Best wishes on your birthday!*, 11; **Ich habe am ... Geburtstag.** *My birthday is on...*, 11
das Geburtstagsgeschenk, -e *birthday present*, 8
die Geburtstagskarte, -n *birthday card*, 11
der Geburtstagskuchen, - *birthday cake*, 12
das Gedächtnis, -se *memory*, 10
gefährdet *endangered*, 11
gefahren (pp) *driven, gone*, 10
gefährlich *dangerous*, 9
gefallen *to be pleasing, to like*, 5; **Er/Sie/Es gefällt mir.** *I like it.*, 5; **Sie gefallen mir.** *I like them.*, 5
gefettet *oiled*, 12
gefühlvoll *full of feeling*, 10
gefüllt *filled*, 12
gegeben *given, supplied*, 10
die Gegend: in der Gegend von *in the vicinity of*, Loc 10
gegenseitig *reciprocal(ly)*, 5
das Gegenteil, -e *opposite*, 4
gegessen (pp) *eaten*, 9
gehackt *chopped*, 8
gehen *to go*, 2; **Das geht nicht.** *That won't work.*, 7; **Es geht.** *It's okay.*, 6; **nach Hause gehen** *to go home*, 3; Geht er noch? *Is it still working?*, 4; **Wie geht's (denn)?** *How are you?*, 6
gehören (zu) *to belong (to)*, Loc 7

der Geist, -er *ghost*, 10
gekauft (pp) *bought*, 8; **Ich habe Brot gekauft.** *I bought bread.*, 8; **Was hast du gekauft?** *What did you buy?*, 8
geknotet *knotted*, 5
gekocht *cooked*, 12
gelb *yellow*, 4; **in Gelb** *in yellow*, 5
das Geld *money*, 4
gelesen (pp) *read*, 10; **Was hast du gelesen?** *What did you read?*, 10
gelten als *to be considered as*, 10
gemacht (pp) *done*, 10; **Was hast du am Wochenende gemacht?** *What did you do on the weekend?*, 10
gemahlen *ground*, 12
gemalt *painted*, 11
gemeinsam *common*, 11
gemischt *mixed*, 8
das Gemüse *vegetables*, 8; **im Obst- und Gemüseladen** *at the produce store*, 8
der Gemüseladen, ⁻ *produce store*, 8
genau *exact(ly)*, 6; genauer lesen *reading for detail*, 6
genießen *to enjoy*, 6
genug *enough*, 9; **Ich habe genug.** *I have enough.*, 9
geöffnet *open*, 6
gepunktet *polka-dotted*, 12
gerade *just*, 8
geradeaus *straight ahead*, 9; **Fahren Sie geradeaus!** *Drive straight ahead.*, 9
das Gericht, -e *dish* (food), Loc 4; *court*, 10
das Gerichtsdrama, -en *courtroom drama*, 10
gern (machen) *to like (to do)*, 2; **gern haben** *to like*, 4; **Gern geschehen!** *My pleasure!*, 9; **Ja, gern!** *Sure!*, 11; **nicht gern (machen)** *to not like (to do)*, 2; **nicht so gern** *not to like very much*, 2; Siehst du gern Horrorfilme? *Do you like to watch horror movies?*, 10; **besonders gern** *especially like*, 10
gesagt (pp) *said*, 10
gesalzen *salted*, 8
der Gesangunterricht *singing lesson*, 4
das Geschäft, -e: ein Geschäft machen *to make a deal*, 7
geschehen: **Gern geschehen!** *My pleasure!*, 9
das Geschenk, -e *gift*, 11
die Geschenkidee, -n *gift idea*, 11
der Geschenkladen, ⁻ *gift shop*, 11
die Geschenkliste, -n *gift list*, 11
die Geschenkwaren (pl) *gifts*, 9
die Geschichte *history*, 4
geschickt *clever, talented*, 12
das Geschirr (pl) *dishes*, 7; **das Geschirr spülen** *to wash the dishes*, 7

der Geschirrspüler, - *dishwasher,* 12; den Geschirrspüler ausräumen *to unload the dishwasher,* 12

geschlossen *closed,* 10

der Geschmack *taste,* 8

die Geschwister (pl) *brothers and sisters,* 3

gesehen (pp) *seen,* 10; **Was hast du gesehen?** *What did you see?,* 10

gesetzt: unter Druck gesetzt werden *to be put under pressure,* 10

das Gespräch, -e *dialogue, conversation,* 7; *phone call,* 11

die Gesprächsnotiz, -en *message,* 11

gesprochen (pp) *spoken,* 10; **Worüber habt ihr gesprochen?** *What did you (pl) talk about?,* 10; Worüber sprichst du mit deinen Freunden? *What do you talk about with your friends?,* 10

die Geste, -n *gesture,* 7

gestern *yesterday,* 8; **gestern Abend** *yesterday evening,* 8; **gestreift** *striped,* 12

gesund *healthy,* 8

das Getränk, -e *beverage,* 11

gewachsen *grown,* 8

gewährleisten *to guarantee,* 4

gewinnen *to win,* 2

das Gewitter, - *thunderstorm,* 7

gewöhnlich *usually,* 11

das Gewürz, -e *spice,* 8

gewürzt *spiced,* 8

gießen *to water,* 7; **die Blumen gießen** *to water the flowers,* 7

die Gitarre, -n *guitar,* 2

Gitarrenklänge *guitar music,* 6

gitterförmig *latticed,* 8

das Glas, ̈er *glass,* 3; **ein Glas Apfelsaft** *a glass of apple juice,* 3; **ein Glas (Mineral) Wasser** *a glass of (mineral) water,* 3; **ein Glas Tee** *a glass of tea,* 6

die Glatze, -n *bald head,* 3; **eine Glatze haben** *to be bald,* 3

glauben *to believe,* 2; **ich glaube** *I think,* 2; ich glaube, dass ... *I think that...,* 9; Ich glaube schon. *I believe so.,* 7

gleich *equal,* 3; *same,* 10

das Gleis, -e *track,* 6

die Globalisierungsfalle, -n *pitfall of globalization,* 10

die Glocke, -n *bell,* 9

das Glück *luck,* 4; **So ein Glück!** *What luck!,* 4

der Glücksklee *clover (symbol for good luck),* 11

das Glücksschwein, -e *good luck pig (symbol for good luck),* 11

das Gold *gold,* 10

das Golf *golf,* 2

der Grad *degree(s),* 7; **zwei Grad** *two degrees,* 7; **Wie viel Grad haben wir?** *What's the temperature?,* 7

das Gramm *gram,* 8

grau *gray,* 3; **in Grau** *in gray,* 5

grausam *cruel,* 10

die Grenze, -n *border,* 11

Griechenland (das) *Greece,* 8

die Griechin, -nen *Greek (female),* 4

der Grill *barbecue,* 9

das Grillfest, -e *BBQ party,* 6

groß *big,* 3

die Größe, -n *size,* 5

die Großeltern (pl) *grandparents,* 3

die Großmutter (Oma), ̈ *grandmother,* 3

der Großvater (Opa), ̈ *grandfather,* 3

grün *green,* 3; **in Grün** *in green,* 5

das Grundstück, -e *piece of land,* 3

grüner *greener,* 8

die Gruppe, -n *group,* 10

der Gruselroman, -e *horror novel,* 10

der Gruß, ̈e *greetings;* liebe Grüße *(many) kind regards; love,* 1

grüßen: **Grüß dich!** *Hi!,* 1

gucken *to watch,* 2

gültig *valid,* 4

die Gültigkeit *validity,* 6

günstig *advantageous, low-priced,* 4

die Gurke, -n *cucumber,* 8

der Gurkensalat, -e *cucumber salad,* 12

der Gürtel, - *belt,* 5

gut *good,* 4; **Gut!** *Good! Well!,* 6; **Gut! Mach ich!** *Okay, I'll do that!,* 7; **Alles Gute!** *Best wishes!,* 11

der Gutschein, -e *gift certificate,* 11

das Gymnasium, die Gymnasien (German secondary school), 4

das Gyros *gyros,* 9

das Haar, -e *hair,* 3

haben *to have,* 4; **er/sie hat** *he/she has,* 4; **gern haben** *to like,* 4; **Haben Sie das auch in Rot?** *Do you have that also in red?,* 5

das Hackfleisch *ground meat,* 8

der Haferbrei *oatmeal,* 9

das Hähnchen, - *chicken,* 8

halb *half,* 6; **halb (eins, zwei, usw.)** *half past (twelve, one, etc.),* 6

halb bedeckt *partly cloudy,* 7

der Halbbruder, ̈ *half brother,* 3

halbieren *to halve,* 12

das Halbjahr, -e *half a year,* 4

die Halbschwester, -n *half sister,* 3

die Hälfte, -n *half,* 12

Hallo! *Hi! Hello!,* 1

der Hals, ̈e *neck,* 8

das Halstuch, ̈er *scarf,* 11

halt (particle), 6

halten *to hold,* 7

der Hamster, - *hamster,* 7

der Handball *handball,* 2

handvermittelt *operator-assisted,* 11

das Handy, -s *cell phone,* 11

die Harmonielehre, -n *harmonics class,* 4

hart gekocht *hard-boiled,* 12

das Hasenfutter *rabbit food,* 8

hassen *to hate,* 9

hässlich *ugly,* 3

der Hauptbahnhof, ̈e *main train station,* 4

hauptsächlich *mainly,* 6

die Hauptstadt, ̈e *capital,* 1

das Hauptwort, -er *noun,* 11

das Haus, ̈er *house,* 3; zu Hause sein *to be at home,* 6; **nach Hause gehen** *to go home,* 3; **zu Hause helfen** *to help at home,* 7

die Hausarbeit, -en *chores,* 7

die Hausaufgaben (pl) *homework,* 2; **Hausaufgaben machen** *to do homework,* 7

der Haushalt, -e *household,* 7

das Haustier, -e *pet,* 3

die Hauswirtschaft *home economics,* 4

He! *Hey!,* 2

das Heft, -e *notebook,* 4

heiß *hot,* 7

heißen *to be called,* 1; **er heißt** *his name is,* 1; **ich heiße** *my name is,* 1; **sie heißt** *her name is,* 1; **Wie heißt das Mädchen?** *What's the girl's name?,* 1; **Heißt sie …?** *Is her name …?,* 1; **Wie heißt der Junge?** *What's the boy's name?,* 1; **Wie heißt du?** *What's your name?,* 1

heiter *clear,* 7

der Held, -en *hero,* 10

helfen *to help,* 7; **zu Hause helfen** *to help at home,* 7

hell *light,* 5

hellblau *light blue,* 5; **in Hellblau** *in light blue,* 5

hellgrau *light gray,* 5

hellgrün *light green,* 5

das Hemd, -en *shirt,* 5

herausnehmen *to take out,* 12

der Herbst *fall* (season), 2; **im Herbst** *in the fall,* 2

der Herd, -e *stove,* 12

Herr *Mr.,* 1

das Herz, -en *heart,* 10

das Herz: im Herzen *in the heart of,* Loc, 7

herzhaft *hearty,* 8

herzlich: Herzliche Grüße! *Best regards!,* 1; Herzlich willkommen bei uns! *Welcome to our home!,* 12; **Herzlichen Glückwunsch zum Geburtstag!** *Best wishes on your birthday!,* 11

heute *today,* 4; **heute Morgen** *this morning,* 8; **heute Nachmittag** *this afternoon,* 8; **heute Abend** *tonight, this evening,* 7

die Hexe, -n *witch,* Loc 10

das Hexenwegle *Witches' Walk,* Loc 10

hier *here*, 3; **Hier bei ...** *The... residence.*, 11; **Hier ist ...** *This is...*, 11; hier vorn *here in front*, 5
hierher *over here*, 11
die Hilfe, -n *help*, 7
hin *to*, 8
hinten *back there*, 4; **da hinten** *there in the back*, 4
hinter *after*, 7
der Hintergrund: im Hintergrund *in the background*, Loc 7
das Hobbybuch, ̈er *hobby book*, 10
hoch *high*, 10
hochbegabt *very talented*, 10
die Hochdruckzone, -n *high-pressure area*, 7
hoffen *to hope*, 9
der Höhepunkt, -e *highlight*, 9
holen *to get, fetch*, 8
das Holz *wood*, 12; **aus Holz** *out of wood*, 12
die Holzbauten (pl) *wooden construction*, Loc 10
hölzern *wooden*, 9
der Honig *honey*, 8
hören *to hear*, 1; Hör gut zu! *Listen carefully*, p. 6; Hört zu! *Listen!*, p. 8; **Musik hören** *to listen to music*, 2
der Hörer, - *receiver*, 11; **den Hörer abheben** *to pick up the receiver*, 11; **den Hörer auflegen** *to hang up (the telephone)*, 11
der Horrorfilm, -e *horror movie*, 10
die Hose, -n *pants*, 5
das Hotel, -s *hotel*, 9
hübsch *pretty*, 5
das Hufeisen, - *horseshoe*, 11
der Hund, -e *dog*, 3
hundert *a hundred*, 3
der Hunger *hunger*, 9

ich *I*, 2; **Ich auch.** *Me too.*, 2; **Ich nicht.** *I don't.; Not me.*, 2
die Idee, -n *idea*, 9
die Idylle, -n *idyll*, 10
ihm *to him, for him* (masc, neuter, dat case), 11
ihn *it, him* (masc, acc case), 5
ihnen *them* (pl, dat case), 12
Ihnen *you* (formal, dat case), 5
ihr *her* (poss adj), 3
ihr *their* (poss adj), 2
ihr *to her, for her* (fem, dat case), 11
ihr *you* (pl, subj pron), 2
im=in dem *in the*, 1; im Fernsehen *on television*, 5; **im Frühling** *in the spring*, 2; **im Herbst** *in the fall*, 2; **im Januar** *in January*, 7; im Kino *at the movies*, 10; im Konzert *at the concert*, 10;

(einmal) im Monat *(once) a month*, 7; **im Sommer** *in the summer*, 2; **im Supermarkt** *at the supermarket*, 8; **im Winter** *in the winter*, 2
der Imbissstand, ̈e *snack stand*, 6
die Imbissstube, -n *snack bar*, 9
immer *always*, 7
in *in*, 1; **in Blau** *in blue*, 5; **in Braun** *in brown*, 5; **in Gelb** *in yellow*, 5; **in Grau** *in gray*, 5; **in Grün** *in green*, 5; **in Hellblau** *in light blue*, 5; **in Rot** *in red*, 5; **in Schwarz** *in black*, 5; **in Weiß** *in white*, 5
der Individualist, -en *individualist*, 9
die Industrie, -n *industry*, Loc 4
die Informatik *computer science*, 4
die Information, -en *information*, 10
der Ingenieur, -e *engineer*, 10
das Inlandsgespräch, -e *domestic telephone call*, 11
die Innenstadt, ̈e *downtown*, 5; **in der Innenstadt** *in the city, downtown*, 9
ins=in das *in the, into the*, 2; *to the*, 6
die Insel, -n *island*, Loc 4
insgesamt *all together*, 8
das Instrument, -e *instrument*, 2
inszenieren *to direct*, 10
intelligent *intelligent*, 10
die Intelligenz *intelligence*, 10
interessant *interesting*, 2
das Interesse, -n *interest*, 2; **Hast du andere Interessen?** *Do you have any other interests?*, 2
interessieren *to interest*, 10
das Internet *Internet*, 2
irgend- *any*, 11
irgendetwas *anything*, 6
irgendwann *anytime*, 11
irgendwelch- *some*, 8
irgendwie *somehow*, 8
der Irrtum, ̈er *error*, 10
ist: er/sie/es ist *he/she/it is*, 1; **sie ist aus** *she's from*, 1
Italien (das) *Italy*, 3

ja *yes*, 1; **Ja klar!** *Of course!*, 1
die Jacke, -n *jacket*, 5
jäh *sudden*, 10
das Jahr, -e *year*, 1; **Ich bin ... Jahre alt.** *I am...years old.*, 1
der Januar *January*, 7; **im Januar** *in January*, 7
die Jeans, - *jeans*, 5
die Jeans-Tasche, -n *denim school bag*, 4
jed- *every*, 5; jeden Abend *every evening*, 10; **jeden Tag** *every day*, 7

jeder: jeder von euch *each of you*, 8
jederzeit *anytime*, 4
jeglich- *any*, 8; jeglicher Art *every kind*, 9
jetzt *now*, 1
joggen *to jog*, 12
der Jogging-Anzug, ̈e *jogging suit*, 5
der Joghurt (Jogurt) *yogurt*, 8
das Joghurteis *frozen yogurt*, 8
die Jugend *youth*, 10
der Jugendclub, -s *youth club*, 9
der Jugendliche, -n *young adult*, 7
das Jugendzentrum, die Jugendzentren *youth center*, 12
der Juli *July*, 7
jung *young*, 10
der Junge, -n *boy*, 1
der Juni *June*, 7

K

der Kaffee *coffee*, 8; **eine Tasse Kaffee** *a cup of coffee*, 6
der Kaiser, - *emperor*, 6
der Kaiserschmarren *(Austrian and southern German dish)*, 8
das Kalb, ̈er *veal*, 8
der Kalender, - *calendar*, 11
die Kalorie, -n *calorie*, 8
kalt *cold*, 7
die Kammer, -n *chamber*, 10
der Kampf, ̈e *struggle*, 10
der Kanal, ̈e *canal*, Loc 4
das Kaninchen, - *rabbit*, 7
das Kännchen, - *small (coffee) pot*, 6
die Kanzlei, -en *law office*, 10
das Kapitel, - *chapter*, 1
kaputt *broken*, 3
die Kapuze, -n *hood (of coat)*, 5
die Karte, -n *card*, 2
das Kartenspiel, -e *card game*, 2
die Kartoffel, -n *potato*, 8
der Kartoffelsalat, -e *potato salad*, 12
der Käse, - *cheese*, 8
das Käsebrot, -e *cheese sandwich*, 6
der Käsekuchen, - *cheese cake*, 6
die Kasse, -n *cashier*, 10
die Kassette, -n *cassette*, 4
die Kastagnette, -n *castanet*, 11
der Kasten, ̈ *box, container*, 9; *word box*, 10
die Kastenform, -en *bread pan*, 12
die Katze, -n *cat*, 3; **die Katze füttern** *to feed the cat*, 7
kaufen *to buy*, 5
das Kaufhaus, ̈er *department store*, 5
die Kavallerie, -n *cavalry*, 10
kegeln *to bowl*, 10
kein *no, none, not any*, 9; **Ich habe keine Zeit.** *I don't have time.*, 7; **Ich habe keinen Hunger mehr.** *I'm not hungry any more.*, 9; **kein(en) ... mehr** *no more...*, 9;

Kein Problem! *No problem!*, 11;
Keine Ahnung! *I have no idea!*,
9; Nein danke, keinen Kuchen
mehr. *No thanks. No more cake.*, 9;
Ich möchte kein(e)(en) ... mehr.
I don't want another…., 9
der Keks, -e *cookie*, 3; **ein paar Kekse**
a few cookies, 3
der Kellner, - *waiter*, 6
kennen *to know, be familiar* or
acquainted with, 10
kennen lernen *to get to know*, 12
die Kerze, -n *candle*, 11
das Kilo=Kilogramm, - *kilogram*, 8
das Kind, -er *child*, 8
der Kindergarten ∺ *kindergarten*, 4
der Kinderhort, -e *day-nursery*, 7
die Kinderkirche *Sunday school*, 8
das Kino, -s *cinema*, 6; im Kino *at the*
movies, 10; **ins Kino gehen** *to go*
to the movies, 6
die Kinokarte, -n *movie ticket*, 9
das Kinoprogramm, -e *movie guide*, 10
die Kirche, -n *church*, 9
die Kirschtorte, -n *cherry cake*, Loc 10
die Kiwi, -s *kiwi*, 8
die Klammer, -n *parenthesis*, 8
die Klamotten (pl) *casual term for*
clothes, 5; **meine Klamotten**
aufräumen *to pick up my clothes*,
7
Klar! *Sure!* 2; *Clear!*, 9; Alles klar!
O.K.!, 10; **Ja, klar!** *Of course!*, 1
die Klasse, -n *grade level*, 4
Klasse! *Great! Terrific!*, 2
die Klassenarbeit, -en *test, exam*, 4
der Klassenkamerad, -en *classmate*, 3
das Klassenzimmer, - *classroom*, p. 8
der Klassiker, - *classicist*, 11
klassisch *classical*, 10
das Klavier, -e *piano*, 2; **Ich spiele**
Klavier. *I play the piano.*, 2
die Klavierschule, -n *piano school*, 4
das Kleid, -er *dress*, 5
klein *small*, 3
kleiner *smaller*, 8
die Kleinigkeit, -en *small thing*, 11
klug *clever*, 9
knackig *crispy, firm*, 7
die Knoblauchzehe, -n *garlic clove*, 8
der Knochen, - *bone*, 8
kochen *to cook*, 5
der Kochschinken *baked ham*, 6
kommen *to come*, 1; **er kommt aus**
he's from, 1; **ich komme** *I come*, 1;
ich komme aus *I'm from*, 1;
Komm doch mit! *Why don't you*
come along?, 7; Komm mit nach ...
Come along to..., 1; es kommt ganz
darauf an *it really depends*, 12; **sie**
kommen aus *they're from*, 1; **sie**
kommt aus *she's from*, 1; **Wie**
komme ich zum (zur) ... ? *How*
do I get to...?, 9; **Wie kommst du**
zur Schule? *How do you get to*
school?, 1; Wie kommt man dahin?
How do you get there?, 9

die Komödie, -n *comedy*, 10
der Komponist, -en *composer*, 11
die Konditorei, -en *pastry shop*, 8
die Konjunktion, -en *conjunction*, 8
können *to be able to*, 7; **Kann ich**
bitte Andrea sprechen? *Could I*
please speak with Andrea?, 11;
Kann ich's wirklich? *Can I really do*
it?, 1; **Was kann ich für dich tun?**
What can I do for you?, 7;
Kann ich etwas für dich tun?
Can I do something for you?, 7
der Kontakt: Kontakt knüpfen *to*
establish contact, 10
das Kontingent, -e *allotment*, 9
das Konzert, -e *concert*, 6; im Konzert
at the concert, 10; **ins Konzert**
gehen *to go to a concert*, 6
der Kopf, ∺e *head*, 1
der Kopfsalat, -e *head lettuce*, 8
die Kopie, -n *copy, imitation*, 5
der Korb, ∺e *basket*, 7
kosten *to cost*, 4; **Was kostet ... ?**
How much does...cost?, 4
köstlich *delicious*, 8
das Kotelett, -s *cutlet*, 8
die Kräuter (pl) *herbs*, 12
der Krautsalat, -e *cabbage salad*, 12
kreativ *creative*, 7
kriegen *to get*, 10
der Kriegsfilm, -e *war movie*, 10
der Krimi, -s *detective movie*, 10;
detective novel, 10; *crime drama*, 10
der Krug, ∺e *jug*, 12
die Kruste, -n *crust*, 8
die Küche, -n *kitchen*, 12; **in der Küche**
in the kitchen, 12
der Kuchen, - *cake*, 3; **ein Stück**
Kuchen *a piece of cake*, 3
die Kuckucksuhr, -en *cuckoo clock*, 12
die Kugel, -n *scoop (of ice cream)*, 6
kühl *cool*, 7
kühler *cooler*, 7
der Kühlschrank, ∺e *refrigerator*, 12
der Kuli, -s *ballpoint pen*, 4
kulinarisch *culinary*, 6
die Kultur, -en *culture*, 10
kulturell *cultural*, 10
der Kümmel *caraway*, 8
die Kunst, ∺e *art*, 4
der Kunststoff, -e: aus Kunststoff *out*
of plastic, 12
der Kurpark, -s *spa park*, 12
kurz *short*, 3
die Kusine, -n *cousin (female)*, 3

lachen *to laugh*, 11
der Laden, ∺ *store*, 8; **im Obst- und**
Gemüseladen *at the produce*
store, 8

die Lampe, -n *lamp*, 12
das Land, ∺er *country*, 3; **auf dem**
Land *in the country*, 3
die Landeshauptstadt, ∺e *state*
capital, Loc 4
die Landschaft *environment*, Loc 10
lang *long*, 3
länger *longer*, 7
der Langlauf *cross-country*, 9
langweilig *boring*, 2
lässig *casual*, 5
die Last, -en *burden*, 7; die Last
abnehmen *to take away a burden*,
7
das Latein *Latin*, 4
laufen *to run*, 2; Rollschuh laufen
to roller skate, 9; **Schlittschuh**
laufen *to ice skate*, 12
das Leben, - *life*, 10
leben *to live*, 10
die Lebensmittel (pl) *groceries*, 8
die Leber *liver*, 9
der Leberkäs (see p. 257), 9
lecker *tasty, delicious*, 6
das Leder *leather*, 12; **aus Leder** *made*
of leather, 12
die Lederhose, -n *leather pants*, Loc 7
die Lederjacke, -n *leather jacket*, 5
legen *to put, lay*, 8
leger *casual*, 5
der Lehrer, - *teacher (male)*, 1
die Lehrerin, -nen *teacher (female)*, 1
leicht *easy*, 10
das Leichtkraftrad, ∺er *light*
motorcycle, 1
Leid: Es tut mir Leid. *I'm sorry.*, 9
das Leiden, - *suffering*, 10
leider *unfortunately*, 7; **Ich kann**
leider nicht. *Sorry, I can't.*, 7
das Leinen *linen*, 5
der Leistungskurs, -e *accelerated*
course, 4
leiten *to manage*, 11
die Lektüre, -n *reading*, 10
lernen *to study, learn*, 8
lesen *to read*, 10; **er/sie liest** *he/she*
reads, 10; richtig lesen *to read*
correctly, 1
der Leserbrief, -e *letter to the editor*, 9
der Lesetrick, -s *reading trick*, 1
letzt *last*, 8; **letzte Woche** *last*
week, 8; **letztes Wochenende** *last*
weekend, 8
die Leute (pl) *people*, 9
das Lexikon, die Lexika *dictionary*, 10
das Licht, -er *light*, p. 8
lieb *nice*, 7
die Liebe *love*, 10
liebenswert *lovable*, 10
lieber (mögen) *to prefer*, 10; Ich
sehe Komödien lieber. *I like*
comedies better., 10
Liebe(r) ... *Dear...*, 1
der Liebesfilm, -e *romance*, 10
der Liebesroman, -e *romance novel*, 10
der Liebling, -e *favorite*, 10
Lieblings- *favorite*, 4

das Lieblingsbuch, ⸚er *favorite book,* 4
das Lieblingsessen, - *favorite food,* 4
der Lieblingsfilm, -e *favorite movie,* 4
das Lieblingsinstrument, -e *favorite instrument,* 4
  liebsten: am liebsten *most of all,* 10
das **Lied, -er** *song,* 10
  liegen *to lie, be located,* 1; liegen bleiben *to stay in bed,* 4
  lila *purple,* 5
die **Limo, -s (Limonade, -n)** *lemon drink,* 3
  link- *left,* 10; **nach links** *to the left,* 9; auf der linken Seite *on the left (side),* 9
der Linseneintopf, ⸚e *lentil soup,* 9
der Lippenpflege-Stift, -e *lip-care stick,* 11
die Liste, -n *list,* 7
der **Liter, -** *liter,* 8
  locker *loose, loose-fitting,* 5
  logisch *logical,* 4
  los: Los geht's! *Let's start!,* 1; Was ist los? *What's happening?,* 5
die Lücke, -en *blank, space,* 8
  lukullisch *sumptuous,* 6
die Lust: Lust haben *to feel like,* 7
  lustig *funny,* 10
  lustigste *funniest,* 10

  machen *to do,* 2; **Das macht (zusammen) ...** *That comes to...,* 6; **Gut! Mach ich!** *Okay, I'll do that!,* 7; **Machst du Sport?** *Do you play sports?,* 2; Macht nichts! *It doesn't matter!* 4; **die Hausaufgaben machen** *to do homework,* 2
das **Mädchen, -** *girl,* 1
  mähen *to mow,* 7; **den Rasen mähen** *to mow the lawn,* 7
die Mahlzeit, -en *meal,* 8
der **Mai** *May,* 7; **im Mai** *in May,* 7
der Maibaum, ⸚e *maypole,* Loc 7
die Maisstärke *corn starch,* 12
der Majoran *marjoram,* 12
  mal *(particle),* 6; *(short for* **einmal***) once,* 9
  malen *to paint,* 2
  man *one, you (in general), people,* 1
  manchmal *sometimes,* 7
die Mandel, -n *almond,* 12
der Mandelkuchen, - *almond cake,* 12
  mangelhaft *unsatisfactory (grade),* 4
der **Mann, ⸚er** *man,* 3
die Männertracht, -en *local custom for men,* Loc 7
der Mantel, ⸚ *coat,* 5

die Maracuja, -s *passion fruit,* 8
die Margarine *margarine,* 12
der Marienkäfer, - *ladybug,* 11
die Mariensäule *St. Mary's Column,* Loc 7
die Mark, - *mark (former German monetary unit)*
das Markenprodukt, -e *trademarked product,* 5
der Markt, ⸚e *market,* 6
der **Marktplatz, ⸚e** *market square,* 9
der Marktplatz, ⸚e *outdoor market,* 8
die Marmelade, -n *jam, jelly,* 8
der **März** *March,* 7; **im März** *in March,* 7
der Maschinenbau *machine building industry, mechanical engineering,* Loc 10
die Masse, -n *mass,* 12
die Mathearbeit, -en *math test,* 4
die **Mathematik (Mathe)** *math,* 4
die Matheprüfung, -en *math exam,* 6
  Mau-Mau *(card game),* 2
die Mauer, -n *wall,* 12
die Maultaschen (pl) *(Southern German dish),* 9
  maurisch *Moorish,* 12
die Maus, ⸚e *mouse,* 7
das Meer, -e *ocean,* 6
das Meerschweinchen, - *guinea pig,* 7
das **Mehl** *flour,* 8
  mehr *more,* 2, 8; **Ich habe keinen Hunger mehr.** *I'm not hungry anymore.,* 9
die Mehrwegflasche, -n *refund bottle,* 7
  mein *my,* 3; **meinem Vater** *to, for my father,* 11; **meiner Mutter** *to, for my mother,* 11
  meinen: **Meinst du?** *Do you think so?,* 5
die Meinung, -en *opinion,* 2
  meisten *most,* 9
  meistens *mostly,* 5
die Melone, -n *melon,* 3
der Mensch, -en *person,* 7; Mensch! *Oh man!,* 2
das Messer, - *knife,* 10
der **Metzger, -** *butcher,* 8; **beim Metzger** *at the butcher's,* 8
die **Metzgerei, -en** *butcher shop,* 8
  mich *me,* 7
die **Milch** *milk,* 8
  mild *mild,* 8
  militärisch *military,* 10
die Million, -en *million,* 7
das **Mineralwasser** *mineral water,* 3
  minus *minus,* 3
die Minute, -n *minute,* 8
  mir *to me,* 3
  miserabel *miserable,* 6
der Mist: **So ein Mist!** *Darn it!,* 2; *That stinks! What a mess!,* 4
  mit *with, by,* 1; **mit Brot** *with bread,* 6; **mit dem Auto** *by car,* 1; **mit dem Bus** *by bus,* 1; **mit dem Moped** *by moped,* 1; **mit dem**

  Rad *by bike,* 1; **mit der U-Bahn** *by subway,* 1; **mit Senf** *with mustard,* 9; **mit Zitrone** *with lemon,* 6
  mitarbeiten (sep) *to work with,* 7
  mitgebracht (pp) *brought with,* 12
das Mitglied, -er *member,* 10
die Mithilfe *cooperation,* 7
  mitkommen (sep) *to come along,* 7
  mitnehmen (sep) *to take with,* 10
der Mitschüler, - *classmate (male),* 1
die Mitschülerin, -nen *classmate (female),* 1
  mitspielen (sep) *to join in, to cooperate,* 1
der Mittag, -e *noon,* 8
die Mittagspause, -n *midday break,* 9
der Mittagstisch, -e *lunch,* 4
  mitteilen *to tell,* 7
die Mitternacht *midnight,* 10
  mittler- *middle,* 9
der **Mittwoch** *Wednesday,* 4; **am Mittwoch** *on Wednesday,* 4
  mitverantwortlich *jointly responsible,* 10
die **Möbel** (pl) *furniture,* 3
  möchten *would like to,* 3; **Ich möchte ... sehen.** *I would like to see...,* 5; **Was möchtest du essen?** *What would you like to eat?,* 3; **Ich möchte noch ein(e) (en) ...** *I'd like another....,* 9; **Ich möchte kein(e)(en) ... mehr.** *I don't want another....,* 9
die **Mode, -n** *fashion,* 10
das Modegeschäft, -e *clothing store,* 5
der Modekenner, - *fashion expert,* 5
  modern *modern,* 5
  modisch *fashionable,* 5
  mogeln *to cheat,* 2
  mögen *to like, care for,* 10
  möglich *possible,* 4
  möglichst ... *as...as possible,* 12
der **Moment, -e** *moment,* 3; **Einen Moment, bitte!** *Just a minute, please.,* 11; **im Moment gar nichts** *nothing at the moment,* 3
der **Monat, -e** *month,* 7; **(einmal) im Monat** *(once) a month,* 7
das **Monster, -** *monster,* 1
der **Montag** *Monday,* 4; **am Montag** *on Monday,* 4
das **Moped, -s** *moped,* 1; **mit dem Moped** *by moped,* 1
  morgen *tomorrow,* 7
der **Morgen, -** *morning,* 2; **Guten Morgen!** *Good morning!,* 1; **Morgen!** *Morning!,* 1
die Mühle, -n *mill,* Loc 10
der **Müll** *trash,* 7; **den Müll sortieren** *to sort the trash,* 7
der Mülleimer, - *trash can,* 12
die Münchner (pl) *residents of Munich,* 9
  mündlich *oral,* 4
die **Münze, -n** *coin,* 11; **Münzen**

einstecken *to insert coins,* 11
das Münztelefon, -e *coin phone,* 11
das Murmeltier, -e *groundhog,* 10
das Museum, die Museen *museum,* 9
die Musik *music,* 2; **klassische Musik** *classical music,* 10; **Musik hören** *to listen to music,* 2
das Musikprogramm, -e *music program,* 10
die Musikstätte, -n *music hall,* Loc 7
das Müsli *muesli,* 8
müssen *to have to,* 7; **ich muss** *I have to,* 7
die Mutter, ̈ *mother,* 3
der Muttertag *Mother's Day,* 11; **Alles Gute zum Muttertag!** *Happy Mother's Day!,* 11
die Mutti *mom,* 3
die Mütze, -n *cap,* 10

Na? *Well?,* 2; Na ja. *Oh well,* 5; na dann *well then,* 9; Na klar! *Of course!,* 5
nach *after,* 2; **nach der Schule** *after school,* 2; **nach links** *to the left,* 9; **nach rechts** *to the right,* 9; **nach der Pause** *after the break,* 4; **nach Hause gehen** *to go home,* 3
die Nachbarschaft *neighborhood,* 8
nacherzählen *to retell,* 3
nachfolgend- *following,* 7
nachher *later, afterwards,* 3
die Nachhilfe *tutoring,* 7
die Nachhilfestunde, -n *tutoring lesson,* 7
der Nachmittag, -e *afternoon,* 2; **am Nachmittag** *in the afternoon,* 2
nächste *next,* 6; **die nächste Straße** *the next street,* 9; **nächste Woche** *next week,* 11
die Nacht, ̈e *night,* 6
die Nähe: **in der Nähe** *nearby,* 3
der Name, -n *name,* 1
der Namenstag, -e *name day,* 11
närrisch *foolish,* 9
nass *wet,* 7
Natürlich! *Certainly!,* 11
der Nebensatz, ̈e *clause,* 8
nehmen *to take,* 5; **er/sie nimmt** *he/she takes,* 5; **ich nehme ...** *I'll take...,* 5; **Nehmt ein Stück Papier!** *Take out a piece of paper.,* p. 8
nein *no,* 1
nennen *to name,* 5
nett *nice,* 2
neu *new,* 3
neuerdings *lately,* 1
neun *nine,* 1
neunundzwanzig *twenty-nine,* 3
neunzehn *nineteen,* 1
neunzig *ninety,* 3

neuste *newest,* 10
nicht *not,* 2; **Nicht besonders.** *Not really.,* 6; **nicht gern haben** *to dislike,* 4; **nicht schlecht** *not bad,* 4; **Ich nicht.** *I don't.,* 2; **Nicht zu lang?** *Not too long?,* 5
nichts *nothing,* 2; **Nichts, danke!** *Nothing, thank you!,* 3; **Nichts mehr, danke!** *Nothing else, thanks!,* 9
nie *never,* 7
niederländisch *Dutch,* 11
noch *yet, still,* 2; **Haben Sie noch einen Wunsch?** *Would you like anything else?,* 8; **Ich brauche noch ...** *I also need...,* 8; **Möchtest du noch etwas?** *Would you like something else?,* 9; **noch ein** *more, another,* 9; **Noch einen Saft?** *Another glass of juice?,* 9; **Noch etwas?** *Anything else?,* 9; **Ich möchte noch ein(e)(en) ...** *I'd like another...,* 9
noch einmal *once again,* 10
nördlich (von) *north (of),* Loc 10
normalerweise *usually,* 10
Notizen machen *to take notes,* 8
die Note, -n *grade,* 4
das Notizbuch, ̈er *notebook,* 1
der November *November,* 7; **im November** *in November,* 7
die Nudelsuppe, -n *noodle soup,* 6
null *zero,* 1
die Nummer, -n *number,* 1
nummeriert *numbered,* 7
nun *now,* 6
nur *only,* 4
nützlich *useful,* 11

ob *whether (conj),* 9
oben *upstairs; up there,* 3
oberflächlich *superficial,* 10
obig *above,* 11
das Obst *fruit,* 3
der Obst- und Gemüseladen, ̈ *fresh produce store,* 8; **im Obst- und Gemüseladen** *at the produce store,* 8
der Obstkuchen, - *fruit cake,* 8
der Obstsalat, -e *fruit salad,* 8
obwohl *although (conj),* 7
oder *or,* 1
der Ofen, ̈ *oven,* 12
öffentlich *public,* 9
öffnen: Öffnet eure Bücher auf Seite ...! *Open your books to page...,* p. 8
oft *often,* 2
ohne *without,* 5
Oje! *Oh no!,* 6
der Oktober *October,* 7; **im Oktober** *in October,* 7

das Öl, -e *oil,* 12
die Oma, -s *grandmother,* 3
der Onkel, - *uncle,* 3
der Opa, -s *grandfather,* 3
die Oper, -n *opera,* 4
die Optik *optics,* Loc 10
die Orange, -n *orange,* 3
der Orangensaft *orange juice,* 3
das Orchester, - *orchestra,* 4
ordnen *to order, put in the right sequence,* 7
Ordnung: in Ordnung, *O.K.,* 11
organisieren *to organize,* 11
die Originalfassung, -en *original version,* 10
der Ort, -e *place, location,* 9
der Ort, -e *site,* 9
das Ortsgespräch, -e *local call,* 11
das Optikunternehmen *optical industry,* Loc 10
das Ostern *Easter,* 11; **Frohe Ostern!** *Happy Easter!,* 11
Österreich (das) *Austria,* 1
österreichisch *Austrian (adj),* 9

das Paar, -e *pair,* 5; **paar: ein paar** *a few,* 3
das Päckchen, - *packet,* 12
das Paddel, - *paddle,* 12
die Pailletten (pl) *beads,* 5
das Papier *paper,* p. 8
das Parfüm, -e *perfume,* 11
der Park, -s *park,* 12; **in den Park gehen** *to go to the park,* 12
das Partizip *past participle,* 10
der Partner, - *partner (male),* p. 7
die Partnerin, -nen *partner (female),* 6
die Party, -s *party,* 11
der Passant, -en *passerby,* 9
passen *to fit,* 5; **der Rock passt prima!** *The skirt fits great!,* 5; Was passt zusammen? *What goes together?,* 1; aufpassen: Passt auf! *Pay attention!,* p. 8; **Pass auf!** *Watch out!,* 6
passend- *suitable,* 7
passen zu *to go with,* 7
passieren: Was passiert hier? *What's happening here?,* 1
die Pastellfarben (pl) *pastel colors,* 5
der Patient, -en *patient,* 10
die Pause, -n *break,* 4; **nach der Pause** *after the break,* 4
das Pech *bad luck,* 4; **So ein Pech!** *Bad luck!,* 4
die Perle, -n *bead,* 5
die Person, -en *person,* 3
persönlich *personally,* 11
der Pfadfinder, - *(similar to Boy Scout),* 6

die Pfarrkirche, -n *parish church*, 9
Pfd.=Pfund (das) *pound*, 8
der Pfeffer *pepper*, 12
der Pfennig, - (smallest unit of the former German currency; 1/100 of a mark)
die Pflanze, -n *plant*, 11
die Pflaume, -n *plum*, 8
pflegen *to do regularly*, 9
die Pflicht, -en *duty*, 7
der Pflichtunterricht *mandatory class*, 4
das Pfund, - (Pfd.) *pound*, 8
phantasievoll *imaginative*, 10
phantastisch *fantastic*, 3
Physik (die) *physics*, 4
die Physikerin, -nen *physicist(f)*, 4
pikant *spicy*, 8
der Pilz, -e *mushroom*, 6
die Pizza, -s *pizza*, 6
der Plan, ⸚e *plan*, 6
planen *to plan*, 6
die Planung, -en *planning*, 10
das Plastik *plastic*, 7
der Platz, ⸚e *place, spot*, 1; **am ...platz** *on ... Square*, 9; **bis zum ...platz** *until you get to ... Square*, 9
der Platz *space*, 8
der Pokalsieg, -e *victory*, 9
die Politik *politics*, 10
die Pommes frites, - *French fries*, 9
populär *popular*, 11
populärste *most popular*, 11
das Portemonnaie, -s *wallet*, 8
die Portion, -en *portion*, 12
die Post *post office*, 9
das Poster, - *poster*, 11
die Postkarte, -n *postcard*, 1
die Praline, -n *fancy chocolate*, 11
der Präsident, -en *president*, 9
der Preis, -e *price*, 4
das Preisplakat, -e *poster with prices*, 8
preiswert *reasonably priced*, 4; **Das ist preiswert.** *That's a bargain.*, 4
Prima! *Great!* 1; Prima Idee! *Great idea!*, 7
die Prise, -n: eine Prise Salz *a pinch of salt*, 12
privat *private*, 10
die Probestunde, -en *practice hour*, 4
probieren *to try* (with foods), 9
das Problem, -e *problem*, 8
der Produzent, -en *producer*, 10
das Pronomen, - *pronoun*, 8
Prost! *Cheers!*, 12
das Prozent, - *percent*, 5
die Prüfungsvorbereitung, -en *preparation for a test*, 7
Pst! *Ssh!*, 12
der Pulli, -s (Pullover, -) *pullover, sweater*, 5
pur *pure*, 8
das Putenschnitzel, - *turkey cutlets*, 8
putzen *to clean*, 7; **die Fenster putzen** *to wash the windows*, 7
das Putzmittel, - *cleaning agent*, 7

Q

der Quadratkilometer, - *square kilometer*, 1
qualifiziert *qualified; competent*, 4
die Qualität *quality*, 5
der Quark (milk product), 8
Quatsch! *Nonsense!*, 7

R

die Rache *revenge*, 10
das Rad, ⸚er *bike*, 1; *wheel*, 10; **mit dem Rad** *by bike*, 1; Wir fahren Rad. *We're riding bikes.*, 10
Rad fahren *to ride a bike*, 2
radeln *to ride a bike*, 7
der Radiergummi, -s *eraser*, 4
das Radieschen, - *radish*, 8
das Radio, -s *radio*, 11
der Radio-Meteorologe, -n *meteorologist*, 10
der Rand, ⸚er *edge*, 7
der Rasen, - *lawn*, 7; **den Rasen mähen** *to mow the lawn*, 7
raten: Rate! *Guess!*, 2; Rate mal! *Guess!*, 1
das Rathaus, ⸚er *city hall*, 9
der Rathausturm, ⸚e *City Hall Tower*, Loc 7
die Raumfahrtindustrie *space industry*, Loc 7
das Rautenmuster *diamond pattern*, Loc 7
die Realschule, -n *secondary school*, 4
der Rechner, - *calculator*, 4
das Recht: Du hast Recht! *You're right!*, 4
rechts: nach rechts *to the right*, 9
die Rechtschreibung *spelling*, 8
reden *to talk*, 5
reduziert *reduced*, 5
das Regal, -e *bookcase*, 3
die Regalreihe, -n *row of shelves*, 11
die Regel, -n *rule*, 2
regelmäßig *regularly*, 7
der Regen *rain*, 7
die Regie *stage-direction* (of a film), 10
regnen: Es regnet. *It's raining.*, 7
regnerisch *rainy*, 7
das Reich, -e *empire*, 6
reich *rich*, 8
die Reihe, -n *row*, 10
der Reim, -e *rhyme*, 11
rein *pure*, 6
das Reisebüro, -s *travel agency*, 9
reiten *to ride horseback*, 2
das Reitturnier, -e *riding tournament*, 12

reizvoll *charming*, Loc 10
die Religion, -en *religion* (school subject), 4
das Relikt, -e *relic*, 10
das Restaurant, -s *restaurant*, 9
der Restbetrag *change*, 11
richtig *correct(ly)*, 1; *right*, 10
die Richtung, -en *direction*, 7
riechen *to smell*, 8
Riesen- *gigantic*, 8
der Rock, ⸚e *skirt*, 5
die Rolle, -n *role*, 9
der Rollschuh, -e *roller skate*, 2; Rollschuh laufen *to roller-skate*, 9; ich laufe Rollschuh *I roller-skate*, 9
die Rollschuhbahn, -en *roller-skating course*, 9
der Roman, -e *novel*, 10
der Rosenkohl *Brussels sprouts*, 9
die Rosine, -n *raisin*, 8
die Rostbratwurst, ⸚e *roasted sausage*, 6
rot *red*, 3; **in Rot** *in red*, 5
die Rückgabe *refund*, 11
Ruhe! *Quiet!*, 4
der Ruhetag, -e *day of rest*, 6
der Rührteig, -e *batter*, 12
rund *round*, 12
runter *down*, 3

S

das Sachbuch, ⸚er *non-fiction book*, 10
die Sache, -n *thing, item*, 5
der Saft, ⸚e *juice*, 3
saftig *juicy*, 6
der Saftstand, ⸚e *juice stand*, 9
sagen *to say*, 2; Sag, ... *Say...*, 1; **Sag mal ...** *Say...*, 2; so sagt man das *here's how you say it*, 1; Was sagst du dazu? *What do you say to that?*, 9; **Was sagt der Wetterbericht?** *What does the weather report say?*, 7; Wie sagt man ... auf Deutsch? *How do you say...in German?*, p. 8
sagenhaft *great*, 6
sagte *said*, 10
die Sahne *cream*, 8
die Saison, -s *season*, 5
der Salat, -e *lettuce*, 8; *salad*, 12
das Salz *salt*, 12
sammeln *to collect*, 2; **Comics sammeln** *to collect comics*, 2; **Briefmarken sammeln** *to collect stamps*, 2
der Samstag *Saturday*, 4; **am Samstag** *on Saturdays*, 4
der Sänger, - *singer (male)*, 10
die Sängerin, -nen *singer (female)*, 10
der Satz, ⸚e *sentence*, 1; Sätze bauen *to form sentences*, 1

sauber *clean*, Loc 7
sauber machen *to clean*, 12
sauberer *cleaner*, 7
sauer *annoyed*, 2
säuerlich *sour*, 12
saugen: Staub saugen *to vacuum*, 7
das **Schach** *chess*, 2
Schade! *Too bad!*, 4
die Schale, -n *serving dish*, 8
schätzen *to value*, 10
schauen *to look*, 2; **Schau!** *Look!*, 4; Schau mal! *Take a look!*, 1; **Schauen Sie!** (formal) *Look!*, 4; Schaut auf die Tafel! *Look at the board!*, 12; **Fernsehen schauen** *to watch television*, 2
der Schauer, - *(rain) shower*, 7
das **Schaufenster**, - *store window*, 12
der **Schauspieler**, - *actor*, 10
die **Schauspielerin, -nen** *actress*, 10
die Scheibe, -n *slice*, 8
scheinbar *seeming*, 10
scheinen *to shine*, 7; **Die Sonne scheint.** *The sun is shining.*, 7
schenken *to give (a gift)*, 11; **Schenkst du deinem Vater einen Kalender zum Geburtstag?** *Are you giving your father a calendar for his birthday?*, 11; **Was schenkst du deiner Mutter?** *What are you giving your mother?*, 11
scheußlich *hideous*, 5
schick, chic *smart (looking)*, 5
schimpfen *to complain*, 7
der Schinken *ham*, 6
das Schlagzeug *drums; percussion*, 2
schlecht *bad(ly)*, 4
der Schlittschuh, -e *ice skate*, 12; **Schlittschuh laufen** *to ice-skate*, 12
das Schloss, ¨er *castle*, Loc 1
schmalzig *corny, mushy*, 10
schmecken: **Schmeckt's?** *Does it taste good?*, 6; **Wie schmeckt's?** *How does it taste?*, 6
der **Schmuck** *jewelry*, 11
der **Schnee** *snow*, 7
schneiden *to cut*, 8
schneien: **Es schneit.** *It's snowing.*, 7
schnell *fast*, 7
das Schnitzel, - *cutlet*, 9
die Schokolade, -n *chocolate*, 11
das Schokoladeneis *chocolate ice cream*, 6
die Schokoladenstücke (pl) *pieces of chocolate*, 12
schon *already*, 1; schon bekannt *already known*, 2; Schon gut! *That's okay!*, 1
schon: schon lange nicht *not in a long time*, 8
schön *pretty, beautiful*, 3
schöner *more beautiful, prettier*, 5
schönste *most beautiful*, 5
der Schornsteinfeger, - *chimney sweep*, 11

der **Schrank, ¨e** *cabinet*, 3
schreiben *to write*, 2; richtig schreiben *to write correctly*, 1; schreib ... ab *copy*, 8 Schreibt euren Namen! *Write your names.*, p. 8; Schreib ... auf! *Write down...!*, 12 schreib ...um *rewrite*, 8
der **Schreibtisch, -e** *desk*, 3
das Schreibwarengeschäft, -e *stationery store*, 11
der Schreibwarenladen, ¨ *stationery store*, 4
schriftlich *written*, 4
der Schritt, -e *step*, 10; auf Schritt und Tritt *all the time*, 10
die **Schule, -n** *school*, 4; **nach der Schule** *after school*, 2; **Wie kommst du zur Schule?** *How do you get to school?*, 1
der Schüler, - *pupil, student (male)*, 3
der Schülerausweis, -e *student I.D.*, 4
die Schülergruppe, -n *group of students*, 9
der Schulhof, ¨e *schoolyard*, 4
das Schuljahr, -e *school year*, 4
die Schulklasse, -n *class, grade*, 1
die **Schulsachen** (pl) *school supplies*, 4
die **Schultasche, -n** *schoolbag*, 4
die Schulter, -n *shoulder*, 8
der Schulverbund, ¨e *school administration*, 4
der Schulzweig, -e *school branch*, 4
die Schüssel, -n *bowl*, 12
der Schutz *protection*, 11
der Schutzumschlag, ¨e *dust jacket (on a book)*, 10
schwach *weak*, 7
schwarz *black*, 3; **in Schwarz** *in black*, 5
der Schwarzwald *Black Forest*, Loc 10
das Schwein, -e *pig*, 8
der Schweinebraten, - *pork roast*, 8
das Schweinschnitzel, - *pork cutlet*, 9
die Schweinshaxe, -n *pork shank*, Loc 7
das Schweinswürstel, - *little pork sausage*, 8
schwer *difficult, hard*, 11
die **Schwester, -n** *sister*, 3
das **Schwimmbad, ¨er** *swimming pool*, 6; **ins Schwimmbad gehen** *to go to the (swimming) pool*, 6
schwimmen *to swim*, 2
der **Sciencefictionfilm, -e** *science fiction movie*, 10
der **Sciencefictionroman, -e** *science fiction novel*, 10
sechs *six*, 1
sechsundzwanzig *twenty-six*, 3
sechzehn *sixteen*, 1
sechzig *sixty*, 3
der See, -n *lake*, Loc 4
segeln *to go sailing*, 2
sehen *to see*, 10; Am liebsten sehe ich Krimis. *I like detective movies the best.*, 10; **er/sie sieht** *he/she sees*, 10; **einen Film sehen** *to see a movie*, 6

sehenswert *worth seeing*, 9
die Sehenswürdigkeit, -en *popular sight*, 9
sehr *very*, 2; **Sehr gut!** *Very well!*, 6
seid: ihr seid *you (pl) are*, 1
die **Seide, -n** *silk*, 12; **aus Seide** *made of silk*, 12
sein *to be*, 1; **er ist** *he is*, 1; **er ist aus** *he's from*, 1; **ich bin aus** *I am from*, 1; **sie sind** *they are*, 1; **sie sind aus** *they're from*, 1; **du bist** *you are*, 1
sein *his*, 3
seit *since, for*, 10
die Seite, -n *page*, 6; *side*, 9; auf der rechten Seite *on the right (hand) side*, 9
selber *myself*, 7
selbst *yourself*, 7
das Selbstgemachte *homemade item*, 11
selten *seldom*, 7
die **Semmel, -n** *roll*, 8
der **Senf** *mustard*, 6; **mit Senf** *with mustard*, 9
sensationell *sensational*, 10
separat *separate*, 7
der **September** *September*, 7
der **Sessel, -** *armchair*, 12
setzen *to sit down*, 6; Setzt euch! *Sit down!*, p. 8
setzen (sich) *to sit*, 9
setzen: setz ...ein *insert*, 8
die **Shorts** *pair of shorts*, 5
sich *oneself*, 5
Sicher! *Certainly!*, 3; **Ich bin nicht sicher.** *I'm not sure.*, 5
sichern *to secure*, 9
sie *she*, 2
sie (pl) *they*, 2
Sie *you* (formal), 2
sie *it* (with objects), 3
sie (pl) *they* (with objects), 3; *them* (with objects), 5
sieben *seven*, 1
siebenundzwanzig *twenty-seven*, 3
siebzehn *seventeen*, 1
siebzig *seventy*, 3
sind: sie sind *they are*, 1; **Sie** (formal) **sind** *you are*, 1; **wir sind** *we are*, 1
singen *to sing*, 10
sinnvoll *meaningful*, 11
die Sitte, -n *custom*, 10
der Sitz, -e *location*, Loc 7
sitzen *to be sitting*, 10
Skat *(German card game)*, 2
Ski laufen *to ski*, 2
skurrilste *most ludicrous*, 10
so *so, well, then*, 2; so groß wie *as big as*, 6; **so lala** *so so*, 6; so oft wie möglich *as often as possible*, 10; so sagt man das *here's how you say it*, 1
sobald *as soon (as)*, 10
die **Socke, -n** *sock*, 5
das **Sofa, -s** *sofa*, 12

der Sohn, ⁻e *son*, 10
sollen *should, to be supposed to,* 8
der Sommer *summer,* 2; **im Sommer** *in the summer,* 2
sommerleicht *summery (clothing),* 5
das Sonderangebot, -e *sale,* 4
sondern *but,* 5
der Sonderpreis, -e *special price,* 6
die Sonne *sun,* 7
sonnig *sunny,* 7
der Sonntag *Sunday,* 4
sonntags *Sundays,* 8
sonst *otherwise,* 2; ansonsten *otherwise,* 11; **Sonst noch etwas?** *Anything else?,* 8
die Sorge, -n *worry,* 8
sorgen *to care (for), to take care of,* 6
sorgen (sich) *to worry,* 10
sortieren *to sort,* 7; **den Müll sortieren** *to sort the trash,* 7
sowie *as well as,* Loc 7
sowieso *anyway,* 5
die Sozialkunde *social studies,* 4
die Spalte, -n *column,* 10
Spanien (das) *Spain,* 8
Spanisch *Spanish* (class), 4; (language), 10
spannend *exciting, thrilling,* 10
der Spargel *asparagus,* 8
sparsam *thrifty,* 7
der Spaß *fun,* 2; Hat es Spaß gemacht? *Was it fun?,* 10; **(Tennis) macht keinen Spaß.** *(Tennis) is no fun.,* 2; **(Tennis) macht Spaß.** *(Tennis) is fun.,* 2; Viel Spaß! *Have fun!,* 9
spät *late,* 6; **Wie spät ist es?** *What time is it?,* 6
später *later,* 2
das Spätprogramm, -e *late show,* 10
das Spatzenbrett, -er (cutting board to make **Spätzle**), 12
die Spätzle (pl) (see p. 338), 12
der Speck *bacon,* 12
die Speisekarte, -n *menu,* 6
spektakulärste *most spectacular,* 10
die Spezialität, -en *specialty,* 9
das Spiel, -e *game,* 10
spielen *to play,* 2; **Ich spiele Fußball.** *I play soccer.,* 2; **Ich spiele Klavier.** *I play the piano.,* 2; **Spielst du ein Instrument?** *Do you play an instrument?,* 2
der Spieler, - *player,* 12
der Spießbraten, - *roast,* 6
der Spinat *spinach,* 9
Spitze! *Super!,* 2
die Spitzenqualität *top quality,* 8
sponsern *to sponsor,* 10
spontan *spontaneous(ly),* 9
der Sport *sports,* 2; *physical education,* 4; **Machst du Sport?** *Do you play sports?,* 2
die Sportanlage, -n *sports arena,* Loc 7
die Sportart, -en *type of sport,* 9

das Sportgymnasium, -ien *secondary school with stress on sports,* 4
die Sporthalle, -n *indoor gym,* 6
sportlich *sporty,* 5
die Sportmode *sportswear,* 9
spottbillig *dirt-cheap,* 11
die Sprache, -n *language,* 5
sprechen: sprechen über *to talk about, discuss,* 10; **er/sie spricht über** *he/she talks about,* 10; **Kann ich bitte Andrea sprechen?** *Could I please speak with Andrea?,* 11
sprengen *to blow up,* 9
das Spülbecken, - *sink,* 12
spülen *to wash,* 7; **das Geschirr spülen** *to wash the dishes,* 7
die Spülmaschine, -n *dishwasher,* 12; die Spülmaschine ausräumen *to unload the dishwasher,* 12
staatlich anerkannt *state-recognized,* 4
die Stadtkarte, -n *city map,* 9
die Stadt, ⁻e *city,* 9; **in der Stadt** *in the city,* 3; in die Stadt fahren *to go downtown (by vehicle),* 11; **in die Stadt gehen** *to go downtown,* 6
die Stadtfahne, -n *city flag,* Loc 7
das Stadtmuseum *city museum,* 9
der Stadtplan, ⁻e *city map,* 9
der Stadtteil, -e *part of the city,* 9
der Standort, -e *location,* 12
stark *great, awesome,* 5
stattfinden: findet statt *takes place,* Loc 7
stattgefunden (pp) *took place,* Loc 7
der Staub *dust,* 7; **Staub saugen** *to vacuum,* 7
stehen: Steht auf! *Stand up!,* p. 8; Wie steht's mit dir? *How about you?,* 10
stehen (vor) *to stand (in front of),* 9
der Stehimbiss, -e *fast-food stand,* 9
stellen *to put,* 10
Stellung beziehen *move into a position,* 10
die Stereoanlage, -n *stereo,* 3
der Stiefbruder, ⁻ *stepbrother,* 3
der Stiefel, - *boot,* 5
die Stiefmutter, ⁻ *stepmother,* 3
die Stiefschwester, -n *stepsister,* 3
der Stiefvater, ⁻ *stepfather,* 3
der Stil, -e *style,* 10
stimmen *to be correct,* 3; **Stimmt (schon)!** *Keep the change.,* 6; **Stimmt!** *That's right! True!,* 2; **Stimmt nicht!** *Not true!; False!,* 2
stimmungsvoll *full of atmosphere,* 6
das Stirnband, ⁻er *headband,* 5
das Stockwerk, -e *floor,* 9
die Straße, -n *street,* 9; auf der Straße *on the street,* 9; **bis zur ...straße** *until you get to ... Street,* 9; **die erste (zweite, dritte) Straße** *the first (second, third) street,* 9; **in der ...straße** *on ... Street,* 3

das Straßenlokal, -e *street restaurant,* Loc 7
das Streichorchester, - *string-orchestra,* 6
der Streifen, - *stripe,* 5
streng *strict,* 7
das Strickkleid, -er *knit dress,* 5
der Strumpf, ⁻e *stocking,* 5
das Stück, -e *piece,* p. 8; **ein Stück Kuchen** *a piece of cake,* 3
das Stückchen, - *small piece,* 8
das Studium, die Studien *study,* 4
die Stufe, -n *level,* 1
der Stuhl, ⁻e *chair,* 3
die Stunde, -n *hour,* 9
der Stundenplan, ⁻e *class schedule,* 4
suchen *to look for, search for,* 5; **ich suche ...** *I'm looking for...,* 5
der Süden *south,* 7
super *super,* 2
der Supermarkt, ⁻e *supermarket,* 8; **im Supermarkt** *at the supermarket,* 8
surfen *to surf,* 2
süß *sweet,* 8
die Süßigkeit, -en *sweets,* 11
die Süßspeise, -n *dessert,* 9
das Süßwarengeschäft, -e *candy store,* 11
die Szene, -n *scene,* 9

die Tafel, -n *(chalk)board,* p. 8; Geht an die Tafel! *Go to the board,* p. 8
der Tag, -e *day,* 2; eines Tages *one day,* 10; **Guten Tag!** *Hello!,* 1; **Tag!** *Hello!,* 1; **jeden Tag** *every day,* 7
täglich *daily,* Loc 7
der Tagesverlauf *duration of the day,* 7
täglich *daily,* 10
die Tante, -n *aunt,* 3
tanzen *to dance,* 2; **tanzen gehen** *to go dancing,* 6
das Taschengeld *pocket money,* 7
der Taschenrechner, - *pocket calculator,* 7
die Tasse, -n *cup,* 3; **eine Tasse Kaffee** *a cup of coffee,* 6
die Taucherausrüstung, -en *scuba gear,* 11
tauschen *to switch, trade,* 9; Tauscht die Rollen aus! *Switch roles.,* 8
die Technik *technology,* 4
der Tee *tea,* 3; **ein Glas Tee** *a (glass) cup of tea,* 6, eine Tasse Tee *a cup of tea,* 3
der Teelöffel (TL) *teaspoon,* 8
der Teig *dough,* 8
der Teil, -e *part,* 9

teilweise *partly*, 12
das Telefon, -e *telephone*, 11
telefonieren *to call*, 11
die Telefonkarte, -n *phone card*, 11
die Telefonnummer, -n *telephone number*, 11
die Telefonzelle, -n *telephone booth*, 11
das Telegramm, -e *telegram*, 11
der Teller, - *plate*, 11
der Temperaturanstieg, -e *rise of temperature*, 7
Tennis *tennis*, 2
der Teppich, -e *carpet*, 12
der Termin, -e *appointment*, 9
teuer *expensive*, 4
der Teufel, - *devil*, 10
der Text, -e *text*, 12
das Theater, - *theater*, 9; **ins Theater gehen** *to go to the theater*, 12
das Theaterstück, -e *(stage) play*, 10
das Thema, die Themen *topic*, 10
Thüringen (das) *Thuringia*, 1
der Thymian *thyme*, 12
der Tibeter, - *Tibetan*, 10
der Tiefstwert, -e *minimum value*, 7
das Tier, -e *animal*, 7
die Tierschutzorganization, -en *organization that protects animals*, 11
der Tisch, -e *table*, 7; **den Tisch abräumen** *to clear the table*, 7; **den Tisch decken** *to set the table*, 7
das Tischtennis *table tennis*, 2
der Titel, - *title*, 10
Tja ... *Hm...*, 2
die Tochter, ⸚ *daughter*, 10
tödlich *deadly*, 10
die Toilette, -n *toilet*, 12
toll *great, terrific*, 2; **Ich finde es toll!** *I think it's great!*, 9
die Tomate, -n *tomato*, 8
das Tor, -e *gate*, 12
die Torte, -n *layer cake*, 8
der Tote, -n *deceased person*, 10
die Touristenattraktion *tourist attraction*, Loc 10
die Tracht, -en *local costume*, Loc 7
traditionsreich *rich in tradition*, Loc 10
das Training *training*, 1
die Traube, -n *grape*, 8
der Traumjob, -s *dream job*, 10
traurig *sad*, 10
traurigste *saddest*, 10
der Treff *meeting place*, 10
treffen *to meet*, 9
der Treffpunkt, -e *meeting place*, 6
treiben: Ich treibe Sport. *I do sports.*, 9
treu *loyal*, 10
der Treuhänder, - *trustee*, 10
der Trimm-dich-Pfad, -e *fitness trail*, 2
trinken *to drink*, 3
trocken *dry*, 7
die Trompete, -n *trumpet*, 2

der Tropfen, - *drop*, 12
trotzdem *nevertheless*, 5; *in spite of it*, 7
trüb *overcast*, 7
Tschau! *Bye! So long!*, 1
Tschüs! *Bye! So long!*, 1
das T-Shirt, -s *T-shirt*, 5
tun *to do*, 7; **Es tut mir Leid.** *I'm sorry.*, 9
die Tür, -en *door*, p. 8
turbulent *turbulent*, 10
die Türkei *Turkey*, 1
der Turnschuh, -e *sneaker, athletic shoe*, 5
tust: du tust *you do*, 9
die Tüte, -n *bag*, 5
typisch *typical*, Loc 7

die U-Bahn=Untergrundbahn *subway*, 1; **mit der U-Bahn** *by subway*, 1
die U-Bahnstation, -en *subway station*, 9
üben *to practice*, p. 9
über *about*, 4
überall *all over the place*, Loc 7
überhaupt: überhaupt nicht *not at all*, 5; **überhaupt nicht gern** *strongly dislike*, 5
überließ *left (to someone else)*, 10
überquellen *to overflow*, 9
die Überraschung, -en *surprise*, 12
die Übersetzung, -en *translation*, 11
übertreffen *to outdo, surpass*, 5
übertrieben (pp) *exaggerated*, 11
überwachen *to supervise*, 4
übrigens *by the way*, 3
die Übung, -en *exercise*, 11
Uhr *o'clock*, 1; **um 8 Uhr** *at 8 o'clock*, 4; **um ein Uhr** *at one o'clock*, 6; **Wie viel Uhr ist es?** *What time is it?*, 6
die Uhrzeit *time (of day)*, 6
um *at*, 1; *around*, 9; **um 8 Uhr** *at 8 o'clock*, 4; **um ein Uhr** *at one o'clock*, 6; **Um wie viel Uhr?** *At what time?*, 6
die Umfrage, -n *survey*, 1
umgeben *to surround*, 10
umhören (sep)(sich) *to listen around*, 7
die Umrechnungstabelle, -n *conversion table*, 5
umsteigen (sep) *to change lines (on a bus, subway, etc.)*, 4
umtauschen *to exchange*, 9
die Umwelt *environment*, 10
unbedingt *absolutely*, 11
unbequem *uncomfortable*, 3
und *and*, 1
unfreundlich *unfriendly*, 11

Ungarn (das) *Hungary*, 2
ungefähr *about, approximately*, 7
ungenügend *unsatisfactory (grade)*, 4
ungewöhnlich *unusual*, 12
unheimlich *incredibly, incredible*, 8
die Uni, -s (Universität, -en), *university*, 2
unlogisch *illogical*, 4
die Unordnung *disorder*, 8
unregelmäßig *irregularly*, 8
uns *us*, 7
unschlagbar *unbeatable*, 8
unser *our*, 4
unten *below, downstairs*, 8
unter *below, under*, 8
unterbrechen *to interrupt*, 10
unterhalten *to entertain*, 11
unterheben *to fold in*, 12
die Unterrichtsveranstaltung, -en *school-sponsored activity*, 4
unterschiedlich *different*, 7
die Unterschrift, -en *signature*, 4
unterstützen *to support*, 10
unterwegs *on the way*, 10
das Urteil, -e *verdict*, 10
usw. = und so weiter *etc., and so forth*, 10

die Vanille *vanilla*, 6
das Vanilleeis *vanilla ice cream*, 6
der Vater, ⸚ *father*, 3; **deinem Vater** *to, for your father*, 11; **meinem Vater** *to, for my father*, 11
der Vatertag *Father's Day*, 11; **Alles Gute zum Vatertag!** *Happy Father's Day!*, 11
verabreden *to make a date*, 6
die Veranstaltung, -en *event*, 10
das Verb, -en *verb*, 7
verbringen *to spend (time)*, 10; **Wie verbringst du deine Freizeit?** *How do you spend your free time?*, 10
verdienen *to earn*, 7
verdünnt *diluted*, 12
veredeln *to refine*, 8
der Verein, -e *club*, 9
verfeinern *to improve*, 8
Verfügung: zur Verfügung haben *to have at one's disposal*, 11
die Vergangenheit *past tense*, 8
vergessen *to forget*, 7; vergiss nicht *don't forget*, 7
vergleichen *to compare*, 11
das Vergnügen, - *pleasure*, 10
die Vergünstigung, -en *benefit, discount*, 10
der Verkauf *sale*, 6
der Verkäufer, - *sales clerk (male)*, 4

die Verkäuferin, -nen *sales clerk (female)*, 4
der Verlag, -e *publishing house*, 7
verlangen *to ask for, to demand*, 7
verlaufen (sich) *to go the wrong way*, 9
verlegt: auf (time expression) verlegt *postponed until*, 6
verlieren *to lose*, 2
verloren *lost*, 9
vermeiden *to avoid*, 7
verrühren *to blend*, 12
der Vers, -e *verse*, 11
verschenkt *given away*, 11
verschieden *different*, 11
verschieden *various*, Loc 7; *different*, 9
verschollen *missing*, 10
versteckt: versteckte Sätze *hidden sentences*, 1
versuchen *to try*, 10
verteilen *to distribute*, 8
der Vertrag, ⁻e *contract*, 10
vervollständigen *to complete*, 8
der Verwandte, -n *relative (male)*, 11
die Verwandte, -n *relative (female)*, 11
die Verwandten (pl) *relatives*, 11
verwenden *to use*, 10
verwerten: wieder verwerten *to recycle*, 7
verzaubern *to transform into*, 10
Verzeihung! *Excuse me!*, 9
das Video, -s *videocassette*, 10
das Videospiel, -e *video game*, 2
die Viehzucht *cattle raising*, Loc 4
viel *a lot, much*, 2; Viel Spaß! *Have fun!*, 9; **viel zu** *much too*, 5;
viele *many*, 2; viele Grüße *best regards*, 9; **Vielen Dank!** *Thank you very much!*, 9
die Vielfalt *diversity*, 5
vielleicht *probably*, 11
vier *four*, 1
viermal *four times*, 7
das Viertel, - *quarter*, 6; **Viertel nach** *a quarter after*, 6; **Viertel vor** *a quarter till*, 6
vierundzwanzig *twenty-four*, 3
vierzehn *fourteen*, 1
vierzig *forty*, 3
der Vogel, ⁻ *bird*, 7
die Volksschule, -n *elementary school*, 4
volkstümlich *popular*, 9
Volleyball *volleyball*, 2
das Vollkornbrot *whole-grain bread*, 8
die Vollkornsemmel, -n *whole-grain roll*, 9
der Vollstrecker, - *executioner*, 10
vom=von dem *from the*, 8
von *of*, 1; *from*, 3; **von 8 Uhr bis 8 Uhr 45** *from 8:00 until 8:45*, 4
vor *before*, 1; *in front of*, 9; vor allem *especially*, 9; **zehn vor ...** *ten till...*, 6
voraus *in advance*, 9
vorbeigehen (sep) *to go by*, 7

vorbeigekommen (pp) *came by*, 8
vorbeikommen (sep) *to come by*, 9
vorbereiten (sep) *to prepare*, 12
die Vorbereitung, -en *preparation*, 12
vorgestern *day before yesterday*, 8
die Vorhersagekarte, -n *weather-forecasting map*, 7
der Vormittag *before noon*, 2
vorn *ahead*, 4; hier vorn *here in front*, 5; **da vorn** *there in the front*, 4
der Vorort, -e *suburb*, 3; **ein Vorort von** *a suburb of*, 3
der Vorschlag, ⁻e *suggestion*, 12
vorstellen (sep) *to introduce*, 1
die Vorstellung, -en *introduction, presentation*, 10
die Vorwahlnummer, -n *area code*, 11
die Vorzeit, -en *prehistory*, 10

wählen *to choose*, 9; **die Nummer wählen** *to dial the (telephone) number*, 11
das Wahlpflichtfach, ⁻er *required elective*, 4
Wahnsinn! *Crazy!*, 11
wahnwitzigste *maddest*, 10
wahr *true*, 11
während *while*, 6
die Wahrheit *truth*, 10
wahrscheinlich *probably*, 11
das Wahrzeichen, - *symbol, emblem*, Loc 7
der Walnusskern, -e *walnut*, 8
wandern *to hike*, 2
wann? *when?*, 2; **Wann hast du Geburtstag?** *When is your birthday?*, 11
das Wappen, - *coat of arms*, Loc 7
war: ich war *I was*, 8; **Ich war beim Bäcker.** *I was at the baker's.*, 8
die Ware, -n *ware*, 5; *merchandise*, 8
waren: wir waren *we were*, 8; **sie waren** *they were*, 8; **Sie** (formal) **waren** *you were*, 8
warm *warm*, 7; warm halten *to keep warm*, 12
die Warmluft *warm air*, 7
warst: du warst *you were*, 8; **Wo warst du?** *Where were you?*, 8
wart: ihr wart *you (plural) were*, 8
warten *to wait*, 2; ich warte auf *I'm waiting for*, 10
warum? *why?*, 7
was? *what?*, 2; Was ist los? *What's up?*, 4; Was gibt's? *What's up?*, 1; Was ist das? *What is that?*, p. 8; **Was noch?** *What else?*, 2

was für? *what kind of?*, 10; **Was für Filme magst du gern?** *What kind of movies do you like?*, 10; **Was für Musik hörst du gern?** *What kind of music do you like?*, 10
die Wäsche *laundry*, 12; die Wäsche aufhängen *to hang up the laundry*, 7
die Waschmaschine, -n *washing machine*, 12
das Wasser *water*, 3; **ein Glas (Mineral)Wasser** *a glass of (mineral) water*, 3
wasserscheu *afraid of water*, 12
Wasserski *(das) waterski*, 4
der Wecken, - *roll*, 8
weder...noch *neither...nor*, 10
weg *away*, 7
der Weg, -e: den Weg zeigen *to give directions*, 9 ·
wegbringen (sep) *to take away*, 7
weggebracht (pp) *taken away*, 7
der Weichkäse *soft cheese*, 8
das Weihnachten *Christmas*, 11; **Fröhliche Weihnachten!** *Merry Christmas!*, 11
weil *because* (conj), 8
weiß *white*, 3; **in Weiß** *in white*, 5
die Weißwurst, ⁻e (southern German sausage specialty), 9
weit *far*, 3; *wide*, 5; **weit von hier** *far from here*, 3
weiter *farther*, 7
weiterhin *further on*, 7
das Weizenmehl *wheat flour*, 12
welch- *which*, 4; an welchem Tag? *on which day?*, 11; **Welche Fächer hast du?** *Which subjects do you have?*, 4
die Welt *world*, 8
der Weltkrieg, -e *world war*, 9
das Weltmeer, -e *ocean*, 11
wem? *whom, to whom?, for whom?*, 11
wen? *whom?*, 7; **Wen lädst du ein?** *Whom are you inviting?*, 12
wenden *to turn (to)*, 9
wenig *few*, 7
weniger *less*, 8
wenn *when, if* (conj), 5
wer? *who?*, 1; **Wer ist das?** *Who is that?*, 1
werben *to advertise*, 8
die Werbung *advertisement*, 4
werden *to become*, 5
Werken (das) *shop (school subject)*, 4
der Wert, -e *value*, 7
die Weste, -n *vest*, 5
der Western, - *western* (movie), 10
das Wetter *weather*, 7; **Wie ist das Wetter?** *How's the weather?*, 7
der Wetterbericht, -e *weather report*, 7
der Wetterdienst *weather service*, 7
die Wetterkarte, -n *weather map*, 7

wichtig *important*, 7
wie? *how?*, 1; **Wie alt bist du?** *How old are you?*, 1; Wie bitte? *Excuse me?*, 8; Wie blöd! *How stupid!*, 4; **wie oft?** *how often?*, 7; **wie viel?** *how much?*, 8; **Wie viel Grad haben wir?** *What's the temperature?*, 7; **Wie viel Uhr ist es?** *What time is it?*, 6
wieder *again*, 9; wieder verwertet *reused*, 7
Wiederhören *Bye!* (on the telephone), 11; **Auf Wiederhören!** *Goodbye!* (on the telephone), 11
Wiedersehen! *Bye!*, 1; **Auf Wiedersehen!** *Goodbye!*, 1
wiegen *to weigh*, 8
das Wiener (Würstchen), - *sausage*, 6
willig *willing*, 10
willkommen: Herzlich willkommen bei uns! *Welcome to our home!*, 12
windig *windy*, 7
der Winter *winter*, 2; **im Winter** *in the winter*, 2
wir *we*, 2
wird *becomes*, 7
wirklich *really*, 5
die Wirkung, -en *effect*, 8
die Wirtschaftsschule, -n *business school*, 4
wischen *to mop*, 12
wissen *to know* (a fact, information, etc.), 9; **Das weiß ich nicht.** *That I don't know.*, 9; **Ich weiß nicht.** *I don't know.*, 5; Weißt du noch? *Do you still remember?*, 7; **Weißt du, wo das Museum ist?** *Do you know where the museum is?*, 9
witzig *funny*, 10
wo? *where?*, 1
wobei *in doing so, in the process of*, 7
die Woche, -n *week*, 6; **(einmal) in der Woche** *(once) a week*, 7
das Wochenende, -n *weekend*, 2; **am Wochenende** *on the weekend*, 2
die Wochenendheimfahrerin, -nen *student (female) who goes home on weekends*, 3
woher? *from where?*, 1; **Woher bist du?** *Where are you from?*, 1; **Woher kommst du?** *Where are you from?*, 1
wohin? *where (to)?*, 6; Wohin geht's? *Where are you going?*, 7
das Wohlbefinden *well-being*, 8
das Wohlergehen *welfare*, 8
wohnen *to live*, 3; **Wo wohnst du?** *Where do you live?*, 3

die Wohnung, -en *apartment*, 3
das Wohnzimmer, - *living room*, 12; **im Wohnzimmer** *in the living room*, 12
der Wolf, ⸚e *wolf*, 12
wolkenlos *cloudless*, 7
wolkig *cloudy*, 7
wollen *to want (to)*, 6
die Wollwurst, ⸚e (southern German sausage specialty), 8
das Wort, ⸚er *word*, 2
das Wörterbuch, ⸚er *dictionary*, 4
der Wortschatz *vocabulary*, 1
die Wortstellung *word order*, 8
worüber? *about what?*, 10; **Worüber habt ihr gesprochen?** *What did you (pl) talk about?*, 10; Worüber sprichst du mit deinen Freunden? *What do you talk about with your friends?*, 10
wunderbar *wonderful*, 4
der Wunsch, ⸚e *wish*, 5; **Haben Sie einen Wunsch?** *May I help you?*, 5; **Haben Sie noch einen Wunsch?** *Would you like anything else?*, 8
würde *would*, 10
würdest: du würdest *you would*, 7
der Würfel, - *cube*, 12
die Wurst, ⸚e *sausage*, 8
das Wurstbrot, -e *bologna sandwich*, 6
das Würstchen, - *sausage link*, 9
das Wüten *raging*, 10

zahlen *to pay*, 6; **Hallo! Ich möchte/will zahlen!** *The check please!*, 6
die Zahlen (pl) *numbers*, p. 9
die Zahnbürste, -n *toothbrush*, 11
zart *tender*, 8
z.B.=zum Beispiel *for example*, 10
zehn *ten*, 1
der Zeichenblock, ⸚e *sketch pad*, 11
die Zeichenerklärung, -en *list of conventional signs*, 7
das Zeichentrickabenteuer, - *cartoon adventure*, 10
zeichnen *to draw*, 2
die Zeichnung, -en *drawing*, 6
zeigen *to show*, 3; den Weg zeigen *to give directions*, 9
die Zeile, -n *line*, 11
die Zeit *time*, 4; die ganze Zeit *the whole time*, 12; **Ich habe keine Zeit.** *I don't have time.*, 7

die Zeitschrift, -en *magazine*, 10
die Zeitung, -en *newspaper*, 10
das Zentrum *center*, Loc 7
das Zeug *stuff*, 4
das Zeugnis, -se *report card*, 4
das Ziel, -e *goal*, 2
ziemlich *rather*, 4
das Zimmer, - *room*, 3; **mein Zimmer aufräumen** *to clean my room*, 7
der Zimt *cinnamon*, 12
die Zitrone, -n *lemon*, 12; **mit Zitrone** *with lemon*, 6
der Zitronensaft, ⸚e *lemon juice*, 8
die Zivilisation, -en, *civilization*, 10
der Zoo, -s *zoo*, 12; **in den Zoo gehen** *to go to the zoo*, 12
zu *too*, 5; *to*, 7; **zu Fuß** *on foot*, 1; zu Hause *at home*, 3; **zu Hause helfen** *to help at home*, 7; zu Hause sein *to be at home*, 6
die Zubereitung, -en *preparation (of food)*, 8
der Zucker *sugar*, 8
zuerst *first*, 4
der Zug, ⸚e *train*, 4
zuhören (sep) *to listen*, p. 6
zuletzt *last of all*, 4
zum = zu dem *to the*, 2; zum Beispiel *for example*, 10
zur = zu der *to the*, 1
zurechtkommen (mit) (sep) *to do well with*, 4
zurück *back*, 4
zurückbekommen (sep) *to get back*, 4
zurückkommen (sep) *to come back*, 12
zusammen *together*, 2
zusammenlegen (sep) *to fold (the wash)*, 12
zusammentun (sep) *to join*, 11
zusätzlich *additional*, 4
der Zuschauer, - *viewer*, 7
die Zutaten (pl) *ingredients*, 8
zwanzig *twenty*, 1
zwei *two*, 1
zweimal *twice*, 7
zweite *second*, 4; **am zweiten...** *on the second:..*, 11
zweiundzwanzig *twenty-two*, 3
die Zwiebel, -n *onion*, 12
zwischen *between*, 9
zwölf *twelve*, 1
zynisch *cynical(ly)*, 5

This vocabulary includes all of the words in the **Wortschatz** sections of the chapters. These words are considered active—you are expected to know them and be able to use them.

Idioms are listed under the English word you would be most likely to look up. German nouns are listed with definite article and plural ending, when applicable. The number after each German word or phrase refers to the chapter in which it becomes active vocabulary. To be sure you are using the German words and phrases in the correct context, refer to the chapters in which they appear.

The following abbreviations are used in the vocabulary: sep (separable-prefix verb), pl (plural), acc (accusative), dat (dative), masc (masculine), and poss adj (possessive adjective).

a, an *ein(e)*, 3
about *ungefähr*, 7
action movie *der Actionfilm, -e*, 10
actor *der Schauspieler, -*, 10
actress *die Schauspielerin, -nen*, 10
adventure movie *der Abenteuerfilm, -e*, 10
after *nach*, 2; **after school** *nach der Schule*, 2; **after the break** *nach der Pause*, 4
after that *danach*, 4
afternoon *der Nachmittag, -e*, 2; **in the afternoon** *am Nachmittag*, 2
again *wieder*, 9
along: Why don't you come along! *Komm doch mit!*, 7
already *schon*, 1
also *auch*, 1; **I also need...** *ich brauche noch ...*, 8
always *immer*, 7
am: I am *ich bin*, 1
and *und*, 1
another *noch ein*, 9; **I don't want any more....** *Ich möchte kein(e)(en) ... mehr.*, 9; **I'd like another....** *Ich möchte noch ein(e)(en) ...*, 9
anything: Anything else? *Sonst noch etwas?*, 8
appear *aussehen (sep)*, 5
apple *der Apfel, ∸*, 8
apple cake *der Apfelkuchen, -*, 6
apple juice *der Apfelsaft, ∸*, 3; **a glass of apple juice** *ein Glas Apfelsaft*, 3
approximately *ungefähr*, 8
April *der April*, 7
are: you are *du bist*, 1; (formal) *Sie sind*, 1; (pl) *ihr seid*, 1; **we are** *wir sind*, 1
armchair *der Sessel, -*, 12
art *die Kunst*, 4
at: at 8 o'clock *um 8 Uhr*, 4; **at one o'clock** *um ein Uhr*, 6; **at the**

baker's *beim Bäcker*, 8; **at the butcher's** *beim Metzger*, 8; **at the produce store** *im Obst- und Gemüseladen*, 8; **at the supermarket** *im Supermarkt*, 8; **At what time?** *Um wie viel Uhr?*, 6
August *der August*, 7
aunt *die Tante -n*, 3
Austria *Österreich*, 1
awesome *stark*, 5; **The sweater is awesome!** *Ich finde den Pulli stark!*, 5
awful *furchtbar*, 5

bad *schlecht*, 4; **badly** *schlecht*, 6; **Bad luck!** *So ein Pech!*, 4
baker *der Bäcker, -*, 8; **at the baker's** *beim Bäcker*, 8
bakery *die Bäckerei, -en*, 8
bald: to be bald *eine Glatze haben*, 3
ballpoint pen *der Kuli, -s*, 4
bank *die Bank, -en*, 9
bargain: that's a bargain *das ist preiswert*, 4
basketball *Basketball*, 2
be *sein*, 1; **I am** *ich bin*, 1; **you are** *du bist*, 1; **he/she is** *er/sie ist*, 1; **we are** *wir sind*, 1; (pl) **you are** *ihr seid*, 1; (formal) **you are** *Sie sind*, 1; **they are** *sie sind*, 1
be able to *können*, 7
be called *heißen*, 1
beautiful *schön*, 3
because *denn, weil*, 8
bed *das Bett, -en*, 3; **to make the bed** *das Bett machen*, 7
believe *glauben*, 9
belt *der Gürtel, -*, 5
best: Best wishes on your birthday! *Herzlichen Glückwunsch zum Geburtstag!*, 11

better *besser*, 8
big *groß*, 3
bike *das Fahrrad, ∸er*, 1; **by bike** *mit dem Rad*, 1
biology *Bio (die Biologie)*, 4
biology teacher (female) *die Biologielehrerin, -nen*, 1
birthday *der Geburtstag, -e*, 11; **Best wishes on your birthday!** *Herzlichen Glückwunsch zum Geburtstag!*, 11; **Happy Birthday!** *Alles Gute zum Geburtstag!*, 11; **My birthday is on....** *Ich habe am ... Geburtstag.*, 11; **When is your birthday?** *Wann hast du Geburtstag?*, 11
black *schwarz*, 3; **in black** *in Schwarz*, 5
blond *blond*, 3
blouse *die Bluse, -n*, 5
blue *blau*, 3; **blue (brown, green) eyes** *blaue (braune, grüne) Augen*, 3; **in blue** *in Blau*, 5
board game *das Brettspiel, -e*, 12
bologna sandwich *das Wurstbrot, -e*, 6
book *das Buch, ∸er*, 4
bookcase *das Regal -e*, 3
boot *der Stiefel, -*, 5
boring *langweilig*, 2
bought *gekauft*, 8; **I bought bread.** *Ich habe Brot gekauft.*, 8
bouquet of flowers *der Blumenstrauß, ∸e*, 11
boy *der Junge, -n*, 1
bread *das Brot, -e*, 8
break *die Pause, -n*, 4; **after the break** *nach der Pause*, 4
broken *kaputt*, 3
brother *der Bruder, ∸*, 3; **brothers and sisters** *die Geschwister (pl)*, 3
brown *braun*, 3; **in brown** *in Braun*, 5
brutal *brutal*, 10
bus *der Bus, -se*, 1; **by bus** *mit dem Bus*, 1
busy (telephone) *besetzt*, 11
but *aber*, 3

butcher shop *die Metzgerei, -en*, 8; **at the butcher's** *beim Metzger*, 8
butter *die Butter*, 8
buy *kaufen*, 5; **What did you buy?** *Was hast du gekauft?*, 8
by: by bike *mit dem Rad*, 1; **by bus** *mit dem Bus*, 1; **by car** *mit dem Auto*, 1; **by moped** *mit dem Moped*, 1; **by subway** *mit der U-Bahn*, 1
Bye! *Wiedersehen! Tschau! Tschüs!*, 1; (on the telephone) *Wiederhören!*, 11

C

cabinet *der Schrank, ⸚e*, 3
café *das Café, -s*, 6; **to the café** *ins Café*, 6
cake *der Kuchen, -*, 3; **a piece of cake** *ein Stück Kuchen*, 3
calendar *der Kalender, -*, 11
call *anrufen* (sep), *telefonieren*, 11
can *können*, 7
capital *die Hauptstadt, ⸚e*, 1
car *das Auto, -s*, 1; **by car** *mit dem Auto*, 1
card *die Karte, -n*, 2
care for *mögen*, 10
carpet *der Teppich, -e*, 12
cassette *die Kassette, -n*, 4
casual *lässig*, 5
cat *die Katze, -n*, 3; **to feed the cat** *die Katze füttern*, 7
cell phone *das Handy, -s*, 11
cent *der Cent, -*, 4
Certainly! *Natürlich!*, 11; *Sicher!*, 3
chair *der Stuhl, ⸚e*, 3
change: Keep the change! *Stimmt (schon)!*, 6
cheap *billig*, 4
check: The check please! *Hallo! Ich möchte/will zahlen!*, 6
cheese *der Käse, -*, 8
cheese sandwich *das Käsebrot, -e*, 6
chemistry *(die) Chemie*, 4
chess *das Schach*, 2
chicken *das Hähnchen, -*, 8
Christmas *das Weihnachten, -*, 11; **Merry Christmas!** *Fröhliche Weihnachten!*, 11
church *die Kirche, -n*, 9
cinnamon *der Zimt*, 12
cinema *das Kino, -s*, 6
city *die Stadt, ⸚e*, 9; **in the city** *in der Stadt*, 3
city hall *das Rathaus, ⸚er*, 9
class schedule *der Stundenplan, ⸚e*, 4
classical music *klassische Musik*, 10
clean: to clean the windows *die Fenster putzen*, 7; **to clean up my room** *mein Zimmer aufräumen* (sep), 7

clear: to clear the table *den Tisch abräumen* (sep), 7
clothes (casual term for) *die Klamotten* (pl), 5; **to pick up my clothes** *meine Klamotten aufräumen* (sep), 7
cloudy *wolkig*, 7
coffee *der Kaffee*, 8; **a cup of coffee** *eine Tasse Kaffee*, 6
coin *die Münze, -n*, 11
cold *kalt*, 7
cold cuts *der Aufschnitt*, 8
collect *sammeln*, 2; **to collect comics** *Comics sammeln*, 2; **to collect stamps** *Briefmarken sammeln*, 2
color *die Farbe, -n*, 5
come *kommen*, 1; **I come** *ich komme*, 1; **That comes to....** *Das macht (zusammen) ...*, 6; **to come along** *mitkommen* (sep), 7
comedy *die Komödie, -n*, 10
comfortable *bequem*, 3
comics *die Comics*, 2; **to collect comics** *Comics sammeln*, 2
computer *der Computer, -*, 3
computer science *die Informatik*, 4
compact disc *die CD, -s*, 11
concert *das Konzert, -e*, 6; **to go to a concert** *in ein Konzert gehen*, 6
cookie *der Keks, -e*, 3; **a few cookies** *ein paar Kekse*, 3
cool *kühl*, 7
corners: with corners *eckig*, 12
corny *schmalzig*, 10
cost *kosten*, 4; **How much does... cost?** *Was kostet ... ?*, 4
cotton *die Baumwolle*, 12; **made of cotton** *aus Baumwolle*, 12
couch *die Couch, -en*, 3 ·
country *das Land, ⸚er*, 3; **in the country** *auf dem Land*, 3
cousin (female) *die Kusine, -n*, 3; **cousin (male)** *der Cousin, -s*, 3
crime drama *der Krimi, -s*, 10
cruel *grausam*, 10

D

dance *tanzen*, 2; **to go dancing** *tanzen gehen*, 6
dancing *das Tanzen*, 2
dark blue *dunkelblau*, 5; **in dark blue** *in Dunkelblau*, 5
Darn it! *So ein Mist!*, 2
day *der Tag, -e*, 1; **day before yesterday** *vorgestern*, 8; **every day** *jeden Tag*, 7
December *der Dezember*, 7
definitely *bestimmt*, 5
degree *der Grad, -*, 7
Delicious! *Lecker!*, 6
desk *der Schreibtisch, -e*, 3

detective movie *der Krimi, -s*, 10
detective novel *der Krimi, -s*, 10
dial *wählen*, 11; **to dial the number** *die Nummer wählen*, 11
dictionary *das Wörterbuch, ⸚er*, 4
different *verschieden*, 11
dining table *der Esstisch, -e*, 12
directly *direkt*, 4
disagree: I disagree. *Das finde ich nicht.*, 2
disco *die Disko, -s*, 6; **to go to a disco** *in eine Disko gehen*, 6
dishes *das Geschirr*, 7; **to wash the dishes** *das Geschirr spülen*, 7
dislike *nicht gern haben*, 4; **strongly dislike** *überhaupt nicht gern*, 10
do *machen*, 2; *tun*, 7; **do crafts** *basteln*, 2; **do homework** *die Hausaufgaben machen*, 2; **Do you have any other interests?** *Hast du andere Interessen?*, 2; **Do you need help?** *Brauchst du Hilfe?*, 7; **Do you play an instrument?** *Spielst du ein Instrument?*, 2; **Do you play sports?** *Machst du Sport?*, 2; **Do you think so?** *Meinst du?*, 5; **Does it taste good?** *Schmeckt's?*, 6; **What did you do on the weekend?** *Was hast du am Wochenende gemacht?*, 10
dog *der Hund, -e*, 3
done *gemacht*, 10
downtown *die Innenstadt*, 9; **to go downtown** *in die Stadt gehen*, 6
draw *zeichnen*, 2
dress *das Kleid, -er*, 5
drink *trinken*, 3
drive *fahren*, 9; **he/she drives** *er/sie fährt*, 9
dry *trocken*, 7
dumb *blöd*, 2; *doof, dumm*, 10

E

Easter *das Ostern, -*, 11; **Happy Easter!** *Frohe Ostern!*, 11
easy *einfach*, 1; **That's easy!** *Also, einfach!*, 1
eat *essen*, 3; **he/she eats** *er/sie isst*, 6; **to eat ice cream** *ein Eis essen*, 6
egg *das Ei, -er*, 8
eight *acht*, 1
eighteen *achtzehn*, 1
eighty *achtzig*, 3
eleven *elf*, 1
enough *genug*, 9
environment *die Umwelt*, 10
eraser *der Radiergummi, -s*, 4
especially *besonders*, 6; **especially like** *besonders gern*, 10
euro *der Euro, -*, 4

evening *der Abend*, 1; **in the evening** *am Abend*, 2
every: every day *jeden Tag*, 7
exciting *spannend*, 10
Excuse me! *Entschuldigung!, Verzeihung!*, 9
expensive *teuer*, 4
eye *das Auge, -n*, 3; **blue (brown, green) eyes** *blaue (braune, grüne) Augen*, 3

F

fall *der Herbst*, 2; **in the fall** *im Herbst*, 2
family *die Familie, -n*, 3
fancy chocolate *die Praline, -n*, 11
fantasy novel *der Fantasyroman, -e*, 10
far *weit*, 3; **far from here** *weit von hier*, 3
fashion *die Mode*, 10
father *der Vater, ∴*, 3; **to, for your father** *deinem Vater*, 11; **to, for my father** *meinem Vater*, 11
Father's Day *der Vatertag*, 11; **Happy Father's Day!** *Alles Gute zum Vatertag!*, 11
favorite *Lieblings-*, 4
February *der Februar*, 7
feed *füttern*, 7; **to feed the cat** *die Katze füttern*, 7
fetch *holen*, 8
few: a few *ein paar*, 3; **a few cookies** *ein paar Kekse*, 3
fifteen *fünfzehn*, 1
fifty *fünfzig*, 3
first *erst-*, 11; **first of all** *zuerst*, 4; **on the first of July** *am ersten Juli*, 11; **the first street** *die erste Straße*, 9
fit *passen*, 5; **The skirt fits great!** *Der Rock passt prima!*, 5
five *fünf*, 1
flower *die Blume, -n*, 7; **to water the flowers** *die Blumen gießen*, 7
foot: on foot (I walk) *zu Fuß*, 1
for *für*, 7; *denn* (conj), 8
forty *vierzig*, 3
four *vier*, 1
fourteen *vierzehn*, 1
for whom? *für wen?*, 8
free time *die Freizeit*, 2
fresh *frisch*, 8
fresh produce store *der Obst- und Gemüseladen, ∴*, 8
Friday *der Freitag*, 4
friend (male) *der Freund, -e*, 1; **(female)** *die Freundin, -nen*, 1; **to visit friends** *Freunde besuchen*, 2
from *aus*, 1; *von*, 4; **from 8 until 8:45** *von 8 Uhr bis 8 Uhr 45*, 4
from where? *woher?*, 1; **I'm from** *ich bin (komme) aus*, 1; **Where are you from?** *Woher bist (kommst) du?*, 1
front: there in the front *da vorn*, 4
fruit *das Obst*, 8; **a piece of fruit** *Obst*, 3
fun *der Spaß*, 2; **(Tennis) is fun.** *(Tennis) macht Spaß.*, 2; **(Tennis) is no fun.** *(Tennis) macht keinen Spaß.*, 2
funny *lustig*, 10
furniture *die Möbel* (pl), 3

G

garden(s) *der Garten, ∴*, 9
geography *die Erdkunde*, 4
German mark (former German monetary unit) *DM = Deutsche Mark*, 4
German teacher (male) *der Deutschlehrer, -*, 1; **(female)** *die Deutschlehrerin, -nen*, 1
Germany *Deutschland*, 1
get *bekommen*, 4; *holen*, 8
gift *das Geschenk, -e*, 11
gift idea *die Geschenkidee, -n*, 11
girl *das Mädchen, -*, 1
give *geben*, 11; **he/she gives** *er/sie gibt*, 11
give (a gift) *schenken*, 11
glass *das Glas, ∴er*, 3; **a glass (cup) of tea** *ein Glas Tee*, 6; **a glass of (mineral) water** *ein Glas (Mineral)Wasser*, 3; **a glass of apple juice** *ein Glas Apfelsaft*, 3
glasses: a pair of glasses *eine Brille, -n*, 3
go *gehen*, 2; **to go home** *nach Hause gehen*, 3
golf *Golf*, 2
good *gut*, 4; **Good!** *Gut!*, 6
Good morning! *Guten Morgen! Morgen!*, 1
Goodbye! *Auf Wiedersehen!*, 1; (on the telephone) *Auf Wiederhören!*, 11
grade *die Note, -n*, 4
grade level *die Klasse, -n*, 4
grades: a 1, 2, 3, 4, 5, 6 *eine Eins, Zwei, Drei, Vier, Fünf, Sechs*, 4
gram *das Gramm, -*, 8
grandfather *der Großvater (Opa), ∴*, 3
grandmother *die Großmutter (Oma), ∴*, 3
grandparents *die Großeltern* (pl), 3
grape *die Traube, -n*, 8
gray *grau*, 3; **in gray** *in Grau*, 5
Great! *Prima!*, 1; *Sagenhaft!*, 6; *Klasse! Toll!*, 2
green *grün*, 3; **in green** *in Grün*, 5
groceries *die Lebensmittel* (pl), 8
ground meat *das Hackfleisch*, 8
group *die Gruppe, -n*, 10

guitar *die Gitarre, -n*, 2
gyros *das Gyros, -*, 9

H

hair *die Haare* (pl), 3
half *halb*, 6; **half past (twelve, one, etc.)** *halb (eins, zwei, usw.)*, 6
hang up (the telephone) *auflegen* (sep), 11
Hanukkah *Chanukka*, 11; **Happy Hanukkah!** *Frohes Chanukka-Fest!*, 11
have *haben*, 4; **he/she has English** *er/sie hat Englisch*, 4; **I have German.** *Ich habe Deutsch.*, 4; **I have no classes on Saturday.** *Am Samstag habe ich frei.*, 4; **I'll have...** *Ich bekomme ...*, 6
have to *müssen*, 7; **I have to** *ich muss*, 7
he *er*, 2; **he is** *er ist*, 1; **he's from** *er ist (kommt) aus*, 1
hear *hören*, 2
Hello! *Guten Tag! Tag! Hallo! Grüß dich!*, 1
help *helfen*, 7; **to help at home** *zu Hause helfen*, 7
her *ihr* (poss adj), 3; **her name is** *sie heißt*, 1
hideous *scheußlich*, 5
hike *wandern*, 2
him *ihn*, 5
his *sein* (poss adj), 3; **his name is** *er heißt*, 1
history *die Geschichte*, 4
hobby book *das Hobbybuch, ∴er*, 10
holiday *der Feiertag, -e*, 11
homework *die Hausaufgabe, -n*, 2; **to do homework** *Hausaufgaben machen*, 2
honestly *ehrlich*, 5
horror movie *der Horrorfilm, -e*, 10
horror novel *der Gruselroman, -e*, 10
hot *heiß*, 7
hotel *das Hotel, -s*, 9
how much? *wie viel?*, 8; **How much does... cost?** *Was kostet ... ?*, 4
how often? *wie oft?*, 7
how? *wie?*, 1; **How are you?** *Wie geht's (denn)?*, 6; **How do I get to...?** *Wie komme ich zum (zur) ... ?*, 9; **How do you get to school?** *Wie kommst du zur Schule?*, 1; **How does it taste?** *Wie schmeckt's?*, 6; **How old are you?** *Wie alt bist du?*, 1; **How's the weather?** *Wie ist das Wetter?*, 7

hunger *der Hunger,* 9
hungry: I'm hungry. *Ich habe Hunger.,* 9; **I'm not hungry any more.** *Ich habe keinen Hunger mehr.,* 9

I *ich,* 2; **I don't.** *Ich nicht.,* 2
ice *das Eis,* 7
ice cream *das Eis,* 6; **a dish of ice cream** *ein Eisbecher,* 6
ice-skate *Schlittschuh laufen,* 12
idea: I have no idea! *Keine Ahnung!,* 9
imaginative *phantasievoll,* 10
in *in,* 2; **in the afternoon** *am Nachmittag,* 2; **in the city** *in der Stadt,* 3; **in the country** *auf dem Land,* 3; **in the evening** *am Abend,* 2; **in the fall** *im Herbst,* 2; **in the kitchen** *in der Küche,* 12; **in the living room** *im Wohnzimmer,* 12; **in the spring** *im Frühling,* 2; **in the summer** *im Sommer,* 2; **in the winter** *im Winter,* 2
insert *einstecken,* 11; **to insert coins** *Münzen einstecken (sep),* 11
instrument *das Instrument, -e,* 2; **Do you play an instrument?** *Spielst du ein Instrument?,* 2
interest *das Interesse, -n,* 2; **Do you have any other interests?** *Hast du andere Interessen?,* 2
interesting *interessant,* 2
Internet *das Internet,* 2
invite *einladen (sep),* 11; **he/she invites** *er/sie lädt ... ein,* 11
is: he/she is *er/sie ist,* 1
it *er, es, sie,* 3; *ihn,* 5

jacket *die Jacke, -n,* 5
January *der Januar,* 7; **in January** *im Januar,* 7
jeans *die Jeans, -,* 5
jewelry *der Schmuck,* 11
jog *joggen,* 12
jogging suit *der Jogging-Anzug, ̈-e,* 5
juice *der Saft, ̈-e,* 3
July *der Juli,* 7
June *der Juni,* 7
just: Just a minute, please. *Einen Moment, bitte!,* 11

keep: Keep the change! *Stimmt (schon)!,* 6
kilogram *das Kilo, -,* 8
kitchen *die Küche, -n,* 12; **in the kitchen** *in der Küche,* 12
know (a fact, information, etc.) *wissen,* 9; **I don't know.** *Ich weiß nicht.,* 5
know (be familiar or acquainted with) *kennen,* 10

lamp *die Lampe, -n,* 12
last *letzt-,* 8; **last of all** *zuletzt,* 4; **last week** *letzte Woche,* 8; **last weekend** *letztes Wochenende,* 8
Latin *Latein,* 4
lawn *der Rasen, -,* 7; **to mow the lawn** *den Rasen mähen,* 7
layer cake *die Torte, -n,* 8
leather *das Leder,* 12; **made of leather** *aus Leder,* 12
left: to the left *nach links,* 9
lemon *die Zitrone, -n,* 12
lemon drink *die Limo, -s,* 3
lettuce *der Salat,* 8
light blue *hellblau,* 5; **in light blue** *in Hellblau,* 5
like *gern haben,* 4; *mögen,* 10; **I like it.** *Er/Sie/Es gefällt mir.,* 5 **I like them.** *Sie gefallen mir.,* 5; **like an awful lot** *furchtbar gern,* 10; **not like at all** *gar nicht gern,* 10; **not like very much** *nicht so gern,* 2
like (to do) *gern (machen),* 2; **to not like (to do)** *nicht gern (machen),* 2
listen (to) *hören,* 2; *zuhören, p.* 6
liter *der Liter, -,* 8
little *klein,* 3; **a little** *ein bisschen,* 5; **a little more** *ein bisschen mehr,* 8
live *wohnen,* 3
living room: in the living room *im Wohnzimmer,* 12
long *lang,* 3
look *schauen,* 2; **Look!** *Schauen Sie!,* 4
look for *suchen,* 5; **I'm looking for** *ich suche,* 5
look like *aussehen (sep),* 5; **he/she looks like** *er/sie sieht ... aus,* 5; **The skirt looks....** *Der Rock sieht ... aus.,* 5; **What do they look like?** *Wie sehen sie aus?,* 3; **What does he look like?** *Wie sieht er aus?,* 3
lot: a lot *viel,* 2
luck: Bad luck! *So ein Pech!,* 4; **What luck!** *So ein Glück!,* 4

made: made of cotton *aus Baumwolle,* 12; **made of leather** *aus Leder,* 12; **made of plastic** *aus Kunststoff,* 12; **made of silk** *aus Seide,* 12; **made of wood** *aus Holz,* 12
magazine *die Zeitschrift, -en,* 10
make *machen,* 2; **to make the bed** *das Bett machen,* 7
man *der Mann, ̈-er,* 3
many *viele,* 2
March *der März,* 7
market square *der Marktplatz, ̈-e,* 9
math *Mathe (die Mathematik),* 4
may: May I help you? *Haben Sie einen Wunsch?,* 5
May *der Mai,* 7
maybe *vielleicht,* 11
me *mich,* 7; **Me too.** *Ich auch.,* 2
meat *das Fleisch,* 8
mess: What a mess! *So ein Mist!,* 4
milk *die Milch,* 8
mineral water *das Mineralwasser,* 3
minute: Just a minute, please. *Einen Moment, bitte.,* 11
miserable *miserabel,* 6
modern *modern,* 12
moment *der Moment, -e,* 3
money *das Geld,* 4
month *der Monat, -e,* 7
moped *das Moped, -s,* 2; **by moped** *mit dem Moped,* 1
more *mehr,* 9
morning *der Morgen,* 1; **Morning!** *Morgen!,* 1
most of all *am liebsten,* 10
mother *die Mutter, ̈-,* 3
Mother's Day *der Muttertag,* 11; **Happy Mother's Day!** *Alles Gute zum Muttertag!,* 11
movie *der Film,* 10; **to go to the movies** *ins Kino gehen,* 6
movie theater *das Kino, -s,* 6
mow *mähen,* 7; **to mow the lawn** *den Rasen mähen,* 7
Mr. *Herr,* 1
Ms. *Frau,* 1
much *viel,* 2; **much too** *viel zu,* 5; **very much** *sehr gern,* 10
museum *das Museum, die Museen,* 9
music *die Musik,* 2; **to listen to music** *Musik hören,* 2
mustard *der Senf,* 6; **with mustard** *mit Senf,* 6
my *mein,* 3; **my name is** *ich heiße,* 1; **to, for my father** *meinem Vater,* 11 **to, for my mother** *meiner Mutter,* 11

N

name *der Name, -n,* 1; **her name is** *sie heißt,* 1; **his name is** *er heißt,* 1; **my name is** *ich heiße,* 1; **What's the boy's name?** *Wie heißt der Junge?,* 1; **What's the girl's name?** *Wie heißt das Mädchen?,* 1; **What's your name?** *Wie heißt du?,* 1
nearby *in der Nähe,* 3
need *brauchen,* 5; **I need** *ich brauche,* 5
never *nie,* 7
new *neu,* 3
newspaper *die Zeitung, -en,* 10
next: the next street *die nächste Straße,* 9; **next week** *nächste Woche*
nine *neun,* 1
nineteen *neunzehn,* 1
ninety *neunzig,* 3
no *kein,* 9; **No more, thanks!** *Nichts mehr, danke!,* 9
non-fiction book *das Sachbuch, ⸚er,* 10
none *kein,* 9
noodle soup *die Nudelsuppe, -n,* 6
not *nicht,* 2; **not at all** *überhaupt nicht,* 5; **not like at all** *gar nicht gern,* 10; **Not really.** *Nicht besonders.,* 6; **Not too long?** *Nicht zu lang?,* 5
not any *kein,* 9
notebook *das Notizbuch, ⸚er,* 1; *das Heft, -e,* 4
nothing *nichts,* 3; **nothing at the moment** *im Moment gar nichts,* 3; **Nothing, thank you!** *Nichts, danke!,* 3
novel *der Roman, -e,* 10
November *der November,* 7
now *jetzt,* 1; *nun,* 6
number *die (Telefon)nummer, -n,* 11; **to dial the number** *die Nummer wählen,* 11

O

o'clock: at 8 o'clock *um 8 Uhr,* 4; **at one o'clock** *um ein Uhr,* 6
October *der Oktober,* 7
Of course! *Ja klar!,* 1; *Ganz klar!,* 4
often *oft,* 2
Oh! *Ach!,* 1; **Oh yeah!** *Ach ja!,* 1
oil *das Öl,* 12
Okay! I'll do that! *Gut! Mach ich!,* 7; **It's okay.** *Es geht.,* 6
old *alt,* 3; **How old are you?** *Wie alt bist du?,* 1
on: on ... Square *am ...platz,* 9; **on ... Street** *in der ...straße,* 3; **on foot (I walk)** *zu Fuß,* 1; **on Monday** *am Montag,* 4; **on the first of July** *am ersten Juli,* 11; **on the weekend** *am Wochenende,* 2
once *einmal,* 7; *mal,* 9; **once a month** *einmal im Monat,* 7; **once a week** *einmal in der Woche,* 7
one *eins,* 1
one hundred *hundert,* 3
onion *die Zwiebel, -n,* 12
only *bloß, nur,* 4
opera *die Oper, -n,* 10
or *oder,* 1
orange juice *der Orangensaft, ⸚e,* 3
other *andere,* 2
oven *der Ofen, ⸚,* 12
over there *dort drüben,* 4; **over there in the back** *da hinten,* 4
overcast *trüb,* 7

P

pants *die Hose, -n,* 5
parents *die Eltern* (pl), 3
park *der Park, -s,* 12; **to go to the park** *in den Park gehen,* 12
party *die Party, -s,* 11
pencil *der Bleistift, -e,* 4
people *die Leute* (pl), 9
perfume *das Parfüm, -e,* 11
pet *das Haustier, -e,* 3
phone card *die Telefonkarte, -n,* 11
physical education *der Sport,* 4
physics *(die) Physik,* 4
piano *das Klavier, -e,* 2; **I play the piano** *Ich spiele Klavier.,* 2
pick up *aufräumen* (sep), 7; **to pick up my clothes** *meine Klamotten aufräumen,* 7; **to pick up the telephone** *abheben* (sep), 11
piece *das Stück, -e,* 3; **a piece of cake** *ein Stück Kuchen,* 3; **a piece of fruit** *Obst,* 3
pizza *die Pizza, -s,* 6
plastic *der Kunststoff, -e,* 12; **made of plastic** *aus Kunststoff,* 12
play *spielen,* 2; **I play soccer.** *Ich spiele Fußball.,* 2; **I play the piano.** *Ich spiele Klavier.,* 2; **to play a board game** *ein Brettspiel spielen,* 12
please *bitte,* 3
pleasure: My pleasure! *Gern geschehen!,* 9
pocket calculator *der Taschenrechner, -,* 4
politics *die Politik,* 10
polka-dot *gepunktet,* 12
post office *die Post,* 9
poster *das Poster, -,* 11
potato *die Kartoffel, -n,* 8
pound *das Pfund, -,* 8
prefer *lieber (mögen),* 10
pretty *hübsch,* 5; *schön,* 3
pretzel *die Brezel, -n,* 8

probably *wahrscheinlich,* 11
produce store *der Obst- und Gemüseladen, ⸚,* 8; **at the produce store** *im Obst- und Gemüseladen,* 8
Pullover *der Pulli, -s,* 5
put on *anziehen* (sep), 5

Q

quarter: a quarter after *Viertel nach,* 6; **a quarter to** *Viertel vor,* 6

R

railroad station *der Bahnhof, ⸚e,* 9
rain *der Regen,* 7; **It's raining** *Es regnet.,* 7
rainy *regnerisch,* 7
rather *ziemlich,* 4
read *lesen,* 10; **he/she reads** *er/sie liest,* 10; **What did you read?** *Was hast du gelesen?,* 10
really *ganz,* 3; *echt,* 5; **Not really.** *Nicht besonders.,* 6
receive *bekommen,* 4
receiver *der Hörer, -,* 11
red *rot,* 3; **in red** *in Rot,* 5
refrigerator *der Kühlschrank, ⸚e,* 12
religion *die Religion, -en,* 4
report card *das Zeugnis, -se,* 4
residence: The ... residence *Hier bei ... ,* 11
right: to the right *nach rechts,* 9
roll *die Semmel, -n,* 8
romance *der Liebesfilm, -e,* 10; **romance novel** *der Liebesroman, -e,* 10
room *das Zimmer, -,* 3; **to clean up my room** *mein Zimmer aufräumen* (sep), 7
round *rund,* 12

S

sad *traurig,* 10
salad *der Salat, -e,* 12
salt *das Salz,* 12
Saturday *der Samstag,* 4
sausage *die Wurst, ⸚e,* 8
say *sagen,* 1; **Say!** *Sag mal!,* 2; **What does the weather report say?** *Was sagt der Wetterbericht?,* 7

school *die Schule, -n,* 4; **after school** *nach der Schule,* 2; **How do you get to school?** *Wie kommst du zur Schule?,* 1

school subject *das Fach, ∺er,* 4

school supplies *die Schulsachen* (pl) 4

schoolbag *die Schultasche, -n,* 4

science fiction movie *der Sciencefictionfilm, -e,* 10

science fiction novel *der Sciencefictionroman, -e,* 10

search (for) *suchen,* 4

second *zweit-,* 11; **the second street** *die zweite Straße,* 9

see *sehen,* 10; **he/she sees** *er/sie sieht,* 10; **See you later!** *Bis dann!,* 1; **to see a movie** *einen Film sehen,* 6; **What did you see?** *Was hast du gesehen?,* 10

sensational *sensationell,* 10

September *der September,* 7

set *decken,* 7; **to set the table** *den Tisch decken,* 7

seven *sieben,* 1

seventeen *siebzehn,* 1

seventy *siebzig,* 3

she *sie,* 2; **she is** *sie ist,* 1; **she's from** *sie ist (kommt) aus,* 1

shine: the sun is shining *die Sonne scheint,* 7

shirt *das Hemd, -en,* 5

shop *einkaufen* (sep), 8; **to go shopping** *einkaufen gehen,* 8

short *kurz,* 3

shortening *das Butterschmalz,* 12

shorts: pair of shorts *die Shorts, -,* 5

should *sollen,* 8

silk *die Seide,* 12; **made of silk** *aus Seide,* 12

singer (female) *die Sängerin, -nen,* 10

singer (male) *der Sänger, -,* 10

sink *das Spülbecken, -,* 12

sister *die Schwester, -n,* 3; **brothers and sisters** *die Geschwister* (pl) 3

six *sechs,* 1

sixteen *sechzehn,* 1

sixty *sechzig,* 3

size *die Größe, -n,* 5

skirt *der Rock, ∺e,* 5

small *klein,* 3

smart (looking) *fesch, schick, chic,* 5

snack bar *die Imbissstube, -n,* 9

sneaker *der Turnschuh, -e,* 5

snow *der Schnee,* 7; **It's snowing** *Es schneit.,* 7

so *so,* 2; **So long!** *Tschau! Tschüs!,* 1; **so so** *so lala,* 6

soccer *der Fußball,* 2; **I play soccer.** *Ich spiele Fußball.,* 2

sock *die Socke, -n,* 5

soda: lemon-flavored soda *die Limo, -s (die Limonade, -n),* 3

sofa *das Sofa, -s,* 12

something *etwas,* 7

sometimes *manchmal,* 7

song *das Lied, -er,* 10

soon *bald,* 11

sorry: I'm sorry. *Es tut mir leid.,* 9; **Sorry, I can't.** *Ich kann leider nicht.,* 7

sort *sortieren,* 7; **to sort the trash** *den Müll sortieren,* 7

spend (time) *verbringen,* 10

sports *der Sport,* 2; **Do you play sports?** *Machst du Sport?,* 2

spring *der Frühling,* 2; **in the spring** *im Frühling,* 2

square *der Platz, ∺e,* 9; **on ... Square** *am ...platz,* 9

stamp *die Briefmarke, -n,* 2; **to collect stamps** *Briefmarken sammeln,* 2

state: German federal state *das Bundesland, ∺er,* 1

stereo *die Stereoanlage -n,* 3

stinks: That stinks! *So ein Mist!,* 4

store *der Laden, ∺,* 8

storm *das Gewitter, -,* 7

stove *der Herd, -e,* 12

straight ahead *geradeaus,* 9

street *die Straße, -n,* 9; **on ... Street** *in der ...straße,* 3

striped *gestreift,* 12

stupid *blöd,* 5

subject (school) *das Fach, ∺er,* 4; **Which subjects do you have?** *Welche Fächer hast du?,* 4

suburb *der Vorort, -e,* 3; **a suburb of** *ein Vorort von,* 3

subway *die U-Bahn,* 1; **by subway** *mit der U-Bahn,* 1

subway station *die U-Bahnstation, -en,* 9

sugar *der Zucker,* 8

summer *der Sommer,* 2; **in the summer** *im Sommer,* 2

sun *die Sonne,* 7; **the sun is shining** *die Sonne scheint,* 7

Sunday *der Sonntag,* 4

sunny *sonnig,* 7

Super! *Spitze!, Super!,* 2

supermarket *der Supermarkt, ∺e,* 8; **at the supermarket** *im Supermarkt,* 8

supposed to *sollen,* 8

Sure! *Aber sicher!, Ja, gern!,* 11

sure: I'm not sure. *Ich bin nicht sicher.,* 5

surf *surfen,* 2

sweater *der Pulli, -s,* 5

swim *schwimmen,* 2; **to go swimming** *baden gehen,* 6

swimming pool *das Schwimmbad, ∺er,* 6; **to go to the (swimming) pool** *ins Schwimmbad gehen,* 6

T-shirt *das T-Shirt, -s,* 5

table *der Tisch, -e,* 12; **to clear the**

table *den Tisch abräumen* (sep), 7; **to set the table** *den Tisch decken,* 7

take *nehmen,* 5; **he/she takes** *er/sie nimmt,* 5; **I'll take** *ich nehme,* 5

talk about *sprechen über,* 10; **he/she talks about** *er/sie spricht über,* 10 **What did you** (pl) **talk about?** *Worüber habt ihr gesprochen?,* 10

taste *schmecken,* 6; **Does it taste good?** *Schmeckt's?,* 6; **How does it taste?** *Wie schmeckt's?,* 6

Tasty! *Lecker!,* 6

tea *der Tee,* 6; **a glass (cup) of tea** *ein Glas Tee,* 6

teacher (male) *der Lehrer, -,* 1; **(female)** *die Lehrerin, -nen,* 1

telephone *das Telefon, -e, der Apparat, -e,* 11; **pick up the telephone** *abheben* (sep), 11

telephone booth *die Telefonzelle, -n,* 11

telephone number *die Telefonnummer, -n,* 11

television *das Fernsehen,* 2; **to watch TV** *Fernsehen schauen,* 2

temperature: What's the temperature? *Wie viel Grad haben wir?,* 7

ten *zehn,* 1

tennis *Tennis,* 2

terrible *furchtbar,* 5

terrific *Klasse, prima, toll,* 2

thank *danken,* 3; **Thank you (very much)!** *Danke (sehr, schön)!,* 3; *Vielen Dank!,* 9; **Thank you!** *Danke!,* 3

that *dass* (conj) 9; **That's all.** *Das ist alles.,* 8; **That's...** *Das ist ... ,* 1

the *das, der, die,* 1; *den* (masc, acc) 5; *dem* (masc, neuter, dat) 11

theater *das Theater, -,* 9

then *dann,* 4

there *dort,* 4

There is/are... *Es gibt...,* 9

they *sie,* 2; **they are** *sie sind,* 1; **they're from** *sie sind (kommen) aus,* 1

think *denken,* 3; **Do you think so?** *Meinst du?,* 5; **I think** *ich glaube,* 2; **I think (tennis) is...** *Ich finde (Tennis) ... ,* 2; **I think so too.** *Das finde ich auch.,* 2; **I think it's good/bad that....** *Ich finde es gut/schlecht, dass ...,* 9; **I think that...** *Ich finde, dass ...,* 9 **What do you think of (tennis)?** *Wie findest du (Tennis)?,* 2

third *dritte,* 9

thirteen *dreizehn,* 1

thirty *dreißig,* 1

this: this afternoon *heute Nachmittag,* 8; **This is...** *Hier ist ...* (on the telephone), 11; **this morning** *heute Morgen,* 8

three *drei,* 1

three times *dreimal,* 7

thrilling *spannend,* 10

Thursday *der Donnerstag,* 4

tight *eng*, 5
till: ten till two *zehn vor zwei*, 6
time *die Zeit*, 4; **At what time?** *Um wie viel Uhr?*, 6; **I don't have time.** *Ich habe keine Zeit.*, 7; **What time is it?** *Wie spät ist es?, Wie viel Uhr ist es?*, 6
to, for her *ihr*, 11
to, for him *ihm*, 11
today *heute*, 4
tomato *die Tomate, -n*, 8
tomorrow *morgen*, 7
tonight *heute Abend*, 7
too *zu*, 5; **Too bad!** *Schade!*, 4
tour *besichtigen*, 12; **to tour the city** *die Stadt besichtigen*, 12
train station *der Bahnhof, ̈-e*, 9
trash *der Müll*, 7; **to sort the trash** *den Müll sortieren*, 7
true: Not true! *Stimmt nicht!*, 2; **That's right! True!** *Stimmt!*, 2
try *probieren*, 9
try on *anprobieren* (sep), 5
Tuesday *der Dienstag*, 4
twelve *zwölf*, 1
twenty *zwanzig*, 1
twenty-one *einundzwanzig*, 3; (see p. 83 for numbers 21-29)
twice *zweimal*, 7
two *zwei*, 1

(see p. 83 for numbers 21-29)

ugly *hässlich*, 3
uncle *der Onkel, -*, 3
uncomfortable *unbequem*, 3
unfortunately *leider*, 7; **Unfortunately I can't.** *Leider kann ich nicht.*, 7
until: from 8 until 8:45 *von 8 Uhr bis 8 Uhr 45*, 4; **until you get to ... Square** *bis zum ...platz*, 9; **until you get to ... Street** *bis zur ...straße*, 9; **until you get to the traffic light** *bis zur Ampel*, 9
us *uns*, 7

vacuum *Staub saugen*, 7
vegetables *das Gemüse*, 8
very *sehr*, 2; **Very well!** *Sehr gut!*, 6
videocassette *das Video, -s*, 10
violent *brutal*, 10
visit *besuchen*, 2; **to visit friends** *Freunde besuchen*, 2
volleyball *Volleyball*, 2

want (to) *wollen*, 6
war movie *der Kriegsfilm, -e*, 10
warm *warm*, 7
was: I was *ich war*, 8; **I was at the baker's.** *Ich war beim Bäcker.*, 8; **he/she was** *er/sie war*, 8
wash *spülen*, 7; **to wash the dishes** *das Geschirr spülen*, 7
watch *schauen*, 2; **to watch TV** *Fernsehen schauen*, 2; **Watch out!** *Pass auf!* 6
water: to water the flowers *die Blumen gießen*, 7
water *das Wasser*, 3; **a glass of (mineral) water** *ein Glas (Mineral)Wasser*, 3
we *wir*, 2
wear *anziehen* (sep), 5
weather *das Wetter*, 7; **How's the weather?** *Wie ist das Wetter?*, 7; **What does the weather report say?** *Was sagt der Wetterbericht?*, 7
Wednesday *der Mittwoch*, 4
week *die Woche, -n*, 7
weekend *das Wochenende, -n*, 2; **on the weekend** *am Wochenende*, 2
weigh *wiegen*, 8
were: Where were you? *Wo warst du?*, 8; **we were** *wir waren*, 8; **they were** *sie waren*, 8; **you** (pl) **were** *ihr wart*, 8; **you** (formal) **were** *Sie waren*, 8
western (movie) *der Western, -*, 10
wet *nass*, 7
what? *was?*, 2; **What can I do for you?** *Was kann ich für dich tun?*, 7; **What else?** *Noch etwas?*, 9
what kind of? *was für?*, 10; **What kind of movies do you like?** *Was für Filme magst du gern?*, 10; **What kind of music do you like?** *Was für Musik hörst du gern?*, 10; **What will you have?** *Was bekommen Sie?*, 6
What's there to eat? *Was gibt's zu essen?*, 9
when? *wann?*, 2
where? *wo?*, 1; **Where are you from?** *Woher bist (kommst) du?*, 1
where (to)? *wohin?*, 6
which *welch-*; 4
white *weiß*, 3; **in white** *in Weiß*, 5
who? *wer?*, 1; **Who is that?** *Wer ist das?*, 1
whole-grain roll *die Vollkornsemmel, -n*, 9
whom *wen*, 7; *wem*, 11
whom? (to whom? for whom?) *wem?*, 11

why? *warum?*, 8; **Why don't you come along!** *Komm doch mit!*, 7
wide *weit*, 5
window *das Fenster, -*, 7; **to clean the windows** *die Fenster putzen*, 7
winter *der Winter*, 2; **in the winter** *im Winter*, 2
with *mit*, 6; **with bread** *mit Brot*, 6; **with corners** *eckig*, 12; **with lemon** *mit Zitrone*, 6; **with mustard** *mit Senf*, 9
woman *die Frau, -en*, 3
wood: made of wood *aus Holz*, 12
work: That won't work. *Das geht nicht.*, 7
would like (to) *möchten*, 3; **I would like to see....** *Ich möchte ... sehen.*, 5; **What would you like to eat?** *Was möchtest du essen?*, 3; **What would you like?** *Was bekommen Sie?*, 5; **Would you like anything else?** *Haben Sie noch einen Wunsch?*, 8
wristwatch *die Armbanduhr, -en*, 11
write *schreiben*, 2

year *das Jahr, -e*, 1; **I am...years old.** *Ich bin ... Jahre alt.*, 1
yellow *gelb*, 5; **in yellow** *in Gelb*, 5
yes *ja*, 1; **Yes?** *Bitte?*, 5
yesterday *gestern*, 8; **yesterday evening** *gestern Abend*, 8; **the day before yesterday** *vorgestern*, 8
you *du*, 2; **you are** *du bist*, 1; (pl) **you are** *ihr seid*, 1; (formal) **you are** *Sie sind*, 1
you (formal) *Sie*, 2
you (plural) *ihr*, 2
you (pl, acc pronoun) *euch*, 7
you (acc pronoun) *dich*, 7
you're (very) welcome! *Bitte (sehr, schön)!*, 3
your *dein*, 3; **to, for your father** *deinem Vater*, 11; **to, for your mother** *deiner Mutter*, 11

zoo *der Zoo, -s*, 12; **to go to the zoo** *in den Zoo gehen*, 12

Page numbers in boldface type refer to **Grammatik** and **Ein wenig Grammatik** presentations. Other page numbers refer to grammar structure presented in **So sagt man das!, Sprachtipp, Lerntrick, Wortschatz,** and **Landeskunde** sections. Page numbers beginning with R refer to the Grammar Summary in this Reference Section.

Grammar Index

question words/interrogatives: wie 22, **23,** 25, 30, 57, 84, 161, 162, 254; **wer 23; woher 23,** 28; **was** 48, 50, 55, 74, 115, 134, 170; **wo 23,** 73, 116; **wann** 107, 164, 314; **worüber 291; wem** 319; *see also* R18

questions: 22; asking and answering questions **23;** questions beginning with a verb **23;** questions beginning with a question word **23;** questions anticipating a yes or no answer **23;** *see also* word order

second person: du, ihr, Sie (formal singular and plural), *see* subject pronouns

sehen: present tense forms of **285,** R21

sein: 25; present tense forms of **26,** R21; simple past tense forms of **231,** R23

separable prefixes: an, aus 143, 144; **auf, ab, mit** 196; **ein** 313; placement of **143, 196**

separable-prefix verbs: definition of **143; anziehen, anprobieren 143; aussehen 143, 144; aufräumen, abräumen, mitkommen 196; abheben, anrufen, auflegen, einstecken** 309; **einladen** 313; *see also* R22

sequencing: 109

Sie-commands: 116, 254, **255;** *see also* command forms

sollen: 222; present tense forms of **223,** R21; *see also* modal auxiliary verbs

sprechen: present tense forms of **291;** with **über** 291, R21

stem-changing verbs: nehmen, aussehen 144; **essen** 170, **171; fahren 255; sehen 285; lesen, sprechen 291;** *see also* R21; present tense verb endings

subject: 25, **135;** placement of **56;** *see also* nominative case

subject pronouns: 22, 25, **26,** 28, 48; plurals **50, 79;** as opposed to direct object pronouns **140**

subordinating conjunctions: denn, weil 230; *see also* word order

superlatives: suffix **-ste** 287

time expressions: 55, 106, 107, 198, 199; **morgen 203;** *see also* word order

third person: er, sie, sie (plural), **Sie** (plural formal) **26,** 28, 48, 79; *see also* subject pronouns

und: 29; *see also* conjunctions

verbs: with separable prefixes, **anziehen, anprobieren, aussehen 143; aufräumen, abräumen, mitkommen 196; einladen** 313; with vowel change in the **du-** and **er/sie-**form, **nehmen, aussehen 144; essen** 170, **171; fahren 255; sehen 285; lesen, sprechen 291;** *see also* R20–R22; present tense and present tense verb endings

verb-final position: in **weil**-clauses **230;** in clauses following **wissen 250,** in **dass**-clauses **260;** *see also* R19

verb-second position: 55, **56,** 167

weil: 230; *see also* conjunctions

wissen: present tense forms of, word order following **250,** R19, R21; **wissen** vs. **kennen** 284

wo: 23, 73, 116

woher: 28

wollen: present tense forms of **166,** R21; *see also* modal auxiliary verbs

word order: 22; questions beginning with a verb **23;** questions beginning with a question word **23,** 55; verb in second position **54;** with separable prefix verbs **143;** using modals **166, 167, 199, 222, 342;** in **denn-** and **weil-**clauses **230;** verb-final in clauses following **wissen 250;** verb-final in **dass**-clauses **260;** with dative case **320;** *see also* R19; infinitive; questions

worüber: 291

ACKNOWLEDGMENTS *(continued from page ii)*

Bertelsmann Club: Advertisement and front cover, "Die Firma," from *Bertelsmann Club*, March 1993, p. 9.

C & A Mode Düsseldorf: Adapted advertisement, "C & A: SCHNUPPER PREISE," from *Süddeutsche Zeitung*, March 1992, p. 18.

Deike-Press-Bilderdienst: Game, "Skat," from *Südwest Presse: Schwäbisches Tagblatt*, Tübingen, July 1990. Copyright © 1990 by Deike Press, Germany.

Winfred Epple: Advertisement, "Gute Laune," by Wertobjekte Immobilien Epple (WIE) from *Südwest Presse: Schwäbisches Tagblatt*, Tübingen, July 14, 1990.

Die Gilde Werbeagentur GmbH: Advertisement, "Das neue Plantaris."

Dr. Rudolf Goette GmbH: Advertisements, "Dienstag, 26. Januar" and "Dienstag, 25. Mai," from *Pro-Arte: Konzerte '93*.

Gräfe und Unzer Verlag, München: "Dallmayr," "Das Wetter" (weather chart), "Der besondere Tip," "Englischer Garten," "Januar Fasching," "Ludwig Beck," "Medizinische Versorgung," "Olympiapark," and "Peterskirche" by H. E. Rübesamen from *Merian live-München*, pp. 30–31, 39, 45, 79, 80, 95, 112, 119 and 120. Copyright © 1993 by Gräfe und Unzer Verlag, München.

Händle & Partner: Advertisement, "Der mit dem Wolf tanzt," from *1. Ludwigsburger: Sommernachts Open Air-Kino*, text by Frank Schneider, illustration by Gernot Händle.

München Hilton Hotel: Advertisement, "Kulinarische Highlights im München City Hilton," (retitled "Hamburg Kulinarische Highlights".)

Immobilien: Advertisement, "Immobilien T. Kurcz," from *Südwest Presse: Schwäbisches Tagblatt*, July 14, 1990.

Institut Rosenberg: Advertisement, "Institut Rosenberg," from *Süddeutsche Zeitung*, July 10–11, 1993, p. 40.

IVT - Immobiliengesellschaft der Volksbank Tübingen mbH & Co., Grundstücks-KG.: "Auf dem Lande" and "2-Zi.-Eigentumswohnung" from "Immobilienverbund-Volksbanken Raiffeisenbanken" from *Südwest Presse: Schwäbisches Tagblatt*, Tübingen, July 14, 1990.

Jahreszeiten Verlag GmbH: "DAS WEISSE HEMD" from *Petra*, May 1992. p. 52.

K + L Ruppert GmbH: Advertisement, "Kurz und Gut!" and "Qualitäts-Garantie."

Karsten Jahnke Konzertdirektion GmbH: Advertisement of upcoming concert tours from *Konzerte: Karsten Jahnke präsentiert Konzertübersicht 1993*, no. 248.

Emil Kriegbaum GmbH & Co. KG: Advertisement, "Stark Reduziert!," from *Südwest Presse: Schwäbisches Tagblatt*, Tübingen, June 27, 1990.

Liberty Diskothek Café: Advertisement, "Liberty Diskothek Café," from *in münchen*, no. 30/31, July 25–August 7, 1991.

Messe Stuttgart Kongress-U. Tagungsbüro. "Hanns-Martin-Schleyer-Halle" from *Veranstaltungskalender der Messe Stuttgart: Programm*, March 1992.

Müller Brot: Advertisements, "Der Mensch ist, wie er ißt" and "HOTLINE."

OK-PUR: From "MTV News" and "OK-PUR TAGESTIP: The Romeos" from *OK-PUR*, June 22, 1993.

QUICK Verlag GmbH: Advertisement, "Milchbars," from *QUICK*, August 8, 1991, no. 33. Copyright © 1991 by QUICK Verlag GmbH.

Dr. Rall GmbH, Reutlingen: Advertisement, "Tübingen-Lustnau am Herrlesberg," from *Südwest Presse: Schwäbisches Tagblatt*, Tübingen, July 14, 1990.

Sator Werbe-Agentur: Advertisement, "Bahrenfelder Forsthaus," from *Hotels und Restaurants 93/94*, D-22761 Hamburg Das Tor zur Welt.

Hartmut Schmid: Game, "Schach," from *Südwest Presse: Schwäbisches Tagblatt*, Tübingen, July 13, 1990.

Schwäbisches Tagblatt: Advertisement, "UNI Sommerfest," from *Südwest Presse: Schwäbisches Tagblatt*, Tübingen, June 23, 1990.

Spar Öst. Warenhandels-AG: From flyer, "Spar Supermarkt: NEUERÖFFNUNG, July 1, 1993."

Stadt Bietigheim-Bissingen: Captions from *Stadt Bietigheim-Bissingen*.

Stuttgart - Marketing GmbH: Captions from *Stuttgart*.

Südwest Presse, Tübingen: Advertisement, "Eninger Hot Jazz Festival," from *Schwäbisches Tagblatt*, Tübingen, June 23, 1990.

Tiefdruck Schwann-Bagel GmbH: Adaption of advertisement, "Hobby" from *JUMA Das Jugendmagazin*, 2/90, February 1990, p. 47. Advertisement, "Mode '91" from *JUMA Das Jugendmagazin*, 3/91, July 1991, p. 31. Caption from "Polo mit Eskimorolle" from *JUMA Das Jugendmagazin*, 1/92, January 1992, pp. 2–3. "Geschenke,"

"Hallo Heiko!," "Hallo Sven!," "Hallo Tina!," "Im Geschenkladen sucht," "Im Supermarkt läuft Ben," "Stefan wird im Schreibwarengeschäft," and "Wem hilfst du?" from *JUMA Das Jugendmagazin,* 2/93, April 1993, pp. 21, 23, 38, 39, 40 and 42.

Tourismus-Zentrale Hamburg GmbH: Advertisement, "Tag u. Nacht," from *Hotels und Restaurants 93/94,* Hamburg Das Tor zu Welt.

United International Pictures GmbH: Advertisement, "Jurassic Park," from *Kino Magazin,* February 1993.

Verlag J.C.B. Mohr (Paul Seibeck) Tübingen: Advertisement, "Wohnung," from *Südwest Presse: Schwäbisches Tagblatt,* Tübingen, July 14, 1990.

Zeiler Möbelwerk GmbH & Co. KG, D-97475 Zeil am Main: Advertisement, "Best in Germany—Best in America (allmilmö®)," from *Metropolitan Home®,* Special Edition, The Best of Winners!, Fall 1991, p. 9.

PHOTOGRAPHY CREDITS

Abbreviations used: (t) top, (c) center, (b) bottom, (l) left, (r) right, (bckgd) background, (i) inset.

All photographs by George Winkler/Holt, Rinehart and Winston, Inc. except:

Border images: Victoria Smith/HRW Photo.

TABLE OF CONTENTS: Page vii (bl), Michelle Bridwell/Frontera Fotos; ix (bl), Victoria Smith/HRW Photo; xi (tl), Michelle Bridwell/Frontera Fotos; xviii (t), Michelle Bridwell/Frontera Fotos; xxi (br), ©European Communities; xxii (bl), Helga Lade/Peter Arnold, Inc.; xxiii (br), Helga Lade/Peter Arnold, Inc.

Preliminary Chapter: Page 1 (cl, tl), Westlight/CORBIS; 1 (br), Bernard Silberstein/FPG International; 4 (tl), DPA/IPOL; 4 (cl), Robert Young Pelton/Westlight/Corbis; 4 (bl), Dallas & John Heaton/Westlight/Corbis; 4 (br), J. Zuckerman/Westlight/Corbis; 4 (tr), Digital imagery® copyright 2003 PhotoDisc, Inc.; 5 (tl), Bettman Archive/Corbis; 5 (tr), AP/Wide World Photos; 5 (tc), Bettman Archive/Corbis; 5 (cl), HRW Photo; 5 (bl), Archive Photos; 5 (cr), AP/Wide World Photos; 9 (all), Victoria Smith/HRW Photo; 10 (bc), AP/Wide World Photos; 10 (tl, cl), Digital imagery® copyright 2003 PhotoDisc, Inc.; 10 (cr), Corbis Images; 11 (bl, bc), Michelle Bridwell/Frontera Fotos.

UNIT ONE: Page 12-13 (all), Jose Fuste Raga/The Stock Market; 14 (tr), Helga Lade/Peter Arnold, Inc.

Chapter One: Page 20 (br), Michelle Bridwell/Frontera Fotos; 21 (bl, cl), Michelle Bridwell/Frontera Fotos; 21 (cr), Viesti Collection, Inc.; 21 (br), Michelle Bridwell/Frontera Fotos; 34-35 (bkgd), Courtesy of Lufthansa German Airlines; 35 (bl), Corbis Images; 36 (c), Michelle Bridwell/Frontera Fotos.

Chapter Two: Page 47 (bl), EyeWire, Inc. Image Club Graphics ©1998 Adobe Systems, Inc.; 47 (bc, br), Digital imagery® copyright 2003 PhotoDisc, Inc.; 48 (tl, tr, cl, br, bl), Digital imagery® copyright 2003 PhotoDisc, Inc.; 51 (l, cl, c, cr), Digital imagery® copyright 2003 PhotoDisc, Inc.; 51 (bcr), John Langford/HRW Photo; 51 (bl), ©1997 Radlund & Associates for Artville; 51 (bcl), Sam Dudgeon/HRW Photo; 51 (r), Digital imagery® copyright 2003 PhotoDisc, Inc.; 51 (bc), Corbis Images; 53 (l, cl, cr, r), Michelle Bridwell/Frontera Fotos; 53 (br), Sam Dudgeon/HRW Photo; 53 (inset), Michelle Bridwell/HRW Photo; 60 (tr), Digital imagery® copyright 2003 PhotoDisc, Inc.; 62 (cr), Michelle Bridwell/Frontera Fotos; 65 (tl, tc, tr), Viesti Collection, Inc.

Chapter Three: Page 73 (c, bl, bc, cr), Michelle Bridwell/Frontera Fotos; 73 (br), Viesti Collection, Inc.; 74 (tl), Richard Hutchings/PhotoEdit; 74 (tcl, tcr), Viesti Collection, Inc.; 75 (tcl, tl), Corbis Images; 75 (bl, bcl), Victoria Smith/HRW Photo; 75 (tcr), ©Stockbyte; 75 (tr), composite - apple (Corbis Images); cherries, banana and pear (Digital Imagery® copyright 2003 PhotoDisc, Inc.; 75 (bcr), Victoria Smith/HRW Photo; 76 (l, cll, cl), Corbis Images; 76 (c, cr), Victoria Smith/HRW Photo; 76 (r), ©Stockbyte; 80 (cl, c, cr, bl), Courtesy of Scandinavia Contemporary Interiors; 80 (bc), Michelle Bridwell/Frontera Fotos; 80 (br), Digital imagery® copyright 2003 PhotoDisc, Inc.; 81 (tl, tr, cl, c, cr, br), Viesti Collection, Inc.; 81 (bl, bc), Michelle Bridwell/Frontera Fotos; 93 (tl, tc, tr, bl, cl, cr, br), Michelle Bridwell/Frontera Fotos.

UNIT TWO: Page 96-97 (all), Helga Lade/Peter Arnold, Inc.; 98 (tr, cr, b), Helga Lade/Peter Arnold, Inc.

Chapter Four: Page 114 (tl, tcl, tcr, tr, cl, c, cr), Victoria Smith/HRW Photo; 115 (tl, tcl, tcr, tr), Michelle Bridwell/Frontera Fotos; 115 (b), ©European Communities; 122 (c), Victoria Smith/HRW Photo; 123 (b), ©European Communities; 124 (bl, br), Victoria Smith/HRW Photo.

Chapter Five: Page 133 (tl, tc, tr, cl, c, cr, bl), Victoria Smith/HRW Photo; 140 (br), Victoria Smith/HRW Photo; 140 (inset), Sam Dudgeon/HRW Photo; 141 (cl, cr, b), Michelle Bridwell/Frontera Fotos; 143 (tl, tcl, tcr, tr), Michelle Bridwell/Frontera Fotos; 149 (tr, cr), Victoria Smith/HRW Photo; 150 (br, cl, cr), Victoria Smith/HRW Photo; 152 (br), David Vance Associates/The Image Bank.

Chapter Six: Page 171 (tl, tcl, tcr), Victoria Smith/HRW Photo; 171 (tr), Michelle Bridwell/HRW Photo; 171 (cl), Digital imagery® copyright 2003 PhotoDisc, Inc.; 171 (ccl, ccr, cr), Victoria Smith/HRW Photo; 178 (cr), Michelle Bridwell/HRW Photo; 178 (bc), Victoria Smith/HRW Photo; 179 (cr), Victoria Smith/HRW Photo.

UNIT THREE:

Chapter Seven: Page 193 (tl, tcr, cl, clc, crc), Michelle Bridwell/Frontera Fotos; 193 (br), Viesti Collection, Inc.; 201 (tl, tr, cl, cr, bl, br), Digital imagery® copyright 2003 PhotoDisc, Inc.; 203 (cr), Viesti Collection, Inc.; 203 (cl), Tony Freeman/PhotoEdit; 203 (cr), Dennis MacDonald/ PhotoEdit; 203 (bl), Vic Bider/PhotoEdit; 203 (bc), David Young-Wolff/PhotoEdit; 207 (tl), Viesti Collection, Inc.; 207 (bl), Michelle Bridwell/Frontera Fotos; 212 (bl), David Madison/Duomo Photography; 212 (clc, bc), Michelle Bridwell/Frontera Fotos.

Chapter Eight: Page 221 (tl, tc, tcr, tr, tlb, tcb), Michelle Bridwell/Frontera Fotos; 221 (crc, cr), Sam Dudgeon/ HRW Photo; 221 (bl, blc, bc, bcr, br, tr), Viesti Collection, Inc.; 226 (tl, cl), Victoria Smith/HRW Photo; 226 (bc), Digital imagery® copyright 2003 PhotoDisc, Inc.; 226 (tr), Victoria Smith/HRW Photo; 226 (cr), ©PhotoSpin, Inc.; 226 (bc), Victoria Smith/HRW Photo; 236 (tr), Sam Dudgeon/HRW Photo; 236 (cr), Michelle Bridwell/ Frontera Fotos; 237 (b), ©PhotoSpin, Inc.; 238 (tr), Digital imagery® copyright 2003 PhotoDisc, Inc.

Chapter Nine: Page 254 (tr, bl), Michelle Bridwell/Frontera Fotos; 260 (tr), Thomas Kanzler/Viesti Collection, Inc.; 265 (c), Michelle Bridwell/Frontera Fotos.

UNIT FOUR: Page 272-273 (all), S.K./Helga Lade/Peter Arnold, Inc.; 274 (c), S.K./Helga Lade/Peter Arnold, Inc.

Chapter Ten: Page 281 (c, cr), Everett Collection; 281 (tl, tc, tr, cl, bl, bc, br), Motion Picture & Television Photo Archive; 283 (bl), Marco Shark/Shark Images Photography; 287 (tl), ©2003/Kennan Ward/Adventure Photo & Film; 288 (c), Michelle Bridwell/Frontera Fotos; 291 (tl, tr, cr, br), Michelle Bridwell/Frontera Fotos; 296 (bc), Motion Picture & Television Photo Archive; 297 (bl), Motion Picture & Television Photo Archive.

Chapter Eleven: Page 304-305 (all), Michelle Bridwell/ Frontera Photos; 309 (bcl), Sam Dudgeon/HRW Photo; 309 (bcr), Digital imagery® copyright 2003 PhotoDisc, Inc.; 311 (cl), Sam Dudgeon/HRW Photo; 317 (tr, cl), Michelle Bridwell/Frontera Fotos; 317 (clc), Viesti Collection, Inc.; 317 (c), Michelle Bridwell/Frontera Fotos; 317 (crc), Viesti Collection, Inc.; 317 (cr, bl, bc, br, tl, tr, cr, tr, cl, c, tc), Michelle Bridwell/Frontera Fotos; 324 (b), Sam Dudgeon/HRW Photo; 325 (tr), Michelle Bridwell/Frontera Fotos; 326 (bl, bc, br), Michelle Bridwell/Frontera Fotos; 328 (tl, c, bl), Michelle Bridwell/Frontera Fotos.

Chapter Twelve: Page 340 (bl), Michelle Bridwell/Frontera Fotos; 340 (bc), Viesti Collection, Inc.; 343 (tr), Michelle Bridwell/Frontera Fotos; 350 (tr, br), Michelle Bridwell/ Frontera Fotos; 350 (c), Digital imagery® copyright 2003 PhotoDisc, Inc.; 351 (tl), Michelle Bridwell/Frontera Fotos; 351 (bl), Digital imagery® copyright 2003 PhotoDisc, Inc.; 351 (c), Corbis Images; 355 (cr), Michelle Bridwell/Frontera Fotos; 355 (br), Sam Dudgeon/HRW Photo.

Reference Section: Page R9 (tl, tc), Digital imagery® copyright 2003 PhotoDisc, Inc.; R9 (tr), EyeWire, Inc. Image Club Graphics ©1998 Adobe Systems, Inc.; R9 (c), Randal Alhadeff/HRW Photo; R9 (cr, brt, bc), Digital imagery® copyright 2003 PhotoDisc, Inc.; R9 (br), Corbis Images; R10 (tl), Corbis Images; R10 (tr), EyeWire, Inc.; R10 (cl, c), Scott Van Osdol/HRW Photo; R10 (br), Digital imagery® copyright 2003 PhotoDisc, Inc.; R11 (cr), Corbis Images; R11 (tl, tr, cl, c, bl, br), Digital imagery® copyright 2003 PhotoDisc, Inc.; R12 (tl, cl), Digital imagery® copyright 2003 PhotoDisc, Inc.; R12 (br), ©Stockbyte; R12 (bc), Sam Dudgeon/HRW Photo; R12 (bl), Corbis Images; R13 (cl), © Digital Vision; R13 (br), Corbis Images; R14 (bl, br), Michelle Bridwell/ Frontera Fotos.

ILLUSTRATION AND CARTOGRAPHY CREDITS

Abbreviated as follows: (t) top, (b) bottom, (l) left, (r) right, (c) center.

All art, unless otherwise noted, by Holt, Rinehart & Winston.

Preliminary Chapter: Page xxii, MapQuest.com; 2, MapQuest.com; 3, MapQuest.com; 6, Holly Cooper; 8, Tom Rummonds.

Chapter One: Page 12, MapQuest.com; 22 (t), George McLeod; 22 (cr), Holly Cooper; 23, George McLeod; 30, George McLeod; 39, Tom Rummonds.

Chapter Two: Page 47 (c) Gail Piazza; 47 (b), Eduard Böhm; 48, Eduard Böhm; 51 (l), George McLeod; 51 (r), Eduard Böhm; 55, Gail Piazza; 64, Holly Cooper.

Chapter Three: Page 74, George McLeod; 78, George McLeod; 81, Holly Cooper; 84, Gail Piazza; 92, Tom Rummonds.

Chapter Four: Page 96, MapQuest.com; 105, Holly Cooper; 107, Holly Cooper; 108, Gail Piazza; 114, Eduard Böhm; 116, George McLeod; 121, Holly Cooper; 124, Eduard Böhm.

Chapter Five: Page 136, Holly Cooper; 137, Holly Cooper; 138, Tom Rummonds; 139, Tom Rummonds; 144, Holly Cooper; 145, Holly Cooper; 152, Holly Cooper; 154, Holly Cooper.

Chapter Six: Page 161 (c), Tom Rummonds; 161 (b), Holly Cooper; 162, Leslie Kell; 164, George McLeod; 165, Tom Rummonds; 172, Holly Cooper; 173, Holly Cooper; 180, Holly Cooper.

Chapter Seven: Page 184, MapQuest.com; 194, George McLeod; 195 (t), Holly Cooper; 195 (b), Eduard Böhm; 199, Tom Rummonds; 200, Tom Rummonds; 201 (t), George McLeod; 204, Tom Rummonds; 214, Holly Cooper.

Chapter Eight: Page 223, Holly Cooper; 224, Tom Rummonds; 232, Tom Rummonds.

Chapter Nine: Page 249, John Wilson; 251 (t), John Wilson; 251 (c), George McLeod; 253 (c), Riki Rushing; 253 (b), Leslie Kell; 256, Holly Cooper; 259, Eduard Böhm; 270, John Wilson.

Chapter Ten Page 272, MapQuest.com; 286, Eduard Böhm.

Chapter Eleven: Page 309, Tom Rummonds; 310, Tom Rummonds; 314, Eduard Böhm; 315 (c), Mike Krone; 315 (b), Eduard Böhm; 320, Mike Krone; 328, George McLeod; 330, Mike Krone.

Chapter Twelve: Page 338 (bl, br), Eduard Böhm; 339, Mike Krone; 342, George McLeod; 344, Holly Cooper; 345 (t), Holly Cooper; 345 (b), Eduard Böhm; 347, Eduard Böhm; 356, Riki Rushing.